T0366510

DUMBARTON OAKS
MEDIEVAL LIBRARY

Jan M. Ziolkowski, General Editor

ON THE LITURGY

VOLUME II

AMALAR OF METZ

DOML 36

# On the Liturgy

## AMALAR OF METZ

### VOLUME II
### BOOKS 3–4

Edited and Translated by

# ERIC KNIBBS

DUMBARTON OAKS
MEDIEVAL LIBRARY

HARVARD UNIVERSITY PRESS
CAMBRIDGE, MASSACHUSETTS
LONDON, ENGLAND
2014

*Library of Congress Cataloging-in-Publication Data*
Amalarius, Archbishop of Lyon, approximately 775–approximately 850,
author.
  On the liturgy / Amalar of Metz ; volume I, books 1–2 edited and
translated by Eric Knibbs.
      2 volumes ; cm.—(Dumbarton Oaks medieval library ; 35–36)
  "Contains final version—the redaction printed and translated here—
On the Liturgy contains 158 chapters divided among four books"—
Introduction.
  Includes bibliographical references and index.
  Latin on the verso, English translation on the recto.
  ISBN 978-0-674-06001-2 (v. 1 : alk. paper)—ISBN 978-0-674-41703-8
(v. 2 : alk. paper) 1. Liturgics—History—Middle Ages, 600–1500.
I. Knibbs, Eric, editor, translator. II. Amalarius, Archbishop of Lyon,
approximately 775–approxinately 850. Opera liturgica omnia.
III. Amalarius, Archbishop of Lyon, approximately 775–approximately
850. Opera liturgica omnia. English. IV. Title.
  BV185.A43 2014
  264—dc23        2014004769

# Contents

# ON THE LITURGY

# LIBER 3

## De Officio Missae

## Praefatiuncula

Domino opitulante, intercedente beato Medardo confessore, cuius festivitas hodie apud nos celebratur, in gaudio sanctorum, prompti sumus animo ad suscipiendum Dei munus, si tamen ipse dignatur purgare et serenare oculum, in quo discamus de officio Missae, quid rationis in se contineat diversitas illa quae ibi agitur, cum satis esset, sine cantoribus et lectoribus et ceteris quae ibi aguntur, sola benedictio episcoporum aut presbyterorum ad benedicendum panem et vinum, quo reficeretur populus ad animarum salutem, sicut primevis temporibus fiebat apud apostolos, ac ideo primum dicendum est de signis.

# BOOK 3

## *On the Office of the Mass*

## Preface

With the Lord's assistance and the intercession of the blessed confessor Medard, whose feast we celebrate today, and in the joy of the saints, our mind is ready to take up God's work, if only he deign to purify and illuminate our sight, that we may learn about the office of the Mass and the purpose behind the variety that we practice during its celebration. For as it was done in ancient times among the apostles, merely the blessing of the bishops or the priests, without the cantors or lectors or the other things that we do during Mass, would suffice to bless the bread and the wine, which refresh the people unto the salvation of their souls. And so we should first discuss bells.

# I

# De signis quibus congregamur in idipsum

Signorum usus a Veteri Testamento sumptus est. Scriptum est in libro Numerorum: "Locutus est Dominus ad Moysen dicens: Fac tibi duas tubas argenteas ductiles, quibus convocare possis multitudinem." Et paulo post: "Quando autem congregandus est populus, simplex tubarum clangor erit et non concise ululabunt. Filii Aaron sacerdotis clangent tubis." Et iterum: "Si quando habetis epulam, et dies festos et kalendas, canetis tubis super holocaustis et pacificis victimis, ut sint vobis in recordationem Dei vestri" [Num 10:1–2, 7–8, 10].

2 Audivimus clangorem tubarum in recordatione Dei nostri resonare, detque nobis Deus ut quicquid boni facere poterimus—sive singulariter in causa nostra, sive communiter in causa fratrum, ut est signa moveri—in memoriam eius faciamus. Audiamus et tubam vocantem nos ad paenitentiam quando in adversis affligimur, dicente Ioel: "Canite tuba in Sion, sanctificate ieiunium, vocate coetum, congregate populum, sanctificate ecclesiam, coadunate senes, congregate parvulos et sugentes ubera" [ Joel 2:15–16].

3 Quod ita Hieronimus in eodem: "Clangite tuba in Sion, et paenitentiam populis praedicate. Sanctificate ieiunium:

I

# On the bells that call us together

The use of bells is derived from the Old Testament. It is written in the book of Numbers: "The Lord spoke to Moses saying: Make two trumpets of beaten silver, with which you may call together the multitude." And a little later: "But when the people are to be gathered together, the sound of the trumpets shall be plain and they shall not make a broken sound. The sons of Aaron the priest shall sound the trumpets." And again: "If at any time you shall have a banquet, and on your festival days and on the first days of your months, you shall sound the trumpets over the holocausts and the sacrifices of peace offerings, that they may be to you for a remembrance of your God."

We have heard that the sound of the trumpets resounds 2 for a remembrance of our God; may God grant us that whatever good we are able to do, we do it in his memory—whether individually and for our own sake, or collectively for the sake of our brothers, as when bells are rung. Let us also hear the trumpet calling us to penitence when we are beaten down by adversities, as Joel says: "Blow the trumpet in Zion, sanctify a fast, call an assembly, gather together the people, sanctify the church, assemble the ancients, gather together the little ones and them that suck at the breasts."

Jerome, on the same passage, as follows: "Sound the trum- 3 pet in Zion and preach penitence to the people. Sanctify a

praedicate curationem sive coetum de quibus iam diximus. Congregate populum, ut qui dispersus peccaverat, congregatus peccare desistat. Sanctificate ecclesiam, ut nullus in ecclesia non sanctus sit, ne forsitan impediantur orationes vestrae et modicum fermentum totam massam corrumpat [1 Cor 5:6]. Et adunate sive eligite senes, ut non aetas in eis, sed sanctitas eligatur. Congregate quoque parvulos et sugentes ubera, ne ulla sit aetas quae non convertatur ad Dominum—parvulos atque lactantes, de quibus in Psalmis et in Evangelio legimus: 'Ex ore infantium et lactantium perfecisti laudem' [Ps 8:3; Matt 21:16]."✝

4  Praedicationem quam significat clangor tubarum, Hieronimo exponente, signat signum quod in nostra ecclesia reboat. Signum nostrum est ex metallo aeris. Aes est metallum durabile et sonorum. Habet idem signum interius plectrum ferreum, quo tunditur ut audiatur, oraque praedicatorum significat Novi Testamenti, quae plus durant quam tubae Veteris Testamenti, atque altius resonant. Ora praedicatorum nostrorum durabunt usque in finem, et auditur longe sonus eorum, usque in fines terrae [Ps 18:5]. Tempore Iudaeorum "notus" tantum erat "in Iudaea Deus" [Ps 75:2], at tunc in omni terra.

5  Vas metalli aeris ora significat, ut diximus, praedicatorum; ferrum interius linguam eorum. Per funem intellegimus mensuram nostrae vitae. Unde dicebat Paulus: "Sed ipsi in nobis nosmet ipsos metientes et comparantes" [2 Cor 10:12]. Mensura meae conversationis nusquam mihi satius ostenditur quam in scriptura, ac ideo funem scripturam intellego. Funis qui habet initium a ligno, scripturam sacram significat Novi Testamenti, descendentem a ligno

6

fast: preach the oversight and the assembly that we have just spoken about. Gather the people, so that he who has wandered astray and sinned may cease sinning once he has been gathered in. Sanctify the church, so that no one in the church is not holy, lest your prayers be obstructed and a little leaven corrupt the whole lump. And assemble or choose the ancients, so that sanctity, and not age, may be chosen in them. And gather the little ones and them that suck at the breasts, lest there be any age not converted to the Lord—the little ones and the sucklings of whom we read in the Psalms and the Gospel: 'Out of the mouth of infants and of sucklings you have perfected praise.'"✝

The bell that resounds in our church, as Jerome explains, 4 indicates the preaching that the sound of the trumpets signifies. Our bell is made of bronze. Bronze is a durable and sonorous metal. The bell has an iron clapper within that strikes it so it may be heard, and this signifies the mouths of the preachers of the New Testament, which outlast the trumpets of the Old Testament and resound more deeply. The mouths of our preachers will last until the end, and their sound is heard from afar, unto the ends of the world. In the time of the Jews, "God was known in Judaea" only, but now he is known throughout the whole earth.

As we said, a bronze cup signifies the mouths of preach- 5 ers; the iron within signifies their tongue. Through the rope we understand the measure of our life. Thus Paul said: "But we measure and compare ourselves by ourselves." Nowhere is the measure of my way of life better revealed to me than in scripture, and so I understand the rope to be scripture. The rope, which hangs from wood, signifies the holy scrip- 6 ture of the New Testament, which descends from the wood

Dominicae crucis. Quod tamen lignum a superioribus continetur, quia Dominica crux a prophetis et antiquis patribus
continetur. Qui funis usque ad manus sacerdotis pertransit;
etenim scriptura ad opera sacerdotum debet transire.

7    De qua dicit Gregorius in libro *De aedificio templi:* "Quisquis hanc legit, in ea semet ipsum metitur—vel quantum in
spiritali virtute proficit, vel quantum a bonis quae praecepta
sunt, longe disiunctus remansit; quantum iam adsurgat ad
bona facienda, quantum adhuc in pravis prostratus iaceat."✝

8    Haec verba novissima valde congruunt operi presbyteri qui
signum movet. Quando funem sequitur sursum, id agit, ut in
se ipso recogitet quantum ad bona opera sit erectus. Quando
deorsum trahit, id considerat, quantum iaceat adhuc in pravis. Qui secundum verba sancti Gregorii semet ipsum metitur, ipse habilis est fratres vocare ad unum cor et ad unam
animam [Acts 4:32]. Ne despiciat presbyter hoc opus agere,
ut in isto imitator sit filiorum Aaron, sicut et in multis ceteris. Qui se cognoscit debitorem esse praedicationis, non debet se retrahere a movendis signis, cum ex eisdem possit
praedicare populo.

9    Vinculum quo plectrum ligatur vasi, quaedam moderatio
est, quae scit ad tempus movere plectrum linguae, ut labia
feriantur. Vinculum ad tactum funis movet plectrum,
quando modestia ad auctoritatem sacrae scripturae linguam
praedicatoris movet.

of the Lord's cross. And this wood is held by higher things, because the Lord's cross is contained in the prophets and the ancient fathers. The rope passes through the priest's hands, and indeed, scripture should pervade the priest's works.

Gregory speaks about this in his book *On the Construction* 7 *of the Temple:* "Whoever reads this measures himself in it— whether the degree to which he is progressing in spiritual virtue, or the degree to which he has remained far removed from the good deeds that have been prescribed. Inasmuch as he is still mired in depravity, he should now rise to do good works."✝ These last words correspond perfectly to the 8 work of the priest who rings the bell. When he follows the rope upward, he considers to what degree he has been elevated to do good works. When he pulls it downward, he considers to what degree he is still mired in depravity. He who measures himself in accordance with the words of Saint Gregory is capable of calling his brothers to one heart and one soul. The priest should not disdain to perform this task, so that through it, as through many other things, he may imitate Aaron's sons. He who recognizes that he is bound to preach should not shrink from ringing bells, since through them he can preach to the people.

The link by which the clapper is tied to the cup is a kind 9 of moderation; it knows to move the tongue's clapper at the right time to strike the mouth. The chain moves the clapper at the operation of the cord, when moderation moves the tongue of the preacher in accordance with the authority of sacred scripture.

## 2

# De situ ecclesiae

Ecclesia est convocatus populus per ministros ecclesiae, ab eo qui facit unanimes habitare in domo [Ps 67:7]. Ipsa domus vocatur ecclesia quia ecclesiam continet. Ipsa vocatur *kyrica,* quia est dominicalis; *kyrius* Grece, Latine "dominus," ac ideo *kyrica,* "dominicalis." Ipsa vocatur basilica, id est regalis, a *basileo. Basileus* rex dicitur, quasi basis populi. *Laos* populus dicitur, *basilaus* basis populi. Unde Isidorus: "Basilicae prius vocabantur regum habitacula, unde et nomen habent. Nam *basileus* 'rex,' et basilicae regiae habitationes. Nunc autem ideo divina templa basilicae nominantur, quia ibi regi Deo cultus et sacrificia offeruntur."✢

2  Iosephus simili modo nominat domum quam aedificavit Salomon ad suum opus dicens: "Post templi fabricam, quam septem annis praediximus fuisse perfectum, aedificium domuum regalium construere coepit, quod tredecim annis vix implevit; non enim huiusmodi erat fervens studium sicut in
3  templo." Et post pauca: "Haec quidem secundum felicitatem Ebraicae regionis ac merito regis aedificata sunt. Quorum totam expositionem et ordinem dicere necessarium est, ut ex hoc omnes conitiant magnitudinem, cum legentes viderint huius rei descriptionem. Erat magna basilica nimis

2

# On church, as a location

A church is a people called together by the ministers of the church, by him who makes those of one mind dwell in a house. That house is called a church because it contains the church. It is called *kyrika* because it is of the Lord; *kyrius* in Greek means "lord" in Latin, and so *kyrika* means "of the Lord.'" It is called a basilica, or royal, from the word *basileus*. *Basileus* means king, as in the basis of the people. *Laos* means people; *basilaus* is the basis of the people. Thus Isidore: "The dwellings of kings were first called basilicas, and they get their name from there. For *basileus* means 'king,' and basilicas are royal dwellings. Today, though, divine temples are called basilicas, because in them worship and sacrifices are offered to God the king."✝

Josephus uses the same term for the house that Solomon   2
built for his work, saying: "After the building of the temple, which we said was completed in seven years, he began to work on the construction of the royal dwellings, which he finished in just thirteen years, for there was no ardent zeal of the sort that accompanied the building of the temple." And   3
after a little: "These were of course constructed in accordance with the fertility of the Hebrew land and by the merit of the king. It is necessary to provide a full explanation and account of them, that all may grasp their magnitude, when, while reading, they see the written representation of the thing. It was a very large and beautiful basilica. It was

et pulchra. Haec innumera columnarum multitudine porta-
batur, quam ad iudicia rerumque cogitationes distribuit."✝

4    Audistis ex auctoritate veteri ideo convenisse populum
ad basilicam, ut audiret iudicia. Audite Apostolum cur conveniatur in ecclesia: "Itaque, fratres mei," inquit, "cum con-
venitis ad manducandum, invicem expectate. Si quis autem
esurit, domi manducet, ut non in iudicium conveniatis" [1
Cor 11:33–34]. Monstrante Paulo, propterea convenimus ad
5    ecclesiam, ut manducemus caenam Domini. Duo audistis
cur conveniat populus: Unum, ex antiqua traditione—ut iudicia rerum et cognitiones accipiat; alterum ex Novo Testamento—ut manducet. Utraque quaerimus ad ecclesiam—
scilicet ut in ea audiamus iudicia nostra, mala sive bona, et
cognitionem Dei, et ut manducemus corpus Domini. Idcirco quae praeter ista sunt, postponamus eo tempore, ut
iudicia Domini percipere et retinere queamus, et panem
Domini manducare, studentes nosmet ipsos probare si
digne possit a nobis manducari.

6    In conventu ecclesiastico seorsum masculi et seorsum feminae stant; quod accepimus a veteri consuetudine, dicente
Beda in tractatu super Lucam: "Quaerit aliquis quomodo
Dei Filius tanta parentum cura nutritus, his abeuntibus,
potuerit obliviscendo relinqui. Cui respondendum quia filiis
Israel moris fuerit, ut temporibus festis, vel Hierosolimam
confluentes vel ad propria redeuntes, seorsum viri, seorsum
autem feminae choros ducentes, incederent, infantesque vel
pueri cum quolibet parente indifferenter ire potuerint;
ideoque beatam Mariam vel Ioseph vicissim putasse puerum

supported by an innumerable multitude of columns, which he apportioned for the judgments and examinations of cases."†

From ancient authority, you have heard that people gath- 4 ered at the basilica to hear judgments. Hear the Apostle explain why they gather in church: "Therefore, my brethren," he says, "when you come together to eat, wait for one another. If any man be hungry, let him eat at home, that you not come together unto judgment." As Paul explains, we come together at church to eat the Lord's supper. You have 5 heard two reasons why people come together: One, from ancient tradition—to receive judgments and examinations of their cases; another, from the New Testament—to eat. We seek both at church—namely to hear our judgment there, whether evil or good, to hear God's examination, and to eat the Lord's body. During that time let us therefore set aside everything else, that we may be able to take up and keep the Lord's judgments and to eat the Lord's bread, striving to examine ourselves, to determine whether we can worthily eat his bread.

When gathered at church, the men and the women stand 6 separately. We have received this practice from ancient custom, as Bede says in his treatise on Luke: "Someone asks how the Son of God, raised through the great care of his parents, could have been forgotten and left behind when they departed. We should respond that it was the custom among the sons of Israel, during the festive seasons, when traveling to Jerusalem or returning home, for the men and the women to travel separately in groups; the babies and children could travel with either parent, as it made no difference. And so it happened that blessed Mary and Joseph

13

Iesum, quem secum comitari non cernebant, cum altero parente reversum."✝

7 Quamvis et aliud hac in re possimus tenere—quod caro viri et mulieris, si propius accesserint, unumquodque ex altero accendatur ad libidinem. Qua de re dicit Salomon: "Longe fac ab ea viam tuam" [Prov 5:8]. Quoniam propterea venimus, ut defleamus carnales delectationes, necesse est

8 vitare fomenta earum. De habitu mulierum docet Paulus ad Corinthios: "Decet mulierem non velatam orare Deum? Nec ipsa natura docet vos quod vir quidem, si comam nutriat, ignominia est illi? Mulier vero si comam nutriat, gloria est illi, quoniam capilli pro velamine ei dati sunt?" [1 Cor 11:13–15] Ambrosius in epistola ad Corinthios: "Mulier," inquit, "idcirco debet velare caput, quia non est imago Dei, sed ut ostendatur subiecta et quia praevaricatio per illam inchoata est, hoc signi debet habere, ut in ecclesia propter reverentiam sacerdotalem non habeat caput liberum, sed velamine tectum. Nec habeat potestatem loquendi, quia sacerdos personam habet Christi. Quasi ergo ante iudicem, sic ante sacerdotem, quia vicarius Domini est, propter reatus

9 originem, subiecta debet videri."✝ Et alio modo: Quia et viri quidam comam nutriebant, et mulieres nudo capite procedebant in ecclesiam, gloriantes in crinibus, quod non solum inhonestum erat, sed etiam concupiscentiae fomenta praestabat.

10 Masculi stant in australi parte et feminae in boreali, ut ostendatur per fortiorem sexum firmiores sanctos semper constitui in maioribus temptationibus aestus huius mundi, et per fragiliorem sexum infirmiores aptiore loco, sicut dicit

each thought that the boy Jesus, whom they did not see traveling with them, had returned with the other parent."✝

Yet we can also keep another point in consideration— 7 that the flesh of man and woman may be inflamed with lust, each by the other, if they come too close. Solomon speaks about this: "Remove your way far from her." Because we come to lament carnal pleasures, we should also avoid the things that inflame them. Paul teaches the Corinthians 8 about the dress of women: "Does it become a woman to pray unto God uncovered? Does not even nature itself teach you that a man indeed, if he grow his hair, it is a shame unto him? But if a woman nourish her hair, it is a glory to her, for her hair is given to her for a covering." Ambrose on the letter to the Corinthians: "A woman should cover her head," he says, "because she is not an image of God; rather, so that she may appear subordinated and because transgression arose through her, she should maintain this symbol, so that in church she may not have an uncovered head, but rather one covered with a veil, out of reverence to the priest. Nor may she have leave to speak, because the priest plays the role of Christ. Because of original sin, she should therefore appear subjected before the priest, as if she were before her judge, since the priest is the Lord's vicar."✝ And for another 9 reason: Because some men also grew their hair, and women came to the church bareheaded, glorying in their hair, which was not only disgraceful, but also inflamed desire.

Men stand in the southern part of the church and women 10 in the northern, to show through the stronger sex that the stronger saints are always stationed amid the greater temptations of the fire of this world, and through the weaker sex that the weaker have a more fitting place, as

Paulus Apostolus: "Fidelis est Deus qui non patietur vos temptari super id quod potestis" [1 Cor 12:13]. Ad hoc quidem pertinet quod Iohannes in Apocalypsi sua vidit "angelum fortem" qui "posuit pedem suum dextrum super mare, sinistrum autem super terram" [Rev 10:1–2]. Fortiora etenim membra in maioribus periculis, et alia in competentibus sistuntur.

11     Locutionem quam homines debent habere in ecclesia, Paulus manifestat dicens ad Ephesios: "Loquentes vobismet ipsis in psalmis et ymnis et canticis spiritalibus" [Eph 5:19].

12  Quod ita Hieronimus in tractatu memoratae epistolae: "Qui se abstinuerit ab ebrietate vini, in quo est luxuria, et pro hoc spiritu fuerit impletus—iste omnia potest accipere spiritaliter: psalmos, ymnos et cantica. Quid aut intersit inter psalmum, ymnum et canticum, in Psalterio plenissime discimus. Hic autem breviter ymnos esse dicendum qui fortitudinem et maiestatem praedicant Dei, et eiusdem semper vel beneficia vel facta mirantur. Quod omnes psalmi continent quibus alleluia vel praepositum vel subiectum est. Psalmi autem proprie ad ethicum locum pertinent, ut per organum corporis quid faciendum et quid vitandum sit noverimus. Qui vero de superioribus disputat, et conventum mundi omniumque creaturarum ordinem atque concordiam subtilis disputator edisserit—iste spiritale canticum canit. Vel certe, ut propter simpliciores manifestius quid volumus eloquamur—psalmus ad corpus, canticum refertur ad mentem; et canere igitur, et psallere, et laudare Deum magis animo quam voce debemus."✝

Paul the Apostle says: "God is faithful who will not suffer you to be tempted above that which you are able." Also relevant to this is the "mighty angel" that John saw in Revelation, who "set his right foot upon the sea, and his left foot upon the earth." For the stronger members are stationed amid greater dangers, and others are stationed in corresponding places.

Paul shows how people should converse in church, saying to the Ephesians: "Speaking to yourselves in psalms and hymns and spiritual canticles." Jerome, in his treatise on the aforementioned epistle, as follows: "He who abstains from the drunkenness of wine, where there is excess, and on that account has been filled with the spirit—he can receive all things in the spirit: psalms, hymns and canticles. We learn most fully in the Psalter about the difference between a psalm, a hymn and a canticle. Here, however, we should say briefly that hymns are those things that preach the strength and majesty of God, and forever marvel over his favors and deeds. All psalms that are either preceded or followed by an alleluia do this. Properly, though, psalms have a moral subject, to let us know what we should do and what we should avoid with the instrument of our body. And he who investigates higher things and sets forth, as a subtle examiner, the concord, order and harmony of the world and all creation—he sings a spiritual canticle. Or actually, to say what we want more clearly for the sake of those who are simpler—the psalm relates to the body and the canticle to the mind. We should therefore sing canticles and psalms and praises to God more in our mind than with our voice."✝

17

13     Quod praetermisimus, quis apostolicorum primus statuerit ut feminae velato capite intrarent in ecclesiam, hic remur intromittere. Linus natione Italus, ut legitur in *Gestis episcopalibus,* "ex praecepto beati Petri constituit ut mulier in ecclesiam velato capite introiret."

# 3

# De choro cantorum

Agustinus in Psalmo centesimo XLVIIII: "Et chorus quid significet multi norunt. Chorum, quia in civitate loquimur, prope omnes norunt. Chorus est consensio cantantium. Si in choro cantamus, corde cantamus. In choro cantantium, quisquis voce discrepuerit offendit auditum et perturbat chorum." Isidorus: "Chorus est multitudo in sacris collecta et dictus chorus, quod initio in modum coronae circum aras starent, et ita psallerent."✝

2     Cantorum ordinem suscipimus ex Davitica institutione, quando reportanda erat arca Domini de domo Obethedom in civitatem David. Praecepit David, ut Verba Dierum narrant, constituere "Levitas de fratribus suis cantores in organis musicorum" [1 Chr 15:16, 17, 19]. Constituerunt Levitae Eman, Asaph, Ethan, ut concreparent in cymbalis aenei. Et

We think we should mention here one point that we have 13
left out—namely, which of the popes first established that
women should enter the church with their heads veiled.
Linus, an Italian by birth, as we read in the *Deeds of the
Bishops,* "ordered that women should enter the church with
veiled head, according to the precept of blessed Peter."

# 3

# On the choir of cantors

Augustine on Psalm 149: "And many know what the choir
signifies. Because we speak in the city, almost everyone
knows the choir. A choir is a band of singers. If we sing in a
choir, we sing with our heart. In the choir of singers, whoever is unharmonious in voice perturbs what is heard and
disrupts the choir." Isidore: "The choir is a group gathered
for sacred matters; and it is called a choir because, origi-
nally, they stood like a crown around the altars and they sang
Psalms this way."✝

We derive our order of cantors from David's instruction, 2
when the ark of the Lord was to be carried from Obededom
to the city of David. As Chronicles tells it, David ordered
"the Levites to appoint some of their brethren to be singers
with musical instruments." The Levites appointed Heman,
Asaph and Ethan to sound with cymbals of brass. And

post reliqua: "Asaph autem ut cymbalis personaret"; Bananias vero et Aciel sacerdotes canere tubis iugiter coram arca foederis Domini. "In illo die fecit David principem ad confitendum Domino Asaph et fratres eius" [1 Chr 16:5–7]. Et iterum: "Emam quoque et Idithun canentes tuba et quatientes cymbala et omnia musicorum organa ad canendum Deo" [1 Chr 16:42]. Et iterum: "Cantores, filii Asaph, stabant in ordine suo iuxta praeceptum David et Asaph et Eman et Idithun, prophetarum regis" [2 Chr 35:15].

3    Cantorum primus, ut Verba Dierum narrant, Eman exstitit: "Hi vero sunt qui assistebant cum filiis suis; de filiis Caath, Eman cantor, filius Iohel, filii Samuhel, filii Elchana, filii Geroan, filii Eliel, filii Tho, filii Sub, filii Elchana, filii Maath, filii Masai, filii Elchana, filii Iohel, filii Azariae, filii Sophoniae, filii Thaath, filii Asir, filii Abisaph, filii Chore, filii Saar, filii Caath, filii Levi, filii Israhel, et fratres eius, qui stabant a dextris eius" [1 Chr 6:33–39].

4    Officii tamen illorum auctor extitit David. De qua re dicit Agustinus in libro XVII *De civitate Dei,* capitulo XIIII: "Erat autem David vir in canticis eruditus, qui armoniam musicam non vulgari voluptate, sed fideli voluntate dilexerit, ea Deo suo—qui verus est Deus—mystica rei magnae figuratione servierit. Diversorum enim sonorum rationabilis et moderatus concentus concordi varietate conpac-

5    tam bene ordinatae civitatis insinuat unitatem."✝ Hinc tractent cantores quid significet simphonia eorum; ea ammonent plebem ut in unitate unius Dei cultus perseverent. Etiamsi aliquis surdus affuerit, idipsum statu illorum

further on: "And Asaph sounded with cymbals"; and the priests Banaias and Jaziel sounded continuously with trumpets before the ark of the Lord's covenant. "In that day David made Asaph the chief to give praise to the Lord with his brethren." And again: "And Heman and Idithun sounded the trumpet and played on the cymbals and all kinds of musical instruments to sing praises to God." And again: "And the cantors, the sons of Asaph, stood in their order according to the commandment of David and Asaph and Heman and Idithun, the prophets of the king."

Heman was the first of the cantors, as Chronicles tells us: 3 "And these are they that stood with their sons; of the sons of Caath, Heman a cantor, the son of Joel, the son of Samuel, the son of Elcana, the son of Jeroham, the son of Eliel, the son of Thohu, the son of Suph, the son of Elcana, the son of Mahath, the son of Amasai, the son of Elcana, the son of Johel, the son of Azarias, the son of Sophonias, the son of Thahath, the son of Asir, the son or Abiasaph, the son of Core, the son of Isaar, the son of Caath, the son of Levi, the son of Israel, and his brothers, who stood on his right hand."

David founded their office. Augustine talks about this in 4 *The City of God,* book 17, chapter 14: "But David was a man skilled in song, who loved musical harmony not with vulgar delight, but with faithful will, and who served his God—who is the true God—through a mystical symbol of great meaning. For a reasonable and moderate concord of diverse sounds, with harmonious variation, signifies the united harmony of a well ordered city."† Let the cantors here consider 5 the meaning of their symphony. Through it, they urge the people to persist in the unity of the worship of a single God. And even if a deaf person were present, the cantors would

in choro ordinatissimo insinuant, ut qui auribus capere non possunt unitatem, visu capiant.

6    Porro cantores laudatores Dei sunt, et ad laudem ceteros excitantes. De quo Hieronimus in tractatu Esaiae libro primo: "Et super choros qui in Libro Dierum plenius descri-buntur, Asaph et Idithun et Eman et filii Chore constituti sunt, ut paulatim a sacrificiis victimarum ad laudes Domini transiret religio." Id frequentissime reperitur in Veteri Testamento, ubi eorum officium narratur, opus eorum esse confessionem Domini. Hic versus sepissime cantoribus im-putatur: "Confitemini Domino quoniam bonus, quoniam in
7    aeternum misericordia eius" [Ps 135:1]. Nostri cantores non tenent cymbala, neque lyram, neque cytharam manibus, ne-que caetera genera musicorum, sed corde. Quanto cor maius est corpore, tanto Deo devotius exhibetur quod per cor fit, quam per corpus. Ipsi cantores sunt tuba, ipsi psalterium, ipsi cythara, ipsi tympanum, ipsi chorus, ipsi cordae, ipsi or-ganum, ipsi cymbala.

8    Unde Agustinus in libro Psalmorum novissimi Psalmi: "Idem ipsi sancti sunt in omnibus musicis organis." Et paulo post: "'Laudate Dominum in sanctis eius': Hoc exequitur varie, significans eosdem ipsos sanctos eius. 'Laudate eum in sono tubae,' propter laudis excellentissimam claritatem. 'Laudate eum in psalterio et cithara' [Ps 150:1, 3]. Psalterium est de superioribus laudans Deum, cithara de inferioribus laudans Deum—tamquam de caelestibus et terrestribus, tamquam eum qui fecit caelum et terram. Iam quippe in

make the very same point through their arrangement in the well-ordered choir, such that those who cannot grasp the unity with their ears may grasp it with their sight.

The cantors also praise God, and they inspire others to 6 his praise. Jerome, in the first book of his treatise on Isaiah, about this: "And Asaph and Idithun and Heman and the sons of Core were placed in charge of the choirs that are described more fully in Chronicles, so that gradually, their piety might progress from the sacrifice of victims to the Lord's praises." We often find in the Old Testament that, where the cantors' office is described, their work is the Lord's praise. This verse is very often attributed to the cantors: "Praise the Lord for he is good, for his mercy endures forever." Our cantors hold neither cymbals nor lyre nor cith- 7 ara nor other kinds of musical instruments in their hands, but in their heart. To the degree that the heart is greater than the body, what comes from the heart is offered to God more piously than what comes from the body. The cantors are themselves the trumpet, they are the psaltery, they are the cithara, they are the timbrel, they are the choir, they are the strings, they are the organ, they are the cymbals.

Thus Augustine, in his book on the Psalms, concerning 8 the last Psalm: "These very saints are in all the musical in- struments." And a little later: "'Praise the Lord in his holy places': The psalmist continues, indicating these same saints of his in different ways. 'Praise him with the sound of the trumpet,' because of the great glory of its praise. 'Praise him with psaltery and cithara.' The psaltery praises God from higher things; the cithara praises God from lower things— as it were, for heavenly and earthly things, and praising, so to speak, him who made heaven and earth. For we already

alio Psalmo exposuimus psalterium desuper habere sonorum illud lignum, cui nervorum series, ut meliorem sonum
9  reddat, incumbit; quod lignum cythara inferius habet. 'Laudate eum in tympano et choro' [Ps 150:4]. Tympanum laudat Deum, cum iam in carne mutata nulla est terrenae corruptionis infirmitas — de corio quippe fit tympanum exsiccato atque firmato. Chorus laudat Deum quando eum laudat pa-
10  cata societas. 'Laudate eum in cordis et organo' [Ps 150:4]. Cordas habet et psalterium et cythara, quae superius commemorata sunt; 'organum' autem generale nomen est vasorum omnium musicorum. Quamvis iam obtinuerit consuetudo ut organa proprie dicantur ea quae inflantur follibus; quod genus significatum hic esse non arbitror. Nam cum organum vocabulum Grecum sit, ut dixi, generale omnibus musicis instrumentis, hoc cui folles adhibentur, alio Greci nomine appellant; ut autem organum dicatur, magis Latina et ea vulgaris est consuetudo. Quod ergo ait 'in cordis et organo,' videtur mihi aliquod organum quod cordas habeat
11  significare voluisse. Non enim sola psalteria et cytharae cordas habent, sed quia in psalterio et cythara propter sonum ab inferioribus et superioribus inventum est aliquid, quod secundum hanc distinctionem possit intelligi, aliud nos in ipsis cordis quaerere admonuit, quia ipsae caro sunt, sed iam corruptione liberata. Quibus ideo fortasse addidit organum, non ut singulae sonent, sed ut diversitate concordissima
12  consonent, sicut ordinatur in organo. Habebunt enim etiam tunc sancti differentias suas consonantes, non dissonantes —

explained, in our discussion of another Psalm, that the psaltery has a sound box on top to which a course of strings is affixed, that it may render a better sound. The cithara has this sound box at the bottom. 'Praise him with timbrel and choir.' The timbrel praises God because in its changed flesh, there is now no weakness of earthly corruption—for the timbrel is made from dried and hardened hide. The choir praises God when its peaceful fellowship praises him. 'Praise him with strings and organ.' The psaltery and the cithara have strings, which we described above; 'organ,' however, is a generic term for all musical instruments. Although it is now the practice for those things that are blown into by bellows to be called 'organs,' I do not think this is the sort of instrument meant here. Since the word 'organ' is a general Greek term, as I said, for all musical instruments, the Greeks call instruments that have bellows by another name. To call this sort of instrument an organ is more a Latin usage, and a vulgar one. 'With strings and organ,' therefore, seems to me to be intended to mean the sort of organ that has strings. For it is not only psalteries and citharas that have strings; but since we have found something symbolic in the psaltery and cithara on account of the sound that is made from below and from above—something that can be understood according to this distinction—the psalmist advised us to seek something else in the strings themselves, because they are made of flesh, but flesh that has now been freed from corruption. To these, therefore, he added the organ, perhaps not to indicate that they ring out individually, but to indicate that they resound together in harmonious diversity, as is the design of the organ. For the saints will also have their harmonious, rather than dissonant, differences—

id est consentientes, non dissentientes—sicut fit suavissimus cantus ex diversis quidem, sed non adversis inter se. 'Stella enim a stella differt in claritate; sic et resurrectio mortuorum' [1 Cor 15:41–42]. 'Laudate eum in cymbalis bene sonantibus, laudate eum in cymbalis iubilationis' [Ps 150:5]. Cymbala invicem tanguntur, ut sonent; ideo a quibusdam labiis nostris comparata sunt. Sed melius intellegi puto in cymbalis quodammodo laudare Deum—dum quisque honoratur a proximo, non a se ipso, et invicem honorantes dant laudem Deo."

# 4

# De vestimento cantorum

Primi cantores vestiti erant byssinis, ut Verba Dierum narrant, dicendo: "Tam Levitae quam cantores, id est qui sub Asaph erant et qui sub Eman et qui sub Idithun, filii et fratres eorum, vestiti byssinis, cymbalis et psalteriis et citharis concrepabant" [2 Chr 5:12]. Ex natura byssi possumus intellegere quam proxima sint inter se haec duo, byssus et linum, quo nostri cantores utuntur. Dicit Beda in libro *De tabernaculo et vasis eius:* "Byssus namque, ut sepius commemoratum est, de terra viridis nascitur, sed eruta de

that is, differences in agreement rather than disagreement —as indeed the sweetest song arises from sounds that are diverse, but not adverse, among themselves. 'For star differs from star in glory; so also is the resurrection of the dead.' 'Praise him on high sounding cymbals, praise him on cymbals of joy.' Cymbals are touched together to make sound; some have therefore compared them to our lips. But I think we do better to recognize, in the cymbals, a way of praising God—since each is honored by its neighbor and not by itself, and through their honoring in turn they give praise to God."

<sub>13</sub>

# 4

# On the vestment of the cantors

The first cantors wore byssus, as Chronicles recounts, saying: "Both the Levites and the cantors, that is, they that were under Asaph and they that were under Heman and they that were under Idithun, with their sons and their brethren, clothed with byssus, sounded with cymbals and psalteries and harps." From the nature of byssus we can understand how closely related byssus is to linen, which our cantors use. In his book *On the Tabernacle and its Vessels,* Bede says: "For byssus, as has often been recounted, sprouts green from the earth, but when it has been pulled out of

<sub>2</sub>

terra siccatur, contunditur, coquitur, torquetur, ac magno et longo exercitio ad candidum de viridi producitur colorem. Sic et caro nostra—ut ad virtutem decoremque castitatis perveniat, artis se necesse est ieiuniorum, orationis, vigiliarum et totius continentiae laboribus subigat, quibus naturales et velut ingenitas eius delectationes exsiccare, atque ad eam quam desideramus dignitatem virtutis accedere queamus." Et in alio loco eiusdem: "Quid per byssum nisi candens decore munditiae corporalis castitas designatur?"✝

3 In significatione non discrepat nostrum linum, quo nostri cantores vestiuntur, a bysso. Ipsi enim labores quos supra diximus non sunt candor, sed per eos pervenitur ad candorem. Ac ideo, ut praetulimus, per casulam possumus intellegere ipsos labores, in camisa vero ipsam munditiam carnis quae splendet ante Dominum. Ex nobis ipsis possumus

4 nis quae splendet ante Dominum. Ex nobis ipsis possumus addiscere aliud esse ieiunium, orationes et vigilias, et aliud munditiam carnis. Multi enim ieiunant et orant ac vigilant et—quod gravius est—delinquunt per carnis appetitum. Unde et Hieronimus in tractatu epistolae ad Ephesios: "Quanti enim diligunt Dominum, parati exilia, parati martyria, parati inopiam et omnia pro eo contumeliarum genera sustinere—et nihilo minus carnis passione superantur?"

the ground it is dried, pressed, heated and spun, and through great and long effort it is brought from green to the color white. Our flesh is similar—in order for it to achieve the virtue and beauty of chastity, we have to subdue it with the hard labors of fasting, prayer, vigils and complete continence; through these we are able to dry out its natural and, as it were, inborn desires, and approach the dignity of virtue that we desire." And in another place, the same author: "What is signified by byssus, except corporal chastity, gleaming with the beauty of cleanness?"✝

The linen that our cantors wear does not differ in meaning from byssus. For those works that we described above are not whiteness, but through them we arrive at whiteness. And therefore, as we said above, we can understand the labors themselves through the chasuble, and in the alb, the purity of flesh that gleams before the Lord. We can further learn, from ourselves, that fasting, prayers and vigils are one thing, and purity of the flesh another. For many fast and pray and keep vigils and—more seriously—sin through the appetite of their flesh. Thus Jerome in his treatise on the epistle to the Ephesians: "For how many love the Lord and are prepared to endure exiles, martyrdoms, poverty and all manner of insults on his behalf—and are nevertheless overcome by the passion of the flesh?"

# 5

# De introitu episcopi ad Missam

Officium quod vocatur introitus Missae habet initium a prima antiphona, quae dicitur introitus, et finitur in oratione quae a sacerdote dicitur ante lectionem. Introitus episcopi ad Missam, qui vicarius est Christi, ipsius adventum nobis ad memoriam reducit et populi adunationem ad eum, sive per suam praedicationem, sive suorum praedicatorum. Introitus episcopi celebratur usque ad sessionem suam; tangit enim ex parte officium quod Christus corporaliter gessit in terra, sive discipuli eius, usquequo ascendit ad sedem paternam.

2  Hoc officium addidit Missae Caelestinus. Ille, ut in *Gestis pontificalibus* continetur: "Constituit ut Psalmi David centum quinquaginta ante sacrificium psallerentur, antiphonatim ex omnibus, quod ante non fiebat, nisi tantum epistola beati Apostoli Pauli recitabatur et sanctum Evangelium, et

3  sic Missa celebrabatur."✝ Quod nos ita intellegimus—ut ex omnibus Psalmis excerperet antiphonas quae psallerentur in officio Missae; nam antea inchoabatur Missa a lectione. Qui mos adhuc retinetur in vigiliis Paschae et in vigiliis Pentecostes. Christus Filius Dei, qui elegit suos ante constitutionem mundi, ut essent sancti et immaculati, misit praecones in Veteri Testamento (ut de aliis taceam), qui suavitate et modulatione vocis populum suum congregarent

# 5

# On the entrance of the bishop at Mass

The office that is called the introit of the Mass begins with the first antiphon, which is called the introit, and ends with the prayer recited by the priest before the reading. The entrance at Mass of the bishop, who is Christ's vicar, calls to mind Christ's coming and the union of the people with him, whether through his preaching or the preaching of his preachers. The entrance of the bishop lasts until he takes his seat; this touches in part on the service that Christ and his disciples performed bodily on earth, until he ascended to the paternal throne.

Celestine added this office to the Mass. As we read in the *Deeds of the Bishops:* "He established that the 150 Psalms of David be sung before the sacrifice, antiphonally out of all. This had not been done before; only a letter of blessed Paul the Apostle was recited, together with the holy Gospel, and Mass was celebrated in that way."✝ We understand this as follows—that he excerpted antiphons from all the Psalms that were then sung for the office of Mass, for previously Mass began with a reading. This custom is still retained on the vigils of Easter and on the vigils of Pentecost. Christ the Son of God, who chose his own before the creation of the world, that they might be holy and immaculate, sent heralds in the Old Testament (among other things), who gathered his people through the sweet harmony of their voice to the

4   ad unius Dei cultum. Quorum auctor fuit David, de quo Agustinum praetulimus dicentem in superioribus: "Erat autem David vir in canticis eruditus, qui armoniam musicam non vulgari voluptate, sed fideli voluntate dilexit," et reliqua.✝ Post eum Eman, Asaph, Ethan et Idithun, de quibus iam praedictum est, et quid significet eorum psalterium, cythara, tympanum, cordae, organum et cetera. Haec omnia sunt in opere et cantu.

5     Unde mos inolevit ut non sedeatur in ecclesia, quamdiu praesens officium agitur, quoniam operi et labori Christi sive praeconum eius deputatur, quo praedestinati ad cultum unius Dei vocantur. De quo statu dicit libellus qui inscribitur *De ordine Romano:* "Pontifex incipit *Gloria in excelsis Deo,* si tempus fuerit, et non sedet ante quam dicant post orati-

6   onem primam: 'Amen.'" Quicumque enim Deo attrahitur, delectatione attrahitur, non necessitate. Unde Agustinus in tractatu super Iohannem, sermone XXIII: "Porro, si poetae dicere licuit: 'Trahit sua quemque voluptas'—non necessitas sed voluptas, non obligatio sed delectatio—quanto fortius nos dicere debemus trahi hominem ad Christum qui delectatur veritate, delectatur beatitudine, delectatur iustitia,

7   delectatur sempiterna vita?"✝ Ac ideo cantorum vox dulcis huic operi dedita est, ut sua dulcedine idonea sit hortari populum ad confitendum Domino. Ita enim scriptum est in libro Paralipemenon: "Igitur cunctis pariter, et tubis et voce, cymbalis, et organis, et diversi generis musicorum concinentibus, et vocem in sublime tollentibus, longe sonitus auditur,

worship of the one God. Their founder was David, about   4
whom we quoted Augustine above, saying: "But David was a
man skilled in song, who loved musical harmony not with
vulgar delight, but with faithful will," and so on.✝ After him
came Heman, Asaph, Ethan and Idithun, whom we discussed above, together with what their psaltery, cithara,
timbrel, strings, organ and so forth signify. All these things
are in their work and their song.

Thus the custom developed that no one should sit in   5
church until this office is finished, because it is reckoned as
the work and labor of Christ and his heralds, by which the
predestined are called to the worship of one God. The manual entitled *On the Roman Order* mentions the fact that we
stand: "The pontiff begins with *Gloria in excelsis Deo,* if it is
the time, and he does not sit before they say 'Amen' after
the first prayer." Now whoever is drawn to God is drawn by   6
pleasure, not necessity. Thus Augustine in his treatise on
John, sermon 23: "Furthermore, if it was appropriate for the
poet to say: 'Each man is pulled by his own desire'—not
necessity but will, not obligation but pleasure—how much
more powerfully should we assert that the man who is pulled
to Christ is enticed by truth, enticed by blessedness, enticed
by justice, enticed by eternal life?"✝ And so the sweet voice   7
of cantors is devoted to this task, that with its sweetness it
may be fit to call the people to confess to the Lord. For it
was written in the book of Chronicles as follows: "So when
they all sounded together, both with trumpets and voice,
and cymbals, and organs, and with the harmonies of diverse
kinds of musical instruments, and lifted up their voice on
high, the sound was heard afar off, so that when they began

33

ut cum Dominum laudare coepissent et dicerent: Confitemini Domino quoniam bonus, quoniam in aeternum misericordia eius, impleretur domus Dei nube. Nec possent sacerdotes stare et ministrare propter caliginem, compleverat
enim gloria Domini domum Domini" [2 Chr 5:13–14].

8 Praeconibus psallentibus, quando placuit Christo, domino psallentium, venire, ascendit super currum suum et
venit in mundum, disponere eundem currum per loca
congrua. De quo curru dicit psalmista: "Currus Dei decem
milium multiplex" [Ps 67:18]. Unde iterum Agustinus in
Psalmo XLVII: "Multitudinem sanctorum atque fidelium,
qui portando Deum fiunt quodammodo currus Dei, signavit
hoc nomine. Hanc inmanendo et regendo perducit in finem,
tamquam currum suum, velut in locum aliquem destina-
9 tum."✝ Multitudo decem milium sanctorum est in ordinibus ecclesiasticis et in auditoribus eorum. Septem gradus
sunt ordinatorum, octavus cantorum, nonus et decimus
auditorum utriusque sexus. Milium additur ad insinuandam
perfectionem eorum.

10 Veniente Domino, ducit secum prophetas, sapientes et
scribas. Hos in Evangelio promittit se mittere ad invitan-
dum populum: "Ecce ego," inquit, "mittam ad vos prophetas
et sapientes et scribas" [Matt 23:34], et reliqua. Diaconi in
loco prophetarum sunt, qui adnuntiant ex Evangelio futuram vitam. Subdiaconi in loco sapientum, qui sciunt ordinate vasa Domini disponere, et quod primum ferendum sit
quodque posterius. Acolyti in loco scribarum, qui accendunt
corda fidelium ex scriptura sacra.

to praise the Lord and to say: Confess to the Lord for he is good, for his mercy endures for ever, the house of God was filled with a cloud. Nor could the priests stand and minister by reason of the cloud, for the glory of the Lord had filled the house of the Lord."

With the psalmists as his heralds, when it pleased Christ, 8 the lord of the psalmists, to come, he climbed upon his chariot and came into the world, to station this same chariot at fitting places. The psalmist speaks about this chariot: "The chariot of God is many tens of thousands." Thus, again, Augustine on Psalm 47: "With this term, he indicated a multitude of saints and faithful who, by bearing God, become in some way God's chariot. By remaining within and ruling this multitude, he drives them to his goal, as if he were driving his chariot to some prearranged location."✝ There is a mul- 9 titude of ten thousand saints in the ecclesiastical orders and their listeners. There are seven ranks of ordained clergy, an eighth rank of cantors, and a ninth and tenth rank of listeners of both genders. A thousand is added to indicate their perfection.

When the Lord comes, he brings prophets, wise men and 10 scribes with him. In the Gospel he promised that he would send them to summon the people: "Behold, therefore," he said, "I will send to you prophets and wise men and scribes," and so on. The deacons, who tell of the life to come through the Gospel, play the role of the prophets. The subdeacons, who know how to arrange the Lord's vessels in good order, and what should be brought first and what later, play the role of the wise men. And the acolytes, who ignite the hearts of the faithful through sacred scripture, play the role of the scribes.

11    Praevenit in turibulo thymiama, quod significat corpus Christi plenum odore bono. Hoc enim corpus primo necesse est praedicari in omnibus gentibus. Unde Paulus dicebat ad rudes Corinthios: "Nihil me iudicavi scire inter vos, nisi Christum Iesum, et hunc crucifixum" [1 Cor 2:2]. Dein ferantur candelabra, ut super fundamentum iam posita luceat lux praedicatorum coram hominibus. Iam eos inluminatos sequantur subdiaconi, ut possit praedicatorum ordo dicere: "Sapientiam loquimur inter perfectos" [1 Cor 2:6].

12    Evangelium illis iungatur, in quo est declarata perfectio: "Si vis," inquit, "perfectus esse, vade, vende omnia" [Matt 19:21], et reliqua. Episcopus et sibi coniuncti Evangelium sequantur, iuxta illud Evangelicum: "Si quis vult post me venire, abneget semet ipsum et tollat crucem suam et sequatur me" [Matt 16:24; Luke 9:23]. Ante oculos habeat sepissime episcopus quod in mente semper oportet retinere.

13    Septem prophetae sive diaconi sunt in ministerio, quia septempliciter dividitur scriptura inter Novum Testamentum et Vetus, quae Evangelio ministrat. Episcopus in medio, vicarius Christi, quasi Evangelium, habet in Novo Testamento ministros historiae, ut Lucam in Actibus Apostolorum; habet ministros in septem epistolis canonicis; habet ministros in XIIII epistolis Pauli; habet ministros in Apocalypsi; in Veteri Testamento, in lege, prophetis et Psalmis. Unde scriptum est in Evangelio Lucae: "Quae scripta sunt in lege Moysi et prophetis et Psalmis de me" [Luke 24:44].

14    At si quinque fuerint, quinque ministros librorum demonstrat Evangelio ministrare. Episcopus in medio, quasi

The incense in its censer leads the way; this signifies 11
Christ's body suffused with a pleasing odor. First it is necessary that this body be preached to all nations. Thus Paul said
to the Corinthians, who were new in their faith: "I judged
not myself to know anything among you, but Jesus Christ,
and him crucified." Then let the candlesticks be brought
in, that the light of the preachers now placed upon a foundation may shine before men. Now let the subdeacons follow those who have been illuminated, that the order of
preachers may be able to say: "We speak wisdom among the
perfect." Let the Gospel join them, where perfection is de- 12
scribed: "If you will be perfect, go sell everything," and so
on. Let the bishop and his companions follow the Gospel,
according to that Gospel verse: "If any man will come after
me, let him deny himself and take up his cross and follow
me." Let the bishop always have before his eyes that which
he should always keep in mind.

There are seven prophets, or deacons, in ministry, be- 13
cause the scripture that ministers to the Gospel is divided
sevenfold between the New Testament and the Old. The
bishop in the middle, Christ's vicar, is like the Gospel; he
has historical ministers in the New Testament, such as Luke
in the Acts of the Apostles; he has ministers in the seven ca-
nonical epistles; he has ministers in the fourteen letters of
Paul; he has ministers in Revelation; and also in the Old Testament, in the law, the prophets and the Psalms. Thus it is
written in the Gospel of Luke: "Which things are written in
the law of Moses and in the prophets and in the Psalms concerning me."

But should there be five deacons, this shows that five 14
books minister to the Gospel as servants. The bishop in the

Evangelium, habet in Novo Testamento primum ordinem
praedicatorum historiae; secundum epistolarum; tertium
prophetarum, ut est Apocalypsis; in Veteri Testamento,
unum legis et alterum prophetiae. Haec duo Philippus in
Iohannis Evangelio ad medium deducit dicens: "Quem
scripsit Moyses in lege et prophetae, invenimus Iesum fi-
lium Ioseph a Nazareth" [John 1:45].

15    At si fuerint tres, tres ministrationes trium librorum.
Fons omnis sapientiae, Evangelium in medio, duos libros in
Novo Testamento, scilicet epistolarum et prophetarum. Liber Actus Apostolorum qui mittitur Theophilo, epistolis
coniungitur: ex una re est epistola quia mittitur alicui homini; ex altera, quia historiam tantum continet, stat per se.
In Veteri Testamento, unum. Omnis scriptura apud veteres
lex nominatur, sicut de Psalmis dicitur: "Et in lege vestra
scriptum est: Quia ego dixi: Dii estis" [John 10:34; Ps 81:6].

16    Unde Agustinus memoratus in tractatu super Iohannem sermone XLIIII: "'Legem' appellavit Dominus generaliter, omnes illas scripturas, quamvis alibi specialiter dicat 'legem,' a
prophetis eam distinguens, sicuti est: 'Lex et prophetae usque ad Iohannem prophetaverunt' [Matt 11:13], et: 'In his
duobus praeceptis tota lex pendet et prophetae' [Matt
22:40]. Aliquando autem in tria divisit easdem scripturas,
ubi ait: 'Oportebat impleri omnia quae scripta sunt in lege
et prophetis et Psalmis de me' [Luke 24:44]."✝

middle, like the Gospel, has a first order of preachers of history in the New Testament; a second order of epistles; a
third order of prophets, as in Revelation; and in the Old Testament, he has one book of law and another of prophecy.
Philip brought these last two to the fore in the Gospel of
John, saying: "We have found him of whom Moses in the
law and the prophets did write, Jesus the son of Joseph from
Nazareth."

But should there be three deacons, that shows three min- 15
istrations of three books. The source of all wisdom, the
Gospel in the middle, has two books from the New Testament, namely the epistles and the prophets. The Acts of the
Apostles, which is directed to Theophilus, is joined to the
epistles; on the one hand it is a letter because it is sent to
someone; on the other, because it contains only history, it
stands on its own. In the Old Testament, there is one book.
Among the ancients all scripture is called law, as is said of
the Psalms: "And is it written in your law: For I said: You are
gods." Thus the aforementioned Augustine, in his treatise 16
on John, sermon 44: "The Lord called all scriptures generally 'law,' though elsewhere he speaks of 'law' more specifically, to distinguish it from the prophets, as in: 'The law and
the prophets prophesied until John,' and: 'On these two
commandments depend the whole law and the prophets.'
But sometimes he divided these same scriptures in three, as
when he said: 'All things must needs be fulfilled which are
written in the law of Moses and in the prophets and in the
Psalms concerning me.'"✝

17    Si unus fuerit, unum praeceptum dilectionis ostendit, ut Apostolus ad Galathas: "Omnis enim lex in uno sermone impletur: Diliges proximum tuum sicut te ipsum" [Gal 5:14; Lev 19:18].

18    Ministerium prophetae est ex memoratis libris Evangelicam veritatem approbare; ut moderate prophetia disponatur, habeat ante se subdiaconorum sapientiam, scilicet ut congruo tempore prophetent et ita ordinate, ut possit capi ab auditoribus quod dicitur. Acolytorum lux doctorum opus expleat, ut in manifestam lucem perducat memoratos libros. Qui enim Christum praecedit ad aliquem locum, ut Evangelium praedicet, ita vero sapienter debet praecedere, ut prosit auditoribus et explanet obscuros sensus scripturarum.

19    Postquam transit vicarius Christi in medio adolescentularum tympanistriarum [Ps 67:26] (de quibus Agustinus qui supra: "In ministerio," inquit, "honorabili, nam ita sunt in medio ministri praepositi ecclesiarum novarum; hoc enim est 'adolescentularum,' carne edomita Deum laudantium"✝)—sapientia, id est subdiaconi, vadunt in medio adolescentularum tympanistriarum, ut doceant quem laudare debeant tympanistriae.

20    Tympanistriae cantores sunt; ministerium cantorum laudem resonat, ut idem in Psalmo LXXII: "Qui enim cantat laudem non solum laudat, sed etiam hilariter laudat; qui cantat laudem non solum laudat, sed et amat eum quem cantat."✝ Notum est quid veteres cantores in lege amabant. De quorum persona dicebat David: "Ut iumentum factus

Should there be one deacon, he reveals the one com-  17
mandment of love, as the Apostle wrote to the Galatians:
"For all the law is fulfilled in one word: You shall love your
neighbor as yourself."

The prophet's ministry is to confirm the truth of the  18
Gospel through the aforementioned books; that his prophecy may be issued in good measure, let the deacon have before him the wisdom of the subdeacons, namely to prophesy
at the right time and in good order, that what is said can
be grasped by the listeners. Let the light of the acolytes fulfill the work of the teachers, that it may bring the aforementioned books into the bright light. For he who precedes
Christ to preach the Gospel somewhere should go with
enough wisdom to benefit his listeners and explain the hidden senses of the scriptures.

After Christ's vicar passes through in the midst of young  19
maidens playing timbrels (about whom Augustine says, in
the same work as above: "They do an honorable service, for
the ministers placed in charge of new churches are in the
middle like they are; and this is the meaning of 'young maidens,' who praise God after taming their flesh"✝)—wisdom,
or the subdeacons, go forth in the midst of the young maidens playing timbrels, to teach the timbrel players whom
they should praise.

The timbrel players are the cantors; the ministry of the  20
cantors resounds with praise, as the same author discusses
with respect to Psalm 72: "For he who sings praise does not
only praise, but also praises joyfully; he who sings praise
does not only praise, but also loves the one he sings about."✝
We know what the ancient cantors loved under the law.
David spoke in their guise: "I am become as a beast before

41

sum apud te" [Ps 72:23] — scilicet ut liberos haberent, opibus habundarent, honore fruerentur et sanitate gauderent. Christo homine novo veniente, cor eorum mutari oportebat ad meliora. Sapientia subdiaconorum innovat eos, ut qui unum antea tantum Deum dicebant, non in tribus personis, dicant nunc: "Gloria Patri et Filio et Spiritui Sancto."

21     Sed expectandum est, usque dum id fiat quod precatur sponsa in Canticis Canticorum: "Osculetur me osculo oris sui" [Song 1:1]. Scitis, dicente Apostolo, Christum semet ipsum exinanivisse se et formam servi accepisse [Phil 2:7]. Quapropter, postquam praesentatus est ecclesiae, inclinatus stat usque ad impletionem suae humilitatis, in qua "factus"

22 est Patri "obediens usque ad mortem" [Phil 3:8]. In ipsa inclinatione dat pacem ministris qui a dextris levaque sunt. Ipse est enim pax per quam reconciliatur ecclesia Deo, sive de Novo Testamento, sive de Veteri. Ipse dextruxit medium parietem inimicitiarum, fecit utrumque unum; pacem dedit his qui longe et pacem his qui prope [Eph 2:14–17; Isa 57:19]. Eandem pacem offert cantoribus qui retro stant, adimplens quae dixit discipulis: "Pacem meam do vobis, pacem meam relinquo vobis" [John 14:27]. Praesentibus dat; absentibus, sive Veteris Testamenti sive Novi, relinquit. Hoc est quod solemus dicere.

23     Innuit episcopus cantori. Quo facto, sapientia Dei, quasi adventu subdiaconorum, intellegunt cantores, mutati iam de Veteri, Trinitatem Deum laudare, et dicunt: "Gloria Patri

you"—namely, in order to have children, abound with riches, delight in honor and rejoice in health. Upon the arrival of Christ, the new man, their heart had to be moved to better things. The wisdom of the subdeacons renews them, so that those who previously spoke of only one God, and not of three persons, may now say: "Glory be to the Father and to the Son and to the Holy Spirit."

But we should wait for this until what the bride begs for 21 in the Song of Songs comes to pass: "Let him kiss me with the kiss of his mouth." You know, as the Apostle says, that Christ emptied himself and took the form of a servant. Thus, after the bishop has been brought to the church, he stands and bows until his act of humility, in which he was "made obedient" to the Father "unto death," is accomplished. In the midst of this bow he gives the kiss of peace 22 to the ministers who are at his right and left. And this is the peace through which the church is reconciled to God, whether in the New Testament or the Old. It destroyed that middle wall of hostilities, and made both one; it gave peace to those who were far away and peace to those who were near. He offers the same kiss of peace to the cantors who stand behind him, fulfilling what he said to his disciples: "My peace I give unto you, my peace I leave with you." He gives it to those who are present; he leaves it with those who are absent, whether in the Old Testament or the New. This is what we are accustomed to say.

The bishop nods to the cantor. After he has done this, the 23 cantors progress from the Old Testament and know through God's wisdom—as it were, through the arrival of the subdeacons—to praise God as the Trinity, and they say: "Glory

et Filio et Spiritui Sancto." Diaconi, quasi chorus propheta-rum, stant cum eo humiliati et dicunt: "Domine, doce nos orare" [Luke 11:1]. Ex spiritu prophetiae, id est spiritu reve-lationis, cognoscunt non se posse habere affectum in orati-one ad Patrem, nisi ab eodem unigenito Filio eius, "qui est in sinu Patris" [ John 1:18], edoceantur.

24   Quod separatim diximus de diaconis et subdiaconis et acolytis, de unoquoque discipulo Christi intellegimus; sed propter quosdam profectus affectuum, unius praedicatoris opus distinguitur per multiplices ordines. Ceterum pro-pheta diaconus, sapiens et scriba; sapiens subdiaconus, pro-pheta et scriba; scriba acolytus, propheta et sapiens.

25   Docet Christus orare discipulos, quapropter cantores — id est laudatores adventus Domini — adnuntiant tempus esse ut corda patrum convertantur in filios [Mal 4:6]. Sicut Abraham tres angelos vidit [Gen 18] et tamen unum Deum adoravit et credidit Trinitatem in unitate, sic et modo filios Abrahae oporteat credere et dicunt: "Sicut erat in principio et nunc et semper," et reliqua. Ecce messis multa, de qua di-citur in Evangelio: "Messis quidem multa, operarii autem pauci. Rogate ergo dominum messis, ut mittat operarios in messem suam" [Matt 9:37–38; Luke 10:2].

26   Christus, dominus messis, mittit operarios in messem suam, ut scriptum est in Luca: "Post haec autem designavit Dominus et alios septuaginta duos, et misit illos binos ante faciem suam in omnem civitatem et locum quo erat ipse

be to the Father and to the Son and to the Holy Spirit." The deacons, like a choir of prophets, stand humbled with the bishop and say: "Lord, teach us to pray." Through the spirit of prophecy, or the spirit of revelation, they understand that they cannot have influence in their prayers to the Father unless they are taught by his only-begotten Son, "who is in the bosom of the Father."

What we said individually about the deacons and sub- 24 deacons and acolytes, we understand as relating to every disciple of Christ; but because of the various progressions of its influence, the work of each preacher is distinguished through diverse ranks. Otherwise the deacon is a prophet, a wise man and a scribe; the subdeacon is a wise man, a prophet and a scribe; the acolyte is a scribe, a prophet and a wise man.

Christ teaches his disciples to pray, and so the cantors— 25 that is, those who praise the coming of the Lord—announce that the time has come for the hearts of the fathers to turn toward their children. Just as Abraham saw three angels and yet adored one God and credited the Trinity in this unity, so also should the sons of Abraham now believe and say: "As it was in the beginning and now and ever," and so forth. Behold the great harvest, about which it is said in the Gospel: "The harvest indeed is great, but the laborers are few. Pray therefore to the Lord of the harvest, that he send forth laborers into his harvest."

Christ, the lord of the harvest, sends laborers to his har- 26 vest, as it is written in Luke: "And after these things the Lord appointed also another seventy-two, and he sent them two and two before his face into every city and place where

45

venturus" [Luke 10:1]. Eodem modo vicissim duo et duo diaconi altrinsecus vadunt osculari latera altaris. Per osculum
eorum demonstratur pax quam eis commendavit Dominus,
dicens: "In quamcumque domum intraveritis, primum dicite: Pax huic domui" [Luke 10:5]. Altare vel, alio modo,
mensa quae osculatur, corda electorum significat, sive in
Hierusalem sive extra Hierusalem. Unde Gregorius in libro
*De aedificio templi:* "Corda itaque sanctorum mensae Dei
27  sunt."✝ Postea revertuntur ad episcopum. Sic, et Evangelio
dicente, legimus fecisse missos illo tempore: "Et reversi,"
inquit, "apostoli nuntiaverunt illi quae fecerunt" [Luke
9:10]. Et in sequentibus: "Et factum est, cum solus esset
orans, erant cum illo et discipuli" [Luke 9:18]. Sunt discipuli
cum Christo; Christus solus orat.

28  Dein, postquam tempus advenit, praeconii Dominicae
passionis, cantores, ut ad memoriam reducant Christi novissimam humiliationem, dicunt versum de psalterio. Psalterium ex inferiori parte percutitur, et ex superiore parte habet in quo reboat. Sic et opus passionis Christi ab inferiore
parte habet percussuram, a superiore parte dulcedinem resurrectionis, quae resultat longe lateque per ora praedicatorum.

29  Adimpleto tempore praeconatus praeconum, vadit Christus ad Hierusalem, in qua est altare, quod osculatur in medio, quoniam ipse est de quo dicitur in Canticis Canticorum: "Media caritate constravit propter filias Hierusalem"
30  [Song 3:10]. Vicarius Christi haec omnia agit in memoriam
primi adventus Christi. Osculatur altare, ut ostendat adventum Christi fuisse Hierusalem; osculatur Evangelium, in
quo duo populi ad pacem redeunt, ut et nos eos diligamus

he himself was to come." In the same way, the deacons go two by two in turn to kiss both sides of the altar. Their kiss signifies the peace that the Lord entrusted to them, saying, "Into whatsoever house you enter, first say: Peace be to this house." The altar, or, in another sense, the table that they kiss signifies the hearts of the elect, whether inside Jerusalem or outside Jerusalem. Thus Gregory in his book *On the Construction of the Temple:* "The hearts of the saints are thus the tables of God."✝ Afterward they return to the bishop. 27 We read in the Gospel that those who had been sent did the same in that time: "And the apostles," it says, "when they returned, told him all they had done." And in a subsequent passage: "And it came to pass, as he was alone praying, his disciples also were with him." The disciples are with Christ; Christ prays alone.

Then, after the time has come, the cantors, as heralds of 28 the Lord's passion, say a verse from the Psalter to commemorate Christ's final humiliation. The psaltery is struck on its lower part, and from its upper part it has a means of resounding. So too does the work of Christ's passion present a beating on the lower part, and on its upper part the sweetness of resurrection, which resounds far and wide through the mouths of preachers.

After the time that the heralds announced has been ful- 29 filled, Christ goes to Jerusalem, where there is an altar that he kisses on its center, because he is the one about whom it is said in the Song of Songs: "He covered the middle with charity for the daughters of Jerusalem." The vicar of 30 Christ does all of this in memory of Christ's first coming. He kisses the altar to show that Christ's coming occurred in Jerusalem; he kisses the Gospel, in which the two peoples

47

qui disiuncti erant a nobis. Oscula vicarii Christi osculo Christi congruunt. Sicut Christus primo osculum his praebuit qui primo crediderunt, sic episcopus ministris primis. Et sicut Christus his se offert ultro, quibus dicit: "Missus sum ad oves quae perierant domus Israel" [Matt 15:24]—sic se episcopus altari, per quod recolimus Hierusalem, in qua Dominus "suos dilexit usque in finem" secundum Iohannem [John 13:1]. Et sicut Christus asscivit sibi postea gentilem populum, qui reconciliatus est Deo in Novo Testamento, sic episcopus Evangelium, quod est Novum Testamentum.

31    Remanet Evangelium in altari ab initio officii usque dum a ministro assumatur ad legendum, quia ab initio adventus Christi Evangelica doctrina resonuit in Hierusalem, et inde exivit ad publicum, sicut scriptum est: "De Sion exivit lex, et verbum Domini de Hierusalem" [Isa 2:3]

32    Dein transit episcopus ad dexteram altaris. Liquet omnibus quod semper Christus egit dexteram vitam postquam resurrexit a mortuis. Diaconi postea stant in ordine; quibus ille praedixit: "Si quis vult post me venire, abneget semet ipsum, et tollat crucem suam et sequatur me" [Matt 16:24]. Qui post eum stant, firmati sunt, ut eum sequantur usque ad

33    mortem et cum eo transeant ad aeternam vitam. Maior pars in dextera parte stat, et minor in sinistra. Quid numerus illorum significet, praedictum est. Ad insinuandum nobis libere Vetus Testamentum legere et tenere (ut Apostolus: "Omnia autem probate . . ." [1 Thess 5:21]), aliqua pars ministrorum in sinistra parte stat, per quam temporalis benedictio designatur. Certe et nostra ecclesia utrumque petit ad Dominum, et temporalem benedictionem et aeternam; temporalem petimus, quando precamur ut Deus conservet dominos

return to peace, that we too may love those who had been separated from us. The kisses of Christ's vicar accord with Christ's kiss. Just as Christ first offered his kiss to those who first believed, so does the bishop kiss his ministers first. And just as Christ offers himself freely to those about whom he says: "I was sent to the sheep that are lost of the house of Israel"—so does the bishop offer himself to the altar, through which we recall Jerusalem, where the Lord "loved his own unto the end," according to John. And just as Christ afterward received the gentiles to himself, who were reconciled to God in the New Testament, so does the bishop receive the Gospel, which is the New Testament.

The Gospel remains on the altar from the start of the office until it is taken up by the minister for reading, because Gospel teaching resounded in Jerusalem from the beginning of Christ's coming, and from there it went out to the people, as it is written: "The law went forth from Zion, and the word of the Lord from Jerusalem." 31

Then the bishop crosses to the right side of the altar. It is clear to all that Christ always led a rightward life after he rose from the dead. Thereafter the deacons stand in order; he preached to them: "If any man will come after me, let him deny himself, and take up his cross and follow me." Those who stand after him are strengthened to follow him unto death and pass over with him to eternal life. The larger group stands on the right, the smaller group on the left. We said above what their number signifies. To invite us to read and hold the Old Testament boldly (as the Apostle says: "But prove all things . . ."), one part of the ministers stands on the left side; through them, temporal blessing is signified. And our church of course asks the Lord for both temporal and 32

33

nostros, filios eorum, fructus terrae et pacem in terra nostra; at aeternam, quando iustitiam, sapientiam et caritatem, et cetera.

34     Inter haec omnia acolyti stant, et tenent cereos in manibus. Quid aliud significat, nisi unumquemque doctorem debere habere in manibus doctrinam suam, ut magis studeat opere docere quam verbis?

# 6

## De *Kyrie eleison*

Hoc opere completo, id est adunato per praedicationem Christi populo Dei ex magna parte (in quo cantores, id est praedicatores, magno certamine laboraverunt), ne aliqua praesumptio inutilis subripiat corda eorum, hortatur eos Dominus dicere: "Dicite: Servi inutiles sumus" [Luke 17:10]. Unde Beda in tractatu super Lucam: "Servi inutiles sumus, quia 'non sunt condignae passiones huius temporis ad superventuram gloriam quae revelabitur in nobis' [Rom 8:18]. Et alibi: 'Qui coronat te in miseratione et misericordia' [Ps 102:4]. Non ait: In meritis et operibus tuis, quia cuius misericordia praevenimur, ut humiliter Deo serviamus, eius

eternal blessing. We seek temporal blessing when we pray that God preserve our lords, their sons, the fruit of the earth and peace in our land; but we seek eternal blessing when we pray for justice, wisdom and charity and the like.

Among all these happenings, the acolytes stand and hold 34 the candles in their hands. What does this signify, if not that every teacher should have his teaching at hand, to strive to teach more through his work than his words?

# 6

# On the *Kyrie eleison*

When this work has been completed, that is when the greater part of God's people has been united through Christ's preaching (a task over which the cantors, or the preachers, labored with great effort), the Lord encourages them to say: "Say: We are unprofitable servants," lest any useless presumption steal away their hearts. Thus Bede in his treatise on Luke: "We are unprofitable servants, because 'the sufferings of this time are not worthy to be compared with the glory to come that shall be revealed in us.' And elsewhere: 'Who crowns you with mercy and compassion.' He did not say: With your merits and works, because his mercy precedes us, that we may serve God humbly; and we are

munere coronamur, ut sublimiter cum illo regnemus. Quod debuimus facere, fecimus re vera. Debuimus, quia qui non venit ministrari, sed ministrare, debitores sibi nos fecit, ne nostris videlicet operibus confidentes, sed de eius semper examine paventes, cum propheta dicamus: 'Quid retribua-

2 mus Domino?' [Ps 115:2]"+ Ac ideo dicant cantores: "Kyrie eleison: Domine Pater, miserere; Christe eleison: Miserere, qui nos redemisti sanguine tuo." Et iterum: "Kyrie eleison: Domine Spiritus Sancte, miserere."

3 Potest et simpliciter intellegi de *Kyrie eleison* necessario constitutum esse a praeceptoribus ecclesiae, ut cantores post finitam antiphonam deprecentur Domini misericordiam, quae deprimat inanem iactantiam quae solet sequi cantores. Habent enim quandam exultationem propter egregiam compositionem melodiarum, et non humiliationem lectionis, qua inluminamur ad studium humilitatis. Qua de re possunt fallaciter decipi per philosophiam et inanem fallaciam secundum traditionem hominum [Col 2:8]. Ubi est vera philosophia, non sequitur inanis fallacia; ubi est pomposa doctrina, sequitur iactantia animi.

4 Et alio modo: Ante omnem orationem specialem sacerdotum necesse est praecedere misericordiam Domini, propter tres causas quae mihi in promptu occurrunt. Una est, ut serenetur mens sacerdotis ad ea intendenda quae ore dicit; altera, ut dignus sit loqui Deo, quantum ad naturam humanam pertinet; tertia, quod si, tedio aliquo corporali affectus, spiritus sine mente oraverit, Dominus non in furore suo respiciat super illum, sed in iudicio misericordiae.

crowned by his favor, that we may reign with him on high. What we were required to do, we did in fact. We were required, because he who did not come to be served, but to serve, made us his debtors, lest we trust in our works while ever fearing his examination, and join the prophet in saying: 'What shall we render to the Lord?'"✝ And so let the cantors say: "Kyrie eleison: Lord Father, have mercy; Christe eleison: You who have redeemed us with your blood, have mercy." And again: "Kyrie eleison: Lord Holy Spirit, have mercy." 2

We can also understand that the *Kyrie eleison* was established simply out of necessity by those in charge of our church, that the cantors might beg the Lord's mercy after finishing the antiphon, to suppress the empty vanity that often accompanies cantors. For they have a certain exultation in the surpassing arrangement of their melodies, and they do not have the lowliness of the reading, through which we are enlightened to strive for humility. For this reason they can be falsely deceived through philosophy and empty artifice according to the tradition of men. Where there is true philosophy, empty deception does not follow; where there is pompous teaching, boasting of the spirit follows. 3

And in another sense: The Lord's mercy must precede each of the priests' private prayers for three reasons that readily occur to me: One is so that the priest's mind may be made calm to attend to those things that he speaks with his mouth; a second is so that he may be worthy to address God, insofar as that is possible for human nature; and a third is so that, if he is afflicted with some bodily nuisance and the breath prays without the mind, the Lord may look down upon him not in anger, but in the judgment of mercy. 4

5 Oportet ut praecedat aliquid tale quod repellat redundantes cogitationes a mente, quae accidunt visu, auditu ceterisque sensibus, ut in oratione mens sola invisibilia cogitet, quoniam invisibili loquitur. Ac ideo in omnibus peractis officiis sequitur *Kyrie eleison* ante orationem Dominicam, ut est in Matutinali et Vespertinali synaxi. Nam quod nos Galli in finitis Psalmis nocturnalibus solemus cantare orationem Dominicam, Romana ecclesia praetermittit.

## 7

## De cereis

Dicentibus cantoribus *Kyrie eleison,* acolyti e manibus ponunt cereos in terram, altrinsecus et unum in medio, quoniam post peracta bona opera ad tantam humilitatem nos deducit Spiritus Sanctus—cuius lumen signatur lumine cereorum, qui superbis resistit et humilibus dat gratiam, ut vere nos cognoscamus esse cinerem et pulverem. Quo lumine inluminatus est patriarcha Abraham, quando post locutionem Domini ad se factam dixit: "Quia semel coepi, loquar ad Dominum meum, cum sim pulvis et cinis" [Gen 18:27]. Cereus in medio stans eum designat qui dixit: "Ubi duo vel tres congregati fuerint in nomine meo, in medio

Something that drives from the mind superfluous thoughts, 5 which occur through sight, hearing and the other senses, should come first, so that in prayer the mind may contemplate only the unseen, because it is speaking to the unseen. And thus, near the end of all our offices, the *Kyrie eleison* precedes the Lord's prayer, as during the gathering for Matins and Vespers. For the Roman church omits the Lord's prayer that we Gauls are accustomed to sing after our nightly psalmody.

# 7

# On candles

As the cantors say the *Kyrie eleison,* the acolytes place the candles on the ground with one in the middle and one on either side, because the Holy Spirit—whose light is signified by the light of the candles and who resists the proud and grants grace to the humble, that we may truly recognize that we are ash and dust—leads us to great humility after the performance of good work. The patriarch Abraham was illuminated with this light when he said, after the Lord had spoken to him: "Seeing I have once begun I will speak to my Lord, whereas I am dust and ashes." The candle that stands in the middle signifies him who said: "Where there are two or three gathered together in my name, there am I in the

2 eorum sum" [Matt 18:20]. Numerus cereostatorum non pertransit septenarium numerum, quoniam septiformi spiritu inluminatur omnis ecclesia. Qui septiformis spiritus singulariter in Christo habitat. Episcopo ascendente ad sedem, cereostata mutantur de locis suis in ordine unius lineae— excepto primo—usque ad altare.

3 Per cereostata varia dona gratiarum Spiritus Sancti figurantur, per quae inluminatur ecclesia. In donis memoratis duo debemus memorari, id est multifaria dona et unitatem spiritus. Per cereostata altrinsecus posita, usque nunc distributa dona per corda electorum signantur; per compositionem unius lineae, unitas Spiritus Sancti in singulis donis. Quae compositio examusin habet a primo cereo, quem diximus significare Christum, a quo procedit Spiritus Sanctus

4 et in quo aeternaliter manet. Ab ipso enim missus est die Pentecostes, ceu usque ad altare—id est usque ad corda electorum apostolorum—in igneis linguis. Ac ideo quod postea agitur in officio Missae illud tempus figurate exprimit quo apostoli apostolorumque successores negotia Domini exercent; quod finitur Evangelio perlecto.

Potest et simpliciter intellegi dispositio cereorum expeditus cursus circa altare ministrandi.

midst of them." The number of candlesticks does not ex-  2
ceed seven, because our whole church is illuminated by
the sevenfold spirit. This sevenfold spirit lives particularly
in Christ. As the bishop ascends to his chair, the candlesticks—excepting the first—are brought from their places
to form a single line up to the altar.

The candlesticks represent the diverse gifts of the Holy  3
Spirit's grace that illuminate the church. We should be
mindful of two points relating to the aforementioned gifts,
namely the multifarious gifts and the unity of the spirit. The
candlesticks placed on either side signify the gifts granted to
the hearts of the elect down to the present time; their arrangement into one line signifies the unity of the Holy Spirit
in each of these gifts. The arrangement has this symbol-
ism precisely from the first candle, which we said signifies
Christ, from whom the Holy Spirit proceeds and in whom
he remains eternally. For he sent the Holy Spirit on Pente-  4
cost, as if to the altar—that is, to the hearts of the chosen
apostles—in tongues of fire. And thus what takes place later
on during the office of the Mass represents figuratively that
time in which the apostles and the apostles' successors performed the Lord's work. This comes to an end when the
Gospel is read.

The placement of the candles can also be simply understood as the preparation of a path around the altar for ministering.

# 8

## De *Gloria in excelsis*

"Telesforus, natione Grecus, ex anachorita, constituit ut ymnus diceretur angelicus, hoc est *Gloria in excelsis Deo,* ante sacrificium." Symmachus, quadragesimus quintus post Telesforum, "constituit ut omni die Dominico et nataliciis martyrum idem ymnus cantaretur."+ Ymnus *Gloria in excelsis Deo* laus Dei est, ut in Evangelio legimus: "Et subito facta est cum angelo multitudo caelestis laudantium Deum et dicentium: Gloria in exelsis Deo" [Luke 2:13].

2    Sacerdos quando dicit *Gloria in excelsis Deo,* orientis partes solet respicere, in quibus ita solemus Dominum requirere, quasi ibi propria eius sedes sit, cum potius eum sciamus ubique esse. Non est ordo ut qui Dominum laudare voluerit, tergum ad eum vertat et pectus ad servos. Ipsum statum ex qualitate loci ubi angeli cecinerunt memoratum ymnum, possumus conicere. Dominus, qui ubique est, secundum formam servi in Bethleem erat; quae Bethleem nostram ecclesiam signat, quae est "domus panis." Angeli ad orientem cecinerunt; de quo statu dicit Micha: "Et tu turris gregis nebulosa filiae Sion, usque ad te venient" [Mic 4:8]. Turris quippe gregis, quae Ebraice dicitur *Turris Ader,* mille circiter passibus a civitate Bethleem ad orientem distat.

# 8

# On the *Gloria in excelsis Deo*

"Telesphorus, a Greek by birth and a former hermit, established that the angelic hymn, that is the *Gloria in excelsis Deo,* would be said before the sacrifice." Symmachus, the forty-fifth pope after Telesphorus, "established that the same hymn would be chanted on every Sunday and on the feasts of the martyrs."† The hymn *Gloria in excelsis Deo* is praise of God, as we read in the Gospel: "And suddenly there was with the angel a multitude of the heavenly army, praising God and saying: Glory to God in the highest."

When the priest says the *Gloria in excelsis Deo,* he is accustomed to look toward the eastern regions, where it is our custom to seek the Lord, as if that were his proper residence, though we know instead that he is everywhere. It is not appropriate for those who want to praise the Lord to turn their backs to him and their chests to his servants. We can conclude that this stance derives from the nature of the place where the angels sang the aforementioned hymn. The Lord, who is everywhere, was in Bethlehem in the form of a servant. Bethlehem, which means "house of bread," signifies our church. The angels sang toward the east; Micah speaks about their stance: "And you, cloudy tower of the flock of the daughter of Zion, unto you shall it come." The tower of the flock, which in Hebrew is called the Tower of Ader, is about a thousand paces to the east of the city of Bethlehem.

3    Diximus superius transitum episcopi de altari in dexteram partem significare Christi transitum de passione ad aeternam vitam. Ac ideo hoc in loco dicimus *Gloria in excelsis Deo* cantandum, quoniam gloria ineffabilis in excelsis facta est, quando Christus transitu suo animas sanctorum copula-

4    vit consortio angelorum. Hoc gaudium adnuntiavit angelus in nativitate eius dicens: "Ecce ego evangelizo vobis gaudium magnum, quia natus est vobis hodie salvator" [Luke 2:10–11]. Manifestum est quibus exstitit salvator: Quando gloria resurrectionis eius caelebrata est, tunc in terra pax hominibus fuit, quibus dicebat: "Pax vobis" [Luke 24:36; John 20:19, 21, 26]. Pax magna est quando sub uno Domino copulantur caelestia et terrena. Ita factum esse post resurrectionem suam denuntiat salvator, dicens: "Data est mihi omnis potestas in caelo et in terra" [Matt 28:18].

9

# De prima oratione Missae

Quando dicimus: "Pax vobiscum," sive "Dominus vobiscum," quod est salutatio, ad populum sumus versi. Quos salutamus, eis faciem praesentamus, excepto in uno, quod est in praeparatione ymni ante *Te igitur.* Ibi iam occupati circa altare, ita ut congruentius sit uno modo versos nos esse

We said above that the bishop's passage across the altar, 3
to its right side, signifies Christ's passage from his passion
to eternal life. And so we say that the *Gloria in excelsis Deo*
should be sung at this point, because there was an ineffable
glory in the highest places when Christ, through his passage, joined the souls of the saints to the community of angels. The angel announced this joy upon Christ's birth, say- 4
ing: "Behold I proclaim to you a great joy, for this day is born
to you a savior." It is clear for whom this savior came: When
the glory of his resurrection was celebrated, there was peace
to men on earth, to whom he said: "Peace be to you." Peace
is great when the heavenly and earthly realms are joined under one Lord. The savior proclaims that this happened after
his resurrection, saying: "All power is given to me in heaven
and on earth."

# 9

# On the first prayer of Mass

When we say: "Peace be with you," or "the Lord be with
you," which is our greeting, we have turned to face the people. We present our face to those whom we greet, with one
exception that occurs during our preparation for the hymn
before the *Te igitur.* At that point we are busy about the altar,
so it is more fitting for us to face one way than it is to look

quam retro aspicere, ad insinuandam intentionem devotissi-
mam quam habemus in offerendo sacrificio, nec debet ara-
tor, dignum opus exercens, vultum in sua terga referre [Luke
9:62].

2    De istis sat est; revertamur ad salutationem. Salutavit
enim in Veteri Testamento angelus Gedeon, dicens: "Dominus tecum, virorum fortissime" [Judg 6:12]. Et iterum:
"Dixit Dominus: Pax tecum" [Judg 6:23]. Et iterum in Ruth:
"Dixit Booz messoribus suis: Dominus vobiscum," et "re-
sponderunt ei: Benedicat te Dominus" [Ruth 2:4]. Nullique
dubium quin in Booz ipse Christus salutasset, qui in lumbis
eius erat. Scriptum est in libro Paralipemenon secundo:
"Audi me Asa, et omnis Iuda et Beniamin: Dominus vobiscum, qui fuistis cum eo" [2 Chr 15:2]. Nostra responsio: "Et
cum spiritu tuo," ex Pauli epistola secunda ad Timotheum
sumpta est. Sic enim in illa scriptum est: "Dominus Iesus
Christus cum spiritu tuo" [2 Tim 4:22].

3    Quando sacerdos dicit: "Pax vobis" secundum Evangelicam scripturam, sive: "Dominus vobiscum," hoc agit quod
Paulus, quando dicit "Dominus Iesus Christus cum spiritu
tuo." Hac salutatione episcopi et responsione populi intellegimus unum debere esse affectum episcopi et populi, sicut
hospitum unius domini. Postquam Christus resurrexit, manifestum est dixisse discipulis: "Pax vobis" [Luke 24:36; John
20:19, 20, 26].

4    Deinde revertitur episcopus ad orientem et dicit: "Oremus." Ac dein sequitur benedictio. Sic et Christus, ante
quam ascenderet ad caelum, benedixit eos, sicut scriptum
est in Evangelio Lucae: "Eduxit autem eos foras in Bethaniam, et, elevatis manibus suis, benedixit eis" [Luke 24:50].

back, to indicate the pious intention that we have in offering the sacrifice. Nor should the plowman, occupied with a worthy task, look back.

Enough about these matters; let us return to the greeting. The angel greeted Gideon in the Old Testament, saying: "The Lord is with you, most valiant of men." And again: "The Lord said: Peace be with you." And again in Ruth: "Boaz said to his reapers: The Lord be with you," and "they answered him: The Lord bless you." And there is no doubt that Christ himself gave this greeting through Boaz; he was in his loins. It is written in the second book of Chronicles: "Hear me Asa, and all Judah and Benjamin. The Lord is with you, you who have been with him." Our response: "And with your spirit," has been taken from Paul's second epistle to Timothy. For there it is written: "The Lord Jesus Christ be with your spirit." 2

When the priest says: "Peace be with you" according to the Gospel, or: "The Lord be with you," he acts as Paul does when he says: "The Lord Jesus Christ be with your spirit." Through the bishop's greeting and the people's response, we understand that the disposition of the bishop and the people should be the same, like the disposition of the guests of a single lord. After Christ rose, it is clear that he said to his disciples: "Peace be with you." 3

Then the bishop turns back to the east and says: "Let us pray." And then the blessing follows. So too did Christ bless his disciples before he ascended to heaven, as it is written in the Gospel of Luke: "And he led them out as far as Bethany, and, lifting up his hands, he blessed them." The priest's 4

Utroque nomine, id est benedictionis et orationis, vocatur oratio sacerdotis. De benedictione dicit Apostolus: "Si benedixeris spiritu, quis supplet locum idiota, quomodo dicit 'Amen' super tuam benedictionem? Quia nescit quid dicas." [1 Cor 14:16] Hanc benedictionem vocat Ambrosius orationem, dicens: "Imperitus enim, audiens quod non intellegit, nescit finem orationis, et non respondit: 'Amen'—id est, 'Verum'—ut confirmetur benedictio. Per hos enim impletur

5    confirmatio precis, qui respondent 'Amen.'"✝ Finis praesentis officii experimento noscitur aliorum officiorum. In fine aliorum solemus dicere *Kyrie eleison* ac deinceps orationem, et sic tandem unumquemque remeare ad sua. Eundem ad demonstrandum finem mutantur cerei de loco in locum.

6    Libet hic proferre auctoritatem Sancti Agustini, quare mos ecclesiae obtineat suas orationes versum orientem dirigere. Dicit in sermone Domini de monte: "Cum ad orationem stamus ad orientem convertimur, unde caelum surgit—non tamquam ibi sit et Deus, quasi ceteras partes mundi deseruerit, qui ubique praesens est, non locorum spatiis sed maiestatis potentia—sed ut ammoneatur animus ad naturam excellentiorem se convertere, id est ad Dominum, cum ipsum corpus eius, quod terrenum est, ad corpus excellentius, id est ad corpus caeleste, convertitur."✝ Ideo dicitur Deus in caelis habitare quia maior cognitio est in caelis illius summae maiestatis et essentiae—in angelis vel in animabus sanctorum—quam in terra habitantibus sanctis, propter gravitudinem carnalis habitationis, quae vix permittit animam ad purum veritatis lumen advolare.

prayer is called by either name, a blessing or a prayer. About this blessing the Apostle says: "If you shall have blessed with the spirit, how will he who holds the place of the unlearned say 'Amen' to your blessing? Because he knows not what you say." Ambrose calls this blessing a prayer, saying: "For the inexperienced person, hearing what he does not understand, does not recognize the end of the prayer and does not reply 'Amen'—that is, 'Truly'—to confirm the blessing. For the prayer is confirmed by those who reply 'Amen.'"✝ We recognize the conclusion of the present office through our experience with other offices. At the end of others it is our custom to say the *Kyrie eleison* and then a prayer, and then finally that everyone should go home. The candles are moved from place to place to indicate this same ending.

It is well to cite the authority of Saint Augustine to explain why our church observes the custom of directing its prayers toward the east. Addressing the Lord's sermon from the mount, he says: "When we stand to pray we turn to the east, where the heavens rise up—not as if God were there, as if he, who is present everywhere, not in space but in the majesty of his power, should have deserted the other regions of the world—but to command our spirit to turn to a more excellent nature, namely to the Lord, when its own body, which is earthly, turns to face a more excellent body, namely the heavenly body."✝ The Lord is said to live in the heavens because there is a greater understanding of his highest majesty and essence in the heavens—whether among the angels or the souls of the saints—than there is among those saints living on earth, because of the weight of dwelling in the flesh, which hardly permits the soul to fly to the pure light of truth.

## 10

# De sessione episcopi

Dein Christus ascendit in caelum, ut sedeat ad dexteram Patris. Episcopus, quia vicarius est Christi, in omnibus memoratis superius debet et hic ad memoriam nobis intronizare Christi ascensionem et sedem. Quapropter ascendit in sedem post opus et laborem ministerii commissi. Christus, disposito curru suo per convenientia loca—id est presbyteros in suo ordine, diaconos in suo, subdiaconos in suo ceterosque gradus in suis, necnon et auditores unumquemque in

2 suo—ascendit ad sedem et sedet. Sedent cum eo quibus promisit: "Cum venerit filius hominis in sede maiestatis suae, sedebitis et vos super sedes duodecim, iudicantes duodecim tribus Israel" [Matt 19:28]. De quibus dicit Paulus Apostolus ad Ephesios: "Et conresuscitavit, et consedere fecit in caelestibus in Christo Iesu" [Eph 2:6]. De his qui ascenderunt secum, aliqui sedent et aliqui stant. Per eos qui sedent, demonstratur membra Christi in pace quiescentia; per eos qui stant, in certamine posita.

3 Caput et membra unum corpus, quoniam Christus in aliquibus sedet, in aliquibus stat, ut illum vidit Stephanus, in certamine positus. Aliqui ascendentium sedent, aliqui stant. Dominus in alto caelorum sedens custodit currum suum—

10

# On the seating of the bishop

Afterward Christ ascended to heaven to sit at the right hand of the Father. The bishop, because he is the vicar of Christ, should enthrone in our memory Christ's ascension and his seat throughout all the things recounted above, and here as well. He therefore ascends to his seat after the work and labor of the ministry entrusted to him. Christ, after he has established his chariot in fitting places—that is, after he has established priests in their order, deacons in theirs, sub-deacons in theirs and the other ranks in theirs, including the listeners, each one in their own—ascends to his seat and sits. Those who sit with him are the ones to whom he promised: "When the son of man shall sit on the seat of his majesty, you also shall sit on twelve seats judging the twelve tribes of Israel." Paul the Apostle speaks about these people to the Ephesians: "And he has raised us up together, and has made us sit together in the heavenly places through Christ Jesus." Of those who ascended with him, some sit and some stand. The members of Christ in restful peace are signified through those who sit; through those who stand are signified the members set for battle.

The head and members are one body, because Christ sits in some and stands in some, as when Stephen, who was set for battle, saw him. Some of those who ascend sit and some stand. The Lord sitting at the height of the heavens guards

id est, civitatem de qua dicit psalmista: "Nisi Dominus custodierit civitatem, frustra vigilat qui custodit eam" [Ps 126:1]. Paulus, quia vice Christi fungebatur, dicente Agustino in Psalmo CXXVI, dicebat: "'Timeo ne forte sicut serpens Evam seduxit astutia sua, sic et vestrae mentes corrumpantur a castitate quae est in Christo' [2 Cor 11:3]. Custodiebat, custos erat; vigilabat, quantum poterat, super eos quibus praeerat—et episcopi hoc faciunt. Nam ideo altior locus positus est episcopis, ut ipsi superintendant et tamquam custodiant populum. Nam et Grece quod dicitur 'episcopus,' hoc Latine 'superintentor' interpretatur, quia superintendat—quia desuper videt. Quomodo enim vinitori altior fit locus ad custodiendam vineam, sic et episcopis altior locus factus est. Et de isto loco alto periculosa ratio redditur, nisi eo corde stemus hic, ut humilitate sub pedibus vestris simus, et pro vobis oremus."

## II

## De officio lectoris et cantoris

Lector dicitur, quia lectione fungitur, ut Isidorus ait: "Lectio dicitur, quia non cantatur, ut psalmus vel ymnus, sed legitur tantum. Illic enim modulatio, hic sola pronuntiatio

his chariot—that is, the city about which the psalmist says: "Unless the Lord keep the city, he watches in vain that keeps it." Paul, because he worked as Christ's vicar, said, as Au- 4 gustine quotes him with respect to Psalm 126: "'I fear lest your minds be corrupted from the chastity that is in Christ, as the serpent seduced Eve by his subtlety.' He kept watch, he was the watchman; he remained vigilant, insofar as he was able, over those in his charge—and bishops also do this. For that reason, a higher position is granted bishops to over- 5 see and, as it were, guard the people. For what is called 'bishop' in Greek is translated 'overseer' in Latin, because he oversees—because he sees from above. In the same way that the vinedresser has a higher position to guard the vineyard, a higher position has also been made for the bishops. And from this high position strict account is rendered, unless we stand here with a heart that places us beneath your feet in humility, and we pray for you."

## II

# On the office of the lector and the cantor

The lector is so-called because he performs the reading, or lection, as Isidore says: "It is called a reading because it is not sung, like a psalm or a hymn, but is only read. For those require melody, but the reading requires only

quaeritur."✝ Cantor multa officia habet. Unumquodque officium ex illo quod efficit, nomen habet. Lectionem quae legitur post sessionem, sequitur cantus qui vocatur responsorius. "Responsorium," ut idem qui supra, "Itali tradiderunt; quos inde responsorios cantus vocant, quod alio desinente, id alter respondeat."✝ Usus lectionis et cantus sumptus est a Veteri Testamento, ut legitur in libro Esdrae—quod ponendum est in Nocturnali Officio, si Dominus dederit.

2    Possumus etiam officio cantoris officium prophetae intellegere. Lectio legis et prophetarum frequentabatur a populo antiquo. Unde scriptum est in Actibus Apostolorum: "Et ingressi synagogam die Sabbatorum, sederunt. Post lectionem autem legis et prophetarum, miserunt principes synagogae ad eos"—id est ad Paulum et Barnabam—"dicentes: Viri, fratres, si quis est in vobis sermo exortationis ad plebem, dicite. Surgens autem Paulus et manu silentium

3    indicens, ait . . ." [Acts 13:14–16] et reliqua. Quamdiu haec duo celebrantur, id est lex et prophetia, solemus sedere more antiquorum. Unde Ambrosius in tractatu ad Corinthios: "Haec traditio synagogae est quam nos vult sectari Apostolus—quia Christianis quidem scribit, sed ex gentibus factis, non ex Iudaeis—ut sedentes disputent: seniores dignitate in cathedris; sequentes in subselliis; novissimi in pavimento super mattas."✝

speech."✝ The cantor has many offices. Each office takes its name from what it accomplishes. A chant called the responsory follows the reading that is read after the bishop sits. "The Italians gave us the responsory," says the same author as above, "and they call these songs responsories because another responds when one leaves off."✝ As we read in the book of Ezra, the practice of reading and song is derived from the Old Testament—which, Lord willing, we will set forth in our commentary on Nocturns.

We can also understand the office of a prophet through 2 the office of the cantor. The reading of the law and the prophets was observed by the ancient people. Thus it is written in the Acts of the Apostles: "And entering into the synagogue on the Sabbath day, they sat down. And after the reading of the law and the prophets, the rulers of the synagogue sent to them"—that is, to Paul and Barnabas— "saying: Men, brethren, if you have any word of exhortation to make to the people, speak. Then Paul, rising up and with his hand bespeaking silence, said . . ." and so forth. For as 3 long as these two things are celebrated, namely the law and prophecy, it is our custom to sit in the manner of the ancients. Thus Ambrose in his treatise on the epistle to the Corinthians: "This is the tradition of the synagogue that the Apostle wants us to follow—for of course he is writing to Christians, but to those converted from the gentiles and not from the Jews—that they should conduct their discussions while sitting: the seniors in rank, upon chairs; their followers on benches; the youngest on the pavement, upon mats."✝

4   Et iterum: Per lectoris officium et cantoris possumus intellegere patrem familias "qui profert de thesauro suo nova
et vetera" [Matt 13:52]. Unde Gregorius in suis omeliis: "In
eo quod veritas dicit: 'Omnis scriba doctus in regno caelorum similis est patri familias' [Matt 13:52], intellegi valet,
quia non de his qui fuerant, sed de his qui esse in ecclesia
poterant, loquebatur. Qui tunc nova et vetera proferunt,
cum utriusque Testamenti praedicamenta vocibus et moribus loquuntur."✝

5   Per lectionem praedicationem Veteris Testamenti, quae
humilior est, possumus intellegere; per responsorium, Novi
Testamenti, quae excelsior est. Haec duo praedicamenta per
Iohannis vitam et Christi designantur. Nam quod ait Lucas
Evangelista: "Lamentavimus et non plorastis" [Luke 7:32] —
ad Iohannem pertinet, cuius abstinentia a cibis et potu luctum paenitentiae significabat. Quod autem ait: "Cantavimus tibiis et non saltastis" [Luke 7:32], ad ipsum Dominum,
qui utendo cum ceteris cibo et potu laetitiam regni figurabat. At Iudaei nec humiliari cum Iohanne, nec cum Christo
gaudere voluerunt. Sicut suavius est Novum Testamentum
Veteri, ita vulgo suavior cantus lectione.

6   Praesentes lectores et cantores, quibus est surgere ad
opus (sicut de Paulo legimus superius) negotia Domini habent. Quibus dicitur: "Negotiamini dum venio" [Luke 19:13].
Lector legem Domini debet tradere auditoribus, quasi
incipientibus in scola Domini exerceri. Nuper vocati sunt
per officia cantorum ad nuptias; neuterici sunt; audiant

And again: Through the office of the lector and the can- 4
tor we can understand the householder "who brings forth
out of his treasure new things and old." Thus Gregory in his
homilies: "Where the truth says: 'Every scribe instructed
in the kingdom of heaven is like a householder,' we understand it to be speaking not about those who had been in the
church, but about those who could have been. Those who
bring forth new things and old preach with the words and
customs of each Testament."✝

Through the reading we can understand the preaching of 5
the Old Testament, which is humbler; through the responsory, the preaching of the New Testament, which is more elevated. These two styles of preaching are signified through
the lives of John and Christ. For where Luke the Evangelist
says: "We have mourned and you have not wept"—that relates to John, whose abstinence from food and drink signified the sorrow of penitence. But where he says: "We have
piped to you and you have not danced"—that relates to
the Lord himself, who gestured toward the happiness of the
kingdom by consuming food and drink with others. But the
Jews wanted neither to be humbled with John nor to rejoice with Christ. Just as the New Testament is sweeter than
the Old, so is song commonly considered sweeter than
reading.

These lectors and cantors, whose duty it is to rise for 6
work (as we read in Paul, above) conduct the Lord's business. To them, it is said: "Trade till I come." The lector
should transmit the law of the Lord to his listeners, as if
they were just beginning their instruction in the Lord's
school. They have just been called to the wedding through
the offices of the cantors; they are new converts; they must

7 doctorem necesse est. Doctor et lector unum sunt. De Esdra enim scriptum est quod ipse legem Dei "et faceret et doceret in Israhel" [1 Ezra 7:10]. Eundem Esdram idem liber inducit postea legentem in gradu ligneo [2 Ezra 8:4]. De doctoribus dicit Ambrosius in epistola ad Corinthios: "Illos dicit doctores"—quin Paulus—"qui in ecclesia litteris et lectionibus retinendis pueros imbuebant more sinagogae, quia traditio illorum ad nos transitum fecit."✝

8 Iterum: Mihi videtur esse inter lectionem et responsorium quod est inter elementa et artes ipsas. Ars quoque musica habet elementa sua, et geometria ab elementis incipit linearum, et dialectica atque medicina habent ΥΣΑΓΟΓΑ suas. Sic elementis Veteris Testamenti, ut ad Evangelicam plenitudinem veniat, sancti vero eruditur infantia. Elementa lex Moysi et omne vetus instrumentum intellegendum est, quibus, quasi elementis et religionis exordiis,

9 Deum discimus. Dent lectores sive doctores precium Domini—id est verba legis—et recipiant scolasticas mentes, scilicet vacantes ab emptione villae, ab emptione boum quinque iugorum, a ductu uxoris [Luke 14:18–20]. "Scola" "vacatio" dicitur. At si adhuc aliquis surdus, obturatis auribus cordis, torpescit, veniat cantor cum excelsa tuba, more prophetarum, sonetque in aures eius dulcedinem melo-

10 diae; forsan excitabitur. Fiat in eo quod de populo narratur factum esse in libro Esdrae. Sic enim scriptum est in eo: "Steterunt sacerdotes in ornatu suo cum tubis, et

listen to the teacher. The teacher and the lector are one. For  7
it was written that Ezra was "to do and to teach" the law of
the Lord "in Israel." This same book guides Ezra later on
when he reads upon the wooden step. Ambrose on the epistle to the Corinthians speaks about teachers: "He"—that is,
Paul—"calls those people teachers who taught boys in the
church through letters and the memorization of readings,
after the manner of the synagogue, since he handed their
tradition down to us."✝

Again: It strikes me that the difference between reading  8
and responsory is the same as that between first principles
and the arts themselves. The musical art has its first principles, and the art of geometry begins from the first principles of lines, and dialectic and medicine have their *eisagōgai*.
So too are holy men, as children, instructed in the first principles of the Old Testament, so that they may arrive at the
fullness of the Gospel. The law of Moses and the entire
ancient record should be understood as first principles,
through which we learn about God, as if through the first
principles and basic ideas of piety. Let the lectors or teach-  9
ers render the Lord's price—that is, the words of the law—
and let them receive scholarly minds, or minds freed from
the buying of a farm, from the buying of five yoke of oxen,
from marrying a wife. "School" means "freeing." But if there
is yet someone who is deaf, and grows listless with the ears
of his heart stopped up, let the cantor come to him with his
sublime trumpet, in the manner of the prophets, and let
him sound a sweet melody in his ears; perhaps he will be
stirred. Let there be in him what we read arose from the  10
people in the book of Ezra. For it is written there: "The
priests stood in their ornaments with trumpets, and the

Levitae filii Asaph in cymbalis, ut laudarent Deum per manus David regis Israhel. Et concinebant ymnis et confessione Domini: Quoniam bonus, quoniam in aeternum misericordia eius super Israhel. Omnis quoque populus
vociferabatur clamore magno in laudando Dominum, in eo
quod fundatum est templum Domini" [1 Ezra 3:10–11]. Et
paulo post: "Multi, vociferantes in laetitia, levabant vocem,
nec poterat quisquam agnoscere vocem clamoris laetan-
tium et vocem fletus populi" [1 Ezra 3:12–13]. Unde Beda in
tractatu Esdrae: "Sacerdotes quidem sanctis ornati vestibus, prout stante adhuc templo consuerant, tubis perso-
nantes et cor populi ad suavitatem supernae laudis ac-
cendentes; Levitae autem in cymbalis bene sonantibus
ymnos Domino concinentes; populus vero clamore communi affectum sui cordis in laudando Dominum ostendens."✝ Cantores qui respondent primo canenti vocem auditorum proferunt—quos testificantur laudare Deum.

12   Non inmerito ipsi cantores agunt causas prophetarum,
quia de filiis principis eorum, id est Asaph, scriptum est in
Paralipemenon: "Filii eius sub manu ipsius erant prophe-
tantes iuxta regem" [1 Chr 25:2]. Ipsi exaltant vocem, ut
tuba; ipsis dicitur in Psalmo LXXXmo: "'Tuba canite' [Ps
80:4]: Hoc est"—ut Agustinus ait—"clarius et fidentius
praedicate, ne terreamini sicut ait propheta quodam loco:
'Exclama et exalta vocem tuam, sicut tuba' [Isa 58:1]."✝

13   Lex enim scripta data est in tabulis. Scriptura enim pertinet ad lectoris officium; prophetia menti inscripta erat,
quam voce fidenti prophetae proferebant; quod pertinet ad
cantoris officium. Fidei praedicatoris officium gerit cantor,

Levites the sons of Asaph with cymbals, to praise God by the hands of David king of Israel. And they sung together hymns and praise to the Lord: Because he is good, for his mercy endures forever toward Israel. And all the people shouted with a great shout praising the Lord, because the foundations of the temple of the Lord were laid." And a little later: "Many, shouting for joy, lifted up their voice, so that one could not distinguish the voice of the shout of joy from the noise of the weeping of the people." Thus Bede in his 11 treatise on Ezra: "And the priests were adorned with holy vestments, as was their custom now that the temple was standing; and they were sounding with trumpets and igniting the hearts of the people to the sweetness of heavenly praise; and the Levites were singing hymns to the Lord with their well-ringing cymbals; and the people, with general shouting, expressed the feeling of their hearts by praising the Lord."✝ The cantors who respond to the first singer bring forth the voice of the listeners, and they attest that these listeners praise the Lord.

It is not inappropriate that these cantors perform the 12 role of prophets, for it is written in Chronicles about the sons of their leader, namely Asaph: "His sons were under his hand prophesying near the king." They lift up their voice like a trumpet; in Psalm 80, they are told: "'Sound with the trumpet.' That is"—as Augustine says—"preach clearly and boldly lest you be frightened, as the prophet remarks at a certain point: 'Cry and lift up your voice like a trumpet.'"✝

Now the written law was handed down on tablets. And 13 scripture pertains to the lector's office. The prophecy that the prophets brought forth with a bold voice had been inscribed in their mind; this relates to the office of the cantor.

quem oportet post oboedientiam auditorum versum cantare.

14    Quid significet versus in officio praedicatoris, ex Evangelica parabola addiscere possum, quae narrat de servo arante, ita dicens: "Quis autem vestrum habens servum arantem, aut pascentem, qui regresso de agro dicit illi statim: Transi, recumbe—et non dicit ei: Para quod caenem?" [Luke 17:7] Arat qui aratro compunctionis scindit corda. Nulli dubium quin per dulcedinem modulationis scindantur corda etiam carnalia, et sese aperiant more sulci in confessione vocis et

15    lacrimarum. Musica habet quandam naturalem vim ad flectendum animum, sicut Boetius in suo libro scribit, quem *De musica* fecit: "Vulgatum quippe est quam saepe iracundias cantilena represserit, quam multa vel in corporum, vel in animorum affectionibus miranda perfecerit."✝ Absit ut vigorem Christiani animi in mollitiem caducam possit conver-

16    tere, quod genus ipsi etiam gentiles vitabant. Unde scriptum est in libro memorato superiore loco: "Idcirco Timotheo Milesio Spartiatas succensuisse, quod, multiplicem musicam reddens, puerorum animis, quos acceperat erudiendos, officeret, et a virtutis modestia praepediret; et quod armoniam, quam modestam susceperat, in genus choromaticum, quod est mollius, invertisset. Tanta igitur apud eos fuit musicae diligentia, ut eam animos quoque obtinere arbitrarentur."✝

17    Sufficiant haec pauca de naturali vi musicae inseruisse; revertendum est ad Evangelicam parabolam. Servus qui arat non debet revertens de agro recumbere, sed parare caenam

The cantor does the work of a faithful preacher, who should sing a verse upon the obedience of his listeners.

I can learn what the verse in the preacher's office signifies 14 from the Gospel parable that tells of the plowing servant, saying: "But which of you having a servant plowing, or feeding cattle, will say to him immediately when he is come from the field: Go, sit down—and not rather say to him: Make ready my supper." He plows who furrows hearts with the plow of compunction. There is no doubt that even our fleshly hearts are furrowed through the sweetness of melody, and that they open themselves like furrows through the confession of the voice and tears. Music has a kind of natu- 15 ral power for moving the spirit, as Boethius writes in the book that he composed *On Music:* "And so everyone knows how often song represses anger, how it brings about marvelous things in the dispositions of bodies and spirits."✝ Heaven forbid that it be able to convert the strength of the Christian spirit to fallen voluptuousness; even the heathens avoided that kind of music. Thus it is written earlier in the 16 aforementioned book that "the Spartans were enraged with Timotheus of Miletus because, in developing a more elaborate style of music, he was impeding the spirits of the boys he had taken in to educate, and hindering them in modest virtue; and because he had converted the harmony, which he had received as temperate, to the chromatic genus, which is softer. Such was their attentiveness to music that they even thought it capable of taking hold of spirits."✝

Let these few remarks that I have included on the natural 17 power of music suffice; we should return to the Gospel parable. The servant who plows should not immediately recline

79

domini. De quo servo dicit Beda in tractatu super Lucam: "Servus de agro regreditur cum, intermisso ad tempus opere praedicandi, ad conscientiam doctor recurrit, atque, a publico locutionis ad curiam cordis rediens, sua secum secretius acta vel dicta retractat."+ Iuxta disciplinam servi arantis, ammonetur cantor ut non ilico post actum opus sui officii requiem spectet, et torpore securitatis torpescat. Perfecit enim opus suum, quando quodammodo sua iubilatione boves in exercitium aratri induxit—id est cantores provocavit, ut scinderent corda aratro compunctionis.

Ac postea versus sequitur. In versu necesse est ut suas cogitationes ad se trahat, et secum cogitet quomodo aut quid a magistro didicisset. Versus timore non est ausus alte levare responsorium; nescit quomodo finiat versum. Et hic imitatur aliud exemplum doctrinae Domini, qua iubetur ut, qui voluerit turrem aedificare, prius sumptus cogitet, si habeat quae necessaria sunt ad perficiendum [Luke 14:28]. Sequitur Beda memoratus: "Post pastum atque agriculturam domi sibi iubet parare quod caenet—hoc est post laborem apertae locutionis, humilitatem quoque propriae considerationis exhibere."+ Hoc facit ille qui versum cantat. In repetitione responsorii exaltat vocem fiducialiter, iam non timens versum. Illum praedicatorem signat qui cursum suum

when he returns from the field; instead, he should prepare his master's dinner. Bede speaks about this servant in his treatise on Luke: "The servant returns from the field when, upon setting the work of preaching aside for a time, the teacher returns to his conscience, and, leaving the public space of his speech for the courtyard of his heart, he considers privately his words and deeds within himself."+ According- to the lesson of the plowing servant, the cantor is advised not to seek rest directly upon completing the work of his office, and not to grow listless with the torpor of security. For he has completed his work when, as it were, he has driven the oxen, through his calls, to move the plow—that is, when he has provoked the other cantors to furrow hearts with the plow of compunction.

And then a verse follows. Upon this verse he must collect his thoughts and consider within himself how or what he has learned from the master. In fear of the verse, he does not dare to raise on high a responsory; he does not know how to finish the verse. And here he follows another example from the Lord's teaching, where it was ordered that he who wants to build a tower should first reckon the charges and determine whether he has what is necessary to finish it. The aforementioned Bede continues: "After the servant has tended to the pasture and the husbandry of the household, the lord orders him to prepare something for him to eat— that is, after the labor of public speaking, he orders him to demonstrate the humility of self-reflection as well."+ The one who sings the verse does this. In repeating the responsory he raises his voice with confidence; now he does not, as he fears the verse. He signifies the preacher who has

consummatum habet, qualis erat Paulus, cum diceret: "Bonum certamen certavi, cursum consummavi, fidem servavi. In reliquo reposita est mihi corona iustitiae" [1 Tim 4:7–8].

20 Diximus quod excitentur per responsorium qui sunt quodammodo surdi ad epistolam; dicamus qualiter oboedientes ilico proficiant per responsorium. In lectione pascitur auditor, quasi quodammodo bos; ad hoc enim pascitur bos, ut in eo exerceatur opus agriculturae. Bos enim praedicator est. Unde scriptum est in libro legis: "Non alligabis os bovi trituranti" [1 Cor 9:9; 1 Tim 5:18; Deut 25:4]. Pastus est enim bos;
21 exerceatur opus. Cantor enim est quasi bubulcus, qui iubilat bubus, ut hilarius trahant aratrum. Cantor est de his de quibus dicit Paulus: "Dei adiutores sumus" [1 Cor 3:9]. Boves sunt qui respondent primo cantori. De quibus iterum dicit: "Dei agricultura estis" [1 Cor 3:9]. Trahentibus bobus aratrum, scinditur terra, quando cantores, intimos anhelitus commoventes, trahunt dulcem vocem et proferunt ad publicum, qua corda suorum sive ceterorum compungunt ad lacrimas, sive ad confitenda peccata, quasi secreta patefaciendo terrae.

22 Et alio modo: Ideo scribuntur litterae, ut per eas memoriae reddatur quod oblivione deletum est. Simili modo ex pictura recordamur quod interius memoriae commendari potest. Ita et responsorio ammonetur praedicator quomodo doctrinam, quae praecessit in lectione, exerceat: Primo, ut dulcedine suae imitationis plurimos sibi asciscat; coniuncti

finished his course, like Paul when he said: "I have fought a good fight, I have finished my course, I have kept the faith. As to the rest, there is laid up for me a crown of justice."

We said that those who are in some way deaf to the epistle are stirred by the responsory; let us explain how the obedient should benefit from the responsory at that moment. During the reading the listener is fed, in a certain sense, like an ox; for the ox is fed to do the work of husbandry. Now the ox is the preacher. Thus it is written in the book of the law: "You shall not muzzle the mouth of the ox that treads out the corn." For the ox has been fed; let the work be done. And the cantor is like the plowman who calls out to the oxen to drag the plow more cheerfully. The cantor is one of those whom Paul speaks about: "We are God's helpers." The oxen are those who respond to the head cantor. Again, Paul speaks of them: "You are God's husbandry." The earth is furrowed as the oxen drag the plow when the cantors, drawing their innermost breath, drag forth a sweet voice and present it to the people. Through this voice they goad their own heart, as well as the hearts of others, to tears and to the confession of sins, as if laying bare the hidden parts of the earth.

And in another sense: Letters are copied so that, through them, what has been lost by forgetfulness might be committed to memory. Similarly, we recall through an image what can be committed to our memory within. In the same way, the preacher is in some sense admonished, through the responsory, to practice the teaching that preceded in the reading: First, so that he may draw the many to himself by the sweetness of his example; and also so that those thus joined

corda multorum excitent ad compunctionem et lacrimas. Et ne se extollere debeat de opere praedicationis, pulsatur versu, quatinus ad memoriam sibi reducat de propriis causis iudicandum ante Dominum.

12

# Quid sit inter responsorium et tractum

Hoc differt inter responsorium, cui corus respondet, et tractum, cui nemo, quod est inter duo sacrificia, scilicet columbarum et turturum. Tractus verba congruentia sui officii habent. Illa quae sunt in Septuagesima tribulationem sonant, ut est illud: *De profundis clamavi ad te, Domine* [Ps 129:1]. Quae in Sexagesima, oportunitatem fugae quaerunt, ut illud: *Ut fugiant a facie arcus* [Ps 59:6], et sic cetera deinceps conicere possumus. *Laudate Dominum omnes gentes* [Ps 116:1] laetitiam neofytorum et nuper ordinatorum significat.

2    De istis sat est; revertendum est ad volucres, scilicet columbas et turtures, quae significant responsorium et

together may inspire the hearts of the many to compunction and tears. And he is struck with the verse, lest he grow proud through the work of his preaching, and that he may remember that he is to be judged before the Lord for his own offenses.

12

# The difference between the responsory and the tract

The difference between the responsory, to which the choir responds, and the tract, to which no one responds, is the same as that between the two sacrifices, namely of doves and turtledoves. The tract has words appropriate for its office. There are those words that sing of tribulation during Septuagesima, as: *De profundis clamavi ad te, Domine.* There are those that seek a chance to flee during Sexagesima, as in: *Ut fugiant a facie arcus,* and we can think of further examples as well. *Laudate Dominum omnes gentes* signifies the rejoicing of the neophytes and the newly ordained.

Enough about these; we should return to the birds, 2 namely the doves and the turtledoves, which represent

tractum. De quibus dicit Beda in tractatu super Lucam: "Volucres hae pro cantu gemitus habent; non inmerito lacrimas humilium designant, quibus plurimum in ipsis etiam bonis operibus indigemus; quia, etsi bona esse quae agimus noverimus, qua tamen districtione a Domino examinanda,

3 qua a nobis perseverantia sint consummanda, nescimus." Et iterum: "Hoc sane inter turturis et columbae significantiam distat, quod columba, quae gregatim conversari, volare et gemere consuevit, activae vitae frequentiam demonstrat, de qua dicitur: 'Multitudinis autem credentium erat cor unum et anima una; nec quisquam eorum quae possidebant, aliquid suum esse dicebat, sed erant illis omnia communia' [Acts 4:32]. Turtur vero, qui singularitate gaudet adeo ut, si coniugem casu perdiderit, solus exinde permaneat, speculativae vitae culmina denuntiat, quia et paucorum est ista vir-

4 tus." Et post pauca: "Item, cum intrans cubiculum clauso hostio oro Patrem in abscondito, turturem offero [Matt 6:6]. At cum eiusdem operis compares quaero, canendo cum propheta: 'Venite adoremus et procidamus ante Deum; ploremus coram Domino qui fecit nos' [Ps 94:6], columbas ad altare deporto." Moyses quasi tractum cantat tribulationis, qui "solus ascendit ad Dominum et, ne idem populus feriatur, lacrimosis precibus impetrat" [Exod 19:32]. Daniel tractum laetitiae cantat quando "solus, fugientibus sociis,

the responsory and the tract. Bede speaks of these in his treatise on Luke: "These birds give out groans for song; it is not inappropriate for them to designate the tears of the humble, which we often need even in the midst of good works. This is because, although we know that what we are doing is good, we do not know how strictly our actions are to be judged by the Lord, and with how much perseverance we should perfect them." And again: "This is the difference 3 between the meaning of turtle doves and doves: The dove, which is accustomed to live, fly and cry out in flocks, signifies the crowding of the active life, about which it is said: 'And the multitude of believers had but one heart and one soul; neither did anyone say that any of the things he possessed was his own, but all things were common unto them.' But the turtle dove, which rejoices in solitude so much that it remains single if it happens to lose its mate, proclaims the heights of the contemplative life, for this is the virtue of the few." And after a little: "Again, when I enter my cham- 4 ber, having shut the door, and pray to my Father in secret, I offer a turtle dove. But when I seek companions in this work by singing along with the prophet: 'Come let us adore and fall down before God; let us weep before the Lord who made us,' I bring doves to the altar." Moses, who "goes up to the Lord alone and begs with tearful prayers that his people not be punished," sings something like a tract of tribulation. Daniel sings a tract of rejoicing when "he remains

inter angelos remanet. Solus Iezechiel quadrigas, cerubin et supernae civitatis aedificia celsa miratur" [Dan 6; Ezek 1, 10, 40–48; etc.].

# 13

# De alleluia

Alleluia quod cantatur per festos dies in recordatione aeternae laetitiae, tam laetitiam electorum, quam laudem Domini ad memoriam reducit; in quo non oportet aliquod sinistrum sonare, sed totum dextrum, quale est in futura vita. Illi sunt recti versus per quos revertimur ad alleluia, qui laetitiam ecclesiae et Domini laudem sine tristitia retinent—sicut sunt: *Dominus regnavit, decorem induit* [Ps 92:1], et: *Dominus regnavit, exultet terra* [Ps 96:1], et: *Lauda anima mea Dominum* [Ps 145:2], et: *Iubilate Deo omnis terra* [Ps 65:1, 99:2], et ceteri tales. In responsorio seminavimus; in alleluia metimus. De qua re dicit psalmista: "Qui seminant in lacrimis, in exultatione metent" [Ps 125:5].

alone with the angels while his companions flee. Ezechiel alone admires the chariots, the cherubim and the lofty buildings of the heavenly city."

## 13

# On the alleluia

The alleluia that is sung on feast days in commemoration of eternal rejoicing, calls to mind both the joy of the elect and the Lord's praise. During the alleluia there should be no leftward singing; instead, all should be rightward, as it is in the life to come. The verses by which we return to the alleluia are rightward; they capture the rejoicing of the church and the praise of the Lord without sorrow—as in: *Dominus regnavit, decorem induit,* and: *Dominus regnavit, exultet terra,* and: *Lauda anima mea Dominum,* and: *Iubilate Deo omnis terra,* and others like these. In the responsory we sowed; in the alleluia we reap. The psalmist speaks of this matter: "They that sow in tears shall reap in joy."

## 14

# Quid sit inter alleluia et tractum

Hoc est inter alleluia et tractum, quod alleluia laetitiam sive laudem Domino, tractus vero aliquando tribulationem, aliquando laetitiam sonat. Tribulationem, ut: *De profundis* [Ps 129:1], ut: *Commovisti* [Ps 59:4], ut: *Qui habitat* [Ps 90:1], ut: *Ad te levavi oculos meos* [Ps 122:1], ut: *Saepe expugnaverunt me* [Ps 128:1, 2], ut: *Deus, Deus meus* [Ps 21:2]. Laetitiam, ut: *Iubilate Domino* [Ps 99:2], ut: *Qui confidunt in Domino* [Ps 124:1], ut: *Laudate Dominum* [Ps 116:1]. Post duos tribulationis tertius occurrit laetitiae, quoniam post duos dies sepulturae, tertius occurrit resurrectionis.

2    Sunt etenim duo genera conpunctionis: unum timoris et alterum amoris. Timor in duobus dividitur, de quibus dicit Isaias: "Ecce ego venio, cogitationes et opera ut congregem" [Isa 66:18]. Verba in cogitationibus comprehenduntur; cogitationes verba sunt animi et radices verborum sonantium. Amor singularis est. Unum scit amare et petere—unum illud de quo propheta dicit: "Unam petii a Domino, hanc requiram: ut inhabitem in domo Domini" [Ps 26:4].

## 14

# The difference between the alleluia and the tract

The difference between the alleluia and the tract is that the alleluia sings of rejoicing and praise to the Lord, while the tract sometimes sings of tribulation and sometimes of rejoicing. Tracts like: *De profundis,* like: *Commovisti,* like: *Qui habitat,* like: *Ad te levavi oculos meos,* like: *Saepe expugnaverunt me,* like: *Deus, Deus meus,* sing of tribulation. Tracts like: *Iubilate Domino,* like: *Qui confidunt in Domino,* like: *Laudate Dominum,* sing of rejoicing. After two tracts of tribulation there occurs a third of rejoicing, because after two days of burial there occurs a third day of resurrection.

And there are two kinds of compunction: one of fear and the other of love. Fear is divided in two, as Isaiah says: "Behold I come that I may gather their thoughts and works." Words are included in thoughts; thoughts are the words of the spirit and the roots of the words that we sing. Love is singular. It knows to love and to seek one thing—the one thing that the prophet talks about: "One thing I have asked of the Lord, this will I seek after: that I may dwell in the house of the Lord." 2

## 15

# De espoliatione casularum

Ministri casula se exuunt quando lectoris sive cantoris officium assumunt. In lectoris officio et cantoris aliquod genus militiae exprimitur; soli enim militant in lectione sive in vocis modulatione. Haec officia agendo extra corum exeunt. Quid hoc aliud significat, nisi iter quod arripuimus pro communi necessitate fratrum? Et iam talia sunt illa opera quae signantur per casulam, ut non possint observari in itinere. Unde Beda in tractatu super Lucam: "At vero famem, sitim, vigilias, nuditatem, lectionem, psalmodiam, orationem, laborem operandi, doctrinam, silentium et cetera huiusmodi, si quis semper exequenda putaverit, non modo se horum fructu privabit, sed et notam indiscretae obstinationis, immo stultitiae pervicacis, incurret."✝

2      Albam sine casula portat lector seu cantor in singulari officio, quando prudenter et strenue agit contra oblectamenta mundi, et talem se praebet fratribus in necessitatibus temporalibus, ut a pluribus possit imitari.

## 15

# On removing chasubles

Ministers take off their chasubles when they take up the office of lector or cantor. A kind of warfare is expressed in the office of the lector and the cantor, for they fight alone in the reading and in melody of the voice. In performing these offices they leave the choir. What does this signify, if not a journey that we have embarked upon for the common need of our brothers? And the works signified by the chasuble are such that now, on this journey, they cannot be observed. Thus Bede in his treatise on Luke: "But if anyone thinks that hunger, thirst, vigils, nakedness, reading, psalmody, prayer, physical labor, teaching, silence and other things of this sort should always be pursued, he will not only deprive himself of their fruit, but he will also incur the distinction of heedless obstinacy, even of stubborn foolishness."✝

The lector and the cantor wear the alb without the chasuble in this solitary office, when they act prudently and vigorously against the delights of the world, and when they offer themselves to their brethren amid their temporal necessities, that they can be imitated by many. 2

# 16

# De tabulis

Scribit Beda in tractatu Esdrae: "Laudabunt autem Dominum Levitae per manus David, sive in organis quae ipse fecit sive Psalmos quos ipse instituit concinentes."✝ Eorum vice cantor, sine aliqua necessitate legendi, tenet tabulas in manibus, ut figurent illud psalmistae: "Laudent nomen eius in coro; et tympano et psalterio psallant ei" [Ps 149:3]. Unde Agustinus in eodem Psalmo: "Quare assumit tympanum et

2 psalterium? Ut non sola vox laudet, sed et opera."✝ Tabulae quas cantor in manu tenet, solent fieri de osse, quia fortem perseverantiam signant bonarum cogitationum et bonorum operum, iuxta Evangelium: "Qui autem perseveraverit usque in finem, hic salvus erit" [Matt 10:22]. Vel signant dilectionem Dei et proximi, quae dilectio, nisi opera habeat, vana est. Quapropter tenentur in manu, ut dilectio vocis exerceatur per opus. Unde idem qui supra, in Psalmo CXLVIIII: "Quando assumit tympanum et psalterium, manus concinunt voci. Sic et tu, si quando cantas alleluia, porrigas et panem esurienti, vestias nudum, suscipias peregrinum—non sola vox sonat, sed et manus consonat, quia verbis facta concordant."✝

# 16

# On the tablets

Bede writes in his treatise on Ezra: "And the Levites praised the Lord through the hand of David, whether through the musical instruments that he made or by singing the Psalms that he created."✝ In the guise of the Levites, the cantor holds tablets in his hands, though he has no need to read, to signify that verse of the psalmist: "Let them praise his name in choir; let them sing to him with the timbrel and the psaltery." Thus Augustine on the same Psalm: "Why does the hand take up the timbrel and psaltery? So that not only the voice, but also works, may praise."✝ The 2 tablets that the cantor holds in his hand are customarily made of bone, because they signify the strong perseverance of good thoughts and good works, according to the Gospel: "But he that shall persevere unto the end, he shall be saved." Or they signify the love of God and neighbor; unless it has works, this love is empty. They are held in the hand so that love of the voice may be expressed through works. Thus the same author as above, on Psalm 149: "When it takes up the timbrel and psaltery, the hand sings with the voice. And so if you also offer bread to the hungry, clothe the naked or receive a stranger when you sing the alleluia—then the voice does not sing alone, but the hand also sings with it, because deeds are in harmony with words."✝

3 Versus alleluia tangit cantorem interius, ut cogitet in quo debeat laudare Dominum, aut in quo laetari. Haec iubilatio, quam cantores "sequentiam" vocant, illum statum ad mentem nostram ducit, quando non erit necessaria locutio verborum, sed sola cogitatione mens menti monstrabit quod retinet in se.

Finitur hic secunda periocha praedicationis; usque ad memoratum statum currit sermo praedicationis. Quae ultra sunt, velata sunt alis Seraphin.

## 17

# De ascensu in pulpitum

Lector et cantor in gradum ascendunt more antiquorum, iuxta quod scriptum est in Esdra: "Stetit autem Esdras scriba super gradum ligneum, quem fecerat ad loquendum," et cetera. Et paulo post: "Super universum quippe populum eminebat" [2 Ezra 8:4, 5].

2 "Huius loci," ut Beda ait in eodem, "videtur meminisse scriptura Paralipemenon, ubi dictum est quia 'stetit Salomon coram altari Domini, ex adverso universae multitudinis Israhel, et extendit manus suas. Siquidem fecerat Salomon basim aeneam et posuerat eam in medio basilicae, habentem quinque cubitos longitudinis et quinque cubitos latitudinis et tres cubitos in altum; stetitque super eam' [2 Chr 6:12–13].

The verse of the alleluia stirs the cantor within to con- 3
sider why he should praise the Lord, or why he should rejoice. This jubilation, which the cantors call *sequentia,* calls
our mind to that state of being where the speaking of words
will not be necessary; rather, one mind will explain to another what it has within by thought alone.

Here the second section of preaching is concluded; the
word of preaching continues up to this point. Those things
that are beyond are veiled by the wings of the Seraphim.

17

# On the ascent to the pulpit

The lector and the cantor ascend a step after the manner
of the ancients, in accordance with what is written in Ezra:
"And Ezra the scribe stood upon a step of wood that he had
made to speak upon," and so forth. And a little later: "For he
was above all the people."

As Bede says about this passage: "Chronicles seems to al- 2
lude to this passage, when it says that Solomon 'stood before the altar of the Lord, in presence of all the multitude of
Israel, and stretched forth his hands. For Solomon had made
a brazen scaffold and had set it in the midst of the basilica;
the scaffold was five cubits long and five cubits broad and
three cubits high; and he stood upon it.' Now 'in the midst

'In medio namque basilicae' in medio dicit atrii sacerdotum. Quae basilica maior atriorum exteriorum omni ex parte templi erat circumdata. De quibus superius in eodem libro scriptum est: 'Fecit etiam atrium sacerdotum et basilicam

3 grandem' [2 Chr 4:9]. Verum quia Salomon, quasi rex, basem fecit aeneam, porro Esdras, quasi minoris potentiae, gradum ad loquendum ligneum constituit—sicut etiam Salomon sive Moyses altare holocausti fecerunt aeneum, pro

4 quo filii transmigrationis reposuerunt lapideum. Sed non est putandum minoris sacramentum perfectionis ligneum gradum, quam basem habere aeneam. Quod enim sepe dictum est: Sicut aes pro diuturnitate perdurandi, vel suavitate sonandi, divinis competit sacramentis, quae nulla saeculorum longitudine deficiunt, et 'in omnem terram exivit sonus eorum' [Ps 18:5]—ita etiam lignum eisdem aptissime congruit,

5 propter videlicet tropheum Dominicae passionis. Super universum ergo populum pontifex eminet, quando is qui gradum doctoris accipit, merito vitae perfectioris actionem vulgi transcendit. Stat autem in gradu ligneo quem fecerat ad loquendum, quando singulari imitatione Dominicae passionis altiorem se ceteris facit; unde merito fiduciam libere verbum Dei praedicandi obtinet. Nam qui passionem Domini pro suo modulo contempnit imitari, necdum gradum ligneum, unde infimis superemineat, ascendit. Ideoque necesse est talis scriba trepidus praecepta Domini praedicet, timens sive erubescens ea quae ipse non fecit, aliis facienda proponere."

of the basilica' means in the midst of the court of the priests. The great basilica was surrounded on every side by the exterior courts of the temple. About these things it is written earlier in the same book: 'He made also the court of the priests and a great basilica.' But since Solomon, as king, 3 made a brazen scaffold, Ezra built a wooden step to speak from later on, as his power was lesser—just as Solomon and Moses made a brazen altar for sacrifice, in place of which the sons of the transmigration relaid one of stone. But we 4 should not suppose that the wooden step is a sacrament of less perfection than the brazen scaffold. For as we have often said: Just as bronze, because of its durability and the beauty of its sound, accords with the divine sacraments that do not weaken over any period of time and 'their sound has gone forth into all the earth'—so does wood aptly accord with these same sacraments, namely because it is a monument to the Lord's passion. The pontiff is therefore above 5 the whole people, when he takes the step of the teacher and transcends the active life of the multitude through the merit of a more perfect life. And he stands on a wooden step that he had made for speaking on, when he raises himself higher than the rest through his singular imitation of the Lord's passion; thus he rightly achieves the courage to preach the word of the Lord freely. For he who neglects to imitate the Lord's passion in his own small way does not yet ascend the wooden step, where he may stand over those beneath him. It is therefore necessary for such a fearful scribe to preach God's precepts, while being afraid and ashamed to tell others to do what he has not done."

## 18

# De diaconi ascensione in tribunal

Sic vocat Cyprianus gradum super quem ascendit diaconus ad legendum, scribens ad clerum et plebem de Quirino confessore lectore ordinato. Estimatum est a mea parvitate, ut satius cognoscatur dignitas diaconi et magnitudo ministerii eius, verba ipsius Cypriani ponenda, ac postea nostrum ordinem:

"Hunc ad nos, fratres dilectissimi, cum tanta Domini dignatione venientem, testimonio et miraculo eius ipsius qui se persecutus fuerat inlustrem—quid aliud quam super pulpitum, id est super tribunal ecclesiae, oportebat imponi, ut, loci altioris celsitate subnixus, et plebi universae pro honoris sui claritate conspicuus, legat praecepta et Evangelium Domini, quae fortiter ac fideliter sequitur? Vox Dominum confessa in his cotidie quae Dominus locutus est audiatur; viderit an sit ulterior gradus ad quem profici in ecclesia possit. Nihil est in quo magis confessor fratribus prosit, quam ut Evangelica ratio de ore eius audiatur. Lectoris fidem quisquis audierit—imitetur. Iungendus in lectione Aurelio fuerat, cum quo et divini honoris societate coniunctus est." Et paulo post: "Hos tamen lectores interim constitutos sciatis,

# 18

# On the deacon's ascent to the tribunal

This is what Cyprian, writing to the clergy and people about the ordination of the confessor Quirinus as lector, calls the step that the deacon ascends to read from. In my inadequacy, I thought I should include Cyprian's words here, and afterward return to the plan of my book, so that the dignity of the deacon and the magnitude of his ministry might be fully understood:

"Beloved brethren, the man who comes to us with so much of the Lord's esteem, made illustrious by the testimony and the miracle of the very person who had persecuted him—where should we station him if not on the pulpit, or upon the tribunal of the church, so that, supported by the height of this higher place and distinguished before all the people for the splendor of his honor, he may read the precepts and the Lord's Gospel, which he so boldly and faithfully follows? May the voice that has confessed the Lord be heard every day in those matters of which the Lord himself spoke; he should see whether there is any higher rank he can advance to in the church. In nothing is a confes- 2 sor of greater use to his brethren than in letting the doctrine of the Gospels be heard from his mouth. Whoever should hear about the lector's faith—let him imitate it. He should have been partnered with Aurelius for the reading, to whom he is joined in the companionship of divine honor." And a little later: "In the meantime, you should know that these

quia oportebat lucernam super candelabrum poni, unde omnibus luceat, et gloriosos vultus in loco altiore constitui, ubi, ab omni circumstante conspecti, incitamentum gloriae videntibus praebeant."✝

3    Nunc revertamur ad ordinem. Usque nunc sedimus more veteris consuetudinis, ut praetulimus; sive ob ammonitionem qua monemur quomodo Deo cantare debeamus secundum Apostolum dicentem: "Canentes et psallentes in cordibus vestris" [Eph 5:19]. Modo surgendum est ad verba Evangelii. "Anastasius, natione Romanus, ex patre Maximo," ut legitur in *Gestis episcopalibus,* "hic constituit ut, quotiescumque Evangelia sancta recitantur, sacerdotes non sede-
4 rent, sed curvi starent."✝ Dein ponit episcopus timiama in turibulum super prunas, ut suavem odorem excitet. Turibulum Christi corpus significat, in quo est ignis—scilicet Spiritus Sanctus—et ex quo procedit bonus odor quem unusquisque electorum ad se vult rapere. Idem odor bonam opinionem de Christo exire demonstrat, quam, qui vivere vult, in suum cor traicit.

5    Post hoc diaconus petit a sacerdote benedictionem. Sacerdos ei dicit: "Dominus sit in corde tuo et in labiis tuis." Intendat diligenter diaconus, ut cor eius cum Dominicis verbis vadat, et non sit infructuosa oratio sacerdotis. Dominum in mente teneat, quem suscipit per benedictionem sacerdotis. Et ut non exhalent verba imposita neu introeant nociva, signo crucis facto manu sacerdotis super caput ipsius munitur.

men have been made lectors, because the lamp had to be placed upon the candlestick to shine on everyone; and glorious faces must be put on high, where they may be seen by all who are present and offer those who stand around them an incitement to glory."✝

Let us now return to our plan. Until now we have been 3 sitting in accordance with ancient custom, as we said; or because of that admonition that warns us about how we should sing to God, according to the Apostle who says: "Singing and making melody in your hearts." Now we should rise for the words of the Gospel. As we read in the *Deeds of the Bishops:* "Anastasius, a Roman by birth, whose father was Maximus, established that priests should not sit, but rather should stand and bow whenever the holy Gospels are recited."✝ Then the bishop places incense over the coals in 4 the censer, to bring forth a sweet odor. The censer signifies Christ's body, in which there is fire—namely, the Holy Spirit —and which produces a good odor that each of the elect wants to take for himself. This same odor signifies the good reputation that comes from Christ, which he who desires to live takes into his heart.

After this the deacon seeks a blessing from the priest. 5 The priest says to him: "May the Lord be in your heart and on your lips." Let the deacon listen carefully, that his heart may go forth with the words of the Lord and that the priest's prayer may not be fruitless. Let him keep in mind the Lord, whom he receives through the priest's blessing. And that he may not breathe out the words he has received or introduce harmful words, he is fortified with the sign of the cross, made over his head by the hand of the priest.

6    Deinde vadit ad altare, ut inde sumat Evangelium ad legendum. Altare Hierusalem potest designare, ut praetulimus, de qua exivit Evangelica praedicatio, sicut scriptum
est: "De Sion exivit lex et verbum Domini de Hierusalem"
[Isa 2:3], vel ipsius Domini corpus, in quo sunt verba Evangelii, videlicet bonae nuntiationis. Ipse praecepit apostolis
praedicare Evangelium omni creaturae. Ipse dixit: "Verba
quae ego loquor vobis, spiritus et vita sunt" [John 6:64].
Christus vita; verba quae locutus est in Evangelio continentur. Diaconus qui portat Evangelium, Christi pes est. Portat
Evangelium in sinistro brachio, per quod significatur temporalis vita, ubi necesse est praedicari Evangelium.

7    Salutante diacono, congruit ut omnis populus ad eum
versus sit. Post hoc sacerdos et omnis populus vertit se ad
orientem, usque dum diaconus incipiat Dominum loqui, et
faciunt crucem in frontibus eorum. Neque hoc frustra acci-
piendum est: Quod infixit sacerdos per suam deprecationem
in corde diaconi, hoc unusquisque fidelis studeat infigere
8    animo suo. Diacono quia non est licitum, propter verba
composita "Sequentia sancti Evangelii secundum (quem-
cumque evangelistam)," orare, praevenit eum maior benedi-
cere, sive quia maiore benedictione indiget qui tradit semina
9    Evangelii, quam qui accipit. Sed populus interim deprecetur
Deum, ne diabolus auferat verba Evangelii de corde eius,
neque petrosa sint corda neu dumosa, sed terra bona, ut
fructum possint accipere et fructificare. Dicat saltim qui
promptior non est—ut capiam verba Evangelii—"Gloria
tibi, Domine" [Luke 14:10]. Hoc orato, muniant se signo

Then he goes to the altar to take up the Gospel book   6
for the reading. The altar can signify Jerusalem, as we said
above, out of which the preaching of the Gospel went forth,
as it is written: "The law has come forth from Zion and the
word of the Lord from Jerusalem." Or it can signify the
Lord's own body, in which are the words of the Gospel, that
is, of good news. He ordered the apostles to preach the Gospel to all creation. He said: "The words that I speak to you
are spirit and life." Christ is life; the words that he spoke are
contained in the Gospel. The deacon who carries the Gospel is Christ's foot. He carries the Gospel in his left arm,
which signifies the temporal life, where it is necessary that
the Gospel be preached.

Upon the deacon's greeting, all the people should turn to-   7
ward him. Afterward the priest and all the people turn to
the east, until the deacon begins to speak of the Lord, and
they make a cross on their foreheads. This should not be
considered purposeless: Each of the faithful strives to fix
upon his own soul the same sign that the priest fixed upon
the heart of the deacon through his prayer. Because the dea-   8
con is not allowed to pray—for he had to read the prescribed
words: "The continuation of the holy Gospel according to
(whichever evangelist)"—one of higher rank first blesses
him. Or this occurs because he who delivers the seeds of the
Gospel requires a greater blessing than he who receives it.
Meanwhile, though, the people ask God that the devil not   9
take the words of the Gospel from their hearts, and that
their hearts not be stony or thorny, but good earth, able to
receive and bear fruit. He who is not very quick should at
least say—I borrow these words from the Gospel—"Glory
to you, Lord." After this prayer, let all fortify themselves

sanctae crucis ad confirmanda ea quae bene cogitando et
loquendo plantavit in mente.

10  Quia mentio facta est de signo crucis in fronte, bonum
est intimare cur eam potissimum in ea parte corporis faciamus. Sedes verecundiae in fronte solet esse. Si quidem Iudaei erubescunt credere in illum quem norunt crucifixum
(ut Apostolus Paulus dicit: "Nos autem praedicamus Christum crucifixum, Iudaeis quidem scandalum" [1 Cor 1:23], et
reliqua), sed nos credimus per crucifixum salvari—de cuius
nomine Iudaei erubescunt, eiusque nos nomine credimus
muniri—atque ideo in fronte signum facimus, ubi sedes verecundiae est, sicut iam diximus.

11  Usque ad istud officium baculis sustentabamur; modo, ut
oportet servos ante Dominum stare, humiliter stamus, de-
ponentes baculos e manibus, quod potest nos separare ab
opere Iudaeorum, qui dabant harundinem in manu Christi
[Matt 27:29]. Sed nostra humilitas per baculorum posi-
tionem demonstretur in conspectu Domini. Duo cerei qui
portantur ante Evangelium, legem et prophetas designant
12  praecessisse Evangelicam doctrinam. Turibulum vero opinionem bonarum virtutum procedentem de Christo. Ipsum
turibulum in tribunal ascendit ante Evangelium, ut ibi suavem odorem ministret. Christi enim bona opera praecesserunt Evangelicam doctrinam, ut Lucas testatur in Actibus
Apostolorum: ". . . Quae coepit Iesus facere et docere" [Acts
1:1]. Prius fecit, et postea docuit.

13  Excellentior locus in quo Evangelium legitur eminentis-
simam doctrinam Evangelicae praedicationis atque mani-
festissimam auctoritatem iudicandi signat. Status cereorum

with the sign of the holy cross to confirm all that they have planted in their mind by thinking and speaking well.

Because we have mentioned the sign of the cross on the 10 forehead, it is a good idea to explain why we make it particularly on that part of our body. The seat of shame is customarily considered to be on the forehead. For if the Jews were ashamed to believe in someone they know was crucified (as Paul the Apostle says: "But we preach Christ crucified, unto the Jews indeed a scandal" and so on), while we believe we have been saved through him who was crucified—the one whose name shames the Jews, and by whose name we believe we are strengthened—we therefore make a sign on our forehead, where the seat of shame is, as we just said.

Until this office we were supported by our staffs; now we 11 stand humbly, as servants should stand before their master, and put our staffs down from our hands. This can distinguish us from the deed of the Jews, who put a reed in Christ's hand. But our humility in the Lord's sight is signified through putting our staffs down. The two candles that are carried before the Gospel show that the law and the prophets preceded the teaching of the Gospel. The censer, mean- 12 while, signifies the renown of good virtues that go forth from Christ. The censer goes up to the tribunal ahead of the Gospel, there to provide a sweet odor. And indeed, Christ's good works preceded the teaching of the Gospel, as Luke attests in the Acts of the Apostles: " . . . Which Jesus began to do and to teach." First he did; afterward he taught.

The more illustrious place where the Gospel is read signi- 13 fies the most eminent doctrine of evangelical preaching and the clearest authority of its judgment. The position of

monstrat inferiorem esse legem et prophetas Evangelio. Evangelio reposito post lectionem in loco suo, cerei exstinguuntur, quia, finita praedicatione Evangelii, lex et prophetia cessabunt. Evangelium, quod a primo tempore adventus episcopi quievit in altari usque ad novissimam tubam diaconi, illud tempus significat quo necesse est illud praedicari.

14 Praecedens officium praedicationem Christi usque ad oram passionis demonstrat, et suorum praedicatorum usque in finem mundi et ultra. Sequens opus passionis Christi et resurrectionis atque ascensionis in caelos, similiter suorum vel sacrificium vel mortificationem et resurrectionem per confessionem, atque suspirium in caelum, ubi audituri sunt: "Venite, benedicti Patris mei, possidete paratum vobis regnum" [Matt 25:34].

## 19

## De officio quod vocatur offerenda

Finitis prioribus officiis superius memoratis, officium introducitur, in quo caelebratur oblatio eorum qui Domino vota sua persolvunt. Primo ad memoriam reducenda est oblatio legalis, ac deinde Christi, postremo nostra.

the candles shows that the law and the prophets are lower than the Gospel. After the Gospel book has been returned to its place following the reading, the candles are put out, because the law and the prophets will be finished when the preaching of the Gospel is finished. The Gospel book, which rested on the altar from the first moment of the bishop's arrival until the final trumpet call of the deacon, signifies that time when the Gospel must be preached.

The preceding office signifies Christ's preaching until the 14 hour of his passion, and the preaching of his preachers until the end of the world and beyond. The following work signifies the work of Christ's passion and his resurrection and ascension to heaven, and also the sacrifice of his preachers and their death and resurrection through their confession, as well as their sighing unto heaven, where they will hear: "Come, blessed ones of my Father, possess you the kingdom prepared for you."

# 19

# On the office that is called the offertory

Now that the earlier offices discussed above have been completed, we begin an office where the offering of those who render their vows to the Lord is celebrated. We should first recall the offering according to the law, and then Christ's offering, and finally our own.

Oblatio legalis habebat duo altaria: unum in introitu tabernaculi, alterum in tabernaculo. Altare in introitu praefigurabat praesens officium, de quo scriptum est in libro
Exodi: "Posuit et tentorium in introitu tabernaculi, et altare
holocausti in vestibulo testimonii, offerens in eo holocaustum et sacrificia, ut Dominus imperarat" [Exod 40:27–28].

2 Pro quibus causis offerebatur Numerorum liber manifestat,
dicens in capitulo XXXVII: "Loquere ad filios Israhel et
dices ad eos: Cum ingressi fueritis terram habitationis vestrae, quam ego dabo vobis, et feceritis oblationem Domino
in holocaustum et victimam pacificam, vota solventes, vel
sponte offerentes munera" [Num 15:2–3].

3 Est et alterum genus sacrificii, quia duae sunt nostrae
oblationes: Una est per mortificationem carnis, altera in
oblatione bonorum operum; quae utraeque offeruntur in
introitu tabernaculi. In praesenti vita mortificare carnem
4 oportet et bona opera reddere. De secundo sacrificio, memoratus liber ita memorat: "Erit sacrificium similae duarum
decimarum, quae conspersa sit oleo tertiae partis hin. Et vinum ad libamentum tertiae partis eiusdem mensurae offe-
ret, in odorem suavitatis Domino" [Num 15:6–7]. Et quod
per sacerdotis manum debeat offerri, manifestatur in Levi-
tico capitulo XXVIIII: "Ideo offerre debent sacerdoti filii
Israhel hostias suas, quas occidunt in agro, ut sanctificentur
Domino ad hostium tabernaculi testimonii, et immolent eas
hostias pacificas Domino" [Lev 17:5].

There were two altars for the offering according to the law: one at the entrance to the tabernacle, the other in the tabernacle. The altar at the entrance prefigured this office, about which it is written in the book of Exodus: "And he put also the hanging in the entry of the tabernacle of the testimony, and the altar of holocaust in the entry of the testimony, offering the holocaust and the sacrifices upon it, as the Lord had commanded." The book of Numbers explains 2 for what reasons the offerings were made, saying in chapter 37: "Speak to the children of Israel and say to them: When you shall have come into the land of your habitation, which I will give you, and shall make an offering to the Lord for a holocaust or a peace offering, paying your vows, or voluntarily offering gifts."

And there is another kind of sacrifice, because our of- 3 ferings are twofold: One occurs through the mortification of the flesh, the other in an offering of good works; both were offered at the entrance to the tabernacle. In this life we should mortify our flesh and render good works. On the 4 second kind of sacrifice, the aforementioned book recounts as follows: "There shall be a sacrifice of flour of two tenths, which shall be tempered with the third part of a hin of oil. And he shall offer the third part of the same measure of wine for the libation, for a sweet savor to the Lord." And in Leviticus, chapter 29, it is shown what should be offered by the hand of the priest: "Therefore the children of Israel shall bring to the priest their victims, which they kill in the field, that they may be sanctified to the Lord before the door of the tabernacle of the testimony, and they may sacrifice them for peace offerings to the Lord."

5    Et iterum, in Paralipomenon, monstratur pro quibus rebus sit offerendum: "Ingressi quoque sunt sacerdotes ad Ezechiam regem et dixerunt ei: Sanctificavimus omnem domum Domini et altare holocausti." Et post pauca: "Consurgensque diluculo Ezechias rex, adunavit omnes principes civitatis et ascendit domum Domini. Obtuleruntque simul tauros VII, arietes VII, agnos VII, et hircos VII, pro peccato, pro regno, pro sanctuario, pro Iuda. Dixit quoque sacerdotibus filiis Aaron, ut offerrent super altare Domino" [2 Chr 29:18, 20–21]. Docti sumus Veteri Testamento pro quibus offerre debeamus sacrificia—scilicet pro votis, pro spontaneis, pro peccato, pro regno, pro sanctuario, pro Iuda. Quando adimplemus ea quae in tribulatione promisimus, pro votis facimus; quando gratias agimus de perceptis, pro spontaneis; quando conpungimur de commissis, pro peccato; quando recta corda petimus regibus, pro regno; quando stabilitatem sacrorum graduum, pro sanctuario; quando pacem et unanimitatem populi, pro Iuda.

7    Interim cantus celebrabatur in templo Domini, dicente eodem Paralipemenon: "Constituit quoque Levitas in domo Domini, cum cymbalis et psalteriis et cytharis, secundum dispositionem David." Et paulo post: "Cumque offerrentur holocausta, coeperunt laudes canere Domino et clangere tubis atque in diversis organis quae David rex reppererat concrepare. Omni autem turba adorante, cantores qui tenebant tubas erant in officio suo donec compleretur holocaustum. Cumque finita esset oblatio, incurvatus est rex et omnes qui erant cum eo et adoraverunt" [2 Chr 25:25, 27–29].

And again, in Chronicles, it is revealed for what things of- 5
ferings are to be made: "And the priests went to king Hezekiah and said to him: We have sanctified all the house of the
Lord and the altar of holocaust." And after a little: "And king
Hezekiah, rising early, assembled all the rulers of the city
and went up to the house of the Lord. And they offered together seven bullocks, and seven rams, and seven lambs, and
seven he-goats, for sin, for the kingdom, for sanctuary and
for Judah. And he spoke to the priests the sons of Aaron, to
offer them upon the altar of the Lord." We have been taught 6
by the Old Testament for what we should offer sacrifices—
namely for vows, for freewill offerings, for sin, for the kingdom, for the sanctuary and for Judah. When we fulfill the
promises we made in our tribulation, we make sacrifices for
our vows; when we give thanks for what we have received,
for freewill offerings; when we are stricken with remorse,
for sin; when we seek upright hearts in our kings, for the
kingdom; when we seek the stability of the holy orders, for
the sanctuary; when the peace and harmony of the people,
for Judah.

Meanwhile, a song was celebrated in the Lord's temple, as 7
the same book of Chronicles says: "And he set the Levites in
the house of the Lord, with cymbals and psalteries and
harps, according to the regulation of David." And a little
later: "And when the holocausts were offered, they began to
sing praises to the Lord and to sound with trumpets and various instruments that David the king of Israel had prepared.
And the whole multitude worshiped, and the singers who
held the trumpets were in their office until the holocaust
was finished. And when the offering was ended, the king
and all that were with him bowed down and worshiped."

8    Sed ante quam ingrederentur sacerdotes ad holocausta, lavabant manus suas, ut scriptum est in libro Exodi capitulo CXIII: "Locutusque est Dominus ad Moysen dicens: Facies et labium aeneum cum basi sua ad lavandum, ponesque illud in tabernaculo testimonii ad altare. Et, missa aqua, lavabunt in ea Aaron et filii eius manus suas et pedes, quando ingressuri sunt tabernaculum testimonii et quando accessuri ad altare" [Exod 30:17–20].

9    Sufficiant ista interim de oblatione veteri; nunc videamus Christi oblationem. Officium quod nos dicimus offerenda ab illo loco inchoatur, ubi sacerdos dicit: "Dominus vobiscum," et finitur circa illum locum ubi excelsa voce dicit: "Per omnia saecula saeculorum." Ideo excelsa voce novissimum profertur, ut audiatur a populo, et populi responsione confirmetur oratio.

10    Christus enim venire dignatus est Hierusalem die palmarum, et ibi expectare diem immolationis suae. Omnis retro immolatio illum praefigurabat; in illo consummata est omnis immolatio. In eo die descendit Dominus de Monte Oliveti, veniente ei obviam turba multa. Non est dubium quin

11  salutaret eam secundum morem bonum antiquae traditionis—quem etiam nostra, non solum perita ecclesia, sed etiam vulgaris tenet. Solet sibi obvianti aliquod bonum optare causa salutationis. Et praecipue propterea dicimus Dominum salutasse turbam venientem sibi obviam, quoniam talis erat consuetudo Iudaeorum, ut Agustinus in Psalmo *Saepe expugnaverunt me* [Ps 128]: "Nostis enim," inquit, "fratres, quando transitur per operantes, est consuetudo ut dicatur illis: Benedictio Domini super vos, et magis

But before the priests entered to the holocaust they 8 washed their hands, as it is written in the book of Exodus, chapter 113: "And the Lord spoke to Moses saying: You shall make also a brazen laver with its foot to wash in, and you shall set it between the tabernacle of the testimony and the altar. And, water being put into it, Aaron and his sons shall wash their hands and feet in it when they are going into the tabernacle of the testimony and when they are to come to the altar."

For now, these remarks on the Old Testament offering 9 should suffice; let us now look into Christ's offering. The office that we call the offertory begins when the priest says: "The Lord be with you," and it ends at the point where he says, with raised voice: "For all the ages of ages." This last is offered in a raised voice so that it may be heard by the people; and the prayer is confirmed by the response of the people.

Now Christ deigned to come to Jerusalem on the Day 10 of Palms, to await there the day of his sacrifice. Every sacrifice before that prefigured him; in him every sacrifice was consummated. On that day the Lord descended from the Mount of Olives and a great crowd came to meet him. There 11 is no doubt that he greeted them according to the good custom of ancient tradition—which is observed not only by our learned church, but also by common habit. It is customary to wish good, by way of greeting, upon anyone who comes to meet you. And we say that the Lord greeted the crowd coming to meet him particularly because this was the custom of the Jews, as Augustine says on the Psalm *Saepe expugnaverunt me:* "For you know, brothers, when we walk past laborers, we are accustomed to say to them: 'May the Lord's blessing be upon you,' and that custom pertained even

ista consuetudo erat in gente Iudaeorum. Nemo transibat et videbat aliquod opus in agro vel in vinea vel in messe vel aliquid eiusmodi—non licebat transire sine benedictione."†

12 Haec consuetudo manet usque hodie in nostra ecclesia. Quando transitum facimus de uno officio ad alterum, quasi nuper introeamus ad operarios, salutamus eos verbis benedictione plenis.

13 Postea dicit sacerdos: "Oremus." Nisi Christi virtus corda replesset turbarum ad orationem, non ei canerent tam magnificas laudes. Oratione enim serenatur cor ad cognoscendum Dominum. Puritas lintei quod ponitur in altari, puritatem mentium eorum signat, qui Domino cantabant. Eandem puritatem qua repleverat corda cantantium, requirebat in templo quando eiecit inde vendentes et ementes, dicens: "Scriptum est: Domus mea domus orationis vocabitur" [Matt 21:12–13; Mark 11:15–17]. Dum enim sacerdos suscipit oblationes, cantores cantant. Quamdiu enim turba cantabat: "Osanna in excelsis" [Matt 21:9; Mark 11:10], Christus vota eorum suscipiebat.

14 Oblatione suscepta, sacerdos redit ad altare, ut in eo disponat, sive ipse seu diaconus, oblationes coram Domino, quas illi immolaturus est in sequentibus Missae. Christus enim, post accepta vota cantantium, Hierusalem et templum Domini intravit, in quo erat altare, ibique se praesentavit sibi Deoque Patri ad immolationem futuram.

15 Postea dicit sacerdos secretam, ut secretae Christi, quae illo tempore agebantur, nobis ad memoriam ducantur. Agustinum legamus super Iohannem, ubi exponit Christum

more among the Jewish people. No one passed by and saw any work in the field or on the vine or at harvest or anything of this sort—it was not permissible to pass by without a blessing."+ This custom persists down to this day in our church. When we pass from one office to the next, as if we were going in among laborers, we greet them with words full of blessing. 12

Then the priest says: "Let us pray." Unless Christ's virtue 13 had reinvigorated the hearts of the crowds for prayer, they would not have sung such magnificent praises to him. For the heart is purified by prayer to understand the Lord. The purity of the linen cloth, or sindon, that is placed on the altar signifies the pure minds of those who sang to the Lord. In the temple, when he expelled the buyers and sellers, he demanded the very purity that had filled the hearts of the singers, saying: "It is written: My house shall be called a house of prayer." For when the priest receives the offerings the cantors sing. And for as long as the crowd sang: "Hosanna in the highest," Christ received their prayers.

After the offering has been received, the priest returns to 14 the altar so that, upon it, either he or the deacon may arrange before the Lord the offerings that will be sacrificed to him later in the Mass. For Christ, after he had received the prayers of the singers, entered Jerusalem and the Lord's temple, where the altar was, and there he presented himself to God the Father for his coming sacrifice.

Then the priest says the secret, so that Christ's secrets, 15 which were kept in that time, may be called to our mind. Let us read Augustine on John, where he explains that Christ

venisse ad diem festum scenophegiae non manifeste, sed quasi in occulto. Ita inquit: "Manifestetur ergo, tollatur velum, appareat quod erat secretum."✝ Omnia quae dicta sunt antiquo populo Israel in multiplici scriptura sanctae legis—quae agerent, sive in sacrificiis sive in sacerdotiis sive in diebus festis, et omnino in quibuslibet rebus quibus Deum colebant—quaecunque illis dicta et praecepta sunt—umbrae fuerunt futurorum. Quorum futurorum? Quae implentur in Christo. Unde dicit Apostolus: "Quotquot enim promissiones Dei in illo 'etiam'" [2 Cor 1:20]—id est, in illo

16   impletae sunt. Ex his dictis possumus intellegere cuius vice secretam dicat sacerdos. Agnus Paschalis latebat in Christo, qui immolandus erat. Hoc erat secretum apostolis; erat secretum ceteris fidelibus qui cum eo erant; erat secretum populo Iudaeorum usque ad diem caenae, quo ipse apertius manifestare dignatus est passionem suam. Usque ad illum diem protenditur secreta sacerdotis.

17   Moraliter: In praesenti officio altare nostrum praefiguratur ab altari holocausti, quo immolabantur victimae, pro peccato, pro regno, pro sanctuario, pro Iuda, pro votis, pro spontaneis. Has oblationes cotidie habemus in nostra ecclesia; easdem per manus sacerdotis offerimus. Altare nostrum designat in praesenti generalem vitam iustorum, qui carnem suam crucifigere cotidie cum vitiis et concupiscentiis, atque in hostiam viventem Deo offerre solent. Si altare, quod praefiguratur ab altari holocausti, significat generalem vitam iustorum, oblationes quae in eo offeruntur eorum cogitationes et bona opera designant.

came on the day of the Feast of the Tabernacles not openly, but as if in secret. He speaks thus: "Let it therefore be revealed, let the veil be lifted, let that which was secret appear."✝ Everything that was said to the ancient people of Israel in the manifold scripture of the holy law—the things that they did, whether in sacrifices or in their priestly offices or on feast days, and in all the matters in which they worshiped God—whatever things they were told and ordered to do—all these were shadows of things to come. Of what things to come? Those things that were fulfilled in Christ. Thus the Apostle says: "For all the promises of God are in him 'indeed'"—that is, they were fulfilled in him. Through these sayings we can understand in whose role the priest says the secret. The Paschal lamb was hidden in Christ, who was to be sacrificed. This was a secret to the apostles; it was a secret to the rest of the faithful who were with him; it was a secret to the Jewish people until the day of the supper, when he deigned to reveal his passion openly. The priest's secret extends until that day. 16

Morally: In this office our altar is prefigured by the sacrificial altar, on which victims were sacrificed for sin, for the kingdom, for the sanctuary, for Judah, for vows and for freewill offerings. We have these offerings daily in our church; we offer the same things through the hands of the priest. Our altar signifies, in the present, the whole life of the just, who are accustomed to crucify their flesh every day with its vices and concupiscences, and to make offerings to God through the living host. If this altar, prefigured by the sacrificial altar, signifies the whole life of the just, the offerings that are offered upon it signify their thoughts and good works. 17

18 Redeamus ad initium praesentis officii. Salutat episcopus populum, deprecando ut Dominus sit cum illo. Populus e contra orat pro sacerdote, ut simul cum suo spiritu sit Dominus cum eis. Haec salutatio introitum demonstrat ad aliud officium. Postea dicit: "Oremus," ammonetque ut unusquisque offerentium sese ad suam conscientiam introducat. Si quis habet ad immolandum, immolet: Id est si quis conscius est proprii vitii, roget ut mucrone invisibili feriatur; si quis habet voluntarium sacrificium, sive spontaneum, sive pro quacunque re sit—precetur ante quam de manu eius exeat, ut acceptabile sit Domino, nec despiciatur, sicut despectum est Cain quia non recte offerebat.

19 Interim ponitur sindo in altare. Sindone, quam solemus corporale nominare, admonetur omnis, scilicet populus et ministri altaris nec non et sacerdos, ut sicut illud linteum castigatum est ab omni naturali viriditate et humore, ita sit mens offerentium ab omni carnali cupiditate. Et, sicut illud nitet suo splendore, ita intentio offerentium simplicitate niteat coram Deo.

20 Dein transit sacerdos ad suscipiendas oblationes. Interim cantores cantant more antiquorum, ut iam praetulimus, sive turbarum, quae cantabant Christo venienti Hierusalem. Populus dat oblationes suas, id est panem et vinum, secundum ordinem Melchisedech [Gen 14:18–20]. Panis quem offert et vinum exprimunt omnia desideria pia intrinsecus latentia, sive sint pro immolatione seu pro hostia viva. Quod

Let us return to the beginning of this office. The bishop   18
greets the people by requesting that the Lord be with them.
The people, for their part, pray for the priest, that the Lord
may be with his spirit and with them. This greeting marks
the beginning of another office. Then he says: "Let us pray,"
and he admonishes each of the offerers to examine his conscience. If anyone has something to sacrifice, let him sacrifice it: That is, if anyone is conscious of his own vice, he
should ask that it be struck with an invisible sword; if anyone has a voluntary or freewill sacrifice, or for whatever reason—he should pray, before it leaves his hand, that it be acceptable to the Lord and that it not be disdained, as Cain's
was disdained because he did not sacrifice property.

Meanwhile, a sindon is placed upon the altar. Through   19
this sindon, which we are accustomed to call the corporal,
everyone, including the people and the ministers of the altar and the priest, is admonished that, just as the linen was
chastised away from its natural greenness and moisture, so
too should the mind of those making the offering be chastised from every desire of the flesh. And, just as the linen
gleams with its own splendor, so should the intention of
those making the offering gleam before God.

Then the priest passes over to receive the offerings. The   20
cantors, meanwhile, sing in the manner of the ancients, as
we just said, or in the manner of the crowd that sang to
Christ as he came to Jerusalem. The people give their offerings, namely the bread and wine, according to the order of
Melchizedek. The bread and the wine that they offer ex-
press all the pious desires that lie hidden within, whether
for the sacrifice or for the living host. That which is done

21 foris agitur, signum est illius quod intrinsecus latet. Unde Agustinus in libro decimo *De civitate Dei,* capitulo XVIIII: "Qui autem putant haec visibilia sacrificia diis aliis congruere, illi vero tamquam invisibili invisibilia, maiora maiori, melioriorque meliora (qualia sunt purae mentis et bonae voluntatis officia)—profecto nesciunt haec ita esse signa illorum, sicut verba sonantia signa sunt rerum. Quocirca, sicut orantes atque laudantes ad eum dirigimus significantes voces, cui res ipsas in corde quas significamus offerimus— ita sacrificantes non alteri visibile sacrificium offerendum esse noverimus, quam illi cuius in cordibus nostris invisibile sacrificium nos ipsi esse debemus."✝

22 Susceptis oblationibus, revertitur sacerdos ad altare, disponente diacono oblatas super altare more primorum septem diaconorum [Acts 6:3–5]. Lavat sacerdos manus more priorum sacerdotum, ut extersae sint a tactu communium

23 manuum atque terreno pane. Quae lavatio manus mundationem cordis signat per lacrimas et compunctiones, sicut Beda in libro *De tabernaculo et vasis eius* refert: "Recte," inquit, "pro altari holocausti labrum ponitur, in quo abluti sacerdotes ingrediantur tabernaculum et thymiama Domino incendant. Duobus namque modis lacrimarum et compunctionum status distinguitur." Et post pauca: "Neque enim quisquam de plebe ibi lavari, sed ipse pontifex iussus est et filii eius (videlicet sacerdotes gradus inferioris) —quia magnorum virorum sicut perfectior vita, sic et compunctio solet esse sublimior." Et iterum: "Quod si in

externally is a sign of what lies hidden within. Thus Augus-    21
tine in *The City of God,* book 10, chapter 19: "Now there are
those who think that these visible sacrifices are suitable for
other gods, while invisible, greater and better sacrifices (like
the services of a pure mind and a good will) befit an invisible, greater and better God. They clearly do not know that
the former sort of sacrifices are signs of the latter sort, just
as the words that we utter are signs of real things. And thus,
just as in prayer and praise we direct our signifying voices to
him, and we offer him the things that we signify in our heart
—so too do we recognize that, while we sacrifice, a visible
sacrifice should be offered to no one except to him, and we
ourselves in our hearts should be his invisible sacrifice."†

Once he has received the offerings, the priest returns to    22
the altar, while the deacon arranges the offerings upon the
altar in the manner of the first seven deacons. The priest
washes his hands in the manner of the first priests, that they
may be cleansed from the touch of common hands and
earthly bread. This hand washing signifies the purification    23
of the heart through tears and compunction, as Bede re-
ports in his book *On the Tabernacle and its Vessels:* "It is
proper," he says, "to place a basin before the altar of the sacrifice; after the priests have been washed in it, let them enter the tabernacle and burn incense to the Lord. For the
state of crying and compunction is marked in two ways."
And after a little: "Nor was just anyone from among the people ordered to wash there, but rather the priest himself and
his sons (that is, the priests of lower rank)—because just as
the life of great men is often more perfect, so too is their
compunction more sublime." And again: "And if we want to

persona Aaron ipsum magnum pontificem Dominum salvatorem accipere volumus, constat etiam eum huius aqua la-
bri, prius quam ad altare oblaturus intraret, esse lotum—
quia, prius quam thymiama sui sacrosancti corporis propter
salutem nostram in altari crucis incenderet, pro nostro
amore etiam lacrimas fudit; quod in resurrectione Lazari
caeleberrime innotuit."✝

24  Cantantibus adhuc cantoribus, vadit sacerdos ad altare et
orat. Quod ceteros praemonuit facere, agit. Orat pro suis
propriis delictis remissionem, ut dignus sit accedere ad altare et ad tactum oblatarum, ne fiat illi quod factum est
Bethsamitibus, qui temere viderunt arcam Domini. De quo
scribitur in libro Samuhelis: "Percussit autem de viris Bethsamitibus, eo quod vidissent arcam Domini; et percussit de
populo LXX viros et quinquaginta milia plebis" [1 Kgs 6:19].

25  Dein suscipit oblationes sacerdotum et diaconorum quibus
licitum est accedere ad altare. Accipit etiam ab archidiacono
duas: unam pro se et alteram pro diacono.

26  Ex turibulo, quod superimponit post orationem, demonstratur per quem ei propitiare possit Dominus, videlicet per
Dominum nostrum Iesum Christum, cuius corpus designat
turibulum. De quo scriptum est in Exodo: ". . . Ut offerant in
ea thymiama Domino, ne forte moriantur" [Exod 30:20–21].
Unde Beda memoratus: "Mors etenim timenda est animae
spiritalis et aeterna, si qui ad ministerium altaris electus thymiama orationum Deo reddere neglegit."✝

accept, in the person of Aaron, that great high priest, our Lord the savior, it is also clear that Jesus was washed with the water of this basin before he proceeded to the altar to sacrifice—because, before burning the incense of his most holy body for our salvation upon the altar of the cross, he also poured out tears out of love for us, as was famously revealed during the resurrection of Lazarus."✝

While the cantors are still singing, the priest goes to the 24 altar and prays. He does what he admonished others to do. He prays for the remission of his own sins, that he may be worthy to approach the altar and touch the offerings, lest what befell the men of Bethshemesh, who looked thoughtlessly upon the ark of the Lord, befall him. About this, it is written in the book of Samuel: "But he slew of the men of Bethshemesh because they had seen the ark of the Lord; and he slew of the people seventy men and fifty thousand of the common people." Then he receives the offerings of the 25 priests and deacons who were allowed to advance to the altar. He also receives two from the archdeacon: one for himself and another for the deacon.

The censer, which he raises up after his prayer, signifies 26 the one through whom the Lord can be rendered favorable, namely through our Lord Jesus Christ, whose body the censer signifies. About this it is written in Exodus: ". . . To offer on it incense to the Lord, lest perhaps they die." Thus the aforementioned Bede: "Indeed, the spiritual and eternal death of the soul should be feared by anyone who has been chosen for service at the altar and fails to render the incense of prayers to God." ✝

27 Diaconus aquam miscet vino. Cur hoc faciat Cyprianus monstrat ad Quirinum, de sacramento Dominici calicis dicens: "Quando autem in calice vino aqua miscetur, Christo populus adunatur, et credentium plebs ei in quem credidit copulatur et iungitur. Quae copulatio et coniunctio aquae et vini sic miscetur in calice Domini, ut commixtio illa non possit ab invicem separari. Unde ecclesiam (id est plebem in ecclesia constitutam, fideliter et firmiter in eo quod credidit perseverantem) nulla res separare poterit a Christo, quomi-

28 nus haereat semper et maneat individua dilectio. Sic autem in sanctificando calice Domini offerri aqua sola non potest, quomodo et vinum solum non potest. Nam, si vinum tantum quis offerat, sanguis Christi incipit esse sine nobis; si vero aqua sit sola, plebs incipit esse sine Christo. Quando autem utrumque miscetur, et adunatione confusa sibi invicem copulatur, tunc sacramentum spiritale et caeleste per-

29 ficitur. Sic vero calix Domini non est aqua sola aut vinum solum, nisi utrumque sibi misceatur—quomodo nec corpus Domini potest esse farina sola aut aqua sola, nisi utrumque adunatum fuerit et copulatum, et panis unius compage solidatum. Quo et ipso sacramento populus noster ostenditur adunatus, ut, quemadmodum grana multa in unum collecta et commolita et commixta panem unum faciunt, sic in Christo, qui est panis caelestis, unum scimus esse corpus, cui coniunctus sit noster numerus et adunatus."✝

30 Omnis populus, intrans ecclesiam, debet sacrificium Deo offerre; at cantores, qui sunt de genere Levitarum propter instantem necessitatem cantandi non habent licentiam huc

The deacon mixes water with wine. Cyprian explains why 27 he does this to Quirinus, speaking about the sacrament of the Lord's chalice: "But when water is mixed with wine in the chalice, the people are made one with Christ, and the multitude of believers are joined and united to him in whom they believed. This joining and uniting of the water and wine is mixed in the Lord's chalice in such a way that their commingling cannot be undone. And so nothing should be able to separate the church (that is, the people established in the church, faithfully and firmly persevering in what they have believed) from Christ, much less hinder love from standing ever fast and remaining undivided. And so, in sanc- 28 tifying the Lord's chalice, water cannot be offered alone, in the same way that wine cannot be offered alone. For if someone should offer wine only, Christ's blood begins to be without us; but if the water were alone, the people begin to be without Christ. But when both are mixed and joined to each other in mingled union, the spiritual and celestial sacrament is accomplished. And so the Lord's chalice is neither 29 water alone nor wine alone; rather, both should be mixed with each other—just as the Lord's body cannot be flour alone or water alone; rather, each should be united and joined with the other, and solidified through union of one bread. Our people are revealed to be joined in this sacrament, so that, just as many grains collected, ground and mixed together make a single loaf of bread, so too do we recognize a single body in Christ, who is our heavenly bread, with which our number is united and joined."✝

All the people, when they enter the church, should offer 30 a sacrifice to God; but the cantors, who are descendants of the Levites, because of their constant singing duties, do not

illucque discurrendi, ut singuli offerant cum ceteris. Statutum est eis, ut penitus non sint extorres a sacrificio, custodire aquam, et hanc unum offerre pro ceteris. Populus offert vinum, cantores aquam. Sicut vinum et aqua unum fiunt in calice, sic populus et cantores in corpore Christi. Cantores more Levitarum antiquorum, qui omnia necessaria tabernaculi providebant, quaerant aquam ad fontem, et servent eam coopertam usque ad tempus sacrificii, et tunc mundam eam offerant.

31    Postea ponit calicem in altari diaconus et sudarium suum in dextro cornu altaris. Est habile ad hoc, ut, quicquid accesserit sordidi, illo tergatur, et sacerdotis mundissimum maneat. Si, per incuriam sacerdotis, ante oram sacrificii aliquae maculae inhaeserunt variarum tentationum, has suo sudario detergat ora sacrificii. Ita vigilet ut nullae possint inhaerere, quantum humana fragilitas sinit, quin ilico repellantur in hostio suggestionis, ac quieta mente pro peccatis aliorum intercedat.

32    Unde Cyprianus in sermone *De oratione Dominica:* "Quando autem stamus ad orationem, fratres dilectissimi, vigilare et incumbere ad preces toto corde debemus. Cogitatio omnis carnalis et saecularis abscedat, nec quicquam tunc animus quam id solum cogitet, quod precatur. Ideo et sacerdos, ante orationem praefatione praemissa, parat fratrum

have leave to move here and there, in order to make offerings with the others. It was established that one of them, that they not be completely excluded from the sacrifice, see to the water and offer it on behalf of the other cantors. The people offer wine, the cantors water. Just as the wine and the water become one in the chalice, so do the people and the cantors become one in the body of Christ. In the manner of the ancient Levites, who provided all that was necessary for the tabernacle, let the cantors procure water at the font and keep it covered until the time of the sacrifice, and then offer it in a pure state.

Then the deacon puts the chalice on the altar and places 31 his maniple at the right edge of the altar. This maniple is useful for wiping away whatever dirt has accumulated, so the priest's maniple may remain as clean as possible. If, through the priest's negligence, the stains of various temptations have clung to him down to the hour of the sacrifice, let him wipe them away with his own maniple at the hour of the sacrifice. He should be so vigilant that no sins can cling to him, insofar as human fragility permits, and so that they are repelled immediately at the door of suggestion, that he may intercede with a peaceful mind for the sins of others.

Thus Cyprian in his sermon *On the Lord's Prayer:* "But 32 when we stand for prayer, beloved bothers, we should be vigilant and exert ourselves toward prayer with our whole heart. Let every carnal and worldly thought depart; nor should the spirit then contemplate anything, except what it prays for. And so the priest, before his prayer and after he has said the preface, prepares the minds of his brothers

mentes dicendo: 'Sursum corda,' ut dum respondet plebs: 'Habemus ad Dominum,' admoneatur nihil aliud se quam

33 Deum cogitare debere. Claudatur contra adversarium pectus et soli Deo pateat, nec ad se hostem Dei tempore orationis adire patiatur. Obrepit enim frequenter et penetrat et subtiliter fallens preces nostras a Deo avocat, ut aliud habeamus in corde et aliud in voce—quando intentione sincera Deum debeat non vocis sonus, sed animus et sensus orare. Quae autem segnitia est alienari et capi ineptis cogitationibus et profanis cum Deum deprecaris, quasi sit aliud quod magis debeas cogitare quam id quod cum Deo loqueris.

34 Quomodo audiri te a Deo postulas, cum te ipse non audias? Vis esse Deum tui memorem, cum rogas, quando tu ipse tui memor non sis? Hoc est de eo hoste in totum non cavere; hoc est, quando oras, Deum et maiestatem Dei neglegentia orationis offendere; hoc est vigilare oculis et corde dormire, cum debeat Christianus, et cum dormit oculis, corde vigilare, sicut scriptum est ex persona ecclesiae loquentis in Cantico Canticorum: 'Ego dormio et cor meum vigilat' [Song 5:2]. Quapropter sollicite et caute Apostolus admonet

35 dicens: 'Instantes orationi, vigilantes in ea,' [Col 4:2]—docens scilicet et ostendens eos impetrare quod postulant de Deo posse, quos Deus videat in oratione vigilare. Orantes autem non infructuosis nec nudis precibus ad Deum veniant. Inefficax petitio est, cum precatur Deum sterilis oratio. Nam, cum omnis arbor non faciens fructum excidatur in ignem mittatur [Matt 3:10, 7:19; Luke 3:9; etc.], utique et

by saying: 'Lift up your hearts,' so that when the people respond, 'We hold them up to the Lord,' they may be advised to think of nothing except God. Let the breast be closed 33 against the adversary and open to God alone; nor should it allow God's enemy to approach it during the time of prayer. For he often approaches in stealth, penetrates and uses quiet deception to call our prayers away from God, that we may have one thing in our heart and another in our voice— while our spirit and senses should pray to God with sincere intention, and not the sound of our voice. What laziness it is to be distracted and seized by improper and profane thoughts while you pray to God, as if there is something you should contemplate more than what you are saying to God. How can you ask to be heard by God when you do not hear 34 yourself? Do you want God to be mindful of you when you make your request, when you are not mindful of yourself? This amounts to not being fully on guard against the enemy; it amounts to offending God and God's majesty in the negligence of your prayer when you pray; it amounts to being vigilant with our eyes while sleeping in our heart, whereas a Christian should be vigilant at heart even when he sleeps with his eyes, as is written through the person of the church that speaks in the Song of Songs: 'I sleep and my heart watches.' Thus the Apostle advises with care and caution, 35 saying: 'Be urgent in prayer, watching in it'—teaching and proving, namely, that those whom God sees being vigilant in prayer can achieve what they ask of God. But those who pray should approach God with neither unfruitful nor naked prayers. A petition becomes unfruitful when the prayer that addresses God is barren. For, since every tree not bearing fruit is cut down and put into the fire, so too is the

sermo non habens fructum promereri Deum non potest, quia nulla operatione fecundus est, et idcirco scriptura divina instruit dicens: 'Bona est oratio cum ieiunio et elemosina' [Tob 12:8]."✝

36    Quo facto, revertitur ad populum sacerdos et precatur ut orent pro illo, quatinus dignus sit universae plebis oblationem offerre Domino. Praesentes adorationes praelibatae sunt in Paralipemenon, ubi orat turba cantantibus levitis. Post holocaustum nempe "incurvatus est rex" [2 Chr 29:28–29] et omnis populus. Audivi dicere quod plebs eadem ora tres versiculos cantet pro sacerdote: "Mittat tibi Dominus auxilium de sancto," et duos sequentes [Ps 19:3–5].

## 20

# De secreta

Sequitur secreta. Secreta ideo nominatur quia secreto dicitur. In hac primo nominatur hostia sive sacrificium, oblatio; in hac precatur sacerdos per eandem hostiam purgari usquequaque. Sacerdotis solius est soli Deo offerre sacrificium, ac ideo, quia Deo cogitationibus loquimur, non est

word that does not bear fruit incapable of being worthy of God, for nowhere in its work is it fruitful, and therefore divine scripture teaches us, saying: 'Prayer is good with fasting and alms.'"+

After this is done, the priest returns to the people and 36 requests that they pray for him, that he may be worthy to render the offering of the entire people to the Lord. These devotions were foreshadowed in Chronicles, where the crowd prays while the Levites sing. Indeed, after the sacrifice, "the king" and all the people "bowed down." I have heard it said that, at this moment, the people should sing three verses on the priest's behalf: "May he send you help from the sanctuary," and the two that follow.

## 20

# On the secret

The secret follows. The secret is so-called because it is said in secret. In it, first of all, the offering is called the victim or the sacrifice; in it the priest prays that this same sacrifice be completely cleansed. It is the priest's duty alone to offer the sacrifice to God alone, and therefore, because we speak to God with our thoughts, no audible voice is

necessaria vox reboans, sed verba ad hoc tantum—ut eisdem
2  ammoneatur sacerdos quid cogitare debeat. In sequenti
namque oratione clamat populum ut quod ipse iam habet,
habeat et ille—hoc est sursum cor ac deinde ut gratias agant
Deo pro serenitate mentis. Igitur haec necessario extollitur
voce. Quod omnibus licet simul agere, id est gratias referre
Deo, hoc adclamatur. Quod ad solum sacerdotem pertinet,
id est immolatio panis et vini, secreto agitur. Quantum enim
victima praestabat in Veteri Testamento ad Domini sacrificium, postquam ducta erat ad hostium tabernaculi—tantum
praestat sacrificium in prima positione altaris. Non potest
iam mutari neque in melius neque in deterius.

## 21

# De ymno ante passionem Domini
# sive praeparatione

Ymnus ideo dicitur quia refertus est gratiarum actione et
laudibus angelorum; praeparatio, quia parat fratrum mentes
ad honestatem decentem conventum sanctorum angelorum, qui solent adesse consecrationi corporis Christi, et ad
ipsam reverentiam tantae consecrationis; ac ideo excelsa

necessary; rather, the words are for this purpose alone—that the priest may be advised, through them, about what he should think. And in the prayer that follows he calls out to 2 the people, that they may have what he now has—namely, that they may lift up their hearts and give thanks to God for their tranquility of mind. It is therefore necessary that this be said aloud. What is proclaimed is what everyone is allowed to do at the same time: namely, offer thanks to God. That which pertains to the priest alone, namely the offering of bread and wine, is done in secret. For as much as the victim for the Lord's sacrifice was present in the Old Testament, after it had been led to the door of the tabernacle—to that same degree is our sacrifice present in its initial position on the altar. It cannot now be altered for better or worse.

## 21

# On the hymn, or preparation, before the Lord's passion

The hymn is so-called because it is filled with the thanksgiving and the praise of the angels; the preparation, because it prepares the minds of the brethren both for the honor befitting the assembly of holy angels, whose custom it is to attend the consecration of Christ's body, and for the dignity of such a consecration. It is therefore sung with raised

voce cantatur. Officium hoc inchoatur a salutatione quae dicitur ante *Sursum corda,* finitur in ymno *Sanctus, sanctus, sanctus.*

2    Praesens officium illud tempus nobis ad memoriam reducit, quando Christus in caena ascendit in "caenaculum magnum stratum" [Mic 14:15; Luke 22:12], et ibi locutus est multa cum discipulis, et ymnum retulit Deo Patri, quem Iohannes commemorat [John 13:31–14:30], usque dum exiret in Montem Oliveti. Ibi gratias egit Deo, ibi ymnum cantavit [Matt 26:30; John 15:1–17:26], in quo precatus est Patrem, ut servaret discipulos suos a malo, dicendo: "Non rogo ut tollas eos de mundo, sed ut serves eos a malo." Et ut sancti permaneant, subiungit: "Sanctifica eos in veritate." Et iterum: "Et pro eis sanctifico meipsum, ut sint et ipsi sanctificati in veritate" Et, ut in caelum transeant, dicit in sequentibus: "Pater, quos dedisti mihi, volo ut ubi ego sum, et illi sint mecum, ut videant claritatem meam quam dedisti mihi" [John 17:15, 17,
3    19, 24]. Iuxta hunc sensum altare est mensa Domini, in qua convivabatur cum discipulis; corporale, linteum quo erat ipse praecinctus; sudarium labor de Iuda proditore.

4    Hunc ordinem sequitur sacerdos: Cum suis auditoribus ascendit in cenaculum quando dicit: "Sursum corda." Auditores respondent: "Habemus ad Dominum." Quod precatus est pro se in praefatione—ut cor suum esset alienum a vinculis mundanis—hoc nunc monet auditores suos, ut pro tanto dono gratias agant Deo. Aditores confirmant "dignum et iustum" ita esse, et cetera usque "Per Christum Dominum
5    nostrum." Per quem reconciliati sumus Deo, per illum nostras gratiarum actiones offerimus. Quia non solum ea renovata sunt per Christum quae sunt in terra, sed etiam quae in

voice. This office begins with the greeting that is said before *Sursum corda,* and it ends in the hymn *Sanctus, sanctus, sanctus.*

This office calls to our mind the time when Christ went 2 up for dinner into "a large furnished dining room," and said many things there together with his disciples, and offered a hymn to God the Father, which John recalls, before he went out to the Mount of Olives. There he gave thanks to God, and there he sang a hymn in which he asked his Father to keep his disciples away from evil, saying: "I pray not that you take them out of the world, but that you keep them from evil." And he prayed that they remain holy, adding: "Sanctify them in truth." And again: "And for them do I sanctify myself, that they also may be sanctified in truth." And that they might go to heaven, saying subsequently: "Father, I will that where I am, they whom you have given me may be with me, that they may see the glory that you have given me." In this sense the altar is the Lord's table, where 3 he feasted with his disciples; the corporal is the linen cloth that he was girded with; the maniple is his suffering over the traitor Judas.

The priest follows this order: With his listeners he goes 4 up to the dining room when he says "Lift up your hearts." Those listening respond: "We hold them up to the Lord." He then tells his listeners about what he requested for himself in the preface—that his heart be free of earthly chains— that they may thank God for this great gift. His listeners confirm that this is "worthy and just," and so on until "Through Christ our Lord." The one through whom we 5 were reconciled to God is the one through whom we offer our thanksgivings. Because not only those things that are on earth were renewed in Christ, but also those things that are

caelis, recolit caelestium laudes. Quia enim de sacrificio agitur, restat ut et gratiarum actiones quas sacerdos offert pro sacrificio eius accipiamus, et ministeria angelorum, quae recoluntur in praesenti ymno, pro eorum sacrificio.

6    Illud intendendum est in omnibus officiis immolationis, tali nomine censendum esse visibile altare, quale est cor offerentium. Tempore quo ymnus ante passionem caelebratur, altare nostrum aptatur altare thimiamatum, quod significat specialem quorundam perfectiorum vitam, eorum scilicet "qui maiori mentis perfectione, exstinctis prorsus ac sopitis inlecebris omnibus carnis, sola Domino orationum vota offerunt, nihil quidem de carne quod se impugnet, nihil de conscientia peccati unde conturbent ac paveant habentes— sed dulcium profusione lacrimarum optantes venire et pa-

7    rere ante faciem Dei."✝ Oblatio quae superposita est in priore officio, Deo deputata est ac per hoc sanctificata, id est a terrenis separata et caelestibus deputata. In isto observatur, usque dum ex ea fiat corpus Domini, ac postea assumatur in caelum.

8    Intimatum est hanc praeparationem, quae caelebratur in altari thimiamatis, sacrificium angelorum ad memoriam nobis reducere, ac ideo quod dicit sacerdos—". . . quam laudant angeli . . ."—angelorum sacrificium est. In angelis archangelos intellegimus; dominationum sacrificium adoratio. In quibus principatus intellegimus; sicut dominationes subiecta sibi habent angelorum agmina, quibus mira potentia praeeminet, sic et principatus spiritus bonorum

in heaven, he recalls the praises of the heavens. Because this is celebrated with respect to the sacrifice, it remains for us to receive the thanksgivings that the priest offers for his sacrifice, together with the ministries of angels for their sacrifice, which are recalled in the present hymn.

We should note that, in all the offices of the sacrifice, the 6 visible altar and the heart of those who make the offering are to be referred to under the same name. At the time when the hymn before the passion is celebrated, our altar is modeled after the altar of incense, which signifies the special life of those who are more perfect, that is, of those who, "with greater perfection of mind, whose every fleshly attraction is dead and completely put to rest, offer only the vows of their prayers to God, retaining nothing assaulting them from the flesh and no consciousness of sin by which they are disquieted and disturbed—desiring, instead, to come and present themselves before God's face with a profusion of sweet tears."✝ The offering that was set up in the earlier office has 7 been counted as God's and on this account sanctified, or separated from the things of this earth and counted among celestial things. It is kept in this state until it becomes the Lord's body, and then it is taken up to heaven.

We have shown that this preparation, which is celebrated 8 upon the altar of incense, reminds us of the sacrifice of the angels. What the priest says, therefore—". . . which the angels praise . . ."—is the sacrifice of the angels. We understand that archangels are among these angels; they adore the sacrifice of the dominions. Among the angels we recognize the principalities. Just as the dominions have armies of angels subjected to themselves, whom they excel in marvelous power, so too do the principalities oversee the spirits of the

angelorum, quibus ad explenda divina ministeria principantur. Qui dominantur principantur; potestatum tremor caelorumque virtutum, ac beatorum seraphin agminum societas sancta. Caelos pro thronis positos intellegimus, quia caelum sedes Dei dicitur [Ps 10:5, 102:19; Isa 66:1; Acts 7:49; etc.]; hisque coniungimus cherubin, super quae dicitur Deus sedere, sicut Psalmus: "Qui sedes," inquit, "super cherubin, appare" [Ps 79:2]. His novem ordinibus praelibatis ordo decimus conditionis humanae adnexus est, ex cuius voce dicit sacerdos: "Cum quibus et nostras voces ut admitti iubeas deprecamur."

9    Ymnus sequens, qui additus est primaevo ymno, a Sixto papa additus est, ut in *Gestis pontificalibus* legitur. Ita enim scriptum est: "Hic constituit ut intra actionem sacerdos incipiens populo ymnum decantaret: Sanctus, sanctus, sanctus Dominus Deus Sabaoth."✝ Idem ymnus horum duorum ordinum voces continet. Ordo angelorum dicit: "Sanctus, sanctus, sanctus, Dominus Deus Sabaoth, pleni sunt caeli et terra gloria tua." Ordo hominum dicit: "Osanna in excelsis, benedictus qui venit in nomine Domini." Quam partem ymni cantavit turba Die Palmarum praecedens Dominum Hierusalem [Matt 21:9; Mark 11:9].

10   Iam diximus de altari quid significet. Dicendum est de sudario. Sudarium iacens in altari significat laborem quem habent angeli in ministerio humano, sive perfecti viri, qui non cessant orare pro nostra fragilitate; corporale vero intentionem non fictam.

good angels, which they govern to perform the divine ministries. Those who are dominated are ruled; the tremor of the powers, of the heavens, of the virtues and of the blessed ranks of seraphim is a holy society. We recognize the heavens in place of the thrones, because heaven is called the seat of God; to these we join the cherubim, over whom God is said to sit, as the Psalm says: "You that sit upon the cherubim, shine forth." To these nine aforementioned orders is joined a tenth order of human creation, in whose voice the priest says: "We ask that you permit that our voices also be received with theirs."

The subsequent hymn, which has been added to the original hymn, was added by Pope Sixtus, as is attested in the *Deeds of the Bishops.* For there it is written: "He established that, during the thanksgiving, the priest should begin to sing a hymn to the people: Holy, holy, holy, Lord God of Sabaoth."✝ This hymn contains the voices of two orders. The order of the angels says: "Holy, holy, holy, Lord God of Sabaoth, the heavens and earth are full of your glory." The order of men says: "Hosanna in the highest, blessed is he who comes in the name of the Lord." The crowd that went before the Lord to Jerusalem sang this part of the hymn on the Day of Palms.

We have already said what the altar signifies. We should speak about the maniple. The maniple lying on the altar signifies the labor that the angels exert in their service of humans, or the labor that perfected men exert, who never stop praying on behalf of our weakness; the corporal signifies unfeigned purpose.

11    Stant interim episcopi, sive sacerdotes, seu diaconi post
pontificem; subdiaconi vero in facie eius. Ibi illud adimple-
tur quod in memorato cenaculo dicit Dominus discipulis
suis secundum Lucam: "Reges gentium dominantur eorum,
et qui potestatem habent super eos benefici vocantur. Vos
autem non sic. Sed qui maior est in vobis, fiat sicut iunior, et
qui praecessor est, sicut minister. Nam quis maior est, qui
recumbit an qui ministrat? Nonne qui recumbit? Ego autem
in medio vestri sum, tamquam qui ministrat" [Luke 22:25–

12    27]. Multos discipulos Christi doctrina habebat, de quibus
erant illi centum viginti qui die Pentecostes simul inventi
sunt in una domo [Acts 1:15, 2:1]. De ipsis erat "Ioseph ab
Arimathia, discipulus Iesu, occultus propter metum Iudeorum" [ John 19:38], et ipse baiulator aquae qui suscepit eum
in cenaculo suo, cui mandavit Dominus: "Dicit tibi magister
. . ." Hi denique sive essent corporali positione in cenaculo,
quando Dominus caenavit, seu non forent, tamen eius obsequio non deerant, sicut is non defuit qui stravit cenaculum
magnum [Mic 14:13–16; Luke 22:10–13; Matt 26:18–19].

13    Hos credimus designari per subdiaconos, qui in facie
stant, sicut ille stetit, sive per praesentiam suam seu per ministerium, cuius erat cenaculum, sive mulieres quae perseve-

14    raverunt in passione Domini. De quibus Gregorius in *Moralibus* scribit: "Sed cum ad crucis oram ventum est, eius
discipulos gravis ex persecutione Iudaeorum timor invasit.
Fugerunt singuli; mulieres astiterunt. Quasi ergo, con-
sumpta carne, os Domini pelli suae adhesit [ Job 19:20], quia
fortitudo passionis tempore, fugientibus discipulis, iuxta se

Meanwhile, the bishops, priests and deacons stand be-  11
hind the pontiff, while the subdeacons face him. At this
point, what the Lord said to his disciples according to Luke
in the aforementioned dining room is fulfilled: "The kings
of the gentiles lord it over them, and they that have power
over them are called beneficent. But you not so. But he that
is the elder among you, let him become as the younger, and
he that is the leader, as he that serves. For which is greater,
he that sits at table or he that serves? Is it not he that sits
at table? But I am in the midst of you, as he that serves."
Christ's teaching had many disciples; among them were  12
those hundred and twenty who were found together in one
house on the day of Pentecost. Among them was "Joseph of
Arimathea, a disciple of Jesus, hidden for fear of the Jews,"
and the water carrier who received him in his dining room,
whom the Lord ordered: "The master says to you . . ." Later
on they would either physically be in the dining room when
the Lord feasted, or they would not be there, though they
were not absent from his service, just as he who prepared
the great dining room was not absent.

We believe that these people are signified by the sub-  13
deacons, who stand facing the pontiff. For the subdeacons
stand just as the man whose dining room it was stood, either
in actual presence or in service; and they stand just as the
women who persevered in the Lord's passion stood. Greg-  14
ory in his *Moralia* writes about them: "But when it came to
the time of the cross, a deep fear of persecution from the
Jews came upon his disciples. They each fled; the women
stood by. It was therefore as if, while his flesh was consumed,
the Lord's bone cleaved to his skin, because in his fortitude
at the time of his passion, as his disciples were fleeing, he

143

mulieres invenit. Stetit equidem aliquandiu Petrus, sed post territus negavit. Stetit etiam Iohannes, cui ipso crucis tempore dictum est: 'Ecce mater tua,' [ John 19:27]; sed perseverare minime potuit, quia de ipso quoque scriptum est quod 'Adolescens quidam sequebatur illum, amictus sindone super nudo, et tenuerunt eum; at ille, reiecta sindone, nudus profugit ab eis' [Mic 14:51–52]. Qui, etsi post, ut verba sui redemptoris audiret, ad oram crucis rediit, prius tamen territus fugit. Mulieres autem non solum non timuisse neque fugisse, sed etiam usque ad sepulchrum stetisse memorantur. Dicit ergo: 'Pelli meae consumptis carnibus adhaesit os meum' [ Job 19:20]: Hoc est hi qui meae fortitudini propinquius inhaerere debuerunt, passionis meae tempore timore consumpti sunt, et eas quas ad exteriora ministeria posui, in passione mea sine formidine inhaerere mihi fideliter inveni."

15

22

# De ymno *Sanctus, sanctus, sanctus*

Post ymnum inchoatum *Sanctus, sanctus, sanctus,* inclinant se et qui retro stant et qui in facie, venerando scilicet maiestatem divinam et incarnationem Domini, quae introducta

found the women nearby him. And Peter also stood by for a time, but afterward he was terrified and denied it. John also stood by; at the time of the cross it was said to him: 'Behold your mother;' but he was unable to persevere, for it is also written about him that 'A certain young man followed him, having a linen cloth cast about his naked body, and they laid hold on him; but he, casting off the linen cloth, fled from them naked.' Although he returned later on to hear the words of his redeemer at the time of the cross, he nevertheless fled earlier in terror. Yet the women are said not only 15 not to have been afraid nor to have fled, but even to have stood by until his burial. It therefore says: 'The flesh being consumed, my bone has cleaved to my skin': That is, those who should have cleaved more closely to my fortitude have been consumed with fear at the time of my passion, and I have found that those whom I placed in more remote ministries cleave to me faithfully in my passion, with no fear."

22

# On the hymn *Sanctus, sanctus, sanctus*

After the hymn *Sanctus, sanctus, sanctus* has begun, those who stand behind and those who stand facing the celebrant bow, namely to venerate the divine majesty and the Lord's incarnation, which were announced by the song of

sunt per cantum angelorum et turbarum. Angelorum concentus, dicendo: "Sanctus, sanctus, sanctus, Dominus Deus Sabaoth" [Isa 6:3], maiestatem divinam introducit; turbarum vero Domini incarnationem, dicendo: "Benedictus qui venit in nomine Domini, Osanna in excelsis" [Matt 21:9].

## 23

# De *Te igitur*

Perseverant retro stantes inclinati usque dum finiatur omnis praesens oratio—id est usque dum dicatur post orationem Dominicam: *Sed libera nos a malo.* Quod enim sequitur usque: *Per omnia saecula saeculorum* expositio est novissimae petitionis Dominicae orationis. Illi enim sunt quibus Dominus dixit: "Vos autem estis qui permansistis mecum in temptationibus meis, et ego dispono vobis, sicut disposuit mihi Pater meus, regnum" [Luke 22:28–29]. Unde Beda in tractatu super Lucam: "Non inchoationi patientiae, sed perseverantia caelestis regni gloria donatur, quia nimirum perseverantia, quae alio nomine constantia vocatur, robur quoddam et fortitudo mentis—cunctarumque, ut ita dixerim, est columna virtutum, quae cum bene recta et firma consistit, nihil est certius, nihil tutius bonis moribus."✠

the angels and the crowds. The choir of the angels, by saying: "Holy holy holy, Lord God of Sabaoth," announces the divine majesty; the harmony of the crowds announces the Lord's incarnation, by saying: "Blessed is he who comes in the name of the Lord, Hosanna in the highest."

23

## On the *Te igitur*

Those who stand behind the celebrant bow until this prayer is wholly finished—that is, until *Sed libera nos a malo* is said after the Lord's prayer. For what follows until *Per omnia saecula saeculorum* is an explanation of the final petition of the Lord's prayer. And those who stand behind are those to whom the Lord said: "And you are they who have continued with me in my temptations, and I dispose to you, as my Father has disposed to me, a kingdom." Thus Bede in his treatise on Luke: "The glory of the heavenly kingdom is granted not at the beginning of patience, but through perseverance, for there is no doubt that perseverance, which is also called constancy, is a kind of mental vigor and fortitude—and, if I may say so, a pillar of the virtues. When it stands straight and firm there is nothing more certain and nothing safer than our virtues."✛

3 Ipsi stant inclinati donec liberentur a malo. Hi enim sunt apostoli qui magna tribulatione erant oppressi; ante quam audirent Domini resurrectionem, non se audebant erigere, ut confiterentur se esse Christi discipulos. Hi, quamvis in passione non forent praesentes, tamen perseverant post Christi resurrectionem in temptationibus. Non enim surgunt ante lucem, de qua psalmista dicit: "Vanum est vobis ante lucem surgere" [Ps 126:2] — id est, vanum est gloriari, ante quam resurgatis a mortuis.

4 At qui in facie stant, signant discipulos occultos propter metum Iudaeorum, sive mulieres quae poterant in facie persistere. Sua declinatione subdiaconi mestitiam eorum signant, de quibus dicit idem qui supra in eodem: "Non autem ideo solus mulierum planctus eum sequebatur, quia non innumerus etiam praesentium virorum coetus de eius erat passione mestissimus — sed quia femineus quasi contemptibilior sexus liberius poterat, praesentibus sacerdotum principibus et magistratibus, quid contra eos senserit osten-

5 tare."✝ Qui poterant non dolere quando eum quem nimio amore dilexerunt et noverunt innocentem, ab impiis comprehendi, ligari, duci ante eos, flagellari, spui in faciem, crucifigi viderunt? Quid significet eorum erectio ante finitam orationem, si Dominus dederit, in congruis locis monstrabitur.

6 Nunc de *Te igitur* dicendum est. Ab initio orationis usque locum ubi dicitur: "Et in electorum tuorum iubeas grege

They stand and bow until they are freed from evil. For 3 they are the apostles who were oppressed with great tribulation; before they heard about the Lord's resurrection, they did not dare stand up straight to confess that they were Christ's disciples. Although they were not present at the passion, they nevertheless persevere amid temptations after Christ's resurrection. For they do not rise before the light that the psalmist speaks about: "It is vain for you to rise before light"—that is, it is vain to boast before you rise from the dead.

Those who stand facing the celebrant, meanwhile, sig- 4 nify the disciples hidden out of their fear of the Jews, or the women who were able to remain facing Christ. Through their bow, the subdeacons signify the mourning of those whom the same author as above speaks about: "But it was therefore not only the mournful cry of the women that followed him, for a not inconsiderable crowd of men were present who were very sorrowful about his passion—but rather because the female sex, which in a way is more despised, was able to show its opposition in the presence of the rulers and magistrates of the priests more freely."✝ Who 5 were they who could not mourn when they saw the one whom they adored with great love, and knew to be innocent, arrested by the impious, bound, led before them, scourged, spat at in the face and crucified? If the Lord grants it, we will reveal, in the relevant section, what it means that those facing the celebrant stand before the prayer is over.

Now we should discuss the *Te igitur.* From the beginning 6 of this prayer to the place where it says: "And may you command that we be counted among the flock of your elect,

numerari, per Christum Dominum nostrum," caelebratur sacrificium electorum, qui non habent in carne quod eis
7 repugnet, neque in conscientia quod conturbet. Sicut enim duo altaria erant in tabernaculo Moysi sive in templo Salomonis—unum thymiamatis, alterum holocausti—ita sunt duo sacrificia sanctae ecclesiae. Unum est in quo omnes carnales motus sopiti sunt, de quo commemoravimus et nunc iterum commemorandum est; alterum est in quo necesse est cotidie carnales motus mactare, de quo in posterioribus dicendum est. In promptu altare thimiamatis est ex utroque officio (scilicet capitis et corporis), usque ad locum de quo superius titulatum est.

8 Nunc vero reddendum est cur oratio praesens et praefatio secreto dicantur, ex sermone Cypriani *De Dominica oratione:* "Sit," inquit, "orantibus sermo et precatio cum disciplina, quietem continens et pudorem. Cogitemus nos sub conspectu Dei stare; placendum est divinis oculis et habitu corporis et modo vocis. Nam, ut impudentis est clamoribus strepere, ita contra congruit verecundo modestis precibus
9 orare. Denique magisterio suo Dominus secreto orare nos praecepit, in abditis et semotis locis, in cubilibus ipsis [Matt 6:6]. Quod magis convenit fidei, ut sciamus Deum ubique esse praesentem, audire omnes et videre, et maiestatis suae plenitudine in abdita quoque et occulta penetrare, sicut scriptum est: 'Ego Deus appropinquans et non Deus de longe. Si absconditus fuerit homo in absconditis, ego ergo non videbo eum? Nonne caelum et terram ego impleo?' [Jer 23:23–24] Et iterum: 'In omni loco oculi Domini speculantur

through Christ our Lord," the sacrifice of the elect is celebrated. They have nothing in their flesh that resists them and nothing in their conscience that disturbs them. For just 7 as there were two altars in the tabernacle of Moses and in the temple of Solomon—one of incense, the other of the burned offering—so there are two sacrifices of the holy church. There is one in which all the impulses of the flesh are put to rest, which we have spoken about and are now about to discuss again; and there is another in which the impulses of the flesh have to be sacrificed every day, which we will discuss later on. The altar of incense is manifest through both offices (that is of the head and the body), down to the passage that was mentioned above.

But now we should return to why the present prayer and 8 the preface are said in secret. From Cyprian's sermon *On the Lord's Prayer:* "Let the words and the request of those who pray be disciplined," he says; "let them have peace and modesty. Let us consider that we stand under God's gaze; the divine eyes should be pleased with the bearing of our body and the manner of our voice. For just as it is the way of the shameless man to cry out with shouts, so is it appropriate for the bashful man to pray with modest prayers. And so 9 in his teaching the Lord ordered us to pray in secret, in hidden and removed places, in our very bedchambers. And this accords better with our faith, that we may know God is present everywhere, that he hears and sees everything, and that he penetrates even secret and hidden places in the fullness of his majesty, as it is written: 'I am a God at hand and not a God afar off. Shall a man be hid in secret places, and I not see him? Do I not fill heaven and earth?' And again: 'The eyes of the Lord in every place behold the good and the evil.'

10 bonos et malos' [Prov 15:3]. Et quando in unum cum fratribus convenimus et sacrificia divina cum Dei sacerdote caelebramus, verecundiae et disciplinae memores esse debemus, non passim ventilare preces nostras inconditis vocibus,
nec petitionem commendandam modesto Deo tumultuosa
loquacitate iactare, quia Deus non vocis, sed cordis auditor
est; nec admonendus est clamoribus, qui cogitationes hominum videt, probante Domino et dicente: 'Quid cogitatis ne-
quam in cordibus vestris?' [Matt 9:4; Luke 5:22] Et alio loco:
'Et scient omnes ecclesiae quia ego sum scrutator renis et
11 cordis' [Rev 2:23; Jer 17:10]. Quod Anna in primo Regnorum
libro, ecclesiae typum portans, custodit et servat; quae
Deum non clamosa petitione, sed tacite et modeste intra
ipsas pectoris latebras precabatur, et loquebatur prece occulta sed manifesta fide. Loquebatur non voce sed corde,
quia sic Deum sciebat audire, et impetravit efficaciter quod
petiit, quia fideliter postulavit [1 Kgs 1:9–20]. Declarat
scriptura divina, quae dicit: 'Loquebatur in corde suo et labia eius movebantur, et vox eius non audiebatur' [1 Kgs 1:13],
et exaudivit eam Dominus. Item legimus in Psalmis: 'Dicite
in cordibus vestris, et in cubilibus vestris compungimini' [Ps
4:5]. Per Ieremiam quoque haec eadem Spiritus Sanctus sug-
gerit, et docet dicens: 'In sensu autem tibi debet adorari
12 Dominus' [Bar 6:5]. Adorans autem, fratres dilectissimi, nec
illud ignoret quemadmodum in templo cum Pharisaeo
publicanus oraverit—non allevatis in caelum impudenter
oculis, nec manibus insolenter erectis, sed pectus suum pul-
sans et peccata intus inclusa contestans, divinae misericordiae implorabat auxilium. Et, cum sibi Pharisaeus placeret,

And when we come together with our brothers as one and 10
celebrate the divine sacrifices with God's priest, we should
be mindful of modesty and discipline; we should not exhale
our prayers at random with confused words, nor hurl the petition we want to commend to our modest God with restless
loquacity, since God does not listen to the voice, but to the
heart. Nor should we petition him who sees the thoughts
of men with cries, as the Lord demonstrates when he says:
'Why do you think evil in your hearts?' And in another place:
'And all the churches shall know that I am he who searches
the reins and hearts.' This is the habit that Hannah, bearing 11
a type of the church, keeps and preserves in the first book of
Kings. She addressed God not with a clamorous petition,
but quietly and modestly within the confines of her heart,
and she spoke with a hidden prayer but in obvious faith. She
spoke not with her voice but with her heart, because she
knew that God hears this way, and she achieved to great effect what she sought, because she asked faithfully. So declares divine scripture, which says: 'Now she spoke in her
heart and her lips moved, and her voice was not heard,' and
the Lord heard her. Again we read in the Psalms: 'The things
you say in your hearts, be sorry for them upon your beds.'
The Holy Spirit advises the very same thing, through Jeremiah, as he teaches when he says: 'But the Lord should be
adored in your mind.' But he who worships, beloved breth- 12
ren, should not overlook how the publican prayed in the
temple with the Pharisee — neither raising his eyes proudly
to heaven nor holding his hands aloft in insolence, but beating his chest and bearing witness to the sins closed inside it,
he implored the help of divine mercy. And while the Pharisee was pleased with himself, the publican deserved more to

sanctificari hic magis meruit, qui sic rogavit. Qui spem salutis non in fiducia innocentiae suae posuit, cum innocens nemo sit, sed peccata confessus humiliter rogavit—et exaudivit orantem qui humilibus ignoscit [Luke 18:9–14].”✝

13    Quia audivimus ex Cypriano modum orationis, audiamus ex *Te igitur* orationes. Primo vice Christi sacerdos tres orationes exercet, sicut Dominus fecit postquam exivit in Montem Oliveti ante traditionem suam, id est pro universali ecclesia, et pro specialibus fratribus, et pro coro sacerdotum. Prima oratio Christi est: “Mi Pater, si possibile est, transeat a me calix iste; verumtamen non sicut ego volo, sed sicut tu” [Matt 26:39]. Transferri calicem a se postulat, non quidem timore patiendi, sed misericordia prioris populi, ne ab illo bibat calicem propinatum. Unde et signanter non dixit: Transfer a me “calicem,” sed “calicem istum”—hoc est

14    populi Iudaeorum. Secunda oratio est Christi: “Pater mi, si non potest hic calix transire, nisi bibam illum, fiat voluntas tua” [Matt 26:42]. Quod ita Hieronimus: “Secundo orat ut, si Ninive aliter salvari non potest nisi aruerit cucurbita, fiat voluntas Patris [ Jonah 4:5–11].”✝ “Tertio oravit” Christus “eundem sermonem” [Matt 26:44], ut ex memorato Hieronimo discimus, qui dicit apostolorum timorem sequenti paenitentia magistrum impetrasse corrigendum. Intellegimus eum pro suo corpore, id est apostolis, nunc orasse.

15    Eodem numero, id est ternario, sacerdos voce electorum complet orationem suam. Sacrificium est electorum ad Deum Patrem per Christum Dominum nostrum: “Haec

be sanctified, for he made his request in this way. He did not place his hope of salvation in presumption of his own innocence, since nobody is innocent, but he confessed his sins humbly and made his request—and he who forgives the humble heard his prayer."✝

Now that we have heard about how to pray from Cyprian, 13 let us hear about prayers from the *Te igitur*. First, the priest, in the role of Christ, recites three prayers, just as the Lord did after he went out to the Mount of Olives before he was handed over. They are for the whole church, for his particular brethren, and for the chorus of priests. Christ's first prayer is: "My Father, if it be possible, let this chalice pass from me; nevertheless not as I will, but as you will." He asks that the chalice be passed from him, of course not in fear of suffering, but out of mercy for the earlier people, lest he drink the chalice offered by them. It is thus significant that he did not say: Take "the chalice" from me, but "this chalice"—that is, the chalice of the Jewish people. Christ's sec- 14 ond prayer is: "My Father, if this chalice cannot pass away, but I must drink it, your will be done." On which, Jerome as follows: "In the second place he prays that the Father's will be done, if Nineveh cannot be saved unless the gourd dries out."✝ Christ "prayed a third time . . . the selfsame word," as we learn from the aforementioned Jerome, who says the master obtained that the apostles' fear be corrected through their ensuing penance. We understand that at this point he prayed for his own body, namely for the apostles.

By the same number, namely three, the priest completes 15 his prayer in the voice of the elect. It is the sacrifice of the elect to God the Father through Christ our Lord: "These gifts, these offerings, these holy unspoiled sacrifices." Gifts

dona, haec munera, haec sancta sacrificia inlibata." Dona et munera unum sunt, iuxta quod Danihel respondit Balthasari, quando ei promisit purpuram et torquem auream: "Munera, inquit, "tua sint tibi, et dona domus tuae alteri da"

16 [Dan 5:17]. Hoc unum bis reperitur, quia duae res offeruntur Deo, id est panis et vinum, quae utraeque non incongruenter possunt plurali numero appellari. Etenim in pane est aqua et farina, in vino aqua et vinum. Idipsum tertio repetitur: "Haec sancta sacrificia inlibata." Singulari repetitione duo superiora recapitulantur, quoniam in uno corpore Christi haec sacramenta continentur.

17 Sed quoniam potius requirit Deus sacrificium cordis, quam hoc quod extrinsecus ministratur, in corde sacerdotis volumus interpretari dona, et munera et sacrificia inlibata. Unde dicit Agustinus in libro X *De civitate Dei,* capitulo III: "Dona eius in nobis, nos quoque ipsos vovemus et reddimus ei. Beneficiorum eius solempnitatibus, festis et diebus statutis, dicamus sacramusque memoriam, ne volumine temporum ingrata subrepat oblivio. Ei sacrificamus hostiam humilitatis et laudis in ara cordis, igne fervidam caritatis."✝ Iuxta eundem Agustinum, si quis dona vult Deo offerre, se ipsum offerat; si quis munera, saepius memoretur beneficiorum eius; si quis sacrificia inlibata, humilitatem laudemque et ca-

18 ritatem offerat. Dicit idem in libro memorato capitulo V:

and offerings are the same thing, according to Daniel's response to Balthazar, when Balthazar promised him the purple and the golden chain: "Your rewards be to yourself," he said, "and the gifts of your house give to another." This single point is repeated twice, because two things are offered to God, namely bread and wine, both of which can be referred to, not inappropriately, in the plural. And indeed, there is water and meal in the bread, and water and wine in the wine. The same line is repeated a third time: "These holy inviolate sacrifices." The two earlier repetitions are recapitulated by this singular repetition, because these sacraments are contained in the single body of Christ. 16

But because God is more interested in the sacrifice of the heart than in what is provided externally, we want the gifts, the offerings and the unspoiled sacrifices to be understood as being in the heart of the priest. Thus Augustine says in book 10 of *The City of God,* chapter 3: "We consecrate and render his gifts in us, together with our very selves, to him. Let us confess and consecrate the memory of his favors on solemnities, feasts and other established days, lest thankless oblivion, through the passage of time, steal them away. To him we offer a sacrifice of humility and praise, burning hot with the fire of charity, on the altar of our heart."✝ According to this same Augustine, if anyone wants to offer gifts to God, he should offer himself; if anyone wants to give offerings, he should be ever mindful of God's benefactions; if anyone wants to offer unspoiled sacrifices, he should offer humility and praise and charity. The same author says in chapter 5 of the aforementioned book: 17

18

"Sacrificium ergo visibile invisibilis sacrificii sacramentum—id est sacrum signum est." Et in sequentibus, in eodem, capitulo XVIIII: "Quocirca, sicut orantes atque laudantes ad eum dirigimus significantes voces, cuius res ipsas
in corde quas significamus offerimus, ita sacrificantes, non
alteri visibile sacrificium offerendum esse noverimus, quam
illi cuius in cordibus nostris invisibile sacrificium nos ipsi
esse debemus."✝

19    Quia, Domino miserante, sacrificium verum invenimus,
sequentia *Te igitur* prosequamur. Sequitur: "In primis quae
tibi offerimus pro ecclesia tua sancta catholica," et reliqua.
Memoratum sacrificium pro tribus offertur, id est pro ecclesia sancta universali; pro specialibus fratribus, quorum ele-
mosinas suscepimus aut munus, aut quorum sponsores sumus facti, vel quorum praesentiam tuemur in officio Missae
nostrae, quorum tamen sacrificium est laus; pro nobis ipsis
sacerdotibus, qui communicamus sanctae Mariae et apostolis in uno Domino, ut in omnibus protectione Domini muniamur.

20    Et iterum: Tria sunt sacrificia iuxta prophetam, quae requirit Dominus a nobis—scilicet facere iudicium et diligere
misericordiam et paratum esse ire cum Domino Deo [Mic
6:8]. Facit iudicium, qui se ei vovet et reddit, cuius totus est,
et omne quod in eo potest esse ex his quae sunt. Idem facit
iudicium, quando indicat primo orandum esse pro pace uni-
versalis ecclesiae. Dein diligit misericordiam qui ex praeteritis beneficiis gratias agendo futura sibi acquirit. Ipse
sibi multam misericordiam adquirit qui Deum ad potiora

"The visible sacrifice is therefore a sacrament of the invisible sacrifice—that is, it is a holy sign." And further on, in the same book, chapter 19: "And thus, just as in prayer and praise we direct our signifying voices to him, and we offer him the things that we signify in our heart—so too do we recognize that, while we sacrifice, a visible sacrifice should be offered to no one except to him, and we ourselves in our hearts should be his invisible sacrifice."✝

Since, through the Lord's mercy, we have found the true 19 sacrifice, let us pursue what comes after the *Te igitur.* There follows: "First of all, those things that we offer you for your holy catholic church," and so forth. The aforementioned sacrifice is offered on behalf of three things, namely on behalf of the holy universal church; for the particular brethren whose alms or offerings we have received, or whose sponsors we have become, or whose presence we behold during the office of Mass and whose sacrifice is simply praise; and for ourselves, the priests, who are in communion with holy Mary and the apostles in one Lord, that we may be strengthened in all things through the Lord's protection.

And again: According to the prophet there are three sac- 20 rifices that the Lord requires of us—namely to give judgment, and to love mercy and to be prepared to walk with the Lord God. He gives judgment, who vows and gives himself over to God, to whom he belongs completely, together with everything that can be in him of those things that exist. And the same person does judgment when he declares that he should first pray for the peace of the whole church. Then, he loves mercy who acquires future favors for himself by first giving thanks for past favors. He who appeals to God for more important things acquires much mercy for himself.

provocat. Idem facit misericordiam circa fratres, quando
21 pro eis specialiter deprecatur Deum. Vult paratus esse ut
eat cum Domino Deo, qui se dicit consortio unius Domini
communicare cum Maria et coro apostolorum. Isti vadunt
quocumque ierit Dominus. Ut non exorbitet mortalis a
recto tramite propter periculum praesentis vitae, rogat ut in
omnibus protectione Domini muniatur.

22 In hac oratione designat sindo, quantum ad caput pertinet, humilitatem Christi, quam assumpsit ex terreno habitu;
in qua oravit Deum Patrem. Sudarium vero, quod iacet in
cornu altaris, laborem suum, quem sustinuit in oratione,
sicut Lucas dicit: "Et factus est in agonia, et prolixius orabat. Et factus est sudor eius sicut guttae sanguinis decurren-
tis in terram" [Luke 22:43–44].

23 His ita praelibatis, dicit pium cor: "Hanc igitur oblationem servitutis nostrae, quaesumus, Domine, ut placide
accipias." In hac oratione deprecatur Deus, ut dignetur vota
electorum suorum suscipere, atque ideo ei praesentantur
per pronomen demonstrativum, dicendo: "Hanc igitur obla-
24 tionem." Quod postea additum est a sancto Gregorio—
"Diesque nostros in tua pace disponas," et cetera—ostendit
nullum securum esse posse in praesenti saeculo de sua stabi-
litate, quamvis perfectus esse videatur, ac ideo necesse fore,
ut semper deprecetur in pace disponi dies suos in praesenti
saeculo, et in futuro eripi ab aeterna damnatione et in electorum grege numerari. De corporali et de sudario dictum
25 est, quantum ad corpus pertinet. Christus, postquam oravit

The same person does mercy for his brothers when he petitions God especially on their behalf. He wants to be prepared to go with the Lord God, who says, in the fellowship of the one Lord, that he is in communion with Mary and the congregation of the apostles. They go wherever the Lord has gone. So that, as a mortal, he may not stray from the right path because of the danger of the present life, he asks to be strengthened by the Lord's protection in all things. 21

In this prayer the sindon, insofar as it relates to the head, signifies Christ's humility, which he took up through his earthly guise and in which he prayed to God the Father. The maniple, on the other hand, which lies at the edge of the altar, signifies the exertion that he sustained in prayer, as Luke says: "And being in an agony, he prayed the longer. And his sweat became as drops of blood trickling down upon the ground." 22

Now that these things have been set forth, the pious heart says: "Therefore we ask, Lord, that you receive this offering of our servitude in a peaceful spirit." In this prayer we ask that God deign to receive the vows of his elect, and these vows are therefore presented to him with the demonstrative pronoun, by saying: "Therefore . . . this offering." What Saint Gregory added next—"And may you guide our days in your peace," and so on—shows that no man can be secure about his stability in this world, although he might seem perfect. It is therefore always necessary that he ask for his days to be guided in peace in this world, and that he be rescued from eternal damnation and counted among the flock of the elect in the world to come. The corporal and the maniple have been discussed, insofar as each pertains to the body. After he prayed for his members, Christ said to his 23 24 25

pro membris suis, dixit discipulis suis: "Surgite, eamus; ecce adpropinquabit qui me traditurus est" [Matt 26:46]. Explanatio Hieronimi: "Non nos inveniant quasi timentes et retractantes; ultro pergamus ad mortem, ut confidentiam et gaudium passuri videant."✝ Praesentat pium cor electorum suorum oblationem suam Deo, praesentat et pius Dominus se ipsum his per quos immolandus erat Deo Patri.

26　　In hac oratione significat sindo subsistens humilitatem maximam, in qua non solum dignatus est orare pro suis, sed etiam tradi in manus impiorum; sudarium vero laborem quem sustinuit ex traditore.

<h1 style="text-align:center">24</h1>

# De institutione Dominica in conficiendo corpus et sanguinem

Immolato priore sacrificio, quod constat orationibus perfectorum et est coniunctum sacrificio angelorum, descenditur ad universale sacrificium, immolationem scilicet Christi, quod caelebratur ante *Nobis quoque peccatoribus.* Etenim Christus pro peccatoribus descendit ad immolandum, dicente Paulo ad Timotheum: "Humanus sermo, et omni acceptione dignus, quia Christus Iesus venit in hunc mun-
2　dum peccatores salvos facere" [1 Tim 1:15]. Ipse est per quem

disciples: "Rise, let us go; behold he is at hand who will betray me." Jerome's explanation: "May they not come upon us as if we are fearful and denying; let us hasten onward to death, that those who are about to suffer may see our confidence and joy."+ The pious heart presents the offering of its elect to God, and the pious Lord presents his very self to those by whom he was to be sacrificed to God the Father.

In this prayer the sindon, as it lies there, signifies the 26 great humility in which he deigned not only to pray for his own apostles, but also to be given over to the hands of the impious. The maniple, meanwhile, signifies the suffering that he endured because of the traitor.

<h1 style="text-align:center">24</h1>

# On the Lord's instruction for consecrating the body and blood

Now that the earlier sacrifice has been offered, which accords with the prayers of the perfected and is joined to the sacrifice of the angels, we come down to the universal sacrifice, namely the offering of Christ, which is celebrated before *Nobis quoque peccatoribus*. And indeed Christ came down to be sacrificed on behalf of sinners, as Paul says to Timothy: "A kind saying, and worthy of all acceptance, that Christ Jesus came into this world to save sinners." He is the 2

omne sacrificium Deo offertur, quia in eo condita sunt omnia quae in caelis sunt et quae in terris [Col 1:16]. Ipse, cum sit Dominus omnium, voluit hostia fieri pro peccatoribus qui non poterant Deo sacrificium offerre, ut sua immolatione reconciliarentur Deo, quatinus et ipsi non forent infructuosi, sed possent offerre sacrificium, quoniam una hostia, Christus, oblatus est pro iustis et iniustis. Idem sacrificium permanet in altari, quod ante positum est.

3    Unde modo dicit sacerdos: "Quam oblationem, tu Deus, in omnibus, quaesumus, benedictam, ascriptam, ratam, rationabilem acceptabilemque facere digneris." Quod sic exponendum arbitror salvo magistrorum intellectu: "Quam oblationem," quae sic oblata est ut ista, id est ea devotione in omnibus, hoc est tota cogitatione, tota vita, toto intellectu. "Benedictam," sicut haec benedicta est, sacerdote dicente: "Uti accepta habeas, et benedicas." "Ascriptam" tibi, ut haec, de qua dictum est: "Quaesumus, Domine, ut placatus accipias." "Ratam," id est fidelem, sicut haec quae tibi porrecta est "per Christum Dominum nostrum." "Tu Deus, quaesumus, rationabilem acceptabilemque facere digneris," quatinus haec "nobis fiat corpus et sanguis Domini nostri Iesu Christi."

4    Quo ordine id perficiendum sit, ex Domini institutione addiscitur. Accipit sacerdos panem manibus suis exemplo Christi, de quo dictum est: "Accepit panem in sanctas ac

one through whom every sacrifice is offered to God, because in him all things that are in heaven and on earth were created. Since he is the Lord of all, he wanted to become a victim on behalf of sinners who were unable to offer sacrifice to God. In this way, sinners might be reconciled to God through his sacrifice, and they might avoid being unfruitful and become capable of offering their sacrifice—for one victim, Christ, was offered on behalf of the just and the unjust. The sacrifice that was earlier placed on the altar remains there.

And so the priest now says: "We ask that you, God, deign to make this offering, in all respects, blessed, included, approved, reasonable and acceptable." I think that this should be explained as follows, saving the understanding of the masters: "This offering," which has been offered as these have, that is with devotion in all things, that is with full thought, full life and full understanding. "Blessed," just as this has been blessed, as the priest says: "That you may consider them accepted, and bless them." "Included" unto you, as these have been, about which it was said: "We ask, Lord, that you receive them in a spirit of peace." "Approved," or faithful, as are these things that have been offered to you "through Christ our Lord." "We ask that you, God, deign to make it reasonable and acceptable," that these things "may become for us the body and blood of our Lord Jesus Christ." 3

We learn from the Lord's instruction in what order this should be done. The priest takes the bread in his hands after the example of Christ, of whom it is said: "He took the 4

5   venerabiles manus suas," et reliqua. "Similiter et calicem" [1 Cor 11:25], dicente Cypriano ad Cecilium *De sacramento Dominici calicis:* "Invenimus non observari a nobis quod mandatum est, nisi eadem quae Dominus fecit, nos quoque faciamus, et, calicem pari ratione miscentes, a divino magisterio non recedamus."✝ Quamvis hoc ille de mixtione vini et aquae conclusisset, tamen de tota institutione Dominica intellegere possumus adimplendum, in quo suum mandatum est et apostolorum observatio.

6   Caeterum de crucibus, quas solemus diverso modo facere super panem et vinum—non est quid dicam cur tali et in tali loco figantur, vel quare plures in aliquo, vel pauciores in aliquo. Si Dominus, quando benedixit panem, fecisset crucis signaculum, ipsi noverunt qui praesentes fuerunt, praeser-

7   tim cum nondum erat erectum vexillum sanctae crucis. At modo scimus quia necessaria est, dicente Agustino in expositione Evangelii Iohannis omelia sexagesima quarta: "Quid," inquit, "quod omnes noverunt, signum Christi, nisi crux Christi? Quod signum nisi adhibeatur, sive frontibus credentium, sive ipsi aquae ex qua regenerantur, sive oleo quo chrismate unguntur, sive sacrificio quo aluntur, nihil horum rite perficitur."✝ Videtur mihi, si semel fuerit facta crux super panem et vinum, posse sufficere, quia semel crucifixus est Dominus.

bread in his holy and venerable hands," and so forth. "Like- 5
wise also the chalice," as Cyprian says to Caecilius in *On the
Sacrament of the Lord's Chalice:* "We find that we do not observe what has been commanded, unless we do the same
things that the Lord did, and, mixing the chalice for the
same purpose, we do not depart from divine teaching."✝ Although he reached this conclusion about the mixing of wine
and water specifically, we can nevertheless understand that
this is to be fulfilled with respect to the whole of the Lord's
instruction, for which we have his commandment, together
with the observance of the apostles.

Otherwise, with respect to the crosses that it is our cus- 6
tom to make over the bread and the wine in varying ways—I
have nothing to say about why they are fixed at this point,
or why in one place more are made, and in another, fewer.
If the Lord had made a sign of the cross when he blessed
the bread, only those who were present know, especially
since the banner of the holy cross had not yet been raised.
But we know that it is necessary now, as Augustine remarks 7
in his commentary on the Gospel of John, in the sixty-
fourth homily: "What," he said, "is the sign of Christ that
everyone recognizes, if not the cross of Christ? Unless this
sign is made on the foreheads of believers, or upon the water through which they are reborn, or upon the oil or chrism
through which they are anointed, or upon the sacrifice
through which they are fed—none of these things is performed correctly."✝ It seems to me that, if a cross is made
over the bread and wine once, that can suffice, for the Lord
was crucified once.

8     Hic concrepant verba Dominicae mensae cum toto officio Missae. Canitur hic *Accipiens panem,* et reliqua, quod ac-
citatur a sacerdote quando suscipit oblatam in secreta Missae, aut quando hic eam elevat. Gratias agit in ymno *Vere
dignum et iustum est.* Benedicit in praesenti loco; frangit circa
communionem; postea dat ad communicandum. Hic credimus naturam simplicem panis et vini mixti verti in naturam
rationabilem—scilicet corporis et sanguinis Christi. Sindo
iacens in altari signat linteum quo erat Dominus praecinctus, et sudarium laborem quem assumpsit in lavatione pe-
dum, sive quem sustinuit pro labore Iudae; altare mensam
Domini.

# 25

# De ascensione Christi in crucem

In sacramento panis et vini, necnon etiam in memoria
mea, passio Christi in promptu est. Dixit ipse: "Haec
quotiescumque feceritis, in mei memoriam facietis" [Luke
22:19–20; 1 Cor 11:23–25]—id est quoties hunc panem et

At this point, the words that were once recited at the  8
Lord's table resound with the whole office of the Mass. Here
*Accipiens panem,* and so on, is sung. This is recited by the
priest when he receives the offering during the secret of
the Mass, or when he raises it. He gives thanks in the hymn
*Vere dignum et iustum est.* At this point he blesses the offering;
he breaks it for communion; afterward he distributes it for
communion. At this point we believe that the simple nature
of the bread and the mixed wine are changed into a rational
nature—namely, that of the body and blood of Christ. The
sindon lying on the altar signifies the linen with which the
Lord was girded, and the maniple signifies the hardship that
he undertook in washing feet, or that he endured on behalf of his hardship over Judas. The altar signifies the Lord's
table.

# 25

# On Christ's ascent to the cross

In the sacrament of the bread and wine, and also in my
memory, Christ's passion is manifest. He himself said:
"However often you do these things, you will do them in my
memory"—that is, however often you bless this bread and

calicem benedixeritis, recordamini meae nativitatis secundum humanitatem, passionis ac resurrectionis. Quare subdit sacerdos ex voce sua et plebis: "Unde et memores sumus, Domine, nos tui servi, sed et plebs tua sancta, Christi Filii tui Domini nostri tam beatae passionis, necnon et ab inferis resurrectionis, sed et in caelos gloriosae ascensionis. Offerimus praeclarae maiestati tuae, de tuis donis ac datis, hostiam puram, hostiam sanctam, hostiam inmaculatam."

2    Sicut in superioribus Christi corpus est vivum in sacramento panis et vini atque in memoria mea, ita in praesenti ascendit in crucem. Cordis sacrificio intendit Deus. Unde Cyprianus in sermone *De oratione Dominica* "Neque enim in sacrificiis quae Abel et Cain primi obtulerunt, munera eorum Deus respexit, sed corda intuebatur, ut ille placeret in munere, qui placebat in corde."✝ De donis Dei ac datis hostiam puram, hostiam sanctam, hostiam inmaculatam offerimus, quando caritate accensi hostiam offerimus de corde puro, et conscientia bona et fide non ficta.

3    De qua hostia in promptu dicat, institutio sacramenti subdendo manifestat: "Panem sanctum vitae aeternae et calicem salutis perpetuae." Panis vitae aeternae et calix salutis perpetuae Christus est; vel, sicut superius dixi, hostia pura est panis, hostia sancta calix, hostia inmaculata utraque simul, quia unum corpus efficiunt. De donis ac datis ita possumus dicere: Dona sunt in re aeterna, data in opere temporali. Et, quoniam a nobis peccatoribus vult Deus offerri sibi

chalice, you remember my birth as a man, and my passion and resurrection. The priest therefore adds, in his own voice and that of the people: "And so, Lord, we your servants and your holy people are mindful of the blessed passion of Christ your Son our Lord, and also of his resurrection from the nether regions, and his glorious ascension into heaven. We offer to your illustrious majesty, from among your gifts and privileges, a pure sacrifice, a holy sacrifice, an immaculate sacrifice."

Just as, above, we saw that Christ's body is alive in the 2 sacrament of the bread and wine and in my memory, so at the present moment does he ascend the cross. God attends to the sacrifice of the heart. Thus Cyprian in his sermon *On the Lord's Prayer:* "Nor, with respect to the sacrifices that Abel and Cain first offered, did God consider their offerings, but he gazed into their hearts, such that he who pleased him in his heart would please him in his offering."+ We offer a pure sacrifice, a holy sacrifice, an immaculate sacrifice from among God's gifts and privileges, when, inflamed with charity, we offer a sacrifice from a pure heart, and in good conscience and with faith unfeigned.

The institution of the sacrament reveals the manifest 3 sacrifice of which it speaks, by adding: "The holy bread of eternal life and the chalice of everlasting salvation." The bread of eternal life and the chalice of everlasting salvation is Christ; or, as I said above, the pure sacrifice is the bread, the holy sacrifice is the chalice, and the immaculate sacrifice is both together, because they make one body. As for the gifts and privileges, we can speak as follows: Gifts are for eternal matters, privileges for our temporal work. And, since God desires that his own gifts be offered to him by us

sua ipsa dona, obnixe precandum est ut dignetur super ea respicere.

4    Unde et subditur: "Supra quae propitio ac sereno vultu respicere digneris, et accepta habere, sicuti accepta habere dignatus es munera pueri tui iusti Abel, et sacrificium patriarchae nostri Abrahae, et quod tibi obtulit summus sacerdos tuus Melchisedech: sanctum sacrificium, inmaculatam hostiam." Rogat sacerdos Deum Patrem ut, sicut illo tempore respicere dignatus est super munera Abel et sacrificium patriarchae necnon et Melchisedech, ita super praesentia vota, quae initium acceperunt per inmolationem Christi.

5    Dein precatur ut suscipiantur, dicendo: "Supplices te rogamus, omnipotens Deus: Iube haec perferri per manus angeli tui in sublime altare tuum, in conspectu divinae maiestatis tuae, ut, quotquot ex hac altaris participatione sacrosanctum Filii tui corpus et sanguinem sumpserimus, omni benedictione caelesti et gratia repleamur, per Christum Dominum nostrum." Precatur sacerdos ut praesens oblatio ita sit accepta in conspectu divinae maiestatis, quatinus sumpturi eam simul fiant caelestes et gratia Dei re-
6    pleti. Mira et magna fides sanctae ecclesiae, quae suis oculis videt quod mortalibus deest, videt quid credere debeat, quamvis nondum videat quod in specie est. Credit sacrificium praesens per angelorum manus deferri ante conspectum Domini, et sentit mandendum esse ab humano ore. Credit namque corpus et sanguinem Domini esse, ac hoc morsu caelesti benedictione repleri animas sumentium.

sinners, we should pray with all our strength that he deigns to look favorably on them.

Thus it is also added: "And may you deign to look favorably on these sacrifices with a propitious and serene countenance, and consider them acceptable, just as you deigned to consider the offerings of your just child Abel acceptable, and the sacrifice of our patriarch Abraham, and that which your high priest Melchizedek offered you: a holy victim, an immaculate sacrifice." The priest asks God the Father that, just as he once deigned to look favorably upon the gifts of Abel and the sacrifice of the patriarch and also of Melchizedek, so also he may look with favor upon the present offerings, which originated with Christ's sacrifice. 4

Then he prays that they be received, saying: "As supplicants we ask you, almighty God: Order that these be brought by the hand of your angel to your sublime altar, in the sight of your divine majesty, so that, however often we receive the sacrosanct body and blood of your Son through this participation at the altar, we may be filled with heavenly blessing and grace, through Christ our Lord." The priest prays that the present offering be received in the sight of divine majesty, so that those who are about to receive it may become at once heavenly and filled with God's grace. The great and marvelous faith of the holy church, which sees with its eyes what is absent for mortals, sees what it should believe, although it does not yet have it in view. It believes that this sacrifice is carried by the hands of angels before the sight of the Lord, and senses that it is to be eaten by the human mouth. For it believes that it is the body and blood of the Lord, and that through this morsel the souls of those receiving it are filled with heavenly blessing. 5 6

7    Nempe Christus oravit in cruce incipiens in Psalmo *Deus, Deus meus* [Ps 21:1; Matt 27:46; Mic 15:34], usque ad versum: "In manus tuas commendo spiritum meum" [Ps 30:6; Luke 23:46]. Postea, "inclinato capite, emisit spiritum" [John 19:30]. Sacerdos inclinat se, et hoc quod vice Christi immolatum est, Deo Patri commendat. Sancita est passio Christi pro nobis usque ad istum locum, ab eo loco ubi dicit: "Unde et memores sumus."

8    Altare praesens altare est crucis; in isto nos peccatores, qui ex gentibus venimus, reconciliati sumus Deo ad offerenda ei sacrificia. Sindo in isto humilitatem illam signat, qua humiliatus est Christus Patri usque ad mortem. Non abhorret a vero, si humilitas designetur per sindonem. Agustinus scribit in Psalmo nonagesimo secundo: "Qui enim tunc humilis fuit, quando linteo praecinctus est et lavit pedes discipulorum."✝ Sudarium vero laborem passionis.

9    Inclinatio subdiaconorum usque modo mestitiam demonstrat eorum discipulorum quibus licitum erat perseverare in praesentia Christi. Quando flagellabatur, omnia illa agebantur quae de eius passione leguntur, tunc potissimum dolebant qui eius erant sectatores; at postquam emisit spiritum, scientes non iam habere persecutores unde rabiem suam amplius in Christi corpus expleant, ut ipse dicit in Evangelio Lucae: "Ne terreamini ab his qui occidunt corpus, et post haec non habent amplius quid faciant" [Luke 12:4], consolantur aliquo modo. Et erigunt se, aspicientes in dilectum sibi corpus, quousque pendet in cruce, maxime cum vident multa miracula fieri. Unde conturbari poterant persecutores, et obsequentes solari.

Christ, of course, prayed on the cross, beginning with the 7
Psalm *Deus, Deus meus,* through the verse: "Into your hands I
commend my spirit." Afterward, "bowing his head, he gave
up his spirit." The priest bows and commends that which
has been sacrificed in Christ's place to God the Father.
Christ's passion is made holy for us up to this passage, and
beginning from that passage where the priest says: "And so
we are mindful."

The present altar is the altar of the cross; upon it we sin- 8
ners, who have come from among the gentiles, are reconciled to God in order to offer sacrifices to him. The sindon
upon it signifies that humility by which Christ was humbled to the Father unto death. It is not contrary to truth,
should humility be designated by the sindon. Augustine
writes on Psalm 92: "For he was humble when he was girded
with a linen cloth and washed the feet of his disciples."✝
The maniple, meanwhile, signifies the labor of the passion.

The bowing of the subdeacons until this point signifies 9
the grief of the disciples who had been allowed to remain in
the presence of Christ. When he was flogged and all those
things took place that are read concerning his passion, those
who were his followers grieved very much; but after he gave
up his spirit, they were in some sense consoled, as they knew
that his persecutors now had no means to further exhaust
their rage upon Christ's body, as he says in the Gospel of
Luke: "Be not afraid of them who kill the body, and after
that have no more that they can do." And they stand up,
looking upon the body that is beloved to them, as long as it
hangs on the cross, especially as they witness the occurrence
of many miracles. Thus could his persecutors be disturbed,
and his followers consoled.

10     In eodem officio lavant diaconi manus, quia omnia opera sordida prioris conversationis Christi passione mundantur. Quod si nihil aliud voluisset ordo ministerii nostri significare, in lavatione manus, quam ut cautiore cura prius actus suos cogitatusque diaconi discuterent, eventilarent, purgarent, ac sic ad participanda fidei sacramenta procederent (quod unusquisque fidelium debet observare, ne manducet et bibat indigne corpus Domini)—nullo modo tali in loco lavarent manus, quia aptius possent eas lavare erecti quam inclinati.

26

# De corpore Domini post emissum spiritum in cruce et nostra mortificatione in idipsum

Christus enim praegustavit mortem, ut nos commoreremur peccatis. Christus mortuus est peccato semel, ut nos moreremur vitiis. Dicit Paulus: "Qui autem sunt Christi carnem suam crucifixerunt cum vitiis et concupiscentiis" [Gal 5:24]. Haec crucifixio praecipue agitur per paenitentiam. Plures sunt qui angustum foramen transeunt ad stabilitatem continentiae, ac ideo—quantum ad moralem

During this same office the deacons wash their hands, 10
because all the unclean actions of their prior way of life
have been cleansed by the passion of Christ. If the order of
our ministry had aimed to signify, through this washing of
hands, nothing more than the fact that the deacons should
scatter, winnow and purge their earlier deeds and thoughts
with great care, and proceed in this way to imparting the
sacraments of faith (as each of the faithful should do, lest
one eat and drink the Lord's body unworthily)—then there
is no way that they would wash their hands here, because
they could wash them while standing more easily than while
bowed.

## 26

# On the body of the Lord after he gave up his spirit on the cross and our mortification through that same body

Christ had a foretaste of death, that we might together
die to sin. Christ died once to sin, that we might die to our
vices. Paul says: "And they who are Christ's have crucified
their flesh with the vices and concupiscences." This crucifixion is accomplished particularly through penance. There
are many who cross the narrow passage to the stronghold
of continence, and thus—insofar as it relates to the moral

sensum pertinet—recte praesens sacrificium sacrificium paenitentiae dicitur, et bene ante sacrificium paenitentum caelebratur passio Christi, ut magis infirmos provocet ad
2   salubrem potionem. Unde dicit Iohannes Chrisostomus in sermone IIII ad Ebreos: "Sicut enim medicus, non habens necessitatem ex cibis qui aegroto praeparantur gustare, sed ille consolans, primus ex illius cibo degustat, ut persuadeat aegroto promptius illos cibos accipere—sic etiam Dominus, quoniam homines mortem timebant, persuadens eis ut fiducialiter ad mortem accederent, et ipse gustavit mortem, nullam habens necessitatem."✝ Ex verbis beati Iohannis ostensum est ideo coniunctim prolatam esse passionem Christi et nostram confessionem peccatorum, ut non timeremus dura pati pro peccatis nostris.
3   Christus iam emisit spiritum, exivit ab eius latere sanguis et aqua. Sine his sacramentis, nemo intrat ad vitam aeternam. De his sacramentis dicit Agustinus in sermone LXV super Iohannem: "Ille sanguis in remissionem fusus est peccatorum; aqua illa salutare temperat poculum; haec et lavacrum praestat et potum." Et post pauca: "Hic secundus Adam, inclinato capite, in cruce dormivit, ut inde formaretur ei coniux, quod de latere dormientis defluxit."✝ Coniux
4   ista illum centurionem signat, de quo narratur in Evangelio: "Videns autem centurio quod factum erat, glorificavit Deum dicens: Vere hic homo iustus erat" [Luke 23:47]. Nisi futurum esset ut sacramento sanguinis et aquae inficeretur gentilitas, non ilico se centurio mutaret ad tantam compunctionem, ut aperte clamaret ex intimo cordis affectu: "Vere hic homo iustus erat."

sense—the present sacrifice is rightly called the sacrifice of penance, and Christ's passion is appropriately celebrated before the sacrifice of the penitent, that it may call the weak to this saving drink all the more. Thus John Chrysostom, in 2 his fourth sermon on the epistle to the Hebrews, says: "For just as a doctor, having no need of the food that is prepared for a sick man to eat, nevertheless first takes a bite of the sick man's food to console him and to persuade him to take the food more readily—so too, because men feared death, did the Lord taste death, though he had no need of it, to persuade them to receive death in confidence."✝ Through the words of blessed John we have been shown that Christ's passion and the confession of our sins were accomplished jointly, that we might not fear to suffer difficulties for our sins.

Christ has now given up his spirit, and blood and water 3 have flowed from his side. Without these sacraments, no one enters into eternal life. Augustine speaks about these sacraments in sermon 65 on John: "The blood was poured out for the remission of sins; water tempers the saving drink; he offers both a bath and a drink." And after a little: "This second Adam, bowing his head, slept on the cross, that a spouse might be made for him from what flowed from his side as he slept."✝ This spouse signifies the centurion, 4 about whom it is said in the Gospel: "Now the centurion, seeing what had been done, glorified God, saying: Indeed this was a just man." Unless it was to happen that the gentiles would be imbued with the sacrament of blood and water, the centurion would not, at that point, have given himself over to such compunction as to openly cry out from the deepest sentiment of his heart: "Indeed this was a just man."

5    Hanc mutationem designat sacerdos per mutationem vocis, quando exaltat vocem suam dicendo *Nobis quoque peccatoribus.* Dicit de eo Beda in tractatu super Lucam: "Notanda distantia gentis et gentis. Et gentiles quippe, moriente Christo, Deum timentes aperta confessionis voce glorificant; Iudaei, percutientes solum pectora, silentes domi redeunt." Percussura pectoris paenitentiae est et luctus indicium.

6    Interim: "'Stabant autem omnes noti eius a longe, et mulieres quae secutae erant a Galilaea haec videntes" [Luke 23:49]. Hoc est quod ipse Dominus in Psalmo, explicata suae passionis serie, Patri queritur dicens: 'Elongasti a me amicum et proximum et notos meos a miseria' [Ps 87:19]."✝ Hos amicos et proximos ad memoriam nobis ducunt subdiaconi erecti et intuentes in presbyteri opus.

7    His ita intuentibus, venit "vir nomine Ioseph, qui erat decurio, vir bonus et iustus (hic non consenserat consilio et actibus eorum) ab Arimathia civitate Iudeae—qui expectabat et ipse regnum Dei. Hic accessit ad Pilatum et petiit corpus Iesu. Et depositum involvit sindone, et posuit eum in monumento exciso, in quo nondum quisquam positus fuerat" [Luke 23:50–53]. Qui quamvis ex numero foret occultorum discipulorum, tamen in promptu omnes transcendit,

8    scilicet et discipulos et apostolos. Discipulis tantummodo a longe stantibus et intuentibus, apostolis latentibus in abditis, Ioseph mercatus est sindonem, ut depositum

The priest represents this change with a change in his 5
voice, when he raises his voice in saying *Nobis quoque pec-*
*catoribus*. Bede speaks about this in his treatise on Luke:
"The difference between the peoples should be noted. For
upon Christ's death the gentiles fearfully glorified the Lord
through an open cry of confession; the Jews returned home
in silence, striking their breasts only." Striking the breast is a
sign of penitence and mourning.

Meanwhile: "'All his acquaintances and the women who 6
had followed him from Galilee stood afar off, beholding
these things.' This is what the Lord complains to his Father
about in the Psalm, after the events of his passion had un-
folded, saying: 'Friend and neighbor and my acquaintances
you have put far from me, because of misery.'"✝ The subdeacons, standing upright and attending to the work of the
priest, call these friends and neighbors to our mind.

As they look on, there comes "a man named Joseph, who 7
was a counselor, a good and just man (he had not consented
to their counsel and doings) from Arimathea, a city of Judea
—who also awaited the kingdom of God. This man went to
Pilate and begged the body of Jesus. And taking him down,
he wrapped him in fine linen, and laid him in a sepulcher
that was hewed in stone, wherein no man had yet been laid."
Although he was from the number of hidden disciples, it is
obvious that he nevertheless surpasses all of them, both disciples and apostles. While the disciples simply stood from 8
afar and watched and the apostles hid in secluded places, Joseph bought a linen cloth or sindon, that he might wrap the

corpus Iesu involveret [Mic 15:46]. Quantae dignitatis foret iste Ioseph, in tractatu Bedae legitur super Lucam, ita dicendo: "Magnae quidem Ioseph iste dignitatis apud saeculum, sed maioris apud Deum meriti fuisse laudatur, ut et per iustitiam meritorum sepeliendo corpore Dominico dignus foret, et per nobilitatem potentiae saecularis idem corpus accipere possit. Non enim quilibet ignotus ad praesidem

9 accedere et crucifixi corpus poterat impetrare."✢ Hunc Ioseph ad memoriam ducit archidiaconus, qui elevat calicem de altari et involvit sudario, scilicet ab aure calicis usque ad aurem. Sicut ille diaconus primatum tenet inter ceteros diaconos qui levat calicem cum sacerdote, ita iste Ioseph tenuit inter ceteros discipulos, qui meruit corpus Domini de cruce deponere, et sepelire in monumento suo. Idem deputatur retro stare cum apostolis, quoniam timore Iudaeorum occultus erat.

10 Sacerdos qui elevat oblatam praesentat Nichodemum, de quo narrat Iohannes dicens: "Venit autem et Nichodemus, qui venerat ad Iesum nocte primum, ferens mixturam myrrae et aloes, quasi libras C. Acceperunt ergo corpus Iesu et ligaverunt eum linteis cum aromatibus, sicut mos Iudaeis est sepelire" [John 19:39–40]. Sacerdos facit oblata duas cruces iuxta calicem, ut doceat eum depositum esse de cruce, qui pro duobus populis crucifixus est. Christi depositionem de cruce monstrat elevatio sacerdotis et diaconi.

11 Sudarium super caput Iesu notum est fuisse, narrante eodem Iohanne quod videret Petrus "linteamina posita et sudarium

body of Jesus after it had been taken down. In Bede's treatise on Luke we read about how great Joseph's dignity was,
where he says: "Indeed, this Joseph was of great dignity in
this world, but he is said to have had even greater merit with
God, such that he was both worthy of burying the Lord's
body through the justice of his merits, and also that he was
able, through the nobility of his worldly power, to get hold
of the same body. For not just any unknown person could
approach the governor and ask for the body of someone
who had been crucified."✝ The archdeacon, who raises the    9
chalice from the altar and covers it with the maniple from
one handle to the other, commemorates this Joseph. Just as
the deacon who raises the chalice with the priest has primacy over the other deacons, so did this Joseph, who was
worthy to take the Lord's body down from the cross and
bury it in his tomb, hold primacy over the other disciples.
He is thought to have lingered behind with the apostles, because he was hidden out of fear of the Jews.

The priest who raises the offering represents Nicodemus,    10
whom John discusses, saying: "And Nicodemus, who at first
had come to Jesus by night, also came, bringing a mixture of
myrrh and aloes, about a hundred pounds in weight. They
therefore took the body of Jesus and bound it in linen cloths
with the spices, as the manner of the Jews is to bury." The
priest makes two crosses with the offering near the chalice,
to teach that he who was crucified for the two peoples has
been brought down from the cross. The elevation by the
priest and the deacon reveals Christ's removal from the
cross. It is known that there was a kerchief, or a maniple,    11
over Jesus's head; the same John says that Peter saw "the
linen cloth lying and the kerchief that had been about

quod fuerat super caput" Iesu [ John 20:6–7]. Oblata et calix Dominicum corpus signant. Quando Christus dixit: "Hic est calix sanguinis mei" [1 Cor 11:25], suum sanguinem signavit. Qui sanguis, sicut vinum est intra calicem, ita erat intra corpus.

12     Hoc peracto, quid agerent quos praesentant subdiaconi, Beda in memorato libro narrat: "Supra legimus," inquiens, "quia stabant omnes noti eius a longe et mulieres quae secutae erant eum [Luke 23:49]. His ergo notis Iesu, post depositum eius cadaver, ad sua remeantibus, solae mulieres, quae arctius amabant, funus subsecutae, quomodo poneretur inspicere cupiebant."✝

13     Haec oratio *Nobis quoque peccatoribus* tendit usque *Per omnia saecula saeculorum*. Usque ad istum locum, quantum pertinet ad exequias sepulturae Christi, altare crucem praesentat. Quantum ad nostram mortificationem, altare holocausti. Sindo et sudarium sunt quae supra memoravi.

14     Moraliter: Voce paenitentium qui confitentur peccata sua, elevat sacerdos vocem, quasi quodam stimulo punctus nimii timoris. Talis compunctio vocatur et vere dicitur "sacrificium spiritus contribulati" [Ps 50:19]. Vox elevata sacerdotis in sacrificio paenitentium signat magnum esse debere clamorem in corde paenitentis. Unde Agustinus in tractatu super Iohannem, sermone XLVI: "Quare 'fremuit,'"—quin Iesus—"'et turbavit se ipsum' [ John 11:33], nisi quia fides hominis sibi merito displicentis fremere quodammodo debet in accusatione malorum operum, ut violentiae paenitendi cedat consuetudo peccandi?" Et iterum in eodem: "Et 'cum haec dixisset, exclamavit voce magna' [ John 11:33]. Fremuit,

Jesus's head." The offering and the chalice signify the Lord's body. When Christ said: "This is the chalice of my blood," he indicated his own blood. This blood was within his body, just as there is wine within the chalice.

Bede explains in his aforementioned book what the peo-   12
ple whom the subdeacons represent did after they had finished this, saying: "Above we read that all his acquaintance and the women that had followed stood afar off. When these acquaintances of Jesus went home after his body was taken down, therefore, only the women, who loved him more firmly, went to his burial and wished to see how he would be laid to rest."✝

The prayer *Nobis quoque peccatoribus* continues until *Per*   13
*omnia saecula saeculorum*. Up to this point, insofar as it relates to Christ's burial, the altar represents the cross. Insofar as it relates to our mortification, it is the altar of the sacrifice. The sindon and the maniple are as they have been described above.

Morally: In the voice of penitents who confess their sins,   14
the priest raises his voice, as if struck by some torment of great fear. Compunction like this is called and is truly said to be "the sacrifice of an afflicted spirit." The raised voice of the priest during the sacrifice of the penitent signifies that there should be a great cry in the penitent's heart. Thus Augustine in his treatise on John, sermon 46: "Why indeed did he 'groan'"—that is, Jesus—"'and trouble himself,' if not because the faith of a man rightly displeased with himself should somehow groan in the accusation of evil works, that the habit of sinning may fall to the violence of doing penance?" And again, in the same work: "And 'when he had said these things, he cried with a loud voice.' He groaned, he

lacrimavit, voce magna clamavit. Quam difficile surgit quem moles malae consuetudinis premit. Sed tamen surgit; occulta gratia intus vivificatur; surgit post vocem magnam."✝

15 Sat est de elevatione vocis; dicendum est de sacrificio. Sacrificium paenitentum est "spiritus contribulatus et cor contritum" [Ps 50:19]. Paenitentia sepeliuntur peccata nostra. Altare paenitentium est altare holocausti; altare holocausti signat cor eorum quibus necesse est carnales motus

16 consummare fervore Spiritus Sancti. Sindo est ipsa castigatio carnis per ieiunia et vigilias ac ceteras virtutes, quibus de genuina carnali delectatione, quasi de umore nativo, perducitur affectus hominis, ceu quoddam linum, ad candorem, ut fiat de eo corporale, in quo possit Dominum recipere. Ille in sindone munda involvit Iesum, qui pura eum mente susceperit. Sudarium est ipsa intentio, qua festinat omnes venientes motus temptationum pristinarum tergere, ante quam oculos sautiant.

17 Postquam vox paenitentum prolata est, impetratio succedit, ut partem sibi societatis concedat Dominus cum sanctis suis. Quibus denominatis, sequitur: "Intra quorum consortium, quaesumus, nos consortium quaesumus nos admitte—

18 tu qui es largitor veniae, non aestimator meriti." In completione prioris sacrificii, quod fungebatur tantummodo orationibus, ibi memoratur communio sanctorum, quorum pene conversatio est aequalis. In isto, quia longe distamus ab eorum conversatione, venia precamur introduci: "Per Christum Dominum nostrum, per quem haec omnia semper,

wept, he cried with a loud voice. How difficult it is for him to rise whom the weight of evil habit oppresses. But he rises nevertheless; within, he is made alive through hidden grace; he rises after a great voice."✝

Enough about the raised voice; we should speak about the sacrifice. The sacrifice of the penitent is an "afflicted spirit and a contrite heart." Through penance our sins are buried. The altar of the penitent is the altar of the sacrifice; the altar of the sacrifice signifies the hearts of those who have to burn away their carnal impulses with the heat of the Holy Spirit. The sindon is the castigation of the flesh through fasts and vigils and other virtues. Through these one's disposition, like a piece of linen, is brought away from its natural carnal pleasure, or its native moisture, to whiteness, that a corporal may be made from it, in which one can receive the Lord. He who has received Jesus with a pure mind wraps him in a pure sindon. The maniple is the resolve through which one hastens to wipe away all the impulses of old temptations that draw near, before they do harm to the eyes.

After the voice of the penitent has been brought forth, a request that the Lord grant them some share in communion with his saints follows. After these saints have been named, there follows: "We ask you to admit us to their company—you who are a granter of pardon, not a judge of merit." Upon the completion of the earlier sacrifice, which was accomplished through prayers alone, the communion of saints is commemorated; their way of life is essentially equal. Since we are far away from their way of life, we pray to be brought into it: "Through Christ our Lord, through whom, Lord, always, all these good things," namely, those which were

187

Domine, bona," scilicet quae retro memorata sunt—"creas,"
ut sint—"sanctificas," tibi ea deputando—"vivificas," ut viva
sint—"benedicis," ut utilia sint nobis—"et praestas," ad fru-
endum. "Per ipsum," eumdemque videlicet per quem superius memorata concedis—"et cum ipso," qui tecum semper
vivit—"et in ipso," in quo restaurata sunt omnia—"est tibi
Deo Patri, in unitate Spiritus Sancti, omnis honor et gloria
per omnia saecula saeculorum." Hoc ipsum volendo tibi
omni nisu monstrare tota fide me ita tenere, elevo praesentia munera ad te—ego indignus sacerdos et diaconus, vice
praepositorum et auditorum, quia tibi ab omni ecclesia tua
omnia bona deputantur.

19    Subdiaconi, qui stant usque modo in facie sacrificii, et
nunc recedunt, ministeria feminarum ad memoriam nobis
ducunt quae recesserunt de monumento sepulto Domino
[Mic 15:47–16:1; Luke 23:55–56]. Non enim ita recesserunt
a sepulchro ut abessent ministerio Domini, sed Sabbato
siluerunt. Quo transacto, paraverunt aromata ut ungerent
corpus eius. Eo modo praesentes subdiaconi recedunt a
praesentia sacrificii, ut Sabbato quidem—hoc est quamdiu
septem petitiones Dominicae orationis dicuntur—sint in
silentio et inclinati, sicut erant apostoli illo in tempore et
sanctae mulieres. Qui postea satagunt cum patenis ad requirendum corpus Domini circa altare, ut mulieres quaesie-
runt corpus Domini circa sepulchrum [Matt 28:1; Mic 16:2;
Luke 24:1].

20    Moraliter: Possumus subdiaconos nos peccatores intellegere, qui faciem, id est conscientiam peccatorum nostrorum, sacerdoti ostendimus, ut nostram confessionem offerat Deo. Quo peracto, non ilico saltum facimus in locum

recounted before—"you create," that they may be—"sanctify," by allotting them to yourself—"enliven," that they may be alive—"bless," that they may be useful for us—"and offer," for enjoyment. "Through him," that is, the same one through whom you concede those things recounted above—"and with him," who lives always with you—"and in him," in whom all things have been renewed—"all honor and glory are yours, Father God, in the unity of the Holy Spirit, for all ages of ages." As this passage demands that I present this to you with all my effort, and hold myself with my complete faith, I raise the present gifts to you—I, an unworthy priest and deacon acting for my leaders and listeners, because all good things are considered by your entire church to come from you.

The subdeacons, who to this point stood facing the sacrifice, and now depart, remind us of the services of the women who left the tomb after the Lord was buried. For they did not leave the tomb to depart from the Lord's service; instead they rested on the Sabbath. After they had done this, they prepared spices to anoint his body. And now these subdeacons depart from the presence of the sacrifice, so that on the Sabbath—or for as long as the seven petitions of the Lord's prayer are recounted—they may bow in silence, just as the apostles and the holy women bowed at that time. Afterward they busy themselves with the patens to seek the body of the Lord at the altar, just as the women sought the Lord's body at his tomb. 19

Morally: We can understand that we, as sinners, are the subdeacons; we show our face, or the conscience of our sins, to the priest, that he may offer our confession to God. When this has been done, we do not immediately leap to 20

magistrorum, sed post diutinam humiliationem, fervore crescente Spiritus Sancti, dilatantur corda nostra, quasi patena, ad suscipienda sacramenta ecclesiae.

## 27

# De praesentatione patenae

Dixit libellus Romanus quem iam memoravimus: "Quando inchoatur canon, venit acolytus sub humero habens sindonem, in collo ligatam, tenens patenam ante pectus in parte dextera, usque medium canonem. Tunc subdiaconus sequens suscipit eam super planetam et venit ante altare, expectans quando eam suscipiat subdiaconus regionarius. Finito vero canone, subdiaconus regionarius stat cum patena post archidiaconum. Quando dixerit: *Et ab omni perturbatione securi,* vertit se archidiaconus, et osculatam patenam dat eam tenendam secundo diacono." Ordo talis est: Subdiaconus sequens non est ausus hostia altaris relinquere, secundum canones Laodicensis concilii, qui dicunt capitulo XLIII quod non oporteat subdiaconum, saltim paululum, ianuas deserere et orationibus vacare. Ac ideo acolytus educit patenam de exedris quando dicitur *Sursum corda.*

the place of the teachers; rather, after a long humiliation, as the heat of the Holy Spirit grows, our hearts are enlarged, like the paten, to receive the sacraments of the church.

27

# On the presentation of the paten

The Roman manual that we have already cited said: "When the canon begins, an acolyte comes and holds a sindon under his upper arm, tied about his neck, and keeps the paten before his chest on the right side, until the middle of the canon. Then the assisting subdeacon receives it on top of his chasuble and comes before the altar, waiting for the regional subdeacon to take it. Then, at the end of the canon, the regional subdeacon stands with the paten behind the archdeacon. When he has said *Et ab omni perturbatione securi,* the archdeacon turns, kisses the paten, and gives it to the second deacon to hold." The order is this: The assisting sub- 2 deacon did not dare abandon the sacrifice of the altar, according to the canons of the Council of Laodicea, which say in chapter 43 that the subdeacon is not permitted—save very briefly—to abandon the gates of the presbytery and leave his prayers. And so the acolyte takes the paten from the apse when the *Sursum corda* is said.

3    Mea humilitas dicit quod sibi videtur rationi congruere, relinquens arbitrio magistrorum quid potissimum tenendum sit. Videtur mihi ut ea ora praesentanda sit patena, qua circa mysteria passionis Domini satagebant discipuli vel mulieres. Postquam enim ivit ad mensam studuerunt circa

4    mysteria passionis. Sequens vero subdiaconus, in medio canone, id est cum dicitur *Te igitur,* suscipit eam ab acolyto et stat ante altare cum patena, usque dum suscipiatur a subdiacono regionario. Suscipitur enim cum dicitur: *Per omnia saecula saeculorum.* Regionarius suscipit illam finito canone, id est ubi dicitur: *Per omnia saecula saeculorum,* et tenet illam usque ad susceptionem diaconi. Potest etiam intellegi simpliciter recessio subdiaconi de facie pontificis, accessio ad patenam.

5    Ubi notandum quod acolytus involutam tenet linteo patenam, subdiaconus nudam. Unde liquido apparet quod consecrata vasa a consecratis clericis merito debeant tantummodo attingi. Hoc denique Esdras sacerdos expressit, quando reversus est de Babilone et vasa sancta sanctis commendavit, dicens: "Separavi de principibus sacerdotum XII." Et paulo post: "Appendique eis argentum et aurum et vasa consecrata domus Dei nostri." Et iterum: "Et dixit eis: Vos sancti Domini, et vasa sancta, et argentum et aurum quod sponte oblatum est Domino Deo patrum nostrorum; vigi-

6    late et custodite" [1 Ezra 8:24, 25, 28–29]. Unde in concilio Cartaginensi, capitulo XXV, scribitur: "Aurelius episcopus

In my humility, I say what seems to me to accord with 3
reason, and leave what should be adhered to most of all to
the judgment of the masters. It seems to me that the paten
should be presented at the moment when the disciples and
women busied themselves with the mysteries of the Lord's
passion. For after he went to the table they struggled with
the mysteries of the passion. And the assisting subdeacon, 4
in the midst of the canon, namely after the *Te igitur* is said,
takes the paten from the acolyte and stands before the altar
with it, until it is taken by the regional subdeacon. And it
is taken when *Per omnia saecula saeculorum* is said. The regional subdeacon receives it when the canon is finished, that
is when *Per omnia saecula saeculorum* is said, and he keeps it
until the deacon takes it. And the subdeacon's withdrawal
from the sight of the pontiff can be understood simply as his
approach to the paten.

Here we should note that the acolyte holds the paten 5
wrapped in a sindon; the subdeacon holds it bare. It is thus
obvious that consecrated vessels should only be touched by
consecrated clergy. The priest Ezra declared as much when
he returned from Babylon and commended the holy vessels
to the holy ones, saying: "And I separated twelve of the chief
of the priests." And a little later: "And I weighed unto them
the silver and gold and the vessels consecrated for the house
of our God." And again: "And I said to them: You are the
holy ones of the Lord, and the vessels are holy, and the silver and gold that is freely offered to the Lord the God of
our fathers; watch and keep them." Thus in chapter 25 of 6
the Council of Carthage, it is written: "The bishop Aurelius

dixit: Addimus, fratres karissimi, praeterea, cum de quorundam clericorum—quamvis lectorum—erga uxores proprias
incontinentia referretur, placuit quod in diversis conciliis
firmatum est: Subdiaconi qui sacra mysteria contrectant, et
diaconi et presbyteri sed et episcopi, secundum propria
statuta, etiam ab uxoribus se contineant."✝ Necnon et:
"Xystus papa, natione Romanus, ex patre Pastore, constituit
7 ut ministeria sacrata non tangerentur nisi a ministris."✝ Verum et in hoc culpavit Danihel Baltasar regem—quia in
consecratis vasis bibebat, sicut scriptum est: "Tu quoque,
Balthasar, filius eius, non humiliasti cor tuum, cum scires
haec omnia, sed adversus dominatorem caeli elevatus es. Et
vasa domus eius allata sunt coram te; tu et optimates tui et
uxores tuae et concubinae tuae vinum bibistis in eis" [Dan
5:22].

8    Patena dicitur eo quod patet; corda ampla caritate significat. Sicut alabastrum in quo portavit unguentum Maria ad
unguendum Dominum significavit cor eius, in quo erat fides
sine impostura—ita et patena potest corda sanctarum feminarum designare, quae patebant latitudine caritatis in obsequio Christi. Nam et ipsae inerant, ut praetuli, non minima
executione in ministerio discipulatus Christi; de quibus dicit Matheus Evangelista: "Erant autem ibi mulieres multae a
longe quae secutae erant Iesum a Galilea, ministrantes ei,
inter quas erat Maria Magdalenae, et Maria Iacobi et Ioseph,
9 mater filiorum Zebedei" [Matt 27:55–56]. Tamen ipsae non

said: Furthermore, dearest brethren, since there has been a report on the incontinence of certain clerics—even if only lectors—regarding their own wives, what has been established in various councils has pleased us: The subdeacons who handle the sacred mysteries, together with the deacons and the priests and also the bishops, should keep themselves from wives, in accordance with their own statutes."✝ And also: "Pope Sixtus, a Roman by birth, whose father was Pastor, established that the sacred vessels should not be handled by anyone but the ministers."✝ Indeed, this was why 7 Daniel found fault with King Balthazar—because he drank in consecrated vessels, as it is written: "You also, his son, O Balthazar, have not humbled your heart, whereas you knew all these things, but have lifted yourself up against the ruler of heaven. And the vessels of his house have been brought before you, and you and your nobles and your wives and your concubines have drunk wine in them."

The paten is so-called because it stands open; it signifies 8 hearts filled with charity. Just as the alabaster box in which Mary carried the ointment to anoint the Lord signified her heart, where there was faith without deceit—so too can the paten designate the hearts of the holy women, which lie open in the breadth of their charity for Christ's service. For, as I said before, they too were involved with and exercised no little effort in the ministry of Christ's discipleship. Matthew the Evangelist speaks about them: "And there were there many women afar off who had followed Jesus from Galilee, ministering unto him, among whom was Mary Magdalene, and Mary the mother of James and Joseph, and the mother of the sons of Zebedee." Yet they did not take the 9

susceperunt corpus Domini de cruce, sed Ioseph [Matt 27:55–56]—sicut nec subdiaconi, sed diaconi, suscipiunt calicem de altari.

28

# De officio quod memorat requiem Domini in sepulchro

Subdiaconus regionarius accipit patenam finito canone, quia laetitiam Dominicae resurrectionis mulieres primo audierunt. Illae huc illucque discurrebant ferventi studio circa sepulturam Domini. Stant diaconi stantque subdiaconi inclinati, usque dum audiant: "Sed libera nos a malo." Ipsa est enim septima petitio de oratione Dominica; septenario 2 enim numero universitas designatur. Septima petitione Dominicae orationis finis signatur totius tristitiae ac perturbationis apostolorum, quam habebant de Domini morte. Sequens oratio quae inchoatur: *Libera nos, quaesumus, Domine, ab omnibus malis,* embolim est Dominicae orationis, ut per illud veniatur ad finem consuetae conclusionis: *Per Dominum nostrum.* Quod apertius in sequentibus demonstrabitur, si Dominus dederit.

3 Quid illo in tempore, hoc est quando Christus quievit in sepulchro, apostoli agerent, non legitur aperte, sed ex

Lord's body from the cross; Joseph did instead—just as it is not the subdeacons, but the deacons, who take the chalice from the altar.

## 28

# On the office that commemorates the Lord's rest in the tomb

The regional subdeacon receives the paten when the canon is over, because the women were the first to hear the rejoicing of the Lord's resurrection. They ran here and there with fervent excitement around the Lord's tomb. The deacons and the subdeacons stand and bow until they hear: "But free us from evil." This is the seventh petition of the Lord's prayer; the whole is signified by the number seven. The end of all the sorrow and confusion that the apostles 2 experienced over the Lord's death is signified by the seventh petition of the Lord's prayer. The following prayer that begins: *Libera nos, quaesumus, Domine, ab omnibus malis,* is an addition to the Lord's prayer, so that through it we may arrive at the customary conclusion: *Per Dominum nostrum.* This will be explained more clearly in what follows, if the Lord grants it.

What the apostles did during this time, that is when 3 Christ rested in the tomb, is not clearly recorded, but from

Iohannis Evangelio metum eorum cognoscimus, qui dicit: "Cum esset ergo sero die illo una sabbatorum, et fores essent clausae ubi erant discipuli congregati, propter metum Iudaeorum . . ." [John 29:19]. Ex quo discimus tristes fuisse apostolos timore. Ipsa tristitia demonstratur per diaco-

4 norum declinationem. Discipulorum vero tristitiam cognoscimus ex Domini sermone, qui dicit, secundum Lucam, ad duos qui ibant in die resurrectionis in castellum Emaus: "Qui sunt hi sermones quos confertis ad invicem ambulantes, et estis tristes?" [Luke 24:17] Ideo et subdiaconi inclinati manent.

5 Secundum modulum lucubrationis meae, demonstratum est quid velit inclinatio diaconorum—excepto quod oratio

6 interna solet demonstrari per habitum corporis. Unde Agustinus in libro ad Paulinum *De cura agenda pro mortuis:* "Nam et orantes de membris sui corporis faciunt quod supplicantibus congruit, cum genua figunt, cum extendunt manus vel etiam prosternuntur solo, et si quid aliud faciunt visibiliter—quamvis eorum invisibilis voluntas et cordis intentio Deo nota sit, nec ille indigeat his indiciis, ut animus ei pan-

7 datur humanus. Sed his magis se ipsum excitat homo ad orandum gemendumque humilius atque ferventius. Et nescio quomodo, cum hi motus corporis fieri, nisi motu animi praecedente, non possint, eisdem rursus exterius visibiliter factis, ille interior invisibilis qui eos facit augetur, ac per hoc cordis affectus, qui, ut fierent ista, praecessit, quia facta

the Gospel of John we know of their fear. It says: "Now when it was late that same day, the first of the week, and the doors were shut where the disciples were gathered together, for fear of the Jews . . ." From this we learn that the apostles were sad and in fear. This sadness is expressed through the bowing of the deacons. And we recognize the sadness of the 4 disciples from the remark that the Lord made, according to Luke, to the two apostles who were going to the town of Emmaus on the day of the resurrection: "What are these discourses that you hold with one another as you walk, and are sad?" Therefore the subdeacons also remain bowed.

The purpose of the bowing of the deacons has been ex- 5 plained, in accordance with the measure of my laborious study—excepting that it is customary for an inner prayer to be expressed through bodily posture. Thus Augustine in 6 his book to Paulinus *On the Care to be Had for the Dead:* "For those who pray arrange their members as befits supplicants, when they kneel, when they extend their hands or even when they lie prostrate on the ground, or whatever else they do that is visible—though their invisible will and the intention of their heart is known to God, and as the human spirit is bent toward him, he does not need these signs. Yet, 7 through these signs, man rouses himself all the more humbly and fervently toward prayer and lamentation. And I do not know how, since these movements of the body cannot come about if not through a preceding movement of the spirit; yet when these same actions have been performed visibly and externally, the interior and invisible disposition that brings them about is increased, and for this reason the disposition of the heart, which preceded so that these external signs might arise, is increased, because these external

sunt, crescit. Verumtamen, si eo modo quisque teneatur, vel etiam ligetur, ut haec de suis membris facere nequeat, non ideo non orat interior homo; et ante oculos Dei in secretissimo cubili, ubi compungitur, sternitur."✝

8    Celebratio huius officii ita currit, ut ostendatur quid illo in tempore actum sit circa passionem Domini et sepulturam eius, et quomodo nos id ad memoriam reducere debeamus per obsequium nostrum, quod pro nobis factum est.

# 29

# De oratione Dominica

Dicendum est quare Dominica oratio dicatur excelsa voce, cum ceterae secreto dicantur. Dicit Cyprianus in sermone *De oratione Dominica:* "Ante omnia pacis doctor atque unitatis magister singulatim noluit et privatim precem fieri; non ut quis, cum precatur, pro se tantum precetur. Non dicimus: 'Pater meus, qui es in caelis,' nec: 'Panem meum da mihi hodie,' nec dimitti sibi tantum unusquisque debitum postulat, aut ut in temptationem non inducatur, atque a malo liberetur pro se solo rogat. Publica est nobis et communis oratio, et quando oramus, non pro uno sed pro toto

signs have been performed. Nevertheless, if someone should be restrained somehow, or even bound, such that he cannot do these things with his limbs, it does not follow that the interior man does not pray; he is stretched out before God's eyes in that most secret room where he feels compunction."✝

The celebration of this office takes place in such a way as 8 to reveal what was done at that time of the Lord's passion and burial, and how we should recall, through our service, that which was done for us.

## 29

# On the Lord's prayer

We should explain why the Lord's prayer is said in a raised voice, since the rest of the prayers are said secretly. Cyprian, in his sermon *On the Lord's Prayer*, says: "Above all, the teacher of peace and the master of unity did not want prayer to be individual and private, so that when praying, one would not pray for oneself only. We do not say: 'My father, who art in heaven,' nor: 'Give me this day my daily bread'; nor does everyone ask that his debt alone be remitted, or that he not be led into temptation, or ask to be freed from evil solely on his own behalf. Our prayer is public and in common, and when we pray, we pray not for one person

populo oramus, quia totus populus unum sumus. Deus pacis et concordiae magister, qui docuit unitatem, sic orare unum pro omnibus voluit, quomodo in uno omnes ipse portavit.

2 Hanc orationis legem servaverunt tres pueri in camino ignis inclusi, consonantes in prece et spiritu consensionis concordes. Declarat scripturae divinae fides; et, dum docet quomodo oraverint, tale dat exemplum quod imitari in precibus debeamus, ut tales esse possimus: 'Tunc,' inquit, 'illi tres quasi ex uno ore ymnum canebant et benedicebant Deum' [Dan 3:51]. Loquebantur quasi ex uno ore, et nondum illos Christus docuerat orare. Et idcirco orantibus fuit impetrabilis et efficax sermo, quia promerebatur Deum pacifica, simplex et spiritalis oratio."✝

3 Quae oratio sic inchoatur: "Oremus. Praeceptis salutaribus moniti et divina institutione formati, audemus dicere . . ." "Praecepta salutaria" dicimus Evangelicam doctrinam; dicimus "institutionem" traditionem quam ipse dignatus est tradere in conficiendo sacramento corporis et sanguinis.

4 Unde idem qui supra in sermone *De sacramento Domini calicis* Caecilio: "Quanquam sciam, frater karissime, episcopos plurimos Dominicis ecclesiis in toto mundo divina dignatione praepositos, Evangelicae veritatis ac Dominicae traditionis tenere rationem, nec ab eo quod Christus magister et praecepit et gessit, humanam et novellam institutionem docere," et reliqua. Et iterum in eodem: "Ab Evangelicis autem praeceptis omnino non recedendum esse et eadem quae magister docuit et fecit discipulos quoque observare et facere debere."✝

but for the whole people, because we, the whole people, are one. The God of peace and the master of harmony, who taught unity, wanted us to pray for all as one, just as he gathered all into one. The three boys shut in the fiery furnace 2 observed this law of prayer, resounding together in their request and concordant in the spirit of harmony. The faith of divine scripture declares it; and, since it teaches how they prayed, it provides the kind of example that we should imitate in our own prayers, that we may be able to be like them: 'Then,' it says, 'these three as with one mouth sang a hymn and blessed God.' They spoke as with one mouth, and Christ had not yet taught them how to pray. And their speech was successful and effective, because a peaceful, simple and spiritual prayer was worthy of God."✝

The prayer begins thus: "Let us pray. Advised by saving 3 precepts and prepared by divine instruction, we dare to say . . ." "Saving precepts" are what we call Gospel teaching; "instruction" is what we call the tradition for preparing the sacrament of the body and blood that he deigned to hand on to us. Thus the same author as above in his sermon *On the Sac-* 4 *rament of the Lord's Chalice,* to Caecilius: "Yet I know, dearest brother, that many divinely esteemed bishops in charge of the Lord's churches throughout the whole world adhere to the plan of Evangelical truth and the Lord's tradition, and do not teach new, human practice in the place of that which our master, Christ, did and commanded," and so forth. And again in the same work: "In no respect should we depart from Evangelical precepts and those things that our master did and taught that his disciples should also do and observe."✝

5    Ubi Cyprianus dicit "Evangelicae veritatis," et in posterioribus, "ab Evangelicis autem praeceptis omnino non recedendum esse," Evangelicam doctrinam monstrat. Ubi dicit: ". . . ac Dominicae traditionis tenere rationem," et in sequentibus "eadem quae magister docuit et fecit," Dominicam institutionem.

6    Qua audatia intrandum sit ad orationem Dominicam, demonstratum est; id est, postquam praecepta salutaria, id est Evangelica, mundaverint cor nostrum, et formaverint divina instituta (quae dicimus in loco ubi scriptum est: "Accipiens panem in sanctas ac venerabiles manus suas," et reliqua), audemus intrare ad orationem Dominicam. Ubi notandum quod non est praesumptuose intrandum ad eum, sed cum reverentia et serenato corde.

7    In recordatione septimae diei, quando Christus quievit in sepulchro, agitur Dominica oratio, quae septem petitiones continet. In quo septimo die laborabant apostoli tristitia ac metu Iudaeorum, et—ni fallor—orabant ut liberarentur a malo, et consecuti sunt quod orabant: resurrectionem Domini. Orat et nunc sancta ecclesia, quasi in septima die, quando—iam quiescentibus animabus sanctorum—instat ieiunando, vigilando, orando, certando in caritate, ne abrumpatur periculis huius mundi a spe caelestium gaudiorum. Quis est qui non deprecetur, quandiu hic est in praesenti saeculo, ut liberetur a malo? Nec hoc negligenter

8    curandum esse, ut ante participationem corporis et sanguinis Domini interveniat oratio, quae nos purget a peccatis, ne indigne manducemus et bibamus corpus Domini.

Where Cyprian speaks of "Evangelical truth," and then later on says "In no respect should we depart from Evangelical precepts," he refers to Evangelical teaching. Where he says ". . . and adhere to the plan of . . . the Lord's tradition" and then "that which our master, Christ, did and commanded," he refers to the Lord's instruction. 5

We have shown with what sort of daring we should enter upon the Lord's prayer; that is, after the saving or Evangelical precepts have cleansed our heart, and divine instructions have prepared it (which we speak of in that passage where it is written: "Taking the bread in his holy and venerable hands," and so on), we dare to enter upon the Lord's prayer. And we should note here that we should not enter upon it presumptuously, but with reverence and a peaceful heart. 6

The Lord's prayer, which contains seven petitions, is celebrated to commemorate the seventh day, when Christ rested in the tomb. On this seventh day the apostles labored in sadness and fear of the Jews, and—if I am not mistaken—they prayed to be freed from evil, and attained what they prayed for: the Lord's resurrection. Today the holy church also prays, as it were on the seventh day, when—now that the souls of the saints are at rest—it requests through fasting, vigils, praying and striving in charity that it not be cut off from the hope of heavenly joys by the dangers of this world. Who is there who does not beg to be freed from evil as long as he is in this world? Nor should we do this carelessly, that a prayer to cleanse us of sin may intervene before we participate in the body and blood of the Lord, lest we eat and drink the Lord's body unworthily. 7 8

9     Quomodo compleatur oratio Dominica in septima petitione, idem qui supra ostendit in libro *De oratione Dominica,*
dicens: "Post ista omnia in consummatione orationis, venit
clausula universas petitiones et preces nostras collecta bre-
vitate concludens. In novissimo enim ponimus: 'Sed libera
nos a malo,' conprehendens adversa cuncta quae contra nos
in hoc mundo molitur inimicus. A quibus potest esse firma
tutela, si nos Deus liberet—si deprecantibus atque implo-
rantibus opem suam praestet. Quando autem dicimus
'Libera nos a malo,' nihil remanet quod ultra adhuc debeat
postulari, quando semel protectionem Dei adversus malum
petamus. Qua impetrata, contra omnia quae diabolus in
mundum operatur, securi stamus et tuti. Quis enim ei de

10   saeculo metus est, cuius Deus tutor est? Quid mirum, fratres
dilectissimi, si oratio talis est quam Deus docuit, qui magisterio suo omnem precem nostram salutari sermone bre-
viavit? Hoc iam per Esaiam prophetam fuerat ante praedictum, cum, plenus Spiritu Sancto, de Dei maiestate ac pietate
loqueretur: 'Verbum consummans,' inquit, 'et brevians in
iustitia; quoniam sermonem breviatum faciet Deus in toto
orbe terrae' [Isa 10:22–23; Rom 9:28]."☩

11   Quando dicit Cyprianus quod illa una petitione conclusa
sit omnis oratio nostra—id est: "Sed libera nos a malo"—in
eo possumus intellegere posse significari per finem orationis
finem nostrae persecutionis.

12   Sequens oratio expositio est novissimae petitionis. Illa
dicit: "Sed libera nos a malo"; ista dicit a quibus malis, scilicet: "Praesentibus, praeteritis et futuris." Et ut non sit domus vacans, precatur pax a Deo intercedentibus sanctis;
igitur subditur: "Et da pacem in diebus nostris." Nulla pax

The same author as above, in his book *On the Lord's Prayer,* 9 explains how the Lord's prayer is completed upon the seventh petition, saying: "After all these things at the end of the prayer, there comes a phrase that concludes all our petitions and requests in collected brevity. For at the end we add: 'But free us from evil,' including all the adversities in this world that the enemy prepares against us. There can be firm protection from these, if the Lord frees us—if, through our begging and imploring, he offers his help. And when we say 'Free us from evil,' there is nothing more we should ask for, once we ask for God's protection against evil. When we have obtained this, we stand safe and secure against all those things that the devil does in the world. For what fear is there for him from this world, who has God as his defender? Is it 10 remarkable, dearest brothers, if this is the sort of prayer that God taught—God who, in his teaching, cuts short our every prayer with his saving word? This had already been foretold through the prophet Isaiah, when, full of the Holy Spirit, he spoke of God's majesty and piety: 'Finishing his word,' he said, 'and cutting it short in justice; because God shall make a word that has been cut short in the midst of all the land.'"✝

When Cyprian says that our entire prayer is concluded 11 with that one petition—namely: "But free us from evil"—we can understand in that statement that the end of our persecution can be signified through the end of the prayer.

The following prayer is a commentary on the last peti- 12 tion. The latter says: "But free us from evil"; what follows explains from which evils, namely: "Of the present, past and future." And lest that house be empty, it asks God for peace through the intercession of the saints; it therefore continues: "And grant peace in our days." No

tutior quam oboedire Domini praeceptis, declinare mala et facere bona. Inde dicit propheta: "Declina a malo et fac bonum" [Ps 36:27]. Et Apostolus: "Odientes malum, adhe-
13   rentes bono" [Rom 12:9]. Replicat in sequentibus eandem orationem. Non se confidit suis meritis hoc posse impetrare apud Deum, quapropter dicit: "Ut ope misericordiae tuae adiuti." Ac deinde subdit apertius a quibus malis precetur erui, videlicet: "Ut a peccato simus liberi." Et quam pacem precetur, subdit iterum: "Et ab omni perturbatione securi." Quod non potest fieri, nisi studeatur virtutibus. Ut diximus, nihil aliud continet sequens, nisi ut exponat memoratam petitionem.

14   Possunt tres articuli praesentis orationis coaptari tempori triduanae sepulturae Domini; ac ideo hoc solum de Missa posse intellegi caelebrari in Parascheve, pro tribus continentibus diebus sepulturae.

## 30

# De praesentatione subdiaconorum, ut suscipiant corpus Domini de altari

Hoc officium ad memoriam ducit devotissimas mentes quae se ipsas praesentaverunt in exequiis sepulturae Domini. Praesentantibus se sanctis mulieribus ad sepulchrum

peace is more secure than obeying the Lord's commandments, avoiding evil and doing good. Thus the prophet says:
"Avoid evil and do good." And the Apostle: "Hating that
which is evil, cleaving to that which is good." In what fol- 13
lows the celebrant repeats the same prayer. He does not
trust that he can achieve this from God through his own
merits, and so he says: "Assisted by the help of your mercy."
And then he adds more clearly from which evils he asks to
be removed, namely: "That we may be free from sin." And
again he speaks of the peace that he requests: "And secure
from all disquiet." This cannot happen unless there is a striving after virtues. As we said, what follows contains nothing
further; it only explains the aforementioned petition.

The three sections of this prayer can be related to the 14
three-day period of the Lord's burial. Thus this alone, of all
the Mass, can be understood to be celebrated on Good Friday, on behalf of the three days of his burial.

## 30

# On the presentation of the subdeacons, to take the Lord's body from the altar

This office recalls the devoted minds that presented
themselves at the Lord's burial. When the holy women present themselves at the Lord's tomb, they find that his spirit

Domini, inveniunt spiritum rediisse ad corpus, et angelorum visionem circa sepulchrum, ac adnuntiant apostolis quae viderant. De quo utilem ammonitionem dat Beda in tractatu super Lucam: "Quomodo," inquit, "posito in sepulchro corpore salvatoris, angeli adstitisse leguntur, ita etiam caelebrandis eiusdem sanctissimi corporis mysteriis tempore consecrationis assistere sunt credendi, monente Apostolo mulieres in ecclesia velamen habere propter angelos [1
2 Cor 11:10].'Cum timerent autem et declinarent vultum in terram, dixerunt ad illas: Quid quaeritis viventem cum mortuis? Non est hic, sed surrexit' [Luke 24:5–6]. Nolite, inquiunt, cum mortuis (hoc est in monumento, qui locus utique est proprie mortuorum) quaerere eum qui ad vitam iam resurrexit a mortuis. Et nos exemplo devotarum Deo feminarum, quoties ecclesiam intramus, mysteriis caelestibus appropinquamus; sive propter angelicae praesentiam virtutis, seu propter reverentiam sacrae oblationis, cum omni humilitate et timore debemus ingredi. Ad conspectum quippe angelorum vultum declinamus in terram, cum, supernorum civium quae sunt gaudia aeterna contemplantes, humiliter nos cinerem esse terramque recolimus."✝

3 Post haec praesentat se subdiaconus cum patena sua ad sepulchrum Domini. Quam accepit a subdiacono sequente, qui ad memoriam—ut supra diximus—reducit sanctarum feminarum studiosissimum affectum circa sepulturam Domini. Non est mirandum, si sanctae feminae iungantur in officio diaconis, cum Paulus eas coniungat in ordinatione eis. Scribit ad Timotheum post ordinationem diaconi:

has returned to its body, and they see a vision of angels at the tomb, and they tell the apostles what they saw. Bede provides useful instruction about this in his treatise on Luke: "Just as we read that the angels attended the body of the savior after it had been placed in the tomb," he says, "so too should we believe that they assist during the consecration, when the mysteries of the same holy body are celebrated. And the Apostle says that the women in church are veiled because of the angels. 'And as they were afraid and bowed down their countenance toward the ground, they said to them: Why do you seek the living with the dead? He is not here, but is risen.' They are saying: Do not look among the dead (that is in the tomb, which is, properly speaking, a place for the dead) for him who has just risen to life from the dead. And whenever we enter church, we approach the heavenly mysteries after the example of those women who were devoted to God; whether because of the presence of angelic virtue, or out of reverence for the holy offering, we should enter with all fear and humility. For within the gaze of the holy angels we should look at the ground, while we contemplate what sorts of joys belong to these heavenly citizens and humbly recall that we are ashes and earth."✝

Afterward, the subdeacon presents himself with his paten at the Lord's tomb. He has taken the paten from the assisting subdeacon, who—as we said above—calls to mind the devoted disposition of the holy women at the Lord's tomb. It is little wonder that the holy women should be associated with the office of the deacon, since Paul joins the women to the deacons in his discussion of ordination. He writes to Timothy after discussing the ordination of the deacon:

"Mulieres similiter pudicas" [1 Tim 3:11], et reliqua. In omni ammonitione ordinationis vult eas similes esse diaconis.

4 Qua de causa sint seiunctae a consortio diaconorum, cum Paulus eas coniungat ordinationi illorum, et subdiaconi succedant (de quibus nihil dixit Paulus), norunt qui caste volunt vivere. Nam et in choro apostolorum legimus feminas fuisse. Unde Paulus ad Corinthios: "Numquid non habemus potestatem mulieres circumducendi, sicut et ceteri apostoli et fratres Domini et Cephas?" [1 Cor 9:5].

5 Postquam sacerdos dicit: "Pax vobis," ponuntur oblatae in patena. Postquam enim Christus sua salutatione laetificavit corda discipulorum, vota feminarum completa sunt percepto gaudio resurrectionis [Luke 24:36; John 20:19, 21, 26].

## 31

# De immissione panis
# in vinum

Immissionem panis in vinum cerno apud quosdam varie actitari, ita ut aliqui primo mittant de sancto in calicem, et postea dicant *Pax Domini.* E contra aliqui reservent immissionem usque dum pax caelebrata sit et fractio panis. Ac

"The women in like manner chaste," and so on. In all of his advice about ordination, he wants the women to be like deacons. Those who want to lead a chaste life know why the   4 women have been separated from the company of the deacons, though Paul joins them to their order, and why the subdeacons (about whom Paul said nothing) follow instead. For we read that there were also women among the band of the apostles. Thus Paul to the Corinthians: "Have we not power to carry about women, as well as the rest of the apostles and the brethren of the Lord and Cephas?"

After the priest says: "Peace be with you," the offerings   5 are placed on the paten. For after Christ delighted the hearts of the disciples with his greeting, the vows of the women upon seeing the joy of the resurrection were fulfilled.

## 31

# On the immersion of the bread in the wine

I see that the immersion of the bread in the wine is practiced in varying ways among certain people, such that some put part of the holy body into the chalice first and afterward say the *Pax Domini*. Others, in contrast, delay this immersion until the peace and the breaking of the bread have been celebrated. And so in my inadequacy, I am eager

ideo studet parvitas mea, ut verba libelli Romani de eadem re ponam, et quod a Domino impetrare potero—ut opinor—in indagine memoratae rei promam. Dicit libellus memoratus: "Cum dixerit: '*Pax Domini* sit semper vobiscum,' mittit in calicem de sancto." Ut reor, non frustra. Corporalis vita ex sanguine constat et carne; quamdiu haec duo vigent in homine, spiritus adest.

2    In isto officio monstratur sanguinem fusum pro nostra anima et carnem mortuam pro nostro corpore redire ad propriam substantiam, atque spiritu vivificante vegetari hominem novum, ut ultra non moriatur qui pro nobis mortuus fuit et resurrexit. Crux quae formatur super calicem particula oblatae, ipsum corpus nobis ante oculos proscribit, quod pro nobis crucifixum est. Ideo tangit quattuor latera calicis, quia per illum hominum genus quattuor climatum ad unitatem unius corporis accessit et ad pacem catholicae

3    ecclesiae. Talia verba sacerdos hoc agendo profert: "Fiat commixtio corporis et sanguinis Domini accipientibus nobis in vitam aeternam." Quae verba precantur ut fiat corpus Domini praesens oblatio per resurrectionem, per quam veneranda et aeterna pax data est, non solum in terra sed etiam in caelo.

4    Tunc cessaverunt murmurare operarii vineae orae primae, tertiae et sextae [Matt 20:8–15]; tunc data est pax quam promiserunt angeli in sacratissima nocte dicentes: "Gloria in excelsis Deo, et in terra pax hominibus bonae voluntatis" [Luke 2:14]. Eandem sacerdos nunc ad memoriam revocat,

to quote the words of the Roman book on this matter, and to set forth what I have been able to learn from the Lord— as I believe—in my investigation of the aforementioned matter. The aforementioned manual says: "When he has said: 'The peace of the Lord *(Pax Domini)* be with you always,' he puts part of the holy body in the chalice." I believe that this is not done in vain. The life of the body consists of blood and flesh; as long as these two live in a person, the spirit is present.

In this office it is shown that the blood that was poured 2 out for our soul and the flesh that died for our body return to their own substance, and that the new man lives through the life-giving spirit, so that he who died and rose for us may die no more. The cross that is made over the chalice with a piece of the offering inscribes the body that was crucified before our eyes. It touches the four sides of the chalice, because through it the human race has come to the unity of one body and to the peace of the catholic church from the four regions of the earth. In doing this, the priest 3 offers these words: "Let this mixing of the Lord's body and blood be for us, who receive it, unto eternal life." These words request that the present offering become the Lord's body through resurrection, through which venerable and eternal peace have been granted, not only on earth but also in heaven.

Then the laborers of the vineyard ceased their grumbling 4 of the first, third and sixth hour; then the peace was granted that the angels promised on that most sacred night, saying: "Glory to God in the highest, and on earth peace to men of goodwill." The priest now commemorates this peace,

dicens: "Pax Domini sit semper vobiscum." Eandem populus insequitur per basia blanda.

5     Estimo, secundum hunc sensum, quod non erret, si quis primo sancta ponat in calicem, et dein dixerit: "Pax Domini sit semper vobiscum"—salvo magisterio didascalorum.

6     Sequitur in libello memorato: "Sed archidiaconus pacem dat episcopo prior, deinde ceteri per ordinem, et populus. Tunc pontifex rumpit oblatam ex latere dextro, et particulam quam rumpit super altare relinquit, reliquas vero oblationes ponit in patenam quam tenet diaconus." Et post pauca: "Tunc acolyti vadunt dextera levaque per episcopos circa altare; reliqui descendunt ad presbyteros ut frangant hostias; patena praecedit iuxta sedem, ferentibus eam duobus subdiaconibus regionariis ad diaconos, ut frangant." Et iterum post aliqua: "Expleta confractione, diaconus minor levata de subdiacono patena fert ad sedem, ut communicet pontifex. Qui dum communicaverit, de ipsa quam momorderat ponit inter manus archidiaconi in calicem."

7     Si hoc ita agitur in Romana ecclesia, ab illis potest addisci quid significet bis positus panis in calicem. Non enim vacat a mysterio quicquid in eo officio agitur iuxta constitutionem patrum. Quid nobis videtur posse significare immissio panis in vinum et pax populo porrecta per vocem sacerdotis, magistris obtulimus ad dilucidandum.

saying: "The peace of the Lord be with you always." The people pursue this peace through gentle kisses.

According to this sense, I think that it is not wrong if one 5 first places the holy offering in the chalice, and then says: "The peace of the Lord be with you always"—though I defer to the instruction of the teachers.

There follows in the aforementioned book: "And the first 6 archdeacon gives peace to the bishop; then the others, according to rank; and then the people. Then the pontiff breaks the offering on the right side, and he leaves the piece that he breaks off on the altar, while he puts the other offerings on the paten that the deacon holds." And after a little: "Then the acolytes follow the bishops, right and left, around the altar; the rest go down to the priests to break the hosts; the paten goes ahead to the chair, carried to the deacons by the two regional subdeacons, that they may break the hosts." And again, after other things: "When it has been broken, the junior deacon takes the paten from the subdeacon and brings it to the chair, that the pontiff may receive communion. When he has received communion, he places the piece that he bit from into the chalice, between the hands of the archdeacon."

If it is done this way in the Roman church, we can learn 7 from them what this twofold placement of the bread in the chalice means. For whatever is done in this office, according to what the fathers established, is not without its mystery. What the immersion of the bread in the wine and the peace offered to the people through the voice of the priest appears capable of signifying to us, we have presented to the masters for elaboration.

# 32

# De pacis osculo

Contentum me oportet esse de pace in eo quod Innocentius de ea scribit ad Decentium episcopum in decretalibus, primo capitulo, propter auctoritatem tanti viri: "Pacem igitur asseris ante confecta mysteria quosdam populis imperare, vel sibi inter sacerdotes tradere—cum post omnia quae aperire non debeo, pax sit necessaria indicenda. Per quam constet populum ad omnia quae in mysteriis aguntur atque in ecclesia caelebrantur, praebuisse consensum; ac finita esse pacis concludentis signaculo demonstrentur."✝ Interrogatus sum ab aliquibus quare non invicem porrigant sibi oscula viri et feminae in officio Missae. Quibus, quamvis tunc non responderem, respondendum nunc fore arbitror. Carnales amplexus quibus iunguntur saepissime viri et feminae vitandi sunt in ecclesiae conventum; ac ideo sequestrantur viri et feminae in ecclesia—non solum ab osculo carnali, sed etiam situ locali. Ab his personis dantur oscula mutua in ecclesia, quae nullam titillationem libidinosae suggestionis cogunt excitare.

## 32

# On the kiss of peace

As for the peace, I have to be content with the first chapter that Innocent wrote about it to the bishop Decentius in his decretals, because of the authority of so great a man: "And so you say that some enjoin peace upon the people before the mysteries have been completed, or that the priests exchange peace among themselves—though the peace must be proclaimed after all the things that I should not go into. The peace shows that the people have offered their consent to everything done in the mysteries and celebrated in the church; through the concluding sign of peace, it is shown that these things are finished."+ Some people have asked  2 me why men and women do not offer kisses to one another in the office of the Mass. Although I did not respond to them at the time, I think I should respond now. The carnal embraces in which men and women are frequently joined should be avoided in the gathering at church, and men and women are therefore sequestered in church—not only with respect to the bodily kiss, but also in their physical location. In church, reciprocal kisses are exchanged only by those persons who do not arouse the excitement of licentious suggestion.

# 33

# De *Agnus Dei*

Sergius papa constituit ut *Agnus Dei* cantaretur, sicut scriptum est in *Gestis pontificatibus:* "Hic statuit ut tempore confractionis Dominici corporis *Agnus Dei* a clero et populo decantetur."✝ Deprecatio est pro populo qui sumpturus est corpus Domini, ut misericordia innocentis agni peccata subitanea et irruentia auferantur (scilicet cogitationum verborumque)—et, sicut passione sua totius mundi tulit offensa, ita et nunc ecclesiae, quae eum susceptura est per Eucharistiam.

2    Antiphona sequens—id est vox reciproca—iura fraternitatis custodit, ut unusquisque alterius utilitati studeat et curet provocare ad gaudia resurrectionis. Quem typum gesserunt illi duo qui Dominum cognoverunt in fractione panis, et ilico perrexerunt Hierusalem et invenerunt congregatos XI, et eos qui cum ipsis erant, dicentes: "Surrexit vere Dominus, et apparuit Symoni. Et ipsi narrabant quae gesta erant in via, et quomodo cognoverunt eum in fractione panis" [Luke 24:30–35]. Illi nempe cantaverunt antiphonam vicissim narrando de resurrectione Domini.

## 33

# On the *Agnus Dei*

Pope Sergius established that the *Agnus Dei* be sung, as it is written in the *Deeds of the Bishops:* "He declared that the *Agnus Dei* be sung by the clergy and the people at the time of the breaking of the Lord's body."+ It is a request on behalf of the people who are about to receive the Lord's body, that, through the mercy of the innocent lamb, sins that invade quickly and without warning may be taken away (that is, sins of thoughts and words)—and also that he may now take away the sins of the church that is about to receive him in the Eucharist, just as he took away the offenses of the whole world through his passion.

The following antiphon—that is, alternating voice—preserves principles of fraternity, that everyone may strive for the advantage of each other and work to call each other to the joys of the resurrection. The two who recognized the Lord upon his breaking of the bread provide an example of this type. They then hastened to Jerusalem and found the eleven gathered together, and those who were with them, and said: "The Lord is risen indeed, and has appeared to Simon. And they told what things were done on the way, and how they knew him in the breaking of the bread." Indeed, they sang an antiphon by telling of the Lord's resurrection in turn.

# 34

# De Eucharistia

Eucharistia sumenda est post osculum pacis. Sicut unus panis sumus in Christo, sic et unum cor debemus habere. Ipsa unitas ut teneatur ammonetur per oscula pacis. Unde Beda in tractatu super Lucam: "Ne quisquam se Christum agnovisse arbitretur, si eius corporis particeps non est—id est ecclesiae—cuius unitatem in sacramento panis commendat Apostolus, dicens: 'Unus panis, unum corpus multi sumus' [1 Cor 10:17]."✝ Per Eucharistiam Christus in nobis manet, et nos in illo per assumptum hominem. Ipse est Deus pacis, per quem pacata sunt caelestia et terrestria.

2  Sunt enim intra sanctam ecclesiam qui raro communicant, et qui cotidie. Quibus utrisque dat aptum consilium sanctus Agustinus ad inquisitionem Ianuarii de eadem re: "Rectius," inquit, "inter eos fortasse quispiam dirimit litem, qui monet ut praecipue in Christi pace permaneant. Faciat autem unusquisque quod secundum fidem suam pie credit esse faciendum. Neuter enim eorum exhonorat corpus et sanguinem Domini, sed saluberrimum sacramentum certatim honorare contendunt. Neque enim litigaverunt inter se, aut quisquam eorum se alteri praeposuit, Zachaeus et ille centurio [Luke 19:6], cum alter eorum gaudens in domum suam susceperit Dominum, alter dixerit: 'Non sum dignus

## 34

# On the Eucharist

The Eucharist is to be received after the kiss of peace. Just as we are one bread in Christ, so too should we have one heart. Through the kiss of peace, we are advised to maintain this unity. Thus Bede in his treatise on Luke: "Nobody should think that he has known Christ if he does not participate in his body—that is, the church—whose unity in the sacrament of bread the Apostle commends, saying: 'We, being many, are one bread, one body.'"+ Christ dwells in us through the Eucharist, and we in him through the human nature that he assumed. This is the God of peace, through whom the heavens and the earth have been pacified.

Now there are those in the holy church who receive communion rarely, and those who receive it daily. Saint Augustine gives good advice to both in response to Januarius's question about the same matter: "Perhaps," he says, "he who advises them above all to remain in Christ's peace cuts through the dispute more correctly. Let everyone do what he piously believes should be done, in accordance with his own faith. For neither of them dishonors the Lord's body and blood; rather, both strive in earnest to honor this most saving sacrament. For Zaccheus and the centurion did not fight among themselves, nor did one place himself before the other, when one of them rejoiced and took the Lord into his house, and the other said: 'I am not worthy

ut sub tectum meum intres' [Luke 7:6; Matt 8:8]—ambo salvatorem honorificantes diverso et quasi contrario modo, ambo peccatis miseri, ambo misericordiam consecuti."✝

3    Idem exponit Apostoli dictum: "Qui enim manducat et bibit indigne, iudicium sibi manducat et bibit" [1 Cor 11:29], in sequentibus ita: "Inde etenim Apostolus indigne dicit acceptum ab eis qui hoc non discernebant a ceteris cibis veneratione singulariter debita. Continuo quippe cum dixisset: 'Iudicium sibi manducat et bibit,' addidit ut diceret: 'non deiudicans corpus Domini.'"✝

4    Ut a ieiunis suscipiatur, idem dicit in eodem libro: "Namque salvator, quo vehementius commendaret mysterii illius altitudinem, ultimum hoc voluit infigere cordibus et memoriae discipulorum, a quibus ad passionem digressurus erat. Et ideo non paecepit quo deinceps ordine sumeretur, ut apostolis, per quos ecclesias dispositurus erat, servaret hunc locum. Nam si hoc ille monuisset, ut post cibos alios semper acciperetur, credo quod eum morem nemo variasset."✝

5    Ex quo tempore debeat se sanctificare homo ad perceptionem tanti muneris, vetus historia docet. Dicit in Exodo Dominus Moysi: "Vade ad populum et sanctifica illos hodie et cras, laventque vestimenta sua, et sint parati in die tertio. In die enim tertio descendet Dominus coram omni

6    plebe super montem Sina" [Exod 19:10–11]. Eodem numero David se et pueros suos sanctificatum dixit, ut comedat panes propositionis. Ita scriptum est in libro Samuelis: Dixit Abimelech sacerdos: "Non habeo panes laicos ad manum, sed tantum panem sanctum—si mundi sunt pueri,

that you should enter under my roof.' Both honored the savior in a different and almost opposite manner; both were wretched in their sins; both attained mercy."✝

The same author explains the Apostle's statement: "For 3 he that eats and drinks unworthily, eats and drinks judgment to himself," in a subsequent passage, as follows: "Then indeed, the Apostle says that it is unworthily received by those who do not distinguish it from other foods, with the particular veneration that it is owed. Thus, right after he said: 'He eats and drinks judgment to himself,' he hastened to add: 'not discerning the body of the Lord.'"✝

The same author remarks, in the same book, that it is to 4 be received by those who are fasting: "And so the savior, to emphasize as forcefully as possible the depth of the mystery, wanted to imprint this final matter upon the hearts and the memory of his disciples, whom he was about to leave for his passion. He thus did not command how they should receive it, in order to leave this decision to his apostles, through whom he would establish his churches. For if he had ordered that it always be received after other foods, I believe that nobody would have deviated from that practice."✝

Ancient history teaches us from what time one should 5 sanctify oneself for the reception of such a gift. The Lord says to Moses in Exodus: "Go to the people and sanctify them today and tomorrow, and let them wash their garments, and let them be ready on the third day. For on the third day the Lord will come down in the sight of all the people upon Mount Sinai." David said that he and his 6 sons were sanctified by the same amount of time, that they might eat the loaves of proposition. Thus is it written in the book of Samuel: Abimelech the priest said: "I have no common bread at hand, but only holy bread—if the young men

maxime a mulieribus? Et respondit David sacerdoti et dixit ei: Et quidem, si de mulieribus agitur, continuimus nos ad heri et nudiustertius quando egrediebamur, et fuerunt vasa puerorum sancta. Porro via haec polluta est, sed et ipsa hodie sanctificabitur in vasis. Dedit ergo ei sacerdos sanctificatum panem" [1 Kgs 21:4–6].

## 35

# De parte oblatae quae remanet in altari

Triforme est corpus Christi, eorum scilicet qui gustaverunt mortem et morituri sunt. Primum videlicet sanctum et immaculatum quod assumptum est ex Maria virgine; alterum, quod ambulat in terra; tertium, quod iacet in sepulchris. Per particulam oblatae inmissae in calicem, ostenditur Christi corpus quod iam resurrexit a mortuis; per comestam a sacerdote vel a populo, ambulans adhuc super terram; per 3 relictam in altari, iacens in sepulchris. Idem corpus oblatam ducit secum ad sepulchrum, et vocat illam sancta ecclesia viaticum morientis, ut ostendatur non eos debere, qui in Christo moriuntur, deputari mortuos, sed dormientes. Unde

be clean, especially from women? And David answered the priest and said to him: Truly, as to what concerns women, we have refrained ourselves from yesterday and the day before when we came out, and the vessels of the young men were holy. Now this way is defiled, but it shall also be sanctified this day in the vessels. The priest therefore gave him hallowed bread."

# 35

# On the part of the offering that remains on the altar

The body of Christ is triform, namely of those who have tasted death and those who are going to die. The first is the holy and immaculate form that was assumed from the virgin Mary; the second is the one that walked on the earth; the third is the one that lies in the tomb. In the particle of 2 the offering dipped in the chalice, the body of Christ that has just risen from the dead is revealed; in the part that was eaten by the priest and the people, that which yet walks upon the earth; in the part left on the altar, that which lies in the tomb. That same body takes the offering with it to the 3 tomb, and the holy church calls it the viaticum of the dying, to show that those who die in Christ should not be considered dead, but asleep. And so the place of tombs is called a

et locus sepulchrorum Grece vocatur *cymiterium,* id est dormitorium. Unde et Paulus ad Corinthios: "Mulier alligata est legi quanto tempore vir eius vivit. Quod si dormierit vir eius, liberata est" [1 Cor 7:39]. Remanetque in altari ipsa particula usque ad finem Missae, quia usque in finem saeculi corpora sanctorum quiescent in sepulchris.

4    Munditiam mentis docet corporale, quod remanet in altari post Domini resurrectionem. Cui debet unusquisque semper studere accipiens corpus Domini, sed praecipue in fine.

# 36

# De ultima benedictione

Etenim Dominus, ante ascensionem in caelos, duxit discipulos in Bethaniam, ibique benedixit eos et ascendit in caelum. Hunc morem tenet sacerdos, ut, post omnia sacramenta consummata, benedicat populo atque salutet. Dein revertitur ad orientem, ut se commendet Domini ascensioni.

2    Dicitque diaconus: "Ite missa est." Singularis etenim legatio, Christus, missa est pro nobis ad Patrem, habens indicia secum suae passionis: Primo, ut per haec discipulis fidem

*cymiterium* in Greek, or a dormitory. Thus also Paul to the Corinthians: "A woman is bound by the law as long as her husband lives. But if her husband fall asleep, she is at liberty." And this particle remains upon the altar until the end of Mass, because the bodies of the saints will rest in their tombs until the end of the world.

The corporal, which remains on the altar after the Lord's  4
resurrection, teaches us about purity of mind. Everyone should always strive for this when receiving the Lord's body, but especially at the end.

# 36

# On the final blessing

Now the Lord, before his ascension to heaven, took his disciples to Bethany, and there he blessed them and ascended into heaven. The priest follows this practice, such that, after all the sacraments have been consummated, he blesses and bids farewell to the people. Then he turns back to the east in order to commend himself to the Lord's ascension.

The deacon says: "Go; it has been sent." And indeed that un-  2
paralleled legation, Christ, was sent on our behalf to the Father, having with him the proofs of his passion: First, that through these proofs he might build up faith in his resurrection

suae resurrectionis astruat. Deinde ut, Patri pro nobis supplicans, quale genus mortis pro mortalium vita pertulerit semper ostendat. Tertio ut sua morte redemptis, quam misericorditer sint adiuti, propositis semper eiusdem mortis innovet indiciis—ideoque misericordias Domini in aeternum cantare non cessent, sed "dicant qui redempti sunt a Domino: Quoniam bonus, quoniam in saeculum misericordia eius" [Ps 106:2, 1]. Postremo ut etiam perfidis in iudicio quam iuste damnentur, ostensa inter alia flagitia, etiam vulnerum quae ab eis suscepit, cicatrice denuntient.

3    De qua legatione dicit Iohannes apostolus: "Sed et si quis peccaverit, advocatum habemus apud Patrem, Iesum Christum iustum" [1 John 2:1]. Ipse Iohannes certe vir iustus erat et magnus, qui de pectore Domini mysteriorum secreta bibebat. Non tamen dixit: "Advocatum me habetis apud Patrem," sed: "Advocatum," inquit, "habemus." Et "habemus" dixit, non "habetis." Maluit se ponere in numero peccatorum, ut haberet advocatum Christum, quam ponere se pro Christo advocatum et inveniri inter damnandos superbos.

4    Nec tamen dicendum quia episcopi vel praepositi non petant pro populo. Orat enim Apostolus pro plebe, orat plebs pro Apostolo, qui dicit: "Orantes simul et pro nobis, ut Deus aperiat nobis hostium verbi" [Col 4:3]. Et pro Petro orabat ecclesia cum esset in vinculis Petrus [Acts 12:5]; exaudita est quomodo et Petrus pro ecclesia—quia omnia pro invicem membra orant, caput pro omnibus interpellat.

5    De quo scriptum est: "Qui est ad dexteram Dei, qui etiam

among the disciples. Second, that, beseeching his Father on our behalf, he might forever show the sort of death he endured for the life of mortals. Third, that he might make known anew to those who have been redeemed by his death how mercifully they were helped, by forever providing proofs this death—and that therefore they might not cease to sing of the Lord's mercies forever, but "they who have been redeemed by the Lord might say: For he is good, for his mercy endures forever." And finally, that he might also announce to the faithless how justly they are damned in his judgment, displaying the scar of his wounds, among the other disgraces that he received from them.

John the apostle speaks about this legation: "But if any  3 man sin, we have an advocate with the Father, Jesus Christ the just." This John was certainly a just and great man, who imbibed the secrets of the mysteries from the Lord's chest. Yet he did not say: "You have me as your advocate with the Father," but rather said: "We have an advocate." And he said "We have," not "You have." He chose to count himself among the sinners that he might have Christ as his advocate, rather than to set himself up as an advocate for Christ and be found among the proud, who are to be damned. Yet this is not to say that bishops and those in au-  4 thority do not make requests on behalf of the people. For the Apostle prays on behalf of the people, and the people pray on behalf of the Apostle, who says: "Praying also for us, that God may open a door of speech for us." And the church prayed for Peter when Peter was in chains; and we have heard how Peter also prayed for the church—because all the members pray for one another, and the head intercedes on behalf of all. About this head, it is writ-  5 ten: "Who is at the right hand of God, who also makes

interpellat pro nobis" [Rom 8:34]. Unigenito enim Filio pro homine interpellare est apud coaeternum Patrem—se ipsum hominem demonstrare, eique pro humana natura rogasse est eandem naturam in divinitatis suae celsitudinem suscepisse. Interpellat igitur pro nobis Dominus non voce, sed miseratione.

6    O utinam quando audimus a diacono: "Ite missa est," mens nostra ad illam patriam tendat quo caput nostrum praecessit—ut ibi simus desiderio, ubi desideratus cunctis gentibus [Hag 2:8] nos expectat cum suo tropheo—quatinus sic desiderando aliquando ad eum pervenire possimus qui ita Patrem supplicat pro nobis: "Volo, Pater, ut ubi ego sum, ibi sit et minister meus" [ John 17:24, 12:26].

7    Solet vulgus indoctum requirere a quo loco totius officii Missa inchoetur, ut, si forte ad totum officium non occurrerit, possit scire quibus officiis se praesentare debeat sine retractatione. Nobis videtur Missa vocari ab eo loco, ubi incipit sacerdos sacrificium offerre Deo, usque ad ultimam benedictionem—id est, ab offerenda usque ad "Ite missa est." A tempore sacrificii Isidorus officium Missae deputat, inquiens in libro *Etymologiarum:* "Missa tempore sacrificii est, quando catecumini foras mittuntur clamante levita: 'Si quis catecuminus remansit, exeat foras. Et inde missa, quia sacramentis altaris interesse non possunt qui nondum

8    regenerati noscuntur."✝ Consuetudo nostra tenet ut catecuminos repellamus ante Evangelium. Non mihi hoc videtur ex ratione incumbere, cum procul dubio praedicatoribus

intercession for us." For it is up to the only begotten Son to intercede on man's behalf with his coeternal Father—to indicate that he is himself a man, as it was his duty to ask, on behalf of human nature, to take that same nature into the lofty heights of his divinity. And so the Lord intercedes on our behalf not with his voice, but with compassion.

If only our mind would strive for that land where our 6 head preceded us, when we hear from the deacon: "Go, it has been sent"—that we may be there in desire, where he, the desired of all nations, waits for us with his victory trophy—so that, through this desire, we may one day be able to go to him who beseeches the Father on our behalf: "Father, I desire that where I am, there my servant might also be."

Unlearned commoners often ask at what point in this 7 whole office the Mass begins, so that, if for some reason they do not attend the whole office, they may be able to know at which offices they should present themselves without being turned away. It seems to us that the Mass, properly called, extends from the place where the priest begins to offer the sacrifice to God, up to the final blessing—that is, from the offering until "Go, it has been sent." Isidore reckons the office of the Mass from the time of the sacrifice, saying in his book of *Etymologies:* "Mass occurs at the time of the sacrifice, when the catechumens are sent out and the deacon proclaims: 'If any catechumen has remained, he should go outside.' And this is therefore the Mass, since those whom we know have not yet been reborn cannot be present at the sacraments of the altar."✝ Our custom is to send the catechumens out before the Gos- 8 pel. This does not strike me as reasonable, since of course

gentium praeceptum sit ut Evangelium eis praedicent. Sed sacrificio omnino interesse non possunt nisi renati, quia neque pro eis oratur a sacerdote in consecratione corporis et sanguinis Domini, neque confectum illis porrigitur. Sic orat sacerdos pro circumstantibus: "Memento, Domine, famulorum famularumque tuarum, et omnium circumstantium quorum tibi fides cognita est et nota devotio." Nondum renati infideles vocantur, non fideles. Igitur non possumus animadvertere pro illis constitutam esse orationem in officio confectionis corporis Christi. Quapropter merito eo tempore recedunt, quo sacrificium caelebratur.

9

## 37

# De ulteriore ultima benedictione

Est ultima benedictio de qua nunc agimus, quam potissimum frequentamus tempore Quadragesimali. Hoc est post illam ultimam continuatam in qua spiritalis refectio commendatur, restat haec ulterior, de qua nunc, ut diximus, agitur. In qua milites Christi commendantur pugnae contra antiquum hostem. Si omni tempore necesse est paratum esse bellicosum adversus insidias sive impetus inimicorum,

those who preach to the heathens are ordered to preach the Gospel to them. But at the sacrifice, of course, only the re-born can be present, since the priest does not pray for the unbaptized during the consecration of the body and blood of the Lord, nor is what he has prepared offered to them. Thus the priest prays for those who are present as follows: 9 "Remember, Lord, your servants and handmaidens, and all those standing here whose faith and devotion are known to you." Those who have not yet been reborn are called un-faithful, not faithful. We are therefore unable to consider the prayer during the office where we prepare Christ's body as having been established for them. It is therefore right that they leave when the sacrifice is celebrated.

# 37

# On the further final blessing

There is another final blessing that we will now dis-cuss, which we employ mostly in the time of Lent. That is, directly after the final blessing in which our spiritual refreshment is commended, there remains this further one that, as we said, is now under discussion. In it, Christ's soldiers are commended to their fight against the an-cient enemy. If we must be prepared at every moment for war against the designs or attacks of our enemies,

2 quanto magis in procinctu? Quadragesimali tempore scit adversarius noster a sancta ecclesia singulare certamen commissum esse contra se, ac ideo instat fortius ad rapiendum et prosternendum, si forte aliquem neglegentem invenerit. Sacerdos noster, ut prudens agonoteta, quantum in maiore periculo videt milites fore, tantum munit eos amplius sua benedictione. Arma nostra contra diabolum sunt humilitas et ceterae virtutes. Vult sacerdos noster ut nostris armis vestiti simus; propterea iubet per ministrum ut humiliemus capita nostra Deo, et ita tandem infundit super milites protectionem benedictionis suae.

3 Benedictio sacerdotis morem antiquum tenet, ut in novissimo porrigatur. Iacob patriarcha, in novissimo vitae suae, benedixit filiis suis. Scriptum est in Genesi: "Benedixit singulis benedictionibus propriis, et praecepit eis, dicens: Ego congregor ad populum meum. Sepelite me cum patribus meis." Et iterum: "Finitisque mandatis quibus filios instituebat, collegit pedes suos super lectum et obiit" [Gen 40:28–29, 32]. Similiter scriptum est de Moyse in libro Deuteronomii: "Haec benedictio qua benedixit Moyses homo Dei filiis Israhel, ante mortem suam" [Deut 33:1]. Denique et ipse Dominus salvator, ut superius praetulimus, ante ascensionem suam in caelum benedixit discipulis suis [Luke 24:50–51].

4 In XII lectionibus non sequitur ista benedictio—sive quia benedictiones praecesserunt plures super consecratos, seu quod officium illud finitur saepe circa noctem Dominicam, in qua non flectimus genua.

how much more should we be prepared when we are under arms? In the season of Lent, our adversary knows that a singular attack has been mounted against him by the holy church, and so he insists more urgently on seizing and striking us down, should he find anyone who is careless. Our priest, like a prudent master of games, fortifies his soldiers with his blessing all the more, to the degree that he perceives they will face great danger. Our weapons against the devil are humility and the other virtues. Our priest wants us to be clad in this armor; therefore he orders, through his minister, that we lower our heads to God, and thus he finally pours out the protection of his blessing upon his soldiers.

The priest's blessing accords with ancient custom, and is therefore offered at the end. The patriarch Jacob, at the end of his life, blessed his sons. It is written in Genesis: "And he blessed every one with their proper blessings, and he charged them, saying: I am now going to be gathered to my people. Bury me with my fathers." And again: "And when he had ended the commandments wherewith he instructed his sons, he drew up his feet upon the bed and died." It is likewise written about Moses, in the book of Deuteronomy: "This is the blessing wherewith the man of God Moses blessed the children of Israel, before his death." And later on, the Lord savior himself, as we said above, also blessed his disciples before his ascension into heaven.

On feasts of twelve lessons this blessing does not occur— whether because many blessings upon the consecrated have preceded, or because that office often ends during Sunday night, when we do not kneel.

## 38

# De Missa in festivitate sancti Iohannis Baptistae, mane prima

Beatus Iohannes Baptista tribus insignibus triumphis excellenter refulsit. Ad hoc enim venit—ut viam Domino praepararet exemplo suae conversationis, qui triumphus caelebratur in vigilia eius. Per baptismi ministerium claruit; insignis huius ministerii triumphus recolitur in prima Missa. Nazareus vero permansit ex utero matris; hoc donum recolitur secunda Missa in die.

## 39

# De offerenda *Vir erat in terra*

Interim occurrit mihi repetitio verborum quae est in versibus offertorii *Vir erat*. Nolui praetermittere quod sensi de illa, quamvis ordo rerum teneat post scriptionem Nativitatis sancti Iohannis Nativitatem Christi scribere. In offertorio non est repetitio verborum; in versibus est. Verba historici

## 38

# On Mass on the feast of Saint John the Baptist, in the early morning

Blessed John the Baptist gleamed brightly with three re-markable triumphs. He came for this reason—to prepare a path for the Lord through the example of his way of life. This triumph is celebrated on his vigil. He shone brightly in the ministry of baptism; the triumph of this remarkable ministry is recalled during the first Mass of his feast. Indeed, he remained a Nazarene from his mother's womb; this gift is recalled on the second Mass of the day.

## 39

# On the offertory *Vir erat in terra*

Meanwhile, I am reminded of the repetition of the words in the verses of the offertory *Vir erat.* I do not want to leave out what I thought about this, although the order of things holds that I should write about Christ's Nativity after writing about the Nativity of Saint John. In the offer-tory there is no repetition of words; in the verses, there is

continentur in offertorio; verba Iob aegroti et dolentis continentur in versibus. Aegrotus cuius anhelitus non est sanus neque fortis, solet verba inperfecta saepius repetere.

2 Officii auctor, ut affectanter nobis ad memoriam reduceret aegrotantem Iob, repetivit saepius verba more aegrotantium. In offertorio, ut dixi, non sunt verba repetita, quia historicus scribens historiam non aegrotabat.

# 40

# De Adventu Domini

In antiquis libris missalium et lectionariorum reperitur scriptum: "Ebdomada quinta ante natale Domini." Totidem enim lectiones habentur in lectionario et totidem Evangelia, a tempore memorato per dies Dominicos usque ad Nativitatem Domini. Antiphonarius habet tria officia diurna et quartum in die Dominico qui vacat post lectiones XII; octurna vero quattuor, ut superius dixi, per dies Dominicos.

2 Auctor lectionarii excitat fidem nostram ad recolendum Domini nostri Iesu Christi venturi in mundum praeconium per quinque aetates mundi. Auctor missalis quod vocatur "Gregorianum," et antiphonarii nos tangit, ut recolamus

repetition. The historian's words are contained in the offertory; the words of Job, ailing and sorrowful, are contained in the verses. His ailing breath is neither healthy nor strong, and he is accustomed to repeat his incomplete statements often. The author of the office, to remind us through feigned    2
imitation of the ailing Job, repeated the words frequently, in the manner of those who are sick. In the offertory respond, as I said, the words are not repeated, because the historian who wrote the history was not sick.

# 40

# On the Lord's Advent

In ancient missals and lectionaries it is found written: "The fifth week before the Lord's birth." For there are that many readings contained in the lectionary and that many Gospel readings, from the aforementioned time on Sundays until the Lord's Nativity. The antiphoner has three daytime offices and a fourth on Sunday, which is empty after the twelve lessons; and there are four night offices, as I just said, on Sundays.

The author of the lectionary excites our faith to recall the    2
heralds of our Lord Jesus Christ through the five ages of the world, as he was yet to enter the world. The author of the missal that is called "Gregorian," and of the antiphoner,

nativitatem Domini caelebratam per tres ordines librorum—scilicet legis, prophetarum et Psalmorum—necnon et
per quartum, id est principium Evangelii. In quo narratur
Gabrihel archangelus missus ad Zachariam, videlicet
nuncius nativitatis praecursoris Domini; verum etiam et
prophetia Zachariae de adventu Domini; et Gabrihel missus
ad Mariam virginem narrans ei conceptionem salvatoris
nostri; et cetera talia usque ad ipsam nativitatem [Luke 1:5–

3    25, 67–79, 26–38]. Nempe et ipsa quarta ebdomada—hoc est
quae proxima est ante Nativitatem Domini, sive in qua caelebratur—singularis est. Habet in Matutinali Officio per
unamquamque feriam antiphonas proprias in Psalmis.

4    Et alio modo: Auctor lectionarii docet nos quam fortis sit
Dominus qui venturus est ad nos et intraturus domum nostram, ut in ea habitet. Quam solemus sordidare quinque
sensibus nostris. Illices formae intrant per oculos, suspicio
mala de fratre per aures, odor libidinosus per nares. Per os
ingluvies polluit, per tactum crudelitas. In sordibus non vult
habitare rex venturus; nisi ita purgetur hospitium, ut nec
saltim pulvis talium fantasmatum remaneat, non dignabitur

5    hospes venturus in illud intrare. Ideo scribit auctor quinque
lectiones quinque ebdomadarum, ut nos hortetur circum-
cidere quinque sensus nostros ab omni vitio, et parare man-
sionem dignam regi et Domino atque singulari prophetae.
De ipso rege dicit prima lectio: "Ecce dies venient, dicit
Dominus, et suscitabo David germen iustum, et regnabit

pushes us to remember the Lord's birth as celebrated through the three orders of books—namely the law, the prophets and the Psalms—and also through the fourth, namely the beginning of the Gospel. There we are told about Gabriel the archangel who was sent to Zechariah, namely to announce the birth of the forerunner of the Lord; and also about Zechariah's prophecy concerning the coming of the Lord; and about Gabriel who was sent to the virgin Mary to tell her about her conception of our savior; and about other such things, up until the birth itself. And of ₃ course the fourth week—that is, the one that comes just before the Nativity of the Lord, or on which it is celebrated— is unique. It has its own antiphons for the Psalms during Matins on each weekday.

And in another sense: The author of the lectionary ₄ teaches us how strong is the Lord who is about to come to us and enter our home, that he may dwell in it. We are accustomed to pollute this home through our five senses. Enticing images enter through our eyes, evil distrust of our brother through our ears, lustful odor through our nose. Gluttony pollutes us through our mouths, cruelty through our touch. The coming king does not wish to dwell in filth; unless the guest house is purged so that not even the dust of such phantasms remains, our guest will not deign to enter. Thus the author prescribes five readings for five weeks, ₅ to encourage us to cut our five senses off from every vice, and to prepare a worthy dwelling for the king and Lord and singular prophet. The first reading speaks about this king: "Behold the days come, says the Lord, and I will raise up to David a just branch, and a king shall reign, and

rex, et sapiens erit." Et iterum, de Domino: "Et hoc est nomen quod vocabunt eum, dominus iustus noster" [Jer 23:5, 6]. Et iterum in Evangelio de propheta: "Quia hic est vere propheta qui venturus est in mundum" [John 6:14].

6      Auctor missalis sive antiphonarii eandem praeparationem hortatur nos facere per quattuor ebdomadas. Sicut enim homo internuntiis quinque sensibus ad animam bene aut male operatur, ita, per quattuor elementa, aut ruit ad mala corporalia aut surgit ad bona. Quapropter, ut dixi, hortatur nos auctor memoratus, ut, si usque modo torpuimus negligentia, dehinc surgamus ad mundandam domum nostram, ut qui non excitatus est in quinta ebdomada saltim

7  surgat in quarta. Ipsud enim sonat lectio quae legitur in quarta ebdomada: "Scimus quia hora est iam nos de somno surgere" [Rom 13:11], et reliqua. Non dubito propterea cantorem in memorata ebdomada cum tuba sua exaltare vocem: "Ad te levavi animam meam" [Ps 24:1]—ut excitet eos qui in quinta ebdomada sopore negligentiae oppressi sunt. Quomodo nostram domum praeparare debeamus, in sequentibus memorata lectio monstrat: "Non in commessationibus et ebrietatibus, non in cubilibus et impudicitiis, non in contentione et emulatione. Sed induite Dominum Iesum

8  Christum" [Rom 13:13–14]. Eandem praeparationem inculcat in aures nostras sacramentorium: "Suscipiamus," inquiens, "Domine, misericordiam tuam in medio templi tui, ut reparationis nostrae ventura solempnia congruis honoribus praecedamus." Si quis voluerit nostra dicta infringere, quasi non sint quattuor ebdomadae plenae a memorata

shall be wise." And again, about the Lord: "And this is the name that they shall call him, the lord our just one." And again, in the Gospel about the prophet: "This is truly the prophet who is to come into the world."

The author of the missal and antiphoner encourages us to  6
make the same preparation in four weeks. For just as man acts well or badly with his five senses as intermediaries for his soul, so too does he, through the four elements, either hasten to carnal evils or rise to the good. Therefore, as I said, the aforementioned author encourages us, if previously we have grown listless with negligence, to stand up hence-forth to clean our house, that he who was not excited in the fifth week may at least rise up in the fourth. Now the read-  7
ing that is read on the fourth week proclaims this very thing: "And we know that it is now the hour for us to rise from sleep," and so forth. I do not doubt that this is why the can-tor raises his voice with his trumpet in the aforementioned week: "To you have I lifted up my soul"—to arouse those who were overwhelmed in the fifth week with the listless-ness of negligence. In subsequent passages the aforemen-tioned reading shows how we should prepare our house: "Not in rioting and drunkenness, not in chambering and im-purities, not in contention and envy. But put on the Lord Jesus Christ." The sacramentary presses this same prep-  8
aration upon our ears, saying: "Let us receive, Lord, your mercy in the midst of your temple, that we may preface the coming solemnities of our renewal with worthy honors." Should anyone want to refute our argument by saying that there are not four full weeks from the aforementioned

Dominica usque in Nativitatem Domini, videtur mihi igna-
rus esse regulae sacrae scripturae, quae a parte totum solet
implere.

9    Vidi tempore prisco *Gloria in excelsis Deo* praetermittere
in diebus Adventus Domini, et in aliquibus locis dalmaticas.
Habet enim et istud aliquid rationis ad insinuandum tempus
Veteris Testamenti? Nulli dubium quin maior gloria sit in
ecclesia Christi tempore Novi Testamenti quam fore Veteris. Et alio modo: Quicquid enim raro fit, preciosius fit, cum
fit. Unde scribitur in libro Samuhelis: "Puer Samuhel minis-
trabat ante Dominum coram Heli, et sermo Domini erat
preciosus" [1 Kgs 3:1]. Ideo dicitur preciosus quia illo in tempore rarus erat. Unde Hieronimus ad Evangelium in epistola
sua: "Omne quod rarum est plus appetitur. Polegium apud
10   Indos pipere preciosius est."✝ Ac ideo, quando intermitti-
tur *Gloria in excelsis Deo* sive alia claritas sacri ordinis ad tempus, multo avidius sumitur quando redditur, et clarius in animis devotorum resplendet, quando ab eruginosis reparatur.
Quasi novum canticum, redditur *Gloria in excelsis Deo* in
nocte Nativitatis Domini, ut eo magis ad memoriam nobis
reducatur tunc primo caelebratum esse eundem canticum
ymnis angelorum.

Sunday to the Lord's Nativity, he strikes me as ignorant of the rule of Holy Scripture, which is accustomed to fill the whole from a part.

Long ago I observed the omission of the *Gloria in excelsis* 9 *Deo* in the days of the Lord's Advent, and the omission, in some places, of the dalmatics. Does this have some purpose in making known the time of the Old Testament? There is no doubt that there is greater glory in Christ's church in the time of the New Testament than there was in the Old. And otherwise: Whatever becomes rare is more precious when it comes about. Thus it is written in the book of Samuel: "Now the child Samuel ministered to the Lord before Eli, and the word of the Lord was precious." It is called precious because it was rare in that time. Thus Jerome in his letter to Evangelus: "Everything that is rare is desired all the more. Among the Indians the pennyroyal is more precious than pepper."✝ And so, when the *Gloria in excelsis Deo* or some other splen- 10 dor of the sacred order is omitted for a time, it is taken up much more avidly when it is restored, and it shines more brightly in the spirits of the devout, when it is recovered from the rust. Like a new song, the *Gloria in excelsis Deo* is restored on the night of the Lord's Nativity, that we may remember all the more that this very song was first celebrated with the hymns of the angels at that time.

## 41

# De Nativitate Domini

M̲issam quam caelebramus in nocte Nativitatis Domini
Telesforus apostolicus constituit. Ita scriptum est in *Gestis
episcopalibus:* "Constituit ut natale Domini noctu Missae
caelebrarentur."✝ Ut opinor, propter recordationem angelorum qui nocte illa cecinerunt *Gloria in excelsis Deo* [Luke
2:14], in eadem Nativitate statuit auctor officii Missam caelebrari mane secundam. Erat enim tempus quando solum
vellus madidum erat, et in circuitu eius terra arida [Judg
6:37–38]. Iste status colitur in prima Missa.

2    Haec caelebratio Missae novam lucem gaudii praestat his
qui ex circumcisione sunt de incarnatione verbi. De qua incarnatione dicit Cyrillus Alexandriae episcopus in epistola
ad Nestorium, episcopum Constantinopolitanae urbis: "Non
enim prius homo communis ex sancta est genitus virgine, et
sic postea verbum supervenit in eo—sed, ex ipsa vulva uni-
tus, nativitatem carnalem creditur et dicitur pertulisse."

## 41

# On the Lord's Nativity

Pope Telesphorus established the Mass that we celebrate on the night of the Lord's Nativity. Thus is it written in the *Deeds of the Bishops:* "He established that Masses be celebrated at night on the Lord's birthday."✝ I believe that, to commemorate the angels who sang the *Gloria in excelsis Deo* on that night, the author of our office established that a second Mass be celebrated in the morning on the same Nativity. For this was the time when only the fleece was damp, with dry ground around it. This state of things is recalled in the first Mass.

This celebration of Mass provides a new light of joy to those of the circumcision concerning the incarnation of the word. Bishop Cyril of Alexandria speaks about this incarnation in his letter to Nestorius, bishop of the city of Constantinople: "For a common man was not first begotten from the holy virgin, and then the word came over him—rather, we say and believe that his two natures accomplished his carnal birth in unity, from the same womb." 2

## 42

# De consueto tempore Missae

Memoratus papa Telesforus scripsit quo tempore primo diei liceret Missam caelebrare. Legitur in *Gestis episcopalibus* dixisse memoratum papam ut ante horae tertiae cursum nullus praesumeret Missas caelebrare, qua hora Dominus

2 noster ascendit in crucem. Si enim propterea aptum est iuxta memoratum papam tempus horae tertiae caelebrationi Missae, quia in eo legitur secundum Marcum crucem Christum ascendisse, et nos possumus convenienter dicere aptum esse tempus horae sextae, quo secundum Matheum crucem ascendit, sed et tempus horae nonae, quando emisit spiritum. Haec tria tempora sacrata sunt Christi fixione linguis Iudaeorum et ligno.

3 Hi qui ante horam tertiam sive post horam nonam necessario offerunt sacrificium Deo, amore divino infecti, ut non praetereat dies sine illorum sacrificio—ut reor, non hoc agunt quasi proterve contra instituta apostolica, sed habent causam seriam, qua excusari probabiliter se possint, ut Dominus discipulos suos defendit reprehensos a Iudaeis quando vellebant spicas, quasi hoc facerent quod non licebat in Sabbatis, exemplo David, quando necessitate famis

## 42

# On the accustomed time of Mass

The aforementioned pope Telesphorus wrote about the earliest time of day that it is appropriate to celebrate Mass. We read in the *Deeds of the Bishops* that the aforementioned pope said no one should presume to celebrate Masses before the third hour, when our Lord ascended the cross. If, 2 according to the aforementioned pope, the third hour is an appropriate time to celebrate Mass, because we read in Mark that Christ ascended the cross at that time, then we can also say, correctly, that the sixth hour, when he ascended the cross according to Matthew, is appropriate, as well as the ninth hour, when he gave up his spirit. These three times have been sanctified by Christ's crucifixion upon the tongues of the Jews and upon the wood.

Those who offer sacrifice to God before the third hour or 3 after the ninth hour out of necessity and filled with divine love, that the day may not pass without their sacrifice—I do not think that they act with impudence against the apostolic institutions. Rather, they have a grave reason for which they can probably be excused, as the Lord defended his disciples who had been seized by the Jews when they wanted grain, as if they were doing something that was not permitted on the Sabbath, by citing the example of David, when he

transgressus est legem, ut manducaret panes consecratos. Fames utique in causa fuit ut probabili excusatione trans-

4 grederetur legem David. Huic rei aliquid simile scribit Innocentius papa capitulo LV: "Ergo quod necessitas pro remedio repperit, cessante necessitate, debet utique cessare pariter quod urgebat—quia alius est ordo legitimus; alia usurpatio, quam ad praesens fieri tempus impellit."✝

5 Namque vidi Leonem apostolicum diluculo intrare ad Missam. Nescio utrum causa necessitatis intercedente hoc ageret, an sola potestate. Quod legimus in *Gestis pontificalibus,* hoc scripsimus. Fulget enim potestas ratione decorata. Protulit enim Telesforus memoratus rationem de hora Missae; qua de re sponte incumbimus suae auctoritati.

# 43

# De Ypopanti

Scriptum est in *Gestis pontificalibus* quod Sergius Papa praeciperet letanias fieri in die Praesentationis Domini in templo. Ita enim scriptum est: "Ut diebus Adnuntiationis Domini, Dormitionis et Nativitatis sanctae Dei genitricis

violated the law by necessity of hunger, in order to eat the consecrated bread. Hunger is surely the reason that David violated the law, most probably with exemption. Pope Inno-  4 cent writes something similar to this, in chapter 55: "There-fore, what necessity procures as a remedy should of course cease to make its demand when necessity ceases—for a le-gitimate order is one thing; the usurpation of that order, which necessity at present forces us to adopt, is another."+

Now I saw Pope Leo enter for Mass at dawn. I do not  5 know whether he did this for some intervening reason of necessity, or by his power alone. What we read in the *Deeds of the Bishops* is what we have written. For power is resplen-dent, decorated by reason. And the aforementioned Teles-phorus provides a reason for the hour of Mass; for this rea-son we freely bow ourselves to his authority.

# 43

# On Hypapante

It is written in the Deeds of the Bishops that Pope Sergius ordered that litanies be celebrated on the Feast of the Lord's Presentation in the temple. For it is written as follows: "That on the feasts of the Lord's Annunciation, and of the Dormition and Nativity of Mary the holy mother of God,

Mariae, ac sancti Symeonis, quod Ypopanti dicitur Grece, cum letania exeat a sancto Adriano et ad sanctam Mariam populus occurrat."‡

2    De qua festivitate dicit Beda, sacerdos et doctor eximius, in libro *De temporibus:* "Secundum dicavit Februo"—quin Numa—"id est Plutoni, qui lustrationum potens credebatur. Lustrarique eo mense civitatem necesse erat, quo statuit ut iura diis manibus solverentur. Sed hanc lustrandi consuetudinem bene mutavit Christiana religio, cum in mense eodem, die sanctae Mariae, plebs universa cum sacerdotibus ac ministris ymnis modulatae vocis per ecclesias perque congrua urbis loca procedit, datosque a pontifice cereos manibus gestant ardentes. Et, augescente bona consuetudine, idipsum in ceteris quoque eiusdem beatae matris et perpetuae virginis festivitatibus agere didicit—non utique in lustrationem terrestris imperii quinquennem, sed in perenni regni caelestis memoria, quando, iuxta parabolam virginum prudentum, omnes electi, lucentibus bonorum actuum lampadibus obviam sponso ac regi suo venientes, mox cum eo ad nuptias supernae civitatis intrabunt."

and on the feast of Saint Simeon, or Candlemas, which is called Hypapante in Greek, the people should leave the church of Saint Hadrian with a litany and proceed to the church of Saint Mary." ✝

The priest and eminent teacher Bede speaks about this 2 feast in his book *On Time*: "He"—that is, Numa—"consecrated the second month to Februs or Pluto, who was thought to be the power that governed lustrations. And the city had to be purified by offerings in that month, so he established that dues be paid to the household gods. But the Christian religion appropriately altered this custom of purification, since in the same month, on the feast of Saint Mary, all the people, with their priests and ministers and hymns sung in melodious voice, proceeded through the churches and through appropriate locations in the city, and they carried in their hands burning candles given to them by the pontiff. And as this good custom grew, the church learned to hold it for other feasts of the blessed mother and ever virgin as well—not, of course, for the five-year purification of the earthly empire, but in perpetual memory of the kingdom of heaven, when, according to the parable of the wise virgins, all the elect will soon come to meet their bridegroom and king, while the lamps of their good actions blaze, and they will enter with him into the nuptials of the eternal city."

# 44

# De Missa pro mortuis

Missa pro mortuis in hoc differt a consueta Missa, quod sine *Gloria* et alleluia et pacis osculo caelebratur. *Gloria* et alleluia suavitatem et laetitiam nostris mentibus inculcant. Quid cogito ex hoc dicere, verbis Origenis explicabo. Scribit idem in omelia quinta Levitici libri: "Sacrificium vero pro peccato non fit in oleo. Dicit enim: 'Non superponit ei oleum, cum iam pro peccato est. Quod ergo pro peccato est, nec oleum laetitiae, nec tus suavitatis inponitur [Lev 5:11]."✝

2 Nulli dubium quin mors sit vindicta primi peccati, ac ideo sine *Gloria* et alleluia caelebratur—quasi sine oleo et ture. Notandum est etiam quod officium pro mortuis ad imitationem agitur officiorum quae aguntur in morte Domini. Iam praetulimus quod novimus, quare in officiis passionis Domini pacis osculum non demus. Hic nescimus aliud proferre nisi quod ibi praelibavimus, quoniam ibi non agitur osculum pacis nec hic agitur.

3 Recordatio mortuorum nuncupativa agitur ante *Nobis quoque peccatoribus.* Ibi finitur memoria mortis Domini, et inchoatur mors nostra per confessionem peccatorum, ac ideo merito ibi agitur memoria transeuntium qui in Domino moriuntur. Christus enim praecessit eos; nos sequimur.

# 44

# On the Mass for the dead

The Mass for the dead differs from the ordinary Mass in that it is celebrated without the *Gloria,* without the alleluia and without the kiss of peace. The *Gloria* and the alleluia impress sweetness and rejoicing upon our minds. I will explain with the words of Origen what I think this means. He writes in his fifth homily on the book of Leviticus: "But sacrifice for sin does not take place in the oil. For he says: 'He does not put oil upon it because it is for sin.' That which is for sin involves neither the imposition of the oil of rejoicing, nor the incense of sweetness."✝ There is no doubt that  2  death is punishment for the first sin, and so this Mass is celebrated without the *Gloria* or the alleluia—as it were, without oil or incense. We should also note that the office for the dead is conducted in imitation of the offices that are conducted for the Lord's death. We have already explained what we know about why we do not give the kiss of peace during offices for the Lord's passion. Here we know of nothing to add beyond what we explained there, since the kiss of peace is not celebrated there and it is not celebrated here.

A commemoration of the dead, by name, is celebrated  3  before *Nobis quoque peccatoribus.* At that point the memorial of the Lord's death is over, and our own death begins through the confession of our sins. It is thus appropriate to commemorate at that point those who passed away and died in the Lord. For Christ preceded them; we follow.

Solemus eorum memorias generaliter caelebrare tertia ac
4   septima et tricesima die. Unde talem habemus auctoritatem, in Veteri Testamento scriptum est, in libro Numerorum, capitulo XLmo septimo: "Qui tetigerit cadaver hominis et propter hoc fuerit inmundus septem dies, aspergetur
ex hac aqua die tertia et septima, et sic mundabitur" [Num
19:11–12]. In caelebratione XXX dierum suffulti sumus
Moysi et Aaron caelebratione. Ita scriptum est in eodem libro, capitulo L: "Omnis autem multitudo, videns occubuisse
Aaron, flevit super eum XXX diebus per cunctas familias
suas" [Num 20:30]. Et iterum in Deuteronomio de Moyse,
capitulo CLIIII: "Fleveruntque super eum filii Israhel in
campestribus Moab XXX diebus" [Deut 34:8].

5   Inmundus propter cadaver hominis pollutam animam
significat mortuis operibus. Purgatio mortui hominis per
sacrificium sacerdotis tertia die et septima congruit naturae
humanae. Constat homo ex anima et corpore; anima tribus
quasi quodammodo columnis erigitur—ut diligat Deum ex
toto corde et ex tota anima et ex tota mente. Corpus vero
6   quattuor notissimis elementis subsistit. Peccatum animae
quae neglexit Dei cultum, in cogitatione, in vita et in intellectu, humiliter confitendo, offerimus sacrificium Deo tertia die, ut ab his peccatis purgetur. Similiter peccatum quod
per corpus gessit, cupimus purgare in quarto die post tertium diem—id est septimo post mortem suam.

7   Duobus modis committitur peccatum—aut faciendo
ea quae non debuimus facere, aut amittendo ea quae debuimus facere. Usque ad septimum diem, in quo numero

It is our custom to commemorate them generally on the third and the seventh and the thirtieth day. In the Old Testament, in the book of Numbers, chapter 47, it is written where our authority to do so comes from: "He that touches the corpse of a man and is therefore unclean seven days, shall be sprinkled with this water on the third day and on the seventh, and so shall be cleansed." We are supported in our celebration of thirty days by the celebrations for Moses and Aaron. Thus it is written in chapter 50 of the same book: "And all the multitude, seeing that Aaron was dead, mourned for him thirty days throughout all their families." And again in Deuteronomy with respect to Moses, chapter 154: "And the children of Israel mourned for him in the plains of Moab thirty days."

Being unclean because of a man's corpse signifies the soul that has been polluted with deadly works. The purification of the dead man through the priest's sacrifice on the third day and the seventh accords with human nature. Man consists of a soul and a body; the soul rests, in some sense, upon three columns—that it love God with its whole heart and its whole soul and its whole mind. The body, on the other hand, consists of the four familiar elements. By humbly confessing the sin of the soul that neglected God's worship in thought, in life and in understanding, we offer sacrifice to God on the third day, that the soul may be cleansed of these sins. We likewise desire to cleanse the sin performed through the body on the fourth day after the third day—that is on the seventh day after the death of the body.

Sin is committed in two ways—either by doing things that we should not have done, or by neglecting to do those things that we should have done. Up to the seventh day,

designatur universitas, omnia peccata quae egit et non debuit agere, deflemus, et pro his rogamus seorsum pro anima et seorsum pro corpore; deinceps usque ad tricesimum, et pro his quae modo in superioribus memoravimus, et pro illis

8 quae debuit facere et non fecit. Triginta enim diebus completur mensis; per mensem designatur curriculus praesentis vitae, ut ex statu lunae facile dignoscitur. Unde Gregorius in *Moralibus Iob,* libro octavo: "Mensium quippe nomine dierum collectio et summa signatur. Per diem ergo unaquaeque actio exprimi potest, per mensem autem actionum finis innuitur."✝ Quando studemus ut opera amicorum nostrorum sint plena coram Deo, triginta diebus pro eis sacrificamus.

9 Non opinor ut aliquis velit dicere quod non liceat nobis orare cotidie et sacrificare Deo pro mortuis, sed quod agitur in tertia et septima et tricesima die, publice agitur, et generaliter ab omnibus amicis, ac convenitur simul ad hoc in precibus Missarum atque elemosinis et ceteris bonis studiis.

10 Legimus in *Historia Anglorum* quendam presbyterum opinatum esse de fratre suo quod mortuus esset in proelio—qui tamen non est mortuus, sed vulneratus ac vinculatus. Mox memoratus presbyter non expectavit tertium diem neque septimum neque tricesimum, sed frequentissime caelebravit pro eo Missas. Tempore Missae cotidie soluta sunt vincula vulnerati. Scriptum est in volumine memorato, libri quarto, capitulo XXIIII: "Cumque vidisset qui emerat eum, vinculis non potuisse cohibere, donavit ei facultatem

which number designates entirety, we lament all the sins that the deceased committed and that he should not have done, and on behalf of these sins we make requests separately for his soul and separately for his body. Then, up to the thirtieth day, we make requests both for those things that we recounted above, and for those things that he should have done and did not do. Now a month is completed in 8 thirty days; through the month the course of this life is signified, as is easily recognized from the phase of the moon. Thus Gregory in book 8 of his *Moralia on Job:* "And so by the name of months the collection and extent of our days is signified. Each action can therefore be expressed by a day, and through the month the end of our actions is suggested."✝ When we long for the works of our friends to be full before God, we sacrifice on their behalf for thirty days.

I do not think that anyone wants to say that we are not 9 permitted to pray and to sacrifice to God on behalf of the dead daily. But that which we celebrate on the third and the seventh and the thirtieth day is done publicly and generally by all the friends, and it takes place alongside the prayers at Mass, the offering of alms and other good pursuits.

In the *History of the English People,* we read of a priest who 10 thought his brother had died in battle—though his brother was not dead, but wounded and in chains. The aforementioned priest did not wait for the third day nor the seventh nor the thirtieth, but celebrated Masses for him very frequently. Every day, at the time of Mass, the wounded man's chains were undone. It is written in the aforementioned volume, book 4, chapter 24: "And when he who bought him saw that he could not restrain him with chains, he gave him the ability to redeem himself if he could. And his chains were

redeundi, si posset. A tertia autem ora, quando Missae fieri solebant, saepissime vincula solvebantur. At ille iureiurando 11 promisit ut rediret, vel pecuniam illi pro se mitteret." Et post pauca: "Qui post haec in patriam reversus, atque ad suum fratrem perveniens, replicavit ex ordine cuncta quae sibi adversa, quaeve in adversis solatia provenissent. Cognovitque referente eo illis maxime temporibus sua fuisse vincula soluta, quibus pro se Missarum fuerant caelebrata solempnia."✝

12 Solet vulgus requirere si pro omnibus Christianis licitum sit Missam caelebrare. Quibus Agustinus respondet in libro *Enchiridion:* "Neque negandum est defunctorum animas pietate suorum viventium posse relevari cum pro illis sacrificium mediatori offertur, vel elemosinae in ecclesia fiunt. Sed eis haec prosunt, qui cum viverent, haec sibi, 13 ut postea possint prodesse, meruerunt. Est enim quidam vivendi modus, nec tam bonus, ut non requirat ista post mortem, nec tam malus, ut ei non prosint ista post mortem. Est vero talis in bono, ut is haec non requirat, et est rursus talis in malo, ut nec his valeat, cum haec vita transierit, adiuvari. Quocirca hic omne meritum comparatur, quo pos- 14 sit post hanc vitam relevari quispiam vel gravari." Et paulo post: "Cum ergo sacrificia, sive altaris sive quarumcumque elemosinarum, pro baptizatis defunctis omnibus offeruntur, pro valde bonis gratiarum actiones sunt, pro non valde malis propitiationes sunt, pro valde malis, etiamsi

most often loosed after the third hour, when the Masses were wont to take place. But he took an oath and promised to return, or to send his captor money for himself." And after a little: "And after this, when he returned to his country and came to his brother, he recounted in order all the adverse things that had befallen him, as well as the comforts that had come to him during his adversities. And he realized, when his brother told him, that his chains were loosed primarily when the solemnities of Mass had been celebrated for him."✝

Commoners often ask if it is permissible to celebrate Mass for all Christians. Augustine responds to them in his book, the *Enchiridion:* "Nor should we deny that the souls of the dead can be relieved by the piety of their living relatives when sacrifice is offered to the mediator on their behalf, or alms are offered in church. But these acts benefit those who merited, while they were alive, that they be beneficial afterward. For there is a certain manner of living that is neither so good that it does not require such actions after death, nor so bad that such actions are of no benefit after death. There is, on the other hand, a kind of life so steeped in good that it does not require these actions, and a kind so steeped in evil that it cannot be helped by these actions when life has passed. All merit is therefore weighed in this world, and through that merit one can receive comfort or further punishment after this life." And a little later: "Therefore, when sacrifices, whether of the altar or of alms, are offered on behalf of all the baptized dead, they are thanksgivings for those who were very good, atonements for those who were not very bad, and a kind of consolation for those who survive those who were very bad, even if they

nulla sint adiumenta mortuorum, qualescumque vivorum consolationes sunt. Quibus autem prosunt, aut ad hoc prosunt, ut sit plena remissio, aut certe ut ea tolerabilior fiat ipsa damnatio."

15    Unde iterum ad Paulinum, *De cura pro mortuis gerenda,* libro secundo: "Quamvis non pro quibus fiunt, omnibus prosint, sed eis tantum pro quibus, dum vivunt, comparatur ut prosint. Sed, quia non discernimus qui sint, oportet ea pro regeneratis omnibus facere, ut nullus eorum praetermittatur, ad quos haec beneficia possint et debeant pervenire. Melius enim supererunt ista eis quibus nec obsunt nec prosunt, quam eis deerunt quibus prosunt."✝

16    Anniversaria dies ideo repetitur pro defunctis, quoniam nescimus qualiter eorum causa habeatur in alia vita. Sicut sanctorum anniversaria dies in eorum honore ad memoriam nobis reducitur super utilitate nostra, ita defunctorum, ad utilitatem illorum et nostram devotionem implendam, credendo eos aliquando venturos ad consortium sanctorum.

17    Alioquin omni tempore bonum est orare pro defunctis. Etiam si nesciatur dies defuncti, per oblivionem seu per ignorantiam, vel praetermittatur propter occupationem aliquam terrenam, agatur tamen eorum solempnitas. Iuxta decretum devotissimarum mentium, credo apud eum apud quem non est vicissitudinis obumbratio acceptam esse, quasi anniversaria sit.

are no help to the dead. But for those whom they benefit, they either provide a complete remission of punishment, or at least make damnation more tolerable."

And so, once again, to Paulinus, *On the Care to be Had for the Dead,* book 2: "Yet they may not benefit everyone for whom they are offered, but rather only those who, while they were alive, obtained that they should be beneficial. But because we do not know who these are, we should do such things for all the baptized, so that nobody who can and should receive these benefits is passed over. For it is better that these things accrue in excess to those whom they neither hurt nor help, than for them to be lacking from those whom they benefit."✝

And so the anniversary day is celebrated on behalf of the dead, because we do not know how their case is progressing in the other life. Just as an anniversary day in honor of the saints commemorates them for our benefit, so should we observe the anniversary of the dead for their benefit and our devotion, through our belief that they will one day arrive in the communion of saints.

Otherwise, it is good to pray at any moment for the dead. Even if the day of death is not known, because of forgetfulness or ignorance, or if it has been neglected because of some earthly preoccupation, a solemnity on their account should nevertheless be observed. In accordance with the declaration of pious minds, I believe that it is accepted by him for whom there is no shadow of change, as if it were an anniversary.

I

# De nomine IHU

Karissimo patri et acutissimo rethori Hieremiae
vati in nostra Hierusalem Amalarius

Scribunt nostri salvatoris nostri Ihu nomen per aspirationem, cuius rationis expers sum. Scio vobis ignotum non esse si alicuius rationis causa postponatur post "I" aspiratio in nomen IHU; quam intimate filio vestro, si assit. Scio, si est, adfore in prumptuario mentis vestrae quod fluat ad me.

Antequam pergeret domnus Karolus Romam novissime, audivi sacerdotes Galliae nostrae sonare "Gisus," quod neque cum Ebreis neque cum Grecis conveniebat. Ab illo tempore audio "Iesus," ut opinor, quod convenit cum Ebreis, quorum ducis nomen legimus "Iesus." Qui Iesus nomine suo praefigurabat nostrum Iesum, ut Sedulius:

. . . Iam tunc famulata videbant
Sidera venturum praemisso nomine Iesum.

I

# On the name of Jesus

To his dearest father and the most acute rhetorician,
the prophet Jeremiah in our Jerusalem, Amalar

Our countrymen write the name of our savior Jesus with the letter "H," and I am puzzled about the reason. I know that, if there is a reason that an "H" in Jesus's name is placed after the "I," it is not unknown to you. If you know, tell your son. If you do know, I am certain that it will be in the storeroom of your mind to pass the reason on to me.

Before the lord Charles entered Rome for the last time, I heard the priests of Gaul saying "Gisus," which agreed neither with the Hebrews nor with the Greeks. Since that time I hear "Iesus," which I think agrees with the Hebrews, the name of whose leader we read was Jesus , or Joshua. This Joshua, through his name, prefigured our Jesus, as Sedulius writes:

... Then the attending stars saw
That Jesus was about to come, with a name that had
come before.

2    Nam Graeci his notis "I" "C" scribunt illud nomen, et legunt "Isus." Unde mihi videtur—si tamen vobis non alias— oportere scribi per "I" et "H" et "C" sive "S," quod legimus "Iesus." Quibus notis memoratum nomen scribere debeam, oro ut mandetis.

## 2

# Responsio Hieremiae archiepiscopi

Porphyrius philosophus nomen Ihu in anacrostica sua Latine scribit hoc modo: "IESUS," quem novimus utriusque linguae peritissimum fuisse. Usus videlicet "Ita" Grecam litteram pro "H" longa—quam Greci in lingua propria pro "I" longa semper sonant, Latini vero pro "E" longa. Alia vero ratione, imitantes Ebraeos, Iesum pronuntiamus, non per aspirationem, sed per "H" Grecum scribentes.

Now the Greeks write that name with the letters "I" 2
and "C," and they read "Isus." Thus it seems to me—if
it does not seem otherwise to you—that what we read as
"Iesus" should be written with an "I" and an "H" and a "C"
or an "S." I ask that you tell me with which letters I should
write the stated name.

## 2

# Response of Archbishop Jeremiah

The philosopher Porphyry, who we know was quite
learned in both languages, writes the name of Jesus in his
Latin acrostic in this way: "IESUS." That is, he represented
with an "E," instead of with a long "H," the Greek letter
eta—which the Greeks always pronounce as a long "I" in
their language, and the Latins as a long "E." And so for
another reason, imitating the Hebrews, we say "Iesus," not
with aspiration, but because we write Greek with "H."

## 3

# Amalarius Ionae venerabili episcopo

Pater intimate nato quibus notis inferius figuratis rectius videatur vobis pingi nomen Iesu: "IHS" an "IHC."

At ille inquit: Sicut "X" et "P" grecis litteris, et alia qualicumque latina convenienti superioribus, scribitur XPI nomen, ita "I" et "H," addita convenienti Latina, scribitur IHS.

## 4

# Epistola ad Rantgarium episcopum

Amalarius Rantgario reverentissimo episcopo
civitatis Noviomensis

Memini me interrogatum a vestra paternitate quomodo intellegerem quod scriptum est in Dominica institutione: "Hic est calix sanguinis mei, Novi et aeterni Testamenti, mysterium fidei." Quia comperi vos velle scire quomodo

# 3

# Amalar to the venerable bishop Jonas

Father, tell your son with which of the following letters Jesus's name strikes you as being more correctly represented: "IHS" or "IHC."

And he said: Just as the name of Christ is written with the Greek letters "X" and "P," along with the relevant Latin letter appropriate for the context, so too is the name of Jesus written with an "I" and an "H," and the relevant Latin letter is appended.

# 4

# Letter to Bishop Rantgar

Amalar to the most reverend bishop
Rantgar of the city of Noyon

I remember that your paternity asked me how I understood what is written in the Lord's instruction: "This is the chalice of my blood, of the New and everlasting Testament, the mystery of faith." Because I realized that you wanted to

intellegerem illud, ideoque scriptis paucis litteris intimo quomodo sentiam.

2    Fuit enim calix Veteris Testamenti, de quo in Exodo scriptum est, capitulo XCVIII: "Tulit itaque Moyses dimidiam partem sanguinis et misit in crateram, partem autem residuam fudit super altare." Et paulo post: "Hic est," inquit, "sanguis foederis quod pepigit Dominus vobiscum super cunctis sermonibus his" [Exod 24:6, 8]. Hunc calicem consummavit Dominus in caena sua secundum Lucam dicentem: "Et accepto calice gratias egit et dixit: Accipite et dividite inter vos. Dico enim vobis quod non bibam de generatione vitis, donec regnum Dei veniat" [Luke 22:17–18]. Calix Veteris Testamenti sanguine animalium irrationabilium redundabat. Ille sanguis figura fuit veri sanguinis Christi.

3    Quem calicem—id est in quo bibimus sanguinem Christi —initiavit nobis ipse in memorata caena post consummatum priorem calicem, ut idem Lucas memorat in sequentibus: "Similiter et calicem postquam caenavit dicens: Hic est calix Novi Testamenti in sanguine meo, qui pro vobis fundetur" [Luke 22:20]. Hic calix est in figura corporis mei, in quo est sanguis qui manavit de latere meo ad complendam legem veterem. Quo effuso, deinceps erit Novum Testamentum. Quoniam novus sanguis et innocens—id est hominis absque peccato—effundetur pro redemptione humana, quod antea non est factum sanguine alicuius animalis.

know how I understood it, I will tell you what I think by writing a few words.

There was a chalice in the Old Testament, which is writ-    2
ten about in Exodus, chapter 98: "Then Moses took half of the blood and put it into a bowl, and the rest he poured upon the altar." And a little later he says: "This is the blood of the covenant that the Lord has made with you concerning all these words." The Lord consummated this chalice during his supper, according to Luke, who says: "And having taken the chalice he gave thanks and said: Take and divide it among you. For I say to you that I will not drink of the fruit of the vine till the kingdom of God come." The chalice of the Old Testament ran over with the blood of unreasoning animals. That blood was a figure of Christ's true blood.

He established for us the use of this chalice—that is, the    3
one from which we drink Christ's blood—during the afore-mentioned supper, after he had consummated the first chal-ice, as the same Luke recounts in what follows: "In like man-ner he took the chalice also after he had supped, saying: This is the chalice of the New Testament in my blood, which shall be shed for you." This chalice is a symbol of my body, in which is the blood that flowed from my side to fulfill the old law. When that has been poured out, there will be a New Testament. Since the blood is new and innocent—that is, it comes from a man without sin—it will be shed for human redemption, which was not accomplished earlier through the blood of whatever animal.

4     Ipse vocatur "aeterni Testamenti," quia Novum Testamentum non mutabitur ad aliud testamentum, sicut mutatum est Vetus in Novum. Ipse vocatur "mysterium fidei," quoniam qui credit se redemptum ab eo sanguine et imitator fit passionis ipsius, ei proficit ad salutem et ad vitam aeternam. Unde ipse Dominus dicit: "Nisi manducaveritis carnem filii hominis et biberitis eius sanguinem, non habebitis vitam in vobismet ipsis" [John 6:54]. Hoc est, nisi participes fueritis meae passionis et credideritis me mortuum pro vestra salute, non habebitis vitam in vobis.

    "Mysterium" Grece, Latine "secretum." Quia fides ista latet in cordibus electorum, propterea vocatur secretum fi-
5 dei. Mysterium fidei fides est, ut Agustinus in epistola ad Bonifacium episcopum: "Sicut ergo secundum quendam modum sacramentum corporis Christi corpus Christi est, sacramentum sanguinis Christi sanguis Christi est—ita sacramentum fidei fides est."✝ Simili modo possumus dicere: "Hic est calix sanguinis mei Novi et aeterni Testamenti," ac si dicat: "Hic est sanguis meus, qui pro vobis datur, ut deinceps Novum et aeternum Testamentum a me accipiatur et teneatur." Sequitur: "mysterium fidei"—hoc credere debetis; id est, hanc fidem habere debetis, ut per illum remissio vobis sit omnium peccatorum.

It is said to be "of the everlasting Testament," because the   4
New Testament will not be converted to another testament,
as the Old was converted to the New. It is called "the mystery of faith," because he who believes that he has been redeemed by that blood and becomes an imitator of that passion is brought by it to salvation and eternal life. Thus the
Lord himself says: "Except you eat the flesh of the son of
man and drink his blood, you shall not have life in you." That
is, unless you have become participants in my passion and
believed that I died for your salvation, you will not have life
in you.

"Mystery" in Greek is "secret" in Latin. Because this faith
lies hidden in the hearts of the elect it is called the secret of
faith. The mystery of faith is faith itself, as Augustine says in   5
his letter to the bishop Boniface: "Therefore, just as in some
sense the sacrament of Christ's body is Christ's body and
the sacrament of Christ's blood is Christ's blood—so the
sacrament of faith is faith."† Likewise, we can say: "This is
the chalice of my blood of the New and everlasting Testament," as if saying: "This is my blood, which is given for you,
that henceforth the New and everlasting Testament may be
received and held from me." There follows: "the mystery of
faith"—you should believe this; that is, you should have this
faith, that through this mystery you may attain remission of
all your sins.

# 5

# Ad Hetdonem abbatem

Dignata est fraternitas vestra nobis mandare ut auctorem illum vobis nominarem qui distinctionem facit inter "seraphin" quando neutri generis est, et quando masculini. Non omnia mihi in promptu possunt occurrere, quae de illis agminibus legistis, et legi. Tamen illum auctorem modo promam qui discernit inter cherubin neutri generis et masculini, nec non et illum qui seraphim per "m" masculi generis dicit et neutri per "n." Opinor quod eisdem finalibus litteris terminetur apud Grecos "cherubin" et "seraphin."

2    Dicit Hieronimus in tractatu Iezechielis tertii libri: "Quanquam plerique *ta cherubin* neutrali genere numeroque plurali dici putent, nos scire debemus singulari numero esse 'cherub' generis masculini et plurali eiusdem generis 'cherubim'—non quo sexus in ministris Dei sit, sed quo unumquodque iuxta linguae suae proprietatem diversis appelletur generibus. Angeli vocantur numero plurali 'malachim' et 'cherubim' et 'seraphim'—eiusdem generis et numeri."✝

3    Ubi sanctus Hieronimus dicit: "nos scire debemus," Latinus Latinis fuit locutus. Ipse erat Latinus, Paula et filia eius Eustochium Latinae erant. Ex hoc intellegere possumus

# 5

# To the abbot Hetto

Your fraternity deigned to command us to name for you the author who distinguishes between "seraphin" when it is in the neuter gender, and when it is in the masculine. Not all the things that you and I have read about these armies of angels come readily to mind. Nevertheless, I will produce the author who distinguishes between cherubin in the neuter and the masculine, as well as the author who refers to seraphim with the "m" of the masculine gender and the "n" of the neuter. I think that "cherubin" and "seraphin" end with the same final letters among the Greeks.

In the third book of his treatise on Ezekiel, Jerome says: 2 "Although many think that they are called *ta cherubin* in the neuter plural, we should recognize that it is 'cherub' in the masculine singular and 'cherubim' in the plural of the same gender—not because there is gender among the ministers of God, but because everything is referred to by different genders, according to the nature of its language. In the plural, angels are called 'malachim' and 'cherubim' and 'seraphim'— all in the same gender and number."✝

When Saint Jerome says: "we should recognize," he 3 was speaking as a Latin to Latins. He was Latin; Paula and her daughter Eustochium were Latins. From this we can

quod nos Latini debemus illorum ministrorum nomina masculino genere tenere, iuxta Ebraicam auctoritatem quam Hieronimus interpretatus est. Et ubi dicit: "Non quo sexus in ministris Dei sit, sed quo unumquodque iuxta linguae suae proprietatem diversis appelletur generibus"—ex hoc intellegimus quod alterius generis sunt ministri memo-

4 rati in peregrina lingua. Dicit Beda in libro primo *De tabernaculo et vasis eius:* "Et quidem numero singulari 'cherub,' plurali autem 'cherubim' dicitur, et est nomen generis masculini. Sed Greca consuetudo neutro genere 'cherubin' posuit, 'm' littera in 'n' mutata. Verum noster interpres Ebreum secutus idioma, masculino genere posuit."✝

5 Monstrabo iterum ubi idem interpres, Hieronimus, ponat "seraphin" neutro genere. Scribit in libro quem fecit de seraphin, quae leguntur in Esaia, inter cetera, "nullum prophetarum extra Esaiam vidisse seraphin circa Deum stantia, et ne ipsa quidem seraphin alibi lectitari."✝ Novit caritas vestra, quando dixit "stantia," et ipsa neutro genere ea protulisse. Habemus et non minimam auctoritatem ex consuetudine ecclesiae, quae solet cotidie in oratione quae fit super mensam, proferre "Beata seraphin."

understand that we Latins should keep the names of these ministers in the masculine, in accordance with the authoritative Hebrew text that Jerome translated. And when he says "not because there is gender among the servants of God, but because everything is referred to by different genders, according to the nature of its language"—from this we understand that the aforementioned ministers are referred to by either gender in that foreign language. Bede says in his 4 first book *On the Tabernacle and its Vessels:* "And indeed it is called 'cherub' in the singular, but 'cherubim' in the plural, and this is a noun of the masculine gender. But Greek custom has put 'cherubin' in the neuter, and changed the letter 'm' to 'n.' Yet our translator followed the Hebrew language and put it in the masculine."✢

I will show again where the same translator, Jerome, puts 5 "seraphin" in the neuter. In the book that he wrote on the seraphin, which we read about in Isaiah, he writes, among other things, that "none of the prophets other than Isaiah saw the seraphin standing around God, and the seraphin are not even mentioned elsewhere."✢ Your charity sees that when he wrote "standing," even he put them in the neuter. We also have no less an authority in the custom of the church, which is accustomed to speak daily of "blessed seraphin" in the neuter, in the prayer that is said over the altar.

# 6

# Amalarius Guntardo dilecto filio in disciplina Christi

F ili mi, recordatus sum percontasse pollens ingenium tuum, quare non me cum maiore cautela custodirem ne ilico post consumptum sacrificium spuerem. Addidisti quod non videres ceteros sacerdotes hoc facere—id est statim spuere post comestam Eucharistiam. Quando hoc audivi a te, nec muttum tibi dixi, neque cogitavi ex hoc tibi respondere.

2 Nauci duxi talem percontationem. Iam in itinere degens, aporiatus sum tua dilectione, ne aliqua suspicio remaneret tibi falsa in pectore—quasi ergo proterve hoc agerem contra nostram religionem et neque remaneres in aliquo errore ignorantiae. Idcirco potissimum, quoniam sensi te sensisse me agere contra consuetudinem religiosorum presbytero-rum, malui ex itinere formare tibi animum meum, quam diutius remanere ardens ingenium tuum in suspicione in-utili.

3 Adtende primo, fili mi, sententiae Pauli dicentis: "Spirita-lis iudicat omnia, ipse autem a nemine iudicatur" [1 Cor 2:15]. Si quod circa spiritum est, in suo ordine manet; ea quae per corpus geruntur recta deputantur, dicente eodem Apos-tolo: "Omnia munda mundis" [Titus 1:15]. Multi sunt qui munditiam corporis observant secundum usum Phariseo-rum, ex quorum tamen mentibus procedunt inmunda quae

# 6

## Amalar to Guntard, his beloved son in Christ's teaching

My son, I remember that you asked me, with your considerable ability, why I do not govern myself with greater caution to avoid spitting directly after I have consumed the sacrifice. You added that you have not seen other priests doing this—that is, spitting right after they have eaten the Eucharist. When I heard this from you, I neither grumbled in reply, nor did I think of responding to you after that. I thought your question was of little importance. Now that I 2 am traveling, I have become worried about your affection and that some false suspicion remains in your heart—as if I were acting wantonly and contrary to our standards of piety, and as if you were not persisting in an error of ignorance. And most of all because I sensed that you thought I had acted contrary to the practice of pious priests, I decided, while on my journey, to explain my thoughts to you, rather than let your intelligence remain aflame with pointless suspicion.

Note first, my son, that saying of Paul, who says: "The 3 spiritual man judges all things, but he himself is judged of no man." If there is something relating to the spirit, it remains in its order; the things that are done by the body are considered upright, as the same Apostle says: "All things are clean to the clean." There are many who observe cleanliness of the body as the Pharisees did, while from their minds proceed

Dominus computat in Evangelio, dicens: "De corde enim exeunt cogitationes malae, homicidia, adulteria, fornicationes, furta, falsa testimonia, blasphemiae. Hace sunt quae

4 coinquinant hominem" [Matt 15:19]. Inter ista non deputatur sputum, nec procedit ex mala cogitatione quae coinquinat hominem. Sputum naturale est nobis; sine peccato procedit ex nobis; sanitati nostrae proficit eius processio. Sine vituperatione religiosorum hominum, agimus quod Christus egit pro salute nostra, docente Evangelio: "Lutum fecit Dominus ex sputo, et linivit oculos caeci nati" [John 9:6]. Et iterum secundum Marcum: "Misit digitos suos in auriculas, et expuens tetigit linguam eius" [Mic 7:33].

5 Corpus Domini saluti hominum consecratum est in aeternum. Eiectio sputi salutem praestat temporalem. Ad hoc deprecamur sanitatem temporalem, ut potius occurramus aeternae saluti. Quod est officium aeternae salutis, non est contra institutionem Domini. Quamvis Apostolus dixisset: "Quando infirmor, tunc fortior sum et potens" [2 Cor 12:10], tamen sanitati studebat, ut novimus ex ammonitione facta ad Timotheum, cum dicat: "Noli aquam bibere, sed modico vino utere propter stomachum et frequentes tuas infirmitates" [1 Tim 5:23].

6 Tu, fili, in redargatione tua non propter aliud ostendisti mihi tibi displicere me spuere, nisi quia ceteros sacerdotes perspexisti a sputo diutius se abstinere post sacrificium. Tu, adhuc puerulus, non vidisti multos sacerdotes. Forsan, quos saepissime vidisti, venatoribus iuncti sunt, qui solent manus lavare a recenti sanguine bubalorum, suum et hyrcorum, sicut et populares faciunt quando ad communem mensam accedunt. Non hoc dico, quod non debeamus venerari

the unclean things that the Lord enumerates in the Gospel, saying: "For from the heart come forth evil thoughts, murders, adulteries, fornications, thefts, false testimonies, blasphemies. These are the things that defile a man." Spit is not 4 included among these, nor does it proceed from the evil thought that pollutes man. Spit is natural for us; it comes out of us without sin; its excretion benefits our health. Without the rebuke of pious men, we do what Christ did for our salvation, as the Gospel teaches: "The Lord made mud from his spit, and he smeared it over the eyes of the man who had been born blind." And again, according to Mark: "He put his fingers into his ears, and spitting, he touched his tongue."

The Lord's body has been consecrated for the eternal 5 health of mankind. Spitting provides temporal health. We request temporal health that we may better arrive at eternal health. That which furthers eternal health is not contrary to the Lord's instruction. Although the Apostle said: "When I am weak, I am stronger and powerful," he nevertheless strove after health, as we know from the advice directed to Timothy, when he says: "Do not still drink water, but use a little wine for your stomach's sake and your frequent infirmities."

Son, in your objection you did not reveal to me that any- 6 thing bothered you about my spitting, except that you have seen other priests who abstain from spitting for some time after the sacrifice. You are still a boy and have not seen many priests. Perhaps those you most often saw were the companions of hunters, whose custom it is to rinse their hands from the fresh blood of oxen, swine and goats, as ordinary people do when they approach the common table. I am not saying

corpus Domini prae omnibus sumptibus, sed quod, si vene-
ratum fuerit ab interiore homine, quicquid naturaliter ab
exteriore agitur Dominico honori deputatur.

7    Quamvis sagacitas infantiae tuae nobilissima mihi quod
displiceret non ostenderet, tamen, ut reor, video quod tibi
displiceat in eo sputo—hoc est, quasi sumptum corpus simul cum sputo proiciam. Fili, non ita retur animus patris
tui. Illum precor cui dicit psalmista: "Fortitudinem meam
ad te custodiam" [Ps 58:10]. Flegmaticus homo, si studuerit
8    sanitati suae, sepius curabit flegma eicere. Non est prohibi-
tus flegmaticus a promotione sacrorum ordinum. Non enim
ignoravit Paulus humores nocivos et nimium abundantes
sepius fore necesse exire ab homine; tamen quando abnegavit episcopum superbum, iracundum, vinolentum, percus-
sorem, turpis lucri cupidum—non abnegavit flegmaticum
[Titus 1:7]. Forte tui animales, inflati munditia corporis,
possunt videre vitia nociva in secreto figmento suo quae
Paulus Apostolus non potuit praevidere in Spiritu Sancto?
Absit.

9    Fili mi, si potuissem me abstinere tamdiu a sputo, quamdiu satisfacerem tuis, ut non haberent quod reprehenderent
in me, hoc ultro curarem, praecipiente Apostolo: "Provi-
dentes bona non tantum coram Deo, sed etiam coram omnibus hominibus" [Rom 12:17; 2 Cor 8:21]. Sed quia hoc mihi
difficile est, tamen confido in Domino, si mens mea pura fuerit et humilis in conspectu eius, ut faciat intrare corpus
suum ad animam meam vivificandam, et, quod exeundum
est propter sanitatem corporis, faciat exire sine dispendio
10    animae. Si quis hoc non credit eum posse, si voluerit, non

that we should not venerate the Lord's body at all costs, but rather that, if it has been venerated by the inner man, whatever is done in accordance with nature by the outer one is put down to the Lord's honor.

Although in the noblest wisdom of your childhood you 7 do did not reveal anything that offended me, I nevertheless think I see what troubled you about that spit—that is, when I spit, it is as if I am ejecting the body that I have consumed. Son, your father's mind does not think this is the case. I call upon him to whom the psalmist says: "I will keep my strength to you." The phlegmatic man, if he is concerned with his health, will often spit out phlegm. Phlegmatics are 8 not prohibited from promotion to holy orders. For Paul was not unaware that it would often prove necessary to expel noxious and overabundant humors from a man; yet when he rejected the proud bishop, the angry one, the one given to wine, the striker, the one greedy for filthy lucre—he did not reject the phlegmatic. Perhaps your sensibilities, puffed up over bodily cleanliness, can perceive in their hidden imagination harmful vices that the Apostle Paul could not discern in the Holy Spirit? Heaven forbid.

My son, if I were able to avoid spitting long enough to 9 satisfy your objections, that they may find no fault in me, I would certainly do so, as the Apostle commands: "Providing good things not only in the sight of God, but also in the sight of all men." But because this is difficult for me, I nevertheless trust in the Lord, that, if my mind should prove pious and humble in his sight, he may allow his body to enter my soul to restore it to life, and that he may cause what ought to be expelled for my bodily health to exit without cost to my soul. If anyone does not believe that God can do 10

285

credit eum omnipotentem esse. Et qui non sperat eum hoc velle, non recipit sententiam Pauli dicentis: "Qui omnes homines vult salvos fieri" [1 Tim 2:4]—id est, illos qui salvationi deputati sunt. Fili mi, recordare quod sepissime solebas mihi proferre: "Nisi Dominus custodierit civitatem, frustra vigilant qui custodiunt eam" [Ps 126:1]. Si aliquod scrupulum tuae menti adhuc haeret de re praelibata, vita comite, noli patri tuo abscondere. Tene quod tenes; Dominus tibi multiplicet sensus praelibatos ultro quam petere scias.

11    De corpore Domini quod sumimus, est mihi dicendum— quamvis sit dispar exemplum praesenti rei—quod Valentinianus imperator dixit militibus qui ei socium adsciscere voluerunt: "Vestrum fuit," inquit, "quod me constituitis imperatorem; meum est socium eligere quem voluero." Ita vero vestrum est velle et precari Dominum cor mundum; suum est corpus suum per artus et venas diffundere ad salutem nobis aeternam. Ipse enim dixit, quando panem tradidit apostolis: "Hoc est corpus meum, quod pro vobis trade-

12 tur" [Luke 22:19]. Suum corpus, quando voluit et quando vult, in terra versatur. Etiam post ascensionem suam non dedignatus est se Paulo Apostolo monstrare in templo Hierosolimis, quod erat in terra. "Domini est terra et plenitudo eius" [Ps 23:1]. Omnis terra, in sua conditione sistens, benedicit Domino. Sola mala voluntas facit vas suum pollutum ad suscipiendum Dominum.

13    Haec propterea dico, ut, si forte me ignorante aut non consentiente exierit de ore meo ex corpore Domini, non me putes alienum a religione Christiana—quasi contemptui

this if he wants, he does not believe that God is omnipotent. And he who does not hope that God wants this does not accept the statement of Paul, who says: "He who will have all men be saved"—that is, those who have been allotted salvation. My son, remember what you often used to tell me: "Unless the Lord keep the city, he watches in vain who keeps it." If some scruple over the things I have set forth still clings to your mind, do not hide it from your father so long as life remains your companion. Hold on to what you have; may the Lord multiply the meaning of what I have set forth to you beyond what you know how to ask for.

With respect to the body of the Lord that we eat, there 11 remains for me to mention—though it is an unworthy example for the present discussion—what the emperor Valentinian said to the soldiers who wanted to appoint him a fellow emperor: "It was your responsibility," he said, "to make me emperor; it is mine to choose the companion I want." Thus it is our responsibility to wish and to beg the Lord for a pure heart; it is his responsibility to pour his body through our cavities and vessels unto our eternal salvation. For when he gave the bread to his apostles, he said: "This is my body, which will be given up for you." His body dwells on earth 12 when he wanted it to and when he wants it to. Even after his ascension he did not deign to reveal himself to Paul the Apostle in the temple at Jerusalem, which was on the earth. "The earth is the Lord's and the fullness thereof." The whole earth, resting in its condition, blesses the Lord. Only an evil will makes its vessel too polluted to receive the Lord.

I say these things so that, if perhaps without my aware- 13 ness or consent some of the Lord's body has left my mouth, you do not think me without Christian piety—as if I were

habeam corpus Domini mei, aut ipsud illuc dirigatur, quo non voluit seu non vult venire. Per hoc corpus anima nostra vivit, dicente eodem Domino: "Nisi manducaveritis carnem Filii hominis et biberitis eius sanguinem, non habebitis vitam in vobismet ipsis" [John 6:54]. Si enim ipsum corpus vita nobis est, non ei aufertur propter nostram separationem—ubicumque fuerit—quod ex se habet et nobis ex se tribuit.

14    Fili mi, dic presbyteris tuis ut caveant ne unum verbum ex his quae Dominus locutus est in Evangelio excedat de corde eorum, quoniam et ipsud vita est nobis, sicut panis consecratus. Dicit Dominus in Evangelio: "Verba quae ego locutus sum vobis spiritus et vita sunt" [John 6:64]. Praeceptum est mihi in lege, si aliquid remanserit de agno, ut igne comburam illud [Exod 12:10]. Ille agnus Christi carnem praefigurabat. Reliquiae agni quae igne conburi videbantur, mysteria sunt divinitatis quae capi non possunt a nobis, sed, Domini praecepto, igne charitatis assumenda sunt in caelesti oblatione. Illo—id est igni caritatis—omnia commendo mea, ut et illo vitia consumantur, et boni affectus assumantur.

15    Ita vero sumptum corpus Domini bona intentione, non est mihi disputandum utrum invisibiliter assumatur in caelum, aut reservetur in corpore nostro usque in diem sepulturae, aut exhaletur in auras, aut exeat de corpore cum sanguine, aut per poros emittatur, dicente Domino: "Omne quod intrat in os in ventrem vadit, et in secessum emittitur" [Matt 15:17]. Hoc solum cavendum est—ne Iudae corde sumam illud et ne contemptui habeatur, sed discernatur saluberrime a communibus cibis.

holding my Lord's body in contempt, or as if it were sent somewhere it did or does not want to go. Through this body our soul lives, as the Lord himself says: "Except you eat the flesh of the son of man and drink his blood, you shall not have life in you." Now if that body is life for us, it is not denied life through separation from us—wherever it is—because it has life through itself and it granted life from itself to us.

My son, tell your priests to beware lest a single word of those that the Lord spoke in the Gospel leaves their heart, since that too is life for us, just like the consecrated bread. The Lord says in the Gospel: "The words that I have spoken to you are spirit and life." In the law I am ordered that, if anything remains from the lamb, I should destroy it with fire. That lamb prefigured Christ's flesh. The remains of the lamb that appear to be destroyed in the fire are the mysteries of divinity that cannot be grasped by us but that, through the Lord's command, are to be received in the heavenly offering with the fire of charity. I entrust all that I do to that— that is, the fire of charity—so that my vices may be consumed by it, and my good dispositions received. 14

And so it is not for me to wonder whether the Lord's body, received with good intention, is taken up to heaven or kept in our body until our day of burial, or is exhaled into the air, or leaves our body with our blood, or is emitted through our orifices, as the Lord says: "Whatever enters into the mouth goes into the belly, and is cast down the drain." This alone is my concern—that I do not receive it with the heart of Judas and that it not be held in contempt, but rather kept wholesomely separate from common food. 15

16   De altero unde redarguisti patrem—non modo respondeo per omnia. Forte dederit Dominus ut te aliquando aliquo modo adhuc videam, et loquar de eo ore ad os. Interim dico: Da, fili, quare non cecinisti patri tuo Virgilianum istud:

Frigidus, o pueri, fugite hinc, latet anguis in herba.

Praecipitur in canonibus ut omnes ingredientes ecclesiam communicent; quod si non communicaverint, dicant causam quare non communicent, et si rationabilis exstiterit, in-
17   dulgeatur illis; sin autem, excommunicentur. Comperi te ancoram mentis tuae fixisse in pelago, et non in portu; fixisti illam in Gennadio Massiliensi episcopo. Hortor ut potius figas illam in portu tutissimo, Agustino scilicet, testificato per universas ecclesias. Hortatus est te Gennadius ut praecipue per dies Dominicos communices. Forte non erat consuetudo illius ut per singulos dies Missam celebraret—si enim esset, non hortaretur per solos Dominicos dies potissimum communicare. Grecorum aliquorum presbyterorum consuetudo est, ut a quinta feria se praeparent et sanctificent ad
18   Missam celebrandam. Potest evenire ut in tertia feria sive quarta feria peccatum committamus, quod non abluatur usque post finitum diem Dominicum; quapropter non rite communicamus per singulos dies Dominicos. Et potest fieri ut Deo placeamus per singulos dies unius ebdomadis, in quibus gustare et videre fas est quam dulcis sit Dominus. A tam dilecto hospite non oportet dilectores diu abesse, quem compulerunt secum hospitari in die resurrectionis eius duo ex discipulis in Emaus.

On the other matter that you complained to your father  16
about—I am not going to respond to all of it now. Perhaps
the Lord should grant that I may still somehow see you at
some point, and I will talk about it face to face. In the meantime, I say: Tell me, son, why you have not sung that verse
from Virgil to your father:

Children, flee: A cold snake lurks in the grass.

In the canons it is ordered that all who enter church should
receive communion. If they do not receive communion,
they should give the reason that they are not receiving it,
and if it is reasonable, they should be given leave; but if not,
they should be excommunicated. I realized that you have  17
fixed the anchor of your mind in the sea, and not at port.
You have fixed it in Bishop Gennadius of Marseille. I urge
you instead to fix it at the safest port, namely Augustine,
known through all churches. Gennadius urged you to receive communion especially on Sundays. Perhaps it was not
his habit to celebrate Mass every day—for if it were, he
would not urge communion particularly and only on Sundays. It is the custom of some Greek priests to prepare and
sanctify themselves from Thursday for celebrating Mass. It  18
can happen that on Tuesday or Wednesday we commit a sin
that is not cleansed until after Sunday is over; we cannot
therefore rightly receive communion every Sunday. And it
can happen that we please God each day of a week, on each
of which it is right to see and taste how sweet the Lord is. It
is not appropriate that lovers be long absent from such a beloved guest, whom two of the disciples compelled to stay
with them on the day of his resurrection in Emmaus.

19     Fuge, fili mi, a pelago ad tutum portum Agustinum; ipse enim dicit ad Ianuarium: "Rectius inter eos fortasse quispiam dirimit litem, qui monet ut in Christi pace permaneant. Faciat unusquisque quod secundum suam fidem pie credit faciendum esse. Neuter eorum exhonorat corpus et sanguinem Domini, sed saluberrimum sacramentum certatim honorare contendunt. Neque enim litigaverunt inter se, aut quisquam eorum se alteri praeposuit, Zacheus et ille centurio [Luke 19:6], cum alter eorum gaudens in domum suam susceperit Dominum, alter dixerit: 'Non sum dignus ut intres sub tectum meum' [Luke 7:6; Matt 8:8]."✝

20     Fili mi, si te cognoscis peccatorem, oportet ut a te non repellas Deum, sed satis ei fac per paenitentiam et in spiritu contrito et humiliato suscipe illum. Si iustus es, gaudens suscipe illum; si infirmus, precare ab illo sanitatem et cade in faciem ante pedes eius, sicut unus de decem leprosis; gratiasque age, ut dicat tibi: "Surge et vade, quia fides tua te salvum fecit" [Luke 17:12–19]. Et ne differas de die in diem converti ad illum, quia quacumque die conversus ingemueris, salvus erit. Iuxta Agustinum, quando videris pium affectum esse in te, sume corpus Domini, ut tibi vitam sempiternam praestet. Noli differre ad diem Dominicum, quia nescis si contingas illum.

Flee, my son, from the sea to the safe port of Augustine. 19
For he says to Januarius: "Perhaps he who advises them to
remain in Christ's peace cuts through the dispute more correctly. Let everyone do what he piously believes should be
done, in accordance with his own faith. Neither of them dishonors the Lord's body and blood; rather, both strive in earnest to honor this most saving sacrament. For Zacheus and
the centurion did not fight among themselves, nor did one
place himself before the other, when one of them rejoiced
and took the Lord into his house, and the other said: 'I am
not worthy that you should enter under my roof.'"✝

My son, if you realize that you are a sinner, you should not 20
push the Lord away from you; rather, you should make satis-
faction to him through penitence and receive him with a
contrite and humble spirit. If you are just, receive him joyfully; if you are weak, beg him for health and fall on your
face before his feet, like one of the ten lepers. And give
thanks, that he may say to you: "Arise, go your way, for your
faith has made you whole." And do not delay to convert to
him from day to day, because on whatever day you have cried
out and are converted, you will be saved. According to Augustine, when you recognize a pious disposition in yourself,
receive the Lord's body, that it may give you eternal life. Do
not wait until Sunday, because you do not know whether you
will reach it.

# LIBER 4

## Praefatiuncula

In hoc quarto libello continentur mota ad investigandum et—iuxta facultatem quam potui precari a misericordia Domini—scripta de cursibus diurnalibus et nocturnalibus, sive in festis diebus seu cotidianis, quatinus, considerato ordine compositionis et numero Psalmorum et lectionum ac responsoriorum convenienti quibusque temporibus, dulcius atque compunctius Deo assistatur in ecclesia, et rogetur atque recordetur—tam pro se qui rogat, quam pro illis quibus necessaria est deprecatio—et recordetur illorum quorum 2 nobis est utilis recordatio. Necnon etiam aliqua recapitulantur de superioribus libellis, quae apertius inventa sunt a mea parvitate post scriptos memoratos libellos.

# BOOK 4

## Preface

This fourth book includes for examination the subject matter and—according to the ability that I have been able to request from the Lord's mercy—the texts for the daytime and nighttime offices, whether on feast days or ordinary days. In this way, when we have considered the arrangement and the number of Psalms and readings and responsories appropriate to each season, God may be attended, beseeched and remembered in church more sweetly and remorsefully—both on behalf of the one who makes requests, and on behalf of those for whom the request is necessary—and we may remember those things that it is useful for us to remember. Also, various matters from the previous books that, in my inadequacy, I understood more fully after having written them, are recapitulated here.

2

I

Ut ea quae Dei sunt Deo reddamus.
Quot oris sol orbem lustrat,
totidem repetitionibus nosmet
ipsos offerimus Deo interdiu
noctuque, exceptis Vespertinis,
Completoriisque et Matutinis
officiis, de quibus seorsum
dicendum est.

Nos qui censemur Christiano nomine redempti sumus a servitute diabolica Christi precioso sanguine. Ideo non sumus nostri, sed redemptoris nostri. De quo pretio dicit Apostolus: "Empti enim estis pretio magno," et ideo quid agere debeamus subiungit: "Glorificate et portate Deum in corpore vestro" [1 Cor 6:20]. Glorificamus illum quando ei gratias referimus de sua redemptione, portamusque in corpore nostro quando in anima nostra, quae portatur a corpore, inhabitat per dilectionem suam—in cogitatu et vita atque intellectu. Ac ideo saepius, per memoriam nostram et suam sanctificationem, portando illum in mente secundum suum beneplacitum, ei, id est corpori, mens memorata praecipit ad oboedientiam, per quam etiam plus placet redemptori nostro inherere ei quae portatur a corpore.

I

# That we should render to God the things that are God's. We offer ourselves to God during the day and the night through just as many sections of psalmody as there are hours in which the sun shines on the world, excepting Vespers, Compline and the Matins, which we will discuss separately.

We who are counted under the Christian name have been redeemed from the devil's servitude by the precious blood of Christ. We are therefore not our own, but our redeemer's. The Apostle talks about the price: "For you are bought with a great price," and so he adds what we ought to do: "Glorify and bear God in your body." We glorify him when we give him thanks for his redemption, and we bear him in our body when he dwells in our soul, which is borne by the body, through his love—in our thought and life and understanding. And thus more frequently, through our memory and his sanctification, by bearing him in our mind according to his pleasure, the aforementioned mind calls the body to obedience, and through obedience it pleases our redeemer to cling even more closely to the soul that is carried by the body.

2    Eidem redemptori, ut fidelis servus domino suo, semper debitores sumus servire—sicut servitur iustitiae et sanctificationi et ceteris bonis moribus per amorem. De qua servitute dicit Zacharias propheta: "Ut sine timore de manu inimicorum nostrorum liberati, serviamus illi, in sanctitate et iustitia coram ipso, omnibus diebus nostris" [Luke 1:74–75].

3    Concessit nobis idem Dominus noster duo volumina temporum, scilicet diei et noctis, ut sol nobis luceret per diem et luna per noctem. Ex his duobus luminibus profectum nostrae fruges assumunt, ut ad utilitatem nostram perveniant. Ex luna habent umorem ut crescant; ex sole temperativum ardorem ut ad maturitatem perveniant. Possumus haec manifestare ex dictis domni Bedae (sit assumptum ab illo a quocunque ipse voluit; mihi sufficit eius auctoritas): "Denique," inquit, "cum serenior nox est et luna pernox, tunc largior ros refertur arva perfundere, et plerique sub aere quiescentes, quo magis sub lumine fuissent lunae, eo

4    plus umoris se capite collegisse senserunt." Et in alio loco de sole: "Tempora sunt anni quattuor quibus sol, per diversa caeli spatia discurrendo, subiectum temperat orbem divina utique procurante sapientia—ut non semper eisdem commoratus in locis, fervoris aviditate mundanum depopuletur ornatum, sed, paulatim per diversa commigrans, terrenis fructibus nascendis maturandisque temperamenta custodiat."✠ Ex frugibus terrae sustentatur corpus nostrum. Corpus animae in obsequio est, ut hic in praesenti saeculo possit servire Deo.

We should always serve this redeemer as a faithful servant serves his master—just as justice, sanctification and other good virtues are served through love. The prophet Zechariah talks about this servitude: "That being delivered from the hand of our enemies, we may serve him without fear, in holiness and justice before him, all our days." 2

Our same Lord gave us two periods of time, namely the day and night, that the sun may shine on us through the day and the moon through the night. Our crops receive their growth from these two lights, that they may become useful for us. From the moon they have moisture to grow; from the sun they have soothing warmth to attain maturity. We can show this through the sayings of the master Bede (he has taken it from whatever source he chose; his authority is enough for me): "And then," he says, "when the night is clear and the moon lasts all night long, more abundant dew is said to moisten the fields, and many resting in the open air have felt more moisture collect on their head the longer they were under the light of the moon." And in another passage, about the sun: "There are four times of the year when the sun, by moving through the various regions of heaven, warms the earth beneath it through the governance of divine wisdom—that it may not destroy the earth's furnishings through its excessive heat by remaining forever in the same place; but rather that, as it gradually moves through different heavenly spaces, it may preserve a moderate climate suitable for begetting earthly crops and raising them to maturity."✝ Our body is sustained from the fruits of the earth. The soul's body is in subjugation, that it may be able to serve God here in this world. 3 4

5    Manifestum est quod, postquam anima per nimiam afflictionem corporis recesserit ab eo, non ei deputetur labor
ad fructum; sed, quamdiu in corpore est, oportet operari
unde placeat Deo. Non enim solum pro his quae nobis mi-
nistrantur in praesenti saeculo, Deo astamus in nostris officiis, sed etiam quia debitores nos esse cognoscimus iugis
servitii eius, ut fidelis servus qui semper vult in servitio
adesse senioris sui.

6    Et ideo duodecim repetitiones facimus per primam, et
tertiam et sextam et nonam oram, ut per unamquamque re-
petitionem Deo praesentes simus in omni ora. Similiter in
nocte per duodecim Psalmos. Et quia pater noster audivit:
"In sudore vultus tui vesceris pane tuo" [Gen 3:19], convertimur nos aliquando ad opera temporalia; atque, ut propter haec necessaria non omittamus servitutem quam Deo
debemus in anima exhibere, statuerunt patres nostri ut tot
orationes psalmodiarum fierent, quot orae sunt nobis datae
ad laborandum pro sustentatione corporis. Et quia non possumus ita semper operari nisi quies aliquando subsequatur,
sequitur nox, in qua non possumus operari, sed quieti otium
damus. Ut et pro ipsa quiete Deo servitium reddamus, can-
7 tamus duodecim Psalmos pro duodecim oris noctis. Tendimus ad tale servitium quale primus Adam pater noster exhi-
buit Deo ante quam peccaret, et quale speramus futurum
post hanc vitam—hoc est ut continui simus in Dei praesentia.

8    Non enim necesse est aliquem in hac discretione musitare propter disparem longitudinem dierum et noctium;
etiam calculatores orarum tempora sic dividunt dierum et
noctium, ut luna per noctem luceat—sive aestivo seu hie-
9 mali tempore—duodecim oris. Unde idem qui supra Beda

It is clear that, after the soul has left the body through 5
great bodily affliction, labor is no longer considered fruitful
for it. But as long as the soul is in the body, it is appropriate
for it to work and thus to please God. For we do not attend
God in our offices only on behalf of those things that are
provided us in this world, but also because we recognize that
we are indebted to the yoke of his service, just like a faithful
servant who always wishes to be in the service of his lord.

And therefore we complete twelve sections of psalmody 6
distributed across the first and the third and the sixth and
the ninth hour, that we may attend God at every hour with
each section. We do likewise with twelve Psalms at night.
And because our father heard: "In the sweat of your face
shall you eat bread," we sometimes turn ourselves to temporal labors; and that we may not neglect the service that we
should show God in our soul because of these necessities,
our fathers established that our prayers of psalmody be as
numerous as the hours that have been provided to us for la-
boring for our bodily sustenance. And because we cannot
always work unless rest sometimes follows, the night follows, when we cannot work; instead, we add leisure to the
quiet. To render service to God for this quiet, we sing twelve
Psalms for the twelve hours of the night. We strive for such 7
service as that which the first Adam, our father, showed to
God before he sinned, and that we hope will come after this
life—that is, the service of being constantly in God's presence.

It is not necessary for anyone to object to this interpreta- 8
tion because of the unequal lengths of days and nights; those
who reckon the hours divide the times of days and nights so
that the moon shines in the night—whether in the summer
or the winter—for twelve hours. And thus the same Bede 9

in libro *De temporibus:* "Verum longissimis in bruma noctibus, vel item aestate brevissimis, quarum alias duodecim orarum spatium longe transcendere, alias nequaquam ad hoc pertingere posse constat, qua ratione lunam duodecim oras lucere credamus? Nisi forte putemus non aequinoctiales oras intellegendas, sed singulas quasque noctes pro suae mensura longitudinis aut brevitatis in duodecim particulas, quas horas vocitamus, aequa distributione findendas."

## 2

# De Prima

Magnificentissime et gloriosissime atque Christianissime imperator: Quoniam professus est se vester servus, quamvis minimus omnium, aliqua pingere de operariis qui omni ora volunt assistere in servitio Dei—videtur parvitati meae per Dei donum quod vestrum animum ad se rapit in prosperis et adversis, ut ab illa hora inchoem qua pater familias conducit operarios in vineam suam. Sancta ecclesia procul dubio est vinea patris familias, quae ita operatur per operarios in vinea sua, ut sibi fructificet. Nos sumus vinea quae colitur per cultores—scilicet praepositos sanctae

as above, in his book *On Time:* "But why do we believe that the moon shines for twelve hours during the longest nights around the winter solstice, and also during the shortest in summer? The length of the winter hours widely exceeds those of the others; clearly the others can by no means be as long. Unless perhaps we consider that the hours are not to be understood as equal in length, but that each night in the measure of its length or brevity is rather divided into twelve equal units, which we call hours."

## 2

# On Prime

Most magnificent, most glorious and most Christian emperor: Because your servant, though the least of all, has promised to explain some matters concerning the laborers who wish to participate in God's service at every hour—it strikes me, in my inadequacy, through the gift of God that takes your spirit to itself in prosperity and adversity, that I should begin with the hour when the householder leads the laborers to his vineyard. The holy church is doubtless that householder's vineyard, which is tilled by the laborers in his vineyard that it may bear him fruit. We are the vineyard that is tilled by the cultivators—that is, those placed in charge of

2

303

ecclesiae—aut per nosmet ipsos. Praepositi ostendunt culturam; nosque simul cum illis exercemus illam. Fodiunt cultores vineam et stercorant quando corda nostra dura per verba increpationis scindunt et fetida peccata nostra infundunt; fodimus et nos terram circa vitem ac facimus fossam quando nostram naturam ad memoriam nobis inducimus et humiliamur sub potenti manu Dei, aspiciendo nos pulverem et cinerem esse. Insuper etiam, quia ipsam naturam corrumpimus peccando, inducimus stercus, ut peccata nostra circa nos sint in praesenti saeculo atque in futuro desint, et per duas res—id est per considerationem nostrae naturae et per paenitentiam nostrorum peccatorum—crescat fructus noster uberius, fiatque vinum per angustiam torcularis et espoliationem carnalium delectationum, quod, quasi per quoddam torcolar, introeat in cellarium aeternae domus.

4 Vinum, quod exprimitur ab uva per pressuram torcolaris, desiderium nostrum fervens est, quod exuitur a carnali desiderio, ut dignum sit recondi in promptuario Domini.

5    Fructui vineae multae adversae ferae insidiantur, ut eum furentur et traiciant in corpus suum. Eisdem feris possunt comparari Zyphei quodammodo, apparitores Saul, qui voluerunt rapere David, ut traderent eum in manus Saul ad interficiendum [1 Kgs 23:19, 26:1]. Non enim desunt nobis idem Zyphei, qui interpretantur "florentes"; quos intellegimus diaboli membra esse, sive ipsum diabolum, qui potest propterea dici "florens," quia prosperitatem caducam suis

6 ostentat. Ipse enim, sive per se sive per membra sua, insidiatur nobis vel aperte persequitur, ut tradat aeternae morti;

the holy church—or by our very selves. Those in charge point out the tillage; together with them, we work it. The cultivators dig up the vineyard and spread manure over it when they cleave our hardened hearts through words of rebuke and pour out our fetid sins; and we dig up the earth around the vine and build a ditch when we recall our nature and are humbled beneath God's potent hand, by seeing that we are dust and ash. And moreover, because we corrupt that 3 nature by sinning, we add manure, that our sins may surround us in this world and depart in the world to come, and that through these two things—that is, through a consideration of our nature and through penance for our sins—our fruit may grow more abundantly, and wine may be made through the distress of the wine press and the stripping away of our fleshly delights—wine which, as if through a wine press, may enter the cellar of our eternal home. Wine, 4 which is squeezed out of the grape through the pressing of the wine press, is our fervent desire, which is stripped away from carnal desire, that it may merit being stowed away in the Lord's storeroom.

Many hostile wild creatures threaten the fruit of the 5 vineyard, that they may steal it away and put it into their body. In a sense the servants of Saul, the Ziphites, can be compared to these wild creatures; they wanted to seize David and hand him over to Saul to be killed. And these same Ziphites, whose name means "blooming," are not absent from us. We understand them to be members of the devil, or the devil himself, who can be called "blooming" because he flaunts a fallen prosperity to his kind. For he threat- 6 ens and openly persecutes us, whether personally or through his members, that he may hand us over to eternal death; and

et fieret, nisi vinea Domini—quae nos sumus—haberet se-
pem circum se atque cultores infra se. Sepes enim custodia
Domini est circa electos suos; cultores enim, ut praediximus, sunt doctores et praepositi ecclesiae. Illa sepe cir-
cumdatus erat David quando Zyphei eum circumdederunt,
ac ideo salvatus est et cecinit Psalmum: "Deus, in nomine
tuo salvum me fac" [Ps 53], et cetera.

7    Quia, Domino miserante, inchoaturi sumus diurnalia officia, ab hora qua pater familias vocavit operarios in vineam
suam, fas nobis videtur ut ab eodem tempore ea inchoemus,
quando illud Evangelium legitur quod ordinationem opera-
riorum continet per competentes horas—id est, Septuage-
8    sima. Sicut enim ovibus (quae nocte custodiuntur in ovili-
bus, et post matutinam custodiam exeuntibus de vico ad
pascua in latitudinem camporum) necesse est ut ilico habeant opilionem qui eas defendat a lupis irruentibus, ita nobis necesse est, mane surgentibus ad mandata Domini, ut
habeamus pastorem et doctorem, qui nos introducat ad eadem mandata et defendat a lupis, de quibus lupis legitur in
Evangelio secundum Iohannem: "Lupus rapit et dispergit
oves" [John 10:12]—ac nihilo minus a leone, qui "rugiens
9    circuit quaerens quem devoret" [1 Pet 5–8]. Quomodo lupus
rapiat sive leo devoret, manifestum est his qui impugnantur
a vitiis. Unusquisque enim qui videt quomodo temptatur a
concupiscentia sua abstractus et inlectus [Jas 1:14], cognoscit quem memoratae ferae per gulam rapiant, quem per
luxuriam, quem per curiositatem nefariarum artium, quem

this would happen unless the Lord's vineyard—which we are —had a hedge around it and cultivators within it. Now the hedge is the Lord's watchfulness over his elect; and the cultivators, as we said above, are the teachers and governors of the church. David had been surrounded by that hedge when the Ziphites surrounded him, and thus he was saved and sang the Psalm: "Save me, O God, by your name," and so on.

Since, with the Lord's mercy, we will start with the day- 7 time offices, from the hour when the householder called the laborers to his vineyard, we thought it right to begin with the season when we read the Gospel passage that contains the appointment of the laborers at their corresponding hours—that is, with Septuagesima. For just as sheep (who 8 are kept at night in the fold, but who leave the village after their early-morning shelter to pasture in the wide fields) must have a shepherd to defend them from ravaging wolves, so must we, upon rising in the morning at the Lord's command, also have a pastor and a teacher to introduce us to his commandments and defend us from the wolves that we read about in the Gospel according to John: "The wolf catches and scatters the sheep"—and no less from the lion, who "roaring goes about seeking whom he may devour." It is clear to those who are beset by vices how the 9 wolf catches and the lion devours. For everyone who sees how he is tempted by his own concupiscence, being drawn away and allured, recognizes whom the aforementioned beasts snatch through gluttony, whom through luxury, whom through curiosity about the evil arts, whom through

per contemplationem spectaculorum turpium et supervacuorum, quem per adquisitionem rerum temporalium, quem per curiositatem inquisitionis sive detractionis vitiorum proximorum, quem per superbiam, quem per iactantiam. Haec sunt vitia quae subiciuntur tribus concupiscentiis quibus totus mundus involvitur, dicente apostolo: "Omne quod in mundo est aut concupiscentia carnis est aut concupiscentia oculorum aut superbia vitae" [1 John 2:16].

10

11 Propter suprascriptas feras, dicit opilio noster: "Deus, in adiutorium meum intende; Domine, ad adiuvandum me festina" [Ps 69:2]. In officii initio precatur ut non possint tantum praevalere, quatenus ab eodem conciliabulo aliquem separent per astutiam suam. Simili modo faciebat Moyses quando arca elevabatur ad portandum; dicebat enim: "Surge, Domine, et dissipentur inimici tui, et fugiant qui oderunt te a facie tua" [Num 10:35]. Nos enim spiritaliter sumus illa arca. Sicut enim cotidie circumdabatur illa ab inimicis, sic et sancta ecclesia usque in finem circumdabitur a persecutoribus, sive apertis sive occultis. Sequitur, post deprecationem nostri opilionis, *Gloria* sanctae Trinitatis, quam deprecamur adesse nostro adiutorio. Recordatur opilio noster sermonis Domini quem dixit: "Sine me nihil potestis facere" [John 15:5]. De additione *Gloria Patri* per diversa loca Hieronimus scripsit in epistola sua ad Damasum papam. Cur in memorato tempore, id est Septuagesima, alleluia non supponatur *Gloriae* sanctae Trinitatis (quae est per omnia saecula saeculorum), sed *Laus tibi, Domine, rex aeternae gloriae,* diximus in libello quem fecimus de Septuagesima, scilicet non ob aliud, nisi ut humiliore lingua Latina Ebrea ammoneamur nos debere informari ad humiliorem conversationem in tempore Septuagesimae quam in alio tempore.

12

13

contemplation of base and empty spectacles, whom through the acquisition of temporal goods, whom through curiosity in uncovering and denouncing the vices of neighbors, whom through pride and whom through boasting. These are the vices that are subject to the three concupiscences that the whole world is enveloped in, as the apostle says: "For all that is in the world is either the concupiscence of the flesh or the concupiscence of the eyes or the pride of life."

Because of the aforementioned wild beasts, our shepherd says: "God, come to my assistance; Lord, make haste to help me." At the beginning of the office he requests that they be unable to succeed to such an extent as to separate someone from our gathering through their cleverness. Moses acted similarly when the ark was lifted to be carried; for he said: "Arise, O Lord, and let your enemies be scattered, and let them that hate you flee from before your face." For, spiritually, we are that ark. And just as it was daily surrounded by enemies, the church will also be surrounded by persecutors, whether open or hidden, until the end. After our shepherd's prayer there follows the *Gloria* of the Holy Trinity, which we request be present for our assistance. Our shepherd recalls the saying that the Lord spoke: "Without me you can do nothing." Jerome wrote in his letter to Pope Damasus about the addition, in various places, of the *Gloria Patri*. We explained in the book that we wrote on Septuagesima why the alleluia is not joined to the *Gloria* of the Holy Trinity (which is to be for all the ages of ages), but rather *Laus tibi, Domine, rex aeternae gloriae*. This is for no other reason than to inform us, through Latin, which is humbler than Hebrew, that we should adhere to a humbler way of life during the season of Septuagesima than we would in any other season.

14    Postea sequitur Psalmus quem David cantavit quando
Zyphei voluerunt eum rapere et tradere in manus Saul.
Quem nobis necesse est cantare in articulo diei, deprecando
tuitionem divinam per omnes horas diei contra machina-
tiones et versutias diabolicae fraudis, de quibus dicit Psalmus: "Quoniam alieni insurgunt super nos qui non propo-
nunt Deum ante conspectum suum"—atque ut ex omnibus
tribulationibus nos eripiat, et super inimicos nostros despiciat oculus noster, ut David suo in tempore fecit [Ps 53:5, 9].

15    Postea sequuntur duae repetitiones Psalmi *Beati inmaculati*
[Ps 118], qui plenus est moribus. Oportet enim ut quos Deus
liberaverit de vinculis et carcere inimicorum, moribus bonis
et piis ei assistant in omni devotione, sicut ex duobus versibus duarum repetitionum possumus conicere. Unus dicit:
"Utinam dirigantur viae meae ad custodiendas iustifica-
tiones tuas." Alter ita: "Revela oculos meos, et considerabo
mirabilia de lege tua" [Ps 118:5, 18]. Istae tres repetitiones
sustentant et defendunt arcam Domini usque ad plenam
tertiam, id est per horam primam et secundam.

16    Dein sequitur versus: "Exsurge, Domine, adiuva nos et
libera nos propter nomen tuum" [Ps 43:26]. Simile quid dicebat Moyses quando arca deponebatur. Sic enim scriptum
est in libro Numerorum capitulo XXVI: "Quando autem
deponeretur aiebat: Revertere, Domine, ad multitudinem
filiorum Israhel" [Num 10:36]. Reversio Dei ad exercitum
Israhel non est aliud quam ut reverti faciat Israhel toto
corde ad se. Deus non habet quo revertatur, cui totum praesens est. Ita enim *Exsurge, Domine* non est aliud intellegendum, quam: "Nos fac exsurgere a somno torporis, et fac
industrios atque strenuos in opere mandatorum tuorum."

Then there follows the Psalm that David sang when the   14
Ziphites wanted to seize him and give him over to the hands
of Saul. Singing this Psalm at this point in the day is necessary for requesting divine protection through all the hours
of the day against the machinations and subtleties of the
devil's deceit, of which the psalmist speaks: "For strangers
rise up against us who do not set God before their eyes"—
and also so that he may remove us from all our tribulations,
and that our eye may look down upon our enemies, as David
did in his time. Then two sections of the Psalm *Beati inmacu-*   15
*lati,* which is filled with virtues, follow. Those whom God
has freed from chains and from the prison of their enemies
should attend him with good and pious virtues in all devotion, as we can gather from two verses of the two sections.
One says: "O, that my ways may be directed to keep your jus-
tifications." The second is as follows: "Open my eyes, and I
will consider the wondrous things of your law." These three
sections support and defend the Lord's ark up to the full
third hour, that is through the first and second hours.

Then a versicle follows: "Arise, O Lord *(Exurge, Domine),*   16
help us and redeem us for your name's sake." This is similar to what Moses said when the ark was set down. For
in the book of Numbers, chapter 26, it is written as follows: "And when it was set down he said: Return, O Lord,
to the multitude of the host of Israel." God's return to Israel's army is nothing but his arrangement that Israel be returned, with its whole heart, to him. God, whose presence is
total, has nowhere to return to. And thus *Exurge, Domine*
should not be understood as meaning anything other than
"Make us rise from the sleep of stupefaction, and make us
vigilant and active in the work of your commandments."

17 Ab ipsa reversione accepit idem cantus "versus"; eandem enim reversionem de qua ammonetur per versum, exercemus statu corporis nostri. Quando audivimus versum ilico vertimus nos ad orientem. Quare hoc, nisi ut omnis cogitatio quae foras exivit aspiciendo et videndo haec temporalia, revertatur infra nos, et dicamus: "Da mihi, Domine, cor ut orem ad te."

18 Postea inchoamus implorare misericordiam Domini per *Kyrie eleison* et *Christe eleison* et iterum *Kyrie eleison*. Tres articulos aliquo modo divinae maiestatis et Trinitatis caelebramus in ecclesia, salvo superiore intellectu. Primus est ante assumptam humanitatem, quando Trinitas invocabatur sine copulatione humanae naturae, ac ideo merito ter dicimus *Kyrie eleison,* sive semel propter unam substantiam. Secundus est post assumptum hominem, quando Christus videbatur in terra et nihilominus a suis credebatur Deus et Filius Dei, ut Petrus: "Tu es," inquit, "Christus Filius Dei vivi" [Matt 16:16], et Paulus de eodem Filio: "Proprio," inquit,

19 "Filio suo non pepercit" [Rom 8:32]. Quoniam propter assumptam naturam vocatur Christus, quae uncta est spiritali oleo, in medio articulorum dicimus: *Christe eleison*. Quando semel dicimus ei *Christe eleison,* ostendimus eum solum fuisse inter homines et neminem habuisse sui similem per omnia; et si tertio, ostendimus numquam eum fuisse separatum a sancta Trinitate propter assumptam humanitatem.

20 Tertius articulus est ex eo tempore quo voluit clarificare illum assumptum hominem plus quam esset, quamdiu

This song is called a versicle because of this very reversion    17
or return. For we perform the very reversion that the versicle teaches us about with the position of our body. When we
have heard the versicle we immediately turn ourselves to the
east. Why do we do this, if not so that every thought that
has gone out of us while we observe and see these temporal
things may return within us, and we may say: "Lord, give me
a heart that I may pray to you."

Afterward we begin to ask for the Lord's mercy through    18
*Kyrie eleison* and *Christe eleison* and again *Kyrie eleison*. We
thereby celebrate in some way three moments of the divine
majesty and the Trinity in church, though there may be a
higher understanding of this prayer. The first moment is before humanity was assumed, when the Trinity was invoked
without being joined to human nature, and therefore we
rightly say *Kyrie eleison* three times, or we say it once because
there is one substance. The second is after man was assumed, when Christ was seen upon the earth and his followers nevertheless believed that he was God and the Son of
God, as Peter said: "You are Christ, the Son of the living
God," and Paul said of the same Son: "He spared not even
his own Son." Since he is called Christ because of the na-    19
ture he assumed, which was anointed with spiritual oil, between these two moments we say: *Christe eleison*. When we
say *Christe eleison* to him once, we show that he alone was
among men and that he had nobody who was like him in
all respects; and if we say it three times, we show that he
was never separated from the Holy Trinity because of the
humanity he assumed. Third is the moment from the time    20
when he wanted to glorify the man he had assumed beyond
what this man was, so long as it remained mortal. Thus he

mortalis erat. Unde ipse dicebat ad Patrem: "Clarifica me, Pater, apud temet ipsum, claritate quam habui prius quam mundus fieret" [ John 17:5]. Ac ideo simili modo ut in primo precamur Deum, ut ignoscat nobis in talibus temptationi-

21 bus sine quibus haec vita non potest transigi. De quibus dicitur in Parabolis Salomonis: "Septies enim cadit iustus in die et resurgit" [Prov 24:16]—id est, per ignorantiam, per oblivionem, per cogitationem, per sermonem, per subreptionem, per necessitatem, per fragilitatem carnis. Singulis diebus, vel inviti vel volentes, frequenter reatum incurrimus, et tamen resurgit iustus, videlicet quia iustitiae eius non praeiudicat lapsus fragilitatis humanae.

22 Ac deinde sequitur oratio Dominica, quam cum magna cautela oportet cantare, ut ipsas res in mente teneamus quas verbis pronuntiamus. Saepissime praecedit *Kyrie eleison,* per quod reconciliatur primo Deus, ut cum sua miseratione et dignatione possimus congruenter illum invocare patrem nostrum, et intendere verbis orationis. Post orationem Dominicam sequitur nostra credulitas, quam sancti apostoli constituerunt de fide sanctae Trinitatis atque dispensatione incarnationis Domini ac statu nostrae ecclesiae.

23 Modus orationis quem praetulimus ad eos aspicit qui de levibus peccatis et cotidianis compunguntur. Sunt enim utrique in nostra ecclesia—scilicet et qui in bonitate permanserunt, et qui corruerunt peccando sed festinant cotidie resurgere per paenitentiam. Ex persona illorum dicitur: "Vivet anima mea et laudabit te, et iudicia tua adiuvabunt me" [Ps 118:175], ac si diceret: Si mortua fuerit anima mea pro erratibus meis, at dein vivet per conversionem; et

said to the Father: "And now glorify me, Father, with yourself, with the glory that I had before the world was." And thus we pray to God just as we did upon the first moment, that he may forgive us for those temptations without which this life cannot be lived. These temptations are discussed in 21 the Proverbs of Solomon: "For a just man falls seven times a day and rises again"—that is, he falls through ignorance, through forgetfulness, in thought, in word, by deception, out of necessity and through the weakness of the flesh. We incur guilt frequently every day, whether willingly or unwillingly, and yet the just man rises, namely because the failing of human fragility is not injurious to his justice.

And then the Lord's prayer follows, which we should sing 22 with great caution, that we may keep in our mind the things that we pronounce with our words. Often the *Kyrie eleison* precedes it; this appeases God first, so that with his mercy and honor we may be able to invoke him appropriately as our father, and to concentrate on the words of our prayer. After the Lord's prayer there follows a statement of our belief, which the holy apostles established concerning faith in the Holy Trinity and the dispensation of the Lord's incarnation and the institution of our church.

The type of prayer that we mentioned above reflects 23 upon those who feel compunction over their light, everyday sins. For there are both kinds in our church—namely, those who have persisted in goodness, and those who have fallen through sin but hasten daily to rise through penance. In their guise, it is said: "My soul shall live and shall praise you, and your judgments shall help me," as if to say: If my soul has died because of my mistakes, it will later live through conversion; and your judgments will help me,

315

iudicia tua adiuvabunt me, quia dixisti: "Nolo mortem peccatoris, sed magis ut convertatur et vivat" [Ezek 33:11]. Et
iterum: Gaudeo "super uno peccatore paenitentiam agente,
quam super nonaginta novem iustis qui non indigent paeni-
24  tentia" [Luke 15:7]. Errorem pristinum illius qui nunc conversus dicit: "Vivet anima mea," monstrat versus sequens:
"Erravi sicut ovis quae periit. Require servum tuum, quia
mandata tua non sum oblitus" [Ps 118:176]. Ex eadem persona sequitur Psalmus quem David cantavit, postquam pae-
nitendo conversus est a malo adulterii et homicidii [Ps 50].

25  Post illum Psalmum commendat se totus grex Deo—pastor simul cum ovibus—et dicit: "Respice in servos tuos et in
opera tua, et dirige filios eorum." Hoc debemus cum his verbis tenere in mente, ut filios nostros cogitemus cogitationes
quae nascuntur ex mente, quatinus illas dirigat Deus secundum suum beneplacitum. Et in sequentibus, ubi dicit: "Et
opera manuum nostrarum dirige super nos," opera proce-
26  dentia ex cogitationibus. Ac dein singularis opilio pro toto
grege precatur dicendo: "Dirige, Domine, corda"—id est
cogitationes—"sensus"—scilicet oculos et aures et nares—
"et sermones nostros"—qui per os offeruntur—"et opera
manuum nostrarum, ut possimus placere in conspectu tuo."
Et sic tandem securi properamus ad opera necessaria.

27  Suprascripto versui *Exurge, Domine* non praeponitur lectio, et ideo non sequitur responsorius ut in ceteris officiis.
Morem sanctae ecclesiae tenet cursus iste, ut primo operari
studeat, et postea docere. Hoc exemplum reliquit nobis
Christus, de quo dicit Lucas: "Quae coepit Iesus facere
et docere" [Acts 1:1]. Psalmi pertinent ad opera, lectio ad

because you said: "I desire not the death of the wicked, but that the wicked turn from his way and live." And again: I rejoice "over one sinner who does penance more than over ninety-nine just who need not penance." The verse that follows reveals the original fault of the one who has now converted and says "My soul shall live": "I have gone astray like a sheep that is lost. Seek your servant, because I have not forgotten your commandments." The Psalm that David sang, after he was converted from the evil of adultery and murder by doing penance, follows in the guise of the same person.

After that Psalm, the whole flock—the pastor together with the sheep—commends itself to God, and says: "Look upon your servants and your works, and guide their sons." With these words we should remember to consider our thoughts, which are born from our mind, as our sons, that God may guide them according to his pleasure. And in the following passage, where it says: "And guide the works of our hands over us," we should remember the works that proceed from our thoughts. And then the single shepherd prays for his whole flock, saying: "Lord, guide our hearts"—that is, our thoughts—"senses"—namely, our eyes and ears and nostrils—"and our words"—which come through the mouth—"and the works of our hands, that we may be able to be pleasing in your sight." And so, finally secure, we hasten to our necessary tasks.

No reading precedes the aforementioned versicle *Exurge, Domine,* and so no responsory follows as in the other offices. This office is in keeping with the custom of the holy church to strive to do work first, and then to teach. Christ left us this example; Luke speaks about it: "The things Jesus began to do and to teach." Psalms pertain to works, and the read-

doctrinam; unde, si Dominus dederit, apertius in sequenti-
28 bus parati sumus dicere. In praesenti cursu precamur Dei
adiutorium ad opera agenda. Operemur primo, et postea
doceamus in cursum tertiae orae. Qua de re, ut opinor, mos
inolevit, ut per monasteria Deo devota legatur lectio in capitulo, quatinus hi qui diebus ac noctibus occupati sunt in
servitio Domini non sint sine lectione. Avidi sunt caelestis
pabuli; non se possunt continere, quin omni ora, quantum-
cumque sit, manducent de cibo scripturarum.

# 3

# De Tertia

Tres orae diei nobis initiatae sunt ad adorandum Deum a
Danihele propheta. De quibus ita scriptum est in libro eius:
"Quod cum Danihel comperisset, id est constituta legum,
ingressus est in domum suam, et fenestris apertis in caena-
culo suo contra Hierusalem, tribus temporibus in die flecte-
bat genua sua" [Dan 6:10]. Unde Hieronimus in explana-
tione eiusdem libri: "Tria autem tempora quibus Deo
flectenda sunt genua: tertiam oram et sextam et nonam,
ecclesiastica traditio intellegit. Denique tertia ora descendit super apostolos Spiritus Sanctus; sexta volens Petrus

ing to teaching; and so, if the Lord grants it, we are prepared
to speak more fully about this in a subsequent passage. In   28
the present office we ask for God's help in doing our work.
Let us work first, and then let us teach in the office for
the third hour. For this reason, I think, in monasteries devoted to God, the custom developed of reading in chapter,
so that those who are occupied with the Lord's service day
and night might not be without the reading. They are hungry for heavenly nourishment; they cannot keep themselves
from eating the food of the scriptures at every hour, whenever it is.

# 3

# On Terce

Daniel the prophet established three hours of the day for
us to adore God. In his book it is written about them as follows: "Now when Daniel knew this, that is to say the estab-
lishments of the laws, he went into his house, and open-
ing the windows in his upper chamber toward Jerusalem, he
knelt down three times a day." Thus Jerome in his explanation of the same book: "Ecclesiastical tradition recognizes
three times when we should kneel before God: the third
hour and the sixth and the ninth. For at the third hour the
Holy Spirit descended upon the apostles; at the sixth, Peter

comedere, ad orationem ascendit in caenaculum; nona Petrus et Iohannes pergebant ad templum" [Acts 2:15, 10:9, 3:1].✠

2     His ita perlectis, invenimus in libro Esdrae, qui post Danihelem fuit, quater in die populum Dei adorasse Dominum et confessum esse peccata sua. Ita enim scriptum est in memorato libro: "Convenerunt filii Israhel in ieiunio et saccis et humus super eos. At separatum est semen filiorum Israhel ab omni filio alienigenae. Et steterunt et confitebantur peccata sua et iniquitates patrum suorum. Et consurrexerunt ad standum, et legerunt in volumine legis Domini Dei sui quater in die, et quater confitebantur et adorabant Dominum 3 Deum suum" [2 Ezra 9:1–2]. Unde Beda sic in tractatu memorati libri: "Quis enim non miretur tantum populum tam eximiam habuisse curam pietatis, ut quater in die—hoc est primo mane, tertia ora, sexta et nonam, quibus orationi sive psalmodiae vacandum erat—auditui se legis divinae contraderent, quo innovata in Deum mente purior ac devotior ad deprecandum eius misericordiam rediret; sed et nocte quater excusso torpore somni ad confitenda peccata sua et postulandum veniam exurgeret. Quorum exemplo reor in ecclesia morem inolevisse pulcherrimum, ut per singulas diurnae psalmodiae horas lectio una de Veteri sive Novo Testamento cunctis audientibus ex corde dicatur; et sic, apostolicis sive propheticis confirmati verbis, ad instantiam orationis genu flectant; sed et oris nocturnis, cum a laboribus cessatur operum, liberas auditui lectionum divinarum aures accommodent."✠

wanted to eat and went up to the dining room for prayer; and at the ninth, Peter and John went into the temple."✝

Having read these things, we find in the book of Ezra, 2 which was written after Daniel, that the people of God adored the Lord and confessed their sins four times a day. For thus it is written in the aforementioned book: "The children of Israel came together with fasting and with sackcloth and earth upon them. But the seed of the children of Israel separated itself from every son of a foreign woman. And they stood and confessed their sins and the iniquities of their fathers. And they rose up to stand, and they read in the book of the law of the Lord their God four times in the day, and four times they confessed and adored the Lord their God." Thus Bede, in his treatise on the afore- 3 mentioned book: "And who is not amazed that this great people had such enormous concern for piety, that four times a day—namely at the first hour of morning, the third hour, the sixth and the ninth, which were set aside for prayer and psalmody—they gave themselves over to hearing the divine law, that their minds might be renewed in God and that they might return purer and more devout to beg for his mercy; and also that they rose four times at night, casting off the torpor of sleep, to confess their sins and beg forgiveness. I think it was after their example that the most beautiful custom developed in our church of pronouncing one reading from the Old or the New Testament at each of the hours of daytime psalmody, while everyone listens from the heart. In this way, they may kneel for prayer encouraged by apostolic and prophetic words; but also during the night hours, when there is a ceasing from the labors of work, they may apply unimpeded ears to the hearing of divine readings."✝

4    Ex inspiratione qua inspiratus est domnus Beda, novimus nostrum cursum diei sive noctis habere exordium a libro Esdrae. Si enim iuxta eorum morem convenimus ad rogandum Deum, oportet nos scire quod habeamus opera murorum aedificandorum ecclesiae nostrae, sicut illi habuerunt urbis Hierusalem—et in circuitu inimicos, sicut illi habuerunt. Murus nostrae ecclesiae habet in fundamento Christum, super quod fundamentum stabiliti sunt apostoli et qui per eos crediderunt, sive credunt, seu credent. Nos sumus hodierna die in structura huius muri, qui semper aedificabitur usque ad finem mundi. Unusquisque sanctorum qui praedestinatus est a Deo ad vitam aeternam lapis est illius muri. Lapis super lapidem ponitur quando magistri ecclesiae assumunt iuniores in proprium studium ad docendum,
5    ad corrigendum et ad stabiliendum in sancta ecclesia. Habet unusquisque super se lapidem, qui laborem fraternum portat. De ipso aedificio dicit Apostolus: "Alter alterius onera portate, et sic adimplebitis legem Christi" [Gal 6:2]. Grossiores lapides ac politi seu quadrati qui ponuntur altrinsecus foris, quorum in medio iacent lapides minores, perfectiores viri sunt, qui continent infirmiores discipulos sive fratres in sancta ecclesia suis monitis atque orationibus.
6    Stabilitas enim muri sine cemento non potest esse. Cementum enim construitur calce et sabulo atque aqua. Calx enim fervens caritas est quae sibi coniungit sabulum, id est terrenum opus de quo dicit Paulus: "Magis autem laboret, operando manibus suis quod bonum est, ut habeat unde tribuat necessitatem patienti" [Eph 4:28]. Caritas enim vera

From the inspiration that inspired Bede, we know that 4 our day and night offices have their origin with the book of Ezra. For if we gather to beseech God according to the custom of that people, we should know that we have the task of building the walls of our church, just as they had the task of building the city of Jerusalem—and we have enemies all around us, just as they had. The wall of our church has Christ at its foundation, and on this foundation the apostles and those who believed, believe or will believe through them, have been established. Every day we are at the construction of this wall, which will always be under construction until the end of the world. Each of the saints who was predestined by God for eternal life is a stone in this wall. Stone is placed upon stone when the teachers of the church take those who are younger into their own school, to teach, correct and establish them in the holy church. Everyone who 5 bears the labor of his brothers has a stone upon himself. The Apostle speaks about this structure: "Bear one another's burdens, and so you shall fulfill the law of Christ." The larger stones that are polished and squared and placed on the outside and the inside, while their lesser stones lie in the middle, are the more perfect men, who hold together their weaker disciples or brothers in the holy church through their advice and prayers.

Now a wall cannot be stable without cement. And ce- 6 ment is made from lime and sand and water. Lime is the burning charity that joins itself to sand, or the earthly labor that Paul speaks about: "But rather let him labor, working with his hands the thing which is good, that he may have something to give to him that suffers need." For true charity

sollicitudinem maximam habet pro viduis et confectis aetate atque aegritudine, sive pupillis seu debilibus, ac ideo
7   studet operari manibus, ut habeat unde eis bene faciat. Recolit dicta Salomonis: "Honora Dominum de tua substan-
tia" [Prov 3:9]. Et iterum: "Redemptio animae viri propriae
divitiae" [Prov 13:8]. Ut enim calx et terra valeat ad aedificium muri, aquae commixtione glutinantur. Aqua Spiritus
Sanctus est, dicente Evangelista Iohanne: "Fluent de ventre
eius aquae vivae. Hoc enim dicebat de spiritu" [John 7:38–
39], et reliqua. Sicut enim sine cemento lapides muri non
iunguntur simul ad stabilitatem muri, sic nec homines ad
aedificium caelestis Hierusalem possunt simul coniungi sine
caritate quam Spiritus Sanctus operatur.

8   Aedificantibus nobis hunc murum asunt Sanabalat et Tobias et Arabes et Amanitae et Azoti, qui volunt impedire
opus nostrum. Per nominatos gentiles videmus diabolum
impugnare nobiscum armis suis, quae sunt vitia sive pravi
homines. At nos iuxta morem populi Iudaici teneamus arma
nostra manibus nostris, et defendamus nos de inimicis nos-
9   tris, clamantes ad Deum. Ita enim scriptum est in libro memorato Esdrae: "Et oravimus Dominum Deum nostrum, et
posuimus custodes super murum die et nocte contra eos."
Et paulo post: "Et factum est a die illa, media pars iuvenum
eorum faciebat opus, et media parata erat ad bellum, et lan-
ceae et scuta et arcus et loricae, et principes post eos in
omni domo Iuda" [2 Ezra 4:9, 16] et reliqua. Nostra arma
sunt protectio Dei. Per scutum fidei et galeam salutis et gla-
dium verbi protegimur.

has the greatest solicitude for widows and those weakened by age and sickness, together with orphans and the infirm, and it therefore strives to work with its hands, to have the means of doing good for these people. It recalls the sayings 7 of Solomon: "Honor the Lord with your substance." And again: "The ransom of a man's life are his riches." And so that lime and earth may be strong enough to build the wall, they are made glutinous by mixture with water. Water is the Holy Spirit, as John the Evangelist says: "Out of his belly shall flow rivers of living water. Now this he said of the spirit," and so forth. For just as the stones of a wall are not joined to make the wall stable without cement, so too are men unable to be joined together for the construction of the heavenly Jerusalem without the charity that the Holy Spirit brings about.

Sanaballat and Tobias and Arabs and Ammonites and Az- 8 otians, all of whom want to obstruct our work, are with us as we build this wall. Through these named gentiles we see the devil fight us with his weapons, which are vices and evil men. Let us, however, keep our weapons in our hands in the manner of the Jewish people, and let us defend ourselves from our enemies, crying out to God. For thus it is written in 9 the aforementioned book of Ezra: "And we prayed to our God and set watchmen upon the wall day and night against them." And a little later: "And it came to pass from that day forward, that half of their young men did the work, and half were ready to fight, along with spears and shields and bows and coats of mail, and the rulers were behind them in all the house of Judah," and so forth. Our armor is God's protection. We are protected through the shield of faith and the helmet of salvation and the sword of the word.

10    Haec teneamus in mente quando sumus congregati simul, et princeps noster sit nobiscum vice Christi, qui dicat: "Deus, in adiutorium meum intende" [Ps 69:2], et doceat nos per lectionem et muniat per orationem suam. Quis scit si sic poterimus evadere de manibus inimicorum nostrorum? Inerant etiam tam studiosi viri in memorato populo Dei, ut una manu arma tenerent pro defensione, alteraque murum facerent. Ita sint et manus nostrae intentionis porrectae, quatinus una resistatur inimicus et altera agatur bo-

11    num opus. Eadem enim resonant aliqui versus de Tertia. In prima periocha dicit versus: "Et respondebo exprobrantibus mihi verbum, quia speravi in sermonibus tuis" [Ps 118:42]. In secunda dicit: "Superbi inique agebant usquequaque; a lege autem tua non declinavi" [Ps 118:51]. Tertia ita: "Multiplicata est super me iniquitas superborum; ego autem in toto corde scrutabor mandata tua" [Ps 118:69].

12    Quid velint tres repetitiones in cursu Tertiae in Prima monstratum est—hoc est ut hic protegamur per tres oras, usque dum iterum conveniatur una (scilicet per tertiam et quartam et quintam); ita tamen ut pertingamus ad sextam cursu orae tertiae, et intrante sexta inchoemus alterum cursum. Si Dominus voluerit, "qui solem suum oriri facit super bonos et malos" [Matt 5:45], dare nobis ut aliquid digne possimus hic dicere de varietate quae fit in cursibus—id est de psalmodia et lectionibus et responsoriis ac versibus—forte

Let us remember these things when we are gathered to-  10
gether, and let our leader be with us in the place of Christ,
saying: "O God, come to my assistance," and let him teach
us through the reading and fortify us through his prayer.
Who knows if we will be able to escape the hands of our enemies in this way? There were also men among the aforementioned people of God who were so zealous that they
held weapons for their defense in one hand, and with the
other they built the wall. So too are the hands of our attention stretched forth, that with one the enemy may be re-
sisted and with the other good work may be done. For some  11
of the verses from Terce proclaim this very thing. In the first
section a verse says: "So shall I answer them that reproach
me, that I have trusted in your words." In the second, one
says: "The proud did iniquitously altogether, but I declined
not from your law." The third, as follows: "The iniquity of
the proud has been multiplied over me, but I will seek your
commandments with my whole heart."

The point of these three sections in the office of Terce  12
was shown in our discussion of Prime—that is, that here we
may be protected through the three hours (that is, through
the third and the fourth and the fifth) until we meet for the
next hour, and so that we may reach the sixth hour through
the office of the third hour, and upon entering the sixth, we
may embark upon another office. If the Lord, "who makes
his sun rise upon the good and bad," wishes to grant us the
ability to say something worthwhile here about the variation that arises in these offices—with respect, that is, to
the psalmody and the readings and responsories and the

13 in sequentibus libere incedemus. Dicit Paulus ad Ephesios: "Propter quod nolite effici inprudentes, sed intellegentes quae sit voluntas Dei; nolite inebriari vino, in quo est luxuria, sed implemini spiritu, loquentes vobismet ipsis in psalmis et ymnis et canticis spiritalibus, cantantes et psallentes
14 in cordibus vestris Domino" [Eph 5:17–19]. Ut de expositione sancti Hieronimi mihi monstratum est, tres mutationes nostri cursus in istis tribus praeceptis apostolicis intellego compleri—videlicet, ut psalmi sint in nostra locutione quando Psalmos cantamus, et ymni quando ex lectione dictorum sanctorum patrum ad laudes Dei compungimur, et cantica quando per cantum responsorii nostra mens sublevatur aliqua laetitia ad concentum supernae patriae. Cantus enim saepissime in laetitia celebratur. Sanctorum mens non habet maiorem laetitiam, quam ut per anagogen sublevetur ad caeleste regnum.

15 Ipsius memorati summi doctoris verba ponenda sunt, ut eius auctoritate figatur in mente audientium quod cupimus disserere. "Quid," inquit, "intersit inter psalmum, ymnum et canticum, in Psalterio plenissime discimus. Hic autem breviter ymnos esse dicendum qui fortitudinem et maiestatem praedicant Dei, et eiusdem semper vel beneficia vel facta mirantur; quod omnes Psalmi continent quibus alleluia vel
16 praepositum vel subiectum est. Psalmi autem proprie ad ethicum locum pertinent, ut per organum corporis quid faciendum et quid vitandum sit noverimus. Qui vero de superioribus disputat, et conventum mundi omniumque creaturarum ordinem atque concordiam subtilis disputator
17 edisserit—iste spirituale canticum canit."✝ Opus psalterii,

versicles—perhaps we will go there openly in what follows. Paul says to the Ephesians: "Wherefore become not unwise, 13 but understanding what is the will of God; be not drunk with wine, wherein is luxury, but be filled with the spirit, speaking to yourselves in psalms and hymns and spiritual canticles, singing and making melody in your hearts to the Lord." As I learned from Saint Jerome's commentary, I rec- 14 ognize that the three modes of celebration of our office are realized in these three apostolic precepts—namely, that there are psalms in our speech when we sing Psalms, and hymns when we are driven to God's praises through reading the sayings of the holy fathers, and canticles when our mind is elevated with joy to the harmony of the heavenly country by singing the responsory. For song is most often practiced in joy. The mind of the saints has no greater joy than being elevated, through anagogy, to the heavenly kingdom.

We should quote the words of this aforementioned su- 15 preme teacher, that what we want to explain may be fixed in the minds of our listeners through his authority: "We learn most fully in the Psalter," he says, "about the difference between a psalm, a hymn and a canticle. Here, however, we should say briefly that hymns are those things that preach the strength and majesty of God and forever marvel over his favors and deeds. All psalms that are either preceded or followed by an alleluia do this. Properly, though, psalms have a moral subject, to let us know what we should do and what we should avoid with the instrument of our body. And he who investigates higher things and sets forth as a subtle examiner the concord, order and harmony of the world and all creation—he sings a spiritual canticle."+ The operation of 17

quod manu percutitur, ut resonet, ad opera nostra pertinet; opera sanctorum sunt mores boni quos exercemus, sive in profectione spiritalis itineris sive in occisione carnalium voluptatum. Hi enim mores sine labore non possunt exerceri. Quapropter, quando Psalmos cantamus, solemus stare. Ex statu corporis demonstramus effectum mentis nostrae—hoc est paratos nos esse sive ad domandam carnem nostram seu ad exercitium operis, in causa nostra et fratrum.

18    Post istam tropologicam locutionem (id est quae de moribus disputat), subsequitur lectio, in qua illa reperiuntur quae sanctus Hieronimus deputavit ymnis, id est quae ad laudem Dei pertinent. Ibi maiestatem Domini invenimus—quomodo incircumscriptus omnia in se contineat; ibi fortitudinem eius—quomodo creatum populum suum redimat in forti manu et brachio extento; ibi beneficia eius—quomodo ipsum quem redemit ditet omnibus bonis; ibi facta eius—quomodo fecit caelum et terram et mare et omnia

19    quae in eis sunt. In illa non deest historia; non deest allegoria; non deest tropologia; non deest anagogen—quamvis tropologia seorsum celebretur, ut praetulimus, in Psalmis. In tropologia Psalmorum nostra opera recolimus, et in tropologia lectionum aliorum. Non enim in Domini maiestate sive in sua fortitudine seu in beneficiis vel factis laboramus; quapropter solemus sedere in recitatione lectionis, aut silendo stare.

20    In responsoriis namque solemus vocem altius levare quam in superioribus, id est Psalmis et ymnis. Per altitudinem vocis altitudinem mentis monstramus, quae se erigit in

the psaltery, which is struck by the hand, that it may resound, pertains to our works; the works of the saints are the
virtues that we practice, whether in the progress of our spiritual journey or when we experience desires of the flesh. For
these virtues cannot be practiced without labor. Thus, when
we sing Psalms, it is our custom to stand. Through our
bodily posture we show the resolve of our mind—namely,
that we are prepared both to dominate our flesh and to perform work, for the sake of ourselves and our brothers.

After this tropological statement (that is, one dealing 18
with virtues), a reading follows in which are found things
that Saint Jerome ascribed to hymns, namely things that
pertain to God's praise. There we find the Lord's majesty—
how, though infinite, he contains everything within himself; there we find his strength—how he redeems his created
people in a strong hand and an outstretched arm; there we
find his favors—how he enriches the one he redeems with
all goods; there we find his deeds—how he made heaven and
earth and the sea and all the things that are in it. History is 19
not absent from the reading; allegory is not absent; tropology is not absent; anagogy is not absent—although tropology is celebrated separately, as we said above, in the Psalms.
In the tropology of the Psalms we remember our works, and
in the tropology of the readings we remember the works of
others. For we do not labor for the Lord's majesty or for his
strength or for his favors or deeds; we are therefore accustomed to sit during the reading, or to stand in silence.

And during the responsories it is our custom to raise our 20
voice more highly than during what preceded, that is during the Psalms and hymns. Through the elevation of our
voice we show the elevation of our mind, which rises to the

gaudium supernae civitatis. Post bona opera et refectionem mentis de sancta scriptura, sequitur gaudium caeleste. Cur

21 responsorius dicatur, in scriptione missae dictum est. Responsorium in isto loco canticis spiritalibus comparamus; cantica sunt quia cantantur, spiritalia quia procedunt ex iubilatione spiritalis mentis. Alia enim sunt cantica quae de singulari munere gaudent, ut sunt ea de quibus scripsimus in baptysterio, ubi gaudium tripudiat neofytorum de singulari innocentia, quibus nemo respondet; et alia sunt ista, quibus unusquisque alterum incitat ad mansiones caelestes, quae multae sunt in domo patris. Quid versus significet responsorii in memorato officio Missae descripsimus — hoc est ut duo sint in ecclesiastico viro, scilicet exortatio ad fratres et singularis deprecatio ad Deum.

22 *Gloria* subsequitur in anagogico officio. Nulli dubium quod nullo in loco tanta gloria referatur Deo, quanta in coetu sanctorum angelorum et eorum sanctorum qui in conspectu Domini sunt. In istis lectionibus — scilicet diurnalibus — non petitur benedictio a maiore, quoniam maior cantat eas, qui solet vicem Christi tenere in ecclesia. Hoc interest inter has lectiones et illam quae ad Missam caelebratur, quod est inter domesticam ammonitionem et il-

23 lam quae ad contionem agitur. Illam enim quam ad Missam agimus ex gradu solemus proferre, ut omnis populus eam audiat. Quam praetulimus in officio de baptysterio

joy of the eternal city. After good works and the restoration of our mind through holy scripture, there follows celestial joy. In discussing the Mass we explained why this is called a responsory. In that place, we compare the responsory to 21 spiritual canticles; responsories are canticles because they are sung, and spiritual because they proceed from the jubilation of a spiritual mind. For there are some canticles that take joy in a particular gift, like those that we wrote about in our discussion of baptism, where our joy dances in the singular innocence of the neophytes; no one responds to these. And there are others in which each urges the other to the heavenly mansions, which are many in the father's house. We described what the verse of the responsory signifies in our aforementioned discussion of the office of the Mass— that is, that there are two things in the man of the church, namely an exhortation to his brothers and a particular prayer to God.

The *Gloria* follows in our anagogical office. Surely such 22 glory is rendered to God nowhere as much as among the gathering of the holy angels and the saints who are in the Lord's sight. In these readings—that is, those during the day—blessing is not sought from the greater one, because the greater one, whose practice is to play the role of Christ in church, sings these. The difference between these readings and that which is celebrated during Mass is the same as the difference between advice offered within a household and that which is offered before an assembly. For we are accustomed to proclaim the reading at 23 Mass from the step, that all the people may hear it. We said earlier in our discussion of the office of baptism,

propter statum temporis, id est diei, ad sapientes fieri. In qua et auctor ad memoriam reducitur, ut si forte aliquis eorum qui congregantur ex universis locis, propter raritatem lectionis incognitam habet historiam—audiat auctorem, qui forte non est incognitus, et ex eius auctoritate firmius infigantur verba lectionis in corde (qui tamen sapientes esse

24 possunt propter rectam conversationem). At hi qui semper in ecclesiasticis rebus insistunt et in lectione divina, ut sunt domestici ecclesiae, non habent necesse audire auctorem, quia ex lectione cognoscunt auctorem. Ut legimus in Esdra [2 Ezra 9:1–2], quattuor lectiones fiebant in die ab antiquo populo Dei, et merito quattuor, quia quattuor elementis constat homo—ut unumquodque elementum per competentes horas se offerat creatori suo.

25 Primam namque iuxta morem nostrum praetulimus sine lectione. Si illa non habuerit lectionem, non erunt nostrae lectiones tot quot fuerunt in illo antiquo populo Dei. Quapropter procuratum est a sanctis patribus ut in capitulo legeretur illa lectio quae silentio praetermissa est in Prima. Et non frustra ibi praetermissa est, sed, quoniam pastor loci doctorem vult insinuare, ideo ibi praetermittit suam doctrinam, ut doceat unumquemque doctorem primo oportere operari et postea docere. De qua dicit Moyses in libro Deuteronomii: "Non arabis in primogenito bovis" [Deut 15:19].

26 Potest etiam in istis tribus varietatibus omne genus musicorum accipi quod antiquus populus exercebat in laude Dei. Triformis est natura musicae artis; aut enim per

that this Mass reading pertains to the wise because of when it takes place, namely during the day. During it the author of the reading is also noted, so that if perhaps someone among those who have gathered from all manner of places (and who can nevertheless be considered wise because of his upright way of life) does not know the story because the reading rarely occurs—he may hear the author, who is perhaps not unknown to him, and through this author's authority the words of the reading may be fixed more firmly in his heart. But those who are always present for ecclesiastical rites and 24 the divine reading, as are the servants of the church, do not need to hear the author, because they recognize the author from the reading. As we read in Ezra, there were four readings a day among the ancient people of God, and it was appropriate that there were four, since man consists of four elements—that each element might offer itself to its creator at the appropriate hours.

Now we said above that it is our custom to have no read- 25 ing at Prime. If it has no reading, the number of our readings will not be as great as the number among that ancient people of God. It was therefore established by the holy fathers that the reading that was passed over in silence during Prime should be read in chapter. And there it was not passed over in vain; rather, since the pastor at that point wishes to suggest the figure of a teacher, he omits his teaching to teach that every teacher should first work and then teach. Moses speaks about this in the book of Deuteronomy: "You shall not work with the firstling of a bullock."

In these three variations we can also recognize each kind 26 of musical instrument that the ancient people employed in God's praise. The nature of musical art is threefold; it

pulsum digitorum fit, ut in psalterio et cythara et ceteris vasis quae pulsu digitorum tanguntur; aut per vocem, ut est
27 cantus; aut per flatum, sicut est in tubis. Haec tria memorantur in Psalterio. Dicit Psalmus tricesimus secundus:
"Confitemini Domino in cithara; in psalterio decem corda-
rum psallite illi. Cantate ei canticum novum; bene psallite ei
in vociferatione" [Ps 32:2–3]. Et iterum in Psalmo tertio:
"Voce mea ad Dominum clamavi" [Ps 3:5]. Ita in Psalmo centesimo quinquagesimo: "Laudate eum in sono tubae, laudate
eum in psalterio et cithara, laudate eum in tympano et coro,
laudate eum in cordis et organo, laudate eum in cymbalis
bene sonantibus" [Ps. 150:3–5], et reliqua. Quando enim
Psalmos cantamus, genus musicae exercemus quod fit per
pulsum digitorum. Nam et Psalterii volumen accepit nomen
a psalterio musicae artis.

28    Quando legimus, genus illud exercemus quod per vocem
fit. Lectionem "voces" vocavit Apostolus Paulus in Actibus
Apostolorum: "Ignorantes," inquit, "Iesum et voces prophetarum, quae per omne Sabbatum leguntur" [Acts 13:27].
Quando responsorios cantamus, quasi per tubam exaltamus
vocem excitando ad altiora fratres, usque adeo ut pervenia-
tur ad laudem sanctae Trinitatis, et dicamus: "Gloria Patri,
29 Filio, et Spiritui Sancto." Quanto enim melius est corpus
nostrum vasis musicis, quae aedificabantur per homines,
tanto acceptius est Deo obsequium in tempore isto, quam

occurs either through the movement of the fingers, as in the psaltery and the cithara and the other instruments that are plucked with a stroke of the fingers; or through the voice, as is the case with song; or through blowing, as is the case with trumpets. These three are commemorated in the Psalter. Psalm 32 says: "Give praise to the Lord on the harp; sing to him with the psaltery, the instrument of ten strings. Sing to him a new canticle; sing well unto him with a loud noise." And again, in Psalm 3: "I have cried to the Lord with my voice." In Psalm 150, as follows: "Praise him with sound of trumpet, praise him with psaltery and harp, praise him with timbrel and choir, praise him with strings and organ, praise him on high sounding cymbals," and so forth. For when we sing Psalms, we perform the sort of music that arises from the movement of fingers. And indeed, the Psalter received its name from the psaltery of musical art. 27

When we read, we perform the kind of music that occurs through the voice. Paul the Apostle called the reading "voices" in the Acts of the Apostles: "Not knowing Jesus," he said, "nor the voices of the prophets, which are read every Sabbath." When we sing responsories, we raise our voice as if through a trumpet by urging our brothers on to higher things, until we arrive at the praise of the Holy Trinity and say: "Glory to the Father and to the Son and to the Holy Spirit." For our body is better than man-made musical instruments to the same degree that our request to God is more acceptable in this age than it was in that prior one. 28 29

esset in prisco. Et quanto melior est lex libertatis quae est per gratiam Novi Testamenti, lege servitutis, tanto dignius est ut in proprio corpore habeamus laudes, quas illi semper et ubique referamus, quam in ligneis vasis et aereis.

30     Hic iterum cupimus dicere de versu. Versus hanc vim habet, ut converti corum totum faciat ad unum, atque totam intentionem illius ad rem pro qua agitur officium. Sicuti est primo mane: "Exsurge, Domine, adiuva nos et libera nos propter nomen tuum" [Ps 43:26]—ac si dicat: Exsurgere nos fac, Domine, ad opera, et adiuva virtute brachii tui ad operandum, et libera de insidiis quae paratae sunt contra nos.

31     Hanc petitionem intentio mentis debet in se retinere in officio Primae, at hic in Tertia dicit versus: "Adiutor meus esto, ne derelinquas me; neque despicias me, Deus salutaris meus" [Ps 26:9]—ac si dicat: Adiuvisti usque ad praesens tempus, adiuva et deinceps. Nondum pervenimus ad id quo tendimus—id est ad meridiem, in quo tu pascis, in quo tu accubas, iuxta Cantica Canticorum [Song 1:6]. Ne derelinquas nos in isto itinere; neque despicias nos, Deus salutaris noster. Deinde sequitur *Kyrie eleison* et *Christe eleison.*

And the law of freedom that we have through the grace of the New Testament is better than the law of servitude to the same degree that it is worthier for us to have praises in our own body that we offer to God always and everywhere, than it would be to have them in wooden and copper vessels.

Here again we wish to discuss the versicle. The versicle 30 has the power to convert the whole chorus into one, and to turn its full attention to the reason we celebrate the office. And so, during the first hour, the versicle is: "Arise, Lord, help us and redeem us for your name's sake"—as if to say: Make us rise, Lord, to our work, and help us to work through the strength of your arm, and free us from the snares that have been laid against us. Our mind's attention should hold 31 onto this petition during the office of Prime, but here in Terce, the versicle says: "Be my helper, forsake me not; do not despise me, God my savior"—as if to say: You have helped us to the present moment; help us from now on. We have not yet arrived where we are going—that is, at noon, when you offer food and when you recline according to the Song of Songs. Do not leave us on this road; do not despise us, God our savior. The *Kyrie eleison* and *Christe eleison* then follow.

# 4

## De oratione quam conventus fratrum celebrat per aliquot cursus diurnos nocturnosque

Est sacerdos in terra, cui necesse est cotidie pro se et pro populo Dei intercedere; est sacerdos in caelo, cui non est necesse intercedere, sed tamen vult, et interpellat cotidie pro nobis. Sacerdos qui est in terra non vult neque potest dicere quod absque peccato sit, dicente Iohanne: "Si dixerimus quoniam peccatum non habemus, nos ipsos seducimus et veritas in nobis non est" [1 John 1:8]. Qui tamen, quamvis sit peccator, non debet a conscientia sua morderi, ut tantum sit peccator quantum multos cognoscit esse in populo terrae. Qui populus in aliquibus est minus obligatus peccatis, in aliquibus magis. Pro his qui minora committunt et pro se orat sacerdos quando dicit *Kyrie eleison* et orationem Dominicam, in qua nemo potest se excusare nisi veraciter dicat: "Et dimitte nobis debita nostra" [Matt 6:12].

3    Dein prosequitur sacerdos modum orationis quem Paulus dinumerat, dicens: "Obsecrationes, orationes, postolationes, gratiarum actiones" [1 Tim 2:1], et cetera quae sequuntur. Unde dicit Ambrosius in tractatu suo super eandem epistolam: "Ante omnia," inquit, "illud obsecro, quod vel maxime vos scire operis esse debet, ut convenientes scire possitis quid fieri conveniens sit. Dicit autem orationes,

## 4

# On the prayer that the community of brethren celebrates on certain day and night offices

There is a priest on earth who must intercede for himself and for God's people every day; there is a priest in heaven who does not have to intercede, but wants to nevertheless, and he intervenes for us every day. The priest who is on earth cannot and does not want to say that he is without sin, as John says: "If we say that we have no sin, we deceive ourselves and the truth is not in us." Yet, though he is a sinner, he should not be troubled by pangs of conscience, inasmuch as he is a sinner to the same degree as he recognizes many on earth to be. People are less burdened by sin in some respects, and more burdened by sin in others. The priest prays for those who commit lesser sins and for himself when he says the *Kyrie eleison* and the Lord's prayer, in which nobody can excuse himself unless he speaks truthfully: "And forgive us our debts."

Then the priest follows the method of prayer that Paul lays out, saying: "Supplications, prayers, intercessions, thanksgivings," and so forth as follows. Thus speaks Ambrose in his treatise on the same epistle: "Above all," he says, "I ask about that portion of your work that you should know above all: that when you gather together you may be able to know what it is proper to do. And he speaks

obsecrationes, postulationes." Et post pauca: "Aut enim bona nobis a Deo dari postolamus, quod orationes vocavit; aut malorum solutionem, quod obsecrationes nuncupavit."

4 Et iterum post pauca: "Illa vero quae ad hoc nobis sunt contraria, multa sunt et assidua—unum quidem, daemonum subreptio varie nos a bono avertere cupit, alterum vero, molestia passionum quae nobis inesse videtur. A quibus et a bonis exclusi contra nostrum propositum, sepe in illis quae nobis non conveniunt, concludimur. Sed necessarium est nos, qui multam super hoc pugnam sustinemus, ad Deum recurrere, qui potens est suo auxilio sedare universa illa quae ad nostram pertinent molestiam. Hoc postolationem dixit."

5 Et iterum infra: "Gratiarum vero actio pro his quae iam praestita sunt, efficitur, et pro quibus haec fieri conveniant doceris: 'Pro omnibus hominibus.' In commune pro omnibus hominibus debere eos sollicitos esse praecepit." Et iterum infra: "Deinde ad illa quae summa esse videntur inter homines, transit: 'Pro regibus,' inquit, 'et omnibus qui in sublimitate sunt' [1 Tim 2:2]. Nostri enim codices habent primo obsecrationes, et postea orationes."✝

6 Hunc ordinem sequitur nostra oratio. Primus versus post orationem Dominicam est "Ego dixi: Domine, miserere mei; sana animam meam, quia peccavi tibi" [Ps 40:5]. In hoc versu obsecratio est, per quam precatur absolutio malorum. Quando dicit: "Sana animam meam, quia peccavi tibi," medicinam Domini precatur, ut a languore absolvatur. Sit secundus versus: "Ostende nobis, Domine, misericordiam tuam, et salutare tuum da nobis" [Ps 84:8]. In eo versu bona
7 nobis postolamus, quod pertinet ad orationem. Sit tertius:

of prayers, supplications, and intercessions." And after a little: "Or indeed we ask that good things be granted us by God, which he called prayers; or for release from evils, which he termed supplications." And again, after a little: "But those things that are opposed to us in this, are many and incessant—on the one hand, demonic deceit wants to turn us in various ways away from the good, while on the other hand, there is the vexation of the passions that seem to be within us. By these we are cut off from good things against our purpose and restrained, often in things that are unsuitable for us. But as we endure a great battle on this account, we must run to God, who is powerful enough to put everything relating to our vexation to rest, through his assistance. He called this postulation." And again, further on: "And thanksgiving is made on behalf of those things that have already been given, and you are taught for whom these things are appropriate: 'For all men.' He ordered them to take responsibility for all men, in common." And again, further on: "Then he moves on to those things that seem most important among men: 'For kings,' he says, 'and for all that are in high station.' Now our manuscripts list supplications first, then prayers."✝

Our prayer follows this order. The first versicle after the Lord's prayer is "I said: Lord, be merciful to me; heal my soul, for I have sinned against you." In this versicle there is supplication, through which we request release from evil. When it says: "Heal my soul, for I have sinned against you," it requests the Lord's medicine, that the soul may be released from its weakness. Let there be a second versicle: "Show us, Lord, your mercy, and grant us your salvation." In this versicle we request good things for ourselves, which pertains to prayer. Let there be a third:

ON THE LITURGY

"Convertere, Domine—usquequo? Et deprecabilis esto super servos tuos" [Ps 89:13]. In eo versu postolamus ut omnia contraria bonis nostris superentur per Domini auxilium; hoc pertinet ad postolationem. De quo versu dicit Agustinus in tractatu suo super Psalmos: "'Convertere, Domine—usquequo? Et deprecabilis esto super servos tuos.' Vox est eorum vel pro eis qui multa persequente isto saeculo mala tolerantes innotescunt 'compediti corde in sapientia' [Ps 89:12]—ut nec tantis malis coacti refugiant a Domino ad huius saeculi bona." Sit quartus: "Confiteantur tibi, Domine" [Ps 144:10]—qui pertinet ad gratiarum actiones.✝

8    Hucusque oratum est secundum Apostolum "pro omnibus hominibus." Dein sequitur "pro regibus et omnibus qui in sublimitate sunt, ut quietam et tranquillam vitam agamus in omni pietate et castitate" [1 Tim 2:1–2].

9    Quoniam sunt intra nostram ecclesiam qui minima committunt, pro his tamen necesse est praecedens oratio. Sunt et qui maiora, pro quibus necesse est addere Psalmum: *Miserere mei, Deus* [Ps 50], qui proprie pertinet ad paenitentes. Alio modo: Oratio praecedens pro minimis peccatis; Psalmus fit pro maximis.

10    Postremo surgit sacerdos, vice illius sacerdotis qui in caelo est et cotidie interpellat pro nobis; et dicit stando orationem. Haec oratio in omni tempore subsequitur, id est Paschali, Pentecostes, Dominicis diebus et festis, ut resurrectionem recolat eius sacerdotis cuius vicem tenet. Surgit ab accubitu et stando dicit hanc orationem, qui tamen prius

344

"Return, O Lord—how long? And be entreated in favor of your servants." In this versicle we ask that all things opposed to what is good for us be overcome through the Lord's help; this pertains to intercession. Augustine speaks about this verse in his treatise on the Psalms: "'Return, O Lord, how long? And be entreated in favor of your servants.' This is spoken by or on behalf of those who endure many evils through the persecution of this world, and make it known that they are 'shackled at heart in wisdom'—that they may not be overwhelmed by these evils and leave the Lord for the good things of this world." Let there be a fourth: "Let them praise you, O Lord"—which pertains to thanksgiving.✝

To this point we have prayed, according to the Apostle, 8 "for all men." We next pray "for kings and for all that are in high station, that we may lead a quiet and peaceable life in all piety and chastity."

Since there are some in our church who commit lesser 9 sins, the preceding prayer was necessary for them. There are also those who commit greater sins; for them it is necessary to add the Psalm: *Miserere mei, Deus,* which properly pertains to the penitent. Put another way: The preceding prayer is for the smallest sins; the Psalm is for the greatest.

Finally the priest stands, acting in the guise of the priest 10 who is in heaven and intercedes for us daily; and he pronounces a prayer while standing. This prayer follows in every season, namely during Easter and Pentecost, and on Sundays and feast days, to commemorate the resurrection of that priest in whose position our priest acts. He who earlier prayed while reclining with the others, now rises from

iacendo orat cum ceteris. Quoniam peccator est, cum peccatoribus prostratus est; et quia vicem tenet Christi, stando
11 dicit specialem orationem. Haec specialis oratio sacerdotum, quae quodammodo libertatem et glorificationem monstrat futuri regni, et tamen semper esse intercessorem ibi
pro nobis, per omnes memoratos dies festos currit. Reliqua
oratio reticetur, quoniam ibi peccator nullus est, neque erit.

12 Si quis voluerit dicere, quoniam haec oratio vicem tenet
interpellationis Christi (qui interpellat pro nobis cotidie Patrem), quare dicat: "Per Dominum nostrum Iesum Christum"—dicatur ei: Christus, qui est in Patre naturaliter et per
quem assumptus homo est in Deum, propter unam eandemque personam Filii Dei, hostium nobis fieri dignatus est per
quod nos et orationes nostrae et omnia bona nostra trans-
13 eant ad Patrem. Idcirco merito sacerdos dicit suam orationem ad Deum Patrem "per Dominum nostrum Iesum
Christum," quia et per illum accepit hanc gratiam, ut vicissitudinem suae interpellationis fratribus atque condiscipulis
ministret, et recolat, atque ad memoriam reducat.

14 Quam orationem praecedit salutatio et subsequitur,
benedictioque et gratiarum actio sequitur. Post resurrectionem suam Dominus salutavit discipulos; salutavit et iterum, benedixitque eos in Monte Oliveti, et illi gratias
referendo adoraverunt "in loco ubi steterunt pedes eius"
[Ps 131:7]. Quod eaedem precum orationes caelebrandae
sint Vespertina ora quae et Nona, in Laodicensi concilio
capitulo octavo decimo scriptum est: "Quod idipsum officium precum Nona et Vespera semper debeat exhiberi."✠

his chair and pronounces this prayer while standing. Because he is a sinner, he laid down with sinners; and because he acts in the guise of Christ, he pronounces this particular prayer while standing. This particular priestly prayer occurs 11 on all the aforementioned feast days; in some sense it reveals the freedom and glorification of the kingdom to come, and that an intercessor is nevertheless always there for us. The other prayer is left unsaid, because there is not, nor will there be, a sinner in that place.

Since this prayer acts in place of the intercession of 12 Christ (who intercedes daily on our behalf with the Father), if anyone wants to ask why it says: "Through our Lord Jesus Christ"—the reply to him should be: Christ, who is by nature in the Father and through whom man was assumed into God, through the selfsame person of God's Son, deigned to become the door through which we and our prayers and all our good deeds pass to the Father. It is therefore appropri- 13 ate for the priest to address his prayer to God the Father "through our Lord Jesus Christ," because through Christ he receives the grace to administer the reward of his intercession to his brothers and codisciples, that he may call it to mind and commemorate it.

A greeting precedes and follows this prayer, and a bless- 14 ing and thanksgiving follow it. After his resurrection the Lord greeted his disciples; and he greeted them a second time and blessed them on the Mount of Olives, and by thanking him they offered adoration "in the place where his feet stood." In the eighteenth chapter of the Council of Laodicea it is written that these same prayers should be celebrated at Vespers and None: "This same office of prayers should always be performed at None and Vespers."+

15 Secundum hoc capitulum in festis et in ceteris diebus uno modo caelebretur oratio in Vespertino et ora Nona. Ut reor, similiter possumus dicere de Tertia et Sexta.

16 Post Vespertinalia et Matutinalia officia quae aguntur pro mortuis, solemus cantare Psalmum, in loco *Miserere mei Deus* [Ps 50], *Domine, ne in furore tuo* [Ps 6]. Ipse est sextus in ordine Psalmorum, et tamen inscribitur pro octava, idcirco quia nos, qui in sexta aetate mundi sumus, debemus pro septima et octava aetate rogare Deum per hunc Psalmum, ut evadamus tormenta quae malis debentur in memoratis aeta-

17 tibus. De quo dicit Agustinus in prologo eiusdem Psalmi: "Veniet octavus iudicii dies, qui meritis tribuens quod debetur, iam non ad opera temporalia, sed ad vitam aeternam sanctos transferet. Impios vero damnabit in aeternum. Quam damnationem metuens orat ecclesia in hoc Psalmo,

18 dicens: 'Domine, ne in ira tua arguas me' [Ps 6:2]." Et Beda in libro *De temporibus:* "Ipsa est octava, pro qua sextus Psalmus inscribitur. Credo, quia in sex huius saeculi aetatibus pro septima vel octava huius saeculi est aetate supplicandum, in qua, quia iusti gaudia, sed reprobi sunt supplicia percepturi, Psalmus hic ingenti pavore incipit, currit, finitur: 'Domine, ne in furore tuo arguas me,'" et cetera.

According to this chapter, the prayer is to be celebrated at 15
Vespers and None in the same way on feasts and other days.
I think that we can say the same thing about Terce and Sext.

After Vespers and Matins that are celebrated for the 16
dead, it is our custom to sing the Psalm *Domine, ne in furore
tuo,* in place of *Miserere mei Deus.* This is the sixth in the order of Psalms, yet it is dedicated to the eighth age, since
we, who are in the sixth age of the world, should beseech
God through this Psalm for the seventh and the eighth ages,
that we may avoid the torments that are destined for the
wicked in these ages. Augustine, writing on the prologue of 17
the same Psalm, speaks about this: "The eighth day of judgment will come; granting what is owed according to merit,
it will no longer bring the saints to their temporal labors,
but rather to eternal life. Yet it will damn the impious for
eternity. The church fears such damnation and prays in this
Psalm, saying: 'O Lord, rebuke me not in your indignation.'"
And Bede, in his book *On Time:* "This is the eighth age, to 18
which the sixth Psalm is dedicated. I believe the reason is
that during the six ages of this world we are to supplicate for
the seventh and eighth age of the world. Because the just are
to receive joys and the reprobate punishment in those ages,
this Psalm begins, continues and ends in great fear: 'O Lord,
rebuke me not in your indignation,'" and so on.

# 5

# De Sexta

De tribus repetitionibus Sextae sive Nonae, prout potui, ministravi in cursu Primae et Tertiae, et de lectionibus atque responsoriis. Praesentes tres repetitiones statuunt nos in famulatu Domini, sive muniunt ab insidiis inimici per sextam oram et septimam et octavam—ita vero ut in Nona habeant initium reliquae tres repetitiones, quae nos perducant usque

2 ad XIIam oram diei. Restat ex statu temporis considerare versum qui dicitur ad Sextam. Status temporis est meridies, quando sol in centro caeli est et ferventissimum ardorem praestat terris. Idem status perfectionem mentium devotorum hominum monstrat, quorum fervor ita coniunctus est igni invisibili, ut ab ipso pascatur delectatione et inluminetur lumine intellegentiae. Eadem hora ascendit Petrus in caenaculum et voluit comedere [Acts 10:9].

3 In Prima sunt initia virtutum, in Tertia profectus, meridie perfectio; quam perfectionem denuntiant nobis aliqui versus cursus Sextae. Prima periocha dicit: "Defecit in salutare tuum anima mea, et in verbo tuo supersperavi. Defecerunt oculi mei in eloquium tuum, dicentes: Quando consolaberis me?" [Ps 118:81–82]. Secunda dicit: "Quomodo dilexi legem tuam, Domine? Tota die meditatio mea est" [Ps 118:97].

# 5

# On Sext

Insofar as I was able, I dealt with the three sections of Sext and None in discussing the offices of Prime and Terce, together with the readings and responsories. The present three sections establish us in the service of the Lord, and they fortify us against the snares of the enemy through the sixth and the seventh and the eighth hours—so that the remaining three sections that lead to the twelfth hour of the day may begin with None. It remains to consider the versi-  2 cle that is pronounced during Sext from the perspective of the time of day. The time of day is noon, when the sun is in the center of the sky and provides the greatest heat to the earth. This time demonstrates the perfection of the minds of devout men; the heat of these minds has been joined to invisible fire, that they might thereby be fed with pleasure and illuminated with the light of understanding. At this hour Peter wanted to eat and went up to the dining room.

The beginnings of virtues come during Prime; their  3 advancement comes at Terce; their perfection comes at noon. Various verses in the office of Sext announce this perfection to us. The first section says: "My soul has fainted after your salvation, and in your word I have very much hoped. My eyes have failed for your word, saying: When will you comfort me?" The second says: "How have I loved your law, O Lord? It is my meditation all the day."

Tertia ita: "Oculi mei defecerunt in salutare tuum et in eloquium iustitiae tuae" [Ps 118:123].

4 Statum talium mentium versus monstrat, dicens: "Dominus regit me et nihil mihi deerit. In loco pascuae ibi me collocabit" [Ps 22:1–2]. Ubi nos dicimus: "Dominus regit me," translatio quae assumpta est a sancto Hieronimo ex Ebraica

5 veritate habet: "Dominus pascit me." Quem Dominus pascit adventu spiritus sui eundem regit; id est, in illis moribus facit eum spiritus Dei delectari qui secundum rationem sunt et deducunt, per rectum iter, ad civitatem munitissimam Hierusalem. Ei nihil deest, sicut Paulus Apostolus dicit: "Omnia possum in eo qui me confortat" [Phil 4:13]. Omnia illi cooperantur secundum Deum, prospera et adversa aequanimiter tolerat, ac ideo subsequitur: "In loco pascuae, ibi me collocabit"—sive in abundantia intellectualium rerum in praesenti, sive in futuro in laetitia et gloria sempiterna, ubi erit satietas omnium gaudiorum sine fine.

# 6

# De Nona

Nona continet nos per nonam oram et decimam et undecimam. Status temporis quando Nona caelebratur designat fervorem studiorum, quem exercebat mens in altitudine virtutum, aliquantulum tepefactum esse propter

The third is as follows: "My eyes have fainted after your salvation and for the word of your justice."

The versicle reveals the state of such minds, saying: "The 4 Lord rules me and I shall want nothing. He will set me in a place of pasture." Where we say: "The Lord rules me," the translation that Saint Jerome derived from the Hebrew truth has: "The Lord feeds me." The Lord rules him whom 5 he feeds through the coming of his spirit; that is, God's spirit causes him to delight in those virtues that accord with reason and that lead, along the straight path, to the most fortified city of Jerusalem. He lacks nothing, as Paul the Apostle says: "I can do all these things in him who strengthens me." All things are combined in him according to God; he endures prosperity and adversity calmly, and so there follows: "He will set me in a place of pasture"—either in an abundance of understanding in the present, or in eternal joy and glory in the future, where there will be an overflowing of all joys without end.

# 6

# On None

None keeps us through the ninth hour and the tenth and the eleventh. The time of day when None is celebrated shows that the heat of eagerness, which the mind practiced at the height of virtues, has cooled somewhat

temptationes accidentes. Unde Gregorius in *Moralibus Iob:*
"Vitia, dum nos temptant, proficientes in nos virtutes humiliant." Sicut tunc sol descendit a centro ad inferiores partes,
ita mens, quando temptatur, descendit ab altitudine intimi
gaudii ad considerandam suam naturam atque fragilitatem,

2  et videt quam facilis sit ad occasum. Temptabatur Paulus
quando dicebat: "Ne magnitudo revelationum extollat me,
datus est mihi stimulus carnis meae, angelus Satanae, qui me
colafizet" [2 Cor 12:7]. Qua de causa temptetur electus,
praesens noster magister Paulus hic demonstrat, atque in
sequentibus molestiam quam patiebatur ex temptatione,
manifestat, dicens: "Propter quod ter Dominum rogavi, ut
discederet a me" [2 Cor 12:8]. Ut opinor, nisi ei molestiam
faceret stimulus satanae, non Deum precaretur ut discederet ab eo.

3  Eandem precationem sonant aliqui versus cursus Nonae.
Prima periocha dicit: "Tribulationes et angustiae invenerunt
me; mandata tua meditatio mea est" [Ps 118:143]. Quod ita
Agustinus in eodem Psalmo: "Seviant, persequantur, dum
tamen mandata Dei non relinquantur; et, ex ipsis mandatis,
etiam qui seviunt diligantur." Secunda dicit: "Multi qui per-
sequuntur me et tribulant me; a testimoniis tuis non declinavi" [Ps 118:157]. Tertia ita: "Erravi sicut ovis quae periit.
Require servum tuum, quia mandata tua non sum oblitus"

4  [Ps 118:176]. Versus praesentis cursus memorat temptationem, quae designatur per solis declinationem: "Ab occultis
meis," inquit, "munda me, et ab alienis parce servo tuo" [Ps
18:13–14]. Quod ita memoratus Agustinus in Psalmo octavo

through the occurrence of temptations. Thus Gregory, in his *Moralia on Job:* "Vices, when they tempt us, humble the virtues that are advancing in us." Just as the sun descends at this time from the center of the sky to its lower parts, so the mind, when it is tempted, descends from the height of its internal joy to a consideration of its nature and fragility, and it sees how easy it is to fall. Paul was tempted when he said: 2 "Lest the greatness of the revelations should exalt me, there was given me a sting of my flesh, an angel of Satan, to buffet me." Our present teacher Paul reveals here why the elect are tempted, and in what follows he reveals the trouble that he suffered through temptation, saying: "For which thing thrice I besought the Lord, that it might depart from me." I think that, unless the sting of Satan had troubled him, he would not have prayed to God that it depart from him.

Some verses in the office of None proclaim this very 3 request. The first section says: "Trouble and anguish have found me; your commandments are my meditation." Augustine, on the same Psalm, explains this as follows: "They rage, they persecute, but they do not abandon God's commandments; and, through these very commandments, even those who rage are loved." The second says: "Many are they that persecute and afflict me; I have not declined from your testimonies." The third is as follows: "I have gone astray like a sheep that is lost. Seek your servant, because I have not forgotten your commandments." The versicle 4 for this course recalls temptation, which is signified through the decline of the sun: "From my secret ones," it says, "cleanse me, and from those of others spare your servant." The aforementioned Augustine, on Psalm 18, explains this

355

decimo: "Tolle mihi ex corde malam cogitationem, repelle a me malum suasorem—hoc est: 'Ab occultis meis munda me, et ab alienis parce servo tuo.'"

# 7

# De Vespertinali synaxi

Legimus in Esdra, quod iam memoravimus, quater in die populum Dei confessum esse Domino et quater in nocte; et ex verbis domni Bedae, qui tractat in eodem Esdra, opinionem esse cognoscimus sanctae ecclesiae iuxta illum morem se quattuor officia caelebrare in die et quattuor in nocte. Non enim inmerito nos, qui militamus Deo, quater in nocte vigilias renovamus, cum hi qui saeculo militabant per quatuor vigilias findebant noctem in castris, ne inrumperentur castra ab inimicis insidiantibus. Nostras quattuor vigilias in nocte solemus vocitare Vespertinum, Completorium, Nocturnum et Matutinum. Ex ethimologia "vespertini" nominis addiscere possumus Vespertinum officium ad noctem pertinere. Dicit Isidorus in libro *Ethimologiarum:* "Vespertinum officium est in noctis initio, vocatum ab stella vespere, quae surgit oriente nocte." Et Agustinus in Psalmo vigesimo nono: "'Vespere demorabitur fletus' [Ps 29:6]. Quid est

2

as follows: "Take evil thought from my heart, drive the evil tempter from me—in other words: 'From my secret ones cleanse me, and from those of others spare your servant.'"

7

# On the gathering for Vespers

As we already noted, we read in Ezra that God's people confessed to the Lord four times a day and four times a night; and from the words of the master Bede, who discusses the same book of Ezra, we understand that the church believes that it celebrates four offices a day and four at night according to that custom. And it is not inappropriate that we, who serve in God's army, should renew our vigils four times a night, since those who serve in worldly armies divide the night in their camps into four watches, that their camps may not be overrun by the wiles of their enemies. It is our custom to call our four nightly vigils Vespers, Compline, Nocturns and Matins. From the etymology of the word "vesper" we can learn that the office of Vespers pertains to the night. Isidore, in his book of *Etymologies,* says: "The office of Vespers is at the beginning of the night, and is so-called after the evening star, which rises in the east at night." And Augustine, on Psalm 29: "'At vesper weeping shall have place.' What does it mean that 'At vesper weeping

'Vespere demorabitur fletus'? Vespera fit quando sol occidit."✝ Hinc possumus conicere, quando feriatos dies observamus, quod eos observare debeamus vespere usque ad vesperam, ut a solis occubitu usque ad eius iterum occasum eos legitime observare necesse sit.

3 Iste status noctis informat fletum eorum peccatorum quibus occidit verus sol. Illis necesse est plorare quinque carnales sensus suos, qui oboedire solent ad peccandum, ut in matutino—id est in evasione peccatorum, quando sol eis iterum inchoat oriri quibus occidit vespere—possint laetari. Unde idem qui supra in memorato Psalmo: "'Vespere demorabitur fletus et in matutino exultatio' [Ps 29:6], quando coeperit oriri fidelibus lux quae occiderat peccatoribus."

4 Informat etiam altero modo statum eorum qui aliqua infirmitate opprimuntur, per quam appropinquant morti. Hi enim, quanto plus timent mori et sententiam percipere veram peccatorum, tanto plus ante oculos mentis suae reducunt carnales motus qui generati sunt per quinque sensus

5 corporis, et eos deflent. Timor solet occupare mentes hominum quando morti appropinquant, sicut de ipso Domino scriptum est—quamvis non timeret infirmitate, sed dispensative "coepit contristari et mestus esse" [Matt 26:37]. Tamen multi sunt qui gaudent de matutino, quando resurgent a mortuis propter consortium Christi resurrectionis.

6 His duobus modis transcursis, debemus venire ad cotidianum usum nostrum. Cotidianus usus noster tenet ut quinque Psalmos cantemus in Vespertinali sinaxi. Quis enim nescit, quamvis per quattuor horas deprecemur Dominum,

will have place'? Vesper occurs when the sun sets."✝ Here we can gather that, when we observe feast days, which we should observe from vesper to vesper, it is necessary and legitimate to celebrate these feasts from the setting of the sun to its second setting.

This time of night reflects mourning over those sinners 3 upon whom the true sun sets. It is necessary for those who are accustomed to obey sin to bemoan their five bodily senses, so that in the morning—that is, upon the avoidance of sins, when the sun begins to rise once again over those on whom it set during the evening—they may be able to rejoice. Thus the same author as above on the aforementioned Psalm: "'At vesper weeping will have place, and in the morning gladness,' when the light that set on sinners has begun to rise over the faithful."

It also reflects, in another way, the position of those who 4 are beset by some infirmity, through which they approach death. For the more these fear to die and to receive the true judgment of sinners, the more they bring before their mind's eye and bemoan the impulses of the flesh that have arisen through the five senses of their body. Fear is accustomed to 5 seize the minds of people when they approach death, as was written about the Lord himself—although he did not fear through his infirmity; it was rather through dispensation that he "began to grow sorrowful and to be sad." Yet there are many who rejoice over the morning, when they rise from the dead in the fellowship of Christ's resurrection.

Now that we have gone over these two means of sym- 6 bolism, we should proceed to our daily practice. Our daily practice holds that we should sing five Psalms at our Vespers gathering. For who is unaware of how great the

quanta impedimenta et quot tristitiae occupent mentem
7  iusti per diem? Oculi adducunt ad eam formas illices, quae,
quia sine voluntate iusti animae intrant ad eam, tedio affici-
tur. Simili modo per aures intrant verba, aut detractionis aut
luxus, quae nihilominus molestiam ingerunt menti. Nares
etiam non sunt alienae ab hoc pestifero internuntio. Os non
se potest excusare, nisi delinquat; unusquisque cognoscit
quando loquatur verba criminalia, quando verba otiosa et
cetera talia, quibus polluitur per os mens. Manus procul dubio et pedes saepe id tangunt, unde anima fit deterior per
8  cogitationem. At quia in istis quinque sensibus tendimus
cotidiano affectu ad tenebras, necesse est ut noctis initio
pro eis veniam Deum precemur. Isti sunt quinque sensus
quos mane commendavimus Domino ad dirigendos, dicendo: "Dirige, Domine, corda, sensus, et sermones nostros
et opera manuum nostrarum." Inter sensus et sermones et
opera conprehenduntur quinque sensus corporis. De cordibus est seorsum dicendum, postquam venerimus (si Dominus dederit) ad ymnum Mariae. Propter hos videlicet quinque sensus—quia forte non fuimus digni ut dirigerentur per
omnia secundum Domini placitum—quinque Psalmi cantantur, ut ignoscatur nobis.

9  Hos quinque Psalmos antiphonatim solemus cantare. Ut
*Tripartita* narrat *historia* in libro Xmo, capitulo VIIII,
ab Ignatio episcopo Antiochae antiphonarum usus in ecclesiis primo coepit actitari. Ita enim narrat: "Dicendum tamen est unde sumpsit initium, ut in ecclesia antiphonae

impediments are and how many sorrows there are that beset the mind of the just man throughout the day, although we beseech the Lord at four times of day? The eyes bring enticing forms into the mind, which is burdened with weariness because they enter it without the consent of the just man's soul. In like manner, words, whether of slander or excess, enter through the ears; they bring no less trouble to the mind. The nostrils, too, are not free of this pestential intermediary. The mouth cannot even excuse itself without lapsing; everyone recognizes when he speaks criminal words, idle words and other such things; through them, his mind is polluted by his mouth. Surely the hands and feet often touch that which, through thought, causes the soul to become weaker. And yet, because we advance in our daily disposition toward the darkness through our five senses, we must beg the Lord for mercy on their behalf at nightfall. These are the same five senses that, in the morning, we commended to the Lord's guidance, saying: "Lord, guide our hearts, senses, and our words and the works of our hands." The five senses of our body are included among our senses and words and works. We will speak about hearts separately, after we come (if the Lord grants it) to Mary's hymn. Because of these five senses—since we were perhaps not worthy that they be directed in all things according to the Lord's pleasure—five Psalms are sung on account of our five senses, that we may be forgiven.

It is our custom to sing these five Psalms antiphonally. As the *Three-Part History* relates, in book 10, chapter 9, the practice of performing antiphons in church began with Bishop Ignatius of Antioch. For it recounts as follows: "Yet it should be said where the singing of antiphons in church

361

decantentur. Ignatius Antiochiae Syriae, tertius post apostolum Petrum episcopus, qui etiam cum ipsis degebat apostolis, vidit angelorum visionem—quomodo per antiphonas sanctae Trinitatis dicebant ymnos—isque modum visionis Antiochenae tradidisse probatur ecclesiae, et ex hoc ad cunctas transivit ecclesias."+

10    Antiphona dicitur vox reciproca. Antiphona inchoatur ab uno unius cori, et ad eius symphoniam Psalmus cantatur per duos coros. Ipsa enim—id est antiphona—coniunguntur simul duo cori. Quanto enim melior est anima corpore, tanto melior est cantus animae quam corporis. Igitur intendendum est quae sit antiphona animae. Videtur nobis virtus dilectionis esse quae coniungit opera duorum fratrum simul.

11    Psalmi ad opera referuntur; antiphona ad illam dilectionem qua unusquisque fratri suo porrigit suum opus. Verbi gratia: Unus legit et discit doctrinam in scola, alter seminat in campo. Tempore fructus doctor seminanti porrigit doctrinam, sator doctori panem. Duobus coris alternatur antiphona quoniam non potest minus esse caritas quam inter duos. Hanc vicissitudinem caritatis significant cantores, qui alternatim ex utraque parte antiphonas levant.

12    Hos duos coros designaverunt pennae animalium invicem porrectae quae vidit Iezechiel in figura adventus Christi et Novi Testamenti. Coniunctio duarum pennarum antiphona est, quae vicem tenet caritatis. Unde Gregorius scribit in omelia septima super eundem Iezechielem: "Nam dum ille verbum praedicationis exhibet et lumine veritatis

originated. Bishop Ignatius of Syrian Antioch, third after Peter the apostle, who also lived among the apostles themselves, had a vision of the angels—how they sang hymns of the Holy Trinity through antiphons—and he is revealed to have handed the method of his vision to the church of Antioch, and from there it went out to all the churches."✝

Alternating voice is referred to as an antiphon. The antiphon is started by one member of one choir, and the Psalm is sung by the two choirs in harmony with him. For in it—that is, the antiphon—two choirs are united at the same time. And the soul is better than the body to the same degree that the song of the soul is better than the song of the body. We should therefore consider what the soul's antiphon might be. It strikes us that the virtue of love is that which unites the works of two brothers. Psalms are related to works; the antiphon is related to that love through which each person offers his work to his brother. For example: One reads and learns the teaching in school, and another sows in the field. At the time of the harvest the teacher offers his teaching to the sower, and the planter offers bread to the teacher. The antiphon is alternated between two choirs because there can be no charity among less than two. The cantors, who raise antiphons alternately on each side, signify this exchange of charity.

The wings of the animals reaching out to one another that Ezekiel saw as symbol for the coming of Christ and the New Testament signified these two choirs. The joining of the two wings is the antiphon, which has the role of charity. Thus Gregory writes in his seventh homily on the same Ezekiel: "For when he reveals the word of his preaching and

ex corde meo ignorantiae tenebras repellit, dumque illi ego (quia fortasse a mundi huius potente opprimitur) solatium meae defensionis impertior atque hunc de violentis manibus evello—vicissim nobis pennas nostras tendimus, ut nos affectu et ope vicaria ex bono quod accepimus tangamus.

13 Unde bene primus pastor ammonet dicens: 'Omnium finis appropinquabit. Estote itaque prudentes et vigilate in orationibus; ante omnia mutuam in vobismet ipsis caritatem continuam habentes, quia caritas operit multitudinem peccatorum' [1 Pet 4:7]."✝

14 Post hoc sequitur lectio a pastore prolata. Ipsa est lectio quam pastor debet domesticis suis solerter amministrare. Audivi olim responsorios cantare apud quosdam post lectionem Vespertinalem, qui continentur in aliquibus antiphonariis; sed apud nonnullos modo, ac pene omnes, post lectionem sequitur coniunctim versus. Saepe enim revolvo apud me—si decantari oportet responsorium post lectionem Vespertinalem, quare non simili modo decantetur post lectionem Matutinalem? In hac revolutione cogitationum occurrit mihi ut, sicut ymnus Zacariae excludit responsorium post Matutinalem lectionem, ita excludat ymnus sanctae Mariae post Vespertinalem lectionem.

15 De versu foret hic dicendum—sed quia nos inchoamus haec officia a Septuagesima, non possumus hic referre aliquid de versu quem solemus dicere in Vespertinali officio, ante quam dicamus aliquid de alleluiaquod cantatur in Sep-
16 tuagesima. In eodem Vespere et in nocte sequenti, alleluia per omnia officia cantoris currit. Ita agimus de alleluia, quando illud recondimus in thesauris suis (id est in cordibus electorum et angelorum vocibus), sicut solet dilectus circa

drives the darkness of ignorance from my heart with the light of truth, and when I provide him with the comfort of my defense and pluck him from the hands of some attacker (for he is perhaps oppressed by some power of this world)— then we extend our wings to each other, to touch in mutual affection and assistance through the good that we have received. Thus the first pastor gives us good advice, saying: 13 'The end of all is at hand. Be prudent therefore and watch in prayers; but before all things have a constant mutual charity among yourselves, for charity covers a multitude of sins.'"†

After this follows a reading proclaimed by the pastor. It is 14 this reading that the pastor should deliver skillfully to his servants. I once heard some people sing responsories, which are contained in some antiphoners, after the Vespers reading. But now among many people, in fact nearly everyone, a versicle follows directly after the reading. And I often wonder to myself—if a responsory should be sung after the Vespers reading, why is one not also sung after the reading for Matins? Amid my churning thoughts, it occurs to me that, just as Zechariah's hymn excludes the responsory after the Matins reading, so too does Mary's hymn exclude the responsory after the Vespers reading.

We should discuss the versicle here—but since we are be- 15 ginning our discussion of these offices from Septuagesima, we cannot relate anything here about the versicle that we are accustomed to recite at the office of Vespers, before we say something about the alleluia that is sung on Septuagesima Sunday. During this Vespers and on the following night, 16 the alleluia occurs in all the offices of the cantor. With respect to the alleluia, when we stow it away in its coffers (that is, in the hearts of the elect and the voices of the angels), we

dilectum agere, qui perrecturus est iter longinquum. Osculatur os eius, collum, oculos, frontem et cetera. Dictum sit strictim de alleluia, quod propterea toties frequentamus quia diligimus illud, et in propinquo recondendum sit.

17    Dicendum est de versibus qui fiunt per Dominicas noctes ceteras et per sex dies ebdomadis. Per Dominicas noctes solemus dicere: "Vespertina oratio ascendat ad te, Domine; et descendat super nos misericordia tua." In ceteris autem noctibus solemus dicere: "Dirigatur oratio mea sicut

18 incensum in conspectu tuo" [Ps 140:2]. Unam orationem habent isti versus. Dominicalis versus ex suis verbis monstrat actitari Vespertinam orationem. Talis enim debet esse omnis versus, ut vel statum officii ad memoriam reducat, vel statum temporis—sicut illi faciunt qui circa passionem Domini et resurrectionem cantantur. At cotidianus versus in posterioribus verbis suis, quamvis non cantentur, eadem aperit dicendo: "Elevatio manuum mearum sacrificium Vespertinum" [Ps 140:2]. Propter haec verba memoratus versus "Dirigatur oratio mea" inchoatur—sed nescio cur non cantentur. Forsan quia cantoribus displicet quod non conve-

19 nit eorum modulationibus. Cum ipso versu offertur incensum, quod Dominus praecepit offerri. De quo scriptum est in libro Exodi: "Ponesque altare contra velum quod ante arcam pendet testimonii, coram propitiatorio quo tegitur testimonium, ubi loquar tibi. Et adolebit incensum super eo Aaron suave flagrans mane. Quando componit lucernas, incendet illud, et quando collocat eas ad vesperam, uret

act just as a beloved is accustomed to act toward his beloved, who is about to set out on a long journey. He kisses his mouth, his neck, his eyes, his forehead and so on. In brief, it may be said about the alleluia that we employ it so frequently because we love it, and it is about to be stored away.

We should discuss the versicles that occur on other Sunday nights and on the six days of the week. On Sunday nights it is our custom to say: "May this Vespers prayer ascend to you, Lord; and may your mercy descend upon us." And on the other nights it is our custom to say: "May my prayer be directed as incense in your sight." These versicles contain one prayer. Through its words, the Sunday versicle shows that the Vespers prayer is being celebrated. Every versicle should be like this, such that it either calls to mind the nature of the office or time of day—as do those versicles that are sung for the Lord's passion and resurrection. And the daily versicle in its following words, although they are not sung, touches on the same matter, saying: "The lifting up of my hands as evening sacrifice." Because of these words, the aforementioned versicle begins with "My prayer be directed"—but I do not know why the words are not sung. Perhaps because it troubled the cantors that it did not accord with their melodies. Incense is offered with this versicle; the Lord ordered that it be offered. About this, it is written in the book of Exodus: "And you will set the altar over against the veil that hangs before the ark of the testimony, before the propitiatory with which the testimony is covered, where I will speak to you. And Aaron shall burn sweet smelling incense upon it in the morning. When he shall dress the lamps, he shall burn it, and when he shall place them in the evening, he shall burn an everlasting

thymiama sempiternum coram Domino" [Exod 30:6–8], et reliqua. Intendat summus sacerdos, qui vicem tenet Aaron in ecclesia, quis debeat incensum offerre Domino super altare.

20 Post hoc sequitur ymnus sanctae Mariae. Sicut quinque Psalmi deplorant quod quinque sensus corporis deliquerant, ita ymnus sanctae Mariae castigat cogitationes quae se inani iactantia extulerunt in prosperitate diei dicendo: "Dispersit superbos mente cordis sui. Deposuit potentes de sede" [Luke 1:51–52].

21 Usque huc modum eorum hominum diximus excepto de versu Dominicali qui aliqua neglegentia percutiuntur, unde habent plangere; at nunc dicendum est de illis qui in Domino triumphant et ei laudem Vespertinalem dicunt per noctes quas vulgo solet appellare Dominicas—verumque, si sol occubuit. Sicut Dominica nox victrix extitit Dominica resurrectione, ita Psalmi qui in ea cantantur victoriam elec-

22 torum Domini et laudem eius resonant. Primus Psalmus, id est *Benedictus Dominus Deus meus* [Ps 143], victoriam continet David contra Goliam. Sequentes Psalmi laudem Dei resonant. De secundo dicit Agustinus in tractatu Psalmorum: "'Exaltabo te, Deus meus, rex meus, et benedicam nomen tuum in saeculum et in saeculum saeculi' [Ps 144:1]. Videtis inchoatam esse laudem Dei, et usque ad finem Psalmi laus ipsa perducitur." De tertio ita: "Ecce Psalmus sonat. Cuius vox est (quae si vultis vestra est) exortantis animam suam ad laudandum Deum et dicentis sibi: 'Lauda, anima mea, Dominum'" [Ps 145:2]. De quarto ita: "Nobis dicitur: 'Laudate Dominum' [Ps 146:1]. Dicitur hoc omnibus gentibus, non solis nobis. Et istam vocem, per loca singula sonantem a

incense before the Lord," and so forth. Let the high priest, who holds the place of Aaron in our church, consider who should offer incense to the Lord over the altar.

After this Saint Mary's hymn follows. Just as the five 20 Psalms lament that the five senses of the body did wrong, so Saint Mary's hymn chastises the thoughts that arose with empty boasting in the day's good fortune, saying: "He has scattered the proud in the conceit of their heart. He has put down the mighty from their seat."

With the exception of the Sunday versicle, we have dis- 21 cussed up to this point the manner of prayer of those men who are afflicted by some negligence and thus have something to lament. Now, however, we should discuss those who rejoice in the Lord and pronounce their Vespers praise to him on what are commonly called Sunday nights—and correctly so-called, if the sun has set. Just as Sunday night was victorious in the Lord's resurrection, so do the Psalms that are sung on that day resound with the victory of the Lord's elect and his praise. The first Psalm, that is *Benedictus Domi-* 22 *nus Deus meus,* contains David's victory over Goliath. The following Psalms resound with the Lord's praise. Augustine speaks about the second Psalm in his treatise on the Psalms: "'I will extol you, O God my king, and I will bless your name for ever and ever.' You see that the praise of God has begun, and this praise continues all the way to the end of the Psalm." About the third, as follows: "Behold, the Psalm cries out. Whose voice is it? It is the voice of someone (your voice, if you so desire) exhorting his soul to praise God and saying to himself: 'Praise the Lord, O my soul.'" About the fourth, as follows: "We are told: 'Praise the Lord.' This is said to all nations, not only to us. And the churches hear

lectoribus, singillatim audiunt ecclesiae. Una vox tamen Dei super omnes non tacet, ut laudemus eum; et quasi quaereremus quare laudare Deum debeamus, videte quam causam attulit: 'Laudate Dominum,' inquit, 'quoniam bonus est'"

23 [Ps 146:1]. Quintus continet laudem Hierusalem, quae restaurata est post peregrinationem. De quo idem qui supra in eodem: "Quid enim factura es, O Hierusalem? Transit certe et labor et gemitus. Quid factura es? Aratura? Seminatura? Novellatura? Navigatura es? Negotiatura es? Quid factura es? An in illis operibus, quamvis bonis et de misericordia venientibus, exerceri te adhuc oportet? Considera numerum tuum; considera undique societatem tuam. Vide utrum aliquis esuriat, cui porrigas panem. Vide si aliquis sitiat, cui des calicem aquae frigidae. Vide utrum aliquis apud te modo peregrinus est, quem hospitio recipias. Vide utrum aliquis aeger, quem visites. Vide utrum aliquis litiget, quem concordes. Vide utrum aliquis moriatur, quem sepelias. Quid ergo factura es? 'Collauda, Hierusalem, Dominum' [Ps 147:1]."✝

24 De ymno sanctae Mariae ita tractat domnus Beda in omeliis suis: "Verba igitur Evangelicae lectionis frequenti meditatione revolvamus. Exempla beatae Dei genitricis semper animo retineamus, ut, et in conspectu Dei humiles inventi et proximis quoque debito honore submissi, mereamur una cum ipsa perpetuo sublimari gaudio. Studeamus sollicite ne nos indebite laudantium favor extollat, cum illam videamus inter verba verae laudationis inconcussam humilitatis

that voice individually, in their respective locations, as it resounds from the lectors. Yet God's singular voice over everyone, that we should praise him, is not silent; and as if we had asked why we should praise God, note the reason he gave: 'Praise the Lord,' he says, 'because it is good.'" The fifth contains the praise of Jerusalem, which was restored after the migration. The same author as above speaks about this in the same treatise: "O Jerusalem, what will you do? Clearly both labor and lamentation have passed. What will you do? Will you plow? Will you sow? Will you till new fields? Will you sail? Will you trade? What will you do? Should you even continue to exert yourself in these labors, though they are good and arise from mercy? Consider your number; consider every part of your community. See if anyone is hungry, to whom you may offer bread. See if anyone is thirsty, to whom you may give a cup of cold water. See if there is anyone among you who is now a stranger, whom you may take in as a guest. See if anyone is sick whom you may visit. See if anyone is fighting, with whom you may be in harmony. See if anyone is dying, whom you may bury. So what will you do? 'Praise the Lord, O Jerusalem.'"✝

The master Bede discusses Saint Mary's hymn in his homilies as follows: "Let us therefore reflect upon the words of the Gospel reading with constant meditation. Let us keep the example of God's blessed mother forever in our mind, so that, once we are found humble in God's sight and have yielded with due honor to our neighbors, we may be worthy of elevation, along with her, to eternal joy. Let us strive with care lest the approval of those who praise us exalt us unduly, since we see that she maintained the unwavering constancy of her humility among words of

25 tenuisse constantiam. Si immoderatus temporalium rerum nos appetitus delectat, reminiscamur quia iudex noster 'divites dimittit inanes.' Si temporalis afflictio forte mentem conturbat, recogitemus quia 'et humiles exaltat.' Numquam de impetranda admissorum venia desperemus, quia 'misericordia eius a progenie in progenies timentibus eum' [Luke 1:50–53]. Nulli inter mala quae fecit gravior impaenitendi culpa subripiat, quia 'Deus superbis resistit' [ Jas 4:6], eosque beatorum sorte secernens, per varia poenarum loca pro

26 peccatorum varietate dispergit. Fit autem, largiente Domino, ut si beatae Mariae semper actus et dicta recolamus, semper in nobis et observantia castitatis, et virtutis opera perseverent. Nam et optimus ac saluberrimus in sancta ecclesia mos inolevit, ut ymnus ipsius cotidie cum psalmodia Vespertinae laudis ab omnibus canatur—quatinus ex hoc animos fidelium et frequentior Dominicae incarnationis memoria ad affectum devotionis accendat, et recogitata saepius exempla genitricis illius in virtutum soliditate confir-

27 ment. Et hoc opportune ad Vesperos fieri complacuit—ut videlicet, fatigata per diem ac distenta diversis cogitationibus mens nostra, incumbente tempore quietis, ad unionem se suae considerationis colligeret, iamque salubriter admonita, quicquid superfluum vel nocivum diurna vagatione contraxisset, totum hoc nocturnis denuo precibus et lacrimis ex tempore mundaret."✝

true praise. Should an immoderate appetite for temporal 25 things seduce us, let us remember that our judge 'sends the rich away empty.' Should some temporal affliction happen to trouble our mind, let us remember that 'he exalts the humble.' Let us never despair of receiving forgiveness for our offenses, because 'his mercy is from generation unto generations to them that fear him.' May the grave fault of impenitence, amid the other evils one has committed, attack nobody, because 'God resists the proud,' and he cuts them off from the lot of the blessed and scatters them through diverse places of punishment according to the diversity of their sins. But may it happen, through the Lord's generosity, 26 if we forever recall the deeds and sayings of blessed Mary, that the observance of chastity and works of virtue remain in us forever. For in our church the great and wholesome custom developed, according to which everyone sings her hymn daily amid the psalmody of praise at Vespers—so that, through this hymn, the more frequent commemoration of the Lord's incarnation may inflame the minds of the faithful to the sentiment of devotion, and the example of the Lord's mother, so often remembered, may encourage these minds in the firmness of their virtues. And it was appropriate and 27 pleasing that this be done at Vespers—namely so that our mind, as a period of quiet approaches, and after it has grown tired and distended with various thoughts through the course of the day, may gather itself to the unity of its own contemplation, now that it has been soundly advised to wash away once again, with its nocturnal prayers and tears, everything superfluous and harmful that it has accumulated in its daytime wandering."✝

28    Post hunc ymnum, per Dominicas noctes aliquibus in locis dicitur *Kyrie eleison,* ut audivi Romae, et postea collecta.
Aliquibus in locis collecta tantummodo sequitur. Sicut genuflexionem amittimus recolendo resurrectionem nostram,
ita et preces flebiles praesentis vitae quas solemus cum ge-
nuflexione promere in eis noctibus amittimus. Ut superius
demonstratum est ex verbis Agustini, in illa caelesti Hierusalem, ubi resurrectio est vera et in re, nulla precatio pro
29    miseriis exercebitur. Quapropter tantum sequitur collecta,
quam solet presbyter stando proferre, ob recordationem
futurae resurrectionis per Dominicas noctes. Quoniam in
praesenti saeculo sumus, necesse est nobis ut muniamur
orationibus sanctorum presbyterorum; et, quia quodammodo recolimus festivitatem civium caelestis Hierusalem,
oportet nos illam caelebrare cum maiori laetitia et securitate quam cum caelebramus nostram peregrinationem.

30    Quoniam in Septuagesima inchoavimus hanc cautionem,
volumus subiungere dicta sancti Agustini de Septuagesima
quae dicit in tractatu Psalmi *Lauda Hierusalem Dominum* [Ps
147]: "Post septuaginta ergo annos, cum prophetavit Hiere-
mias reparari civitatem Hierusalem, et factum est ut ibi sig-
nificaretur imago futurorum. Significatum est nobis post
omnem istam volubilitatem temporis quae septenario numero volvitur, futuram illam civitatem nostram in aeterni-
tate in uno die. In illa quippe habitatione tempus non vol-
31    vitur, quia habitator ibi non labitur."✝ Ex verbis beati
Agustini, docemur per Septuagesimam designari praesens
tempus, quod volvitur septenario numero; et per Paschales
dies, qui sequuntur Septuagesimam, futuram patriam.

In some places, the *Kyrie eleison* is said on Sunday nights 28 after this hymn, as I heard it done at Rome; and then the collect. In some places only the collect follows. Just as we omit kneeling in recalling our resurrection, we also omit the mournful prayers of the present life that we are accustomed to offer along with kneeling on these nights. As was shown above through the words of Augustine, in that heavenly Jerusalem, where there is true and actual resurrection, no prayer will be offered for our miseries. Therefore only the 29 collect follows, which the priest is accustomed to recite while standing, in commemoration of our future resurrection on Sunday nights. Because we are in this world, we must be fortified with the prayers of holy priests; and, because in some sense we are commemorating the jubilation of the citizens of the heavenly Jerusalem, we should celebrate it with greater rejoicing and confidence than we do when we commemorate our exile.

Because we began this admonition with Septuagesima, 30 we want to include the statements that Saint Augustine makes on Septuagesima in his treatise on the Psalm *Lauda Hierusalem Dominum:* "After seventy years, therefore, when Jeremiah prophesied that the city of Jerusalem would be rebuilt, it also happened that a vision of the future was imparted there. We were shown that, after the full period of time that revolves upon the number seven, we will have that future city for eternity and for a single day. And indeed, in that dwelling place time does not pass, because he who dwells there will not pass away."✝ Through the words of 31 blessed Augustine, we are taught that this world, which revolves around the number seven, is signified through Septuagesima; and that the future country is signified through the days of Easter that follow Septuagesima.

# 8

# De Completorio

Completorium ideo dicitur, quia in eo completur cotidianus usus cibi sive potus, qui necessario sumitur ad sustentationem corporis, seu locutio communis. Unde et apud monachos tenetur usus ex regula Sancti Benedicti, ut ab eo officio claustra oris muniant, et ea aliena faciant a communi colloquio usque dum iterum ad opera redeant. Non enim inmerito potest haec pars noctis conticinium vocari, in qua conticescunt omnia. Apud eos qui noctem dividunt in septem partibus, prima pars vocatur crepusculum, secunda vesperum, tertia conticinium, de qua nunc agimus; quam ideo sic posse vocari opinor, quia in eo conticescunt omnia. In eo officio quattuor Psalmi recoluntur usque ad versum. In quattuor Psalmis quattuor elementa corporis nostri commendamus Domino, quod versus aperte dilucidat dicens: "Custodi me, Domine, ut pupillam oculi. Sub umbra alarum tuarum protege me" [Ps 16:8]. Quot pericula possint hominem invadere dormiendo extrinsecus plus quam vigilando, unusquisque recognoscit—qui vel tenuiter sapit.

3    Aptatur quodammodo hoc officium commendationi qua se commendat homo Deo quando transit de saeculo. Somnus est imago mortis. Sicut enim alienatur mens mortui hominis ab istis mortalibus et miseriae huius saeculi oblivioni

# 8

# On Compline

Compline is so-called because at that point our daily consumption of food and drink, which are necessarily consumed for the sustenance of the body, together with ordinary speech, is complete. And thus monks, in accordance with Saint Benedict's rule, see to the closing of their mouths and keep them distant from ordinary conversation from the time of this office until they return to work again. And it is not inappropriate that this time of night, in which all things are silent, can be called quietude. Among those who divide the night into seven parts, the first part is called twilight, the second vespers, and the third quietude, which we are now discussing. And I think that it is so-called because, at this moment, all things are quiet. In this office four Psalms 2 are recounted before the versicle. In the four Psalms we commend the four elements of our body to the Lord, as the versicle makes clear, saying: "Keep me, Lord, as the apple of your eye. Protect me under the shadow of your wings." Everyone—even those with tenuous understanding—recognizes how many more external dangers can befall a man when he is asleep than when he is awake.

In some sense this office corresponds to that commendation 3 through which man commends himself to God when he leaves this world. Sleep is the image of death. And just as the mind of the dead man is withdrawn from mortal things and given over to forgetfulness of the suffering of this

traduntur, ita quodammodo animus dormientis alienatur a cogitationibus consuetis et ab omni officio temporali.

4     Quod monstrat Agustinus, in uno versu primi Psalmi qui cantatur in Completorio, dicens: "'In pace in idipsum dormiam et somnum capiam' [Ps 4:9]. Recte enim a talibus speratur omnimoda mentis abalienatio a mortalibus rebus et miseriarum saeculi huius oblivio. Quae nomine 'obdormitionis' et 'somni' decenter et prophetice significatur, ubi summa pax nullo tumultu interpolari potest. Sed hoc iam non tenetur in hac vita, sed post hanc vitam sperandum

5 est."✝ Secundus Psalmus transit usque ad illum versum in quo Christus spiritum suum posuit in cruce. In quo cupimus conformari dormitioni eius—hoc est ut membra quiescant

6 et cor vigilet. Tertius Psalmus, *Qui habitat in adiutorio* [Ps 90], plenus est verbis orationum quae deprecantur Domini protectionem. Qui et secundum Romanum usum cantatur in Parascheve post lectionem, in qua (secundum Osee) nostra mortificatio ad exemplum Christi demonstratur et resurrectio post duos dies. Ammonet nos per hunc Psalmum compositor Officii ut in omnibus periculis et tribulationibus, secundum verba eius, mens nostra intenta sit ad deprecandum Deum; ac ideo, quia somnus noster aliquam similitudinem habet dormitionis eorum qui sub protectione Domini transierunt de praesenti saeculo, idem Psalmus re-

7 citatur in Completorio nostro. Nec non et quartus Psalmus aliquo modo recolit intentionem illorum qui in tribulatione sunt et tamen de tribulatione transeunt in pacem, dicendo: "In noctibus extollite manus vestras in sancta" [Ps 133:2]. Unde Agustinus in tractatu eiusdem Psalmi: "Nox enim

world, so in some sense is the spirit of the sleeping man withdrawn from its usual thoughts and from every temporal occupation.

Augustine, writing on a verse from the first Psalm that is 4 sung during Compline, explains this: "'In peace in the self-same I will sleep and I will take rest.' For it is right that such people hope for all manner of mental withdrawal from mortal affairs, and for forgetfulness of the miseries of this world. This is properly and prophetically indicated by the words 'unconsciousness' and 'sleep,' where the highest peace can be interrupted by no disturbance. This is not, however, available in this life, though it is to be hoped for after this life."✝ The second Psalm continues up to the verse in which 5 Christ laid down his spirit on the cross. In that verse, we desire that we be brought into conformity with his sleep—that is, that our members rest while our heart is vigilant. The 6 third Psalm, *Qui habitat in adiutorio,* is filled with words of prayers that request the Lord's protection. In Roman usage it is also sung on Good Friday after the reading, where (according to Hosea) our mortification after the example of Christ is revealed, together with our resurrection after two days. Through this Psalm, the author of the Office advises us, in accordance with its words, that our mind should be intent on beseeching God amid all our dangers and difficulties; and thus, because our sleep has some likeness to the sleep of those who have left this world under the Lord's protection, the same Psalm is recited at Compline. In some 7 sense the fourth Psalm also recalls the intention of those who are in difficulty and nevertheless pass from this difficulty to peace, saying: "In the nights lift up your hands to the holy places." Thus Augustine in his treatise on the same Psalm: "For the night is a sorrowful thing, and the day is a

tristis res est, dies laeta res est." Et paulo post: "'Benedicite' ergo 'Dominum' [Ps 133:1–2]. Quando? In noctibus. Quando benedixit Iob, quam tristis erat nox! Ablata sunt omnia quae possidebantur, ablati filii quibus servabantur. Quam tristis nox! Sed videamus si non in noctibus benedicit: 'Dominus dedit, Dominus abstulit. Sicut Domino placuit, ita factum est. Sit nomen Domini benedictum' [Job 1:21]."✝

8   Versus qui sequitur, ut praetulimus, totum opus officii monstrat—hoc est postulationem custodiae Domini circa pericula noctis. Et quam pacem desiderat anima orantis, sequens ymnus sancti Symeonis monstrat—hoc est ut ab omni tumultu huius saeculi quiescat. Hoc precabatur Symeon quando cupiebat transire de hac vita ad alteram vitam, et dicebat: "Nunc dimitte servum tuum, Domine, secundum verbum tuum in pace" [Luke 2:29]. Ex praesenti ymno manifeste edocemur quod, in praesenti commendatione, conformemur illis qui in Domino mortui sunt.

9   Igitur non est congruum, post hanc commendationem, bibere aut comedere aut tale aliquid agere quod non pertineat ad quietem membrorum et abalienationem status quieti corporis. Et quia non est deinceps conlatio habilis invicem referentium et disputatio, quae necessaria est post lectionem, dormitantibus palpebris oculisque somnum trahentibus, cessat lectio. Tempus illud significat de quo scriptum est: "Et erunt omnes docibiles Dei" [John 6:45]. Et illud Apostoli: "Sive prophetiae evacuabuntur, sive linguae cessabunt, sive scientia destruetur" [1 Cor 13:8].

joyful thing." And after a little: "Therefore, 'Bless the Lord.' When? At night. When Job blessed him, what a sorrowful night it was! All his possessions were taken away; the sons who had kept them were taken away. What a sorrowful night! But let us see if he does not give his blessing during the night: 'The Lord gave, and the Lord has taken away. As it has pleased the Lord, so was it done. Blessed be the name of the Lord.'"✝

The versicle that follows, as we said above, clarifies the full task of the office—namely, a request for the Lord's protection amid the dangers of the night. And the subsequent hymn of Saint Symeon reveals the peace that the soul of the one praying desires—namely, that it may rest without any disturbance from this world. This is what Symeon prayed for when he wished to pass from this life to the other life, and said: "Now dismiss your servant in peace, Lord, according to your word." Through the present hymn we are clearly informed that, through the present commendation, we are brought into conformity with those who have died in the Lord.

It is therefore inappropriate, after this commendation, to drink or to eat or to do any such thing that does not relate to the rest of our members and the withdrawal of our body's state of quiet. And since subsequently there is no gathering and discussion suitable for people talking to each other, which is necessary after a reading, and the eyelids become drowsy and the eyes pull us toward sleep, there is no reading. It signifies that time about which it is written: "And they shall all be taught of God." And that line from the Apostle: "Whether prophecies shall be made void, or tongues shall cease, or knowledge shall be destroyed."

381

10    Et quia ex ordine Esdrae necessaria est lectio in isto officio, ut quater in nocte legatur, solent religiosi viri ante
praesens officium lectionem legere. Sicut Maria, quae unxit
Dominum unguento, praevenit facere quod faciendum erat
in sepultura eius si inveniretur corpus eius [Mic 14:8; Matt
26:12; John 12:7], ita lectio sua doctrina ungit animas devotas
ante commendationem dormitionis.

9

# De Nocturnali officio per Dominicas noctes

In Nocturnali officio dicimus primo: "Domine, labia mea
aperies et os meum adnuntiabit laudem tuam" [Ps 50:17];
deinde sequitur *Gloria.* Quando pridem in nocte conventi
fuimus, commendavimus nos Domino et conclusimus ora,
atque post singuli, quasi quodammodo in singulis sepulchris, quievimus, et soli Domino mente astitimus, cui non
sunt verba necessaria, quia omnes cogitationes novit. At
nunc, quia iterum convenimus ad confitendum Domino,
precamur eum, ut sua directione labia nostra aperiat et ad
2    suam laudem os nostrum fatiscat. Dein sequitur invitato-
rius. In eo communis coetus fratrum convocat omnes

And since, according to the arrangement of Ezra, this  10
office must have a reading, that we may read four times a
night, pious men are accustomed to read the reading before
this office. Just as Mary, who anointed the Lord with ointment, went forth to do what ought to have been done at his
tomb were his body found there, so does the reading anoint
devout souls with its teaching before commending them to
sleep.

# 9

# On Nocturns during
# Sunday nights

During Nocturns, we first say: "Lord, you will open my
lips and my mouth shall declare your praise"; the *Gloria* then
follows. The last time we gathered at night, we commended
ourselves to the Lord and closed our mouths, and then each
of us were quiet, as if we were all somehow in our graves,
and mentally we were present before God alone, for whom
words are unnecessary, since he knows all our thoughts.
But now, since we have again gathered to confess the Lord,
we ask him to open our lips under his direction and to
widen our mouths for his praise. Then the invitatory fol-  2
lows. In it, the public gathering of brethren calls everyone,

degentes undique, ut excitentur et veniant ad confitendum Domino. Iuxta quod versus secundus sonat invitatorii: "Praeoccupemus faciem eius in confessione et in Psalmis iubilemus ei" [Ps 94:2]. Deinde sequuntur duodecim Psalmi sine antiphona, cum tribus glorificationibus sanctae Trinitatis per ternas divisiones quattuor Psalmorum.

3 Dominica nox Dominicam resurrectionem ad memoriam nostram reducit; quae ideo vocatur Dominica, quia Dominus eam clarificavit sua resurrectione. Non enim solus resurrexit a mortuis, sed omnes sui electi—sive qui fuerunt ab initio mundi ante suam incarnationem, sive qui futuri sunt usque ad finem mundi. Quapropter dicit Paulus Apostolus: "Qui praedestinatus est Filius Dei in virtute, secundum spiritum sanctificationis, ex resurrectione mortuorum Iesu Christi Domini nostri" [Rom 1:4]. Quoniam in sua resurrectione voluit resurrectionem omnium electorum designare, propterea dixit: "ex resurrectione . . . mortuorum." Horum omnium resurrectionem recolimus in Dominicis noctibus.

4 Status ecclesiae nostrae tribus articulis distinguitur—id est sub lege naturali, et sub lege Mosaica, et sub lege evangelicae gratiae. Quamvis multi sancti essent sub naturali lege, tamen maxime duodecim patriarchae viguerunt—scilicet intantum ut ab his duodecim tribus postea fierent. Sicut ex duodecim apostolis in Novo Testamento propagatus est Christianus populus, ita in Veteri Testamento

5 populus peculiaris Deo ex duodecim patriarchis. Isti duodecim Psalmi recolunt annum primum visitationis vineae, in quo ficus inutilis stetit [Luke 13:6–9]. Ut nos non simus

everywhere, to awaken and come to confess the Lord. Accordingly the second verse of the invitatory calls out: "Let us come before his face in confession and make a joyful noise to him with Psalms." Then twelve Psalms follow without antiphons, with three glorifications of the Holy Trinity for each threefold grouping of four Psalms.

The Lord's night reminds us of the Lord's resurrection. It ₃ is called the Lord's night because the Lord ennobled it with his resurrection. For he did not rise from the dead alone, but did so together with all his elect—whether those who lived before his incarnation from the beginning of the world, or those who are still to come until the end of the world. Thus Paul the Apostle says: "Who was predestinated the Son of God in power, according to the spirit of sanctification, by the resurrection of our Lord Jesus Christ from the dead." Because he wanted to indicate the resurrection of all the elect through Christ's own resurrection, he said: "by the resurrection . . . from, or of, the dead." We recall the resurrection of all of these elect on Sunday nights.

The state of our church is divided into three periods— ₄ namely, under the natural law, and under the Mosaic law, and under the law of evangelical grace. Although there were many saints under the natural law, the most prominent were the twelve patriarchs—so much so that the twelve tribes of Israel later arose from them. Just as the Christian people were begotten through the twelve apostles in the New Testament, so in the Old Testament were God's special people begotten through the twelve patriarchs. These twelve ₅ Psalms recall the first year that the vineyard was visited, when the fig tree stood useless. That we not be useless,

inutiles, recolimus duodecim Psalmos instar bonorum morum sanctorum patriarcharum.

6     Quos divisos cantamus per quaternarium numerum, quia quattuor virtutes sunt quibus credimus sanctos patriarchas coluisse sanctam Trinitatem—scilicet, prudentia, fortitudo, iustitia et temperantia. Istae virtutes non separantur ab invicem, sed ubi una ex illis est, tres semper oportet adesse.

7 Unde Agustinus in epistola ad Hieronimum: "Porro si prudentia tunc erit, si et fortis et iusta et temperans sit, profecto ubi fuerit, secum habet ceteras. Sic et fortitudo inprudens esse non potest vel intemperans vel iniusta; sic et temperantia necesse est ut prudens, fortis et iusta sit; sic iustitia non est, si non sit prudens, fortis et temperans. Ita ut ibi vera est aliqua eorum, et aliae similiter sint; ubi autem aliae desunt, vera illa non est, etiam si aliquo modo similis esse videatur."✝

8     Sequentes tres Psalmi cum antiphonis recolunt secundum annum, in quo Dominus per legem visitavit vineam suam permanente adhuc ficu inutili. Ut nos non simus inutiles, cantamus tres Psalmos, quatinus consortes simus ordini trium electorum qui fuerunt sub lege Mosaica, scilicet

9 legislatorum, psalmistarum et prophetarum. Hoc est inter duodecim Psalmos qui sine antiphona cantantur et tres qui cum antiphona, quod erat inter duodecim patriarchas qui peregrini erant et sperabant hereditatem quam posteri eorum possederunt, et eosdem posteros qui hereditaverunt terram promissam patribus eorum. Gloriati sunt XII patriarchae de promissis, sed posteri eorum magis de perceptis.

we recount the twelve Psalms as a token of the virtues of the holy patriarchs.

We sing these Psalms divided into groups of four, because 6 there are four virtues through which we believe that the holy patriarchs worshiped the Holy Trinity—namely prudence, fortitude, justice and temperance. These virtues are not distinct from one another; instead, where one of them exists, the other three should always be present. Thus Augustine in his letter to Jerome: "And if prudence only exists 7 if it is strong and just and temperate, wherever it exists it certainly has the other virtues with it. And fortitude likewise cannot be imprudent or intemperate or unjust; and temperance must also be prudent, strong and just; and there is no justice if it is not prudent, strong and temperate. Thus, where one of these virtues truly exists, the rest are also there; but where the others are lacking, it is not a true virtue, even if it somehow seems like one."✝

The next three Psalms with antiphons recall the second 8 year, when the Lord visited his vineyard through the law and the fig tree still remained useless. That we may not be useless, we sing three Psalms to associate ourselves with the order of the three bodies of elect that existed under the Mosaic law, namely the givers of the law, the psalmists and the prophets. The difference between the twelve Psalms that 9 are sung without antiphons and the three that are sung with antiphons is the same as that between the twelve patriarchs who were without a country and hoped for the inheritance that their progeny possessed, and their progeny who inherited the land that was promised to their fathers. The twelve patriarchs rejoiced in what was promised them, but their progeny rejoiced more in what was given them.

10 Tres novissimi Psalmi cum alleluia recolunt tertium annum in Novo Testamento, ficu inutili manente, coruscante iam Evangelica gratia. Laudamus Dominum in primitiva ecclesia ex Iudaico populo; laudamus in sequenti ex gentilitate. Simili modo, in revocatione populi Iudaici, ut nostra ficus fructum pariat—noster videlicet populus—verbis et

11 moribus colimus illam per exempla sanctorum patrum. Hoc enim distat inter illos tres Psalmos qui cum antiphonis cantantur, et istos tres qui cum alleluia, quod est inter illos qui habuerunt testamentum mutandum, et eos qui habent testamentum non mutandum. Maior clarificatio est in Novo Testamento quam in Veteri. Horum omnium resurrectionem celebramus in Dominica nocte; horum participes nos

12 credimus futuros. Tres articulos memoratorum temporum dicit Sanctus Gregorius in omelia sua significatos esse in tribus annis quibus Dominus quaesivit fructum ficulneae et non invenit. Quando eorum recordamur qui migraverunt de mundo, fodimus fossam circa ficulneam, quia humiliamus nos usque ad pulverem mortis; et stercus addimus quoniam peccata nostra recolimus.

13 Hic dicendum est quid sit inter statum praesentium lectionum et earum quae per pastores domesticis amministrantur. Lectiones quae per pastores cantantur, domesticos et scientes ammonent ut non deficiant. Sicut ligna in focis adduntur lignis, ut non deficiat ignis, ita ignitis sensibus domesticorum adduntur verba ignita pastorum, ut non deficiant. Lectiones in Nocturnali officio typum gerunt earum

The three last Psalms, together with the alleluia, recall 10 the third year in the New Testament, when the fig tree remained useless even as the grace of the Gospel shone forth. We praise the Lord in the early church through the Jewish people; in the later church we praise him through the gentiles. Similarly, in calling back the Jewish people so that our fig tree—that is, our people—may bear fruit, we cultivate the tree with words and virtues after the example of the holy fathers. And the difference between those three Psalms that 11 are sung with antiphons, and these three that are sung with the alleluia, is the same as that between those who had a testament that was to be changed, and those who have a testament that is not to be changed. There is greater glory in the New Testament than in the Old. We celebrate the resurrection of all these people on Sunday night; we believe that we will be their companions. Saint Gregory, in his homily, says 12 that the three aforementioned periods of time were signified in the three years when the Lord sought fruit from the fig tree and did not find it. When we are mindful of those who have left the world, we dig a trench around the fig tree, because we are humbled unto the dust of death; and we add dung because we recall our sins.

Here we should discuss the difference between the na- 13 ture of the present readings and those that are provided by pastors to their household servants. The readings that are declaimed by the pastors advise their household servants and those who are knowledgeable not to fail. Just as, in a fire, wood is added to wood that the flame may not fail, so are the fired words of the pastor added to the fired sentiments of the household servants that they may not fail. The readings for Nocturns follow the example of the

lectionum quae solebant fieri in scolis patrum, in quibus nescientes imbuebantur et licitum erat eis interrogare in quibus dubitabant. Quarum exempla praetulimus in libello *De officio Missae,* et hic unum proferimus. Scriptum est in Actibus Apostolorum: "Hi autem erant nobiliores eorum qui sunt Thessalonicae, qui susceperunt verbum cum omni aviditate, cotidie scrutantes scripturas si haec ita se haberent" [Acts 17:11]. Ipsa enim dubitatio quae est in mentibus audientium, ante quam ad plenam cognitionem veniant, designatur per statum noctis.

14

15 Est varietas una de versu, qui fit altero ordine in isto officio quam in ceteris officiis. In ceteris officiis post lectionem sequitur versus, in isto praecedit. Versus causa est ut ostendat totam intentionem quam gerit corus in officio suo. Igitur, quia finis continet futurum effectum—sive in malo seu in bono—merito post completum officium, ante specialem orationem, versus ponitur; at in isto officio, quoniam sedetur ad lectionem post Psalmos, praecedit versus lectionem.

16 Nulli dubium quin aliqua quies sit fessis sessio, et quasi aliqua praesumptio de otio. Ac ideo, quia Deus non spernit preces afflictorum, constitutum est ut ilico post afflictionem corporum sequatur oratio versus. Coniungunt nos novem lectiones conversationi novem ordinum angelorum; coniungunt nos novem responsorii gaudiis eorundem novem ordinum angelorum. Et quoniam orandum est ante quam ad illorum societatem perveniamus, caelebratur versus orationis communis cori ante lectionem.

readings that used to be offered in the schools of the fathers, where the ignorant were trained and allowed to question the fathers where they had doubts. We laid out these examples above, in our book *On the Office of the Mass,* and we include one here. It is written in the Acts of the Apostles: "Now these were more noble than those in Thessalonica, who received the word with all eagerness, daily searching the scriptures whether these things were so." For the doubt that is in the minds of listeners before they come to full understanding is signified by the time of night.

There is one variation with respect to the versicle, which occurs in a different order in this office than it does in our other offices. In our other offices the versicle follows the reading; in this office, it precedes. The point of the versicle is to show the full intention that the choir exercises in its duty. Thus, because the end contains the future effect—whether for evil or for good—it is appropriate to place the versicle after the office has been completed, and before the special prayer. But in this office, because we sit for the reading after the Psalms, the versicle precedes the reading. There is no doubt that sitting provides some rest for the tired, and a kind of anticipation of leisure. Therefore, because God does not spurn the prayers of the afflicted, it was established that the prayer of the versicle should follow immediately after the affliction of our bodies. Nine readings join us in fellowship to the nine orders of angels; the nine responsories join us to the joys of these same nine orders of angel. And because we have to pray before we enter their ranks, the choir's common versicle of prayer is celebrated before the reading.

17    Primus versus dicit: "Memor fui nocte nominis tui" [Ps 118:55], et reliqua. Ipsa verba ostendunt cur surreximus de strato nostro. Secundus versus: "Media nocte surgebam" [Ps 118:62]. Iste ostendit qua ora noctis oporteat surgere; sed, quoniam neglegentes sumus de tempore quo soliti erant surgere patres nostri, non audemus mentiri; mutamus versum istum et dicimus alterum: "Quoniam tu inluminas lucernam meam" [Ps 17:29]. Tertius versus dicit: "Exaltare, Domine" [Ps 20:14]. Iste aperte Novum Testamentum recolit, in quo Christus exaltavit hominem assumptum ad caelos in virtute sua.

18    Quia diximus quod media nocte surgendum esset in Nocturnali officio, ex verbis Sancti Agustini et Hieronimi oportet nos confirmare nostra. David dicit in Psalmo *Beati inmaculati* [Ps 118] quo tempore ipse solitus esset surgere ad confitendum Domino: "Media nocte surgebam" [Ps 118:62]. Et in alio loco: "Praeveni inmaturitate et clamavi" [Ps 118:147].

19    Quod ita Agustinus: "'Praeveni intempesta nocte et clamavi.' Plures codices non habent: 'intempesta nocte,' sed: 'inmaturitate.' Vix autem unus inventus est qui haberet geminatam praepositionem, id est: 'in immaturitate.' Immaturitas itaque hoc loco nocturnum tempus est, quod non est maturum, id est oportunum, ut agatur aliquid vigilando; quod etiam vulgo dici solet hora importuna. 'Nox' quoque 'intempesta,' id est media, quando quiescendum est, hinc procul dubio nuncupata est, quia inportuna est actionibus vigilantium. 'Tempestivum' enim dixerunt veteres opportunum, et 'intempestivum' importunum, a tempore ducto vocabulo, non ab illa tempestate quae consuetudine Latinae linguae caeli perturbatio iam vocatur; quamquam isto verbo

The first versicle says: "In the night I have remembered 17 your name," and so forth. These words show why we arose from our bed. The second versicle: "I rose at midnight." This shows at what hour of the night we should rise; but, because we neglect the time when our fathers were accustomed to rise, we dare not lie; we change the versicle and pronounce another: "For you light my lamp." The third versicle says: "Be exalted, O Lord." This openly commemorates the New Testament, where Christ, through his virtue, raised to heaven the man that he assumed.

Because we said that we should rise for Nocturns at mid- 18 night, we should confirm our words with the words of Saint Augustine and Jerome. In the Psalm *Beati inmaculati,* David says at what time he was accustomed to rise to confess to the Lord: "I rose at midnight." And in another place: "I rose with immaturity and cried."

Augustine explains this as follows: "'I rose in an intem- 19 pestuous night and cried.' Many books do not have 'in an intempestuous night,' but: 'with immaturity.' But none has been found that doubles the preposition, as in: 'in immaturity.' In this passage, then, 'immaturity' is the time of night that is not mature or opportune for doing something while awake; it is also commonly called an importune hour. And here 'intempestuous night,' or midnight, doubtless refers to the time when there should be quiet, because it is importune for the actions of those who are awake. Now the ancients called that which was opportune 'tempestuous,' and that which was importune 'intempestuous,' deriving their terminology from the time of day and not from the tempest that, in the custom of the Latin tongue, means a disturbance of the sky. Yet historians freely use this words,

libenter utantur historici, ut dicant: 'ea tempestate,' quod
volunt: 'eo tempore' intellegi."

20    Unde et Hieronimus in libro *De vita Paulae:* "Post alleluia
cantatum, quo signo vocabantur ad collectam, nulli residere
licitum erat; sed prima vel inter primas veniens, ceteras
operiebatur, pudore et exemplo ad laborem eas provocans—
non terrore. Mane, ora tertia, sexta, nona, vespere, noctis

21    medio per ordinem Psalterium canebant." Item eiusdem ad
Demedriadem virginem: "Nunc tantum ad virginem loquar,
id est non ea quae extra te, sed in te sunt, tantum conside-
rans. Praeter Psalmorum et orationis ordinem quod tibi ora
tertia, sexta, nona, ad vesperum, noctis medio, et mane semper est exercendum, statue quot oris sanctam scripturam
ediscere debeas, quanto tempore legere—non ad laborem,
sed ad delectationem et instructionem animae. Cumque
haec finieris spatia et frequenter te ad figenda genua sollici-
tudo animi suscitaverit, habeto lanam semper in manibus,
vel staminis pollice fila deducito, vel ad torquenda subteg-
mina in alveolis fusa vertantur; aliarumque neta aut in glo-

22    bum collige aut texenda compone," et reliqua. Et iterum eiusdem ad Aleam de institutione filiae: "Praeponatur ei
probae fidei, ac morum ac pudicitiae virgo veterana, quae illam doceat et assuescat exemplo ad orationes et Psalmos
nocte consurgere, mane ymnos canere, tertia, sexta, nona
ora stare in acie, quasi bellatricem Christi, accensaque lu-
cernula reddere sacrificium vespertinum. Sic dies transeat;

saying 'in that tempest,' when they want 'in that time' to be understood."

And so Jerome, in his book *On the Life of Paula:* "After 20 singing the alleluia, the sign by which they were called to the gathering, nobody was allowed to remain behind; but when the first or one of the first came, she waited for the others, calling them to work by her modesty and example— not with fear. They sang the Psalter in order in the morning, at the third hour, the sixth, the ninth, at vespers and midnight." Again, from the same author to the virgin Deme- 21 trias: "I will now speak only to the virgin; that is, I will consider only what is within you, and not what is outside you. Beyond the order of Psalms and prayer that you should always observe at the third hour, the sixth, the ninth, at vespers, midnight and morning, establish for how many hours you should study Holy Scripture, and how long you should read—not as work, but for the delight and instruction of your soul. And when you have finished these periods of time and care for your spirit has often driven you to kneel, keep the wool ever in your hands, and form it into strings of thread with your thumb, and let the scattered cross-threads be turned and wound onto the shuttles; and either gather what others have spun into a ball or arrange it for weaving," and so on. And again, from the same author to Alea on the 22 instruction of her daughter: "Let an experienced virgin of excellent faith, morals and modesty be put in charge of her, to teach and accustom her by example to rise for prayer and Psalms at night, to sing hymns in the morning, to stand ready for battle like Christ's warrior at the third, sixth and

sic nox inveniat laborantem; orationi lectio, lectioni succedat oratio."✝

23 Sufficiant nobis haec exempla ad demonstrandum qua
ora surgendum sit in Nocturnali officio. Et hic habeant finem tres stationes vigilum quae per ternas oras divisae exer-
citae sunt. Et in quarta, oriente iam lucifero, excussis torpo-
ribus tedii nostri, sobrie et strenue praestolemur adventum
Domini nostri Iesu Christi, qui sua resurrectione nos laetificavit et informavit ad resurrectionem nostram, quam desi-
deraverunt patres sed in nobis completa est, "in quos fines
saeculorum devenerunt" [1 Cor 10:11]. Quos fines recoluntur in Matutinali officio usque ad resurrectionem corporum.

## 10

# De Matutinali officio per
# Dominicas noctes

Matutinale officium tempus Novi Testamenti mentibus
nostris intimat—hoc est ab initio baptismi usque ad plenam
remunerationem quam promisit Deus cum iure iurando
Abrahae et filiis suis in aeternum [Luke 1:73]. Eo enim tempore—id est matutinali—baptizati sunt filii Israhel in Mari

ninth hour, and to render the evening sacrifice with a lit lamp. Let the day pass in this way; let the night find her at work in this way; let reading follow prayer and prayer follow reading."✝

May these examples suffice to show us at what hour we    23 should rise for Nocturns. And let the three gatherings of vigils that we celebrated in divisions of three hours have their end here. And in the fourth, as the morning star rises and we cast off the torpor of our weariness, let us await with prudence and eagerness the coming of our Lord Jesus Christ, who has delighted us with his resurrection and informed us of our resurrection, which the fathers desired but which has been completed in us, "upon whom the ends of the world are come." These ends are recalled in Matins until the resurrection of our bodies.

## 10

# On Matins during Sunday nights

Matins puts us in mind of the era of the New Testament—that is, the era from the establishment of baptism to the full reward that God promised with his oath to Abraham and his sons in eternity. For in that time—that is, the morning—the sons of Israel were baptized in the

Rubro, ut Exodus narrat: "Factum est," inquiens, "in vigilia matutina, et ecce respiciens Dominus super castra Aegyptiorum per columnam ignis et nubis, et interfecit exercitum eorum et subvertit rotas curruum" [Exod 14:24–25], et reliqua. Quando isti sunt interfecti, tunc baptizati sunt filii Israhel.

2    Quae sit vigilia matutina, Beda monstrat in tractatu super Marcum, ubi disputat de quarta vigilia noctis: "'Et circa,'" inquit, "'quartam vigiliam noctis venit ad eos ambulans super mare' [Mic 6:48]. Stationes et vigiliae militares in terna horarum spatia dividuntur. Quando ergo dicit quarta vigilia noctis venisse ad eos Dominum, ostendit tota nocte periclitatos, et extremo noctis tempore eis auxilium praebitum."

3    Et paulo post: "Cum vero mentem"—quin nisi iustus?—"ad superni lumen praesidii et perpetuae dona retributionis erexerit, quasi inter umbras noctis repente exortum luciferi conspicit quod diem proximum nuntiat—lucifer namque, cum plurimum tres horas noctis, id est totam vigiliam matutinam, inluminare perhibetur. Aderitque Dominus qui, sopitis temptationum periculis, plenam libertatis fiduciam suae protectionis attribuat."+

4    Quod tempus, id est baptismi, praefiguratum est in arca Noe, in qua pauci, id est octo animae, salvae factae sunt. Docet Petrus apostolus hoc praecessisse in forma nostri baptismatis, dicens: "In qua pauci, id est octo animae, salvae factae sunt per aquam; quod et nos nunc similis formae sal-

5    vos baptysma facit" [1 Pet 3:20–21], et reliqua. Sicut tunc octo animae fuerunt in arca, ita possumus invenire octo

Red Sea, as Exodus relates, saying: "And now the morning watch was come, and behold the Lord, looking upon the Egyptian army through the pillar of fire and of the cloud, slew their host and overthrew the wheels of the chariots," and so forth. When the Egyptians were killed, the sons of Israel were baptized.

In his treatise on Mark, Bede explains what the morning 2 vigil is while discussing the fourth watch, or vigil, of the night: "'And,'" he says "'about the fourth watch of the night, he comes to them walking upon the sea.' Military posts and watches are divided into three-hour periods. And so when he says that the Lord came to them at the fourth watch of the night, he shows that they struggled the whole night, and at the last moment of the night help was offered them." And 3 a little later: "But when he has raised his mind"—who, if not the just man?—"to the light of heavenly protection and the gifts of eternal recompense, it is as if he suddenly sees, amid the nighttime shadows, the rising of the morning star that proclaims the coming day—the morning star, since it is often seen shining for three hours of the night, or the whole of the morning vigil. And the Lord, who bestows the full confidence of the freedom of his protection after he has laid to rest the dangers of temptation, will be there."✝

This era, namely the era of baptism, was prefigured in 4 Noah's ark, wherein a few, namely eight souls, were saved. Peter the apostle teaches that this preceded as a symbol of our baptism, saying: "In which a few, namely eight souls, were saved by water; and baptism, being of the like form, now saves us also," and so forth. Just as there were 5 eight souls at that time in the ark, so can we find eight

ordines electorum sub tempore baptismi. Primus ordo est primitivae ecclesiae, versantis in populo Iudaico; secundus, eiusdem primitivae ecclesiae, intrantis ad gentes; tertius, credentis gentilitatis; quartus, resipiscentis populi Iudaici; quintus, eorum qui futuri sunt sub tempore antichristi; sextus et septimus ac octavus, eorum qui universaliter colligendi sunt ex Asia et Europa ac Africa. Et fruentur maiori pace quam nunc fruatur ecclesia. Unde Gregorius: "Quae sagina scilicet tunc universaliter repletur, cum in fine suo humani generis summa concluditur."✝

6   Primus Psalmus [Ps 92] monstrat primitivam ecclesiam, quae reformata et aedificata est Christi praedicatione, eo iam regnante, sicut ipse dicit: "Data est mihi omnis potestas in caelo et in terra" [Matt 28:18]. Quod primus et secundus versus dilucidant: "Dominus regnavit, decorem induit; induit Dominus fortitudinem et praecinxit se" [Ps 92:1]. Iste regnantem Christum monstrat; at secundus, aedificationem membrorum suorum, dicens: "Etenim firmavit orbem terrae, qui non commovebitur" [Ps 92:1]. Quid iste Psalmus in

7   se contineat, addiscimus verbis sancti Agustini in expositione tituli ipsius. Ita enim infit: "In titulo enim tamquam ammonemur in limine quid intus quaeramus. Inscriptus ergo est ita: 'Laus cantici ipsi David in die ante Sabbatum, quando fundata est terra.'" Et post aliqua: "Cum omnes qui credunt per universam terram immobiles sunt in fide, fundata est terra; tunc fit homo ad imaginem Dei, quod significat sextus ille dies de Genesi. Sed quomodo illum fecit Deus? Quomodo fundata est terra? Christus venit ut

orders of the elect in the era of baptism. The first is the order of the early church, living in the Jewish people; the second is of the same early church, going forth to the gentiles; the third, of the believing gentiles; the fourth, of the returning Jewish people; the fifth, of those who will live in the time of the antichrist; the sixth and seventh and eighth, of those who are to be gathered from all of Asia and Europe and Africa. And they will enjoy a greater peace than the church enjoys now. Thus Gregory: "And that net is completely filled when the fullness of the human race is included in its bounds."✝

The first Psalm reveals the early church, which was re- 6 formed and built through the preaching of Christ as he reigns now, as he himself says: "All power is given to me in heaven and in earth." The first and the second verse proclaim this: "The Lord has reigned, he is clothed with beauty; the Lord is clothed with strength and has girded himself." This reveals that Christ reigns, while the second verse reveals the building of his members, saying: "For he has established the world, which shall not be moved." We 7 learn what this Psalm contains through Saint Augustine's words in explanation of its title. For he begins as follows: "For in the title it is as if we are advised on the threshold about what we seek within. Thus it is inscribed as follows: 'Praise in the way of a canticle for David himself on the day before the Sabbath, when the earth was founded.'" And somewhat further: "When all those who believe throughout the whole earth are immovable in their faith, the earth has been founded; then man is in God's image, which is what that sixth day signifies in Genesis. But how did God make it? How was the earth founded? Christ came to

fundaret terram. 'Fundamentum enim nemo potest ponere praeter id quod positum est, quod est Christus Iesus' [1 Cor 3:11]."✝

8    Super hoc fundamentum apostolica ecclesia primo fundata est. Ipsa venit ad ceteras nationes, adnuntians eis Christi adventum et praecipiens ut ei iubilarent et servirent. Unde idem qui supra dicit in tractatu Psalmi nonagesimi noni: "'Iubilate ergo Domino, universa terra' [Ps 99:1]. Numquid modo vocem meam audit universa terra? Et tamen hanc vocem audivit universa terra. Iam iubilat Domino universa terra—et quod adhuc non iubilat, iubilabit. Pertendens enim benedictio, incipiente ecclesia ab Hierusalem per omnes gentes," et reliqua.✝ Ex his verbis Iudeorum vo-

9    cationem sentimus, in secundo Psalmo [Ps 99], per praedicationem apostolorum; ac in tertio [Ps 62] nostram benivolentiam offerimus apostolorum vocationi et dicimus: "Deus, Deus meus, ad te de luce vigilo. Sitivit in te anima mea; quam multipliciter tibi et caro mea" [Ps 62:2]. Titulus Psalmi monstrat praesentem Psalmum cantatum esse ex persona gentilitatis. Titulum habet ipse Psalmus: "Ipsius David, cum esset in deserto Idumeae." Quod ita idem Agustinus in tractatu Psalmi eiusdem: "Per 'Idumeae' nomen intellegitur saeculum istud. Idumea enim gens erat quaedam errantium hominum ubi idola colebantur."✝

10    Arca enim Noe, quae octo animas continebat, bicamerata erat. De qua re scribit idem qui supra in libro quinto decimo *De civitate Dei:* "Et fieri quidem potest ut et nobis

found the earth. 'For other foundation no man can lay beyond that which is laid, which is Christ Jesus.'"✝

The apostolic church was founded upon this foundation 8 in the beginning. It went out to the other nations, telling them about Christ's coming and commanding that they sing joyfully to Christ and serve him. Thus the same author as above says in his treatise on Psalm 99: "'Sing joyfully to the Lord, all the earth.' Does the whole earth really hear my voice right now? And yet the whole earth did hear this voice. Now the whole earth sings joyfully to the Lord—and whatever does not now sing joyfully, will sing joyfully. For the blessing is ongoing as the church goes out from Jerusalem to all the gentiles," and so forth.✝ In these words we hear, 9 in the second Psalm, the calling of the Jews through the preaching of the apostles; and in the third Psalm we offer our goodwill to the apostles' call and say: "O God, my God, to you do I watch at break of day. For you my soul has thirsted; for you my flesh, oh how many ways." The title of the Psalm shows that the present Psalm was sung in the guise of a gentile. This Psalm has the title: "A Psalm of the same David while he was in the desert of Edom." The same Augustine, in his treatise on the same Psalm, explains this as follows: "Through the name 'Edom' we understand that age. For Edom was a nation of men who wandered where idols were worshiped."✝

Now the ark of Noah, which contained eight souls, had 10 two stories. The same author as above writes about this matter in the fifteenth book of the *City of God:* "And it can happen that one person explains these things more aptly

quispiam, et alius alio exponat haec aptius, dum tamen ea quae dicuntur ad hanc de qua loquimur Dei civitatem, in hoc saeculo maligno tamquam in diluvio peregrinantem, omnia referantur—si ab eius sensu, qui ista conscripsit, non vult longe aberrare, qui exponit. Exempli gratia, velut si quispiam quod hic scriptum est—'inferiora, bicamerata et tricamerata facies ea' [Gen 6:16]—non quod ego in illo opere dixi velit intellegi, quia ex omnibus gentibus ecclesia congregatur, bicameratam dictam propter duo genera hominum, circumcisionem scilicet et praeputium, quos Apostolus et alio modo dicit Iudaeos et Grecos . . ." et reliqua.✝

11 Quia futurum est ante persecutionem antichristi, ut populus ex praeputio et circumcisione unum sint in fide, ideo duo Psalmi [Ps 62, 66] in tertio ordine continentur, sub una antiphona. Quae continentur in Psalmo *Deus misereatur nostri* [Ps 66] utrumque populum designant—scilicet Iudaeum et gentilem.

12 Postquam hi fuerint coniuncti, veniet tribulatio antichristi, in cuius figuram praecessit Nabuchodonosor, et mittet in caminum tribulationis tres filios Noe, quasi tres pueros, quos non solum liberabit Deus de eius malignitate, quia electi sunt, sed et benedicent Domino ad similitudinem trium puerorum [Dan 3]. Quapropter cum in ceteris Psalmis solemus dicere alleluia, in ista benedictione Latinis verbis utimur ad commendandam tribulationem quam passuri sunt sancti in diebus memorati antichristi, sive modo

13 patiuntur a membris eius. Et non est necesse ibi cantare

to us, and another person explains them more aptly to someone else, while the things being said all nevertheless relate
to this city of God that we are speaking about, as it wanders
in this evil world, as if in a flood—so long as the one offering the explanation does not wish to wander far from the
thought of the one who wrote these things. For example: If
someone wants to understand the passage I quoted—'with
lower, second and third stories shall you make it'—not as I
explained in that work, where I maintained that the church
was gathered from all the gentiles and called two-storied because of the two races of man, namely those who were circumcised and those with foreskin, as in another sense the
Apostle calls the Jews and the Greeks . . ." and so on.✝ Since,   11
before the persecution of the antichrist, it will come about
that the people of foreskin and of circumcision become one
in faith, two Psalms are contained in the third position, under one antiphon. The contents of the Psalm *Deus misereatur
nostri* designate both peoples—namely, the Jewish and the
gentile.

After these peoples have been united, the tribulation of   12
the antichrist will come. Nebuchadnezzar was his forerunner, and he will send the three sons of Noah, like the three
boys, into the furnace of tribulation. And God will not only
free them from his wrath because they are the elect, but
they will also bless the Lord like the three boys did. Therefore, while we are accustomed to sing the alleluia with the
other Psalms, in this blessing we use Latin words to commemorate the tribulation that the saints will suffer in the
days of the aforementioned antichrist, or that they now
suffer at the hands of his members. And at that point it is   13

*Gloria Patri et Filio,* quia in ipsa benedictione commemoramus eandem sanctam Trinitatem, dicendo: "Benedicamus Deo Patri et Filio et Spiritui Sancto." Diximus de *Gloria Patri* quod eius usum scripserit beatus Hieronimus ad papam Damasum. Post hoc, secundum Danielem, erit quies aliqua. Qui ita dicit: "Beatus qui expectat et pervenit usque ad dies mille trecentos triginta quinque" [Dan 12:12]. Quod beatus Hieronimus sic exponit: "Beatus, inquit, qui, interfecto antichristo, supra mille ducentos nonaginta dies (id est tres semis annos) dies quadraginta quinque praestolatur, quibus est Dominus atque salvator in sua maiestate venturus."✝

14    In qua quiete celebrabitur laus Dei, quae continetur in tribus Psalmis, scilicet: *Laudate Dominum de caelis* [Ps 148] et *Cantate Domino canticum novum* [Ps 149] et *Laudate Dominum in sanctis eius* [Ps 150], ab universo genere humano quod evadet de tribulatione. Quod genus humanum a tribus filiis Noe propagatum est. Unde Agustinus in libro memorato quinto decimo *De civitate Dei:* "Tricamerata vero"—quin arca— "erat, eo quod omnes gentes de tribus filiis Noe post diluvium
15 reparatae sunt." Sive alio modo, ut idem Agustinus in libro *Quaestionum Evangeliorum,* titulo XLVII: "Ad ipsa tria genera quae assumuntur, arbitror pertinere etiam illa tria nomina virorum sanctorum quos solos liberatos vir Ezechiel propheta praenuntiat—Noe, Daniel et Iob [Ezek 14:14; Luke 17:34–35]. Videtur enim Noe pertinere ad eos per quos ecclesia regitur, sicut per illum in aquis arca gubernata est, quae figuram gestabat ecclesiae [Gen 6–8]. Daniel autem, quia elegit celebem vitam (id est nuptias terrenas contempsit [Dan 1:3] ut, sicut dicit Apostolus, sine sollicitudine

not necessary to sing the *Gloria Patri et Filio,* because in that blessing we commemorate this same Holy Trinity by saying: "Let us bless God the Father and the Son and the Holy Spirit." We said of the *Gloria Patri* that blessed Jerome wrote about its use to Pope Damasus. After this, according to Daniel, there will be some rest. He speaks thus: "Blessed is he who waits and comes unto a thousand three hundred thirty-five days." The blessed Jerome explains this as follows: "Blessed, he says, is he who, upon the death of the antichrist, waits forty-five days beyond the one thousand two-hundred and ninety days (that is, three and a half years), in which the Lord and savior will come in his majesty."✝

God's praise will be celebrated during this peace. It is 14 contained in three Psalms, namely: *Laudate Dominum de caelis* and *Cantate Domino canticum novum* and *Laudate Dominum in sanctis eius.* It will be celebrated by the whole of the human race that avoids the tribulation. This human race was begotten from the sons of Noah. Thus Augustine, in the aforementioned fifteenth book of the *City of God:* "But it had three stories"—that is, the ark—"because all nations were restored from the three sons of Noah after the flood." Or in 15 another sense, as the same Augustine writes in his book of *Questions on the Gospels,* title 47: "I think that the names of the three holy men, the only ones whom the man and prophet Ezekiel announces were freed—Noah, Daniel and Job—also relate to the three categories of people who are taken up. For Noah seems associated with those through whom the church is governed, just as the ark, which was a symbol of the church, was steered by Noah in the waters. And Daniel, because he chose a celibate life (that is, he held earthly nuptials in contempt so that, as the Apostle says, he

viveret cogitans quae sunt Dei [Dan 1:3; 1 Cor 7:32–34]), genus eorum significat qui sunt in ocio, sed tamen fortissimi in
temptationibus, ut possint assumi. Iob autem, quia et uxo-
rem habuit et filios et amplas terrenas rerum copias, ad illud
genus pertinet cui molendinum deputatum est, sed tamen
ut sint fortissimi in temptationibus, sicut ille fuit—non
enim aliter assumi poterunt. Nec puto alia esse genera ho-

16 minum quibus constat ecclesia, quam ista tria."✝ Quoniam
futura sunt haec unius virtutis, scilicet patientiae, consortia
et communia, sub una antiphona sive alleluia canuntur tres
Psalmi qui nos invitant ad eorum societatem.

17     Dein sequitur lectio quae pro ammonitione fraterna reci-
tatur in coro; quae semper placita erit quamdiu in praesenti
saeculo deget ecclesia. Postea sequitur versus aptus tempori
tali, dicit enim: "Dominus regnavit" [Ps 92:1], et cetera. Tunc
fiet illud quod Apostolus dicit: "Cum tradiderit regnum Deo
et Patri" [1 Cor 15:24]. Quando regnum Deo tradit—sibi
ipsi, qui Deus est—coniungit illud ad perpetuum regnum

18 suum. At ymnus Zachariae remunerationem recolit promissam Abrahae—id est, ut serviamus Domino sine timore in
sanctitate et iustitia omnibus diebus [Luke 1:74–75]. Tale
servitium reperitur modo in raris qui sunt iam perfecti; sed
tunc ab electis omnibus caelebrabitur, quia omnes erunt
perfecti.

might live without solicitude, considering those things that are of God), signifies the category of those who are at peace, but are nevertheless the strongest in the face of temptation, that they may be able to be taken up. And Job, because he had a wife and sons and abundant lands full of possessions, is associated with that category that is allotted the mill, that they may nevertheless be strong in the face of temptations, just as he was—for otherwise they could not be taken up. I do not think that the church consists of other categories of men beyond these three."✝ Because their future fellowship and community will have one virtue, namely patience, the three Psalms that invite us to their society are sung with a single antiphon or alleluia.

Then follows the reading that is recited in the choir for fraternal admonition; this will always be pleasing so long as the church dwells in this world. Then a versicle, appropriate for such a time, follows; it says: "The Lord has reigned," and so on. Then that which the Apostle speaks of will come about: "When he shall have delivered up the kingdom to God and the Father." When he delivers the kingdom to God —to himself, for he is God—he joins it to his eternal kingdom. And the hymn of Zechariah recalls the reward promised to Abraham—that is, that we may serve the Lord without fear in sanctity and justice for all our days. Such service is found today among those rare people who are already perfected; in the world to come, however, it will be celebrated by all the elect, because they will all be perfected.

## 11

# De Nocturnali officio per cotidianas noctes

Ut enim Dominica nox recolit cives Hierusalem ab initio mundi usque in finem, cotidianae noctes peregrinationem mortalium et abalienationem a patria inter inimicos degentem. Et quia duodecim horae sunt noctis in quibus necesse habemus custodia Domini muniri, duodecim Psalmos cantamus. Et quia haec custodia seria est per sex aetates mundi, sex antiphonis coniungimus Psalmos. Et quia sex aetates mundi tribus temporibus concluduntur—scilicet naturalis legis, legis litterae et legis gratiae—tres lectiones leguntur et tres responsorii canuntur.

## 12

# De Matutinali officio per cotidianas noctes, de secunda feria

In Dominicis noctibus, per quinque antiphonas, recolimus statum ecclesiae ab initio apostolicae stabilitatis usque ad perfectionem electorum, qui in fine mundi venturi sunt.

## 11

# On Nocturns during
# ordinary nights

As Sunday night recalls the citizens of Jerusalem from the beginning of the world to the end, the ordinary nights recall the exile of mortals and their alienation from their country as they dwell among enemies. And because there are twelve hours of the night when we need to be fortified by the Lord's protection, we sing twelve Psalms. And because this protection is necessary through the six ages of the world, we join the Psalms to six antiphons. And because the six ages of the world are gathered into three periods of time—namely, of natural law, the law of the letter and the law of grace— three readings are read and three responsories are sung.

## 12

# On Matins during ordinary
# nights, from Monday

On Sunday nights, through five antiphons, we recall the state of the church from the origin of its apostolic establishment to the perfection of the elect who will come at the end

At cotidianis noctibus altero modo eundem statum recolimus—per mutationem Psalmorum et canticorum a secunda
2 feria usque in Sabbato. Primus Psalmus, *Miserere mei Deus*
[Ps 50], continet paenitentum conversionem. Iudaei conversi qui deputantur in primitiva ecclesia istius Psalmi
vigorem frequentabant, quando ad praedicationem Petri
paenitentiam egerunt et conpuncti sunt corde. De quibus
scriptum est in Actibus Apostolorum: "His auditis, compuncti sunt corde et dixerunt ad Petrum et ad reliquos apostolos: Quid faciemus, viri fratres? Petrus vero ait ad illos:
Paenitentiam, inquit, agite et baptizetur unusquisque vestrum in nomine Iesu Christi" [Acts 2:37–38]. Simili modo,
per sequentes noctes, idem Psalmus nos, qui de gentili conversatione conversi sumus, ad paenitentiam provocat.

3 Sufficit de praesenti Psalmo. De ceteris, id est *Deus, Deus
meus* [Ps 62] et *Deus misereatur nostri* [Ps 66] et *Laudate Dominum de caelis* [Ps 148] ac *Cantate Domino* [Ps 149] atque *Laudate Dominum in sanctis eius* [Ps 150], iam dictum est. Restat
ordo, ut ad secundam feriam revertamur et transeamus per
mutationem Psalmorum et canticorum. Illud primo oportet
intueri, ut Psalmus et canticum, sicut sunt in uno officio deputata unius noctis, ita sunt in rebus similia et significa-
4 tionibus. Psalmus *Verba mea* habet hunc titulum: "Pro ea
quae hereditatem accepit" [Ps 5:1]. Quem ita exponit Agustinus: "Intellegitur ergo ecclesia, quae accepit hereditatem,
vitam aeternam, per Dominum nostrum Iesum Christum,
ut possideat ipsum Deum, cui adherens, beata sit secundum

of the world. On ordinary nights, however, we recall this state in another way—through changing Psalms and canticles from Monday through Saturday. The first Psalm, *Miserere mei Deus,* contains the conversion of the penitent. The converted Jews who were counted among the early church often contemplated the force of this Psalm, when they did penance in response to Peter's preaching and had compunction in their heart. About them it is written in the Acts of the Apostles: "Now when they had heard these things, they had compunction in their heart and said to Peter and to the rest of the apostles: What shall we do, men and brethren? But Peter spoke to them: Do penance, he said, and be baptized every one of you in the name of Jesus Christ." In a similar fashion, on the following nights, the same Psalm calls us, who were converted upon the conversion of the gentiles, to penance.

That is enough on the present Psalm. We have already discussed the others, namely *Deus, Deus meus* and *Deus misereatur nostri* and *Laudate Dominum de caelis* and *Cantate Domino* and *Laudate Dominum in sanctis eius.* There remains the requirement that we return to Monday and move on to the changing of Psalms and canticles. It should first be observed that the Psalm and the canticle, just as they are assigned to a single office on a single night, are also similar in contents and meaning. The Psalm *Verba mea* has this title: "For her that obtained the inheritance." Augustine explains this as follows: "It is understood, therefore, that this refers to the church, which obtained the inheritance of eternal life through our Lord Jesus Christ, that it might possess this same God, and, clinging to him, be blessed according to that

illud: 'Beati mites, quoniam ipsi hereditate possidebunt terram' [Matt 5:4]."✝

5   Hanc hereditatem primitiva ecclesia accepit, quae simul
cum apostolis in praesenti saeculo vixit. Ex eius persona
cantatur canticum Isaiae prophetae: "Confitebor tibi, Domine, quoniam iratus es mihi. Conversus est furor tuus et
consolatus es me" [Isa 12:1], et reliqua. Canticum istud illud
tempus recolit quando primo vexillum sanctae crucis erectum est. Unde in superioribus partibus in eodem propheta
scriptum est: "Et levabit signum in nationes, et congregabit
6   profugos Israel" [Isa 11:12], et reliqua. Quod sic Hieronimus
in eodem exponit: "In die illa, hoc est in illo tempore de quo
et supra dictum est, cum resurrexerit radix Iesse in signum
populorum sive ut dominetur gentium, apponet Dominus
secundo manum suam—ut nequaquam, iuxta eos nostros
Iudaizantes, in finem mundi cum intraverit plenitudo gentium tunc omnis Israhel salvus fiat; sed haec omnia in primo
intellegamus adventu." Et paulo post: "Levabit igitur signum crucis in universas nationes, et de sinagogis Iudaeorum
primum Israhel populos congregabit, ut apostoli praeceptum salvatoris implerent, qui dixerat: 'Ite ad oves perditas
7   domus Israhel' [Matt 10:6]." Idem in sequentibus in memorato libro monstrat de quibus canticum narret, dicens: "Qui
prius in solitudine dixeratis—quando ascendistis de terra
Aegypti et Mare siccatum est Rubrum: 'Cantemus Domino,
gloriose enim magnificatus est' [Exod 15:1]. Et nunc, per-
cussa lingua maris Aegypti et flumine illius arefacto atque
consciso et humiliato, glorificate Dominum et dicite: Confitebor tibi, Domine, quoniam iram merui et furorem. Tuam

verse: 'Blessed are the meek, for they shall possess the land.'"✝

The early church, which lived together with the apostles 5 in this world, obtained this inheritance. The canticle of the prophet Isaiah is sung in the guise of this church: "I will confess to you, Lord, for you were angry with me. Your wrath has turned away and you have comforted me," and so forth. This canticle recalls that time when the banner of the holy cross was first erected. Thus, in earlier passages of the same prophet, it is written: "And he shall set up a sign unto the nations, and shall assemble the fugitives of Israel," and so on. Jerome, on the same prophet, explains this as follows: "On 6 that day, that is in the time discussed above, when the shoot of Jesse was set up as a sign for the people and also to govern the gentiles, the Lord will stretch out his hand for a second time—but not, according to those Judaizers among us, so that all of Israel may be saved at the end of the world when the fullness of the gentiles has gone in; rather, we should understand all of this in light of the first coming." And a little later: "He will therefore raise the sign of the cross over all nations, and he will first gather the people of Israel from the Jewish synagogues, that the apostles may fulfill the command of the savior, who said: 'Go rather to the lost sheep of the house of Israel.'" Further on, the same author in the 7 aforementioned book reveals whom the canticle speaks of, saying: "You who had first spoken in the desert—when you went forth from the land of Egypt and the Red Sea was drained: 'Let us sing to the Lord, for he is gloriously magnified.' And now that the tongue of the sea of Egypt has been struck and its water dried up and destroyed and humbled, glorify the Lord and say: I will confess to you, Lord, because

misericordiam consecutus sum. Tu es enim salvator meus—
id est Iesus. Et nequaquam fiduciam habebo in idolis, nec
timebo quae non sunt timenda; sed tu es fortitudo mea et
laus mea."✝

8 Hoc est inter Psalmum et canticum, quod est inter opera
iusti et gratiarum actionem—ut Psalmus demonstret opera
iusti post conversionem, ut est in praesenti Psalmo ("Quoniam ad te orabo, Domine, mane exaudies vocem meam.
Mane adstabo tibi" [Ps 5:4–5], et reliqua), et canticum laudem Dei pro eodem opere.

9 Versus post lectionem per cotidianas noctes illud tempus
ad memoriam reducit, quando merces recompensabitur
post laborem praesentis saeculi iustis a Domino. Versus dicit: "Repleti sumus mane misericordia tua" [Ps 89:14], et re-
10 liqua. Quem ita exponit Agustinus in eodem Psalmo, unde
sumptus est: "Deinde," inquit, "illa bona quae futura sunt
spe anticipans, et velut facta iam deputans: 'Repleti sumus,'
inquit, 'mane misericordia tua.' Ergo in his velut nocturnis
laboribus et doloribus prophetia nobis accensa est, sicut lu-
cerna in obscuro loco, 'donec dies illucescat, et lucifer oriatur in cordibus vestris' [2 Pet 1:19]. 'Beati' enim 'mundo
corde, quia ipsi Deum videbunt' [Matt 5:8]. Tunc replebun-
tur eo bono iusti quod nunc esuriunt et sitiunt, cum, per fidem ambulantes, peregrinantur a Domino. Unde et illud dicitur: 'Replebis me laetitia cum vultu tuo' [Ps 15:10]. Mane
adstabunt et contemplabuntur [Ps 5:5]; et, sicut alii dixerunt interpretes: 'Satiati sumus mane misericordia tua'
[Ps 89:14]. Tunc satiabuntur; sicut enim alibi ait: 'Satiabor

I have deserved your anger and fury. I have pursued your mercy. For you are my savior—that is, Jesus. And I will have no faith in idols, nor will I fear what should not be feared; but you are my strength and my praise."✝

The difference between a Psalm and a canticle is the same 8 as that between the works of a just man and his thanksgiving—such that the Psalm demonstrates the works of the just man after conversion, as in the present Psalm ("For to you will I pray, Lord, in the morning you shall hear my voice. In the morning I will stand before you," and so forth), and the canticle demonstrates God's praise for the same work.

On ordinary nights, the versicle after the reading brings 9 to mind that time when the wages will be paid by the Lord to the just, after the labor of this world. The versicle says: "We are filled in the morning with your mercy," and so forth. Augustine, on the very Psalm from which the versicle was 10 taken, explains this as follows. "Then," he says, "anticipating with hope the good things that are to come, and considering them as already granted, he says: 'We are filled in the morning with your mercy.' It is therefore as if, in the midst of these nightly labors and sorrows, the prophecy has been set alight for us, like a lamp in a dark place, 'until the day dawns and the morning star arises in your hearts.' For 'Blessed are the clean of heart, for they shall see God.' Then the just will be filled with the good after which they now hunger and thirst, while they wander in faith, exiled from the Lord. Thus it is also said: 'You shall fill me with joy with your countenance.' In the morning they will stand before you and they will see; and, as other translations have it: 'We are satisfied in the morning with your mercy.' Then they will be satisfied; for as it says elsewhere: 'I shall be satisfied

cum manifestabitur gloria tua' [Ps 16:15]. Unde dicitur:
'Ostende nobis Patrem et sufficit nobis' [John 14:8]. Atque
ipse Dominus: 'Ostendam me ipsum illi' [John 14:21]. Quod
donec fiat, nihil boni nobis sufficit, nec sufficere debet, ne

11  desiderium nostrum in via remaneat." Et post pauca: "'Repleti sumus mane misericordia tua, et exultavimus et laetati
sumus in omnibus diebus nostris' [Ps 89:14]. Dies ille dies
est sine fine; simul sunt illi omnes dies."✝

12  Quod per cotidianas noctes sequitur post ymnum Zachariae (qui nos introducit post resurrectionem corporum in
aeternam vitam)—oratio consueta—hoc innuit: Quod omnia illa bona peccatores per paenitentiam sperant.

# 13

# De tertia feria

Tertia feria illud tempus recolit quando ab impiis imperatoribus persequebatur ecclesia, qui conabantur auferre
lucrum apostolorum, ne filios spiritales generarent. Tempus illud praecipue fuit a prima persecutione Neronis usque ad tempus Diocletiani et Maximiani. Quid sancti eo
tempore passi sunt, Psalmus monstrat, dicens: "Iudica me,
Deus, et discerne causam meam de gente non sancta" [Ps
42:1], et cetera. Sequentia non minus demonstrat tristitiam

when your glory shall appear.' Thus it is said: 'Show us the Father and it is enough for us.' And the Lord himself: 'I will manifest myself to him.' Until this occurs, no good is enough for us; nor should it be enough, lest our desire remain on the path." And after a little: "'We are filled in the morning with your mercy, and we have exulted and rejoiced all our days.' That day is the day without end; all those days occur at once."✝ 11

What follows on ordinary nights after the hymn of Zechariah (which leads us, through the resurrection of our bodies, into eternal life)—the customary prayer—suggests this: That sinners, through penance, hope for all these good things. 12

# 13

# On Tuesday

Tuesday recalls the time when the church was persecuted by the impious emperors, who tried to steal the wealth of the apostles and prevent them from begetting spiritual sons. That time extended primarily from the first persecution of Nero to the time of Diocletian and Maximian. The Psalm shows what the saints suffered in that time, saying: "Judge me, God, and distinguish my cause from the nation that is not holy," and so forth. The program no less reveals the

sanctae ecclesiae, quam habebat quia non ei aperte licebat
2 Christum generare in cordibus electorum. Evasit sancta
ecclesia de hac tribulatione, et cantat canticum quod cantavit Ezechias, postquam liberatus est de Senacerib et postquam eum Deus visitavit per flagellum infirmitatis, ne ele-
varetur cor eius de victoria concessa [Isa 38:10–20]. Unde
et dicit: "Vivens, vivens, ipse confitebitur tibi, sicut et ego
hodie. Pater filiis notam faciet veritatem tuam" [Isa 38:19].
Nam et ipse ideo flebat, quia dolebat orbitatem filiorum.


## 14

## De feria quarta

Feria quarta tempus illud recolit in quo sancta ecclesia
exaltata est super inimicos suos. Quod ex titulo Psalmi
qui in ea cantatur, cognoscere possumus. Titulus talis est:
"In finem Psalmus David; canticum Hieremiae et Ezechiel ex populo transmigrationis, cum inciperent exire"
[Ps 64:1]. Iste Psalmus ex persona eorum cantatur qui in-
tuentur reditum ad Hierusalem et libertatem Dei populi.
Sicut Iudaei quondam liberati sunt de Babylonia et traducti
in Hierusalem, ita et ecclesia nostra liberata est de manu

sorrow that the holy church endured because it was not permitted to propagate Christ openly in the hearts of the elect. The holy church emerged from this tribulation, and it sings ₂ the canticle that Hezekiah sang after he was freed from Sennacherib and after the Lord punished him with the scourge of sickness, that his heart would not be elevated to pride over the victory he had been granted. And so it says: "The living, the living, he shall give praise to you, as I do this day. The father shall make your truth known to the children." For he mourned because he was sorrowful over the loss of the children.


## 14

# On Wednesday

Wednesday recalls that time when the holy church was exalted over its enemies. We can recognize as much from the title of the Psalm that is sung on that day. This is the title: "To the end a Psalm of David; the canticle of Jeremiah and Ezekiel to the people of the captivity, when they began to go out." This Psalm is sung in the guise of those who observed the return of God's people to Jerusalem and to freedom. Just as the Jews were once freed from Babylon and brought to Jerusalem, so too was our church freed from the

2  impiorum imperatorum et donata libertati tempore Constantini imperatoris. Unde exultat in cantico quod cantavit Anna, Samuelis mater, postquam liberata est de afflictione Fennenae, emulae suae: "Exultavit," inquit, "cor meum, et exaltatum est cornu meum in Deo meo" [1 Kgs 2:1]. Ab illo enim tempore, postquam res publica et potestas Romanorum subdita est apostolicis viris et Christianis imperatoribus, dilatatum est os ecclesiae super inimicos suos [1 Kgs 2:1], scilicet paganos et perfidos Iudaeos. Ista dilatatio hodierna die permanet. Det Deus, ut diu permaneat et adimpleatur illud Apostoli, donec plenitudo gentium introierit, et sic omnis Israel salvus fiet [Rom 11:25].

## 15

# De quinta feria

Iste articulus sub una virga, id est sub uno regimine, suscipit populum Iudaicum et populum gentilem. Quia in isto articulo recipiendus est populus Iudaicus, cantatur Psalmus in quinta feria qui praetitulatur ex oratione Moysi. Talis est titulus: "Oratio Moysi hominis Dei" [Ps 89:1]. Sequitur canticum *Cantemus Domino* [Exod 15:1–9]. Quod olim cantavere in figura futurae victoriae, percipient, quando adimplebitur

hands of the impious emperors and granted freedom in
the time of the emperor Constantine. Thus it rejoices in the     2
canticle that Samuel's mother Anna sang after she was freed
from the affliction of Phennena, her rival: "My heart has rejoiced in the Lord," she said, "and my horn is exalted in my
God." For from that time, after the republic and the power
of the Romans was subjected to the popes and the Christian
emperors, the mouth of the church was increased over its
enemies, namely the pagans and the faithless Jews. This increase continues today. May the Lord grant that the Apostle's statement persist and be fulfilled, until the fullness of
the gentiles comes in, and thus will all of Israel will be saved.


# 15

# On Thursday

This period receives the Jewish people and the gentile
people under one staff, or under one rule. Because the Jewish people are to be received in this period, the Psalm that
bears the title of Moses's prayer is sung on Thursday. This is
the title: "A prayer of Moses the man of God." There follows
the canticle *Cantemus Domino*. They will achieve what they
once sang of as a symbol of future victory, when that which

quod Dominus in Evangelio dixit: "Amodo non me videbitis donec dicatis: Benedictus qui venit in nomine Domini" [Matt 23:39].

16

## De sexta feria

Sexta feria caelebratur in memoriam passionis salvatoris nostri. Psalmus qui in ea cantatur, hunc titulum habet: "Ipsi David, quando eum filius eius persequebatur" [Ps 142:1]. De quo titulo ita dicit Agustinus in prologo eiusdem Psalmi: "Agnoscamus ergo quemadmodum Christum persequebatur filius suus. Habebat enim filios, de quibus dicebat: Non ieiunant filii sponsi quamdiu cum eis est sponsus; cum autem ab eis ablatus fuerit sponsus, tunc ieiunabunt filii sponsi [Matt 9:15]. Ergo filii sponsi apostoli, et inter hos persecutor—diabolus—Iudas. Passionem itaque suam in hoc Psalmo praedicaturus est Christus."+ Canticum passionem eius nihilominus sonat, dicens: "Cornua in manibus eius, ibi abscondita est fortitudo eius" [Hab 3:4]. Quod sic Hieronimus exponit: "Vexilla et trophea crucis: Et in ipsis cornibus abscondita est fortitudo eius." Et paulo post: "In cruce ergo paulisper abscondita est fortitudo eius, quando dicebat ad Patrem: 'Tristis est anima mea usque ad mortem' [Matt 36:38; Mic

the Lord said in the Gospel is fulfilled: "You shall not see me henceforth until you say: Blessed is he who comes in the name of the Lord."

# 16

# On Friday

Friday is celebrated in memory of our savior's passion. The Psalm that is sung then has this title: "A Psalm of the same David, when his son Absalom pursued him." Augustine, in his prologue on the same Psalm, speaks about the title as follows: "Let us therefore understand how Christ's son persecuted him. For he had sons, about whom he said: The sons of the bridegroom do not fast as long as the bridegroom is with them; but when the bridegroom is taken away from them, the sons of the bridegroom will fast. The sons of the bridegroom are therefore the apostles, and the persecutor among them—the devil—is Judas. And so Christ will preach of his passion in this Psalm."☨ The canticle 2 also sings of his passion, saying: "Horns are in his hands, there is his strength hid." Jerome explains this as follows: "The standard and the banner of the cross: On these very horns his strength was hidden." And after a little: "Thus his strength was hidden for a short while on the cross, when he said to the Father: 'My soul is sorrowful even unto death.'

14:34]. Et: 'Pater, si possibile est, transeat a me calix iste' [Matt 26:39]. Et in ipsa cruce: 'Pater, in manus tuas commendo spiritum meum' [Luke 23:46]."☩

3    Ista est quinta nox a secunda feria. Sicut in quinto Psalmo per Dominicas noctes caelebratur contemptus Nabochodonosoris et victoria trium puerorum, inter quos erat quartus aspectus filii hominis [Dan 3:92] — ita et nunc in quinto loco contemptus totius mundi, et victoria summi et solius triumphatoris illius, cuius aspectus olim videbatur inter tres pueros. Digneque in sexta feria memoratur eius passio prae ceteris noctibus, quia in ea peracta est.

# 17

# De Sabbato

Sabbatum recolit memoriam electorum Iudaeorum qui erunt iuncti ecclesiae in fine mundi. Sabbatum quod fingebant et fingunt Iudaei carnales se observare, Iudaei fideles in

2    veritate custodient in fine. Psalmus qui in eo cantatur, talem titulum habet: "Psalmus cantici in die Sabbati" [Ps 91:1]. Ex titulo Psalmi conveniens est Psalmus Sabbato. Quomodo congruat populo Iudaico, versus quidam demonstrat dicens: "In decacordo psalterio, cum cantico et cithara" [Ps 91:4].

And: 'My Father, if it be possible, let this chalice pass from me.' And on the cross itself: 'Father, into your hands I commend my spirit.'"✝

This is the fifth night after Monday. Just as in the fifth ₃ Psalm on Sunday nights we commemorate the disgrace of Nebuchadnezzar and the victory of the three boys, among whom there was the fourth figure of the son of man—so do we now, in the fifth place, commemorate our contempt for the whole world, and the victory of that highest and only conqueror, whose figure once appeared among the three boys. And it is appropriate that his passion is remembered before all other nights on Friday, because it was accomplished on that day.

# 17

# On Saturday

Saturday commemorates the chosen Jews who will be joined to the church at the end of the world. At the end, the faithful Jews will keep in truth the Sabbath that carnal Jews pretended and pretend to observe. The Psalm that is sung ₂ on this day has this title: "A psalm of a canticle on the Sabbath day." According to its title, it is an appropriate Psalm for Saturday. One verse shows how it relates to the Jewish people, saying: "Upon the ten-stringed psaltery, with a

Quod ita Agustinus: "Decacordum psalterium non modo audistis. Decacordum psalterium significat decim praecepta legis. Sed cantare in illo opus est, non portare psalterium. Nam et Iudaei habent legem; portant; non psallunt. Qui sunt qui psallunt? Qui operantur. Qui operantur cum tristitia nondum psallunt. Qui sunt qui psallunt? Qui cum hilaritate faciunt bene," et reliqua.✝ Hoc credimus futurum esse in populo Iudaico, quando unus populus erit cum sancta ecclesia, quod modo beatus Agustinus narrat de sancta ecclesia.

3    Canticum quod sequitur, *Audite caeli* [Deut 32:1], quomodo Sabbato conveniat et populo Iudaico, dominus Beda explanat in secundo libro tractatus super Lucam: "Confluebant autem die Sabbati in sinagogis, ut, iuxta quod Dominus praecepit—'Vacate et videte quoniam ego sum Deus' [Ps 45:11]—feriatis mundi negotiis, ad meditanda legis monita quieto corde resident. Cuius eo die devotionis agendae actenus in ecclesia perdurat indicium, quia, ad memoriam priscae religionis canticum Deuteronomii, in quo universus veteris populi status, quid videlicet offenso, quid propitio Deo meruerit, continetur, nonnullis in locis Sabbato dicere consuevit. Alioquin esset praeposterum ut in prioribus septimanae diebus, prophetarum dictis carminibus, Moysi ultimum diceretur."✝

4    Valet enim ad opusculum huiusce fabricationis, si consideremus ex sensibus et intellectu Psalmorum Dominicae noctis in Matutinali officio, quomodo eis colligentur Psalmi

canticle and harp." About this, Augustine as follows: "You have not just now heard about the ten-stringed psaltery: The ten-stringed psaltery signifies the ten commandments of the law. But one must sing upon the psaltery, not carry it. For the Jews have the law as well; they carry it; they do not sing. Who are those who sing? Those who work. Those who work in sadness do not yet sing. Who are those who sing? Those who do work joyfully and well," and so forth.✠ We believe that what Augustine relates here about the holy church will come about for the Jewish people, when they become one with the holy church.

In the second book of his treatise on Luke, the master 3 Bede explains how the canticle that follows, *Audite caeli,* relates to the Sabbath and the Jewish people: "And on the day of the Sabbath they went to the synagogues, so that, in accordance with the Lord's command—'Be still and see that I am God'—they might stay there to meditate on the commands of the law, with a quiet heart and while resting from worldly business. To this day a token of the devotion that we should observe on this day remains in the church, since, in memory of that early religion, some places have the custom of pronouncing the canticle of Deuteronomy on Saturday. That canticle contains the full circumstances of the ancient people: namely what they deserved from an offended God and what they merited from a forgiving God. Otherwise it would be absurd for the canticle of Moses to be pronounced last, after the songs of the prophets had been pronounced on the earlier days of the week."✠

Now it is worthwhile for a work structured like this one 4 to consider how the Psalms and canticles for the six days of the week cohere with the Psalms for Matins on Sunday

5 et cantica quae sunt per sex dies ebdomadis. Primus Psalmus, *Dominus regnavit* [Ps 92], Domini regnum demonstrat
post eius resurrectionem, de quo ipse dicebat: "Data est
mihi omnis potestas in caelo et in terra" [Matt 28:18]. Et e
contra, *Miserere mei, Deus* [Ps 50:1] paenitentiam mortui hominis peccato, sed etiam respirantis per bonum odorem
quem accepit a nuntiis verborum Dei. Pro illo enim venit
Christus mori et resurgere a mortuis, ut ipse manifestat in
Evangelio: "Non veni vocare iustos, sed peccatores" [Matt
9:3]. Et iterum: "Veni enim salvare quod perierat" [Matt
18:11]. Et, ut manifestius dicam, propterea surrexit ut nos
resurgeremus. Sua resurrectio extitit per corpus inmortale;
6 nostra extat per paenitentiam. Unde non inmerito, sicut,
vice resurrectionis suae, *Dominus regnavit* [Ps 92:1] cantamus
in Dominicis et in festivis noctibus, ita congruit, vice nostrae resurrectionis, in sequentibus noctibus *Miserere mei,*
*Deus* [Ps 50:1] cantare.

7 Quoniam duo continet memoratus Psalmus *Dominus reg-*
*navit*—Christi regnum acceptum per triumphum crucis, et
firmationem sanctae ecclesiae non commovendam a statu
suo—Psalmus de secunda feria et canticum huic (id est,
Psalmo *Dominus regnavit*) propter constructionem ecclesiae
8 adnectuntur. Psalmus *Verba mea* [Ps 5] vocem ecclesiae
continet quae in primo tempore coniuncta est apostolis. De
qua dicit Agustinus in Psalmo quinto: "Vox ecclesiae est in
hoc Psalmo, vocatae ad hereditatem Domini. 'Verba mea:
Exaudi me, Domine' [Ps 5:2]. Vocata invocat Dominum, ut,
eodem opitulante, pertranseat nequitiam saeculi huius et ad

night, according to their meanings and our understanding of them. The first Psalm, *Dominus regnavit,* reveals the Lord's ₅ kingdom after his resurrection, about which he said: "All power is given to me in heaven and in earth." On the other hand, *Miserere mei, Deus* reveals the penance of the dead man for his sin, as well as the penance of the one who breathes in the good odor that he received from the heralds of God's word. And it was for him that Christ came to die and rise from the dead, as Christ reveals in the Gospel: "I did not come to call the just, but sinners." And again: "For I came to save that which was lost." And, to put it more openly, he rose that we might rise again. His resurrection was accomplished through an immortal body; ours is accomplished through penance. Thus, just as it is not inappropriate for us ₆ to sing *Dominus regnavit* from the perspective of his resurrection, on the nights of Sundays and feasts, it is also appropriate for us to sing *Miserere mei, Deus* from the perspective of our resurrection, on the nights that follow.

Since the aforementioned Psalm, *Dominus regnavit,* cov- ₇ ers two points—Christ's kingdom as received through the triumph of the cross, and the holy church's foundation, which is not to be pushed from its place—the Psalm and the canticle from Monday are joined to it (that is, the Psalm *Dominus regnavit*), because of the construction of the church. The Psalm *Verba mea* contains the voice of the church that ₈ was joined to the apostles in that earlier period. Augustine, on the fifth Psalm, speaks about this: "The voice of the church, which is called to the Lord's inheritance, is in this Psalm. 'My words: Hear me, Lord.' The church has been called and it calls upon the Lord so that, through his help, it may cross through the evil of this world and come to

eum perveniat."✝ Canticum *Confitebor tibi, Domine* [Isa 12:1–6], ut superius demonstratum est, eandem ecclesiam praesentat.

9    Psalmus *Iubilate Domino, omnis terra* [Ps 99] corum praedicatorum continet qui non timentes minas principum, exciverunt ecclesiam de Babylone ad serviendum Domino soli. Quid idem corus passus sit a civibus Babyloniae civitatis, Psalmus *Iudica me, Deus, et discerne causam meam de gente non sancta* [Ps 42] dilucidat. Canticum minime latet angustiam Ezechiae regis, qui dixit: "Ego dixi: In dimidio dierum meorum, vadam ad portas inferi" [Isa 38:10], et cetera quae sequuntur. Ezechias, bonus et iustus rex, in corpore praedicantium adnumeratur. Satis indicat praesens canticum angustiam praesentis ecclesiae, de qua angustia dicit versus: "Recogitabo omnes annos meos in amaritudine animae meae" [Isa 38:15].

10   Psalmus *Deus, Deus meus* [Ps 62] continet vocem gentilis populi, qui a somno animae evigilat post introductam inluminationem praedicatorum. Quis sit somnus de quo evigilat, quando dicit: "Deus, Deus meus, ad te de luce vigilo" [Ps 62:2], Agustinus memoratus dilucidat in tractatu eiusdem Psalmi: "Illud autem," inquiens "cavere debemus, ne ipsa anima nostra dormiat. Malus enim est somnus animae, bonus somnus corporis, quo reparatur valitudo corporis. Somnus autem animae est oblivisci Deum suum. Quaecunque anima oblita fuerit Deum suum, dormit." Et infra: "'Deus, Deus meus, ad te de luce vigilo. Sitivit in te anima mea.' Ecce illud desertum Idumeae. Videte quomodo hic sitit." Et paulo post: "Quando anima sitit, fontem sapientiae sitit. De ipso

him."✝ The canticle *Confitebor tibi, Domine,* as was shown above, reveals this same church.

The Psalm *Iubilate Domino, omnis terra* contains the band 9 of preachers who do not fear the threats of princes, and who have summoned the church out of Babylon and into the Lord's sole service. The Psalm *Iudica me, Deus, et discerne causam meam de gente non sancta* explains what that same band suffered at the hands of the citizens of the city of Babylon. The canticle does not hide the difficulty of the king Hezekiah, who said: "I said: On the midst of my days I shall go to the gates of hell," and so forth as follows. Hezekiah, the good and just king, is counted among the body of preachers. The present canticle reveals the difficulty of the present church well enough; one of its verses speaks about this difficulty: "I will recount to you all my years in the bitterness of my soul."

The Psalm *Deus, Deus meus* contains the voice of the gen- 10 tiles, who awaken from the sleep of the soul after the light of the preachers has been brought in. The aforementioned Augustine explains, in his treatise on the same Psalm, what sleep the gentiles awake from when the Psalm says: "O God, my God, to you do I wake at break of day": "But we should on guard," he says, "lest our soul sleep. For the sleep of the soul is evil, while the sleep of the body, which restores the body's health, is good. But the sleep of the soul amounts to forgetting its God. Whatever soul has forgotten its God, sleeps." And further: "'O God, my God, to you do I wake at break of day. For you my soul has thirsted.' Behold that desert of Edom. See how it thirsts." And after a little: "When the soul thirsts, it thirsts for the font of wisdom. Our souls

fonte inebriabuntur animae nostrae, sicut dicit alius Psalmus: 'Inebriabuntur ab ubertate domus tuae, et torrente deliciarum tuarum potabis eos' [Ps 35:9]. Sitienda ergo est sapientia; sitienda iustitia."✝

11     Eandem reversionem sonat Psalmus in quarta feria [Ps 64]—id est de oblivione Dei ad eius recordationem, quasi de Babylone ad Hierusalem. In eodem Psalmo aliqua sitis memoratur similis de Psalmo *Deus, Deus meus.* Infit iste Psalmus: "Sulcos eius inebria, multiplica generationes eius" [Ps 64:11]. Unde idem qui supra in tractatu Psalmi *Te decet ymnus, Deus* [Ps 64]: "Videmus: Credunt, et ex credentibus alii credunt, et ex illis alii credunt, et non sufficit uni homini ut, factus ipse fidelis, unum lucretur."✝ Canticum *Exultavit cor meum in Domino* [1 Kgs 2:1–10] liquide monstrat sanctam ecclesiam superiorem esse Babylonia.

12     Psalmus *Deus misereatur nostri* [Ps 66]—in quo per voces praedicatorum colligitur populus Iudaicus dicentium: "Confiteantur tibi populi, Deus" [Ps 66:4]—convenit cum Psalmo de quinta feria: *Domine, refugium factus es nobis* [Ps 89], qui habet titulum: "Oratio Moysi hominis Dei." Cui apte respondet canticum *Cantemus Domino* [Exod 15:1–19].

13     Ymnus trium puerorum, *Benedicite* [Dan 3:57–88, 56], passionem Domini ac triumphum eius ad memoriam nobis reducit. Nabochodonosor diabolum significat; ministri eius, qui incenderunt flammam ignis in fornace, Iudaeos clamantes: "Crucifige, crucifige" [Luke 23:21; John 19:6]. Missi sunt tres pueri in caminum ignis, futurum enim erat ut furorem incendii Iudaeorum sustineret Christus. Tres fuerunt pueri qui una voce confitebantur Domino; tria pura sacramenta exierunt de homine Christo in passione

will become inebriated from this fountain, as another Psalm says: 'They shall be inebriated with the plenty of your house, and you shall make them drink of the torrent of your pleasure.' Wisdom should therefore be thirsted after; justice should be thirsted after."✝

The Psalm for Wednesday proclaims this same return— 11 that is, from forgetting God to remembering him, as if from Babylon to Jerusalem. In this Psalm a thirst similar to that from the Psalm *Deus, Deus meus* is commemorated. This Psalm says: "Fill up plentifully its streams, multiply its fruits." And so the same author as above in his treatise on the Psalm *Te decet ymnus, Deus*: "We see: They believe, and through these believers others believe, and through those others believe, and it is not enough for one man, once he has been made faithful, to gain just one more."✝ The canticle *Exultavit cor meum in Domino* clearly shows that the holy church is superior to Babylon.

The Psalm *Deus misereatur nostri*—in which the Jewish 12 people are called together by the voices of preachers saying: "Let people confess to you, O God"—relates to the Psalm for Thursday: *Domine, refugium factus es nobis,* which has the title: "A prayer of Moses the man of God." The canticle *Cantemus Domino* offers an appropriate response to it.

The hymn of the three boys, *Benedicite,* reminds us of the 13 Lord's passion and his triumph. Nebuchadnezzar signifies the devil; his servants, who lit the flame of the fire in the furnace, signify the Jews crying: "Crucify him, Crucify him." The three boys were sent into the fiery furnace, for it was to come about that Christ would endure the fury of the Jews' fire. There were three boys who confessed to the Lord with one voice; three pure sacraments went forth from the man

435

sua—spiritus, aqua et sanguis—quae tria unum monstrant Christum [1 John 5:8]. Erat in fornace aspectus quarti, quasi similitudo Filii Dei [Dan 3:92]; etenim pendebat sive sepeliebatur corpus Christi assumptum ex Maria virgine. Puerorum corpora non sunt corrupta in fornace; futurum erat ut Christi corpus non corrumperetur putredine mortis. Liberati sunt de camino tres pueri; liberatus Christus de ore leonis. Propter hoc sacramentum, ut opinor, audivi cantari in vigiliis Paschae in ecclesia Turonensi post lectiones "Benedicite."

14    "Omnes qui pie volunt vivere persecutionem patiuntur" [1 Tim 3:12], et pertinent ad corpus trium puerorum qui missi sunt in caminum; cuius corporis caput est Christus. At hi qui persecutiones ingerunt, ad corpus diaboli; cuius membrum extitit Nabochodonosor, et omnes persecutores us-

15 que ad maximum membrum, antichristum. Et merito in quinto ordine recolitur evasio electorum de persecutoribus, quia corpus, quod quinque sensibus regitur, possunt occidere, amplius autem quid faciant, non habent. Psalmus de sexta feria [Ps 142], ut praetulimus, et canticum [Hab 3:2–19], Christi passionem detinent.

16    *Laudate Dominum de caelis* [Ps 148] et *Cantate Domino canticum novum* [Ps 149] et *Laudate Dominum in sanctis eius* [Ps 150] actum sanctae ecclesiae monstrant post transactam persecutionem. Quem continet versus: "Bonum est confiteri Domino et psallere nomini tuo altissime" [Ps 91:2]. At canticum *Audite caeli quae loquor* [Deut 32:1–43], quamvis duo in se contineat, id est remunerationem Domini pro bonis et retributionem pro offensis, tamen propter Sabbati

Christ during his passion—spirit, water and blood—and these three reveal the one Christ. In the furnace there was the form of a fourth person, as if a likeness of the Son of God; and indeed, Christ's body, assumed from the virgin Mary, was hung on the cross and buried. The bodies of the boys were not destroyed in the furnace; it was to come about that Christ's body would not be destroyed by the rottenness of death. The three boys were freed from the furnace; Christ was freed from the mouth of the lion. I think it was because of this sacrament that I heard *Benedicite* sung in the church at Tours, after the readings on the Easter vigil.

"And all that will live piously in Christ Jesus suffer perse- 14 cution," and they pertain to the body of the three boys who were sent into the furnace; the head of this body is Christ. But those who inflict persecutions pertain to the body of the devil; Nebuchadnezzar was his member, as are all perse- cutors down to the greatest member, the antichrist. And it 15 is appropriate that the escape of the elect from their perse- cutors is recalled fifth in order, because persecutors can kill the body, which is governed by the five senses; but they can- not do more than that. The Psalm and the canticle for Fri- day, as we said above, contain Christ's passion.

*Laudate Dominum de caelis* and *Cantate Domino canticum no-* 16 *vum* and *Laudate Dominum in sanctis eius* demonstrate the ac- tion of the holy church after its persecution was completed. The versicle contains as much: "It is good to give praise to the Lord and to sing to your name, O most high." But, because of the peace of the Sabbath on which it is sung, we direct the canticle *Audite caeli quae loquor* to those who

quietem in qua cantatur, ad eos illud dirigimus, qui bona
pace utentur post persecutionem in ecclesia nostra. De quibus dicit versus: "Pars autem Domini populus eius, Iacob
funiculus hereditatis eius" [Deut 32:9].

## 18

# De Dominicis noctibus in Matutinali officio a Septuagesima usque in Pascha

Per Dominicas noctes a Septuagesima usque in Pascha
Domini, in Matutinali officio duo Psalmi mutantur, *Miserere
mei, Deus* [Ps 50] et *Confitemini Domino* [Ps 117]. Per hos duos
Psalmos informantur hi qui nondum sunt perfecti, etiam illo
modo quo homines hic perfecti esse possunt. De quibus dicebat Paulus: "Quicumque perfecti, hoc sapite" [Phil 3:15].
Quibus non congruit praeceptoribus et doctoribus auferre
2 timorem et spem. Timorem quem oportet nobis peccatoribus habere in praesenti peregrinatione de vindicta Dei, inculcat Psalmus *Miserere mei, Deus,* qui resultat vocem peccatoris paenitentis. Plangamus peccata in Psalmo *Miserere mei,
Deus;* post planctum aderit caritas, quae foras mittit timorem per spiritum qui consolatur corda lugentium. Ac ideo,

enjoy good peace in our church following their persecution, although it contains two things, namely the Lord's reward for good deeds and his punishment for offenses. A verse from this canticle speaks about those who enjoy peace: "But the Lord's portion is his people, Jacob the lot of his inheritance."

# 18

# On Matins for Sunday nights from Septuagesima to Easter

On Sunday nights from Septuagesima to the Lord's Easter, two Psalms are changed in Matins: *Miserere mei, Deus* and *Confitemini Domino.* These two Psalms represent those who have not yet been perfected, even in the sense that men can be perfect here. Paul spoke about them: "As many as are perfect, know this." It is not appropriate for their directors and teachers to take fear and hope away from them. The Psalm *Miserere mei, Deus,* which resounds with the voice of the repentant sinner, emphasizes the fear of God's wrath that we, as sinners, should have in our current exile. Let us bemoan our sins in the Psalm *Miserere mei, Deus;* after this lament there will be charity, which drives out fear through the spirit that consoles the hearts of mourners. And therefore,

439

quia post dolorem cordis et indignationem reatus solet caritas praebere fiduciam accedendi ad Dominum, ascendamus
spe sortis electorum ad bona opera laudandi Deum; et dicamus ad alterutrum: "Confitemini Domino quoniam bonus"
[Ps 117:1].

3    De his duobus gradibus scribitur in Deuteronomio: "Non
accipies loco pignoris inferiorem et superiorem molam, quia
animam suam apposuit tibi" [Deut 24:6]. Quod sic Sanctus
Gregorius exponit: "Accipere namque aliquod—dicimus auferre. Unde et aves illae quae rapiendi sunt avidae, 'acci-
pitres' vocantur." Et paulo post: "Pignus vero debitoris est
confessio peccatoris. A debitore enim pignus accipitur cum
a peccatore iam peccati confessio tenetur. Superior autem
et inferior mola est spes et timor." Et iterum post pauca: "In
peccatoris itaque confessione incessanter debet spes et for-
mido coniungi, quia incassum misericordiam sperat, si non
etiam iustitiam timeat; incassum iustitiam metuit, si non
etiam de misericordia confidit." Et iterum: "Tollit enim superiorem, si flenti peccatum dicat: 'Non habebis veniam de
commissis.' Tollit inferiorem, si peccantem palpet et dicat:
'Age mala, inquantum vis—nam Deus pius est et ad indul-
gentiam paratus," et reliqua.✝

4    Psalmus *Dominus regnavit* [Ps 92] perfectos informat,
quales fuerunt apostoli; *Miserere mei, Deus* [Ps 50], fragiles et
infirmos quos oportet plorare et plangere; quod significat
tempus Septuagesimae. Videtur parvitati nostrae congruere
propter numerum septuaginta qui tenet peregrinationem

because charity is accustomed to offer the comfort of approaching the Lord after the heartfelt sorrow and regret of the accused, let us ascend to the good work of praising the Lord in our hope for the lot of the elect; and let us say to one another: "Confess to the Lord for he is good."

These two degrees are written about in Deuteronomy: 3 "You shall not get the lower and the upper millstone in place of a pledge, for he has pledged his soul to you." Saint Gregory explains this as follows: "Now receiving something—we call that taking. And so those birds that are eager to snatch things away are called raptors, or 'takers.'" And a little later: "And the debtor's pledge is the confession of the sinner. For a pledge is taken from the debtor when the confession of a sin is held from a sinner. And the upper and the lower millstone are hope and fear." And again, after a little: "In a sinner's confession, therefore, hope and fear should always accompany each other, because one hopes in vain for mercy if one does not also fear justice; and one has feared justice in vain if one does not also trust in mercy." And again: "For he takes away the upper millstone, if he says to him who mourns his sin: 'You will not receive mercy for what you did.' He takes away the lower millstone, if he caresses the sinner and says: 'Do however much evil you want—for God is honorable and ready to indulge,'" and so forth.✝

The Psalm *Dominus regnavit* represents the perfected, 4 as the apostles were; *Miserere mei, Deus* represents the fragile and infirm who should bewail and mourn; this is what the season of Septuagesima signifies. In our inadequacy, it strikes us as appropriate, because of the number seventy

nostram, ut cum alleluia et cum altitudine Psalmi *Dominus regnavit, Gloria in excelsis Deo* introducatur in thesauros suos, usque ad diem exultationis ecclesiae per resurrectionem capitis nostri.

## 19

# De versibus qui in Quadragesima sunt usque in passionem Domini

Saepe dictum est quod Psalmus *Qui habitat in adiutorio altissimi* [Ps 90] mentionem eorum informet, qui, in certamine positi, in Domino ponunt spem suam et omne adiutorium ab eo deprecantur. Est enim sancta ecclesia in maiori certamine constituta diebus Quadragesimae quam in alio tempore. Ideo hunc Psalmum eo tempore frequentat in versibus, qui Domini protectionem insinuat et adiutorium.

that contains our exile, that the *Gloria in excelsis Deo* should be returned to its store rooms together with the alleluia and the elevation of the Psalm *Dominus regnavit,* until the day that the church rejoices through the resurrection of its head.

## 19

# On the versicles for Lent, up to the Lord's passion

It has been said repeatedly that the Psalm *Qui habitat in adiutorio altissimi* represents those who, set for battle, put their hope in the Lord and seek all assistance from him. For the holy church is positioned in a greater struggle during the days of Lent than at any other time. In that season, therefore, it revisits this Psalm, which references the Lord's protection and assistance, in versicles.

20

# De passione Domini

Dies passionis Domini computantur duabus ebdomadibus ante Pascha Domini. Neque enim ab re est, quod in duabus ebdomadibus recolitur eius passio, quoniam in duobus temporibus huius mundi scribitur et informatur idem passio—quale est illud primi temporis de Noe, qui inebriatus est vino et denudatus iacuit et ab uno filio dehonestatus, a duobus vero veneratus [Gen 9:21–23]; et illud iam sub lege: "Et erit vita tua quasi pendens ante te. Timebis nocte et die,

2 non credes vitae tuae" [Deut 28:66]. In illis diebus amittimus per XI dies in solis responsoriis *Gloriam* sanctae Trinitatis, quoniam per humilitatem veniendum est ad passionem Christi. Passio et persecutio humiliant, quantum ad praesens cernitur, massam quae ex Adam sumpta est. Hanc imitationem humilitatis designant turbae quae obviam venerunt Domino die Palmarum ad descensum Montis Oliveti. Ymnus, scilicet *Gloria Patri et Filio et Spiritui Sancto,* gloriam

3 sanctae Trinitatis recolit. Quoniam una est persona Filii Dei et filii hominis, qui pati venerat, conformat se sancta ecclesia capiti suo et de glorificatione eius reticet usque dum exaltetur per triumphum victoriae. Haec humiliatio prius et iterum exaltatio per unum versum Psalmi centesimi noni monstratur qui dicit: "De torrente in via bibet; propterea

444

20

# On the Lord's passion

The days of the Lord's passion are reckoned for two weeks before the Lord's Easter. Nor is it inappropriate to recall his passion during these two weeks, since the same passion was written about and represented in the two eras of this world—as in the episode in the first era concerning Noah, who was drunk with wine and lay naked and was disgraced by one son but honored by two; and as in that remark already under the law: "And your life shall be as if it were hanging before you. You shall fear night and day, neither shall you trust your life." In those days we omit the *Gloria* of 2 the Holy Trinity, in the responsories only, for eleven days, because we should approach Christ's passion with humility. Passion and persecution, inasmuch as we experience them in the present, humble the lump that has been handed down from Adam. The crowds who came to meet the Lord on the Day of Palms upon his descent from the Mount of Olives signify this imitation of humility. The hymn, namely *Gloria Patri et Filio et Spiritui Sancto,* recalls the glory of the Holy Trinity. Because the Son of God and the son of man who 3 came to suffer are one person, the holy church imitates its head and is silent about his glorification until he is exalted by the triumph of victory. This initial humiliation and subsequent exaltation is revealed by a verse from Psalm 109 that says: "He drinks of the torrent in the way; therefore he has

exaltavit caput" [Ps 109:7]. De hoc torrente Dominus in via bibit quia mortem in transitu gustavit, atque ideo exaltavit caput, quia hoc quod moriendo in sepulcro posuit, surgendo super angelos elevavit.

4 Quamvis rite congruat, ut propter humiliationem capitis nostri proximam, amittamus glorificationem sanctae Trinitatis, in qua honoratur filius hominis propter unitatem personae Filii Dei (unde et ipse praecepit apostolis, ne alicui diceret transfigurationem suam in monte, ante quam resurgeret a mortuis [Matt 17:9; Mark 9:9])—potest tamen et simpliciter intellegi, quatinus ad memoriam nobis reducat, quod aliquando esset tempus quando memoratus ymnus non dicebatur in ecclesia nostra. A sancto Hieronimo scriptum est de eodem ymno ad Damasum papam.

5 Ab illo die quando amittimus *Gloria Patri,* duae ebdomadae sunt, hoc est quattuordecim dies, usque in Pascha Domini. Dies Paschae iam de tertia ebdomada est, in qua restauratur omnis amissa glorificatio. In tertio tempore legis gratiae, omnia beneficia redduntur ecclesiae quae expectaverunt patres nostri, qui tenebantur in claustris inferni,

6 tempore naturalis legis et tempore legis litterae. Neque abhorret a vero, si dies passionis Domini, qui per duas hebdomadas caelebrantur, quasi per duo tempora eorum murmurationem nobis ad memoriam reducant, qui meritis suis caeleste regnum promerebant, et tamen humiliati erant in claustris inferni usque ad tertiam ebdomadam legis gratiae.

lifted up his head." The Lord drinks of this torrent in the way because he tasted death on his journey, and he raised his head because what he put into the tomb by dying, he raised above the angels by rising.

Although it is appropriate for us, because of the coming 4 humiliation of our head, to omit our glorification of the Holy Trinity, in which the son of man is honored because of his unity in person with the Son of God (and thus he ordered his apostles to speak to nobody about his transfiguration on the mountain before he rose from the dead)—it can also be simply understood that we do so to remember that there was once a time when the stated hymn was not said in our church. Saint Jerome wrote about this hymn to Pope Damasus.

From the day when we omit the *Gloria Patri,* there are 5 two weeks, or fourteen days, until the Lord's Easter. And the day of Easter is already the beginning of the third week; at that point, every omitted glorification is restored. In the third period of the law of grace, all benefits are rendered to the church that our fathers awaited—our fathers, who were confined to hell in the period of the natural law and the period of the law of the letter. Nor is it contrary to the truth, 6 if the days of the Lord's passion, which are celebrated over two weeks, should in some sense remind us of the wailing, through two eras, of those who earned the heavenly kingdom through their merits, but had nevertheless been humbled in the confines of hell until the third week of the law of grace.

21

# De Caena Domini et Parascheve ac Sabbato Sancto

Hic notandum est quod duo officia diurnalia quae caelebrantur in quarta et in quinta feria ante passionem Domini, vicem teneant eorum officiorum quae congruenter potuissent celebrari in Parascheve et in Sabbato, si Missae his diebus celebrarentur. Introitus de quarta feria evidenter ostendit quod factum est in sexta feria, quando oboedivit Christus

2 Patri suo usque ad mortem [Phil 2:8]. Nam et responsorii et offertorium et communio de humilitate Christi sonant, qua factus est oboediens usque ad mortem. Sequens vero officium exaltationem ecclesiae notat quam percepit per humilem oboedientiam Christi, in quo ipsa gloriatur post passionem Domini. Hac ratione orationes sextae feriae, quae dicuntur ante venerationem crucis, coluntur in quarta feria—sed mos obtinuit ut hae solummodo dicerentur a sacerdote in Parascheve.

3 Quantum potuit institutor Officii, conformari nos voluit sua ammonitione Christi passioni et causis apostolorum, qui obstricti erant tempore passionis, nec non et disiungi

4 moribus persecutorum. Primo dicendum est quod omnis doctrina pastoris taceatur in ecclesia his diebus, id est

## 21

# On Holy Thursday and Good Friday and Holy Saturday

Here it should be noted that the two daytime offices, celebrated on the Wednesday and Thursday before the Lord's passion, take the place of the offices that could well have been celebrated appropriately on Good Friday and Saturday, if Masses were celebrated on those days. The introit for Wednesday clearly shows what was done on Friday, when Christ was obedient to his father unto death. And the responsories and the offertory and the communion hymn sing of Christ's humility, through which he was made obedient unto death. The following office, meanwhile, in which the church rejoices after the Lord's passion, declares the exaltation that the church received through Christ's humble obedience. For this reason the prayers for Friday, which are said before the veneration of the cross, are also recited on Wednesday—but the custom has developed that, on Good Friday, they be said by the priest alone.

The founder of our Office, insofar was he was able, wanted, through his admonition, to bring us into conformity with Christ's passion and the position of the apostles, who had been yoked together at the time of his passion; he also wanted us to be divided from the vices of persecutors. First, we should say that the whole of the pastor's teaching is silenced in church during these days,

caena Domini et Parascheve ac Sabbato Sancto. Non dicitur
*Domine, labia mea aperies* [Ps 50:17]; non datur benedictio
legentibus; ammonitio lectionis non ministratur in Matutinali officio; post ymnum Zachariae non gubernatur oratio
5 solito more a pastore. Ideo haec non fiunt quia pastor noster
Christus recessit, et arietes gregis, qui iam praedestinati
erant ut pastores fierent ecclesiae, dispersi sunt. Minores
quique faciunt suum officium typo discipulorum, qui forsan
minus cogniti erant discipuli esse Christi, et typo mulierum,
quae praesentes adesse poterant humiliationi Christi. Solent enim aliqui cantores amittere versum ante *Benedictus
Dominus Deus Israhel* [Luke 1:68–79], quia non praecedit lectio. Quod non oportet illis facere; suum officium illi caele-
brant, sed pastoris officium reticetur.

6    Invitatorium non cantant, ut doceant malum conventum
vitare suos, qualis fuit apud Iudaeos de nece Christi. Quanto
propius instant passioni, tanto se plus humiliant in officio
suo. Igitur in istis noctibus sive diebus penitus amittunt *Gloria Patri et Filio et Spiritui Sancto*. Omnis salutatio deest in
istis tribus diebus sive noctibus, ad vitandam salutationem
7 pestiferam, qualem diabolus Iudas exercuit. Necnon etiam
altitudo signorum, quae fiebat per vasa aerea, deponitur, et
lignorum sonus, usquequaque humilior aeris sono, necessario pulsatur, ut conveniat populus ad ecclesiam. Potest et in
hoc humilior usus ecclesiae Romanae designari antiquis
temporibus, quam nunc sit—et praecipue tunc, quando lati-
tabat per criptas propter persecutores. Nam adhuc iunior
Roma, quae antiquis temporibus sub uno dominio cum

that is on Holy Thursday and Good Friday and Holy Saturday. *Domine, labia mea aperies,* is not said; the lectors are not blessed; the admonition of the reading is not delivered at Matins; after the hymn of Zechariah the pastor does not lead a prayer in the usual manner. These things do not occur 5 because our pastor, Christ, has left, and the rams of the herd, who had already been predestined to become pastors of the church, have been scattered. Lessers perform their duty after the example of the disciples, who were probably not well known as Christ's disciples, and also after the example of the women, who were able to be present at Christ's humiliation. And some cantors are accustomed to omit the versicle before *Benedictus Dominus Deus Israhel,* because a reading does not precede it. They should not do this; they do their duty, but the pastor's duty is left undone.

They do not sing the invitatory, to teach that evil com- 6 pany shuns its own, as was the case among the Jews upon Christ's murder. The nearer they come to the passion, the more they humble themselves in their office. On these days and nights, therefore, they completely omit the *Gloria Patri et Filio et Spiritui Sancto.* Every greeting is left out during these three days and nights, to avoid a pestilential greeting like the one that the devil Judas employed. Furthermore, 7 the high pitch of the bells, made by bronze vessels, is also put aside, and wood is struck as necessary to gather the people to church; in every way the sound is more humble than the sound of bronze. This can also signify the usage of the Roman church in ancient times, humbler then than now— and especially when it hid in crypts because of persecutors. For the younger Rome, which in ancient times was ruled by

antiqua Roma regebatur, usum lignorum tenet—non prop-

8 ter aeris penuriam, sed propter vestutatem. Et quia salvatoris nostri humiliatio per sepulturam triduo caelebratur, convenit ut per tres dies, id est quintam feriam et sextam et
septimam, humiliatio nostri officii subsequatur.

9 Novem Psalmi et novem lectiones ac novem responsorii
qui caelebrantur per tres noctes insinuant quod Dominus,
descendens ad inferiora loca terrae, inde tria genera hominum rapuit et transvexit ad societatem novem ordinum angelorum. Haec tria genera distinguntur in Evangelio per eos
qui in agro sunt et per eos qui in molendino sunt atque per
eos qui in lecto sunt. Et quia haec tria genera creduntur
fuisse in naturali lege et in tempore legis litterae, seu tempore prophetarum, merito per tres noctes recoluntur. Et
propter novem ordines angelorum, quorum nomina legimus
per novenarium numerum, eorum reductio colitur ad societatem eorundem angelorum.

10 Memorata tria genera electorum Agustinus ita dilucidat
in libro *Quaestionum Evangeliorum,* titulo quadragesimo septimo: "Qui sunt 'in illa nocte duo in lecto' et 'duae molentes
in unum' et 'duo in agro' [Luke 17:34–35]—de quibus omnibus binis singuli assumentur et singuli relinquentur? Tria
11 genera hominum hic videntur significari. Unum eorum qui
otium et quietem eligunt, neque negotiis saecularibus neque
negotiis ecclesiasticis occupati; quae illorum quies 'lecti' nomine significata est. Alterum eorum qui in plebibus constituti, reguntur a doctoribus, agentes ea quae sunt huius

the same power as ancient Rome, still maintains the use of wood—not because it lacks brass, but because of its antiquity. And because our savior's humiliation in the tomb is celebrated for three days, it is appropriate that we adhere to the humiliation of our office for three days, namely on Thursday and Friday and Saturday. 8

The nine Psalms and nine lessons and nine responsories that are celebrated during these three nights suggest that the Lord, descending to the depths of the earth, removed three categories of men and brought them into fellowship with the nine orders of angels. These three categories are defined in the Gospel as those who are in the field and those who are in the millworks and those who are in bed. And because these three categories are believed to have existed under the natural law and in the time of the law of the letter, or the time of the prophets, they are rightly commemorated for three nights. And because of the nine orders of angels, whose names we gather from the number nine, their return to fellowship with these same angels is commemorated. 9

Augustine explains the aforementioned three categories of elect in his book of *Questions on the Gospels,* title 47: "'On that night,' who are the 'two men in bed' and 'two women grinding together' and 'the two men in the field'—from each of which pairs one will be taken and one left? Three categories of people seem to be signified here. One consists of those who choose peace and quiet, and are occupied neither by worldly nor ecclesiastical business; their quiet is indicated by the word 'bed.' A second consists of those who are established among the people, are governed by teachers, 10 11

saeculi; quos et 'feminarum' nomine significavit, quia consi-
liis, ut dixi, peritorum regi eis expetit. Et molentes dixit,
propter temporalium negotiorum orbem atque circuitum;
quas tamen in uno molentes dixit, in quantum de ipsis rebus
et negotiis suis praebent usibus ecclesiae. Tertium eorum
qui operantur in ecclesiae ministerio, tamquam in agro Dei,
de qua agricultura Apostolus loquitur [1 Cor 3:9]."

12    Quoniam ista tria genera non afuisse credimus in omnibus articulis temporum, quae tamen, quamvis electa essent,
descendebant ad inferni claustra, et ea in istis diebus descendit Dominus inde auferre et sociare actioni et cogni-
tioni et gaudio scilicet angelorum—non immerito per novem Psalmos, qui pertinent ad actionem; et novem lectiones,
quae pertinent ad cognitionem operum Dei; et novem responsorios, qui pertinent ad cantica sanctorum angelorum,
Nocturnalia officia caelebrantur.

## 22

# De extinctione luminum

Accenduntur in quinta et sexta et septima feria, per singulas noctes XXIIIIor lumina, et extinguntur per singulas
antiphonas et responsorios. Et fiunt simul LXX duae in-
luminationes et extinctiones. Totidem enim oris iacuit

and do things that are of this world; and he called them 'women,' because, as I said, he ordered that they be governed by the advice of the learned. And he said that they were grinding because of the circuity and revolution of temporal business; and he said that they were grinding together, insofar as they provide for the uses of the church from their own possessions and their business. The third consists of those who work in service of the church, as if in God's field; the Apostle speaks of this husbandry."

Since we believe that these three categories were present 12 in all periods of time, though they descended to the confines of hell despite being the elect, where the Lord also descended to remove them and place them among the action and understanding and joy of the angels—it is not inappropriate to celebrate Nocturns with nine Psalms, which pertain to action; and nine lessons, which pertain to understanding God's works; and nine responsories, which pertain to the songs of the holy angels.

## 22

# On putting out the lights

On Thursday and Friday and Saturday, twenty-four lights are lit each night, and they are put out during each of the antiphons and responsories. Altogether, that makes seventy-two lightings and extinguishings. Now it was for this many

Christus in sepulchro. Lumen et cantus gaudii et laetitiae participes sunt; extinctio enim luminum signat defectum laetitiae septuaginta duorum discipulorum, et mestitiam eorum quam habuerunt quamdiu Christus iacuit in sepulchro—sive mestitiam apostolorum quam pertulerunt per septuaginta duas oras quae consecratae sunt Christi sepulturae.

2    In Romana ecclesia, extinguitur totus ignis in sexta feria et reaccenditur. In hoc facto imitatur ignis, fotus et conservatus per congesta lignorum, principalem ignem—id est solem corporeum—qui ab humanis obtutibus se abscondit tempore passionis Domini, a sexta ora usque ad oram nonam, ne suo lumine fruerentur qui male gaudebant de ignominia domini sui et creatoris. Hac ratione ignis iste qui nostris usibus procuratur, potest extingui in sexta feria circa

3    sextam oram diei, et renovari circa nonam oram diei. De quo igne dicit Gregorius in *Moralibus:* "Ignis namque corporeus, ut esse ignis valeat, corporeis indiget fomentis. Qui, cum necesse est ut servetur, per congesta ligna procul dubio nutritur; nec valet nisi succensus esse, et nisi refotus subsistere."✝

4    Quod enim praecipitur in libello qui vocatur *De Romano ordine*—ut quinta feria et sexta feria atque Sabbato remaneat ignis circa oram nonam, non est mihi in aperto quid rationis in se contineat, unde mihi aliqua materies tribuatur scribendi, praecipue cum archidiaconus sanctae Romanae ecclesiae retulisset mihi ignotum sibi fore utrum in aliquo loco urbis idem ordo servaretur necne.

hours that Christ lay in the tomb. Light and song are companions of joy and rejoicing, and putting out lights signifies the lack of rejoicing among the seventy-two disciples and their grief that they felt for as long as Christ lay in the tomb—and also the grief that the apostles felt for the seventy-two hours that were consecrated for Christ's burial.

In the Roman church, all fire is extinguished on Friday 2 and then relit. In this action, the fire, maintained and conserved through the piling of wood, imitates the primary fire —that is, the corporeal sun—which hid itself from the sight of men at the time of the Lord's passion, from the sixth hour to the ninth hour, lest those who took evil delight in the disgrace of its master and creator enjoy its light. For this reason the fire that is cultivated for our use can be put out on Friday at the sixth hour of the day, and relit at the ninth hour of the day. Gregory speaks about this fire in his *Moralia:* "For cor- 3 poreal fire, in order to be fire, needs corporeal kindling. Since it is necessary to maintain fire, it is surely nourished through piling up wood; nor can it exist unless it has been lit; and it cannot subsist unless it is revived."✝

I do not know the purpose behind what is prescribed in 4 the small book that is entitled *On the Roman Order*—that on Thursday and Friday and Saturday the fire should persist to the ninth hour. Thus I have nothing to write about it, especially since an archdeacon of the holy Roman church told me that he did not know whether this usage was observed anywhere in the city or not.

## 23

# De tribus Psalmis qui cantantur in Nocturnali officio per septem dies baptismales

Tres Psalmi qui cantantur in Dominica nocte resurrectionis Domini, opera trium dierum monstrant quae Dominus secundum Lucam promisit se perficere in praesenti saeculo. Dicit Lucas: "In ipso autem die accesserunt quidam Phariseorum, dicentes illi: Exi et vade hinc, quia Herodes vult te occidere. Et ait illis: Ite, dicite vulpi illi: Ecce eicio daemonia et sanitates perficio hodie et cras, et tertia die consumor. Verumtamen oportet me hodie et cras et sequenti ambulare, quia non capit prophetam perire extra Hierusalem" [Luke 13:31–33]. Haec tria opera—id est daemonia eicere et sanitates perficere et tertia die consummari—promisit se acturum, et statim subiecit de sua passione, quae futura erat in Hierusalem.

2 De daemoniis eiciendis, dicit secundum Ioannem: "Nunc iudicium mundi est" [John 12:31]. Quod sic exponit Sanctus Agustinus in sermone quadragesimo nono super eundem Iohannem: "Servato illo in fine iudicio, ubi novissime vivi et mortui iudicandi sunt, possidebat ergo diabolus genus humanum, et reos suppliciorum tenebat chirographo peccatorum. Dominabatur in cordibus infidelium; ad creaturam colendam deserto creatore deceptos captivosque

## 23

# On the three Psalms that are sung at Nocturns during the seven baptismal days

The three Psalms that are sung on the Sunday night of the Lord's resurrection reveal the works of the three days that the Lord, according to Luke, promised to perform in this world. Luke says: "The same day there came some of the Pharisees, saying to him: Depart and go hence, for Herod has a mind to kill you. And he said to them: Go and tell that fox: Behold I cast out devils and do cures today and tomorrow, and the third day I am destroyed. Nevertheless I must walk today and tomorrow and the day following, because it cannot be that a prophet perish out of Jerusalem." He promised to perform these three works—that is, casting out demons and doing cures and being consummated on the third day—and immediately he went on to discuss his passion, which was to happen in Jerusalem.

On casting out demons, he says according to John: "Now 2 is the judgment of the world." Saint Augustine explains this in his forty-ninth sermon on the same John, as follows: "The devil therefore possessed the human race, and he held those who deserve punishment under the bond of their sins—excepting that final judgment, where the living and the dead are to be judged for the last time. He ruled in the hearts of the unfaithful; he forced his captives and those

pertrahebat. Per Christi autem fidem, quae morte eius et resurrectione firmata est, per eius sanguinem, qui in remissionem peccatorum fusus est, milia credentium a dominatu diaboli liberantur. Christi corpori copulantur, et sub uno capite, uno eius spiritu fidelia membra vegetantur. Hoc vocabat iudicium—discretionem hanc, a suis redemptis diaboli
3  expulsionem."✝ De eadem expulsione dicit idem Iohannes Evangelista in sequentibus: "Nunc princeps mundi huius eicietur foras" [John 12:31]. Ipsa est prima dies de qua Dominus dicit, secundum Lucam: "Ecce daemonia eicio hodie" [Luke 13:32].

4    Ipsam diem monstrat prima antiphona, quae dicit: "Ego sum qui sum et consilium meum non est cum impiis." Hoc est iudicium, id est discretio, de qua dicit Iohannes—ut separati sint fideles, cum quibus est consilium Domini, ab impiis. Eandem monstrat primus Psalmus, *Beatus vir* [Ps 1], qui describit primo quid beatitudo debeat fugere et quid appetere, ac postea expulsionem impiorum nihilominus describit, dicendo: "Non sic impii, non sic, sed tamquam pulvis quem proicit ventus a facie terrae" [Ps 1:4], et cetera quae sequuntur.

5    Secunda antiphona monstrat quod in crastino dixit Dominus se perficere, secundum Lucam—hoc est sanitates. Quae sint istae sanitates, Iohannes continuatim, postquam dixit: "Ecce princeps mundi eicietur foras," subiunxit dicens: "Et ego si exaltatus fuero a terra, omnia traham post
6  me" [John 12:31–32]. Quod ita Agustinus in sermone memorato: "Non itaque hoc ad universitatem hominum retulit,

he had deceived to worship creation without its creator. But through faith in Christ, which was secured through his death and resurrection, and through his blood, which was poured out for the remission of sins, thousands of believers are freed from the dominion of the devil. They are joined to Christ's body, and these faithful members are given life under his one head and his one spirit. This is what he called judgment—this division and the expulsion of the devil from his redeemed."✝ John the Evangelist himself speaks about 3 this very expulsion in what follows: "Now shall the prince of this world be cast out." This is the first day that the Lord speaks about, according to Luke: "Behold, I cast out devils and do cures today."

The first antiphon reveals this day; it says: "I am who am 4 and my counsel is not with the impious." This is the judgment, or separation, that John speaks about—that the faithful, who are accompanied by the Lord's counsel, are separated from the impious. The first Psalm, *Beatus vir,* reveals the same thing; it first describes what happiness should flee from and what it should seek, and then it also describes the expulsion of the impious, saying: "Not so the wicked, not so, but like the dust that the wind drives from the face of the earth," and so forth as follows.

The second antiphon reveals what the Lord said he ac- 5 complished on the next day, according to Luke—that is, cures. Right after John said "Now shall the prince of this world be cast out," he continued to explain what these cures were, saying: "And I, if I be lifted up from the earth, will draw all things after myself." Augustine, in his aforemen- 6 tioned sermon, explains this as follows: "For he did not address this to the varieties of all mankind, but to the entirety

sed ad creaturae integritatem, aut certe omnia hominum genera, sive in linguis omnibus, sive in aetatibus omnibus, sive in gradibus honorum omnibus." Et post paululum: "Ut sit caput eorum, et illi membra eius."✝ De qua re dicit antiphona secunda: "Postulavi Patrem meum; dedit mihi gentes in hereditatem." Quae traxit post se, sunt gentes, quas Pater dedit Filio in hereditatem.

7    Tertia antiphona tangit consummationem quam Dominus se promisit perfecturum in tertia die. Tertia dies est quando eos de quibus diabolum eiecit et sanitati restituit, per coniunctionem corporis sui, perducit ad societatem

8    sanctorum angelorum. Antiphona dicit: "Ego dormivi et somnum coepi et resurrexi." Resurrexit Christus, sed non solus. Hoc testificati sunt illi qui in die resurrectionis eius per resurrectionem apparuerunt multis in sancta civitate [Matt 27:52–53]. Caput surrexit; necesse est ut membra sequantur. Propterea non dixit Paulus: "Qui praedestinatus est Filius Dei in virtute, secundum spiritum sanctificationis ex resurrectione mortui Iesu Christi Domini nostri," sed

9    dixit: "Ex resurrectione mortuorum" [Rom 1:4]. Institutor Officii congruentius non potuit singula opera trium dierum monstrare quam per tres Psalmos et tres antiphonas. In resurrectione Domini omnia haec impleta sunt: Diabolus eiectus est a fidelibus, ipsi coniuncti sunt capiti, caput surrexit, humana natura, in sua resurrectione, coniuncta est naturae angelorum, quamvis nimis exaltata sit super omnes

10    angelos. Angeli ubique possunt esse citato transitu, et in caelo et in terra; et illa humana natura, a sua ipsa persona, iuxta quod ipsa eademque persona disposuit, potuit, quando

of creation, and also of course to all the races of men, in all their languages, ages and ranks." And after a little: "That he may be their head, and they his members."+ The second antiphon speaks on this subject: "I have asked my Father; he gave me the nations as inheritance." The things that he drew after himself are the nations, which the Father gave the Son as inheritance.

The third antiphon touches on the consummation that 7 the Lord promised to accomplish on the third day. The third day is when he leads those from whom he has cast out the devil and whom he has restored to health, through union with his body, to the fellowship of the holy angels. The anti- 8 phon says: "I lay down and I began to sleep and I rose." Christ rose, but not alone. Those who appeared upon their own resurrection to many in the holy city, on the day of his resurrection, bore witness to this. The head rose; the members must follow. Therefore Paul did not say: "Who was predestined the Son of God in power, according to the spirit of sanctification, by the resurrection of our Lord Jesus Christ from his death"; but instead: "By the resurrection . . . from the dead." The founder of our Office could not reveal the 9 individual works of this three-day period more appropriately than through three Psalms and three antiphons. Upon the Lord's resurrection all these things were fulfilled: The devil was cast out from the faithful, they were joined to their head, their head rose, and human nature, upon its resurrection, was joined to the nature of the angels, though it was exalted far beyond all the angels. Angels can be everywhere 10 through their swift travel, both in heaven and on earth; and that human nature, through its own person and in accordance with what that same person decided, was able, when

voluit, esse in terra et sublimari in caelum per immortalitatis triumphum. Angelorum natura non eget cibo, nec eget potu, non vestimento, neque vehiculo aliquo quo discurrat; neque eguit ista postea illa humana natura. Quapropter dixit Apostolus: "Et si noveramus Christum secundum carnem, sed nunc iam non novimus" [2 Cor 5:16].

11 Per istos tres dies, informantur catecumini nostri in membris Christi—primo quando per exorcizationem et abrenuntiationem expellitur diabolus; deinde per fidem perficitur sanitas in eis; postremo per manus impositionem episcoporum iustificantur. Resurrectio Christi nostra iustificatio est; ibi resurgimus cum Christo, ubi iustificamur. Nempe per istos tres dies, quasi per tres antiphonas—scilicet primam, quae nos disiungit ab impiis; et postea alteram, quae coniungit capiti Christo; atque tertiam, quae nos facit surgere per iustificationem—ingressi sumus in ecclesiam. Ex persona neofytorum dico.

12 Sequentes dies et noctes baptismales ostendunt qualiter in ipsa ecclesia secundum Christi doctrinam vivere debeamus. Dies ostendunt resurrectionem Christi. Igitur quia una die resurrexit Dominus, sic currunt officia nostra per illos septem dies, quasi adhuc sit dies Dominica. In sacramentorio cantamus: "Vere dignum et iustum est, aequum et salutare, te quidem omni tempore, sed in hac potissimum die gloriosius praedicare." Cantores cotidie cantant: "Haec

13 dies quam fecit Dominus" [Ps 117:24]. Unam eandemque diem per sacramenta baptismalia septem dierum caelebramus, quando electi, per omne curriculum huius vitae, non

it wanted, to be on earth and to be raised on high in heaven through the triumph of immortality. The angelic nature does not require food, nor does it require drink, nor clothing, nor any vehicle to move about in; and subsequently human nature, too, did not require these things. Thus the Apostle said: "And if we had known Christ according to the flesh, but now we know him so no longer."

On these three days, our catechumens are signified in Christ's members—first, when the devil is expelled through exorcism and renunciation; later, when they are cured through their faith; and finally, when they are justified through the bishop's laying on of hands. Christ's resurrection is our justification; we rise with Christ where we are justified. For indeed, we went to church on these three days as if through three antiphons—namely the first, which divides us from the impious; and then the second, which joins us to Christ, our head; and the third, which causes us to rise through our justification. I speak in the guise of the neophytes. 11

The following baptismal days and nights show how we ought to live in this same church according to Christ's teaching. The days show Christ's resurrection. And because the Lord rose on one day, our offices continue for seven days, as if each day were still Sunday. In the sacramentary, we sing: "It is truly worthy and just, right and wholesome, to preach you in every season, but it is especially glorious to do so on this day." On each day the cantors sing: "This is the day that the Lord has made." We celebrate one and the same day through the baptismal sacraments of seven days, when the elect, through the whole course of this life, do not depart 12 13

declinant per opera tenebrarum a capite suo, quod ita surrexit ut ultra non moriatur.

14    Sicut dies recolit resurrectionem Domini, ita nox sepulturam eius. Si fecimus de septem diebus unum diem propter
iugem resurrectionem bonorum operum, debemus noctes
praecedentes quasi uni diei aptare. Triduana sepultura praecessit resurrectionem Domini, et triduana sepultura praecedit iustificationem nostram. "Consepulti enim sumus cum
illo," dicit Apostolus, "per baptismum in morte, ut quomodo surrexit Christus a mortuis per gloriam Patris, ita et
nos in novitate vitae ambulemus" [Rom 6:4]. Qui enim mo-
15    ritur ac sepelitur, nullum peccatum potest operari. Per noctem enim designatur tempus quietis, ut Dominus in Evangelio: "Veniet autem nox quando nemo potest operari" [John
9:4]. Quamvis hic dicatur mixtim de bonis et malis operibus,
possumus tamen noctem intellegere, quando quiescit homo
a pravis operibus.

16    Hanc quietem in qua cessamus a malis et vigilamus in bonis, recolimus per tres Psalmos qui fiunt Nocturnali officio
per dies baptismales. Quando mergimur ter in aqua, conse-
pelimur Christo triduano sepulchro. Ille enim cantat tres
Psalmos in nocte, qui mente retinet consepultum se esse
Christo, et idcirco mortuum esse peccato. Ille mortuus est
peccato, qui non operatur peccatum. Ille enim cantat in die:
"Haec est dies quam fecit Dominus, exultemus et laetemur
in ea" [Ps 117:24], qui perseverat in innocentia et in bonis
moribus. Et quia haec certatim debemus meditari et satagere, quamdiu in praesenti saeculo sumus—id est usque
dum veniat septima dies, in qua separatur anima a corpore—

through works of darkness from their head, who rose that there might be no more dying.

While the day commemorates the Lord's resurrection, 14 the night commemorates his burial. If we made one day out of seven because of the perpetual resurrection of good works, we should bring the preceding nights into conformity, as it were, with one day. A three-day burial preceded the Lord's resurrection, and a three-day burial precedes our justification. "For we are buried together with him by baptism into death," the Apostle says, "that as Christ is risen from the dead by the glory of the Father, so we also may walk in newness of life." He who dies and is buried can perform no sin. Night signifies a time of quiet, as the Lord says 15 in the Gospel: "The night will come when no man can work." Although we are discussing both good and bad works here, we can nevertheless understand night as the time when man rests from evil works.

We commemorate this rest, when we cease from evil 16 works and remain awake for good works, through the three Psalms that occur in Nocturns on the baptismal days. When we are submerged three times in water, we are buried for three days with Christ. For he who remembers that he has been buried with Christ, and thus that he is dead to sin, sings three Psalms at night. He who does not sin is dead to sin. And he who perseveres in innocence and virtues sings during the day: "This is the day which the Lord has made, let us be glad and rejoice in it." And because we should earnestly contemplate and consider these things as long as we are in this world—that is, until the seventh day comes, when our soul is separated from our body—

cantemus in die: "Haec dies quam fecit Dominus," et in
17 nocte caelebremus sepulturam Domini. Et si in nobis pluribus non recolimus hanc mortificationem carnis quae designatur per tres Psalmos, et iustificationem quae designatur
per unius coloris officium, saltim in his qui nuper baptizati
sunt recolamus.

18 Aliter: Qui baptizantur simplici corde septiformem spiritum percipiunt, quem Esaias propheta decantat super Dominum nostrum Iesum Christum singulariter requiescere
[Isa 1:2–3]. Nisi crederetur percipi posse ab eis idem spiritus
qui baptizantur, non deprecaretur ab episcopis qui manus
19 impositionem exercent mitti in neofytos. Ut eidem septiformi spiritui concinamus, per septem dies religiosius, cum
maiore cautela solito, nostros conventus caelebramus. Per
singulos dies singulis donis satagimus concinere. Vitamus
pigritiam, ne iuxta Domini vocem corripiamur, qui dixit:
"Cantavimus vobis, et non saltastis" [Luke 7:32]. Advenit
Spiritus Sanctus novus hospes; exercet canticum laetitiae
inenarrabilis, scilicet sapientiae et intellectus, consilii et fortitudinis, scientiae et pietatis, ac timoris Domini. Hospes
suscipiens debet saltare huic cantico fide et spe et caritate.

20 Propter hanc vicissitudinem per singulos dies cantamus
aliquid, sive in responsorio seu in alleluia, de Psalmo *Confite-*
*mini Domino* [Ps 117], qui recolit bonitatem et misericordiam
Dei in saeculum, et in nocte tres antiphonas, sive alleluia
cum tribus Psalmis. Unusquisque Christianus Spiritum
Sanctum debet colere fide, spe et caritate. Has tres sorores
habet unumquodque donum Spiritus Sancti, et omnium

let us sing during the day: "This is the day which the Lord has made," and at night let us celebrate the Lord's burial. And if the greater part of us do not commemorate the mortification of the flesh that is designated through the three Psalms, and the justification that is designated through an office of one type, let us at least commemorate this mortification in those who have been recently baptized. 17

Otherwise: Those who are baptized with a simple heart receive the sevenfold spirit, which, the prophet Isaiah proclaims, rests particularly upon our Lord Jesus Christ. Unless it were believed that this same spirit can be received by those who are baptized, the bishops who perform the laying on of hands would not request that it be sent into the neophytes. On these seven days, to harmonize with the sevenfold spirit, we conduct our celebrations more piously and with greater care than usual. On each of the days we strive to be in harmony with each of the spirit's gifts. We avoid indolence, lest we be chastised according to the statement of the Lord, who said: "We sang to you, and you have not danced." The Holy Spirit comes as a new guest; he performs a song of indescribable rejoicing, namely a song of wisdom and understanding, of knowledge and piety, and of fear of the Lord. The host who receives him should dance to this song with faith and hope and charity. 18 19

Because of this exchange, on each day, whether in the responsory or the alleluia, we sing something from the Psalm *Confitemini Domino,* which recalls God's goodness and mercy in the world, and at night we sing three antiphons, or an alleluia with three Psalms. Every Christian should worship the Holy Spirit with faith, hope and charity. Each of the Holy Spirit's gifts has these three sisters, and these 20

21 septem sunt hae tres sorores et singulorum. Quod in nostro usu possumus experire, si septem fratres habuerint tres sorores, et omnium sunt et singulorum. Ut recolamus unum spiritum qui haec omnia operatur, unum diem ducimus in religione per septem dies; et ut recolamus septem dona eius, dies multiplicantur per septenarium numerum; et ut recolamus nostram fidem, spem et caritatem, quae usque in finem mundi nobiscum manere debent (secundum Apostolum, qui dicit: "Nunc autem manent fides, spes, caritas" [1 Cor 13:13]), usque in septimum diem tres Psalmos in nocte cantamus.

22 Baptismalia sacramenta usque ad conpletionem dierum septem tendunt, quia septiformi spiritu ditantur nuper baptizati—sive quia universitas temporis, quae fine septem dierum volvitur, significatur per septem dies (in qua necesse est satagere ut nullus Christianus a fide et spe ac caritate alienus sit, quamvis cetera omnia dona non possit capere)—seu quia unaquaeque anima electa, recedens de corpore, ilico invenit Sabbatum, et habet suum opus completum, quia Deus

23 septimo die complevit opus suum. Deinceps in sequenti tempore, quasi crescentium arborum frondes, multiplicantur et recoluntur mores boni diversorum operum per plures Psalmos. Agimus Deo gratias, qui dedit in corde servorum suorum ut eo ordine statuerent officia nostra, quo possit populus Dei praedicari ex eo, propemodum sicut ex lectione.

24 Habemus scriptum in Romano ordine ut non dicatur *Kyrie eleison* sive *Christe eleison* ad ullum cursum in memoratis

three are sisters of each and every one of the seven gifts. We   21
can understand this through our own experience by suppos-
ing that seven brothers have three sisters, and that they are
brothers of each and every one. That we may recall the one
spirit that does all these things, we spend one day in reverence over seven days; and that we may recall this spirit's
seven gifts, the days are increased to seven; and that we may
recall our faith, hope and charity, which should remain with
us until the end of the world (according to the Apostle, who
says: "And now there remain faith, hope, and charity"), we
sing three Psalms at night until the seventh day.

The baptismal sacraments last for seven days, because   22
the newly baptized are enriched by the sevenfold spirit—or
because the fullness of time, which revolves around a period
of seven days, is signified by seven days (in which we must
strive to ensure that no Christian be without faith and hope
and charity, though he may not be able to take hold of all the
other gifts)—or because each elect soul finds its Sabbath as
it leaves the body, and has finished its work, because the
Lord finished his work on the seventh day. Then in the fol-   23
lowing season, the good virtues of diverse works are multiplied and recalled through many Psalms, like the branches
of growing trees. We give thanks to God, who put it in the
heart of his servants to establish our offices in such a way
that God's people can receive preaching through their arrangement, just as they do through the reading.

We have it written in the Roman order that neither   24
*Kyrie eleison* nor *Christe eleison* should be said at any of
the offices on the aforementioned days; rather, we should

diebus, sed sine retractatione cantemus: "Haec dies quam fecit Dominus; exultemus et laetemur in ea" [Ps 117:24]. Collectam solam solet sacerdos dicere in fine officii. Si esset iam in re quod agimus, non ea diceretur; quoniam est in spe, oratio sacerdotis subsequitur, ut firmetur quod tenetur, et

25 quod nondum tenetur, accipiatur. De qua re dicit Agustinus in tractatu Psalmi centesimi quadragesimi octavi: "Laus nostra laetitiam habet, oratio gemitum. Promissum est nobis aliquid quod nondum habemus, et quia verax est qui promittit, in spe gaudemus. Quia tamen nondum habemus, in desiderio gemimus. Bonum est perseverare in desiderio, donec veniat quod promissum est, et transeat gemitus, succedat sola laudatio."+ Quicquid orationis fit ab his qui veraciter Pascha celebrant, sive in collecta seu in cubiculo cordis, propterea fit ut quod promissum est et nondum tenetur, adveniat. Vice desiderii, quod sanctus Agustinus memorat, caelebratur oratio sacerdotis.

26 Idem in sequentibus ostendit quam laetitiam recolat sancta ecclesia in diebus omnibus Pentecostes. "Propter haec," inquit, "duo tempora, unum quod nunc est in tribulationibus et temptationibus huius vitae, alterum quod tunc erit in securitate et exultatione perpetua—instituta est nobis etiam caelebratio duorum temporum: ante Pascha et post Pascha. Illud quod est ante Pascha significat tribulationem in qua modo sumus; quod vero nunc agimus post

unhesitatingly sing: "This is the day which the Lord has made; let us be glad and rejoice therein." At the end of the office the priest is accustomed to say only the collect. If that which we celebrate were already achieved, it would not be said; because we hope for it, the priest's prayer ensues, that what we have may be strengthened and what we do not yet have may be obtained. Augustine speaks about this in his 25 treatise on Psalm 148: "Our praise expresses rejoicing, our prayer lamentation. Something has been promised to us that we do not yet have, and because he who makes the promise is truthful, we rejoice in our hope. Yet because we do not yet have it, we lament in our desire. It is good to persevere in desire until what was promised arrives, our lamentation passes and only our rejoicing remains."✝ Whatever prayer arises from those who truly celebrate Easter, whether in the collect or in the confines of their hearts, it arises so that what was promised and is not yet realized may come about. The priest's prayer is celebrated from the perspective of the desire that Saint Augustine speaks of.

In a later passage, the same author shows what sort of re- 26 joicing the holy church cultivates on all the days of Pentecost. "Because of these two times," he says, "the one in the tribulations and temptations of this life that we have now, and the other in security and eternal exultation that will come—a celebration of two seasons has also been established for us: before Easter and after Easter. The one before Easter signifies the tribulation that we are in now; but the

27 Pascha significat beatitudinem in qua postea erimus. Ante Pascha ergo quod caelebramus, hoc et agimus; post Pascha autem quod caelebramus, significamus quod nondum tenemus. Propterea illud tempus in ieiuniis et orationibus exercemus, hoc vero tempus relaxatis ieiuniis in laudibus agimus. Hoc est enim alleluia quod cantamus; quod Latine interpretatur, ut nostis, 'Laudate Dominum.' Ideo illud tempus ante resurrectionem, hoc tempus post resurrectionem Domini est. Quo tempore significatur vita futura, quam nondum tenemus, quia quod significamus post resurrectionem Domini, tenebimus post resurrectionem nostram.

28 In capite enim nostro nobis utrumque figuratum est, utrumque demonstratum est. Passio Domini ostendit nobis vitam praesentis necessitatis, quia oportet et laborare et tribulari et ad extremum mori. Resurrectio vero et clarificatio Domini ostendit nobis vitam quam accepturi sumus, cum venerit retribuere digna dignis, mala malis, bona bonis. Et qui-

29 dem modo mali omnes cantare nobiscum possunt alleluia. Si autem in malitia sua perseveraverint, canticum vitae nostrae futurae labiis poterunt dicere, ipsam vero vitam quae tunc erit in ea veritate quae nunc significatur, obtinere non possunt, quia noluerunt meditari, ante quam veniret, et tenere quod venturum erat. Nunc ergo, fratres, exortamur vos ut laudetis Deum. Et hoc est quod omnes dicimus quando dicimus 'alleluia': Laudate Deum."✝

one after Easter that we are now observing signifies the happiness that we will experience later on. Before Easter, therefore, what we celebrate we also do; after Easter, however, we show that we do not yet have what we celebrate. We therefore spend the former time in fasting and prayer, but we celebrate the latter season in praise, by lifting the fast. For this is the alleluia that we sing; in Latin, as you know, it means 'Praise the Lord.' And so the former time comes before the resurrection, and this time comes after the Lord's resurrection. In this time the life to come, which we do not yet have, is signified, because after our resurrection we will have what we signify after the Lord's resurrection. For both times were prefigured for us in our head; each was signified. The Lord's passion shows us the life of our present necessity, since we must work and suffer and ultimately die. Yet the Lord's resurrection and his glorification show us the life that we will receive when he comes to give worthy things to the worthy, evil things to the evil, and good things to the good. And indeed, now all the evil can sing the alleluia with us. But if they persist in their evil, they will be able to sing the song of our future life with their lips, but they cannot obtain the life that is to come in that truth which is now signified, because they refused to consider it and to obtain what was to come before it came. Therefore, brothers, we now encourage you to praise God. And this is what we all say when we say 'alleluia': Praise God."✝

27

28

29

475

## 24

# Repetitio de Laetania Maiore

Quando scripsi de Laetania Maiore in superioribus, id est in primo libello huiusce operis, nondum legeram illam statutam esse a sancto Gregorio. Dixi illam statutam esse ob duas causas, scilicet propter imminentia bella, quae eo tempore excitari possunt, et propter fruges conservandas. At postquam legi statutum sancti Gregorii, curavi illud hic interponere, eodem modo ut legitur in volumine epistolarum

2 eius. Post quod similiter curavi epistolam quandam ad Phocam imperatorem subnectere, in qua demonstratur a Longobardorum gente eo tempore dibacchari terminos Romanorum.

## 25

# Sequuntur dicta ex epistolis sancti Gregorii

"In nomine Dei, salvatoris nostri Iesu Christi, per indictionem sextam, die vicesima tertia mensis Novembris, temporibus domni et beatissimi papae Gregorii, coronatus est Phocas et Leontia Augusta in septimo in palatio qui dicitur

## 24

## Addendum on the Greater Litany

When I wrote about the Greater Litany above, that is in the first book of this work, I had not yet read that it was established by Saint Gregory. I said that it was established for two reasons, namely because of imminent wars, which can arise at that time, and to protect the crops. But after I read that it had been established by Saint Gregory, I inserted it here, just as it reads in the book of his letters. After it I likewise inserted a letter to the emperor Phocas, in which it is shown that the lands of the Romans were being ravaged by the race of the Lombards at that time.

2

## 25

## Here follow statements from the letters of Saint Gregory

"In the name of God, our savior Jesus Christ, in the sixth indiction, on the twenty-third day of the month of November, in the time of the most blessed lord pope Gregory, Phocas and Empress Leontia were crowned at the Hebdo-

477

Secundianas. Et occisus est Mauricius imperator cum omnibus filiis suis masculis, id est Theodosio, iam coronato, Tiberio, Petro, Paulo et Iustiniano; simul et Petro, fratre suprascripti Mauricii Augusti, sed et aliqui procerum qui ei cohaerebant, id est Constantinus, patricius et curator de
2 Placidias, sed et Georgius, notarius principis. Venit autem icona suprascriptorum Phocae et Leontiae Augustae Romae septimo Kalendarum Maiarum; et acclamatum est eis in Lateranis in Basilica Iuliana ab omni clero vel senatu: 'Exaudi, Christe: Phocae Augusto et Leontiae Augustae vita.' Tunc iussit ipsam iconam domnus beatissimus et apostolicus Gregorius papa reponi in oratorio Sancti Caesarii intra palatium.

3   "Oportet, fratres karissimi, ut flagella Dei, quae metuere ventura debuimus, saltim praesentia et experta timeamus. Conversionis nobis aditum dolor aperiat, et cordis nostri duritiam ipsa iam quam patimur poena dissolvat. Ut enim propheta teste praedictum est: 'Pervenit gladius usque ad
4 animam' [Jer 4:10]. Ecce etenim: Cuncta plebs caelestis irae mucrone percutitur; et repentina singuli cede vastantur, nec languor mortem praevenit—sed languoris moras, ut cernitis, mors praecurrit. Percussus quisque ante rapitur quam ad lamenta paenitentiae convertatur. Pensate ergo qualis ad conspectum districti iudicis pervenit, cui non vacat flere quod fecit. Habitatores quique non ex parte subtrahuntur, sed pariter corruunt. Domus vacuae relinquuntur; filiorum

mon in the palace called Secundianas. And Emperor Maurice was killed together with all his male children, namely Theodosius, already crowned, Tiberius, Peter, Paul and Justinian; and also Peter, brother of the aforementioned emperor Maurice, and various nobles who were associated with him, namely Constantine, patrician and curator of Placidia, and also George, notary to the emperor. And a portrait of 2 the aforementioned Phocas and Empress Leontia came to Rome on the seventh day before the Kalends of May; and for them acclamation was made in the Lateran, by the entire clergy and senate in the Julian Basilica: 'Hear us, Christ: Life for Emperor Phocas and Empress Leontia.' Then the most blessed lord and apostolic pope Gregory ordered that the same portrait be placed in the oratory of Saint Cesarius within the palace.

"Dearest brethren, at the least, let us fear even the expe- 3 rience and presence of God's scourges, whose approach we should dread. May sorrow open for us a path to conversion, and may the penalty we now suffer soften the hardness of our hearts. For as it has been said, with the prophet as witness: 'The sword reaches even to the soul.' And indeed, be- 4 hold: All the people are struck down by the sword of heavenly anger; and they are laid waste by this sudden and singular slaughter, nor does weariness precede their death— rather, as you can see, death precedes the delays of weariness. One is struck down and seized before one turns to the laments of penance. Ponder, therefore, how one who had no time to lament what he did comes to the sight of a severe judge. The inhabitants are not carried off in part; rather, they fall all together. Houses are left empty; parents watch

funera parentes aspiciunt, et sui eos ad interitum heredes praecedunt.

5    "Unusquisque ergo nostrum ad paenitentiae lamenta confugiat, dum flere ante percussionem vacat. Revocemus ante oculos mentis quicquid errando commisimus, et quod nequiter egimus, flendo puniamus. 'Praeveniamus faciem eius in confessione' [Ps 94:2]. Et, sicut propheta admonet: 'Levemus corda nostra cum manibus ad Deum' [Lam 3:41]. Ad Deum quippe corda cum manibus levare est orationis

6 nostrae studium cum merito bonae operationis erigere. Dat profecto, dat tremori nostro fidutiam, qui per prophetam clamat: 'Nolo mortem peccatoris; sed convertatur et vivat' [Ezek 18:32]. Nullus autem de iniquitatum suarum immanitate desperet. Veternosas namque Ninivitarum culpas triduana paenitentia abstersit, et conversus latro vitae premia etiam in ipsa sententia suae mortis emeruit [ Jonah 3; Luke 23:40–43]. Mutemus igitur corda et praesumamus nos iam percepisse quod petimus. Citius ad precem iudex flectitur si a pravitate sua petitor corrigatur.

7    "Imminente ergo tantae animadversionis gladio, nos inportunis fletibus insistamus. Ea namque quae ingrata esse hominibus inportunitas solet, iudicio veritatis placet—quia pius ac misericors Deus vult a se precibus veniam exigi, qui, quantum meremur, non vult irasci. Hinc etenim per psalmistam dicit: 'Invoca me in die tribulationis tuae, et eruam te, et magnificabis me' [Ps 49:15]. Ipse ergo sibi testis

the funerals of their children, and their heirs precede them to destruction.

"Let each of us therefore flee to the lamentation of penance, since there is time to weep before we are struck down. Let us call before our mind's eye whatever we did in wandering astray, and let us endure punishment in our mourning for our vile actions. 'Let us come before his face in confession.' And, as the prophet advises: 'Let us lift up our hearts with our hands to God.' And in fact raising our hearts with our hands to God amounts to raising the desire of our prayer together with the merit of our good work. And indeed he provides assurance for our trembling, who cries out through the prophet: 'I do not want the death of the sinner; rather let him be converted and live.' But let no one despair over the vastness of their sins. For he wiped away the faults of the indolent Ninevites with a penance of three days, and the converted thief earned the reward of life even upon the sentence of his death. Let us therefore change our hearts and presume that we have already achieved what we seek. The judge is persuaded more readily by a request if the petitioner is chastised by his own depravity.

"And so, as the sword of this great tribulation approaches, let us press on with our grievous laments. For the importunity that is accustomed to disturb mankind pleases the judgment of truth—since the pious and merciful God wants pardon to be extracted from him through prayers; he does not want to be angered, as much as we deserve it. Thus he says through the psalmist: 'Call upon me in the day of trouble, and I will deliver you, and you shall glorify me.' He is therefore

est, quia invocantibus misereri desiderat, qui ammonet ut

8 invocetur. Proinde, fratres karissimi, contrito corde et correctis operibus crastina die primo diluculo ad septiformem laetaniam, iuxta distributionem inferius designatam, devota cum lacrimis mente veniamus. Nullus vestrum ad terrena opera in agro exeat, nullus quodlibet negotium agere praesumat, quatenus ad sanctae genitricis Domini ecclesiam convenientes, qui simul omnes peccavimus, simul omnes male quae fecimus deploremus—ut districtus iudex, dum culpas nostras nos punire considerat, ipse a sententia propositae damnationis parcat."

9 Sequitur: "Laetania clericorum exeat ab ecclesia beati Iohannis Baptistae; laetania virorum, ab ecclesia sancti martyris Marcelli; laetania monachorum, ab ecclesia martyrum Iohannis et Pauli; laetania ancillarum Dei, ab ecclesia beatorum martyrum Cosmae et Damiani; laetania feminarum coniugarum, ab ecclesia beati Petri et martyris Stephani; laetania viduarum, ab ecclesia beati martyris Vitalis; laetania pauperum et infantum, ab ecclesia beatae martyris Caeciliae."✝

10 In sequenti epistola monstrabitur quod pro inportunitate bellorum potest procul dubio videri laetania instituta esse. Et ex qualitate temporis, colligimus eam necessariam esse ad fruges conservandas.

11 "Gregorius Phocae Augusto: Considerare cum gaudiis et magnis actionibus gratiarum libet quantas omnipotenti Domino laudes debemus, quod remoto iugo tristitiae ad libertatis tempora sub imperiali benignitatis vestrae pietate pervenimus. Nam quod permanere in palatio, iuxta antiquam

his own witness, for he who advises that he be called upon wants to have mercy on those who call upon him. And so, 8 dearest brethren, let us with contrite heart and corrected deeds proceed at dawn tomorrow to the sevenfold litany, in the divisions outlined below, with a devout mind and tears. May none of you go out to do earthly works in the field, and let nobody presume to conduct any business, so that as we gather at the church of the Lord's holy mother, we, who have all sinned together, may deplore together the evil things that we have done—that our severe judge, while he considers punishing us for our sins, may spare us from the sentence of damnation that has been proposed for us."

There follows: "Let the litany of the clergy go forth from 9 the church of blessed John the Baptist; the litany of men, from the church of the holy martyr Marcellus; the litany of monks, from the church of the martyrs John and Paul; the litany of God's maidservants, from the church of the martyrs Cosmas and Damian; the litany of married women, from the church of blessed Peter and the martyr Stephen; the litany of widows, from the church of the blessed martyr Vitalis; the litany of children and the poor, from the church of the blessed martyr Cecilia."✠

In the following letter it will be shown, beyond doubt, 10 that the litany seems to have been instituted because of the grievousness of wars. And from the nature of the season, we gather that the litany is necessary to protect crops.

"Gregory to Emperor Phocas: We should consider with 11 joy and great thanksgiving how many praises we owe to our almighty Lord, that we have arrived at times of liberty under the imperial piety of your favor, now that the yoke of sorrow has been lifted. And it was not out of neglect on my part

consuetudinem, apostolicae sedis diaconem vestra serenitas non invenit, non hoc meae negligentiae, sed gravissimae necessitatis fuit: Quia dum ministri omnes huius vestrae ecclesiae tam contrita asperaque tempora cum formidine declinarent atque refugerent, nulli eorum poterant imponi, ut ad urbem regiam in palatio permansurus accederet.

12    "At postquam vestram clementiam omnipotentis Dei gratia disponente ad culmen imperii pervenisse cognoverunt, ipsi quoque suadente laetitia ad vestra vestigia venire festinabant, qui illuc prius accedere valde timuerant. Sed quia eorum quidam ita senectute sunt debiles ut laborem ferre vix possint, quidam vero ecclesiasticis curis vehementer implicantur, et lator praesentium, qui primus omnium defensorum fuit, bene mihi ex longa assiduitate compertus est, vita, fide ac moribus approbatus; hunc aptum pietatis vestrae

13 vestigiis esse iudicavi. Unde eum, auctore Deo, diaconem feci et sub celeritate transmittere studui, qui, cuncta quae in iis partibus aguntur, invento opportuno tempore, valeat clementiae vestrae suggerere. Cui rogo ut serenitas vestra pias aures inclinare dignetur, ut tanto nobis celerius valeat misereri, quanto afflictionem nostram verius eius relatione cognoverit.

14    "Qualiter enim cotidianis gladiis et quantis Langobardorum incursionibus—ecce iam per triginta et quinque annorum longitudinem—premimur, nullis explere suggestionibus vocibus valemus. Sed in omnipotente Deo confidimus quia ea quae coepit consolationis suae nobis bona perficiet, et qui suscitavit in republica pios dominos exstinguet

that your highness has not found a deacon of the apostolic see dwelling in your palace, in accordance with ancient custom; this is rather because of the gravest necessity: Since all the ministers of your church have fled in terror and taken refuge from these difficult and downtrodden times, none of them could be imposed upon to enter the royal city and stay in the palace.

"But after they realized that your clemency had ascended 12 to the summit of the empire through the grace of almighty God, those who had earlier greatly feared going forth, were persuaded by joy and they hastened to follow in your footsteps. But because some of them are so frail in their old age that they can hardly bear the work, and others are much burdened by ecclesiastical duties, I judged the bearer of this letter suitable to follow in the footsteps of your piety; he was the first of all the defenders, is well known to me for his lasting constancy, and he is proven in his faith and virtue. And so, with God's guidance, I made him a deacon and 13 sent him off in haste, that he might be able to bring to the attention of your clemency, when he has found a good moment, all that occurs in these parts. I ask that your serenity deign to bend pious ears to him, that you may take pity on us more quickly, the more accurately you understand our affliction through his account.

"And we cannot describe in what way and by how many 14 daily murders and assaults from the Lombards we are oppressed—now for the space of thirty-five years. But we trust in almighty God that he will perfect the consoling favors that he has begun for us, and that he who has raised up pious

crudeles inimicos. Sancta itaque Trinitas vitam vestram per tempora longa custodiat, ut de bono vestrae pietatis quod tarde suscepimus diutius gaudeamus."

26

## Repetitio de alleluia quod cantatur in Missa, et de vestimento subdiaconorum, et *Kyrieleison,* ac Dominica oratione, ex epistola sancti Gregorii

Quando scripsit nostra parvitas de officio Missae, simili modo me latebant quae sequuntur, ut ea quae superius dixi de Laetania Maiore. Nondum legeram quod postea inveni in epistola sancti Gregorii, quo tempore alleluia in Missa primo cantatum esset in ecclesia Romana, et caetera quae manifestabuntur verbis ipsius epistolae ad Iohannem Siracusanum. Quibus inventis non potui praeterire nisi ea hic introducerem, quamvis non in competenti loco, quia magis competebat ea scribi in officio Missae, quam in officio Nocturnali. Sequitur textus epistolae:

masters of the republic will destroy our cruel enemies. May the Holy Trinity therefore long preserve your life, that we may rejoice all the longer over the good of your piety that we have lately received."

## 26

## Addendum on the alleluia that is sung during Mass, and on the vesting of subdeacons, and the *Kyrie eleison* and the Lord's prayer, from a letter of Saint Gregory

When, in our inadequacy, we wrote about the office of the Mass, the following things escaped me, as did those things that I set forth above on the Greater Litany. I had not yet read what I found later on in a letter of Saint Gregory, about when the alleluia was first sung during Mass in the Roman church, and the rest of the things that will be clarified through the words of his letter to John of Syracuse. When I discovered these things I could not pass over them without adding them here, although this is not an appropriate place, since it was more appropriate that these things be copied into our discussion of the office of Mass, than into our discussion of Nocturns. The text of the letter follows:

2    "Gregorius Iohanni episcopo Siracusanae. Veniens quidam de Sicilia dixit mihi quod aliqui amici eius, vel Greci
vel Latini nescio, quasi sub zelo sanctae Romanae ecclesiae,
de meis dispositionibus murmurarent, dicentes: 'Quomodo
ecclesiam Constantinopolitanam disponit comprimere, qui
eius consuetudines per omnia sequitur?' Cui cum dicerem:
'Quas consuetudines eius sequimur?' responsum est: 'Quia
alleluia dici ad Missas extra Pentecosten tempora fecistis;
quia subdiaconos spoliatos procedere, quia *Kyrieleison* dici,
quia orationem Dominicam mox post canonem dici statuis-
3 tis.' Cui ego respondi quia in nullo eorum aliam ecclesiam
secuti sumus.

   "Nam ut alleluia hic diceretur de Hierosolimorum ecclesia, ex beati Hieronimi traditione, tempore beatae memo-
4 riae Damasi papae traditur tractum." Et paulo post: "Subdiaconos autem ut spoliatos procedere facerem, antiqua
consuetudo ecclesiae fuit; sed placuit cuidam nostro ponti-
fici, nescio, qui eos vestitos procedere praecepit. Nam vestrae ecclesiae numquid traditionem a Grecis acceperunt?
Unde habent ergo hodie ut subdiaconi in eis in tonicis pro-
cedant, nisi quia hoc a matre sua Romana ecclesia percepe-
5 runt? *Kyrieleison* autem nos neque diximus, neque dicimus,
sicut a Grecis dicitur, quia in Grecis simul omnes dicunt,
apud nos autem a clericis dicitur, a populo respondetur,
et totidem vocibus etiam *Christe eleison* dicitur, quod apud
Grecos nullo modo dicitur. In cotidianis autem Missis,
alia quae dici solent, tacemus; tantummodo *Kyrieleison* et

"Gregory to Bishop John of Syracuse. Someone coming ₂ from Sicily told me that some of his friends, whether Greek or Latin I do not know, apparently beset by zeal for the holy Roman church, were complaining about my arrangements, saying: 'How does he manage to keep the church of Constantinople in check—he who follows its customs in all things?' When I replied: 'What customs do we follow?' the response was: 'That you have the alleluia said at Masses beyond the season of Pentecost, and that you have required the subdeacons to process unvested, the *Kyrie eleison* to be said, and the Lord's prayer to be said right after the canon.' I answered him that in none of these matters have ₃ we followed another church.

"Saying the alleluia here is a usage held to have been derived from the church of Jerusalem, through the instruction of blessed Jerome, in the time of Pope Damasus of blessed memory." And after a little: "It was in accordance with an ₄ ancient custom of the church that I had the subdeacons process unvested; it was rather some previous pontiff—I do not know who—who thought it pleasing to have them process in their vestments. But have your churches really never received a tradition from the Greeks? From where, then, do your subdeacons have the custom of processing in your churches in tunics, if not because they got it from their mother, the Roman church? And we have not said, nor do ₅ we say, the *Kyrie eleison* as the Greeks say it, since among the Greeks they say it all together, while among us it is said by the clergy and the people respond, and the same number of voices say *Christe eleison,* which the Greeks do not recite at all. But in our daily Masses we omit the other things that they are accustomed to say; we say only *Kyrie eleison* and

*Christe eleison* dicimus, ut in his deprecantibus vocibus paulo

6 diutius occupemur. Orationem vero Dominicam idcirco mox post precem dicimus quia mos apostolorum fuit, ut ad ipsam solummodo orationem oblationis hostiam consecrarent. Et valde mihi inconveniens visum est ut precem quam scolasticus composuerat super oblationem diceremus, et ipsam traditionem quam redemptor noster composuit, super eius corpus et sanguinem non diceremus. Sed et Dominica oratio apud Grecos ab omni populo dicitur, apud nos vero a solo sacerdote. In quo ergo Grecorum consuetudines secuti sumus, quia aut veteres nostras reparavimus, aut novas et utiles constituimus, in quibus tamen alios non probamur imitari?

7 "Ergo vestra caritas, cum occasio dederit ut ad Catanensem civitatem pergat vel in Syracusana ecclesia, eos quos credit aut intellegit quia de hac re murmurare potuerunt, facta collocutione, doceat, et quasi alia ex occasione eos instruere non desistat. Nam de Constantinopolitana ecclesia quod dicunt—quis eam dubitet sedi apostolicae esse subiectam? Quod et piissimus domnus imperator et frater noster,

8 ter, eiusdem civitatis episcopus, assidue profitentur. Tamen si quid boni vel ipsa vel altera ecclesia habet, ego et minores meos, quos ab illicitis prohibeo, in bono imitari paratus sum. Stultus est enim qui in eo se primum existimat, ut bona quae viderit discere contempnat."

9 Ex praesenti epistola docemur, ut quidquid boni ab aliis ecclesiis discere possumus, non ea contempnamus. Simulque edocemur quod aliquo tempore cantabatur Missa in Romana ecclesia absque alleluia. Si eo tempore cantabantur tractus per omnes Dominicos dies et, post alleluia

*Christe eleison,* that we may be occupied a little longer with these prayerful words. And we say the Lord's prayer right af- 6 ter the canon because it was the custom of the apostles to consecrate the host accompanied by this prayer alone. And it struck me as very inappropriate for us to say a prayer that a scholar had composed over the offering, and not to say the traditional prayer that our redeemer composed, over his body and blood. But among the Greeks the Lord's prayer is said by the entire people, while among us it is said by the priest alone. In what respect, then, have we followed Greek customs, since we have either restored our own ancient customs, or established new and useful ones, for which there is no proof that we imitate others?

"And so in your charity, when you happen to travel to the 7 church at Catania or the church at Syracuse, you should start a conversation with those whom you know or believe were capable of complaining about this matter, and you should teach them and, as it were, not fail to instruct them on a further occasion. For what they say about the church of Constantinople—who doubts that it is subject to the apostolic see? Our most pious lord emperor and our brother, the bishop of the same city, repeatedly attest as much. Yet if 8 that or another church has some good observance, I am prepared to imitate even my lessers, whom I prohibit from illicit practices, in that good observance. For he is a fool who considers himself to be the first in goodness, such that he disdains to learn from the good things that he sees."

This letter teaches us not to disdain whatever good we 9 can learn from other churches. And we also are taught that, at one time, Mass was sung in the Roman church without the alleluia. I do not know whether, at that time, tracts were sung on all Sundays and, after the alleluia was

assumptum, in solis Dominicis diebus de Septuagesima re-
servarentur, nescio. Unum habeo notum, ex eo quod alleluia
divulgatum sit, cantatum esse apud sanctum Agustinum et
apud Romanam ecclesiam atque Constantinopolitanam
priscis temporibus—per dies Pentecostes debere alleluia
decantari, ad recordandum de laetitia resurrectionis sanctorum.

10    Restat adhuc quod pulsat intentionem ad requirendum—
hoc est ut sicut per Dominicos dies et festos cantatur alleluia ad Missam, ita debeat cantari per communes dies, an
non. Nisi forte imbui possimus ex praesenti scriptura sancti
Gregorii. Nam ex eo ubi sanctus Gregorius dicit: "Alia quae
dici solent, in cotidianis Missis tacemus, tantummodo *Kyrieleison* et *Christe eleison* dicimus," possumus intellegere
quod non alleluia cantabatur apud illum per cotidianos dies
in officio Missae.

27

# De completione dierum
# Pentecostes

Praecepit Dominus discipulis suis, quando ascendit in
caelum, "ne ab Hierosolimis discederent, sed expectarent
promissionem Patris quam audierunt per os eius. Quia Iohannes quidem baptyzavit aqua, vos autem baptyzabimini

taken up, they were reserved only for the Sundays of Septuagesima. I noted one point from that passage where it
emerged that the alleluia was sung in Saint Augustine's
church, and in the Roman church and the church of Constantinople in ancient times—that the alleluia should be
sung throughout the days of Pentecost, to commemorate
the rejoicing of the resurrection of the saints.

There still remains something that provokes us to inquire    10
further—namely, whether or not the alleluia should be sung
during Mass on ordinary days, just as it is sung on Sundays
and feast days. Unless, perhaps, we could learn the answer
from this text by Saint Gregory. For in the passage where
Saint Gregory says: "In our daily masses we omit the other
things that they are accustomed to say; we say only *Kyrie eleison* and the *Christe eleison,*" we can understand that his
church did not sing the alleluia during the office of Mass on
ordinary days.

## 27

# On the fulfillment of the days
# of Pentecost

When he ascended to heaven, the Lord ordered his disciples "that they should not depart from Jerusalem, but
should wait for the promise of the Father that they have
heard from his mouth. For John indeed baptized with water,

Spiritu Sancto non post multos hos dies" [Acts 1:4–5]—id est post decem dies. Merito expectant decem dies, quia futurum erat ut mysterium denarii numeri post decim dies

2 perfectius, Spiritu Sancto veniente, perciperent. Ita Lucas narrat: "Vos autem sedete hic in civitate quoadusque induamini virtute ex alto. Eduxit autem eos foras usque in Bethaniam, et elevatis manibus suis benedixit eis. Et factum est, dum benediceret illis, recessit ab eis et ferebatur in caelum. Et ipsi adorantes eum regressi sunt in Hierusalem cum gaudio magno. Et erant semper in templo laudantes Deum et benedicentes Dominum" [Luke 24:49–53]. In civitate sedere est aliquem tacita mente et quieta cogitare de promissis Domini, et a statu perpetuae pacis non recedere—firmare sensus corporis, ne mors per eos introeat, et cogitare quod se ipsum debeat totum integrum reddere Deo.

3 Hoc est habere integra quatuor elementa in se, qualia illi Deus ea praestitit—totum se versum esse in dilectionem Dei ex toto corde et ex tota anima et ex tota mente, et scire imaginem sanctae Trinitatis signatam in se. Si quis istum denarium desiderat in se habere, et cognoscit minus aliquid habere ab eo, debet adorare Dominum et precari ut sibi concedat illum. Et si senserit per caritatem quae foras mittit timorem posse eum impetrare, maneat in templo, laudans et

4 benedicens Deum. Hoc est expectare per decim dies promissum Patris, desiderare iugiter integritatem suae creationis et creatoris sui cognitionem. Hunc denarium percepe-

but you shall be baptized with the Holy Spirit not many days hence"—that is, after ten days. It was appropriate that they wait ten days, since it would come about that they would receive the mystery of the number ten more perfectly after ten days, upon the coming of the Holy Spirit. Luke tells it as 2 follows: "But stay in the city till you are filled with power from on high. And he led them out as far as Bethania, and lifting up his hands he blessed them. And it came to pass, while he blessed them, he departed from them and was carried up to heaven. And they adored him and went back into Jerusalem with great joy. And they were always in the temple praising God and blessing the Lord." To stay in the city is to ponder the Lord's promises with a quiet and peaceful mind, and not to depart from this state of perpetual peace—to reinforce the bodily senses, lest death enter through them, and to consider that you should render your whole self to God.

This is having the fullness of the four elements in your- 3 self, as God offered them to you—to have turned your whole self to love of God through your whole heart and your whole soul and your whole mind, and to know that the image of the Holy Trinity has been inscribed on you. Should anyone desire to have the number ten within himself, while recognizing that he has something less of it, he should adore the Lord and pray that the Lord grant it to him. And should he sense through the charity that drives out fear that he can obtain it, let him remain in the temple, praising and blessing God. This is awaiting the Father's promise for ten days, con- 4 tinually desiring the fullness of his creation and an under-

runt apostoli amplius et perfectius, quam prius haberent, in die Pentecostes. Eodem praecepto ammonitus est sanctus Agustinus a Spiritu Sancto, ante quam transiret de corpore, qui postulavit ut spatium ei daretur per decem dies

5 meditandi se et sua. Ita scriptum est in eius *Vita:* "Nam sibi iusserat Psalmos Daviticos—qui sunt paucissimi—de poenitentia scribi. Ipsos quaterniones, iacens in lecto, contra parietem positos, diebus suae infirmitatis intuebatur et legebat, et ubertim ac iugiter flebat. Et ne intentio eius a quoquam impediretur, ante dies ferme decim quam exiret de corpore, a nobis postolavit praesentibus ne quis ad eum ingrederetur, nisi his tantum oris quibus medici ad inspiciendum intrabant vel cum ei refectio inferretur."✝ Usque huc, de *Vita sancti Agustini.*

6 Aliter: Scribit idem sanctus Agustinus in sermone septimo decimo super Iohannem: "Ieiunium autem magnum et generale est abstinere ab iniquitatibus et illicitis voluptatibus saeculi; quod est perfectum ieiunium, ut abnegantes impietates et saeculares cupiditates, temperanter et iuste vivamus in hoc saeculo. Huic ieiunio quam mercedem addit Apostolus, sequitur, et dicit: 'Expectantes illam beatam spem et manifestationem gloriae beati Dei et sal-

7 vatoris nostri Iesu Christi' [Titus 2:13]. In hoc ergo saeculo quasi Quadragesimam abstinentiae caelebramus, cum bene vivimus, cum ab iniquitatibus et illicitis voluptatibus abstinemus. Sed quia haec abstinentia sine mercede non erit, 'expectamus beatam illam spem et revelationem gloriae magni Dei et salvatoris nostri Iesu Christi.' In illa spe—cum fuerit de spe facta res—accepturi sumus mercedem

standing of its creator. On the day of Pentecost the apostles received the number ten more fully and perfectly than they had it before. Saint Augustine, who, before leaving his body, asked that he be given the space of ten days to contemplate himself and his affairs, was advised by the Holy Spirit according to the same precept. Thus it is written in his *Life:* 5 "Now he ordered that the Psalms of David on penance—which are very few—be copied out for him. He gazed upon and read from those quaternions, placed against the wall as he was lying in bed, through the days of his sickness, and he cried continually and abundantly. And lest anything distract his concentration, for nearly ten days before he left his body, he demanded of those of us present that nobody go in to him, excepting only the hours when doctors entered to examine him and when refreshment was brought in to him."✝ Up to here, from the *Life of Saint Augustine.*

Otherwise: The same Saint Augustine writes in his seven- 6 teenth sermon on John: "But the great and general fast is abstinence from the evils and forbidden desires of the world; that is the perfect fast, that by denying impieties and worldly desires we may live temperately and justly in this world. The reward that the Apostle adds to this fast follows, and he says: 'Looking for the blessed hope and the manifestation of the glory of the blessed God and our savior Jesus Christ.' In this world, therefore, we celebrate a sort of Lent 7 of abstinence, when we live well and when we abstain from evils and forbidden desires. But because this abstinence will not be without reward, 'we look for the blessed hope and revelation of the glory of the great God and our savior Jesus Christ.' In that hope—when the event that we have hoped for has occurred—we will receive the reward of the

denarium." Et paulo post: "Denarius ergo, qui accepit nomen a numero decim, redditur, et coniunctus quadrage-
8 nario, fit quinquagenarius. Unde cum labore caelebramus
Quadragesimam ante Pascha, cum laetitia vero, tamquam
accepta mercede, quinquagesimam post Pascha. Nam huic
tamquam salutari labori boni operis, qui pertinet ad quadra-
genarium numerum, additur quietis et felicitatis denarius,
ut quinquagenarius fiat. Significavit hoc ipse Dominus Iesus
multo apertius, quando post resurrectionem, quadraginta
diebus conversatus est in terra cum discipulis suis; quadragesima autem die cum ascendisset in caelum, peractis
9 decem diebus, misit mercedem Spiritus Sancti."✝ Nam in
decima die post Ascensionem Domini—hoc est in vigiliis
Pentecostes—caelebrat sancta ecclesia baptysterium et laetaniam exercet ante solempnia Missarum. Orat enim, sive
ut ipsa mereatur frui adventu Spiritus Sancti, sicut apostoli
fructi sunt, qui baptyzati sunt ab eo in Pentecoste; seu ut
neofyti perseverent in unitate ecclesiae. Cantat postea memorata ecclesia *Gloria in excelsis Deo,* more apostolorum qui,
prius quam acceperint Spiritum Sanctum, in templo erant
semper laudantes Deum et benedicentes Dominum.

10 Quamvis de Missae officio non proponerem aliquid dicere in istis litteris, tamen—quia occurrit in hac festivitate
de baptysmo scribere—desideravi voluntarium me demonstrare de his quae circa baptisteria aguntur, scire aliquid.
Nunc transeo ad Psalmos tres qui cantantur in nocte Pen-
11 tecostes [Ps 47, 67, 103]. Ut mihi videtur, hoc differt inter istos tres Psalmos qui in Pentecostes cantantur, et inter tres

penny." And after a little: "And so the penny, or the denarius, which derives its name from the number ten, is paid, and joined to forty, it makes fifty. Thus we celebrate Lent before 8 Easter in labor, but we celebrate the fifty days following Easter in rejoicing, as if the reward had been received. For it is as if the denarius of peace and happiness is added to this saving labor of good work that relates to the number forty, to make fifty. The Lord Jesus indicated this much more openly when, after his resurrection, he lived on the earth for forty days with his disciples; but ten days from the fortieth day when he ascended into heaven, he sent the reward of his Holy Spirit."+ For on the tenth day after the Lord's Ascen- 9 sion—that is, on the vigil of Pentecost—the holy church celebrates baptism and performs a litany before the solemnities of Mass. And it prays both that it may be worthy of enjoying the coming of the Holy Spirit, as the apostles who were baptized by the Holy Spirit enjoyed its coming on Pentecost; and that the neophytes may persevere in the unity of the church. Afterward the aforementioned church sings the *Gloria in excelsis Deo,* after the manner of the apostles who, before they received the Holy Spirit, were in the temple constantly praising God and blessing the Lord.

Although I would not propose to say anything about 10 the office of the Mass in this discussion, nevertheless—because it happens that in the course of commenting on this feast I am writing about baptism—I wanted, of my own choice, to show that I know something about the things that are done with respect to baptism. Now I move on to the three Psalms that are sung on the night of Pentecost. It strikes me that the difference between those 11 three Psalms that are sung on Pentecost, and the three that

qui in Pascha Domini, quod est inter baptismum quem acceperunt apostoli per aquam, et baptismum quem acceperunt per Spiritum Sanctum in die Pentecostes. De quo eis
dixit Dominus: "Vos autem baptizabimini Spiritu Sancto"
[Acts 1:5]. Iam baptizati erant aqua; iam acceperunt Spiritum Sanctum. Tamen dicitur eis postea: "Vos autem baptyzabimini Spiritu Sancto."

12    De baptysmo aquae dicit Agustinus in epistola ad Seleu-
tianum: "Tunc ergo, quando Hierosolimis exiit cum discipulis suis in Iudaeam et illic morabatur cum eis, baptyzabat
non per se ipsum sed per discipulos suos. Quos intellegimus
iam fuisse baptizatos, sive baptismo Iohannis (sicut non-
nulli arbitrantur), sive, quod magis credibile est, baptysmo
Christi. Neque enim ministerium baptizandi defugeret,
ut haberet baptyzatos servos per quos ceteros baptyzaret,
qui non defugit memorabilis illius humilitatis ministerio,
13    quando eis lavit pedes."✝ Quod ante diem Pentecostes acceperint Spiritum Sanctum, Iohannes manifestat, dicens:
"Cum ergo esset sero die illa, una sabbatorum, et fores
essent clausae." Et post pauca: "Sicut misit me Pater, et ego
mitto vos. Hoc cum dixisset, insufflavit et dicit eis: Accipite
Spiritum Sanctum; quorum remiseritis peccata, remittuntur
14    eis" [John 20:19, 21–23], et reliqua. Iam acceperunt Spiritum
Sanctum in remissione peccatorum, sed adhuc restabat donum quod nondum acceperant, sed accepturi erant in die
Pentecostes—id est, ut praedicationem suam firmarent signis miraculorum, et ut non timerent rabiem persequen-
tium; neque inretiri possent vinculo terreni desiderii neque

are sung on the Lord's Easter, is the same as the difference between the baptism that the apostles received through water, and the baptism that they received through the Holy Spirit on the day of Pentecost. The Lord spoke to them about this: "But you shall be baptized with the Holy Spirit." They had already been baptized with water; now they received the Holy Spirit. Yet afterward it is said to them: "You shall be baptized with the Holy Spirit."

Augustine speaks about baptism with water in his letter 12 to Seleucianus: "And then, when he went out from Jerusalem with his disciples into Judaea and stayed there with them, he baptized not through himself but through his disciples. We understand that they had already been baptized, whether by the baptism of John (as some think) or, as is more likely, by the baptism of Christ. For he who did not shun that ministry of memorable humility, when he washed his apostles' feet, also did not shun the ministry of baptism, that he might have baptized servants through whom he might baptize others."✝ John shows that they received the Holy Spirit 13 before the day of Pentecost, saying: "Now when it was late the same day, the first of the week, and the doors were shut." And after a little: "As the Father has sent me, I also send you. When he had said this, he breathed on them and said to them: Receive the Holy Spirit; whose sins you shall forgive, they are forgiven them," and so on. They had already re- 14 ceived the Holy Spirit for the remission of their sins, yet there still remained a gift that they had not yet received, but that they would receive on the day of Pentecost—that is, that they would fortify their preaching through signs of miracles, and that they would not fear the rage of persecutors; nor could they be snared by the chain of earthly desire or

labefactari errore aliquo. Credimus Petrum iam baptizatum fuisse quando negavit ad vocem ancillae; simili modo et Thomam, qui dubitavit de Domini resurrectione.

15 Sicut tunc duo baptisteria leguntur in apostolis—unum per aquam et alterum per baptysmum Spiritus Sancti—ita sunt hodie in nostra ecclesia duo genera electorum qui baptyzati sunt. Unum genus est in activa vita, alterum in contemplativa. Quae duo genera Martha et Maria, soror eius, significabant. Optima pars Mariae deputata est a Domino,

16 sed et Marthae non est reprehensa, quia bona est. Haec distinctio potest inveniri in antiphonis quae dicuntur in Pascha Domini et in Pentecoste. In Pascha Domini dicit prima antiphona: "Consilium meum non est cum impiis." Prima de Pentecoste dicit: "Factus est repente de caelo sonus tamquam advenientis spiritus vehementis." Spiritus vehemens pulverem terrae solet dispergere. Distat multum inter donum Dei quod separat fideles ab impiis, et illud donum quod

17 terrenas cogitationes expurgat de pectore. Ibi dicit secunda antiphona: "Postulavi patrem meum et dedit mihi gentes in hereditatem." Hic dicit secunda: "Confirma hoc, Deus, quod operatus es in nobis, a templo sancto tuo quod est in Hierusalem, alleluia, alleluia." Simili modo distat inter eos qui in hereditate Domini deputantur quia fideles sunt, et tamen in actuali vita, et inter eos qui omnia terrena respuerunt, et precantur Deum, ut ad haec non revertantur, sed confirmet donum suum in eis, ut possint Deo semper a tem-

shaken by any error. We believe that Peter had already been baptized when he denied the suggestion of the handmaiden; we similarly believe that Thomas, who doubted the Lord's resurrection, had been baptized.

Just as we read that there were two baptisms among the apostles at that time—one through water and the other through the baptism of the Holy Spirit—so today in our church are there two categories of elect who are baptized. One category is in the active life, the other in the contemplative. Martha and Mary, her sister, signified these two types. The best part was allotted by the Lord to Mary, but Martha was not rebuked, for she was good. This distinction can be found in the antiphons that are said on the Lord's Easter and Pentecost. On the Lord's Easter the first antiphon says: "My counsel is not with the impious." The first from Pentecost says: "Suddenly there came a sound from heaven as of a mighty wind coming." A mighty wind is wont to scatter the dust of the earth. There is a great difference between the gift of God that separates the faithful from the impious, and the gift that scatters earthly thoughts from the heart. The second antiphon on Easter says: "I have called upon my father and he gave me the nations for an inheritance." The second on Pentecost says: "Confirm this, God, what you have wrought in us, from your holy temple in Jerusalem, alleluia, alleluia." Similarly, there is a difference between those who are counted in the Lord's inheritance because they are faithful, though they are in the active life, and those who have spat out all the things of this world, and call upon God that they may not return to these things, but that he may confirm his gift in them, that they may always be capable of singing alleluia to God from the temple that is in

18 plo quod est in Hierusalem, alleluia cantare. Ibi dicit tertia antiphona: "Ego dormivi et somnum coepi, et resurrexi." Hic dicit tertia: "Emitte spiritum tuum et creabuntur, et renovabis faciem terrae." Christus enim resurrexit a morte, et nos cotidie possumus resurgere a vitiis, et potest nobis veraciter dici: "Nolite contristare spiritum Dei" [Eph 4:30].

19 Haec antiphona quae dicit: "Emitte spiritum tuum et creabuntur," spiritum Dei precatur obnixe advenire, ut neque in cogitationibus neque in verbis regnet spiritus superbiae, sed spiritus Dei utrimque deducat per suam creationem, ut scriptum est in Evangelio: Cum vos coeperint et adduxerint, "nolite cogitare quomodo aut quid loquamini. Non enim vos estis qui loquimini, sed spiritus Patris vestri qui loquitur in vobis" [Matt 10:19–20]. Precatur renovari faciem terrae, ut novus homo sit confitens se iustificatum non a se, sed gratia Dei.

20 Sicut in Pascha Domini tres Psalmi recolunt opera Christi trium dierum, sic et in adventu Spiritus Sancti eadem opera. Ut demonstretur unum opus esse in potentia miraculorum totius sanctae Trinitatis, unus ordo Psalmorum continetur et in resurrectione Domini et in adventu Spiritus Sancti. Sed in aliquibus minus operatur Christus, et in aliquibus plus. "Stella enim a stella differt in claritate" [1 Cor 15:41].

21 Quod in Pascha diximus de sequentibus noctibus baptismalibus, hoc et hic dicimus: ut tres Psalmi recolant sepulturam Domini triduanam, in his praecipue qui nuper consepulti sunt Domino. Hoc agitur per septem dies propter sacramentum praesentis vitae et propter septimam diem,

Jerusalem. The third antiphon on Easter says: "I have slept    18
and begun to sleep, and I have risen." The third on Pentecost says: "Send forth your spirit and they shall be created,
and you shall renew the face of the earth." For Christ rose
from death, and we can daily rise from our vices, and it can
truly be said to us: "Grieve not the spirit of God."

The antiphon that says: "Send forth your spirit and they    19
shall be created," calls insistently upon God's spirit to come,
that the spirit of pride may reign neither in our thoughts nor
in our words, but rather that God's spirit may guide both
our thoughts and words through his creation, as it is written
in the Gospel: When they have seized and brought you in,
"take no thought over how or what to speak. For it is not
you that speak, but the spirit of your Father that speaks in
you." It asks that the face of the earth be made new, that the
new man may trust that he has been justified not through
himself, but by God's grace.

Just as the three Psalms on the Lord's Easter recall the    20
three days' works of Christ, the Psalms for the coming of
the Holy Spirit recall these same works. In order to show
that there is a single action in the miraculous faculty of the
entire Holy Trinity, both the Lord's resurrection and the
coming of the Holy Spirit contain a single order of Psalms.
But in some things Christ works less, and in others more.
"For star differs from star in glory."

We also add here what we said while discussing Easter,    21
concerning the baptismal nights that follow: that the three
Psalms recall the Lord's three-day burial, especially with respect to those who have recently been buried in the Lord.
This is celebrated for seven days because of the sacrament
of the present life and because of the seventh day, which the

quam animae sanctorum recipiunt exutae a corporibus; vel propter septiformem Spiritum Sanctum, qui per unumquemque diem diverso cibo alit suos. Possunt et tres Psalmi recolere tres virtutes, id est fidem, spem et caritatem, sine quibus nemo potest placere Deo.

22 Adnectimus etiam convivium quod unum quodque donum, quasi unusquisque frater, parat suis convivis per septem dies; et tres virtutes, quasi tres sorores convivantes—ex

23 libro sancti Gregorii primo *De moralibus:* "Ut enim," inquit, "haec ipsa dona breviter septiformis spiritus replicem, alium diem habet sapientia, alium intellectus, alium consilium, alium fortitudo, alium scientia, alium pietas, alium timor. Neque enim hoc est sapere quod intellegere, quia multi aeterna quidem sapiunt sed haec intellegere nequaquam pos-

24 sunt. Sapientia ergo in die suo convivium facit, quia mentem de aeternorum spe et certitudine reficit. Intellectus in die suo convivium parat, quia in eo quod audita penetrat, reficiendo cor, tenebras eius inlustrat. Consilium in die suo convivium exhibet, quia, dum esse praecipitem prohibet, ratione animum replet. Fortitudo in die suo convivium facit, quia, dum adversa non metuit, trepidanti menti cibos confidentiae apponit. Scientia in die suo convivium parat, quia in ventre mentis ignorantiae ieiunium superat. Pietas in die suo convivium exhibet, quia cordis viscera misericordiae operibus replet. Timor in die suo convivium facit, quia, dum premit mentem, ne de praesentibus superbiat, de futuris illam spei cibo confortat.

souls of the saints receive, having have cast off their bodies; and because of the sevenfold Holy Spirit, which each
day nourishes its own with a different food. The three
Psalms can also recall the three virtues, namely faith, hope
and charity, without which no one can please God.

We also add the banquet that each gift, as a brother, pre-   22
pares for its fellows over seven days; and the three virtues,
as three fellow sisters—from the first book of Saint Gregory's *Moralia:* "To reflect briefly upon these gifts of the seven-   23
fold spirit," he says, "wisdom has one day, understanding
another, counsel another, fortitude another, knowledge another, piety another and fear another. For wisdom is not the
same as understanding, since many people indeed have wisdom about eternal things but are unable to understand
them. Wisdom, therefore, makes a banquet on its day, be-   24
cause it refreshes the mind with the hope and certainty of
eternal things. Understanding prepares a banquet on its day,
because it penetrates what it hears and, by refreshing the
heart, it illuminates the heart's darkness. Counsel puts forth
a banquet on its day, because it fills the spirit with reason,
while preventing it from being hasty. Fortitude makes a banquet on its day, because, as it does not fear adversity, it offers
the food of confidence to the fearful mind. Knowledge prepares a banquet on its day, because it overcomes the hunger
of ignorance in the stomach of the mind. Piety puts forth a
banquet on its day, because it fills the interior of the heart
with works of mercy. Fear makes a banquet on its day, because, while it presses upon the mind not to take pride in
present things, it comforts it over the things to come with
the food of hope.

25    "Sed illud in hoc filiorum convivio illud perscrutandum video—quod semet ipsos invicem pascunt. Valde enim singula quaelibet destituitur si non una alii virtus virtuti suffragetur. Minor quippe est sapientia si intellectu careat, et valde inutilis intellectus est si ex sapientia non subsistat— quia cum altiora sine sapientiae pondere penetrat, sua illum levitas, gravius ruiturum, levat. Vile est consilium cui robur fortitudinis deest, quia quod tractando invenit, carens viribus, usque ad perfectionem operis non perducit. Et valde fortitudo destruitur nisi per consilium fulciatur, quia quo plus se posse conspicit, eo virtus, sine rationis moderamine, deterius in praeceps ruit. Nulla est scientia si utilitatem pietatis non habet, quia, dum bona cognita exequi neglegit, sese ad iudicium artius stringit. Et valde inutilis est pietas si scientiae discretione caret, quia, dum nulla hanc scientia inluminat, quomodo misereatur, ignorat. Timor quoque ipse, si non has etiam virtutes habuerit, ad nullum opus procul dubio bonae actionis surgit—quia, dum ad cuncta trepidat,

26    ipsa sua formidine a bonis omnibus torpens vacat. Quia ergo alternato ministerio virtus a virtute reficitur, recte dicitur quod apud se vicissim filii convivantur. Cumque una aliam sublevanda sublevat, quasi per dies suos numerosa soboles pascenda convivium parat.

27    "Sequitur: 'Et mittebant et vocabant tres sorores suas, ut comederent et biberent cum eis' [Job 1:4]. Cum virtutes nostrae, in omne quod agunt, spem, fidem et caritatem sciunt, quasi operatores, filii tres ad convivium sorores

"But I see that we should consider this aspect of the sons' 25
banquet—that they feed one another in turn. For each virtue is surely forsaken if one virtue does not support the
other. Wisdom is surely lesser if it lacks understanding, and
understanding is surely useless if it does not depend on wisdom—for when it penetrates higher matters without the
weight of wisdom, its levity lightens the understanding, and
it will tumble the more gravely to ruin. Counsel that lacks
the strength of fortitude is trifling, for what it finds in consideration it does not bring to completing the work, as it
lacks strength. And fortitude surely falls unless it is supported by counsel, because the more it sees that it can do,
the worse this virtue, without the moderation of reason,
rushes into haste. There is no knowledge if it does not have
the benefit of piety, for it binds itself the more tightly to
judgment as it neglects to pursue good thoughts. And piety
is surely useless if it lacks the discretion of knowledge, because it does not know how to show mercy when no understanding illuminates it. And fear itself, if it does not also
have these virtues, doubtless rises to no worthy task—since,
as it is fearful of everything, it lies empty of all good works
being benumbed by its fright. Since, therefore, virtue is re- 26
freshed by virtue through mutual service, it is rightly said
that the sons feast in turn among themselves. And when one
virtue, in supporting another, supports itself, it is as if the
numerous progeny to be fed prepare a banquet, each on his
own day.

"There follows: 'And they sent for and called their three 27
sisters, to eat and drink with them.' When our virtues,
like laborers, know hope, faith and charity in all that they
do, the sons call their three sisters to the banquet, so that

vocant, ut fides, spes et caritas gaudeant in opus bonum quod unaquaeque virtus administrat. Quae quasi ex cibo vires accipiunt, dum bonis operibus fidentiores fiunt; et dum, post cibum, contemplationis rore infundi appetunt, quasi ex poculo ebriantur."✝

Non abhorret a vero, si sive propter sepulturam Domini, ut memoravimus, tres Psalmi in nocte cantentur in diebus neofytorum; seu propter fidem, spem et caritatem, quae unusquisque Christianus debet tenere ab ipso initio intellectus sui.

## 28

# De ora baptisterii in die Sancto Sabbato sive in vigilia Pentecostes

Notandum est quod ea ora diei nunc caelebret sancta ecclesia baptysmum, qua hora angelus Domini venit ad Cornelium, adnuntians ei quod orationes eius et elemosinae ascenderint in memoriam in conspectu Dei [Acts 10:4–6], et ut mitteret ad Petrum, qui eum baptizaret. Eadem hora venit baptysta Petrus ad eundem Cornelium baptyzandum. Ita enim interrogavit Petrus Cornelium, ut in Actibus Apostolorum scriptum est: "Interrogo ergo ob quam causam accersisti me? Et Cornelius ait: A nudiusquartana

faith, hope and charity may rejoice in the good work that each virtue prepares. They derive strength, as if from food, as they become more confident in good works; and when, after eating, they desire to be filled with the dew of contemplation, they become, as it were, intoxicated from this cup."✠

It is not contrary to the truth, whether the three Psalms are sung at night on the days of the neophytes because of the Lord's burial, as we said; or rather because of faith, hope and charity, which every Christian ought to have from the very beginning of his understanding.

# 28

# On the hour of baptism on Holy Saturday and on the vigil of Pentecost

It should be noted that the holy church now celebrates baptism at the very hour of the day when the angel of the Lord came to Cornelius, announcing to him that his prayers and alms ascended for a memorial in the sight of God, and that he should send for Peter, who would baptize him. At 2 this very hour the baptist Peter came to the same Cornelius to baptize him. And Peter questioned Cornelius, as it is written in the Acts of the Apostles, as follows: "I ask, therefore, for what cause you have sent for me? And Cornelius

die usque ad hanc oram, orans eram ora nona in domo mea,"
et reliqua. Quem continuo imbuit Petrus symbulo fidei, ut
in memoratis Actibus continetur: "Moxque cecidit Spiritus
Sanctus super omnes qui audiebant verbum." Quo peracto,
respondit Petrus: "Numquid aquam quis prohibere potest,
ut non baptizentur hi qui Spiritum Sanctum acceperunt,
sicut et nos? Et iussit eos in nomine Iesu Christi baptizari"
[Acts 10:4–6, 24–30, 44–48].

3    Igitur eo in tempore circa primitivam ecclesiam ora nona
baptysmus caelebratus est, ut et ipsa et imitatrix eius, quae
hodierna die est, retineret in mente quod in morte Christi,
qui ora nona emisit spiritum, oporteat eam baptizare. Hunc
morem tenet nunc nostra ecclesia in vigilia Pentecostes—
quem praesignavit Cornelius, qui, ut mereretur accipere
baptysmum, ora nona erat orans et ieiunans in domo sua.

# 29

# De octavis Pentecostes

Quinquaginta dies post Pascha Domini—hoc est totum
tempus Pentecostes—figurant illam laetitiam quae erit in
alia vita. Sive quia quadragenarius numerus, partibus suis
multiplicatus, quinquaginta facit; seu quod quadraginta

said: Four days ago up to this hour, I was praying in my house at the ninth hour," and so forth. Peter immediately instructed him with the symbol of faith, as is related in the aforementioned Acts: "And then the Holy Spirit fell on all them who heard the word." When this was done, Peter responded: "Can any man forbid water, that these should not be baptized who have received the Holy Spirit, as well as we? And he commanded them to be baptized in the name of Jesus Christ."

At that time in the early church, therefore, baptism was celebrated at the ninth hour, so that its imitator, as it exists today, might keep in mind that it should perform baptism upon the death of Christ, who gave up his spirit at the ninth hour. Today our church observes this custom on the vigil of Pentecost—which Cornelius, who prayed and fasted in his house at the ninth hour, that be might be worthy of receiving baptism, prefigured.

## 29

# On the octave of Pentecost

The fifty days after the Lord's Easter—that is, the entire season of Pentecost—represent the rejoicing that will come in the next life. Whether because the number forty, multiplied by its parts, makes fifty; or because the forty days

habent in se perfectionem bonorum operum, cui numero si addatur denarius, qui tenet remunerationem operum, quinquaginta facit; seu quacumque alia ratio sit—hoc procul dubio tenetur, quod praesentes quinquaginta dies futuram

2 quietem et securitatem atque laetitiam significant. Septem dies qui sequuntur recolunt adventum septiformis spiritus, sive nostram laetitiam in qua congratulamur nuper baptizatis, qui nimirum informantur in corpore Christi.

3 Habemus in nostris libris officialibus scriptum: "Post octavas Pentecostes." Ideo de eodem scripto tractare debemus. Satis manifestum est "Pentecoste" exprimere numero quinquagesimum. Non enim mea simplicitas novit quas octavas habeat Pentecoste; sed quoniam haec festivitas, quae, ut diximus, recolit adventum Spiritus Sancti et remunerationem nuper baptyzatorum, nomen obtinuit "Pentecoste," ipsae octavae quae huic mysterio possunt congruere, retinuerant nomen quod habet prima dies huius festivitatis.

4 Quomodo adventui Spiritus Sancti octavae conveniant, vel regenerationi novi hominis, ex verbis sancti Agustini *De sermone Domini in monte,* aliquam scintillam luminis carpimus. Post enumeratas sententias octo beatitudinum, dicit inter cetera: "Octava tamquam in caput redit, quia consummatum perfectumque ostendit et probat." Et paulo post: "Septem sunt ergo quae perficiunt, nam octava clarificat et quod perfectum est demonstrat, ut per hos gradus perficiantur et ceteri—tamquam a capite rursus exordiens. Videtur ergo mihi etiam septiformis operatio Spiritus Sancti de quo

5 Esaias loquitur his gradibus sententiisque congruere." Et

have within themselves the perfection of good works, and if the number ten, which contains the recompense for these works, is added to this number, it makes fifty; or for some other reason—we assert without doubt that these fifty days signify the peace, security and rejoicing to come. The seven 2 days that follow recall the coming of the sevenfold spirit, or our rejoicing wherein we congratulate the newly baptized, who have surely been shaped in the body of Christ.

In our office books it is written: "After the octave of Pen- 3 tecost." We should therefore discuss this line. It is clear enough that "Pentecost" expresses the number fifty. And in my simplicity I do not know what sort of octave Pentecost can have; but because this feast, which, as we said, recalls the coming of the Holy Spirit and the reward of the recently baptized, obtained the name of "Pentecost," the octave that can coincide with this mystery retained the name that the first day of this feast has.

We gather some spark of insight about how the octave 4 corresponds to the coming of the Holy Spirit, and to the re-birth of the new man, from the words of Saint Augustine's *On the Lord's Sermon on the Mount*. After having enumer-ated the teachings of the eight beatitudes, he says, among other things: "It is as if the eighth beatitude returns to the beginning, because it shows and demonstrates what has been fulfilled and perfected." And a little later: "There are therefore seven beatitudes that perfect, while the eighth ennobles and demonstrates what has been perfected, so that through these degrees the others may also be made per-fect—arising, as it were, once again from the head. And so it seems to me that even the working of the sevenfold Holy Spirit that Isaiah speaks of adheres to these steps and teach-ings." And again: "This eighth teaching, which returns to 5

515

iterum: "Haec octava sententia, quae ad caput redit perfectumque hominem declarat, significat fortasse et circumcisionem octava die in Veteri Testamento, et Domini resurrectionem post Sabbatum (qui est utique octavus, idem qui primus dies), et caelebrationem octavarum feriarum quas in regeneratione novi hominis caelebramus."✝ Hucusque Agustini.

6    Octavus dies est qui et primus, secundum formam octo beatitudinum. Prima beatitudo dicit: "Beati pauperes spiritu, quoniam ipsorum est regnum caelorum." Octava: "Beati qui persecutionem patiuntur propter iustitiam, quoniam ipsorum est regnum caelorum" [Matt 5:3, 10]. Ad regeneratos pertinent hae sententiae—ut, qui pauperes sunt, in hac vita propter regnum caelorum usque ad finem vitae perseverantes sint, ut accipiant regnum pro quo laboraverunt

7    hic. Baptysmus neofytorum, quamvis in Sabbato agatur, ad illum baptysmum pertinet quem apostoli acceperunt in die Pentecostes, cuius octava dies est Dominica sequens, quam solemus appellare octavas Pentecostes. Istae sunt feriae quas beatus Agustinus memorat superius, octavarum feriarum regenerati hominis.

8    Hoc est inter nostrum baptysma et apostolorum, quod illi primo aqua baptizati sunt; deinde acceperunt semel per insufflationem Christi Spiritum Sanctum adhuc in terra Christo sistente, postremo de caelo in die Pentecostes. Nos vero, praesente episcopo, simul baptizamur et per imposi-

9    tionem manus episcopi Spiritum Sanctum accipimus. Imitando Christi mortem et eius resurrectionem, debemus consummationem nostri baptysmatis in die Dominico

the beginning and declares that man has been perfected, perhaps also signifies the circumcision on the eighth day in the Old Testament, and the Lord's resurrection after the Sabbath (which is also the eighth day, the same as the first day), and the celebration of the eight days that we celebrate upon the rebirth of the new man."+ Thus far, from Augustine.

The eighth day is the same as the first, after the example 6 of the eight beatitudes. The first beatitude says: "Blessed are the poor in spirit, for theirs is the kingdom of heaven." The eighth: "Blessed are they that suffer persecution for justice's sake, for theirs is the kingdom of heaven." These teachings pertain to the reborn—that, as they are poor, they may persevere in this life until the end of their life because of the kingdom of heaven, and that they may receive the kingdom that they have labored for here. The baptism of the neo- 7 phytes, although celebrated on Saturday, pertains to the baptism that the apostles received on the day of Pentecost; the eighth day after it is the following Sunday, which we are accustomed to call the octave of Pentecost. These are the days that the blessed Augustine recounts above, the eight days of the reborn man.

The difference between our baptism and the baptism of 8 the apostles is that they were first baptized with water; then they received the Holy Spirit once through Christ's breath while Christ was still on earth, and a final time from heaven on the day of Pentecost. We, however, are baptized and receive the Holy Spirit through the bishop's laying on of hands, all at once and in the bishop's presence. By imitat- 9 ing Christ's death and resurrection, we should contemplate the fulfillment of our baptism on Sunday, lest the members

cogitare, ne praecedant membra caput, et, secundum modum primitivae ecclesiae, donationem Spiritus Sancti in eadem die ora tertia. Quamvis non eisdem diebus vel oris, propter aliquas occasiones fluctuantis mundi, caelebretur aliquando baptysmus vel impositio manus, tamen propter sacramentum quod in se continent, eisdem diebus et oris deputantur. Si enim propterea acceperunt apostoli Spiritum Sanctum ora tertia, quia fidem sanctae Trinitatis praedicaturi erant, volvamus et nos in mente eadem ora percepisse eundem spiritum, in quo copulatur Trinitas, quae monstrat eandem Trinitatem.

10     Propius pertinet nostrum baptisma aliquo modo ad baptysmum apostolorum quam ad baptysmum Christi. Non propter sua abluenda peccata baptizatus est Christus, sed propter formam membrorum suorum, quia esse in futuro poterant aliqui qui sibi placerent de sua innocentia, et cogitarent non sibi esse necessarium baptysma. Ac ideo praecessit Christi baptysmus, qui sine peccato fuit, ut nemo, de-

11  ceptus per stultam securitatem, periret sine baptismo. Non propterea advenit Spiritus Sanctus in columbae specie super Christi baptysmum, ut daret tunc ei donum quod non habebat [Matt 3:16], sed ut nobis in nostro baptismate suam praesentiam monstraret adesse, et per columbae simplicitatem demonstraret Christi simplicitatem et puritatem.

12  Apostoli propterea baptizati sunt, ut peccata eorum delerentur in baptysmo, sicut et nostra delentur; et ideo venit Spiritus Sanctus per ignem ad eos, quia rubigo ex eorum fragilitate potuit eis inhaerere, et hanc voluit vis Spiritus Sancti in perpetuum consumere. Vis enim ignis unam materiam

precede the head; and, in accordance with the custom of the early church, we should contemplate the gift of the Holy Spirit on the same day at the third hour. Although, for various reasons in this uncertain world, baptism and the laying on of hands are sometimes not celebrated on these days or at these hours, they are nevertheless ascribed to these days and hours because of the sacrament that they contain within themselves. For if the apostles received the Holy Spirit at the third hour because they were about to preach faith in the Holy Trinity, let us consider that we, too, have in our mind received the same spirit, in which the Trinity is united, at the very hour that indicates this selfsame Trinity.

In some sense our baptism relates more closely to the 10 baptism of the apostles than to the baptism of Christ. Christ was not baptized to wash away his sins, but as an example for his members, because there could be some in the future who would be pleased with their innocence, and would think that baptisms were not necessary for them. And therefore the baptism of Christ, who was without sin, preceded, that nobody might be deceived through foolish security and perish without baptism. The Holy Spirit did 11 not come over Christ's baptism in the form of a dove to give him a gift that he did not then have, but to reveal to us his presence at our baptism, and to demonstrate the simplicity and purity of Christ through the simplicity of a dove. The 12 apostles were baptized that their sins might be wiped away in baptism, as ours are wiped away; and the Holy Spirit came to them through fire, because rust was able to cling to them through their fragility, and the force of the Holy Spirit wished to consume this rust for eternity. For the power of fire consumes one material and renews and warms another;

consumit et alteram reficit et fovet; ligna consumit et materiem nostri corporis reficit. Ita et ignis Spiritus Sancti rubiginem peccatorum consumit et animam nostram calefacit

13   ad amorem Dei et proximi. Isti duo effectus sunt duo denarii quos Dominus dedit stabulario iuxta Lucam Evangelistam altera die—id est secunda die—postquam alligavit vulnera semivivi: quasi secunda die post baptysmum [Luke 10:35]. Bene duo sunt qui significant ordinem dilectionis, quia Deum non potest diligere qui non diligit proximum, neque recte diligit proximum qui non eum propter Deum diligit.

14   Sicut in baptysmate conformamur Christi morti et sepulturae, ita in acceptione Spiritus Sancti spiritui vivificanti, qui operatur in nobis rectum ordinem dilectionis. Propter mortem Christi, quae memoratur ora nona esse peracta, ora nona baptizantur qui in Christi morte baptizantur. Propterque mysterium consepulturae Christi, quae recolitur in Sabbato, baptizatur Christi corpus in Sabbato, ut post hanc sepulturam in die Dominica resurgat. Initium enim resurrectionis a Dominica die debemus caelebrare.

15   Sit illa Dominica dies initium novi hominis qui resurrexit a mortuis, et iterum sepultura eius, quando anima transit in requiem sine corpore, in Sabbato die, quando vestimenta mutantur baptizatorum, et receptio eorum corporum caelebretur in octavis Pentecostes. Vel ideo caelebretur octava Pentecostes quia septiformis spiritus opus tunc perficitur, quando perfectum hominem monstrat, de quo dicebat Apostolus: "Si quis autem in verbo non offendit, hic perfec-

16   tus est" [Jas 3:2]. Caelebretur per septem dies opus septiformis spiritus, et in octava die consummatio et declaratio

it consumes wood and renews the material of our body. So too does the fire of the Holy Spirit consume the rust of sins and warm our soul for love of God and neighbor. These two 13 effects are the two pennies that the Lord gave to the host according to Luke the Evangelist, on the next day—that is, the second day—after he bound the wounds of the one who was half alive: as it were, on the second day after baptism. And it is appropriate for two pennies to signify the order of love, because he who does not love his neighbor cannot love God, and he does not love his neighbor properly who does not love him because of God.

Just as we are molded after Christ's death and burial in 14 baptism, so too upon receiving the Holy Spirit are we molded after the living spirit, who creates the correct order of love in us. Because of Christ's death, which is said to have happened at the ninth hour, those who are baptized in Christ's death are baptized at the ninth hour. And because of the mystery of burial with Christ, which is recalled on Saturday, Christ's body is baptized on Saturday, that it may rise on Sunday after this burial. For we should celebrate the beginning of the resurrection from Sunday.

Let that Sunday be the beginning of the new man who 15 rose from the dead, and let his second burial be on Saturday, when the soul passes on to rest without the body, when the baptized change their clothing, and let the reception of their bodies be celebrated on the octave of Pentecost. And let the octave of Pentecost be celebrated because the work of the sevenfold spirit is perfected when it reveals the perfected man whom the Apostle speaks about: "If any man offend not in word, the same is a perfected man." Let the work 16 of the sevenfold spirit be celebrated for seven days, and let

atque glorificatio eiusdem operis. Quod si ita est, merito eandem glorificationem in nostris officiis recolit octava dies, quae redit ad caput, quam et prima dies. Itaque sicut caelebravimus maiestatem Spiritus Sancti in Pentecoste, caelebremus et in octavis eiusdem festivitatis, quatinus saepissime recolendo eius dona, dignetur caritas eius se profusius infundere cordibus nostris, usque dum, secundum Evangelicum sensum, tria sata farinae fermententur in unum [Luke 13:21], et totum quod cogitamus, aut intellegimus, aut vivimus, ad eius dilectionem referatur. In commemoratione harum trium mensurarum farinae, cantamus in eadem nocte tres Psalmos in nocturnis, et usque ad finem diei praesentis Dominici alleluia cantamus. Sic enim caelebratur auctoritate divinae legis festivitas—a vespera usque ad vesperam, id est a solis occubitu usque ad solis occubitum.

17

## 30

# De Adventu Domini

Scripsimus in superioribus libellis in quinta ebdomada ac quarta ante Nativitatem Domini inchoari praeparationem Adventus Domini: In quinta ebdomada propter quinque aetates mundi, in quibus fuerunt tales electi qui crediderunt et speraverunt et dilexerunt adventum Domini; in

the fulfillment and declaration and glorification of this same work be celebrated on the eighth day. If it is done in this way, it is appropriate for the eighth day in our offices, which returns to the beginning and is like the first day, to recall this same glorification. And thus just as we celebrated the majesty of the Holy Spirit on Pentecost, let us also celebrate it on the octave of the same feast, that by recalling his gifts as often as possible, his charity may deign to fill our hearts all the more abundantly until, as the Gospel has it, three measures of flour are leavened as one, and all of what we think, understand and live relates to his love. To commemorate 17 these three measures of flour, we sing three Psalms in our nocturns on the same night, and until the end of the day on this Sunday we sing the alleluia. For thus is a feast celebrated by the authority of divine law—from evening to evening, or from the setting of the sun to the setting of the sun.

# 30

# On the Lord's Advent

We wrote in previous books that our preparation for the Lord's Advent begins in the fifth and fourth weeks before the Lord's Nativity: In the fifth week because of the five ages of the world, in which there were such elect as those who believed in and hoped for and loved the Lord's coming;

quarta, propter quattuor ordines librorum, scilicet legis, Psalmorum, prophetarum, et initium Evangelii. Quamvis liber Moysi narret electos viros extitisse in prima et secunda et tertia aetate mundi, tamen eo tempore scripsit illum

2 Moyses totum, in quo deputatur legislatio. Addidimus etiam alterum sensum posse initiari Adventum Domini in quinta seu quarta ebdomada, sequendo auctores lectionarii et antiphonarii ac missalis, cuius auctorem credimus esse beatum papam Gregorium. Quae utraque tempora intimant nobis rationabilem praeparationem, propter quinque sensus hominis qui insunt corpori nostro et quattuor elementa quibus constat corpus nostrum. At nunc tertium intellectum addimus, qui non minus convenit praeparationi Adventus Domini.

3 Dicimus duos ordines esse iustorum in ecclesia nostra qui student se praeparare ad recipiendum venturum Dominum. Unus ordo in saeculari conversatione studet, alter in spiritali. De ordine saecularium possumus intellegere quod lectio dicit in quinta ebdomada ante Nativitatem Domini: "Propter hoc ecce dies veniunt, dicit Dominus, et non dicent ultra: Vivit Dominus qui eduxit filios Israhel de terra Aegypti. Sed vivit Dominus qui eduxit et adduxit semen do-

4 mus Israhel de terra aquilonis" [ Jer 23:7–8]. Adduxit Dominus filios Israhel de terra aquilonis, quando de Babilonia reversi sunt in Iudaeam; sed melius adducit nostros bonos saeculares Dominus ad Iudaeam, id est ad veram confessionem, de confusione Babyloniae, quando eos liberat de potestate diaboli et de corpore eius. Hoc fit per baptysmum,

and in the fourth, because of the four orders of books, namely of the law, the Psalms, the prophets and the beginning of the Gospel. Although the book of Moses relates that the elect existed in the first and second and third ages of the world, Moses nevertheless wrote all of it in the time that is considered to include the giving of the law. We also added 2 the further interpretation that the Lord's Advent could commence on the fifth or fourth week, according to the authors of the lectionary and the antiphoner and the missal, whose author we believe to be the blessed pope Gregory. Both time periods suggest rational preparation to us, because of the five human senses that are present in our body and the four elements that our body consists of. But now we add a third understanding, which is no less appropriate in preparing for the Lord's Advent.

We say that there are two orders of the just in our church 3 who strive to prepare themselves for receiving their coming Lord. One order strives in secular life, the other in spiritual life. What the reading says in the fifth week before the Lord's Nativity we can understand in relation to the secular order: "Therefore behold the days come, says the Lord, and they shall say no more: The Lord lives who brought up the children of Israel out of the land of Egypt. But the Lord lives who has brought out and brought here the seed of the house of Israel from the land of the north." The Lord brought the sons of Israel from the land of 4 the north, when they returned from Babylon to Judaea. But it is even better that the Lord leads our good secular faithful to Judaea, or to true confession, out of the confusion of Babylon, when he frees them from the power of the devil and the devil's body. This occurs in baptism,

quem habent saeculares fideles et spiritales communem. Qui in animo patiuntur aquilonis rigiditatem, membra diaboli sunt. Quanto peior est diabolus totus cum capite in suo corpore, quam unum membrum eius, tanto melius nos liberati sumus a diaboli potestate, quam essent filii Israhel a regibus Caldeorum.

5    De ipsis saecularibus memorat Evangelium quod in quinta memorata ebdomada legitur; narrat enim quinque milia hominum Dominum pavisse ex quinque panibus. Quod ita Beda exponit in Evangelio super Lucam: "'Erant autem fere viri quinque milia' [Luke 9:14]. Quia quinque sunt exterioris hominis sensus, quinque milia viri Dominum secuti designant eos qui, in saeculari adhuc habitu positi, exterioribus quae possident bene uti noverunt. Qui recte quinque panibus aluntur, quia tales necesse est legalibus adhuc praeceptis instituti."✝

6    Officia cantorum et presbyterorum quae celebrantur in sacramentorio, et habent initium in quarta ebdomada ante Nativitatem Domini, spiritales per quattuor Evangelia ad potiorem perfectionem excitant. Unde dicit epistola quae in eodem die legitur: "Scientes quia hora est iam nos de somno surgere, nunc autem propior est nostra salus quam cum

7    credidimus" [Rom 13:11]. De eisdem spiritalibus dicit memoratus Beda in memorato libro: "Nam qui mundo ad integrum renuntiant, et quattuor sunt milia, et septem panibus refecti—hoc est Evangelica refectione sublimes, et spiritali sunt gratia docti. Cuius significandae distantiae

which the secular and spiritual faithful have in common. Those who suffer the hardness of the north in their spirit are members of the devil. It is better for us to be liberated from the devil's power than for the sons of Israel to have been liberated from the kings of the Chaldeans, to the same degree that the whole devil, with his head upon his body, is worse than one of his members.

The Gospel reading that is read on the aforementioned 5 fifth week commemorates these secular faithful, for it relates that the Lord fed five thousand people from five loaves. Bede, on the Gospel of Luke, explains this as follows: "'Now there were about five thousand men.' Because the exterior man has five senses, the five thousand men who followed the Lord represent those who, though still stationed in the secular life, know how to use the exterior senses that they possess for good. It is appropriate that they are fed from five loaves, because it is still necessary that such men be instructed in the precepts of the law."✝

The offices of the cantors and the priests that are pro- 6 claimed in the sacramentary, and that begin in the fourth week before the Lord's Nativity, excite the spiritual faithful to greater perfection through the four Gospels. Thus the epistle that is read on that day says: "And knowing that it is now the hour for us to rise from sleep, for now our salvation is nearer than when we believed." The aforementioned Bede 7 speaks of these same spiritual faithful in his aforementioned book: "For those who renounce the world entirely, and are four thousand, and are fed with seven loaves—that means that they were uplifted by the food of the Gospel and were taught with spiritual grace. I think that, for the purpose of demonstrating this difference mystically, it was ordered that

causa mystice, reor in introitu quidem tabernaculi quinque columnas deauratas, ante oraculum vero, id est sancta sanctorum, quattuor fieri iussas—quia videlicet incipientes per legem castigantur, ne peccent; perfecti autem per gratiam, ut devotius Deo vivant, admonentur."+

8  Typice: Per cantum qui renovatur in quarta ebdomada ante Nativitatem Domini, gaudium mentium perfectorum intellegimus. Si per quinque ebdomadas illi intelleguntur qui adhuc paenitentia deplorant recentia peccata, merito per quattuor ebdomadas eos intellegimus qui gaudio spiritali proficiunt de virtute in virtutem, in qua videbitur Deus deorum in Sion [Ps 83:8]. Isti duo ordines fuerunt in Veteri Testamento, isti sunt modo.

9  Renovatio cantus significat gaudium electorum, qui gaudent plurimum in adventu dilecti Domini. Ad eos dicit versus qui canitur in Vespertinali officio: "Rorate caeli, desuper, et nubes pluant iustum. Aperiatur terra et germinet salvatorem" [Isa 45:8]. Ipsi perfecti sunt caeli; ipsi sunt nubes; ipsi subtilia adnuntiant instar roris de incarnatione Domini, quando exponunt: "Verbum caro factum est et habitavit in nobis" [John 1:14]. Ipsi pluunt grossiora quando narrant quomodo Ioseph desponsavit Mariam, et Christus natus est in Bethleem et inventus est in praesepio, et cetera talia.

10  Aperta est terra—uterus scilicet sanctae Mariae virginis sine damno virginitatis; et protulit germen totius mundi odoris: qui bonus odor redolet per universum mundum. At nunc multa corda fidelium ad vocem praedicatorum calefiunt et germinant fidem rectam in Christo. Proferunt gaudium,

five gilded columns be placed in the entrance to the tabernacle; and it was ordered that four be placed before the mercy seat, or the holy of holies—namely because beginners are chastised according to the law, lest they sin; but the perfected are admonished through grace, that they may live more devoutly for God."†

Figuratively: Through the song that is taken up anew before the Lord's Nativity on the fourth week of Advent, we understand the joy of the minds of the perfected. If by five weeks are understood those who still deplore their recent sins through penance, it is appropriate that by four weeks we understand those who, in spiritual joy, go from virtue to virtue, in which the God of gods will be seen in Zion. These two orders existed in the Old Testament, as they do now.

Our return to the song signifies the joy of the elect, who greatly rejoice in the coming of their beloved Lord. The versicle that is sung at Vespers speaks to them: "Drop down dew, heavens, from above, and let the clouds rain on the just. Let the earth be opened and bud forth a savior." The perfected are the heavens; they are the clouds; they announce subtle things about the Lord's incarnation in the form of dew, when they proclaim: "And the word was made flesh and dwelt among us." They rain down blunter matter when they relate how Joseph was betrothed to Mary, and how Christ was born in Bethlehem and was found in the manger, and other such things. The earth is opened—that is, the womb of the holy virgin Mary, without the loss of her virginity; and she brought forth the shoot of perfume for the entire world: a good odor that is redolent through the whole world. But now the many hearts of the faithful warm to the words of the preachers and bud forth right faith in Christ. They bring

pacem, longanimitatem et cetera germina, quae fecundat

11 Spiritus Sanctus. Alter versus in Matutinali officio dicit: "Vox clamantis in deserto: Parate viam Domino, rectas facite semitas eius" [Isa 40:3], quod est dicere: Et bona opera satagite et cogitationes pias. Hoc ministerium quod praedicatores debent satagere in diebus Adventus Domini, memorati versus recolunt.

12 Quamvis cum gaudio boni servi expectent adventum Domini sui, tamen maximum gaudium recolunt in praesentia eius. Idcirco aliqua de nostro officio reservamus usque ad praesentiam Nativitatis Domini—hoc est, *Gloria in excelsis Deo* et clarum vestimentum dalmaticarum—si forte nunc ita agitur, ut vidi actitari in aliquibus locis.

13 Praeparationem nobis necessariam insinuat Paulus Apostolus in memorata epistola, quae legitur quarta ebdomada ante Nativitatem Domini: "Nox," inquiens, "praecessit, dies autem appropinquabit. Abiciamus ergo opera tenebrarum et induamus arma lucis. Sicut in die honeste ambulemus— non in commessationibus et ebrietatibus, non in cubilibus et impudicitiis, non in contentione et emulatione. Sed in-

14 duimini Dominum Iesum Christum" [Rom 13:12–14]. Sicut per plures et frequentiores nuntios movetur magis ac magis animus subditi ad sollicitudinem suscipiendi praelatum, ita renovatione cantus movemur magis ac magis ad curam nostrae praeparationis in susceptionem Domini. Ideo octo dies ante Nativitatem Domini renovantur ferme cata nocte responsorii et antiphonae, ut per hoc frequentius nos excitemur ad purgandas omnes quisquilias turpium cogitationum

forth joy, peace, forbearance and other shoots, which the Holy Spirit makes fruitful. Another versicle for Matins says: 11 "The voice of one crying in the desert: Prepare the way of the Lord, make straight the paths," which is to say: Practice both good works and pious thoughts. The aforementioned versicles recall the ministry that preachers should practice in the days of the Lord's Advent.

Although good servants await their Lord's coming with 12 joy, they nevertheless cultivate the greatest joy in the Lord's presence. For that reason we reserve some elements of our office until the presence of the Lord's Nativity—namely the *Gloria in excelsis Deo* and the white dalmatics—that is to say, if celebrations are now conducted as I saw them practiced in some places.

In the aforementioned epistle, which is read on the 13 fourth week before the Lord's Nativity, Paul the Apostle tells us that preparation is necessary: "The night is past," he says, "and the day will come. Let us therefore cast off the works of darkness and put on the armor of light. Let us walk honestly as in the day—not in rioting and drunkenness, not in beds and lewdnesses, not in contention and envy. Put on instead the Lord Jesus Christ." Just as a subject's spirit is 14 moved by abundant and frequent messengers more and more toward solicitude for receiving his master, so too are we moved, by the renewal of the chant, more and more toward care in our preparation for receiving the Lord. And so during the eight days before the Lord's Nativity responsories and antiphons are taken up anew almost every night, that on this account we might be moved more frequently to purge all the refuse of our filthy and terrestrial thoughts;

ac terrenarum; et dignum habitaculum, ornatum videlicet piis cogitationibus, paremus regi regum et domino dominantium.

## 31

# De Nativitate Domini

Dei Filius, cum esset unigenitus filius, voluit sibi fratres adiungere. Descendit ad humanum genus et assumpsit hominem ut faceret sibi fratres, nullum despiciens in fraterno loco suscipere quem cognovit oboedientem iri praeceptorum suorum. Ut saepe dictum est, tempus saeculi praesentis tribus temporibus distinguitur, videlicet naturalis legis, et

2 legis litterae, et Novi Testamenti. Praecipui viri naturali lege extiterunt tres: Abraham, Isaac et Iacob. Quanquam multi forent similes illis, tamen eorum se esse Deum specialiter Deus idem saepissime memorat per scripturas, dicens: "Ego sum Deus Abraham et Deus Isaac et Deus Iacob" [Exod 3:6, etc.].

3 Istis tribus tres Psalmos primae periochae Nocturnalis officii deputamus [Ps 2, 18, 23]—praecipue cum hi tres primi ponantur in genealogia Christi, et per hos ad memoriam reducimus omnes electos patres qui in naturali lege fuerunt, et

and that we might prepare a worthy dwelling, namely one adorned with pious thoughts, for the king of kings and lord of lords.

## 31

# On the Lord's Nativity

The Son of God, since he was an only-begotten son, wanted to join brothers to himself. He descended to the human race and took on manhood that he might make brothers for himself; and as his brother he disdained to receive nobody whom he recognized would follow his precepts in obedience. As often noted, the time of this world is divided into three periods, namely the natural law, the law of the letter, and the New Testament. There were three men who 2 excelled under the natural law: Abraham, Isaac and Jacob. Although many were like them, God often relates in the scriptures that he was their God in particular, saying: "I am the God of Abraham and the God of Isaac and the God of Jacob."

We allot the three Psalms of the first nocturn of Noc- 3 turns to these three—especially since these three are placed first in Christ's genealogy, and through them we call to mind all those fathers who were elect under the natural law, and who were joined to the choir of holy angels through

per Christi adventum sociati sunt coro sanctorum angelorum, ut, sicut angeli sanctae Trinitati congaudent, ita et illi
4    congaudeant. Secunda periocha recolit eos quos sibi Christus fratres fecit ex lege Mosaica, qui exercebantur per legem
et Psalmos et prophetas. Eos nihilominus perduxit ad societatem sanctorum angelorum, ut et illi congaudeant sanctae
5    Trinitati. Ascivit sibi etiam fratres in Novo Testamento per
primitivam ecclesiam, et per gentilitatis oboedientiam et
Iudaicam recognitionem. Quoniam istos plus honoravit
suus adventus quam praecedentes patres (ita ut, si digni ha-
beantur, quando transeunt de mundo ilico transferantur in
caelum et coniungantur societati sanctorum angelorum—
quod longo tempore expectaverunt patres murmurantes infra claustra inferni), ideo in illis antiphonis quae eos recolunt, alleluia caelebratur, sicuti est: "Ipse invocabit me, alleluia." Et iterum: "Notum fecit Dominus, alleluia."

# 32

# De octavis in Nativitate Domini

Octavae ideo caelebrantur quia primis diebus concur-
runt, sicut unus Dominicus dies ad alterum qui eodem ritu
caelebratur. Quando sequentia opera bona ad prima recur-
runt, aliquo modo octavas exercemus. Tanta miseria fuit in

Christ's coming, that they might rejoice in the Holy Trinity just as the angels rejoice in it. The second nocturn recalls 4 those whom Christ made his brothers through the Mosaic law, and who were active through the law and the Psalms and the prophets. He nevertheless led them to fellowship with holy angels, that they also might rejoice in the Holy Trinity. He also acquired brothers for himself in the New Testament 5 through the early church, both through the obedience of the gentiles and the recognition of the Jews. Because his coming honored these more than it did the fathers who came before (such that, if they were held worthy, when they left the world they would be brought directly to heaven and joined to fellowship with holy angels—something that the fathers long awaited while grumbling in the confines of hell), in the antiphons that recall them an alleluia is celebrated, as in: "He will call me, alleluia." And again: "The Lord made it known, alleluia."

## 32

# On the octave of the Lord's Nativity

Octaves are celebrated because they accord with the first days of their feasts, just as one Sunday accords with another that is celebrated in the same season. When our later good works return to our first good works, we observe, in some sense, an octave. So great were the miseries among

hominibus ante Christi adventum, ut nemo ad eandem innocentiam perveniret quam habuit primus homo ante quam peccaret. Nam et circumcisio quae octava die caelebrabatur, in recordatione primae innocentiae agebatur—id est ut mens circumcisa esset ab omni cogitatione carnali—quamvis sit et ipsa umbra futurorum verorum. Christus per baptysmum restituit in genere humano eandem innocentiam, ideoque octava die, id est Dominica, ex baptismo re-

2 surrectio recolitur. Hoc est inter istos qui primi innocentiam hominis imitantur, et illos qui in Veteri Testamento erant, quod, quamvis illi iusti essent, tamen detinebantur infra claustra inferni ante Christi adventum; isti penetrant regna caelorum. Et, quoniam ad meliorem statum vult nos perducere redemptor noster quam haberet primus Adam, adhuc expectatur octava dies quae erit in resurrectione corporum. Primus Adam ita erat innocens, ut posset peccare si vellet. Et nos ita accipimus innocentiam per baptysmum, ut possimus peccare et possimus velle; sed post receptionem corporum nemo poterit, nemo volet peccare.

3 Igitur quia ad hoc institutae sunt octavae, ut redeant ad primum, oportet considerare quid in octavis Domini redeat ad primum diem Nativitatis. Primo die nativitatis exivit de utero virginis et inventus est in praesepio pannis involutus. Numquid octava die iterum exivit de utero virginis, et inventus est in praesepio, et caelebrata sunt ea quae de angelorum affatu leguntur prima die acta. Possumus tamen invenire in quo congruenter octava dies congruat primae.

men before Christ's coming that nobody could return to the same innocence that the first man enjoyed before he sinned. For even the circumcision that was celebrated on the eighth day was carried out in commemoration of that first innocence—that is, that the mind might be circumcised of every carnal thought—although it was also the foreshadowing of truths to come. Through baptism Christ restored this innocence in the human race, and therefore our resurrection through baptism is recalled on the eighth day, or Sunday. The difference between those who imitate the innocence of 2 the first man, and those who lived under the Old Testament, is this: Although the latter were just, they were nevertheless detained within the confines of hell before Christ's coming; the former enter the kingdoms of heaven. And, because our redeemer wants to bring us into a better state than the first Adam enjoyed, we continue to await the eighth day that will occur upon the resurrection of our bodies. The first Adam was innocent in such a way that he could sin if he wanted. And through baptism we receive innocence such that we are able to sin and to desire to sin; but after we receive our bodies, nobody will be able and nobody will desire to sin.

Because octaves were established to return to the first 3 day of their feasts, we should consider what in the octave of the Lord's Nativity accords with the first day. On the first day of his birth the Lord emerged from the virgin's womb and was found in a manger wrapped in swaddling clothes. Surely he did not emerge from the virgin's womb a second time on the eight day, and he was not found a second time in the manger, and all those things that we read were celebrated with respect to the angels' speech on the first day did not happen again. Yet we can nevertheless discover in what respect the eighth day accords appropriately with the first.

4    Duas causas intellegimus in Christi nativitate: scilicet primam, Christum venisse ad homines; secundam, homines venisse ad Christum. De qua re dicit Agustinus in libro primo *De doctrina Christiana:* "Non enim ad eum qui ubique praesens est, locis movemur, sed bono studio bonisque moribus. Quod non possemus, nisi ipsa sapientia tantae etiam nostrae infirmitati congruere dignaretur, ut vivendi nobis praeberet exemplum, non aliter quam in homine, quoniam

5    et nos homines sumus. Sed quia nos, cum ad illam venimus, sapienter facimus, ipsa, cum ad nos venit, ab hominibus superbis quasi stulte fecisse putata est. Et quoniam nos, cum ad illam venimus, convalescimus, ipsa, cum ad nos venit, quasi infirma existimata est. Sed 'quod stultum est Dei sapientius est quam homines, et quod infirmum est Dei for-

6    tius est quam homines' [1 Cor 1:25]. Cum ergo ipsa sit patria, viam se quoque nobis fecit ad patriam. Et cum sano et puro interiori oculo ubique sit praesens, eorum qui oculum illum infirmum inmundumque habent, oculis etiam carneis apparere dignata est. 'Quia enim in sapientia Dei non poterat mundus, per sapientiam, cognoscere Deum, placuit Deo per stultitiam praedicationis salvos facere credentes' [1 Cor 1:21]. Non igitur per locorum spatia veniendo, sed in carne mortali mortalibus apparendo, venisse ad nos dicitur. Illuc ergo venit ubi erat, quia 'in hoc mundo erat, et mundus per eum factus est' [John 1:10]."✝

7    Christi adventum ad homines colimus in die Nativitatis eius, hominum adventum ad Christum colimus in octavis eius. Quod facile dinoscitur ex antiphonis quae can-

8    tantur in Matutinali officio. Prima antiphona in Nativitate

We understand two aspects of Christ's birth: the first is 4
that Christ came to men; the second is that men came
to Christ. Augustine writes on this subject in his first book
*On Christian Doctrine:* "For we are not brought to him who
is present everywhere, through space, but rather through
good effort and good virtues. We would not be able to do
this, unless wisdom had deigned to conform even to our
great infirmity, that it might provide us with an example of
how to live in no other way than in the guise of a man, since
we are also men. But because we act wisely when we come to 5
that wisdom, wisdom itself, when it comes to us, is thought
by proud men to have acted foolishly. And because we regain
our health when we come to it, wisdom, when it comes to
us, is thought to be almost weak. But 'the foolishness of
God is wiser than men, and the weakness of God is stronger
than men.' Since therefore wisdom is our homeland, it has 6
also made itself a path for us to the homeland. And since it is
present everywhere to the pure and healthy interior eye, it
also deigned to appear to the carnal eyes of those whose interior eye is infirm and unclean. 'For since in the wisdom
of God the world, by wisdom, was not able to know God,
it pleased God by the foolishness of our preaching to save
them that believe.' He is therefore said to have come to us
not by moving through space, but by appearing to mortals
in mortal flesh. Thus he came to a place where he already
was, because 'he was in the world and the world was made
through him.'"✝

We commemorate Christ's coming to men on the feast of 7
his Nativity, and the coming of men to Christ on the octave
of his nativity. This is easily recognized through the antiphons that are sung for Matins. The first antiphon for the 8

Domini, *Genuit puerpera regem,* de pura nativitate Domini narrat. Prima in octavis Domini dicit: "O admirabile commercium." Quando dicit "commercium," ostendit aliud dari et aliud accipi. Dedit Christus suam deitatem et accepit nostram humanitatem. Quod dedit, colimus in Nativitate eius, et quod accepit, in octavis. Membra, iuncta capiti, congratulantur in praesenti festivitate.

9    De sequentibus antiphonis—si quis considerare voluerit, potest agnoscere quod antiphonae de Nativitate Domini suam nativitatem specialiter monstrant, et de octavis Domini, membrorum suorum copulationem. In antiphona secunda, *Rubem quem viderat Moyses,* sic loquitur ex persona membrorum ad Dei genetricem: "Intercede pro nobis." Tertia habet in fine: "Te laudamus, Deus noster." Quarta est in Romano antiphonario, *Nato Domino, angelorum chori canebant dicentes: Salus Deo nostro,* quae concinit laudi trium puerorum. In quinto loco est una de Romano antiphonario et altera de nostro, quae tenet verba Iohannis Baptistae, quibus demonstravit utilitatem nostram, quae data est nobis ex adventu Christi, dicentis: "Ecce agnus Dei, ecce qui tollit peccata mundi" [John 1:29, 36].

10    Antiphona quae in Evangelio dicitur et Domini praesentiam ad homines monstrat, et hominis assumptionem ad eum. Sic enim dicit: "Mirabile mysterium declaratur hodie; innovantur naturae." Quomodo innovantur natu-

11  rae Gregorius Nazanzenus manifestat in libro *De secundis Epiphaniis,* dicens: "Quid de nobis agitur, vel pro nobis? Nova quaedam et inaudita efficitur permutatio naturarum, et Deus homo fit." Et paulo post: "Dei Filius coepit

Lord's Nativity, *Genuit puerpera regem,* tells of the Lord's pure birth. The first for the Lord's octave says: "O admirable exchange." When it speaks of "exchange," it shows that something is given and something received. Christ gave his divinity and received our humanity. We commemorate what he gave on his Nativity, and what he received, on the octave. The members, joined to the head, are commended in this feast.

As for the antiphons that follow—should anyone want to 9 consider them, he can recognize that the antiphons for the Lord's Nativity reveal the Lord's birth in particular, while those for the Lord's octave reveal the joining of his members. In the second antiphon, *Rubem quem viderat Moyses,* it speaks in the guise of God's members to his mother: "Intercede for us." The third has at the end: "We praise you, our God." The fourth in the Roman antiphoner is *Nato Domino, angelorum chori canebant dicentes: Salus Deo nostro,* which resonates with the praise of the three boys. In the fifth place is one from the Roman antiphoner and another from ours, which contains the words of John the Baptist, through which he revealed the benefit that we have been granted through Christ's coming, saying: "Behold the lamb of God, who takes away the sins of the world."

The antiphon sung with the Gospel canticle reveals both 10 the Lord's presence among men, and mankind's reception unto the Lord. For it says: "A marvelous mystery is revealed today; nature is made new." Gregory of Nazianzus shows 11 how nature is made new in his book *On the Second Epiphany,* saying: "What is done regarding us, or on our behalf? A new and unheard-of exchange of natures is brought about, and God becomes man." And a little later: "The Son of God

esse filius hominis, non conversus ex eo quod erat, sed assumens quod non erat, ut capi possit qui capi non poterat, et per mediantem carnem, sicut velamine quodam interposito, alloqui nos possit. Quoniam quidem ferre sinceram divinitatis eius naturam non erat corruptibilis huius nostrae fragilisque naturae, idcirco ergo incommixta miscentur, et non solum nativitati nostrae Deus, vel carni superna mens, vel tempori illud quod ante omne tempus est—verum etiam virginitati partus imponitur, et inpassibili passio conciliatur, et immortali mortis poculum propinatur."✝

12    Sequitur in antiphona: "Id quod fuit, permansit." Hoc est verbum, quod se nobis voluit demonstrare per materiam carnis; ut fuit incommutabile lumen et Deus aeternus, sic permansit, non mutatum in aliquam creaturam.

13    Sequitur: "Et quod non erat, assumpsit." His verbis monstratur assumptio hominis. Quoniam Christus hominem dignatus est assumere in unam eandemque personam Dei, merito membra capitis dicuntur transisse in Dominum.

14    Unde Agustinus in sermone vicesimo sexto super Iohannem: "Quid est ergo credere in eum? Credendo amare, credendo diligere, credendo in eum ire et eius membris incorporari."✝

Sequitur: "Non commixtionem passus neque divisionem." Scilicet non est passus illam commixtionem quam dicit Sabellius in unam personam Patris et Filii, neque illam divisionem quam blaterat Arius. De circumcisione Domini me abunde facit securum lucubratio sanctorum interpretum.

began to be the son of man, not through transformation from what he was, but by assuming what he was not, so that he who could not be possessed might be able to be possessed, and through the mediation of flesh, as though a veil had been interposed, he might be able to speak to us. For indeed, as it was not in our corruptible and fragile nature to carry the pure nature of his divinity, the unmixed are therefore mixed, and God is not only imposed upon our birth, and the supreme mind upon flesh, and that which was before all time upon time—but birth is also imposed upon virginity, passion is united with unsuffering, and the cup of death is extended to an immortal."✝

There follows the antiphon: "That which was, remained." 12 This is the word, which desired to show itself to us through the stuff of flesh; as it was unchangeable light and God eternal, it thus persisted and was not changed into any creature.

There follows: "And he took on that which he was not." 13 In these words the assumption of man is indicated. Because Christ deigned to take on man in one and the selfsame person of God, the members of the head are rightly said to have gone over to the Lord. Thus Augustine in his twenty-sixth 14 sermon on John: "What is it, therefore, to believe in him? Believing is to love him, believing is to be fond of him, believing is to go to him and be joined to his members."✝

There follows: "He suffered neither commingling nor division." That is, he did not suffer the commingling in a single person of the Father and the Son that Sabellius proclaims, nor the division that Arius babbles about. The labor of the holy commentators leaves me supremely untroubled about the Lord's circumcision.

# 33

# De Theophania et Ypopanti

Unum amittimus in Theophania ex his quae caelebramus in Nativitate Domini, id est invitatorium. Saepe dictum est quod institutor officii, in quantum potuit, actionem omnem illius temporis, quando illa agebantur quae recolimus in usitato officio, voluit ad memoriam nobis reducere. Igitur quia voluit in isto distinguere nostram bonam invitationem, qua invitantur et excitantur fideles ad Deum deprecandum, ab invitatione Herodis, qui propterea congregavit scribas et principes Iudaeorum, ut sciret ubi Christus nasceretur—quem cogitabat interficere—invitatorium praesentis officii amisit.

2 Praesens officium Nocturnale certat intimare tria insignia nobis manifestata per adventum Christi, id est adventum Magorum et baptysmum Christi et miraculum ex aqua factum a Christo. De secundo et tertio summatim memoratur in tertia nocturna et in antiphona *Hodie caelesti sponso iuncta est ecclesia.* Aperte vero et plene de adventu Magorum

3 canit in duabus superioribus nocturnis. Nam et hoc videtur ordini potissimum congruere ceterorum officiorum: Verum officium quod in nocte Nativitatis eius canitur de infantia eius resonat; memoria quae recolit per officia cantorum de octavis Domini et circumcisionem eius et scintillas mittit de infantia; similique modo quod agitur in Ypopanti.

## 33

# On Epiphany and Hypapante

On Epiphany we omit one point from among the things that we celebrate on the Lord's Nativity, namely the invitatory. It has often been said that the founder of our office, insofar as he was able, wanted to remind us of all that happened in the time when the things that we recall in our customary office were done. He therefore left the invitatory out of the present office, because in it he wanted to distinguish our good invitation, through which the faithful are invited and urged to pray to God, from the invitation of Herod, who gathered the scribes and princes of the Jews, to find out where Christ—whom he had in mind to kill—was born.

The office of Nocturns for this feast strives to suggest 2 the three signs that were revealed to us upon Christ's coming, namely the coming of the Magi and the baptism of Christ and the miracle that Christ performed through water. The second and third are briefly recalled in the third nocturn and in the antiphon *Hodie caelesti sponso iuncta est ecclesia.* In the two previous nocturns, meanwhile, there is open and clear singing about the coming of the Magi. For 3 this too seems to cohere most of all with the order of the other offices: For the office sung on the night of his Nativity resounds with his infancy; the commemoration that, through the offices of the cantors for the Lord's octave, recalls his circumcision, also sends forth glimmerings of his infancy; the celebration for Hypapante is conducted similarly.

Idcirco congruebat ut praesens officium plurimum illa tan-
4 geret quae circa infantiam eius gesta sunt. Nec non et apos-
tolici viri satagebant baptysmum generale transferre de
praesenti festivitate in festivitatem Paschae et Pentecostes;
quem propterea multi certabant frequentare in ista festivitate, quia in ipsa a multis creditur Dominus baptyzatus esse
a Iohanne. Unde potest videri ab officio praesenti summatim dictum esse de baptysmo eius, et plene de adventu
Magorum.

5    Ut plenius haec clarescant, insero quod sanctus Leo papa
scripsit de memoratis festivitatibus, dicens in capitulo VIII
decretalium: "Ordo rerum per Iesum Christum Dominum
nostrum temporaliter gerendarum in incarnatione verbi
sumpsit exordium. Unde aliud tempus est quo, adnuntiante
angelo, beata virgo Maria fecundandam se per Spiritum
Sanctum credidit et concepit; aliud quo, salva integritate
virginea, puer editus, exultante gaudio caelestium ministrorum, pastoribus indicatur; aliud quo infans circumciditur;
aliud quo hostia pro eo legalis offertur; aliud cum tres Magi,
claritate novi sideris incitati, in Bethleem ab Oriente perve-
niunt, et adorant parvulum, mistica munerum oblatione ve-
6 nerantur. Nec idem sunt dies quibus impio Herodi, ordinata
divinitus in Aegyptum translatione, subtractus est, vel quibus ab Aegypto in Galileam, mortuo persecutore, vocatus
est. Inter has autem dispensationum varietates accedunt
augmenta corporea. Crescit Dominus, sicut evangelista testatur, profectibus aetatis et gratiae."✠

It was therefore appropriate that the present office should touch mostly upon what occurred during his infancy. The popes have also worked to move the common baptism from this feast to the feasts of Easter and Pentecost; many strive to celebrate baptism on this feast because many believe that the Lord was baptized by John on this day. Thus it can be seen, from the present office, that the Lord's baptism is treated of briefly, and the coming of the Magi at length.

To make these matters clearer, I include what Saint Leo, the pope, wrote about the aforementioned feasts, saying in chapter eight of his decretals: "The order of temporal celebrations for our Lord Jesus Christ originated with the incarnation of the word. Thus it is at one time that, upon the angel's announcement, the blessed virgin Mary believed she would be made fruitful by the Holy Spirit, and she conceived; at another that she brought forth a boy without loss of her virginity, and notice was given to the shepherds through the exultant joy of heavenly ministers; at another that the child is circumcised; at another that a sacrifice is offered on his behalf according to the law; and at another that the three Magi, encouraged by the splendor of the new star, come to Bethlehem from the East, adore the small child and venerate it with the mystical offering of gifts. Nor are these days the same as those when he was withdrawn from the wicked Herod through his divinely ordained passage to Egypt, or when he was called from Egypt to Galilee upon the death of his persecutor. And among these various dispensations his body was growing. The Lord grows, as the evangelist tells it, and advances in age and grace."✝

7    Tertia nocturna praesentis festivitatis recolit tres terminos credentium—id est populi Iudaici ante receptionem gentilium, gentilis populi post repulsionem Iudaicae plebis,

8    iterum populi Iudaici in finem mundi. In prima nocturna recolitur intellectus Magorum, qui Christum intellexerunt Deum esse; in secunda nocturna idem intellectus, qui conspicit Christum regem esse; in tertia, qui conspicit Christum ad hoc venisse, ut doceret homines suo baptismo necessarium eis esse baptizari, et per baptismum mori patri diabolo et operibus eius et pompis eius. In baptismo mors ·Christi et sepultura eius recolitur.

9    Hanc tertiam periocham recolimus per introitus Missae ab octavis Theophaniae usque in Praesentationem Domini, nisi forte anticipet nos tempus Septuagesimae. Primus introitus est post octavas Teophaniae, iuxta ordinem antiphonarii nostri: "In excelso throno vidi sedere virum quem adorat multitudo angelorum." Apostolorum et apostolicorum virorum est ista visio—hoc est ut mente intellegant eundem Dominum, qui a Magis adoratus est quasi infans, et cuius praesentatio isto in tempore expectatur usque ad quadragesimam diem nativitatis, gubernare virtutes caelorum et

10    ab his adorari. Secundus est: "Omnis terra adoret te, Deus" [Ps 65:4], qui pertinet ad multitudinem credentium, ut quem primo adoraverunt tres Magi, postea adorent omnes credentes ex Asia et Africa et Europa.

The third nocturn of the present feast recalls the three 7
divisions of believers—that is, the Jewish people before the
reception of the gentiles, the gentile people after the re-
jection of the Jewish people, and again the Jewish people at
the end of the world. In the first nocturn the understanding 8
of the Magi, who understood that Christ was God, is commemorated; in the second nocturn, the understanding of
those same Magi, who saw that Christ was king; in the third,
the one who saw that Christ came to teach men, through his
baptism, that it was necessary for them to be baptized, and
through baptism to die to their father, the devil, together
with his works and his pomps. In baptism Christ's death and
his burial are recalled.

We commemorate this third category in the introits for 9
Mass from the octave of Epiphany to the feast of the Lord's
Presentation, unless the season of Septuagesima intervenes
for us. The first introit is after the octave of Epiphany, according to the order of our antiphoner: "I saw a man sitting upon an exalted throne whom the multitude of angels
adores." This is the vision of the apostles and their apostolic successors—that is, that they understand in their
minds that this same Lord, who was adored by the Magi as
an infant, and whose presentation at that time was awaited
until the fortieth day after his birth, governs the powers of
heaven and is adored by them. The second is: "Let all the 10
earth adore you, God"; it pertains to the multitude of believers, such that all the believers from Asia, Africa and
Europe may later adore him whom the three Magi first
adored.

11 Iam circa ebdomadam in qua celebratur Praesentatio Domini, cantatur *Adorate Deum, omnes angeli eius* [Ps 96:7–8]. Unde dicit Apostolus: "Ut in nomine Iesu omne genu flectatur, caelestium, terrestrium et infernorum" [Phil 2:10]. Quod ita exponit Ambrosius, in epistola ad Philipenses: "Hoc enim illi donavit: ut omnes illum adorent et ut omnes Deum confiteantur Iesum Christum in gloria Dei Patris effectum—hoc est, talem potitum gloriam qualem fas est illum qui sibi patrem ascribit Deum potiri, propter illam copulationem quam habet ad unigenitum." Et post pauca: "'Caelestium' quidem invisibilium virtutum." Et Petrus de eodem Filio Dei: "Profectus," inquit, "in caelum, subiectis

12 sibi angelis et potestatibus et virtutibus" [1 Pet 3:22]. Unde Beda in tractatu epistolae eiusdem Petri: "Nulli dubium quin Filio Dei semper erant angeli et omnes patriae caelestis virtutes ac potestates subiectae, quem cum Patre et Spiritu Sancto unum sine initio Deum laudant, tremunt, adorant. Sed necessario ammonendum beatus Petrus estimavit quod assumpta humanitas in tantam sit gloriam resurgendo sublimata, ut incomparabili culmine omni angelicae dignitatis

13 potentiae praeferatur."+ Iste introitus aut intra se habet Ypopanti, aut initium possidet infra octo dies eiusdem Ypopanti, nisi per anticipationem Paschae praecurrat Septuagesima.

14 Memorati introitus beneficia Christi insinuant, praestita nobis ad laetificanda corda nostra. Idcirco cum duobus cantamus offertoria *Iubilate*. Laetari enim nos oportet, quia non solum de inferno inferiore beneficia Christi nos liberant, sed etiam de claustris inferni, et perducunt usque ad

During the week when the Lord's Presentation is cele- 11
brated, *Adorate Deum, omnes angeli eius* is sung. Thus the
Apostle says: "That in the name of Jesus every knee should
bow of those that are in heaven, on earth and under the
earth." Ambrose, on the letter to the Philippians, explains
this as follows: "And he granted him this: that all the nations
would adore him and that all would confess that Jesus Christ
has been made God in the glory of God the Father—that is,
he acquired the sort of glory that it is right for one who calls
God his father to acquire, because of the connection that he
has to the only-begotten." And after a little: "And indeed,
'those that are in heaven' are the invisible powers." And Peter on the same Son of God: "Being gone into heaven," he
says, "the angels and powers and virtues being made subject
to him." Thus Bede in his treatise on the same letter of 12
Peter: "There is no doubt that the angels and all the virtues
and powers of the heavenly country were always subject to
God's Son, whom they forever praise, tremble before and
adore, together with the Father and the Holy Spirit, as one
God without a beginning. But blessed Peter thought it necessary to remind us that the assumed humanity was raised to
such glory through the resurrection, that in its incompara-
ble summit it exceeded all the might of angelic dignity."+
This introit either encompasses Hypapante, or it begins be- 13
fore the octave of Hypapante, unless Septuagesima precedes in anticipation of Easter.

The aforementioned introits proclaim the favors of 14
Christ that have been granted to us to delight our hearts.
We therefore sing the offertory *Iubilate* with both of them.
And we should rejoice, since Christ's favors free us not only
from the lower hell, but also from the lockups of hell, and

15 visionem sempiternae gloriae. Unde versus responsorii qui cantatur in ebdomada Ypopanti dicit: "Quoniam aedificavit Dominus Sion et videbitur in gloria sua" [Ps 101:17]. De quo ita Agustinus in tractatu Psalmorum: "At vero cum venerit iudicare cum angelis suis, quando congregabuntur ante eum omnes gentes. . . ." Et post pauca: "'Aedificavit Dominus Sion et videbitur in gloria sua'—qui in illa primo visus est in infirmitate sua."✝

16 Ex hoc versu possumus conicere institutorem officiorum insinuare voluisse praesentationem Domini in templo, excitare nos ad praesentationem nostram sibi et Patri. Quadraginta dies in quibus expectatur Domini praesentatio, omnem statum sanctae ecclesiae demonstrant hic in praesenti saeculo, quamdiu necesse est ei per quattuor partes mundi satagere, ut impleat decim praecepta legis—hoc est, ut iuste et pie vivat in hoc saeculo, expectans beatam spem: quando videat Dominum in gloria sua et corum angelorum adorantem Deum.

17 Eandem perseverantiam in bono studio figurat tonica talaris quam induit Ioseph in praefiguratione corporis Christi, et nos clerici eam portamus sive in cotidiano usu sive in ecclesiastico. Ex ea nempe ammonemus populum Dei ut usque ad finem mundi satagat se operire bonis operibus. Unde Gregorius in primo libro *De moralibus:* "Nam quid est talaris tonica, nisi actio consummata? Quasi enim propensa tonica talum corporis operit, cum bona actio ante Dei oculos usque ad vitae terminum tegit."✝

they lead us into the sight of eternal glory. Thus the verse of 15
the responsory that is sung on the week of Hypapante says:
"For the Lord has built up Zion and he shall be seen in his
glory." About which, Augustine in his treatise on Psalms, as
follows: "But when he comes with his angels to judge, when
all the nations will be gathered before him . . ." And after a
little: "'The Lord has built up Zion and he shall be seen in
his glory'—he who was first seen in his infirmity."✝

From this verse we can gather that the founder of our of- 16
fices wanted to suggest the Lord's presentation in the temple, and to urge us on to our own presentation before him
and his Father. The forty days during which we await the
Lord's presentation signify the full state of the holy church
here in this world, for as long as it must labor through the
four regions of the world to fulfill the ten precepts of the
law—that is, to live justly and piously in this world while it
awaits what it happily hopes for: when it may see the Lord
in his glory and the choir of angels adoring God.

The ankle-length tunic that Joseph put on in prefigura- 17
tion of Christ's body recalls this same perseverance in vir-
tuous striving, and as clerics we wear this tunic both in everyday use and in church. Through it, of course, we
admonish God's people to work to cover themselves with
good works until the end of the world. Thus Gregory in
the first book of his *Moralia:* "For what is the ankle-length
tunic, if not consummated action? For a low-hanging tunic
covers the ankles of one's body, in some sense, when good
action covers one, in God's eyes, to the end of one's life."✝

18    Hoc est cereos accensos manibus portare in Ypopanti, quod est in praesentatione sui unumquemque secum habere opera sua, in quibus clarus et lucidus appareat in coetu sanctorum angelorum, in quorum commemoratione caelebratur in Nocturnali officio Ypopanti novenarius numerus. Post commemorata officia, veniente Septuagesima, mutamus cantum laetitiae in tribulationem, ut ex eo trahamus ad nostram memoriam cui affectui debitores simus ex nostris meritis, et ut educatu humilitatis perveniamus ad passionem Domini.

# 34

# De octavis Theophaniae

Natus est Christus ex Maria virgine temporaliter—non propter se, ut tunc inciperet esse, quasi non antea esset (ante omnia tempora fuit cum Patre, per quem haec omnia tempora creata sunt)—sed ut mentibus nostris nova lux appareret, per quam reverteremur ad creatorem nostrum, 2  qui eramus in tenebris. Simili modo baptyzatus est, non quod eguerit baptisterio ut in eo ablueret sua peccata, quae nulla erant, sed ut formam daret suae ecclesiae, quomodo

Carrying lit candles in our hands on Hypapante amounts 18
to each of us having his own works with him on his own presentation, in the midst of which he appears clear and bright
in the fellowship of the holy angels, in whose commemoration nine lessons are celebrated in the office of Nocturns for
Hypapante. After these offices have been celebrated, upon
the coming of Septuagesima, we exchange our song of rejoicing for one of tribulation, that through it we may call to
mind the disposition to which we remain indebted because
of our merits, and that through the guidance of humility we
may arrive at the Lord's passion.

# 34

# On the octave of Epiphany

Christ was born temporally of the virgin Mary—not
for himself, that he might at that time begin to be, as if he
did not exist before (before all time he was with the Father, through whom all time was created)—but rather so
that a new light might appear before our minds, through
which we who were in darkness might return to our creator. Similarly, he was baptized not because he needed 2
baptism to wash away his sins, which were nothing,
but rather to provide an example to his church of how

quaereret ablui sua peccata. Unde ipse dicebat in Evangelio: "Sic enim decet nos omnem iustitiam implere" [Matt 3:15]. Mortuus est Christus, ut suum corpus, quod est sancta ecclesia, morti moriretur. Erat prius genus humanum Deo mortuum, quia morti oboediebat; vivebamus morti cum ei serviebamus. Morimur morti cum ei renuntiamus.

3    Ut ad memoriam reducamus quod Christus propterea passus sit ut nos moreremur peccato, in quarta feria ante caenam Domini et nostra mortificatio recolitur in aliquibus officiis et Domini passio legitur—unde dictum est in iam scripto libello de quinta varietate. Si sequerentur dies post sextam feriam in quibus oporteret tristari, forte octavas passionis Domini caelebrassemus—hoc est per caelebrationem officii ad memoriam reduceremus morti obnixae mori nos debere. Moritur homo luxuriae qui castitatem servat; moritur invidiae qui caritate pollet; moritur incredulitati cuius cor fide mundatur.

4    In duabus lectionibus quae leguntur in sexta feria passionis Domini, animadvertimus duas mortes in eo die caelebratas. Lectio de Exodo Christi mortem manifestat, de Osee vero, membrorum suorum. De quibus dicit Paulus: "Qui autem sunt Christi carnem suam crucifixerunt cum vitiis et concupiscentiis" [Gal 5:24]. Tractus qui sequitur post lectiones, *Qui habitat in adiutorio altissimi* [Ps 90:1], informat omne praesidium quo adiuvantur a Domino sancti in certa-
5    mine positi. Hunc Psalmum congruit potissimum meditari, cum quis periculis appropinquat et circumdatur insidiis ac angustiis, velut bestia multis laqueis inretita, ut possit audiri a Domino: "Invocavit me et ego exaudiam eum;

its sins should be washed away. Thus he said in the Gospel: "For so it becomes us to fulfill all justice." Christ died so that his body, which is the holy church, would die to death. At first the human race was dead to God, because it obeyed death; we lived for death when we were in service to it. We die to death when we renounce it.

So that we may call to mind that Christ suffered so we 3 would die to sin, on the Wednesday before Holy Thursday, our mortification is also commemorated in various offices and the Lord's passion is read out—thus was our discussion in a previously written book, concerning the fifth variation. If, after Friday, there followed days when it was appropriate to mourn, perhaps we would have celebrated the octave of the Lord's passion—that is, we would recall in celebrating such an office that we ought to die to the death that has struggled against us. The man who dies to depravity preserves his chastity; he dies to envy who prevails in charity; he dies to doubt whose heart is cleansed with faith.

In the two readings that are read on Good Friday, we con- 4 sider the two deaths celebrated on that day. The reading from Exodus reveals Christ's death, while the one from Hosea reveals the death of his members. Paul speaks about this: "And they that are Christ's have crucified their flesh with the vices and concupiscences." The tract that follows the readings, *Qui habitat in adiutorio altissimi,* represents every protection by which those saints who are mired in struggle are helped by the Lord. It is appropriate to contemplate 5 this Psalm especially when one draws near to dangers and is surrounded by ambushes and difficulties, like a beast caught in many snares, that one may be able to hear from the Lord: "He cried to me and I will hear him; I am with him

cum ipso sum in tribulatione" [Ps 90:15]. Idcirco nunc cantatur ex persona membrorum, quia affectum illorum non
dedignatus est Dominus in se assumere. Cantatur et per singulas noctes propter timores nocturnos, vel quia somnus

6 habet imaginem mortis. In passione salvatoris nostri, paries
inimicitiarum ruptus est, et coniuncti sunt duo populi in
uno lapide angulari, quod non potuit fieri, nisi gentilitas
prius moreretur morti vitiorum.

7 Quoniam ista non proposuimus hic inquirere, sed precamur supplices ut ab eo spiritu inserta sint qui ubi vult spirat.
Nunc ad propositum redeundum est.

8 In Teophania celebramus quomodo Dominus a Magis sit
inquisitus et inventus ac adoratus, et partim sit baptizatus,
quomodo laetati sint convivae in nuptiis. Quae omnia possumus dinoscere ex antiphonis quae cantantur in Matutino.
Quia summatim cantatum est de baptismo Christi in Teophania, in octavis eius integre atque aperte decantatur et
memoratur de eo, nam et profectus nostri baptismatis in eis
celebratur. Quod monstratur ex prima antiphona in octavis
Teophaniae: "Veterem hominem renovans salvator." Et in
secunda: "Te, qui in spiritu et igne purificas humana conta-
gia." Idipsum poterit reperire diligens inquisitor in sequentibus.

9 Quia duo praecepta sunt dilectionis—Dei scilicet et
proximi—sicut honorando baptysmum Christi Dei et salvatoris nostri caelebravimus in Teophania, caelebremus
et nostrum, initiatum iam in capite nostro, in octavis Teophaniae. Hoc est ad memoriam reducamus qua de causa

in tribulation." This is now sung in the guise of the members, because the Lord has not deigned to take their state of mind upon himself. It is also sung each night because of our nocturnal fears, and because sleep is the image of death. Upon our savior's passion, the wall of our enemies was broken down, and two peoples were conjoined in one corner stone, which could not have happened unless the gentiles first died to the death of vices.

Since we have not proposed to inquire into these things here, we beg instead in supplication that they may be imparted by that spirit who breathes where he wishes. We should now return to our purpose.

On Epiphany we celebrate how the Lord was sought after and found and adored by the Magi, and to some extent how he was baptized, and how the guests rejoiced at the wedding. We can learn all of this from the antiphons that are sung at Matins. Because there is brief singing about Christ's baptism on the Epiphany, on its octave there is full and open declamation and commemoration of this theme, for our progress with baptism is also celebrated on the octave. This is revealed in the first antiphon for the octave of Epiphany: "The savior renewing the old man." And in the second: "You, who in spirit and fire purify human impurities." The careful inquirer will be able to find the same theme in subsequent passages.

Because there are two commandments of love—namely of God and neighbor—let us also celebrate our baptism, as already established in our head, on the octave of Epiphany, just as we celebrated Epiphany by honoring the baptism of Christ our God and savior. That is, let us remember for what

559

Christus baptizatus sit: scilicet quia necesse erat ut baptiza-
remur. Et quid prosit baptysmus, antiphonae monstrant in
octavis Teophaniae. Unde dicit una ex illis: "Baptizato Domino, facta est peccatorum nostrorum remissio." Ypopanti
non habet octavas, quoniam legaliter praesentatus est in
templo Christus. Ad quod nullus doctor nos coartat, ut in-
fantes nostri quadragesima die nativitatis suae praesenten-
tur in templo.

## 35

# De natalitiis sanctorum

Quae sint natalicia sanctorum, ex uno responsorio qui
cantatur in festivitate beati Stephani, cognoscere possumus. Dicit responsorius: "Hesterna die Dominus natus est
in terris, ut Stephanus nasceretur in caelis." Natalitia sanctorum nativitates eorum monstrant quibus nascuntur in societatem novem ordinum angelorum, et in societatem sanctorum patrum naturalis legis, et legis litterae et Novi
Testamenti. Propter gloriam Novi Testamenti, continent
antiphonae de tertia periocha alleluia, veluti sunt: "Exalta-
buntur cornua iusti, alleluia," "Lux orta est iusto, alleluia,"

purpose Christ was baptized: namely because it was necessary that we be baptized. And the antiphons for the octave of Epiphany reveal the benefit of baptism. Thus one of them says: "Now that the Lord has been baptized, the remission of our sins has been accomplished." Hypapante does 10 not have an octave because Christ was presented in the temple according to the law. No teacher compels us to present our children in the temple on the fortieth day after their birth.

## 35

# On the feasts of the saints

We can understand what the feasts of the saints are from one responsory that is sung on the feast of blessed Stephen. The responsory says: "Yesterday the Lord was born on the earth, that Stephen might be born in heaven." The feasts of the saints reveal the births by which they are born into the fellowship of the nine orders of angels, and into the fellowship of the holy fathers of the natural law, the law of the letter and the New Testament. Because of the glory of 2 the New Testament, the antiphons for the third nocturn contain the alleluia, as follows: "The horns of the just shall be exalted, alleluia," "Light is risen to the just, alleluia,"

"Custodiebant testimonia eius et praecepta eius, alleluia."
In festivitatibus quas recolimus per novenarium numerum,
stantes oramus, recolendo sanctam societatem angelorum
et patrum sanctorum, qui iam sunt in laetitia sempiterna.

# 36

# De octavis nataliciorum sanctorum

Solemus octavas nataliciorum aliquorum sanctorum caelebrare, eorum scilicet quorum festivitas apud nos clarior
habetur, veluti est in octavis apostolorum Petri et Pauli, et
ceterorum sanctorum quorum consuetudo diversarum ecclesiarum octavas caelebrat. Si non valemus omnium sanctorum natalicia caelebrare, quanto minus octavas eorum.
Non est nobis disserendum quae ecclesiae colant illas vel
illas octavas, sed quid nobis innuant ipsae octavae. In nataliciis sanctorum frequentamus receptiones illas in quibus animae sanctorum recipiuntur, quando exeunt de corpore.

2      De his receptionibus dicit Agustinus in sermone quadragesimo sexto super Iohannem: "Sicut ergo diversae custodiae agentium in officio, sic diversae custodiae mortuorum, et diversa merita resurgentium. Receptus est pauper,

"They kept his testimonies and his commandments, alleluia." In those feasts that we celebrate with nine lessons, we pray while standing, to recall the holy fellowship of the angels and the holy fathers, who are already in eternal joy.

# 36

# On the octaves of saints' feasts

It is our custom to celebrate the octaves of the feasts of certain saints, namely those whose feast is particularly distinguished for us, as is the case for the octaves of the apostles Peter and Paul, and of the other saints whose octaves it is the custom of various churches to celebrate. If we are unable to celebrate the feasts of all the saints, still less are we able to celebrate all their octaves. It is not for us to explain which churches celebrate which octaves, but rather what the octaves themselves suggest to us. On the feasts of the saints we observe the receptions into which the souls of the saints are received, when they leave the body.

Augustine speaks of these receptions in his forty-sixth 2 sermon on John: "For just as there are various kinds of custody for those in official positions, there are also different kinds of custody for the dead, and varying merits among those who rise again. The pauper has been received

receptus est dives, sed ille in sinu Abrahae, ille ubi sitiret et guttam aquae non inveniret [Luke 16:19–31]. Habent ergo omnes animae—ut ex hac occasione instruam caritatem vestram—habent omnes animae, cum de saeculo exierint, diversas receptiones suas; habent gaudium bonae et malae

3 tormenta. Sed cum facta fuerit resurrectio, et bonorum gaudium amplius erit et malorum tormenta graviora, quando cum corpore torquebuntur. Recepti sunt in pace sancti patriarchae, prophetae, apostoli, martyres, boni fideles, omnes tamen adhuc in fine accepturi sunt quod promisit Deus. Promissa est enim resurrectio etiam carnis, mortis consumptio, vita aeterna cum angelis. Hoc omnes simul accep-

4 turi sumus. Nam requiem quae continuo post mortem datur, si ea dignus est, tunc accipit quisque, cum moritur. Priores acceperunt patriarchae—videte ex quo requiescunt; posteriores prophetae, recentius apostoli, multo recentiores martyres sancti, cotidie boni fideles. Et alii in ista requie iam diu sunt, alii non tam diu, alii annis paucioribus, alii nec recenti tempore. Cum vero ab hoc somno evigilabunt simul omnes, quod promissum est accepturi sunt."✝

5     In nataliciis sanctorum, memoratae requiei congratulamur; in octavis vero eorum, resurrectioni corporum. Quo honore digna sit octava dies, liber Leviticus monstrat, et quid habeat in mysterio, Esicius presbyter tractat super eundem Leviticum in libro sexto. Dicit Leviticus: "Et locutus est Dominus ad Moysen, dicens: Loquere filiis Israhel: A

and the rich man has been received, but one into the bosom of Abraham and the other into a place where he thirsts and finds not a drop of water. And so all souls have—if I may take this occasion to inform your charity—all souls have, when they leave the world, their various receptions; they have the joy of the good reception and the torments of the evil reception. But when the resurrection has occurred, the 3 joy of the good will be greater and the torments of the evil more onerous, since they will then experience bodily torture. The holy patriarchs, prophets, apostles, martyrs and the good faithful have been received in peace, and all will yet receive in the end what God has promised. For the resurrection of their flesh has also been promised, and the destruction of death, and eternal life with the angels. All of us will receive this. For upon dying everyone receives the rest that 4 is granted immediately after death, if he is worthy of it. The early patriarchs received it—see through whom they rest; later on the prophets, more recently the apostles, and very recently the holy martyrs received it; and every day the good faithful receive it. And some have already been in this rest a long time, others not so long, others for a very few years, and still others not even for a short time. But when they all wake together from this sleep, they will receive what they have been promised."✝

On the feasts of the saints, we commend their afore- 5 mentioned rest; on their octaves, we commend the resurrection of their bodies. The book Leviticus shows the honor that the eighth day is worthy of, and the priest Hesychius discusses what mystery it contains in his sixth book on the same Leviticus. Leviticus says: "And the Lord spoke to Moses, saying: Say to the children of Israel: From

quinto decimo die mensis huius septimi erunt feriae taber-
naculorum septem diebus Domini. Dies primus vocabitur
caeleberrimus atque sanctissimus. Omne opus servile non
facietis, et septem diebus offeretis holocausta Domino.
Dies quoque octavus erit caeleberrimus atque sanctissimus"
[Lev 23:33–36].

6      Unde dicit memoratus Esicius: "Et primam autem septem dierum caeleberrimam atque sanctissimam appellavit—
qui enim scit praesentibus tamquam tabernaculo uti; prima
dies, id est initium et principium, a sanctificatione vocatio-
nis incipit. Propterea et nimis consequenter ait: 'Omne opus
servile non facietis,' quia nulli in saeculo serviunt qui, tamquam tabernaculum et transitoria, ea quae in eo sunt, inten-
dunt. Sed et septem diebus holocausta offerri praecepit,
ostendens oportere per omne tempus perfectam conversationem sequi. Quando ergo istam praesentem vitam percurre-
rimus, tunc caeleberrimum atque sanctissimum octavum
7      diem—saeculum videlicet futurum—habebimus." Et infra:
"Die autem primo requies, et in octava die requies—non
iam septimo, cum numero septem dierum festivitatem agi
proposuisset—sed octavo. Primum quidem, quia his qui secundum litteram legem tenent, festivitatem caelebrare non
licet; novo enim segregatus est populo, qui scit legem secundum spiritum accipere et octavum honorare, quem diximus
significare mortuorum resurrectionem."

the fifteenth day of this same seventh month shall be kept the feast of tabernacles for seven days of the Lord. The first day shall be called most solemn and most holy. You shall do no servile work, and for seven days you shall offer holocausts to the Lord. The eighth day also shall be most solemn and most holy."

Thus the aforementioned Hesychius says: "And he called the first of the seven days most solemn and most holy—he who knows to treat the present life as a tabernacle; the first day, that is the beginning and the origin, begins with the sanctification of his calling. Therefore he also says, quite importantly: 'You shall do no servile work,' because those who regard this world as a tabernacle and the things that are in it as transitory serve nobody in this world. And he also ordered that holocausts be offered for seven days to show that one should pursue a perfect way of life at all times. When we have passed through this present life, therefore, we will have a most solemn and holy eighth day—namely, the world to come." And further on: "But on the first day there is rest, and on the eighth day there is rest—not yet on the seventh, since he had declared that the feast was to be celebrated for seven days—but on the eighth. In the first place, this is because those who keep the law according to the letter are not allowed to celebrate the feast; they have been set apart from the new people, who know to receive the law according to the spirit and to honor the eighth day, which we have said signifies the resurrection of the dead."

## 37

# De observatione dierum per annum

Ubi sanctus Hieronimus exponit illud ad Galatas—"Dies observatis, et menses, et tempora, et annos. Timeo vos, ne forte sine causa laboraverim in vobis" [Gal 4:10–11]—ibi sententiam Christianorum subnectit contra eos qui volunt nobis opponere quod observemus dies et tempora (unde arguti sunt a Paulo neuterici Christiani).

2 Dicit inter alia ita: "Dicat aliquis: Si dies observare non licet et menses et tempora et annos, nos quoque similiter crimen incurrimus, quartam sabbati observantes et Parascheven et diem Dominicam et ieiunium Quadragesimae et Paschae festivitatem et Pentecostes laetitiam et, pro varietate regionum, diversa in honore martyrum tempora 3 constituta. Ad quod qui simpliciter respondebit, dicit non eosdem Iudaicae observationis dies esse, quos nostros. Nos enim non azimorum pascha caelebramus, sed resurrectionis et crucis. Nec septem iuxta morem Israhel numeramus ebdomadas in Pentecoste; sed Spiritus Sancti veneramur adventum. Et ne inordinate congregati populi fides minueretur in Christo, propterea dies aliqui constituti sunt, ut in unum omnes pariter veniremus—non quo caelebrior sit dies illa qua convenimus, sed quo quacumque die conveniendum sit, ex conspectu mutuo laetitia maior oriatur. 4 Qui vero oppositae quaestioni acutius respondere conatur,

568

## 37

# On observing days throughout the year

Where Saint Jerome explains that verse to the Galatians
—"You observe days and months and seasons and years. I
am afraid of you, lest perhaps I have labored in vain among
you"—he includes a Christian reply to those who want to
oppose us because we observe days and seasons (for which
reason the new Christians were denounced by Paul).

Among other things, he says the following: "Someone 2
may say: If it is not permitted to observe days and months
and seasons and years, we likewise commit a crime when we
observe Wednesday and Friday and Sunday and the Lenten
fast and the Easter feast and the joy of Pentecost and the different seasons established in various regions in honor of the
martyrs. He who will answer this simply says that the days 3
the Jews observed are not the same days that we observe.
For we do not celebrate the pasch of unleavened bread, but
the pasch of the resurrection and of the cross. Nor do we include seven weeks in Pentecost, or the Feast of Weeks, after
the custom of Israel; instead we venerate the coming of the
Holy Spirit. And to prevent the faith of the people in Christ
from being diminished by irregular gatherings, certain days
were established, that we might come together equally, as
one—not so that the day when we gather might be more distinguished, but so that on whatever day we gather, greater joy
might arise from the sight of one another. But he who aims 4
to respond to the question that has been posed more keenly,

illud affirmat, omnes dies aequales esse, nec Parascheve tantum Christum crucifigi et die Dominica resurgere, sed semper sanctum resurrectionis esse diem, et semper eum carne
vesci Dominica. Ieiunia autem et congregationes inter dies
propter eos a viris prudentibus constituta, qui magis saeculo
vacant quam Deo, nec possunt—imo nolunt—toto in ecclesiam vitae suae tempore congregari, et ante humanos actus
Deo orationum suarum offerre sacrificium.

5    "Quotus enim quisque est qui saltim haec pauca quae statuta sunt—vel orandi tempora vel ieiunandi—semper exerceat? Itaque, sicut nobis licet vel ieiunare semper vel semper
orare, et diem Dominicam accepto Domini corpore inde-
sinenter caelebrare gaudentibus—non ita et Iudaeis fas est
omni tempore immolare agnum, Pentecosten agere, taber-
nacula figere, ieiunare cotidie."✝

6    Post enumerationem temporum quae observabantur
tempore in illo quando beatus Hieronimus haec scripsit, il-
lata est causa quare Christiani, tempora memorata observantes, crimen non incurrant. Hoc est: "Qui simpliciter respondebit, dicit non eosdem Iudaicae observationis dies
esse quos nostros," et cetera quae sequuntur. Et iterum
infra: "Qui vero oppositae quaestioni acutius respondere
conatur, illud affirmat, omnes dies aequales esse, nec Parascheve tantum Christum crucifigi et die Dominica resurgere, sed semper sanctum resurrectionis esse diem, et semper eum carne vesci Dominica."

affirms that all days are equal, and that Christ is not crucified only on Friday and he does not rise only on Sunday; instead, the holy day of his resurrection is always, and he always partakes of the Lord's flesh. But the fasts and the gatherings on various days were established by prudent men for the sake of those who have more time for the world than for God, and are unable—indeed, unwilling—to be assembled in church for the full space of their lives, and to offer the sacrifice of their prayers to God before engaging in human affairs.

"Indeed, how many always perform even these few things 5 that have been established—either the times of prayer or fasting? And so, while it is always appropriate for us to fast or to pray, and, upon receiving the Lord's body, to celebrate Sunday with those who rejoice unceasingly—it is not right for the Jews to sacrifice a lamb, to observe the Feast of Weeks, to fix tabernacles or to fast daily in every season."✝

After enumerating the seasons that were observed at the 6 time when blessed Jerome wrote these things, the reason why the Christians do not commit a crime in observing the aforementioned seasons is introduced. That is: "He who will answer this simply says that the days the Jews observed are not the same days that we observe," and so forth as follows. And again, further on: "But he who aims to respond to the question that has been posed more keenly, affirms that all days are equal, and that Christ is not crucified only on Friday and he does not rise only on Sunday; instead, the holy day of his resurrection is always, and he always partakes of the Lord's flesh."

7    Superior excusatio, in qua dicitur non eosdem dies esse in observatione apud nos qui apud Iudaeos observantur, aliquod supplementum nobis accommodat, qui propterea tempore passionis Domini amittimus salutationem solitam quia Iudas salutavit Dominum falso; et genuflexionem in orationem die Parascheves (quae fit pro Iudaeis, quia Iesu illudendo genuflectebant), et in oratione duodecim lectionum, quando memoratur passio trium puerorum in fornace, quia nolebant poplite flexo adorare statuam Nabochodonosoris cum perfidis; et invitatorium in diebus passionis Domini, quando Iudaei congregabantur ad pessima consilia de

8    nece Domini. Similiter in Teophania invitatorium amittimus, quando Herodes congregavit sapientes Iudaeorum pravo animo ad inquirendum ubi Christus nasceretur.

9    Quartam feriam et Parascheven et diem Dominicam et ieiunium Quadragesimae et Paschae festivitatem et Pentecostes laetitiam et, pro varietate regionum, diversa in honore martyrum tempora constituta observamus. Quartam feriam observamus, quia, ut Agustinus ait ad Casulanum, in ea die congregati sunt Iudaei, et consiliati sunt de nece salvatoris; Parascheven, quia in eo passus est idem salvator.

10   Quoniam isti dies antiquitus erant in observatione, ritus Romanae ecclesiae obtinuit ut isdem diebus mutaret officia et Missam caelebraret ora nona, per quod forinsecus populus congregaretur in unum quando aliqua causa nova imminebat ad deprecandum, in quibus observatio caelebrabatur.

11   Unde dicit Hieronimus memoratus in superioribus: "Ieiunia autem et congregationes inter dies propter eos sunt a viris

The earlier excuse, where it is said that the days that the   7
Jews observed are not the same days that we do, provides
some reinforcement for us, as we omit the customary greeting in the season of the Lord's passion because Judas greeted
the Lord falsely; and we omit kneeling both during prayer
on Good Friday (which we do because of the Jews, for they
knelt while mocking Jesus), and also during the prayer of
twelve lessons, when the suffering of the three boys in the
furnace is recounted, because they refused to adore the
statue of Nebuchadnezzar on bended knee with the other
faithless; and we omit the invitatory during the days of the
Lord's passion, when the Jews gathered for their detestable
conspiracies concerning the Lord's murder. We likewise   8
omit the invitatory on Epiphany, when Herod called together the wise men among the Jews for the evil purpose of
inquiring where Christ was born.

We observe Wednesday and Friday and Sunday and the   9
Lenten fast and the feast of Easter and the joy of Pentecost
and various seasons established in different regions in honor
of the martyrs. We observe Wednesday because, as Augustine said to Casulanus, on that day the Jews gathered and
conspired about the murder of the savior. We observe Friday because on that day the same savior suffered. Because   10
these days have been in observance since ancient times, the
rite of the Roman church prevailed in adjusting its offices
on the days when an observance was celebrated and celebrating Mass at the ninth hour; in this way the people outside, among whom the observance was celebrated, would be
gathered together when a new occasion for praying was im-
pending. Thus the aforementioned Jerome says, above: "But   11
the fasts and the gatherings on various days were established

prudentibus constituta, qui magis saeculo vacant quam Deo, nec possunt—imo nolunt—toto in ecclesiam vitae suae tempore congregari, et ante humanos actus Deo orationum suarum offerre sacrificium. Quotus enim quisque est qui saltim haec pauca quae statuta sunt, vel orandi tempora vel ieiunandi, semper exerceat?" et reliqua.

12    Habemus ex Romano ordine Sabbati diem in observatione, quem non computavit Hieronimus in ordine dierum observationis. Novimus enim ex multis auctoribus quod dies sabbati, sicut quarta sabbati et sexta, inclusa erat ieiunio apud Romanos, et in eo officium mutatum habemus saepe, sicut in quarta et sexta sabbati. Et praecipue in ea benedictio datur, quia ipsa est quam benedixit Dominus, et proprie significatio ad Sanctum Spiritum pertinet, qui est septiformis. Unde, cum et Pater spiritus sit et Filius spiritus sit, quoniam Deus spiritus est; et Pater sanctus et Filius sanctus sit, proprio tamen nomine amborum spiritus vocatur Spiritus Sanctus.

13    De eodem Sabbato diverso modo observatum est apud Orientes, et apud aliquos Occidentes, nec non et apud Romanam urbem. De qua re sufficienter tractatum est a sancto Agustino in epistola ad Casulanum presbyterum, de quibus pauca hic inseram. De varietate, inquit, ad Casulanum de Urbico: "Non tibi persuadeat urbem Christianam sic laudare Sabbato ieiunantem, ut cogaris orbem Christianum damnare prandentem." Et iterum ex responsione sancti Ambrosii in eadem epistola, qui inquit: "Quando hic sum, non ieiuno Sabbato; quando Romae sum, ieiuno Sabbato. Et ad quamcumque ecclesiam veneritis, eius morem servate,

by prudent men for the sake of those who have more time for the world than for God, and are unable—indeed, unwilling—to be assembled in church for the full space of their lives, and to offer the sacrifice of their prayers to God before engaging in human affairs," and so forth.

According to the Roman rite we keep Saturday in observance, which Jerome did not list it among his days of observance. For we know from many authors that the Romans included Saturday, along with Wednesday and Friday, in fasting, and on that day we often adjust our offices as on Wednesday and Friday. And blessing is bestowed on that day in particular, because that is the day that the Lord blessed, and it is particularly significant for the Holy Spirit, who is sevenfold. Thus, although the Father is spirit and the Son is spirit, because God is spirit; and the Father is holy and the Son is holy, the spirit of both is nevertheless referred to, by its proper name, as the Holy Spirit.

This same Saturday is observed differently among those in the East, some in the West, and also in the city of Rome. This matter was discussed well enough by Augustine in his letter to the priest Casulanus, from which I will insert a few points here. He speaks to Casulanus about Urbicus, concerning the variation: "Do not let him persuade you that a Christian city promotes fasting on Saturday, to the extent that you are forced to condemn the rest of the Christian world that breaks its fast on Saturday." And again, from the reply of Saint Ambrose in the same letter, who says: "When I am here I do not fast on Saturday; when I am at Rome, I fast on Saturday. Observe the custom of whatever church

14 si pati scandalum non vultis aut facere."✝ Scriptum est in *Vita beati Ambrosii* quod ipse Ambrosius ieiunaret ceteros dies ebdomadae, Sabbato et Dominico pranderet. Quare prandio uteretur in Sabbato aut in Dominica, memoratus Agustinus monstrat in memorata epistola, scribens de Sabbato sic: "Quibus autem diebus non oporteat ieiunari et quibus oportea praecepto Domini vel apostolorum non invenio definitum. Ac per hoc sentio quidem—non ad obtinendam veritatem (quam fides obtinet) atque iustitiam (in qua est pulchritudo filiae regis intrinsecus)—sed tamen ad significandam requiem sempiternam, ubi est verum Sabbatum, relaxationem quam constrictionem ieiunii aptius con-

15 venire." Et infra: "Duo quippe sunt quae iustorum beatitudinem et omnis miseriae finem sperare faciunt: mors et resurrectio mortuorum. In morte requies est de qua dicitur per prophetam: 'Plebs mea: intra in cellaria tua, abscondere pusillum, donec transeat ira Domini' [Isa 26:20]. In resurrectione autem in homine toto—id est, in carne et spiritu— perfecta felicitas. Hinc factum est ut horum duorum utrumque non significandum putaretur labore ieiunii, sed potius refectionis hilaritate—excepto Paschali uno Sabbato, quo discipulorum, sicut diximus, luctus propter rei gestae memoriam fuerat ieiunio prolixiore signandum."✝

16    Huic enim sensui potest congruere, quando festivitates sanctorum caelebramus, ut in prioribus festivitatibus congratulemur animabus sanctorum, et in octavis eorundem

you come to, if you do not wish to endure or cause a scandal."✝ It is written in the *Life of Blessed Ambrose* that Ambrose himself fasted on the other days of the week; on Saturday and Sunday he broke his fast. The aforementioned Augustine shows in the aforementioned letter why he partook of breakfast on Saturday and Sunday, writing on Saturday as follows: "I have not found that the Lord or the apostles established by precept on which days it is not permitted to fast and on which days it is permitted. And for this reason I feel that relaxing the fast, rather than maintaining it, is more apt and appropriate—not for obtaining truth (which faith obtains) and justice (which has the beauty of the king's daughter within it)—but rather for signifying eternal rest, where there is a true Sabbath." And further on: "For there are two things that cause us to hope for the happiness of the just and the end of all misery: death and the resurrection of the dead. In death there is the rest that the prophet speaks about: 'My people: enter into your chambers, hide for a moment, until the Lord's anger pass away.' But in the resurrection there is perfect happiness in the whole man—that is, in the flesh and the spirit. And thus it happened that both of these were thought to be signified not by the labor of fasting, but rather by the joy of refreshment—with the exception of one Saturday during Easter, when the mourning of the disciples, as we said above, was to be signified by a longer fast in memory of what had occurred."✝

And it can coincide with this interpretation, when we celebrate the feasts of the saints, that on their initial feasts we rejoice in the souls of the saints, and on the octaves of

sanctorum resurrectioni corporum. Pro hac re solebant omnes Romani omnia Sabbata ieiunare, quam modo dixit beatus Agustinus in uno Sabbato observari. Propterea dico praeteritum quia nescio quomodo nunc agant.

17    Si quis voluerit episcoporum Ambrosium imitari, usquequaque non erit extorres a consortio sanctorum. Ponatur populus in doctrina sancti Agustini, ubi dicit in memorata epistola: "Libenter acquiescas episcopo tuo in hac re; noli resistere, et quod facit ipse sine ullo scrupulo vel disceptatione sectare."✝ Ut omnis disceptatio discolis absit propter
18
diversa haec ieiunia, dummodo teneatur fides, spes et caritas in idipsum (quibus omnis doctrina prophetarum et scientia scripturarum servit), repetit versum saepe sanctus Agustinus in memorata epistola: "Astitit regina a dextris tuis in vestitu deaurato, circumamicta varietate" [Ps 44:10].

19    Observatur etiam apud nos in aliquibus locis unus dies, id est secunda feria; qui non deputatus est in observatione a memoratis auctoribus, id est a sancto Innocentio et sancto Ambrosio et sancto Agustino nec non et beato Hieronimo. Quem adhuc solent nostri principes in ieiunio ligare, quando indicitur triduanum ieiunium instar Ninivitarum. Quod, ut reor, potest habere normam a praedicatione Pauli, qui dixit: "Alius iudicat diem inter diem, alius iudicat omnem diem"
20    [Rom 14:5]. Tamen exponens illud Ambrosius, de ceteris silet, quartam et sextam sabbati introducit, iuxta morem quem tenebat populus qui ei tunc notus erat. Verius tamen implent quod dicit Paulus qui, inter Dominicum diem et

these same saints we rejoice in the resurrection of their bodies. For this reason it was the custom of the Romans to fast on all Saturdays, as the blessed Augustine just now said was done on one Saturday. I speak of the past because I do not know how they do things now.

If any of the bishops should want to imitate Ambrose, he 17 will not be completely out of company with the saints. Let the people be instilled in the teaching of Saint Augustine, when he says in the aforementioned epistle: "You should freely acquiesce to your bishop in this matter; do not resist, and do what he does without any anxiety or disagreement."✝ To avoid any ill-tempered disagreement over these 18 different fasts, while keeping hold of faith, hope and charity (which all the teaching of the prophets and the knowledge of scriptures are in service of), Saint Augustine often repeats a verse in his aforementioned letter: "The queen stood on your right hand in gilded clothing, surrounded with variety."

One day, namely Monday, is also observed among us in 19 some locations. It is not included in observation by the aforementioned authors, that is by Saint Innocent and Saint Ambrose and Saint Augustine and also the blessed Jerome. Still, it is the custom of our leaders to bind it with the fast, when a three-day fast after the example of the Ninevites is proclaimed. I think that it can depend on the precept preached by Paul, who said: "One judges between day and day, and another judges every day." While explaining this 20 verse, Ambrose is nevertheless silent about the other days, but mentions Wednesday and Friday, according to the custom that the people who were known to him at the time observed. Nevertheless, they fulfill Paul's statement more truly

tertiam sabbati refectionis medium ieiunant secundam sabbati; iterum inter tertiam sabbati et quintam refectionis ieiunant quartam; et iterum inter quintam sabbati et septimam refectionis ieiunant sextam.

21    Dies Dominicus interdictus est ad ieiunandum in libro qui proprie vocatur *Canones.* Rationem interdictionis sanctus Agustinus aperit in memorata epistola ad Casulanum: "Die," inquit, "Dominico ieiunare scandalum magnum est, maxime postea quam innotuit detestabilis multumque fidei catholicae scripturisque divinis apertissime contraria haeresis Manicheorum, qui suis auditoribus ad ieiunandum istum tamquam legitimum constituerunt diem, per quod factum est ut ieiunium diei Dominici horribilius haberetur."✝

22    Sanctus Hieronimus unam Quadragesimam ponit in observatione. Nos observamus tres quadragesimas—id est ante Pascha Domini, circaque festivitatem sancti Iohannis, et ante Nativitatem Domini. Sit a piis mentibus frequentatum apud nos. Apud sanctum Hieronimum manifestum est quod Montanus hereticus illam observationem trium quadragesimarum statuerit apud suos—id est tres qua-

23    dragesimas per annum. Apud nos quoque non est dubium quin praeparare nos debeamus in Adventu Domini multis piis operibus. Natalicia sanctorum observantur apud nos, de quibus dicit beatus Agustinus in memorata epistola: "Diebus Dominicis omnibus et quinquaginta post Pascha, et per diversa loca diebus solemnibus martyrum, et festis quibusque prandetur."✝ Solemus post octavas Nativitatis Domini octavas caelebrare sancti Stephani et Iohannis Evangelistae atque Innocentum, ut earum octavarum cantu

who, between eating on Sunday and Tuesday, fast in between on Monday; and also between eating on Tuesday and Thursday, fast on Wednesday; and also between eating on Thursday and Saturday, fast on Friday.

It is forbidden to fast on Sunday in the book that is enti- 21 tled the *Canons*. Saint Augustine reveals the reason for this prohibition in his aforementioned letter to Casulanus: "It is a great scandal to fast on Sunday," he says, "especially since the detestable heresy of the Manicheans, greatly and openly opposed to the catholic faith and divine scriptures, has gained notoriety. They established this day among their followers as one legitimate for fasting, and on that account it has happened that fasting on Sunday is considered dreadful."✝

Saint Jerome places one forty-day fast, Lent, in obser- 22 vance. We observe three forty-day fasts—that is, before the Lord's Easter, for the feast of Saint John, and before the Lord's Nativity. Let this be the practice of pious minds among us. For Saint Jerome, it is clear that the heretic Montanus established the observance of three forty-day fasts among his followers—that is, three forty-day fasts in one year. For us there is likewise no doubt that we should pre- 23 pare ourselves for the Lord's Advent with many pious works. And we observe the feasts of the saints, which the blessed Augustine speaks about in his aforementioned letter: "The fast is broken on all Sundays and on the fiftieth day after Easter, and in various regions on the solemnities of the martyrs and on other feasts."✝ It is our custom to celebrate the octaves of Saint Stephen and John the Evangelist and the Innocents after the octave of the Lord's Nativity, that by

24 perveniamus ferme usque ad vigilias Teophaniae. De ieiunio quod facimus ante Ascensionem Domini, manifestum est a quo auctore habeat exordium—de quo nihil dicendum est— quoniam dicit idem beatus Agustinus: "In his enim rebus de quibus nihil certi statuit scriptura divina, mos populi Dei et instituta maiorum pro lege tenenda sunt."✝ Tamen non possumus dicere quod de laetitia dierum Pentecostes non sit scriptum a sanctis auctoribus.

# 38

## Qua reverentia et metu standum sit in ecclesia, quando caelebrantur mysteria divina

Quoniam de nataliciis sanctorum pauca praelibavimus, iuvat subnectere verba Iohannis Chrisostomi, ut his ammonear quomodo me ipsum debeam coercere a superfluis verbis et risu, quatenus coram sancto altari astitero. Dicit idem in tractatu duodecimo super epistolam ad Ebreos: "Stat sacerdos Dei orationem offerens cunctorum—tu autem rides, nihil timens? Et ille quidem tremens pro te orationem offert—tu autem contemnis? Non avertis scripturam

singing these octaves we may nearly arrive at the vigil of
Epiphany. As for the fast that we observe before the Lord's   24
Ascension, it is clear with whom it originated—about whom
there is nothing to say—since the same blessed Augustine
says: "For in those matters about which divine scripture has
established nothing certain, the custom of God's people and
the traditions of our forefathers are to be held as law."☩ Yet
we cannot proclaim what has not been written by the holy
authors concerning rejoicing on the days of Pentecost.

## 38

# On the reverence and fear with which we should stand in church, when the divine mysteries are celebrated

Because we set forth a few points on the feasts of the
saints, it is helpful to add the words of John Chrysostom,
that through them I may be advised about how I should
keep myself from excess words and laughter, for as long
as I assist at the holy altar. In his twelfth tract on the letter
to the Hebrews, the same author says: "God's priest stands
and offers the prayer of all—but you laugh and fear nothing? And he trembles in offering prayers on your behalf—
while you are disdainful? Do you not turn to the scripture

dicentem: 'Ve contemptoribus'? Non contremiscis? Non
2 colligis temet ipsum? Et in aulam quidem regiam intraturus,
et habitu et oculis et incessu et cunctis aliis componis et or-
nas temet ipsum. Huc autem ingressurus, ubi vere aula est
regia—et talis qualis caelestis est—rides. Et tu quidem
nescis quia non vides. Audi tamen quia angeli praesentes
sunt ubique, et maxime in domo Dei astant regi, et omnia
plena sunt incorporeis illis virtutibus.

3 "Iste mihi sermo etiam ad mulieres dicitur. Et ante viros
quidem non citius hoc audent facere, ac si faciunt non tamen semper, sed in tempore remissionis. Hic autem et velas
et obnubis caput tuum. Dic mihi—et rides, o mulier, in
ecclesia sedens? Ingressa es confiteri peccata tua, procidere
Deo, postulare et deprecari pro delictis tuis, et cum risu hoc
facis? Quomodo ergo eum propitiare poteris? Et quid ma-
4 lum est risus? inquis. Non est malus risus. Itane non est malum? Sed valde malum, importuno tempore, inmoderate.
Risus enim inest nobis, ut, quando amicos viderimus post
multum temporis, hoc faciamus; quando aliquos delinquen-
tes et timentes, ut foveamus eos risu—non ut cogamus nos
ipsos et semper rideamus. Risus inest animae nostrae, ut remissionem habeat aliquando anima—non ut diffundatur."

that says 'Alas, despisers'? Do you not tremble? Do you not collect yourself? And when you are about to enter a royal court, you compose and adorn yourself with respect to your dress and your eyes and your gait and in all else. But when you are about to enter here, where there is truly a royal court—and one that is heavenly—you laugh. And of course you do not know because you do not see. But take it from me that angels are present everywhere, and they assist the king especially in God's house, and all things are full of these incorporeal powers.

"My sermon is also directed to the women. Of course, before men they do not readily dare do this, and if they do so it is not all the time, but during the season of penance. But here you veil and cover your heads. Tell me, woman—do you also laugh as you sit in church? You have entered to confess your sins, to fall prostrate before God, to beg and plead for your transgressions, and you do this with laughter? How then will you be able to appease him? And you say: What evil there is in a laugh? Laughter is not evil. So it is not evil? To the contrary, it is a great evil in immoderation and at an unfit time. For laughter is in us, that we may use it when we see friends after a long time, and that we may encourage those who have done wrong and are afraid with laughter—not that we may always laugh when we gather together. There is laughter in our soul, that our soul may sometimes have release—not that it may be dissipated."

# 39

# Iterum de tonsura clericorum

Memini me dixisse in superioribus dubitando, utrum corona clericorum nostrorum formam primo acciperet a sancto Petro an a successoribus eius, scilicet episcopis urbis Romae. Repperi postea auctoritatem huiusce rei Bedae famuli Dei in *Historia Anglorum,* capitulo vigesimo primo, ex epistola Ceolfrid abbatis ad Aitanum regem Pictorum:

2    "Verum, etsi profiteri nobis liberum est quia tonsurae discrimen non noceat quibus pura in Deum fides et caritas in proximum sincera est, maxime cum numquam patribus catholicis, sicut de Paschae vel fidei diversitate conflictus, ita etiam de tonsurae differentia legatur aliqua fuisse contro-

3    versia: Inter omnes tamen quas vel in ecclesia vel in universo hominum genere repperimus tonsuras, nullam magis sequendam nobis amplectendamque iure dixerim ea, quam in capite suo gestabat ille cui se confitenti Dominus ait: 'Tu es Petrus, et super hanc petram aedificabo ecclesiam meam, et portae inferi non praevalebunt adversus eam. Et tibi dabo claves regni caelorum' [Matt 16:18–19]; nullam magis abominandam detestandamque merito cunctis fidelibus crediderim ea quam habebat ille, cui gratiam Spiritus Sancti comparare volenti idem Petrus ait: 'Pecunia tua tecum sit in perditione, quoniam donum Dei existimasti

## 39

# Again, on the clerical tonsure

I remember that, above, I spoke in doubt about whether the crown of our clergy first received its shape from Saint Peter or from his successors, namely the bishops of the city of Rome. I later found an authority for this question in the *History of the English,* by Bede, the servant of God, chapter 21, quoting from a letter of the abbot Ceolfrith to Nechtan, king of the Picts:

"And although we freely acknowledge that differences in tonsure are not harmful to those who have pure faith in God and sincere charity toward one another, especially since no controversy among the catholic fathers, like the conflicts concerning differences in Easter or in faith, has ever been read of concerning differences in tonsure: Nevertheless, among all the tonsures that we have seen, either in church or in the entire human race, I would say that we should follow and embrace none more rightly than the one he wore, to whom the Lord said in answer to his confession of belief: 'You are Peter, and upon this rock I will build my church, and the gates of hell shall not prevail against it. And I will give to you the keys of the kingdom of heaven.' And I would say that it is appropriate for none to be more despised and accursed among all the faithful, than that which he who wanted to buy the grace of the Holy Spirit wore, and to whom Peter said: 'Keep your money to yourself to perish with you, because you have thought that the gift of God

per pecuniam possideri. Non est tibi pars neque sors in sermone hoc' [Acts 8:20–21].

4    "Neque vero ob id tamen in coronam attondimur quia Petrus ita attonsus est, sed quia Petrus in memoriam Dominicae passionis ita attonsus est, idcirco et nos, qui per eandem passionem salvari desideramus, ipsius passionis signum cum illo in vertice—summa videlicet corporis nostri parte—

5    gestamus. Sicut enim omnis ecclesia, quia per mortem sui vivificatoris ecclesia facta est, signum sanctae crucis eius in fronte portare consuevit, ut crebro vexilli huius munimine a malignorum spirituum defendatur incursibus, crebra huius admonitione doceatur se quoque carnem suam cum vitiis et

6    concupiscentiis crucifigere debere. Ita etiam oportet eos qui, vel monachi votum vel gradum clericatus habentes, artioribus se necesse habent pro Domino continentiae frenis astringere, formam quoque coronae quam ipse in passione spineam portavit in capite, ut spinas ac tribulos peccatorum nostrorum portaret, id est exportaret et auferret a nobis, suo quemque in capite per tonsuram proferre, ut se etiam inrisiones et obprobria pro illo libenter ac prompte omnia sufferre ipso etiam frontispitio doceant, ut coronam vitae aeternae, quam repromisit Deus diligentibus se, semper expectare, proque huius perceptione et adversa se mundi et prospera contempnere designent."

may be purchased with money. You have no part nor lot in this matter.'

"But we are not tonsured with our crown because Peter    4
was so tonsured, but rather because Peter was tonsured thus
in memory of the Lord's passion; and so we, too, who wish
to be saved through the same passion, wear the sign of that
passion on the top of our head—that is, on the highest part
of our body—with him. For it is the custom of every church    5
to bear the sign of his holy cross on its facade, because the
church was founded through the death of him who gave it
life, that through the repeated protection of this banner
it might be defended from the attacks of evil spirits, and
through its repeated admonition it might be taught that it
should crucify its flesh, together with its vices and desires.
In the same way, those who have either vows, as monks, or    6
rank, as clerics, must bind themselves with tighter cords of
continence on the Lord's behalf, and each must bear on his
head, as a tonsure, the likeness of the crown that the Lord
wore during his passion upon his head as a crown of thorns,
to carry the thorns and thistles of our sins—to carry them
off, that is, and take them away from us. In this way the
mockery and contempt that they receive because of their
tonsure may teach them, through their very front, to suffer
all things freely and readily, and they may show that they are
ever awaiting the crown of eternal life that God promised to
those who love him; and with a view toward receiving this,
they may hold the adversities and prosperities of the world
in contempt."

7    Dicit idem Beda de tonsura in *Vita venerabilis et sanctissimi
Cuthberti episcopi:* "Postquam servitutis Christi iugum ton-
suraeque Petri formam, in modum coronae spineae caput
Christi cingentis, Domino adiuvante, susceperat."+ Suffi-
ciant haec ad demonstrandum quid memoratus Dei famulus
Beda sentiret de auctore coronae nostrae.

## 40

# Mentio iterum qua hora diei Missa caelebranda sit a libere vacantibus

Retulimus in huiusce operis verbis prohibitum esse ab
apostolicis viris Missam caelebrari ante horam tertiam, et
tamen indidi quod vidi—hoc est Leonem nuperum Missam
caelebrare diluculo. Additum est in *Gestis pontificalibus* qua
de re Missa caelebranda sit circa horam tertiam—scilicet,
quia eadem hora Dominus crucifixus est linguis Iudaeorum.
Addidimus etiam propter nostram consuetudinem inolitam,
sexta hora rationabiliter posse Missam caelebrari, quia sexta
hora diei Dominus crucifixus est manibus persecutorum;
similiter et hora nona, quia tunc emisit spiritum.

The same Bede speaks about the tonsure in his *Life of* 7
*the Venerable and Holy Bishop Cuthbert:* "Afterward, with the
Lord's help, he received the yoke of Christ's servitude and
the form of Peter's tonsure, after the manner of the crown
of thorns that bound Christ's head."+ These points are suf-
ficient to demonstrate what the aforementioned servant of
God, Bede, thought about the inventor of our crown.


40

# Again, mention about the hour of the day when Mass is to be celebrated by those who are otherwise unoccupied

We related in the words of this work that the popes for-
bade the celebration of Mass before the third hour, but I
also included what I saw—that is, that the recent pope Leo
celebrated Mass at daybreak. In the *Deeds of the Bishops* it is
added why Mass should be celebrated around the third hour
—namely, because the Lord was crucified by the tongues of
the Jews at that hour. Because of our established conven-
tion, we also added that it is reasonable to celebrate Mass at
the sixth hour, because the Lord was crucified by the hands
of his persecutors at the sixth hour of the day; and likewise
at the ninth hour, because he gave up his spirit then.

2    Manifestum est Missam caelebrari praecipue in recordatione passionis Domini nostri Iesu Christi. In cuius commemoratione agatur, ex ipsis verbis quae in canone leguntur
manifeste liquet: "Haec," inquit, "quotiescumque feceritis,
in mei memoriam facietis. Unde et memores sumus, Domine, nos tui servi, sed et plebs tua sancta, Christi Filii tui
Domini Dei nostri tam beatae passionis nec non et ab inferis resurrectionis sed et in caelos gloriosae ascensionis."

3    Quae aguntur in caelebratione Missae post initiatum canonem, Domini passionem et resurrectionem ac in caelos
ascensionem recolunt. De quibus omnibus quae mihi occur-
rerunt tetigi, quando de officio Missae scripsi.

4    Postea recordatus sum sanctum Gregorium insinuasse
nobis Cassium Narniensem episcopum accedere hora tertia
ad Missarum solempnia, quod diligenti cura studui hic inse-
rere, ut me ipsum ammonerem—quamvis vidissem apostolicum Leonem diluculo caelebrasse Missam seu caeteros
presbyteros in Romana ecclesia—non tamen excidisse a
sancto Gregorio, quod hora tertia caelebranda esset Missa,
praesertim cum idem papa referat in omelia sua habita in
basilica sancti Sebastiani, die festivitatis ipsius, memorato
Cassio episcopo mandatum esse ut instaret operi quod
operabatur, per presbyterum quemdam Domino nostro Iesu
Christo dicente: "Age quod agis, operare quod operaris; non
cesset manus tua; non cesset pes tuus; natali Apostolorum

5    venies ad me et reddam tibi mercedem tuam." Quid idem
episcopus ageret idem sanctus Gregorius manifestat in eadem omelia—scilicet, Missam cotidie caelebravit. Et qua

It is clear that Mass is celebrated primarily in commem- 2
oration of the passion of our Lord Jesus Christ. In whose
commemoration it is celebrated is abundantly obvious from
the very words that are read in the canon: "However often
you do these things," it says, "you will do them in my memory. And so we your servants, Lord, together with your holy
people, are mindful of the blessed passion of Christ your
Son our Lord God, and also of his resurrection from the
dead and his glorious resurrection into heaven." Those 3
things that are done during the celebration of Mass after the
beginning of the canon recall the Lord's passion and resurrection and ascension into heaven. I touched on all these
things as they occurred to me, when I wrote on the office of
the Mass.

Afterward, I remembered that Saint Gregory had in- 4
formed us that Cassius, the bishop of Narni, proceeded
to the solemnities of Mass at the third hour. With dili-
gent care I strove to include that here, to remind myself—
though I saw Pope Leo and other priests in the Roman
church celebrate Mass at daybreak—that I nevertheless
did not depart from Saint Gregory, because Mass was to
be celebrated at the third hour. This is especially so, as
the same pope relates in the homily he delivered in Saint
Sebastian's basilica, on the day of his feast, that the aforementioned bishop Cassius was ordered to attend closely
to the work that he was performing. Our Lord Jesus Christ
spoke to him through a certain priest: "Do what you are doing, work what you are working; do not stop your hands;
do not stop your feet; on the feast of the apostles you will
come to me and I will give you your reward." The same Saint 5
Gregory reveals in the same homily what the same bishop
was doing—namely, he was celebrating daily Mass. And in

hora ad Missam iret, in sequentibus aperit, dicens: "Quibus auditis, episcopus in oratione se cum magna cordis contritione prostravit; et qui oblaturus sacrificium ad horam tertiam venerat, hoc pro extensae orationis magnitudine ad horam nonam usque protelavit."✠

6    Ut opinor, sanctus Gregorius eamdem horam voluit caelebrare in caelebratione suae Missae quam cognovit acceptabilem esse Domino per exhortationem factam ab eo ad illum episcopum, quem dixit ad horam tertiam venisse ad Missarum solempnia—salvo tamen constituto circa oram nonam per dies abstinentiae.

7    Si enim in ceteris oris ex constituto agitur Missa, ratio quaedam adest qua defendatur eadem hora, veluti est in Nativitate Domini, in qua nocte caelebratur Missa propter nativitatem panis qui nunc cotidie manditur ex altari, sive propter concentum angelorum; quod iam retulimus. In eodem mane caelebratur Missa propter exortum novae lucis, seu propter visitationem pastorum ad praesepe Domini, in quo invenerunt pabulum unde cotidie animae sanctorum

8    reficiuntur. Similiter habemus officia constituta in festivitate Iohannis Evangelistae et Iohannis Baptystae primo diluculo, qui utrique ex utero matris—id est ab accepto lumine huius mundi—in semet ipsis sacrificium singulare quoddam Deo obtulerunt. Iohannes Evangelista obtulit ab initio huius lucis virginitatis sacrificium; Iohannes Baptysta sacrificium abstinentiae, qui nec vinum bibit nec siceram, et

the following passage he reveals at what hour he went to Mass, saying: "When he heard these things, the bishop prostrated himself in prayer with great contrition of heart; and he who had come to offer sacrifice at the third hour put it off to the ninth hour because of the magnitude of his extended prayer."✝

I believe that Saint Gregory wanted to celebrate, in his 6 celebration of Mass, the very hour that he understood to be acceptable to the Lord, through the exhortation that the Lord made to that bishop, whom he said arrived to the solemnities of Mass at the third hour—though with an exception for the ninth hour on days of abstinence.

And if, according to established principle, Mass is cel- 7 ebrated at other hours, there is some reason by which this other hour is defended. This is the case on the Lord's Nativity, when Mass is celebrated at night because of the birth of the bread that is now daily eaten from the altar, or because of the choir of angels; we have already discussed this. Mass is celebrated that same morning because of the rising of the new light, or because of the visitation of the shepherds to the Lord's manger, where they found the fodder from which the souls of the saints are daily refreshed. We 8 likewise have offices established at dawn for the feast of John the Evangelist and John the Baptist, both of whom offered in themselves a singular sacrifice to God through the womb of their mother—that is, by having received the light of this world. John the Evangelist offered the sacrifice of virginity from the beginning of this light; John the Baptist, who drank neither wine nor strong drink, and remained a

9   Nazareus permansit omni tempore. In nocte sancta resurrectionis Domini Missam caelebramus propter eandem resurrectionem quae in ea completa est, et propter visitationem sanctarum mulierum ad sepulchrum Domini

# 41

# De exequiis mortuorum

Aperte domnus Beda declarat, in exequiis sancti Cuthberti, quomodo vestiri oporteat sacerdotem defunctum. Ita enim scribit de eius exequiis: "Postquam ergo sanctae memoriae Cuthbertus episcopus, peracta communione, elevatis oculis et manibus ad Deum, commendans ei animam suam emittens spiritum sedensque sine gemitu, obiit in via patrum, a navigantibus ad insulam nostram delatus, toto corpore levato, capite sudario circumdato, oblata super pectus sanctum posita, vestimento sacerdotali indutus, in obviam Christi calceamentis suis praeparatus, in sindone cereata involutus, animum habens cum Christo gaudentem."✝

2   Non est dubitandum quin ipse mos esset apud Romanam ecclesiam in hac re qui apud Anglos fuit, praesertim cum ex illa primum episcopum Agustinum haberent Angli Saxones, et eo tempore quando celeberrima fuit Romana ecclesia,

Nazirite for all time, offered the sacrifice of abstinence. We 9
celebrate Mass on the holy night of the Lord's resurrection
because of the very resurrection that was accomplished on
that night, and because the holy women visited the Lord's
tomb.

## 41

# On funeral ceremonies for the dead

The master Bede, on the funeral ceremony of Saint Cuthbert, clearly explains how a dead priest should be clothed.
For he writes as follows about his funeral: "And therefore,
after the bishop Cuthbert of holy memory had received
communion, he raised his eyes and hands to God, and commended his soul to him as he sat and breathed his last without a groan. Then he went the way of his fathers. He was
brought by sailors to our island; his whole body was washed,
his head was covered in a cloth, the offering was placed
upon his holy chest, he was dressed in his priestly vestments,
prepared for the path of Christ with his shoes, and wrapped
in fine waxed linen as his mind rejoiced with Christ."+
There is no doubt that the same custom was in force among 2
the Roman church as among the English in this matter, especially since the Anglo-Saxons had their first bishop, Augustine, from that church, at a time when the Roman church

propter auctoritatem doctissimi eius episcopi Gregorii. Et postea ex eadem ecclesia habuerunt archiepiscopum Theodorum in utraque lingua, scilicet Greca et Latina, peritissimum.

3     Sed mirari coepi quid vellet domnus Beda dicere, ubi dixit "in obviam Christi calceamentis suis praeparatus"— utrum vellet dicere quod cum eodem vestimento resurrecturus esset Cuthbertus, an moribus bonis, qui designantur

4 per vestimenta. Interim occurrit mihi cogitare de Christo, utrum ille vestitus esset vestimentis aliquibus postquam resurrexit a mortuis, et si fuit, utrum cum ipsis ascenderet in caelum, an solo naturali corpore, quod spiritale erat. Coepi cogitare utrum illis duobus qui eum in via conspexerunt apparuit vestitus, quando eum cogitabant peregrinum esse, etiam et Mariae Magdalenae, quando eum credebat hortulanum esse, similiter et discipulis, quando cum eis comedit et bibit vel ubicunque apparuit eis.

5     Similiter cogitavi quod angeli apparuissent vestiti. Unde legitur de illis secundum Iohannem, "Vidit angelos in albis sedentes" [ John 20:12]. Et in die assumptionis eius ad caelos legitur: "Ecce duo viri astiterunt iuxta illos in vestibus albis, qui et dixerunt: Hic Iesus, qui assumptus est a vobis in caelum, sic veniet quemadmodum vidistis eum euntem in caelum" [Acts 1:10–11]. Et hic nescio utrum tunc vestitus esset an non. Scimus enim dixisse angelos eum in ea forma venturum esse ad iudicium, qua tunc ascendit ad caelos. Simili modo, cogitavi quod, quando transfiguratus est in monte, non amisisse eum vestimenta sua, sed ea facta esse alba sicut

6 nix. Post hoc occurrit quod primi homines, Adam et Eva,

was quite illustrious, as it was then under the authority of its most learned bishop Gregory. And later on they had their archbishop Theodore, who was well learned in both languages, that is Greek and Latin, from the same church.

But I have begun to wonder what the master Bede meant 3 to say when he said "prepared for the path of Christ with his shoes"—whether he meant to say that Cuthbert would be resurrected with this actual clothing, or rather with his virtues, which are symbolized by his clothing. Meanwhile it oc- 4 curs to me to consider whether Christ was dressed in any clothes after he rose from the dead, and if he was, whether he ascended to heaven with them, or with his natural body only, which was spiritual. I also wondered whether he appeared in clothing to those two people who saw him on the path, when they thought he was a pilgrim; and also to Mary Magdalene, when she believed he was a gardener; and likewise to his disciples, when he ate and drank with them and wherever he appeared to them.

I also considered that the angels appeared in clothing. 5 Thus we read about them according to John: "And she saw angels sitting in white." And on the day of his assumption into heaven, we read: "Behold two men stood by them in white garments, who said: This Jesus, who is taken up from you into heaven, shall so come as you have seen him going into heaven." And at this point I do not know whether he was clothed or not. For we know that the angels said he would come for judgment in the same form in which he then ascended into heaven. Similarly, I also considered that, when he was transfigured on the mountain, he did not put off his clothes; they rather became white as snow. After 6 this it occurred to me that the first people, Adam and Eve,

nudi erant antequam peccarent; ad quorum conditionem nos venit revocare redemptor noster, sed multo meliorem. Quibus postquam peccaverunt, "fecit Deus tunicas pelliceas" [Gen 3:21]. Salva fide—quamvis nesciam utrum ita vestiti visuri sint homines, ut Christus apparuit post resurrectionem et angeli visi sunt, an ita nudi, ut primi homines fuerunt—credo tamen nullam deformitatem iri in spiritalibus corporibus quae possit offendere vel nausiam facere spiritalibus oculis.

7    Inter has ambiguitates occurrit mihi ut legerem Agustinum *De civitate Dei,* et ad Paulinum *De cura pro mortuis gerenda.* Pauca inde excerpsi, quibus tamen intellegi potest exequias nos debere facere circa mortuos nostros, potius pro nostra salute quam illorum; et, si non fuerint exequiae, ipsis qui in Christo mortui sunt nihil obesse; et quod qui eis facit exequias ob amorem illius facit qui promisit corpora

8    resurrectura. Dicit idem in primo libro *De civitate Dei,* capitulo duodecimo: "Multa itaque corpora Christianorum terra non texit, sed nullum eorum quisquam a caelo et terra separavit, quam totam impleret praesentia sui, qui novit unde resuscitet quod creavit. Dicitur quidem in Psalmo: 'Posuerunt mortalia servorum tuorum escas volatilibus caeli, carnes sanctorum tuorum bestiis terrae. Effuderunt sanguinem eorum sicut in circuitu Hierusalem, et non erat qui se-

9    peliret' [Ps 78:2–3]." Et paulo post: "Quamvis enim haec in conspectu hominum dura et dira videantur, sed 'pretiosa est in conspectu Domini mors sanctorum eius' [Ps 115:15]. Proinde omnia ista—curatio funeris, conditio sepulturae,

were naked before they sinned; and our redeemer came to return us to their condition, though a much better version of it. After they sinned, "God made garments of skins" for them. Allowing for faith—and though I do not know whether men will appear clothed, as Christ appeared after his resurrection and as the angels appeared, or whether they will appear naked, as the first men were—I nevertheless believe that no deformity capable of offending or revolting our spiritual eyes will come upon our spiritual bodies.

Amid these uncertainties it occurred to me to read Augustine on the *City of God,* and his letter to Paulinus *On the Care to be Had for the Dead.* I excerpted a few points from these works; through them we can understand that we should perform funeral ceremonies for our dead, though more for our salvation than theirs; and, if there were no funeral ceremonies, it would do no harm to those who have died in Christ; and that he who performs such ceremonies does so out of love for him who promised that our bodies will rise again. The same author says in the twelfth chapter of his first book on the *City of God:* "And so the earth has not covered many Christian bodies, but nobody has separated any of them from heaven and earth, all of which his presence fills—he who knows from where he will raise what he created. Indeed, it is said in the Psalm: 'They have given the dead bodies of your servants to be meat for the fowls of the air, the flesh of your saints for the beasts of the earth. They have poured out their blood as water round about Jerusalem, and there was none to bury them.'" And a little later: "For although these matters seem hard and fearful in the sight of men, 'precious in the sight of the Lord is the death of his saints.' Likewise all these things—conducting a

pompa exequiarum—magis sunt virorum solatia, quam subsidia mortuorum."

10    Iterum in eodem libro, capitulo decimo tertio: "Nec ideo tamen contempnenda et abicienda sunt corpora defunctorum, maxime iustorum atque fidelium, quibus tamquam organis et vasis ad omnia opera bona sancte usus est spiritus. Si enim paterna vestis et anulus ac si quid huiusmodi tanto carius est posteris, quanto erga parentes maior affectus, nullo modo ipsa spernenda sunt corpora, quae utique multo familiarius atque coniunctius quam quaelibet indumenta gestamus. Haec enim non ad ornamentum vel adiutorium quod adhibetur extrinsecus, sed ad ipsam naturam hominis

11    pertinent. Unde et antiquorum iustorum funera officiosa pietate curata sunt, exequiae caelebratae et sepultura provisa, ipsique mundi ipsique cum viverent de sepeliendis vel etiam transferendis suis corporibus filiis mandaverunt. Et Tobis sepeliendo mortuos Deum promeruisse teste angelo commendatur [Tob 12:12]. Ipse quoque Dominus, die tertio resurrecturus, religiosae mulieris bonum opus praedicat praedicandumque commendat, quod unguentum pretiosum super membra eius effuderit atque hoc ad eum sepeliendum fecerit [Matt 26:12; Mic 14:8–9; John 12:7]. Et laudabiliter commemorantur in Evangelio qui corpus eius de cruce acceptum diligenter atque honorifice tegendum sepeliendum-

12    que curarunt [Matt 27:59–61, etc.]. Verum istae auctoritates non hoc admonent quod insit ullus cadaveribus sensus, sed ad Dei providentiam cui placent etiam talia pietatis officia, corpora quoque mortuorum pertinere significant, propter fidem resurrectionis astruendam. Ubi et illud salubriter discitur: Quanta possit esse remuneratio pro elemosinis quas viventibus et scientibus exhibemus, si neque hoc apud

funeral, the manner of burial, the funeral procession—are solace for the living more than they are help for the dead."

Again in the thirteenth chapter of the same book: "Yet the bodies of the dead, especially those of the just and faithful, which the spirit has used piously as organs and vessels for all good works, should not be neglected and cast aside. For if a father's clothing or ring or something else of this sort is all the dearer to those progeny who have greater love for their parents, then these bodies, which we obviously carry with much more familiarity and intimacy than any garment, should on no account be spurned. For they pertain not to some ornamentation or support exhibited externally, but to human nature itself. Thus even the funerals of the righteous ancients were conducted with due piety, and their rites were celebrated and their burials were seen to, and they gave orders about their burial and even about transferring their bodies to their sons while still of the world and still alive. And, as an angel witnesses, Tobit was commended and found merit with God for burying the dead. Even the Lord himself, who would rise on the third day, praised and recommended for our praise the good work of the pious woman, when she poured precious ointment on his members and did so for his burial. And those who took his body down from the cross and had it covered and buried carefully and honorably are remembered with praise in the Gospel. Yet authorities do not teach us that cadavers are at all sensible; but they do reveal that the bodies of the dead are also included in God's providence; and these pious offices please him, because they increase faith in the resurrection. And it is well to learn another point here: How great can our reward be for the alms that we offer to the living and sensible,

Deum perit quod exanimis hominum membris officii dili-
gentiaeque persolvuntur?"✝

13    Ex istis verbis sancti Agustini apparet quod propterea
debeamus exequias caelebrare circa mortuorum hominum
corpora, quia Deus vult ea resuscitare. Ecce: Manifestae
sunt exequiae mortuorum, manifestusque est affectus hominis qui debet esse circa exequias mortuorum. Nunc dicendum est de officiis Vespertinalibus et Nocturnalibus
atque Matutinalibus.


# 42

# De officiis mortuorum

Habemus scriptum in quodam sacramentario quod officia mortuorum agenda sint circa tertiam diem et septimam
et tricesimam. Quod non ita intellego, quasi ille qui in tertia
die vult agere officia mortuorum debeat praetermittere
priores duos dies sine supplicationibus, aut qui in septima
die sex priores debeat tenere in otio, aut qui in tricesima, viginti et novem vacare otio; sed quod tertia die dicuntur caelebrari officia mortuorum, duobus modis possit intellegi: Id
est ut tertia die infra septem, sive septima infra triginta,
caelebrius agatur circa officia mortuorum quam in ceteris

if not even the service and care that is bestowed upon the dead members of men is wasted upon God?"†

From these words of Saint Augustine it appears that we 13 should celebrate funeral ceremonies over the bodies of the dead, because God wants to raise these bodies. Behold: The funeral ceremonies for the dead have been explained, and the mental disposition of the one who attends to the ceremonies of the dead has been explained. Now we should speak about Vespers and Nocturns and Matins.

# 42

# On offices for the dead

We have it written in a sacramentary that offices for the dead are to be celebrated on the third, seventh and thirtieth days. I do not understand this as meaning that he who wishes to celebrate offices for the dead on the third day should leave the first two days without supplication, or that he who wishes to celebrate offices on the seventh day should keep the previous six days free, or that he who wishes to celebrate offices on the thirtieth day should wait for twenty-nine days. Rather, that the offices for the dead are said to be celebrated on the third day can be understood in two ways: Namely, that on the third day within seven, or on the seventh day within thirty, offices for the dead are celebrated

2 diebus; sive ut tertia die consumat illa. Simili modo dicimus de septima et tricesima. De his tribus terminis ponemus auctoritatem sanctarum scripturarum.

3 Dicitur in libro Sapientiae de exequiis: "Fili, in mortuum produc lacrimas et quasi dira passus incipe plorare, et secundum iudicium contege corpus illius et non despicias sepulturam illius. Propter delaturam autem amare fer luctum illius una die, et consolare propter tristitiam, et fac luctum secundum meritum eius uno die vel duobus propter detrac-

4 tionem" [Eccl 38:16–18]. Ubi primo dixit propter delaturam, una die ferre luctum, et postea, propter detractionem, uno vel duobus diebus, tres dies introduxit in luctum. Possumus per tertiam diem commendati defuncti tertiam diem resurrectionis Domini ad memoriam reducere, ut eo dierum numero deprecemur pro nostro defuncto, quatenus mereatur per remissionem peccatorum particeps fieri resurrectionis Christi.

5 Pro qua re triduanum ieiunium Ninivitae fecerunt secundum Septuaginta, ut in Christi glorificatione per resurrectionem ex mortuis delerentur peccata eorum [ Jonah 3].

6 Unde dicit Agustinus in *Libro Quaestionum Genesis:* "Nec septuaginta interpretes, quos legere consuevit ecclesia, errasse credendi sunt, ut non dicerent quadraginta dies sed triduum, et Ninive evertetur." Et post pauca: "Triduum posuerunt, quamvis non ignorarent quod dies quadraginta in Ebreis codicibus legerentur, ut in Domini Iesu Christi clarificatione intellegerentur dissolvi abolerique peccata, de quo dictum est: 'Qui traditus est propter delicta nostra et

more solemnly than on the other days; or that one exhausts these celebrations on the third day. We speak likewise of the 2 seventh and thirtieth days. We will include the authority of the holy scriptures on these three periods.

In the book of Wisdom it is said of funeral ceremonies: 3 "My son, shed tears over the dead and begin to lament as if you had suffered some great harm, and according to judgment cover his body and neglect not his burial. And to avoid accusation weep bitterly for a day, and then comfort yourself in your sadness, and make mourning for him according to his merit for a day or two to avoid detraction." Where it 4 first said that to avoid accusation, one should weep for a day, and then, to avoid detraction, for a day or two, it brought three days into mourning. Through the third day of commemoration for the dead, we can call to mind the third day of the Lord's resurrection, that we may pray for our dead for the same number of days, and through the remission of our sins become worthy participants in Christ's resurrection.

For this reason the Ninevites fasted for three days ac- 5 cording to the Septuagint, that their sins might be abolished in Christ's glorification through his resurrection from the dead. Thus Augustine, in his book of *Questions on Genesis,* 6 says: "Nor should we believe that the seventy interpreters, whom the church is accustomed to read, erred by saying that Nineveh would be destroyed not in forty days, but in three." And after a little: "They put down three days, though they were not unaware that the Hebrew codices read forty days, that it might be understood that sins would be dissolved and abolished upon the glorification of the Lord Jesus Christ, about whom it is spoken: 'He was delivered up

resurrexit propter iustificationem nostram' [Rom 4:25]. Clarificatio autem Domini et in resurrectione et in caeli ascen-
sione cognoscitur."✝

7     Secunda igitur caelebratio pro defuncto in septimo die
habet auctoritatem in memorato libro Geneseos: "Habuit
quoque," inquit, quin Ioseph "in comitatu currus et equites,
et facta est turba non modica. Veneruntque ad aream quae
sita est trans Iordanem, ubi, caelebrantes exequias planctu
magno atque vehementi, impleverunt septem dies" [Gen
50:9–10]. Unde memoratus Agustinus in memorato *Libro
Quaestionum* scribit: "'Et fecit luctum patri suo septem dies'
8 [Gen 50:10]. Nescio utrum inveniatur alicuius sanctorum in
scripturis caelebratum esse luctum novem dies, quod apud
Latinos novendial appellant. Unde mihi videntur ab hac
consuetudine prohibendi, si qui christianorum istum in
mortuis suis numerum servant, qui magis est in gentilium
9 consuetudine. Septimus vero dies auctoritatem in scripturis
habet. Unde alio loco scriptum est: 'Luctus mortui septem
dierum, fatui autem omnes dies vitae eius' [Eccl 22:13]. Sep-
tenarius autem numerus, propter Sabbati sacramentum,
praecipue quietis indicium est. Unde merito mortuis tamquam requiescentibus exhibetur."✝

10     Tertia agitur tricesimo die, quam nobis Aaron et Moyses
in auctoritatem ducunt [Num 20:30; Deut 34:8], de quo dictum est in scriptione de Missa.

for our sins and rose again for our justification.' And the Lord's glorification both in his resurrection and in his ascension to heaven is understood."✝

The second celebration for the dead, then, on the seventh day, derives its authority from the aforementioned book of Genesis: "He had also in his train chariots and horsemen," it says, speaking of Joseph, "and it was a great company. And they came to the threshing floor that is situated beyond the Jordan, where, celebrating the funeral with a great and vehement lamentation, they spent a full seven days." Thus the aforementioned Augustine writes in his aforementioned *Book of Questions:* "'And they mourned their father for seven days.' I do not know whether it is found anywhere in scripture that mourning for any holy person was celebrated for nine days, which among the Latins they call the novendial. Thus it seems to me that Christians are prohibited from this custom, if indeed any observe this period with respect to their dead, which is rather an observance among the heathen. The seventh day, however, derives its authority from the scriptures. And so it is written in another place: 'The mourning for the dead is seven days, but for a fool all the days of his life.' And the number seven, because it is a sacrament for the Sabbath, is above all a sign of rest. And so it is rightly extended to the dead, who are, as it were, at rest."✝

The third celebration occurs on the thirtieth day, which Aaron and Moses made authoritative for us, as we said in our discussion of the Mass.

7

8

9

10

11     Quoniam sic certamus pro nostris defunctis, quatenus possint participes fieri eorum quos Christus revocavit a claustris inferni, in ea commemoratione simili modo caelebramus officia pro ipsis, quomodo caelebrantur in illis diebus, quando Christus descendit ad inferna et in quibus creditur mortuus. Non enim possumus intellegere de omnibus qui sint qui ilico, postquam recesserint de corpore, penetrent regna caelorum, aut qui in aliis custodiis recipiantur. Igitur uno modo facimus mortuorum officia.

12     Sunt etiam loca in quibus generaliter pro omnibus defunctis omni tempore, excepto Pentecostes et festis diebus, oratur in officio Vespertinali et Matutinali. Sunt et alia in quibus Missa pro isdem cotidie caelebratur. Sunt etiam et alia in quibus in initio mensis novem Psalmi, novem lec-

13     tiones totidemque responsorii pro eis cantantur. Quid hoc valeat, Agustinus in libro ad Paulinum *De cura gerenda pro mortuis* monstrat: "Non sunt," inquit, "praetermittendae supplicationes pro spiritibus mortuorum, quas faciendas pro omnibus in christiana societate defunctis, etiam tacitis nominibus eorum, sub generali commemoratione suscepit ecclesia—ut quibus in ista desunt parentes aut filii aut qualescunque cognati vel amici, ab una eis exhibeatur pia matre communi. Si autem deessent istae supplicationes, quae fiunt recta et pia fide ac pietate pro mortuis, puto quod nihil prodesset spiritibus eorum quamlibet locis sanctis exanima corpora ponerentur."

Because we labor on behalf of our dead, that they may be   11
able to join those whom Christ has recalled from the depths
of hell, we celebrate offices for them that are similar to the
ones celebrated on the days when Christ descended to hell
and is held to be dead. Of all the dead, we cannot know
which enter the kingdom of heaven immediately after they
have left their bodies, and which are received into other cus-
todies. Thus we celebrate offices for the dead in uniform
fashion.

There are also places in Vespers and Matins, in all seasons   12
excepting Pentecost and feast days, where we pray for all the
dead generally. There are also times when the daily Mass is
celebrated for them. And there are also times, at the beginning of the month, when nine Psalms, nine lessons and the
same number of responsories are sung for them. Augustine   13
reveals the purpose of this in his book to Paulinus, *On the
Care to be Had for the Dead*: "We should not neglect supplications for the spirits of the dead," he says. "The church un-
dertakes the celebration of these supplications, in general
commemoration, on behalf of all who have died in Christian
fellowship, even if their names are not mentioned—so that
a celebration may be provided in this fellowship by a single,
common, pious mother for those who are without parents
or children or any relatives or friends. But if these supplications, which arise out of upright and pious faith and respect
for the dead, are lacking, I think that, whatever the holy
places where their dead bodies are interred, they are of no
benefit to their spirits."

# 43

# Repetitio de tribus
# Psalmis baptysmalibus

Diximus in superioribus tres Psalmos baptysmales per noctes nobis ad memoriam reducere tria opera Christi, hoc est repulsionem daemonum, effectum sanitatum et resurrectionem nostram, simulque sepulturam triduanam Domini; atque, altero modo, officia dierum baptysmalium, Spiritus Sancti deductionem in terra recta, et tres Psalmos noctium, fidem, spem et caritatem.

2    At nunc addimus in operibus tenebrarum, ceu in nocte, tria esse vitia originalia: id est suggestionem diaboli, carnis delectationem et consensum animi. Propter haec tria vitia, vice trium virtutum, scilicet fidei, spei et caritatis, tres Psalmos cantamus, quibus memorata vitia repellantur de nostris

3    catecumenis. Qualiter caelebrandum sit officium in Dominica nocte, quae est octava post Pascha Domini, demonstratum est ab ipsa Romana ecclesia, matre nostra: id est, per decem et octo Psalmos, et novem lectiones, et novem responsorios. Nam et requies animarum et octava dies resurrectionis eius in Sabbato adimplentur. Octava enim officia Paschalia in eo adimplentur, et summa septimae quietis in eo caelebratur.

## 43

# Addendum on the three
# baptismal Psalms

Above, we said that the three baptismal Psalms at night remind us of Christ's three works, namely his expulsion of demons, his performance of cures and our resurrection; and they also remind us of the Lord's three-day burial. And in another sense, we said that the daytime baptismal offices recall the Holy Spirit's guidance to the upright land, and that the three Psalms at night recall faith, hope and charity.

But now we add that the three original vices are among 2 our works in the darkness, or at night: namely the suggestion of the devil, the pleasure of the flesh and the consent of the spirit. Because of these three vices, we sing three Psalms in the guise of the three virtues, namely faith, hope and charity; through them the aforementioned vices are cast out of our catechumens. The Roman church, our mother, has 3 shown how the office should be celebrated on Sunday night, which is the eighth day after the Lord's Easter: namely, with eighteen Psalms, nine readings and nine responsories. For the rest of souls and the eighth day of his resurrection are both accomplished on Saturday. The eight Easter offices are fulfilled on that day, and the conclusion of the seventh day of rest is celebrated then.

## 44

# Repetitio de antiphona *Fluminis impetus,* quae cantatur in Theophania

Solent musitare de Psalmo *Deus noster refugium* [Ps 45], quare praepostero ordine ponatur in tertia periocha. De qua re ita dicimus, sequentes ordinem Evangelii: Prius venerunt magi adorare Dominum quam baptyzatus esset. Magi edocti erant a doctrina Balaam per stellam novam recognoscere ducem novum et regem [Num 24:17]; hi venerunt primo adorare Dominum, et postea baptyzatus est ipse. Et apostoli atque ipsi baptyzaverunt, quorum officium perspicue dilucidatur, et praecipue in antiphona *Fluminis impetus,* quae cantatur in tertia nocturna.

2    Satis apertum est ex officiis ceterarum nocturnarum Novum Testamentum recoli in tertia nocturna, praecedentibus duabus nocturnis quae habent in se memoriam sanctorum patrum qui fuerunt in Veteri Testamento repleti Spiritu Sancto, sive de circumcisis sive de gentilibus. Sequitur tertia nocturna, cum antiphonis quae habent alleluia solito more, et perspicue demonstrant Novum Testamentum et

3    baptismi sacramenta recolunt. Unde ad responsorios *Hodie in Iordane* et *In columbae specie* propterea in ea cantamus, quia ipsi baptismum Christi praescribunt nobis ante oculos, et

# 44

# Addendum on the antiphon *Fluminis impetus,* which is sung on Epiphany

Cantors are wont to mutter about why the Psalm *Deus noster refugium* is placed out of order, in the third nocturn. We say this on the matter, following the order of the Gospel: The Magi came to adore the Lord before he was baptized. The Magi had been instructed by the teaching of Balaam to recognize a new leader and king in the new star; they came to adore the Lord first, and later he was baptized. Both they and the apostles performed baptism, and their action is especially evident, above all in the antiphon *Fluminis impetus,* which is sung in the third nocturn.

It is obvious enough from the offices for the other nocturns that the New Testament is recalled in the third nocturn, while the two that precede it commemorate the holy fathers who were filled with the Holy Spirit in the Old Testament, whether circumcised or gentiles. The third nocturn follows, with antiphons that have the alleluia in the usual manner, and that clearly reveal the New Testament and recall the sacraments of baptism. And so for the third nocturn we sing the responsories *Hodie in Iordane* and *In columbae specie,* because they place Christ's baptism before our eyes; and

in ea memoriam facimus, per responsorium *Dicit Dominus: Implete ydrias aqua,* de miraculo quod eadem die fecit Dominus. Antiphona monstrat quomodo Spiritus Sanctus laetificavit apostolos, ut sanctificarent tabernaculum Domini per baptysmum.

4    Ceteri versus sonant quid homines mundi contra hoc agerent, sicuti sunt isti: "Propterea non timebimus dum turbabitur terra et transferentur montes in cor maris" [Ps 45:3], "Sonuerunt et turbatae sunt aquae eorum, conturbati sunt montes in fortitudine eius" [Ps 45:4]. Psalmus *Cantate Domino* [Ps 95] monstrat quod omnes dii gentium sunt daemonia. Et iterum de atrocitate gentilium infidelium et laetitia credentium dicit: "Commoveatur mare et plenitudo eius; gaudebunt campi et omnia quae in eis sunt; tunc exultabunt omnia ligna silvarum ante faciem Domini" [Ps 95:11–13]. *Dominus regnavit, exultet terra, laetentur insulae multae* [Ps 96:1] praedicationem apostolorum monstrant, nihilominus et subversionem idolorum. Ita inquiunt versus: "Alluxerunt fulgura eius orbi terrae, vidit et commota est. Montes sicut cera fluxerunt a facie Domini." Et in sequentibus: "Confundantur omnes qui adorant sculptilia" [Ps 96:4–7].

in that nocturn we commemorate the miracle that the Lord performed on that same day, through the responsory: *Dicit Dominus: Implete ydrias aqua.* The antiphon reveals how the Holy Spirit delighted the apostles, that they might sanctify the Lord's tabernacle through baptism.

The other verses proclaim what the people of the world 4 did in opposition; they are as follows: "Therefore we will not fear when the earth shall be troubled and the mountains shall be removed into the heart of the sea," "Their waters roared and were troubled, the mountains were troubled with his strength." The Psalm *Cantate Domino* reveals that all the gods of the gentiles are demons. And again, it speaks of the hatefulness of the unfaithful gentiles and the joy of believers: "Let the sea be moved and the fullness thereof; the fields and all things that are in them shall be joyful; then shall all the trees of the woods rejoice before the face of the Lord." *Dominus regnavit, exultet terra, laetentur insulae multae* reveals the preaching of the apostles, and also the overthrow of idols. The verses speak as follows: "His lightnings have shone forth to the world, the earth saw and trembled. The mountains melted like wax at the face of the Lord." And in what follows: "Let them be all confounded who adore graven things."

# 45

# Repetitio de versu, et de Pentecoste et de calice

Versus hoc habet singulare, ut excitet corda cantantium ad requirendam faciem Domini in oratione. Idcirco saepissime ante orationem praecedit. Versus qui dicitur in Nocturnali officio, ante orationem quae praecedit lectionem, intenta vult facere corda praesentium ad lectionem. Notum est quod sessio plus pertinet ad securitatem quam statio. Securitas enim parit negligentiam inter ignavos. Ideo praecedit oratio ante sessionem, ut Domini protectio nostra corda eripiat ab omni securitate fallaci.

2    Ante ymnos *Magnificat* [Luke 1:46–52] et *Benedictus Dominus Deus Israel* [Luke 1:68–79] praecedit versus, quoniam sic debemus esse vigilantes et intenti ad verba ymnorum memoratorum ut in oratione. In ceteris cursibus ante novissimam orationem praecedit.

3    Oratio et benedictio semper in fine sunt, ante quam disiungantur fratres singuli ad propria. Morem tenet iste usus antiquae ecclesiae. Ita legitur in Actibus Apostolorum de Paulo, quando recessit ab Epheso et Ephesiis praedixit iam faciem suam non eos visuros amplius [Acts 20:25]: "Et cum haec dixisset, positis genibus suis cum omnibus illis oravit" [Acts 20:36]. Similiter quando de Tyro recessit:

## 45

# Addendum on the versicle, and on
# Pentecost and on the chalice

The versicle has this peculiarity: It encourages the hearts
of those who sing it to seek the Lord's face in prayer. Therefore it most often precedes prayer. The versicle that is said
at Nocturns, before the prayer that precedes the reading,
aims to direct the hearts of those present to the reading. It
is known that sitting relates to heedlessness more than
standing. And heedlessness gives birth to negligence among
the lazy. Therefore a prayer precedes sitting, that the Lord's
protection may remove our hearts from all fallacious heedlessness.

A versicle precedes the hymns *Magnificat* and *Benedictus*  2
*Dominus Deus Israel,* because we should be as vigilant and intent on the words of the aforementioned hymns as we are in
prayer. In our other offices it precedes the last prayer.

A prayer and blessing are always at the end, before each of  3
the brethren departs to his own duties. This usage follows
the custom of the ancient church. Thus we read in the Acts
of the Apostles about Paul, when he left Ephesus and proclaimed to the Ephesians that they would see his face no
more: "And when he had said these things, kneeling down,
he prayed with them all." And likewise when he left Tyre:

"Deducentibus nos omnibus cum uxoribus et filiis, usque foras civitatem; et positis genibus in littore orabamus. Et cum valefecissemus invicem, ascendimus in navem; illi autem redierunt in sua" [Acts 21:5–6]. Oratio novissima ideo communiter caelebratur in novissimo, ut unusquisque tali scuto—id est communi oratione—rediens ad sua, muniatur contra omnia adversa. Hanc orationem vocavit sanctus Ambrosius postulationem. Postulationem namque Agustinus deputat in oratione Missae quam solet sacerdos dicere post communionem.

4

5 Quam orationem ubique subsequitur benedictio et gratiarum actio; hoc enim sonant verba "Benedicamus Domino" et "Deo gratias." Haec enim utraque ad gratiarum actionem referenda sunt, qua oratione Paulus concludit caeteras orationes [1 Tim 2:1].

# 46

# Repetitio de Pentecoste

Post superiora descripta, inveni iterum autenticum perspicuum Ambrosianum de quinquaginta diebus post Pascha. Quod malui hic introducere, quamvis non in suo loco, quam

"They were bringing us on our way with their wives and children, until we were out of the city; and we kneeled down on the shore and we prayed. And when we had bid one another farewell, we took ship; and they returned home." A final 4 prayer is therefore celebrated collectively at the end, so that everyone, as he returns to his own duties, may be fortified against all adversities by such a shield—that is, by common prayer. Saint Ambrose called this prayer an intercession. And Augustine considers the intercession to be that which the priest, during the prayer of Mass, is accustomed to say after communion.

In every case, blessing and thanksgiving follow this 5 prayer; this is what the words "Let us bless the Lord" and "Thanks be to God" proclaim. And both should be related to thanksgiving, with which prayer Paul concludes his list of the other prayers.

# 46

# Addendum on Pentecost

After the above was copied, I then found a genuine and clear statement from Ambrose about the fifty days after Easter. I wanted to include it here rather than pass over it in

pigritia praeterire. Dicit Ambrosius in tractatu super Lucam: "Maiores tradidere nobis Pentecostes omnes quinquaginta dies, ut Paschae, caelebrandos." Et post pauca: "Ergo per hos quinquaginta dies ieiunium nescit ecclesia, sicut Dominica qua Dominus resurrexit; et sunt omnes dies tamquam Dominica."

# 47

# De situ corporis Domini et calicis in altari

Nuperrime monstratum est mihi (ut puto ab eo qui quod aperit nemo claudit) quid rationabiliter possit dici de corpore Domini posito in altari et de calice ex latere eius— salvo magisterio eorum qui alias et melius mihi volunt aperire, quomodo et quare aliter panis ponendus sit in altari et calix iuxta eum.

2    Altare crux Christi est ab eo loco ubi scriptum est in canone: *Unde et memores sumus,* usque dum involvitur calix de sudario diaconi, vice Ioseph, qui involvit corpus Domini sindone et sudario [Matt 27:59, etc]. De quo altari dicit Beda

indolence, though this is not its proper place. In his treatise on Luke, Ambrose says: "Our ancestors handed down to us that all fifty days of Pentecost, like Easter, are to be celebrated." And after a little: "The church therefore does not know fasting during these fifty days, just as on the Sunday when the Lord rose again; and all these days are like Sunday."

# 47

# On the position of the Lord's body and chalice on the altar

Very recently it was revealed to me (I think by the one who opens that which no one closes) what can reasonably be said about how the Lord's body is positioned on the altar and how the chalice is placed to its side—saving the teaching of those who wish to reveal to me, otherwise and in better fashion, the issue of how and why the bread is to be placed on the altar in one way, and the chalice next to it in another.

The altar is the cross of Christ, beginning from the place 2 where it is written in the canon: *Unde et memores sumus,* up to the moment when the chalice is wrapped in the maniple of the deacon, who acts in the guise of Joseph, who wrapped the Lord's body with a cloth and kerchief. Bede speaks

secundo libro super Apocalypsin: "Alia editio habet: 'super aram,' eo quod super altare crucis turibulum suum aureum — id est corpus inmaculatum et Spiritu Sancto conceptum —

3 obtulerit Patri pro nobis."✝ Panis extensus super altare corpus Domini monstrat extensum in cruce, quod nos manducamus. Vinum et aqua in calice monstrant sacramenta quae de latere Domini in cruce fluxerunt, id est sanguinem et aquam, quibus nos potat Dominus noster.

4 De quo potu mystico dicit memoratus Ambrosius in libro memorato: "Quaero etiam cur ante mortem non inveniamus esse percussum, post mortem inveniamus — nisi forte ut voluntarius magis quam necessarius exitus eius fuisse doceatur, et ordinem mysticum noverimus — quia non ante altaris sacramenta quam baptysmum, sed baptysmum ante, sic poculum." Et paulo post: "Aqua enim et sanguis exivit; illa quae diluat, iste qui redimat. Bibamus ergo precium nostrum, ut bibendo redimamur."

about this altar in his second book on Revelation: "Another version has: 'upon the altar,' because he offered to his Father on our behalf his golden censer—that is, his immaculate body conceived of the Holy Spirit—upon the altar of the cross."† The bread extended on the altar reveals the  3
Lord's body extended on the cross, which we eat. The wine and water in the chalice reveal the sacraments that flowed from the Lord's side on the cross, namely the blood and water, which our Lord gives us to drink.

The aforementioned Ambrose in his aforementioned  4
book speaks about this mystical drink: "I also ask why we do not find that he was pierced before death, but we find that he was pierced after death—unless perhaps, to teach that his death was voluntary rather than unavoidable, and that we may recognize the mystical order—for the sacraments of the altar do not precede baptism; rather, baptism goes before, like the cup." And after a little: "For water and blood poured forth; the former cleanses, the latter redeems. Let us therefore drink our reward, that in drinking we may be redeemed."

# Note on the Text

The Latin text printed and translated in this volume is derived from Jean-Michel Hanssens's monumental critical edition of 1948, which synthesizes the evidence of over seventy-four medieval manuscripts. The orthography is Hanssens's throughout and reflects his careful efforts to represent Amalar's own habits as closely as possible. The punctuation has been thoroughly reworked to conform with modern English usage and decisions made in the translation.

The Notes to the Text track all of the emendations that Hanssens made to his own edited text as well as further changes undertaken for this edition. The vast majority of these additional changes are corrections that resolve corruptions in Amalar's patristic quotations, particularly those of Augustine. In every case, these revisions reflect the standard modern editions of the patristic texts in question, they were undertaken only when necessary for the translation, and they have not changed the meaning or force of Amalar's arguments.

# Abbreviations

*Antiphonale Missarum* = R.-J. Hesbert, ed., *Antiphonale Missarum Sextuplex*

*Antiphonalia Officii* = R.-J. Hesbert, ed., *Corpus Antiphonalium Officii*

*Canon Romanus* = B. Botte, ed., *Le canon de la messe romaine*

*Capitulare* = T. Klauser, *Das römische Capitulare Evangeliorum*

CCCM = Corpus Christianorum: Continuatio Mediaevalis

CCSL = Corpus Christianorum: Series Latina

CSEL = Corpus Scriptorum Ecclesiasticorum Latinorum

*Gelasianum* = L. C. Mohlberg, L. Eizenhöfer, and P. Siffrin, eds., *Sacramentarium Gelasianum*

*Gellonense* = A. Dumas, ed., *Liber Sacramentorum Gellonensis*

*Hadrianum* = J. Deshusses, ed., *Sacramentarium Gregorianum*

MGH = Monumenta Germaniae Historica

    Conc. = Concilia

    Epp. = Epistolae

    PL = Poetae Latini

    SS rer. Germ. = Scriptores rerum Germanicarum

    SS rer. Merov. = Scriptores rerum Merovingicarum

*Paduense* = A. Catella, F. Dell'Oro, and A. Martini, eds., *Liber Sacramentorum Paduensis*

PG = J.-P. Migne, *Patrologia Graeca Cursus Completus*

PL = J.-P. Migne, *Patrologia Latina Cursus Completus*

# Notes to the Text

23.18    dirigimus significantes voces *corrected from* dirigimus sacrifican-
         tes voces

24.7     nisi crux Christi *corrected from* nisi crucifixi Christi
         sacrificio quo aluntur *corrected from* sacrificium quo aluntur

34.2     exhonorat corpus . . . honorare contendunt *corrected from* exhor-
         reat corpus . . . honorare contendat

36.2     cicatrice denuntient *corrected from* cicatrices denuntient

36.3     "Advocatum," inquit, "habemus" *corrected from* "Advocatum," in-
         quit, "habemus" dixit

41.2     gaudii praestat *corrected from* gaudii; sunt de incarnatione *cor-
         rected from* est de incarnatione, in both cases following Paris, Bib-
         liothèque nationale de France Ms. lat. 12033*

43.2     ymnis modulatae vocis *corrected from* ymnis modula devotis

44.8     actionum finis innuitur *corrected from* actionum finis innititur

44.10    iureiurando promisit *corrected from* iureiurando, *following Hans-
         sens*

44.11    referente eo *corrected from* revertente eo

44.13    nec his valeat *corrected from* nec his valeant

44.14    Cum ergo sacrificia *corrected from* Cum de sacraficio

## Letters

2        "Ita" Grecam litteram pro "H" longa *corrected from* "H" Grecam
         litteram; porro "H" longam (*following MGH Epp 5, 260*)

6.19     exhonorat corpus . . . honorare contendunt *corrected from* exhor-
         reat corpus . . . honorare contendant; *see note to 3.34.2*

## Book 4

1.3      mihi sufficit eius auctoritas *corrected from* mihi sufficit eius auc-
         toritatis

2.16     Quando autem deponeretur *corrected from* Quando autem depo-
         nerentur

3.3      quo innovata in Deum *corrected from* quae innovata in Deum
         aures accommodent *corrected from* aures accommodentur

4.4      daemonum subreptio *corrected from* quia daemonum subreptio

4.7    qui multa persequente isto saeculo mala tolerantes innotescunt compediti . . . nec tantis malis coacti *corrected from* qui multas persecutiones in isto saeculo malas tolerantes innotescunt compeditos . . . nec tamen malis coacti

4.17    damnabit in aeternum *corrected from* dampnet in aeternum

7.12    tenebras repellit *corrected from* tenebras expello

7.23    aliquis esuriat . . . aliquis sitiat *corrected from* aliquis esuriet . . . aliquis sitiet

7.24    sublimari gaudio *corrected from* sublimari

7.30    prophetavit . . . habitator ibi *corrected from* prophetat . . . habitatoribus

9    per Dominicas noctes *added by Hanssens*

9.7    similis esse videatur *corrected from* similes esse videantur

9.18    Praeveni inmaturitate *corrected from* Praeveni in maturitate *to make sense of what follows*

9.19    sed: 'inmaturitate' *corrected from* sed: 'in maturitate' *to align with Augustine's text*

        geminatam praepositionem *corrected from* geminata in praepositione

9.22    fidei, ac morum *corrected from* fidei ac murum

10    per Dominicas noctes *added by Hanssens*

10.8    Pertendens enim benedictio *corrected from* Praetendens enim benedictio

10.15    sine sollicitudine viveret *corrected by Hanssens from* sine sollicitudine vivere

12    de secunda feria *added by Hanssens*

12.10    Satiati sumus mane misericordia tua] *On this variant* (satiati sumus *in place of* repleti sumus): *Pierre Sabatier,* Bibliorum sacrorum latinae versiones antiquae *(Paris, 1751), 2:182*

23.6    universitatem hominum . . . honorum omnibus *corrected from* diversitatem hominum . . . bonorum omnibus

23.29    veniret, et tenere *corrected from* veniret tenere

25.3    iam quam patimur *corrected from* iam quae patimur

26.2    Cui cum dicerem *corrected from* Cum dicerent

26.6    non probamur imitari *corrected from* non probamus imitari

27.25    quia quo plus se posse *corrected from* quia quod plus se posse

27.26    una aliam sublevanda sublevat *corrected from* unam alia sublevan-
dam sublevat

28.2     aquam quis prohibere *corrected from* aqua quis prohibere

32.4     Quod non possemus *corrected from* Quod non possumus

33.3     et circumcisionem eius *corrected from* et circumcisione eius

36.2     agentium in officio *corrected from* agentium in officia

36.4     iam diu sunt *corrected from* tam diu sunt

37.3     quo caelebrior . . . quo quacumque *corrected from* quod caelebrior
. . . quacumque

37.15    non significandum putaretur *corrected from* ad significandum non
putaretur

38.3     quid malum est risus? inquis *corrected from* quid malum est risus?
inquit

42.13    tacitis nominibus eorum *corrected from* tacitis nominibus quorum

spiritibus eorum quamlibet locis *corrected from* spiritibus eorum
si quamlibet locis

47.4     voluntarius magis quam necessarius exitus *corrected from* potus;
quam baptysmum *corrected from* post baptysmum

# Notes to the Translation

Amalar's commentary incorporates excerpts from over eighty different Latin and Greek patristic sources. For the current editions of these texts, see Eligius Dekkers and Emil Gaar, eds., *Clavis Patrum Latinorum,* 3rd ed. (Turnhout, 1995); and Mauritius Geerard et al., eds., *Clavis Patrum Graecorum,* 6 vols. (Turnhout, 1983–1998). All titles in the Notes to the Translation are given in Latin and standardized according to their *Clavis* entries.

  These notes also include glosses to the third book of Amalar's *On the Liturgy* (listed below), contributed by an anonymous member of the Lyon clergy sometime during Amalar's tenure as bishop of the archdiocese, from 835 to 838. (Glosses to the first two books are included in DOML 35, volume 1 of this translation.) As discussed in the Introduction (pp. xxv–xxvi), the glosses occur exclusively in Paris, Bibliothèque nationale de France, MS nouv. acq. lat. 329.

| | |
|---|---|
| 3.4.3 | 3.5.24 |
| 3.5.1 | 3.7.1 |
| 3.5.8 | 3.8.2 |
| 3.5.15–19 | 3.10.4 |
| 3.5.20 | 3.11.3 |
| 3.5.22 | 3.11.18 |

## Book 3

pref.  "Medard, whose feast we celebrate today": June 8.

1.3  "Sound the trumpet . . . perfected praise": Jerome, *Commentarius in Ioelem,* 2.

"you have perfected praise.✝": For Amalar's use of the cross to distinguish his words from those of the authorities he quotes, see Preface, 6.

1.7    "Whoever reads . . . good works": Gregory I, *Homiliae in Hiezechielem,* 2.1.14.

2.1    *"kyrika":* Amalar appears to be discussing the Greek adjective κυριακή.

"The dwellings . . . God the king": Isidore, *Etymologiae,* 15.4.11.

2.2–3  "After the building . . . examinations of cases": Josephus, *Antiquitates Iudaicae,* 8.5.

2.6    "Someone asks . . . the other parent": Bede, *In Lucae Evangelium expositio,* 1.2.

2.8    "A woman . . . the Lord's vicar": Ambrosiaster, *Commentarius in epistulam ad Corinthios primam,* 11.

2.10   "Men stand in the southern part . . . women in the northern": See, for example, *Ordo Romanus V,* 36.

2.12   "He who abstains . . . with our voice": Jerome, *Commentarius in epistulam ad Ephesios,* 3.5.

2.13   "ordered that women . . . blessed Peter": *Liber pontificalis,* 2.

3.1    "And many know . . . disrupts the choir": Augustine, *Enarrationes in Psalmos,* 149.7.

"The choir is . . . psalms this way": Isidore, *Etymologiae,* 6.19.5.

3.3.7  "they are the choir": In Latin, *chorus*—a term that Amalar has gotten from the Psalms, and that for him indicates a band of singers. Yet in the Middle Ages, a *chorus* could also be a musical instrument. See Mary Remant, "Chorus (iii)," in *The New Grove Dictionary of Music and Musicians* (New York, 2001).

3.4    "But David was . . . well ordered city": Augustine, *De civitate Dei,* 17.14.

3.6    "And Asaph . . . the Lord's praises": Jerome, *Commentarius in Esaiam,* 1.1.

3.8–13 "These very saints . . . praise to God": Augustine, *Enarrationes in Psalmos,* 150.5–8.

3.11   "something that can be understood according to this distinction": That is, according to the categories of above and below.

4.1    "byssus": A kind of fine linen cloth.

4.2    "For byssus . . . that we desire": Bede, *De tabernaculo,* 2.13.

"What is signified . . . beauty of cleanness": Bede, *De tabernaculo,* 3.4.

4.3    Fragmentary gloss: [. . .] *ana ex* [. . .] *o.*

4.4    "For how many . . . of the flesh": Jerome, *Commentarius in epistulam ad Ephesios,* 3.6.

5.1    "The office . . . the reading." Gloss: *Rogandum si fuit unquam ullus hominum doctorum qui tales ineptias adinvenire videretur.* (It should be asked if there has ever been anyone among learned men who was seen to devise such absurdities.)

"The entrance at Mass of the bishop": For example, *Ordo Romanus V,* 1–24.

5.2    "Celestine": Celestine I, pope from 422 to 432.

"He established . . . celebrated in that way": *Liber pontificalis,* 45.

"antiphonally out of all": The meaning of this phrase *(antiphonatim ex omnibus)* is disputed; my translation follows Edward Nowacki, "The Latin Antiphon and the Question of Frequency of Interpolation," *Plainsong and Medieval Music* 21 (2012): 34 and passim.

5.4    "But David . . . faithful will": Augustine, *De civitate Dei,* 17.14; and above, 3.3.4.

5.5    "The pontiff begins . . . the first prayer": *Ordo Romanus I,* 53 (long recension); *Ordo Romanus V,* 24.

5.6    "Furthermore . . . enticed by eternal life": Augustine, *Tractatus in Evangelium Ioannis,* 26.6.4.

"Each man is pulled by his own desire": Virgil, *Eclogues,* 2.65.

5.8    "With the psalmists . . . fitting places." Gloss: *Si de omni sermone otioso redditurus est homo rationem in die iudicii, hoc et tu facturus es de omnibus quae dicis, qui licet verba scripturarum convolvas et sanctorum doctorum illa omni aedificatione facis vacua et merito otiosa computentur.* (If man will give account for each of his superfluous statements on the day of judgment, you will have to do so for all the things that you say here. Although you weave together the words of scripture and learned men, you deprive them of all edification, to the point that they are rightly reckoned superfluous.)

"With this term . . . prearranged location": Augustine, *Enarrationes in Psalmos,* 67.24.

5.15–19    Gloss: *Quasi violentus tirannus, omnes scripturas Veteris et Novi Testamenti ad tuum argumentum servire compellis.* (Like an impetuous tyrant, you force all the scriptures of the Old and New Testament to serve your argument.)

5.15    "But should . . . the prophets." Gloss: *O praesumptio vanissima, unde plenus es.* (Vain presumption; you are full of it.)

"on the one hand . . . on its own." Gloss: *Si liber Actus Apostolorum epistola est quia uni homini, id est Teophilo, scribitur, quare non ergo et Evangelium secundum Lucam, quod ad eundem mittitur?* (If the book of the Acts of the Apostles is a letter because it is written to one man, namely Theophilus, why is the Gospel according to Luke, which is directed to the same person, therefore not also a letter?)

5.16    "The Lord . . . concerning me": Augustine, *Tractatus in Evangelium Ioannis,* 48.9.

5.19    "They do . . . taming their flesh": Augustine, *Enarrationes in Psalmos,* 67.34.

5.20    "For he who sings . . . sings about": Augustine, *Enarrationes in Psalmos,* 72.1.

"those who previously spoke of only one God." Gloss: *Aperta blasphemia et scelestum mendacium; frequentissime ipsi cantores in Psalmis unum Deum dicebant in tribus personis.* (An open blasphemy and a wicked lie; these cantors quite often proclaimed one God in three persons through the Psalms.)

5.22    "This is what we are accustomed to say." Gloss: *Non tam admirabilis scientia tua quam dicis.* (Your knowledge is not as admirable as you say it is.)

5.24    "What we said . . . and a wise man." Gloss: [. . .] *rabido ore inextricabilia vincula conaris inicere cervicibus simplicium.* ([. . .] with your raving mouth you aim to cast inextricable chains upon the necks of the simple.)

5.25    "Abraham": See the responsory *Dum staret Abraham* for Vespers on Quinquagesima Sunday: *Antiphonalia Officii,* 56a.

5.26 "The hearts of the saints are thus the tables of God": Gregory I, *Homiliae in Hiezechielem*, 2.9, 8.

5.28 "Psalter . . . psaltery": In Latin, *psalterium* indicates both the book of Psalms (the Psalter) and the psaltery (the musical instrument).

5.33 "But prove all things": ". . . hold fast that which is good."

6 "On the *Kyrie eleison*": *Ordo Romanus I,* 51–52; *Ordo Romanus V,* 21–22.

6.1 "We are unprofitable . . . to the Lord": Bede, *In Lucae Evangelium expositio,* 5.17.

6.5 "And thus . . . nightly psalmody": See Amalar, *De ordine antiphonarii,* prol.6 (ed. Hanssens, *Opera liturgica omnia,* 3).

7 "on candles: *Ordo Romanus I,* 52; *Ordo Romanus V,* 23.

7.1 "that we may truly recognize that we are ash and dust." Gloss: *Si ad tantam humilitatem pervenisses ut te cognosceres cinerem et pulverem, istam ingredereris promptior.* (If you had arrived at such humility that you recognized that you were ash and dust, you would embark upon this subject more quickly.)

8 "On the *Gloria in excelsis Deo*": *Ordo Romanus I,* 53 (long recension); *Ordo Romanus V,* 24.

8.1 "Telesphorus, a Greek . . . the sacrifice": *Liber pontificalis,* 9. Telesphorus was pope from ca. 125 to 136.

   "established that . . . the martyrs": *Liber pontificalis,* 53. Symmachus was pope from 498 to 514.

8.2 "It is not appropriate . . . chests to his servants." Gloss: *Ille vertit tergum ad Deum qui conversus non est prece ad eum. Nam corporis tergum nequaquam possumus vertere ad Deum, qui non est localis.* (He turns his back to God who has not turned toward him in prayer. For we cannot turn the back of our body to God, who does not subsist in space.)

9 "on the first prayer of Mass": *Ordo Romanus I,* 53; *Ordo Romanus V,* 25.

9.1 "the hymn before the *Te igitur*": the *Sanctus.*

9.4 "For the inexperienced . . . Amen": Ambrosiaster, *Commentarius in epistulam ad Corinthios primam,* 14. Quoted by Hrabanus Maurus, *Enarrationes in epistulas Pauli,* 11.14.

9.6      "When we stand . . . heavenly body": Augustine, *De sermone Domini in monte,* 2.5.18.

         "The Lord is said . . . light of truth": Alcuin, *De fide sanctae Trinitatis,* 2.5 (ed. Eric Knibbs and E. Ann Matter, CCCM 249 [Turnhout, 2012]).

10.1      "He therefore ascends to his seat": *Ordo Romanus V,* 27.

10.2–3    "set for battle": That is, ready for martyrdom.

10.4–5    "I fear lest . . . pray for you": Augustine, *Enarrationes in Psalmos,* 126.3.

10.4      "the chastity that is in Christ": Augustine's text of Paul's epistles varies from the Vulgate. In the Vulgate version Paul fears lest "your minds should be corrupted from the simplicity that is in Christ."

         "bishops also do this." Fragmentary gloss: *Numquid omnes* [. . .] (Do all [. . .]).

11        "the lector and cantor": *Ordo Romanus I,* 56–57; *Ordo Romanus V,* 29–30.

11.1      "It is called . . . only speech": Isidore, *Etymologiae,* 6.19.9.

         "The Italians . . . leaves off": Isidore, *Etymologiae,* 6.19.8.

         "our commentary on Nocturns": See below, 4.9: though as Hanssens also notes, there is no discussion of Ezra.

11.3      "This is the tradition . . . upon mats": Ambrosiaster, *Commentarius in epistulam ad Corinthios primam,* 14. Gloss: *Non hoc dicit ille Ambrosius omni ecclesiae notissimus doctor.* (Ambrose, that teacher who is extremely familiar to every church, does not say this.)

11.4      "Where the truth . . . each Testament": Gregory I, *Homiliae in Evangelia,* 1.2.4.

11.7      "He . . . calls . . . down to us": Ambrosiaster, *Commentarius in epistulam ad Corinthios primam,* 12.

11.8      *"eisagōgai":* That is, introductory teachings.

11.11     "And the priests . . . praising the Lord": Bede, *In Ezram et Neemiam prophetas allegorica expositio,* 1.4.

11.12     "Sound with . . . like a trumpet": Augustine, *Enarrationes in Psalmos,* 80.6.

11.13     "upon the obedience of his listeners": That is, upon the response.

11.15 "And so everyone . . . bodies and spirits": Boethius, *De musica,* 1.1.

11.16 "the Spartans . . . hold of spirits": Boethius, *De musica,* 1.1.

11.17 "The servant returns . . . within himself": Bede, *In Lucae Evangelium expositio,* 5.17.

11.18 "In fear of the verse . . . finish the verse." Gloss: *Vaga levicula, futilia fragilia, quae adamat animula similis eis erit.* (Vague vanities, futile fragilities: the little soul that covets such things will be like unto them.)

11.19 "After the servant . . . self-reflection as well": Bede, *In Lucae Evangelium expositio,* 5.17.

12.1 *"De profundis . . . Domine":* Out of the depths I have cried to you, O Lord.

*"Ut fugiant a facie arcus":* That they may flee from before the bow.

*"Laudate Dominum omnes gentes":* Praise the Lord, all nations.

12.2–4 "These birds . . . heavenly city": Bede, *In Lucae Evangelium expositio,* 1.2.

13 *"Dominus regnavit, decorem induit":* The Lord has reigned, he is clothed with beauty.

*"Dominus regnavit, exultet terra":* The Lord has reigned, let the earth rejoice.

*"Lauda, anima mea Dominum":* Praise the Lord, O my soul.

*"Iubilate Deo omnis terra":* Shout with joy to God, all the earth.

14.1 On these tracts: *Antiphonale Missarum,* 34, 35, 40a, 53, 67a, 73b, 36b, 60, 79b, 105, and 192.

*"De profundis":* Out of the depths.

*"Commovisti":* You have moved.

*"Qui habitat":* He that dwells.

*"Ad te levavi oculos meos":* To you I have lifted up my eyes.

*"Saepe expugnaverunt me":* Often have they fought against me.

*"Deus, Deus meus":* O God, my God.

*"Iubilate Domino":* Sing joyfully to God.

*"Qui confidunt in Domino":* Those who trust in the Lord.

*"Laudate Dominum":* Praise the Lord.

15.1 "But if anyone . . . stubborn foolishness": Bede, *In Lucae Evangelium expositio,* 6.22.

16.1 "And the Levites . . . he created": Bede, *In Ezram et Neemiam prophetas allegorica expositio,* 1.4.

"Why does . . . may praise": Augustine, *Enarrationes in Psalmos,* 149.8.

16.2 "When it takes . . . with words": Augustine, *Enarrationes in Psalmos,* 149.8.

16.3 "which the cantors call *sequentia*": The *sequentia* was an extended melisma added to the end of the alleluia.

17 On the ascent of lector and cantor: *Ordo Romanus I,* 56; *Ordo Romanus V,* 29. By pulpit, Amalar means the ambo.

17.2–5 "Chronicles seems . . . has not done": Bede, *In Ezram et Neemiam prophetas allegorica expositio,* 3.26.

18.1–2 "Beloved brethren . . . incitement to glory": Cyprian, *Epistula* 34, 4–5.

18.1 "Quirinus": The name is garbled; the letter is actually about the ordination of Celerinus.

"the pulpit . . . or . . . tribunal": That is, the ambo.

18.3 "Anastasius . . . Gospels are recited": *Liber pontificalis,* 41.

18.5 "After this . . . on your lips": *Ordo Romanus I,* 59.

18.6 "then he goes to the altar to take up the Gospel book for the reading": *Ordo Romanus I,* 59; *Ordo Romanus V,* 32.

18.7 "until the deacon begins to speak of the Lord": Presumably, Amalar is indicating the *Dominus vobiscum* (The Lord be with you).

18.10 "Because we have . . . as we just said": Compare Amalar's letter to Charlemagne on baptism, ed. MGH Epp. 5, 243–44.

18.13 "the candles are put out": *Ordo Romanus V,* 40.

19.9 "The office that we call the offertory": *Ordo Romanus I,* 67–87; *Ordo Romanus V,* 43–58.

19.11 "For you know . . . without a blessing": Augustine, *Enarrationes in Psalmos,* 128.13.

19.13 "Then the priest says: 'Let us pray'": *Ordo Romanus I,* 53; *Ordo Romanus V,* 25.

19.15 "Let it therefore . . . secret appear": Augustine, *Tractatus in Evangelium Ioannis,* 28.8.

"Everything that was . . . fulfilled in him": Augustine, *Tractatus in Evangelium Ioannis* 28.9.

19.17 "Our altar signifies . . . good works": Bede, *De tabernaculo,* 3.11.

19.18 "the beginning of this office": *Ordo Romanus I,* 53; *Ordo Romanus V,* 25.

19.20 "in the manner of the ancients": As described in the Old Testament.

19.21 "Now there are . . . invisible sacrifice": Augustine, *De civitate Dei,* 10.19.

19.23 "It is proper . . . resurrection of Lazarus": Bede, *De tabernaculo,* 3.14.

19.25 "the archdeacon": The archdeacon was first in rank among the college of deacons. From the later ninth century, archdeacons took on increasingly important administrative roles in the diocese.

19.26 "Indeed . . . prayers to God": Bede, *De tabernaculo,* 3.14.

19.27–29 "But when water . . . united and joined": Cyprian, *Epistula* 63, 13.

19.32–35 "But when we . . . fasting and alms": Cyprian, *De Dominica oratione,* 31–32.

20 "On the secret": *Ordo Romanus I,* 87; *Ordo Romanus V,* 58.

21 "On the hymn": *Ordo Romanus I,* 87; *Ordo Romanus V,* 58.

21.6 "with greater . . . of sweet tears": Bede, *De tabernaculo,* 3.11.

21.8 "We have shown . . . sacrifice of the angels": Compare the possibly-Amalarian *Canonis missae interpretatio,* 3–11 (ed. Hanssens, *Opera liturgica omnia,* 1).

"archangels . . . dominions . . . principalities": The angelic hierarchy, which depends upon Pseudo-Denis's elaboration of Eph 1:21 and Col 1:16, distinguishes nine orders of angels divided across three spheres. In the lowest are angels, archangels, and principalities; in the middle are powers, virtues, and dominions; at the summit are thrones (or, as Amalar prefers, heavens), cherubim, and seraphim.

21.9 "He established . . . Sabaoth": *Liber pontificalis,* 8.

21.14–15 "But when . . . with no fear": Gregory I, *Moralia,* 14.49.57.

22 "On the . . . *Sanctus*": *Ordo Romanus I,* 87–88; *Ordo Romanus V,* 58–59.

23     "*Te igitur*": You therefore.

23.1    "Those who stand . . . bow until this prayer is wholly finished": *Ordo Romanus I*, 88; *Ordo Romanus V*, 59–67.

    "*Sed libera nos a malo*": But free us from evil.

    "*Per omnia saecula saeculorum*": For all ages of ages.

23.2    "The glory . . . than our virtues": Bede, *In Lucae Evangelium expositio*, 6.22.

23.4    "But it was . . . more freely": Bede, *In Lucae Evangelium expositio*, 6.23.

23.6    "the *Te igitur*": *Canon romanus*, 3.

23.8–12    "Let the words . . . heard his prayer": Cyprian, *De Dominica oratione*, 4–6.

23.11    "bearing a type of the church": That is, Hannah is an Old Testament symbol for the church.

23.13    "He asks . . . Jewish people": Bede, *In Lucae Evangelium expositio*, 6.22.

23.14    "In the second . . . dries out": Jerome, *Commentarius in Evangelium Mathaei*, 6.26.

23.17    "We consecrate . . . the altar of our heart": Augustine, *De civitate Dei*, 10.3.

23.18    "The visible sacrifice . . . holy sign": Augustine, *De civitate Dei*, 10.5.

    "And thus . . . his invisible sacrifice": Augustine, *De civitate Dei*, 10.19; also quoted above, 3.18.20.

23.24    "What Saint Gregory added next": see the *Liber pontificalis*, 66.

23.25    "May they not . . . confidence and joy": Jerome, *Commentarius in Evangelium Mathaei*, 4.26.

24.1    "which accords . . . of the angels": Above, 3.21.8 and 3.23.6.

    "*Nobis quoque peccatoribus*": Likewise for us sinners.

24.5    "Likewise also . . . divine teaching": Cyprian, *Epistula* 63, 10.

24.7    "What . . . performed correctly": Augustine, *Tractatus in Evangelium Ioannis*, 118.5.

24.8    "*Accipiens panem*": Taking the bread.

    "*Vere dignum et iustum est*": It is truly right and just.

25.1    "However often . . . in my memory": *Canon romanus*, 9.

"And so, Lord . . . immaculate sacrifice": *Paduense,* 217 (882); *Hadrianum,* 1 (11).

25.2    "Nor, with respect . . . in his offering": Cyprian, *De Dominica oratione,* 24.

25.7    *"Deus, Deus meus":* O God, my God.

"And so we are mindful": Above, 3.25.1.

25.8    "For he was . . . of his disciples": Augustine, *Enarrationes in Psalmos,* 92.3.

26.2    "For just as . . . in confidence": John Chrysostom, *Homilia XXXIV in epistulam ad Hebraeos.*

26.3    "The blood was . . . as he slept": Augustine, *Tractatus in Evangelium Ioannis,* 120.2.

26.5–6  "The difference . . . because of misery": Bede, *In Lucae Evangelium expositio,* 6.23.

26.8    "Indeed, this Joseph . . . had been crucified": Bede, *In Lucae Evangelium expositio,* 6.23.

26.11   "kerchief": Amalar denotes the maniple with the same word *(sudarium)* that is used to describe Jesus's head covering in the Gospel accounts.

"This is the chalice of my blood": *Canon romanus,* 9.

26.12   "Above we read . . . laid to rest": Bede, *In Lucae Evangelium expositio,* 6.23.

26.14   "Why indeed . . . a great voice": Augustine, *Tractatus in Evangelium Ioannis,* 49.19, 24.

26.19   "The subdeacons . . . now depart. . . . Afterward they busy themselves with the patens": *Ordo Romanus I,* 91–92; *Ordo Romanus V,* 67–69.

27.1    "regional subdeacon": That is, one of the seven subdeacons, from the seven regions of Rome, who assisted with the stational Roman liturgy.

*"Et ab omni perturbatione securi":* And safe from all disquiet.

"the archdeacon turns, kisses the paten, and gives it to the second deacon to hold": *Ordo Romanus I,* 91–93; *Ordo Romanus V,* 68–70.

27.2     "according to the canons of the Council of Laodicea": Council of Laodicea, 43; in the *Collectio Dionysio-Hadriana,* Codex Canonum Ecclesiasticorum, 125.

27.6     "The bishop Aurelius . . . their own statues": Fifth Council of Carthage, 3; in the *Collectio Dionysio-Hadriana,* Canones Concilii Africani, 25. Lectors, as members of the lower clergy, were free to marry in the medieval church. Despite the decrees at Carthage, subdeacons were not firmly and finally assigned to the higher clergy (and therefore required to maintain celibacy) until the High Middle Ages.

         "Pope Sixtus . . . the ministers": *Liber pontificalis,* 8.

27.8     "The paten is so-called because it stands open": The Latin word for paten, *patena,* reminds Amalar of the Latin verb *patere,* "to be open."

28.1     "The deacons and subdeacons stand and bow": *Ordo Romanus V,* 67.

28.2     *"Libera nos, quaesumus, Domine, ab omnibus malis":* Free us, we ask you, Lord, from all evil.

         *"Per Dominum nostrum":* Through our Lord.

28.6–7   "For those who . . . feels compunction": Augustine, *De cura pro mortuis,* 5.7.

29.1–2   "Above all . . . worthy of God": Cyprian, *De Dominica oratione,* 8.

29.4     "Yet I know . . . do and observe": Cyprian, *Epistula* 63, 1.

29.9–10  "After all these . . . of all the land": Cyprian, *De Dominica oratione,* 27–28.

30       "on the presentation of the subdeacons": *Ordo Romanus I,* 100–101; *Ordo Romanus V,* 75–76.

30.1–2   "Just as we . . . ashes and earth": Bede, *In Lucae Evangelium expositio,* 6.24.

30.5     "the offerings are placed on the paten": *Ordo Romanus I,* 95–97; *Ordo Romanus V,* 72–74.

31.1     *"Pax Domini":* Peace of the Lord.

         "he puts part of the holy body in the chalice": *Ordo Romanus I,* 95; *Ordo Romanus V,* 72.

31.6     "And the first archdeacon . . . the hands of the archdeacon": *Ordo*

*Romanus I,* 96–97, 102–3, 106–7; *Ordo Romanus V,* 73–74, 77–78, 81–82.

32.1    "And so you . . . things are finished": Innocent I, *Epistula* 25, 1.1; in the *Collectio Dionysio-Hadriana, Decreta Innocentii,* 1.

33.1    *"Agnus Dei":* Lamb of God.
        "He declared . . . Lord's body": *Liber pontificalis,* 86.

34.1    "Nobody should . . . one body": Bede, *In Lucae Evangelium expositio,* 6.24.

34.2    "Now there are . . . receive it daily": The frequency of communion among the faithful declined broadly after Late Antiquity, though encouragement of weekly communion accompanied the Carolingian reforms.

34.2–3  "Perhaps . . . of the Lord": Augustine, *Epistula* 54, 3.4.

34.4    "And so . . . from that practice": Augustine, *Epistula* 54, 6.8. Cited at 1.20.3.

36      "On the final blessing": *Ordo Romanus I,* 123; *Ordo Romanus V,* 95.

36.2    "First, that through . . . received from them": Bede, *In Lucae Evangelium expositio,* 6.24.

36.3–5  "This John was . . . but with compassion": Bede, *Super epistulas septem catholicas: In primam epistolam Ioannis,* 2.

36.7    "Mass occurs . . . of the altar": Isidore, *Etymologiae,* 6.19.

36.8    "the reborn": That is, the baptized.

37      "On the further final blessing": See de Puniet's overview of sacramentaries, 30*–67* (oratio 6).

38      "Mass on the feast of Saint John the Baptist": June 24, Nativity of Saint John.

39      "the offertory *Vir erat in terra*": *Antiphonale Missarum,* 196a; There was a man in the land.

39.1    "The historian's words": The offertory consists of the words of the narrator of the book of Job.

40.1    "In ancient missals and lectionaries": See de Puniet's overview of sacramentaries, 164*–65*, 166*–75*; Capitulary of Würzburg, 170–74; Lectionary of Murbach, 147–56; Epistolary of Corbie, 139–46; Epistolary of Alcuin: Supplement, 50–51; *Capitulare,* D, 307. Roman sources attest to only four weeks of

Advent: *Capitulare,* A, from 233; B, from 258; C, from 262. The Gregorian sacramentary also contains only four weeks of Advent: de Puniet, 164*–75*, and Epistolary of Alcuin, 176–82.

"The antiphoner has three daytime offices and a fourth on Sunday . . . and there are four night offices": *Antiphonale Missarum,* 1a–7bis; and *Antiphonalia Officii,* 1a–8a.

40.2   "and of the antiphoner": *Antiphonalia Officii,* 9–18.

40.7   "the reading . . . on the fourth week": Epistolary of Alcuin, 176 (Rom 13:11–14).

"To thee have I lifted up my soul": *Antiphonale Missarum,* 1a.

40.8   "Let us receive . . . worthy honors": *Paduense,* 295 (783); *Hadrianum,* 185 (780).

40.9   "Everything . . . than pepper": Jerome, *Epistula* 146, 2.

41.1   "He established . . . the Lord's birthday": *Liber pontificalis,* 8.

41.2   "This celebration . . . incarnation of the word": See the Latin annotation; this passage is corrupt.

"For a common . . . the same womb": Cyril of Alexandria, *Epistula* 4.

42.1   "We read in the *Deeds of the Bishops*": *Liber pontificalis,* 9.

42.4   "Therefore . . . is another": Innocent, *Epistula* 17, 5.9; in the *Collectio Dionysio-Hadriana,* Decreta Innocentii, 55.

42.5   "Pope Leo": Leo III, pope from 795 to 816.

"For power is resplendent, decorated by reason": Cicero, *De natura deorum,* 1.5.10.

43.1   "That on the feasts . . . church of Saint Mary": *Liber pontificalis,* 86.

43.2   "He consecrated . . . the eternal city": Bede, *De temporum ratione,* 12.

44.1   "But sacrifice . . . incense of sweetness": Origen, *In Leviticum homiliae,* 5.6.

44.8   "And so by . . . actions is suggested": Gregory I, *Moralia,* 8.8.16.

44.10–11   "And when he . . . celebrated for him": Bede, *Historia ecclesiastica,* 4.22.

44.12–14   "Nor should we . . . more tolerable": Augustine, *Enchiridion,* 110.

44.15   "Yet they may . . . whom they benefit": Augustine, *De cura pro mortuis,* 18.22.

## Letters

I      "the prophet Jeremiah": Archbishop Jeremy of Sens (818–827).

1.1    "Our countrymen write the name of our savior Jesus with the letter 'H'": In Latin manuscripts, the name of Jesus was typically represented via a three-letter abbreviation, either as IHS or IHC. The "H" that puzzles Amalar is actually the Greek letter eta, as Amalar proceeds to learn from his correspondent.

       "the name of whose leader we read was Jesus, or Joshua": That is, Joshua: Jesus and Joshua are alternative renderings of the same Hebrew name, and the Latin tradition represents both as *Iesus.*

       "Then the . . . came before": Sedulius, *Carmen Paschale,* 1.168–69.

2      "Porphyry . . . writes the name of Jesus in his Latin acrostic": Publilius Optatianus Porfyrius, *Carmina: Carmina litteris capitalibus expressa,* 8 (ed. Giovanni Polara, *Corpus Scriptorum Latinorum Paravianum* [Turin, 1998]). Here Jeremy refers to Porfyrius's poem as an *anacrostica,* an unusual term apparently chosen because Prorphyry's poems are not simply acrostics, but *carmina figurata;* that is, their letters align to form graphical images. See Bayerische Akademie der Wissenschaften, *Das Mittellateinische Wörterbuch* 1: A–B (Munich, 1967), 606, article "*anachrostichis."

3      "Jonas": Bishop Jonas of Orléans (818–841).

4      "This is the . . . mystery of faith": *Canon Romanus,* 9.

4.5    "Therefore . . . faith is faith": Augustine, *Epistula* 98, 9.

5.2    "Although many . . . gender and number": Jerome, *Commentarius in Ezechielem,* 3.9.

       *"ta cherubin":* τὰ χερουβίν.

5.4    "And indeed . . . the masculine": Bede, *De tabernaculo,* 1.5.

5.5    "none of the . . . mentioned elsewhere": Jerome, *Epistula* 18, 10.

       "standing": The Latin participle *stantia* has the neuter plural inflection.

       "the church, which is accustomed to speak daily of 'blessed seraphin'": *Paduense,* 217 (875): seraphim; *Hadrianum,* 1 (3): serafin; *Gellonense,* 325 (1931): seraphyn; *Canon romanus,* 2: seraphim.

6.11    "It was your . . . companion I want": Ammianus Marcellinus, *Res*

> gestae 26.2 (ed. Wolfgang Seyfarth, *Rerum gestarum libri qui supersunt* [Leipzig, 1978], 2). Also *Historia tripartita*, 7.7.

6.16 "Children, flee . . . grass": Virgil, *Eclogues*, 3.93.

"In the canons": *Canones apostolorum*, 9, in the *Collectio Dionysio-Hadriana*.

6.17 "You have fixed it in Bishop Gennadius of Marseille": See Gennadius, *Libri ecclesiasticorum dogmatum*, 53.

6.19 "Perhaps he . . . under my roof": Augustine, *Epistula* 54, 3.4; see above, 3.34.2.

## Book 4

1 "sections of psalmody": Amalar uses the Latin word *repetitio* (English, very roughly, "repetition") generally to indicate the twelve sections of psalmody (and especially the eleven sections of Ps 118) that are recited through the daylight hours.

1.3 "And then . . . of the moon": Bede, *De temporum ratione*, 18.

1.4 "There are four . . . to maturity": Bede, *De temporum ratione*, 35.

1.9 "But why do . . . we call hours": Bede, *De temporum ratione*, 24.

2.7 "the Gospel passage that contains the appointment of the laborers": *Capitulare* A, 51 (Matt 20:1–16); B, 58; C, 55; D, 62; P, 57.

2.12 "Jerome . . . in his letter to Pope Damasus": Pseudo-Jerome, *Epistula* 47.

"*Gloria Patri*": Glory be to the Father.

2.13 "*Laus tibi, Domine, rex aeternae gloriae*": Praise to you Lord, king of eternal glory.

"This is for . . . any other season": See 1.1.16–17.

2.15 "*Beati inmaculati*": Blessed are the undefiled.

2.26 "Lord, guide our hearts . . . necessary tasks": See below, 4.7.8.

3.1 "Ecclesiastical tradition . . . into the temple": Jerome, *Commentarius in Danielem*, 6.

3.3 "And who is . . . divine readings": Bede, *In Ezram et Neemiam prophetas allegorica expositio*, 3.28.

3.11 "the first section . . . the second . . . The third": The psalmody at Terce, Sext, and None consisted of three sections, or *periochae*, of verses taken from Ps 118.

3.15–16   "We learn most . . . spiritual canticle": Jerome, *Commentarius in epistulam ad Ephesios*, 3.5. Also quoted above, 3.2.11.

3.20   "In discussing the Mass": Above, 3.11.

3.21   "in our aforementioned discussion": See above, 3.11.19.

3.22   "the greater one": That is, the hebdomadarian.

3.23   "We said earlier": Above, 1.21.

4.3–5   "Above all . . . then prayers": Not Ambrose, but rather Theodore of Mopsuestia, *Commentarii in epistulas Pauli minores;* quoted in Hrabanus Maurus, *Enarrationes in epistulas Pauli,* 23.2.

4.7   "Return, O Lord . . . of this world": Augustine, *Enarrationes in Psalmos,* 89.14.

4.8   *"Miserere mei, Deus":* Have mercy on me, O God.

4.14   "This same . . . Vespers": Council of Laodicea, 18; in the *Collectio Dionysio-Hadriana, Codex Canonum Conciliorum,* 121.

4.16   *"Domine, ne in furore tuo":* O Lord, not in your indignation.
   *"Miserere mei Deus":* Have mercy on me, O God.

4.17   "The eighth day . . . in your indignation": Augustine, *Enarrationes in Psalmos,* 6.2–3. By "prologue," Amalar means the introductory verse at Ps 6:1 ("Unto the end, in verses, a psalm for David, for the octave"), which Augustine discusses at some length.

4.18   "This is the eighth . . . in your indignation": Bede, *De temporum ratione,* 10.

5.3   "The first section . . . The second . . . The third": See the note to 4.3.11, above.

6.1   "Vices . . . advancing in us": Gregory I, *Moralia,* 22.25.51.

6.3   "They rage . . . are loved": Augustine, *Enarrationes in Psalmos,* 118.28.6.
   "The first section . . . The second . . . The third": See the note to 4.3.11, above.

6.4   "Take evil thought . . . spare your servant": Augustine, *Enarrationes in Psalmos,* 18.2.13.

7.2   "The office of . . . east at night": Isidore, *Etymologiae,* 6.19.2.
   "At vesper . . . when the sun sets": Augustine, *Enarrationes in Psalmos,* 29.2.16.

7.3   "At vesper . . . over the faithful": Augustine, *Enarrationes in Psalmos,* 29.2.16.

7.8      "The five senses of our body": See above, 4.2.26.

        "We will speak about hearts separately": Below, 4.7.20.

7.9      "Yet it should . . . all the churches": *Historia Tripartita,* 10.9.

7.10      "Alternating voice is referred to as an antiphon": See Isidore, *Etymologiae,* 6.19.7.

7.12–13      "For when he . . . multitude of sins": Gregory the Great, *Homiliae in Hiezechielem,* 7.21.

7.14      "responsories . . . after the Vespers reading": See the antiphoner of Compiègne, *Antiphonalia Officii,* 144d; the responsories in question are ed. PL 78, 725–850. See also Amalar, *De ordine antiphonarii,* 80 (ed. Hanssens, *Opera liturgica omnia,* 3).

7.16      "the alleluia occurs": *Antiphonalia Officii,* 52; Amalar, *De ordine antiphonarii,* 30 (ed. Hanssens, *Opera liturgica omnia,* 3).

7.21      *"Benedictus Dominus Deus meus":* Blessed be the Lord my God.

7.22      "I will extol . . . end of the Psalm": Augustine, *Enarrationes in Psalmos,* 144.2.

        "Behold, the Psalm . . . my soul": Augustine, *Enarrationes in Psalmos,* 145.2.

        "We are told . . . it is good": Augustine, *Enarrationes in Psalmos,* 146.1.

7.23      "O Jerusalem . . . O Jerusalem": Augustine, *Enarrationes in Psalmos,* 147.6.

7.24–27      "Let us therefore . . . daytime wandering": Bede, *Homiliae,* 1.4.

7.30      *"Lauda Hierusalem Dominum":* Praise the Lord, O Jerusalem.

        "After seventy years . . . not pass away": Augustine, *Enarrationes in Psalmos,* 147.5.

8.1      "in accordance with Saint Benedict's rule": Benedict, *Regula,* 42.

8.4      "In peace . . . after this life": Augustine, *Enarrationes in Psalmos,* 4.9.

8.6      *"Qui habitat in adiutorio":* He who dwells in the aid.

8.7      "For the night . . . name of the Lord": Augustine, *Enarrationes in Psalmos,* 133.2.

8.10      "that we may read four times a night": See above, 4.3.2–3 and 4.7.1.

9.3      "the resurrection . . . from, or of, the dead": The Latin has "dead"

in the genitive plural; this passage therefore indicates, for Amalar, "the resurrection of all the elect."

9.7 "And if prudence . . . seems like one": Augustine, *Epistula* 167, 5.

9.12 "Saint Gregory, in his homily": Gregory I, *Homiliae in Evangelia,* 2.31.2–3.

9.13 "the difference between the nature of the present readings and those that are provided by pastors to their household servants": That is, the difference between Office readings and Mass readings. See 1.21, and above, 3.11.

9.14 "We laid out these examples above": 3.11.8–9.

9.18 "with immaturity": That is to say, "early."

9.19 "I rose in . . . to be understood": Augustine, *Enarrationes in Psalmos,* 118.29.3.

9.20 "After singing . . . vespers and midnight": Jerome, *Epistula* 108, 19.

9.21 "I will now speak . . . arrange it for weaving": Jerome, *Epistula* 130, 15.

9.22 "Alea": That is, Laeta; Amalar corrupts the name.

"Let an experienced . . . follow reading": Jerome, *Epistula* 107, 9.

10.2–3 "And . . . about the fourth . . . will be there": Bede, *In Marci Evangelium expositio,* 2.6.

10.5 "And that net . . . in its bounds": Gregory, *Homiliae in Evangelia,* 1.11.4.

10.7 "For in the title . . . is Christ Jesus": Augustine, *Enarrationes in Psalmos,* 92.1.

10.8 "Sing joyfully . . . all the gentiles": Augustine, *Enarrationes in Psalmos,* 99.3.

10.9 "Through the name . . . idols were worshiped": Augustine, *Enarrationes in Psalmos,* 62.3.

10.10 "And it can happen . . . and the Greeks": Augustine, *De civitate Dei,* 15.26.2.

"the passage I quoted . . . as I explained in that work": Augustine is discussing his use of Gen 6:16 in an earlier treatise, *Contra Faustum.*

10.11 *"Deus misereatur nostri":* May God have mercy on us.

10.13 "We said of the *Gloria Patri*": Above, 4.2.12.

   "Blessed, he says . . . in his majesty": Jerome, *Commentarius in Danielem,* 12.

10.14 *"Laudate Dominum de caelis":* Praise the Lord from the heavens.

   *"Cantate Domino canticum novum":* Sing to the Lord a new canticle.

   *"Laudate Dominum in sanctis eius":* Praise the Lord in his holy places.

   "But it had . . . after the flood": Augustine, *De civitate Dei,* 15.26.2.

10.15 "I think that . . . beyond these three": Augustine, *Quaestiones Evangeliorum,* 2.44.

12.2 *"Miserere mei Deus":* Have mercy on me, O God.

12.3 *"Deus, Deus meus":* O God, my God.

   *"Deus misereatur nostri":* May God have mercy on us.

   *"Laudate Dominum de caelis":* Praise the Lord from the heavens.

   *"Cantate Domino":* Sing to the Lord.

   *"Laudate Dominum in sanctis eius":* Praise the Lord in his holy places.

12.4 *"Verba mea":* My words.

   "It is understood . . . possess the land": Augustine, *Enarrationes in Psalmos,* 5.1.

12.6 "On that day . . . house of Israel": Jerome, *Commentarius in Esaiam,* 4.11.

12.7 "You who had . . . and my praise": Jerome, *Commentarius in Esaiam,* 4.12.

12.10–11 "Then . . . anticipating with hope . . . days occur at once": Augustine, *Enarrationes in Psalmos,* 89.15.

15 "Cantemus Domino": Let us sing to the Lord.

16.1 "Let us therefore . . . in this Psalm": Augustine, *Enarrationes in Psalmos,* 142.2.

16.2 "The standard and . . . commend my spirit": Jerome, *Commentarius in Abacuc,* 2.3.

17.2 "You have not . . . joyfully and well": Augustine, *Enarrationes in Psalmos,* 91.5.

17.3 *"Audite caeli":* Here, O heavens.

"And on the day . . . days of the week": Bede, *In Lucae Evangelium expositio,* 2.4. See 1.38.4.

"the custom of pronouncing the canticle of Deuteronomy on Saturday": Bede is discussing the Saturday before Pentecost.

17.5    *"Dominus regnavit":* The Lord has reigned.

*"Miserere mei, Deus":* Have mercy on me, O God.

17.8    *"Verba mea":* My words.

"The voice of . . . come to him": Augustine, *Enarrationes in Psalmos,* 5.1–2.

17.9    *"Confitebor tibi Domine":* I will confess to you, O Lord.

"as was shown above": 4.12.5.

*"Iubilate Domino, omnis terra":* Sing joyfully to the Lord, all the earth.

*"Iudica me, Deus, et discerne causam meam de gente non sancta":* Judge me, God, and distinguish my cause from the nation that is not holy.

17.10   *"Deus, Deus meus":* Oh God, my God.

"But we should . . . be thirsted after": Augustine, *Enarrationes in Psalmos,* 62.4–6.

17.11   *"Te decet ymnus, Deus":* A hymn, O God, becomes you.

"We see . . . one more": Augustine, *Enarrationes in Psalmos,* 64.15.

*"Exultavit cor meum in Domino":* My heart has rejoiced in the Lord.

17.12   *"Deus misereatur nostri":* May God have mercy on us.

*"Domine, refugium factus es nobis":* Lord, you have been our refuge.

*"Cantemus Domino":* Let us sing to the Lord.

17.13   *"Benedicite":* Bless.

17.16   *"Laudate Dominum de caelis":* Praise the Lord from the heavens.

*"Cantate Domino canticum novum":* Sing to the Lord a new canticle.

*"Laudate Dominum in sanctis eius":* Praise the Lord in his holy places.

*"Audite caeli quae loquor":* Hear, O heavens, the things I speak.

18.1    *"Miserere mei, Deus":* Have mercy on me, O God.

*"Confitemini Domino":* Confess to the Lord.

18.3 "Now receiving . . . ready to indulge": Gregory I, *Moralia*, 33.12.24.

18.4 *"Dominus regnavit"*: The Lord has reigned.

19 *"Qui habitat in adiutorio altissimi"*: He who dwells in the aid of the most high.

20.4 "Saint Jerome . . . Pope Damasus": Above, 4.2.12 (with annotation).

21.1 "The introit for Wednesday": *Antiphonale*, 76.

21.4 *"Domine, labia mea aperies"*: O Lord, you will open my lips.

21.5 *"Benedictus Dominus Deus Israhel"*: Blessed be the Lord God of Israel.

21.7 "For the younger Rome": Constantinople.

21.10–11 "On that night . . . this husbandry": Augustine, *Quaestiones Evangeliorum*, 2.44. For a related citation, see above, 4.10.15.

22.1 "twenty-four lights are lit . . . and they are put out": *Ordo Romanus XXVI*, 13; *Ordo Romanus XXVII*, 5; *Ordo Romanus XXVIII*, 30 and 49; *Ordo Romanus XXXA*, 5 and 12; *Ordo Romanus XXXII*, 5.

22.2 "For corporeal fire . . . it is revived": Gregory I, *Moralia*, 15.29.35.

23.2 "The devil therefore . . . from his redeemed": Augustine, *Tractatus in Evangelium Ioannis*, 52.12.6.

23.4 *"Beatus vir"*: Blessed is the man.

23.6 "For he did . . . they his members": Augustine, *Tractatus in Evangelium Ioannis*, 52.12.11.

23.8 "Therefore Paul did not say . . .": For the same point, see above, 4.9.3, and the note to that passage.

23.12 "It is truly worthy . . . on this day": *Paduense*, 75 (329).

  "This is the day which the Lord has made": *Antiphonale Missarum*, 80–86.

23.20 *"Confitemini Domino"*: Confess to the Lord.

  "Every Christian . . . hope and charity": See Gregory I, *Moralia*, 1.32–33.

23.24 "We have it written in the Roman order": *Ordo Romanus XXXA*, 2–3; *Ordo Romanus XXVIII*, 10.

23.25 "Our praise expresses . . . our rejoicing remains": Augustine, *Enarrationes in Psalmos*, 148.1.

23.26–29 "Because of these . . . Praise God": Augustine, *Enarrationes in Psalmos,* 148.1–2.

24.1 "When I wrote about the Greater Litany above": 1.37.

25.1–2 "In the name . . . within the palace": Gregory I , *Registrum epistularum,* 13.1.

25.1 "the Hebdomon in the palace called Secundianas": The Hebdomon was a coastal habitation, seven miles (hence the name) outside the city of Constantinople, home to an imperial residence.

"Emperor Maurice": Flavius Mauricius Tiberius Augustus, who began his reign as emperor of Byzantium in 582, was overthrown by Phocas in 602 and was executed along with his six sons on November 27 of that year.

"Constantine, patrician and curator of Placidia": Constantine Lardys (d. 602), a senior official in the reign of Maurice, is here identified as *curator domus divinae,* or an administrator of imperial property. For more on Constantine and the conflicting information on the estates that were subject to him, see John Robert Martindale, Arnold Hugh Martin Jones, and John Morris, eds., *The Prosopography of the Later Roman Empire* (Cambridge, 1992), 3:347–8.

25.2 "the seventh day before the Kalends of May": April 25.

25.3–9 "Dearest brethren . . . blessed martyr Cecilia": Gregory I, *Registrum epistularum,* 13.2.

25.9 "God's maidservants": That is, nuns.

25.11–14 "Gregory to Emperor Phocas . . . have lately received": Gregory I, *Registrum epistularum,* 13.38.

25.12 "he was the first of all the defenders": The *defensores regionarii* were municipal officials assigned administrative duties in the seven regions of Rome.

26.2–8 "Gregory to Bishop John . . . things that he sees": Gregory I, *Registrum epistularum,* 9.12.

27.5 "Now he ordered . . . brought in to him": Possidius, *Vita Augustini,* 8.11.3.

27.6–8 "But the great . . . of his Holy Spirit": Augustine, *Tractatus in Evangelium Ioannis,* 17.5.4–5.

27.8    "Thus we celebrate Lent before Easter in labor, but we celebrate the fifty days following Easter in rejoicing": Lent, in Latin, is Quadragesima, or "fortieth"; hence Augustine's connection to the progression from forty to fifty, and from Lent to Eastertide.

27.12   "And then, when . . . might baptize others": Augustine, *Epistula* 265, 5.

27.21   "what we said while discussing Easter": Above, at 4.23.12–15.

27.23–27 "To reflect briefly . . . from this cup": Gregory I, *Moralia,* 1.32.44–33.46.

29.1    "the number forty, multiplied by its parts, makes fifty": See 1.36.1.

29.3    "In our office books it is written . . .": See, for example, the sacramentary of Monza (ed. Alban Dold and Klaus Gamber, *Das Sakramentar von Monza* [Beuron, 1957], 36, n. 110); and *Antiphonale Missarum,* 173–98.

        "I do not know what sort of octave Pentecost can have": That is, Amalar wonders how Pentecost, a feast that is supposed to consist only of fifty days, can be prolonged with an octave.

29.4–5  "It is as if the eighth . . . of the new man": Augustine, *De sermone Domini in monte,* 3.10–4.12.

30.1    "We wrote in previous books": Above, 3.40.1–8.

30.3    "the reading . . . in the fifth week": Epistolary of Corbie, 139 (Jer 23:5–8); Capitulary of Würzburg, 171.

30.5    "The Gospel reading . . . on the . . . fifth week": *Capitulare* D, 307 (John 6:5–14); also A, 233; B, 258; C, 262; P, 282.

        "Now there were . . . precepts of the law": Bede, *In Lucae Evangelium expositio,* 3.9.

30.6    "The offices of the cantors and the priests": *Antiphonale Missarum,* 1, 2, 4, 7 bis; *Paduense,* 195, 196, 198, 202. For the Gospel readings, see *Capitulare* A, 238 (Matt 21:1–9); 239 (Luke 21:25–33); 240 (Matt 11:2–10); 241 (John 1:19–28).

        "the epistle that is read on that day": Epistolary of Alcuin, 176 (Rom 13:11–14); Capitulary of Würzburg, 179; Epistolary of Corbie, 140.

"But when he comes . . . in his infirmity": Augustine, *Enarrationes in Psalmos,* 101.18.

33.17   "For what is . . . end of one's life": Gregory I, *Moralia,* 1.27.55.

34.3   "our mortification is also commemorated in various offices and the Lord's passion is read out": *Ordo Romanus XXIV,* 5–7; *Ordo Romanus XXVII,* 18–20; *Ordo Romanus XXVIII,* 4–6. *Capitulare,* B, 102 (Luke 22:1–23, 53); C, 92. Hanssens notes the different usage outlined at *Capitulare* A, 88; D, 111; P, 111.

"our discussion in a previously written book": At 1.11.

34.4   "The reading from Exodus . . . the one from Hosea": Epistolary of Alcuin, 79 (Hos 6:1–6); 80 (Exod 12:1–11); Capitulary of Würzburg, 83–84; Epistolary of Corbie, 86–86a.

"The tract that follows the readings": *Ordo Romanus XXIV,* 24; *Ordo Romanus XXVIII,* 33; *Ordo Romanus XXVII,* 37; compare *Antiphonale Missarum* 40a and 70a, and 1.13.9.

*"Qui habitat in adiutorio altissimi":* He who dwells in the aid of the most high.

35.1   "The feasts of the saints reveal the births": The Latin word here translated "feast" is *natalitia*—literally, "birthday celebration."

36.2–4   "For just as . . . have been promised": Augustine, *Tractatus in Evangelium Ioannis,* 49.9–10.

36.6–7   "And he called . . . resurrection of the dead": Hesychius, *Commentarius in Leviticum,* 6.23.

37.2–5   "Someone may say . . . to fast daily": Jerome, *Commentarii in epistolam ad Galatas,* 2.4.

37.7   "when the suffering of the three boys . . . is recounted": Epistolary of Alcuin, 40, 120, 181.

37.9   "as Augustine said to Casulanus": Augustine, *Epistula* 36, 13, and 30.

37.13   "Do not let him . . . cause a scandal": Augustine, *Epistula* 36, 8.20 and 14.32.

37.14   "It is written in the *Life of the Blessed Ambrose*": Paulinus of Milan, *Vita sancti Ambrosii,* 38.

37.14–15   "I have not found . . . what had occurred": Augustine, *Epistula* 36, 11.25, and 13.31.

37.17 "You should . . . or disagreement": Augustine, *Epistula* 36, 14.32.

37.20 "While explaining this verse, Ambrose . . .": Ambrosiaster, *Commentarius in epistulam ad Romanos,* 14.

37.21 "It is forbidden to fast on Sunday in the book that is entitled the *Canones*": *Canones apostolorum,* 25, in the *Collectio Dionysio-Hadriana.*

   "It is a great scandal . . . considered dreadful": Augustine, *Epistula* 36, 12.27.

37.22 "Saint Jerome places. . . . For Saint Jerome, it is clear . . .": Above, 4.37.2; and Jerome, *Epistula* 41, 3.

37.23 "The fast . . . on other feasts": Augustine, *Epistula* 36, 9.21.

37.24 "For in those . . . held as law": Augustine, *Epistula* 36, 1.2.

38.1–3 "God's priest stands . . . may be dissipated": John Chrysostom, *In epistulam ad Hebraeos,* 9, homilia 15. See also 1.1.22, for a related citation.

39.2–6 "And although we . . . world in contempt": Bede, *Historia ecclesiastica,* 5.21.

39.7 "Afterward, with . . . bound Christ's head": Not Bede, but rather the anonymous *Vita Cuthberti,* 2.2. The *Vita* is edited and translated by Bertram Colgrave, *Two Lives of Saint Cuthbert* (New York, 1940).

40.1 "We related in the words of this work . . .": Above, 3.42.

40.2 "However often . . . into heaven": *Canon romanus,* 9–10.

40.4 "Do what you . . . his extended prayer": Gregory the Great, *Homiliae in Evangelia,* 2.37.9.

41.1 "And therefore, after . . . rejoiced with Christ": Again, not Bede but the anonymous *Vita Cuthberti,* 4.13 (ed. and trans. Colgrave, *Two Lives of Saint Cuthbert*).

41.8–9 "And so the earth . . . help for the dead": Augustine, *De civitate Dei* 1.12.

41.10–12 "Yet the bodies . . . wasted upon God": Augustine, *De civitate Dei* 1.13.

42.1 "We have it written in a sacramentary": See, for example, the *Paduense,* 245.

42.6 "Nor should we . . . heaven is understood": Augustine, *Quaestiones in Heptateuchum I: Quaestiones in Genesim,* 169.

42.7–9    "And they mourned . . . as it were, at rest": Augustine, *Quaestiones in Heptateucham I: Quaestiones in Genesim*, 172.

42.10    "as we said in our discussion of the Mass": Above, 3.44.4.

42.13    "We should not . . . to their spirits": Augustine, *De cura pro mortuis*, 4.6.

43.1    "Above, we said . . .": 4.23.1–21.

44    *"Fluminis impetus":* The stream of the river.

44.1    *"Deus noster refugium":* God is our refuge.

44.3    *"Hodie in Iordane":* Today in the Jordan.

    *"In columbae specie":* In the form of a dove.

    *"Dicit Dominus: Implete ydrias aqua":* The Lord says: Fill the water pots with water.

44.4    *"Cantate Domino":* Sing to the Lord.

    *"Dominus regnavit, exultet terra, laetentur insulae multae":* The Lord has reigned, let the earth rejoice, let many islands be glad.

45.2    *"Magnificat":* (My soul) magnifies.

    *"Benedictus Dominus Deus Israel":* Blessed be the Lord God of Israel.

45.4    "Saint Ambrose called this prayer an intercession": Actually Theodore of Mopsuestia, *Commentarii in epistulas Pauli minores: Commentarius in epistolam primam ad Timotheum*, on 1 Tim 2:1; as quoted in Hrabanus Maurus, *Enarrationes in epistulas Pauli: In epistulam primam ad Timotheum*, 2.

    "And Augustine considers": Augustine, *Epistula* 149, 2.16, and passim.

46    "Our ancestors . . . are like Sunday": Ambrose, *Expositio Evangelii secundum Lucam*, 8.25.

47.2    *"Unde et memores sumus":* And so we are mindful; *Canon Romanus*, 10.

    "Another version . . . of the cross": Bede, *Explanatio Apocalypsis*, 2.8.

47.4    "For water and . . . may be redeemed": Ambrose, *Expositio Evangelii secundum Lucam*, 10.135.

# Bibliography

AMALAR, *ON THE LITURGY:* EDITIONS AND TRANSLATION

Cochlaeus, Johann. *Speculum antiquae devotionis circa Missam et omnem alium cultum Dei . . .* Mainz, 1549. This *editio princeps* contains only the Preface and part of Book 3. It was reprinted by Niccolò Bonfigili at Venice in 1572.

Hittorp, Melchior. *De divinis catholicae ecclesiae officiis . . .* Cologne, 1568, 101–262, 589, 594–98. This is a full edition, lacking only Amalar's epistolary appendix to Book 3. Reprinted nine times, including PL 105, 985–1242, with the addition of the appended letters at 1333–39.

Hanssens, Jean-Michel. *Amalarii Episcopi Opera liturgica omnia.* 3 vols. Vatican, 1948–1950, at 1:120–202 (introduction) and 2 (full edition). For more on the early editions of Amalar's commentary, see Hanssens, *Opera liturgica omnia,* 1:131–3.

Raftery, Paul K. "Amalar of Metz on the Mass: A Translation of Book III, Chapters 1–18 of the *Liber Officialis.*" Thesis, Jesuit School of Theology at Berkeley, 1998.

AMALAR'S SOURCES

Legal, Historical, and Biblical

*Collectio Dionysio-Hadriana:* Pithou, F., ed. *Codex canonum vetus Ecclesiae Romanae restitutus.* Paris, 1687.

*Historia tripartita:* Jacob, Walter, and Rudolf Hanslik, eds. CSEL 71. Vienna, 1952.

Hrabanus Maurus, *Ennarationes in epistolas Pauli:* Ed. PL 111, 1273–1616, and 112, 9–834.

663

*Liber pontificalis:* Duchesne, L., ed. *Le Liber Pontificalis: Texte, introduction et commentaire.* vol. 1. Paris, 1886.

*Statuta ecclesiae antiqua:* Munier, Charles, ed. *Les Statuta Ecclesiae Antiqua: édition, études critiques.* Paris, 1960.


## Liturgical Readings

Epistolary of Alcuin: Described in Leclercq, Henri, "Épitres." In *Dictionnaire d'archéologie chrétienne et de liturgie* 5.1, edited by Fernand Cabrol and Henri Leclercq, 300–310. Paris, 1922.

Epistolary of Corbie: Described in Frere, W. H., *Studies in Early Roman Liturgy III: The Roman Epistle-Lectionary,* 1–24. Oxford, 1935.

Lectionary of Murbach: Described in Leclercq, "Épitres," 316–21.

Capitulary of Würzburg: Described in Leclercq, "Épitres," 312–16.

Gospel pericopes, or *Capitulare evangeliorum:* Collected in Klauser, Theodor. *Das römische Capitulare Evangeliorum.* Münster, 1935.


## Sung Texts for the Liturgy

Mass antiphoner: Hesbert, René-Jean, ed. *Antiphonale Missarum Sextuplex.* Brussels, 1935.

Office antiphoners: Hesbert, René-Jean, ed. *Corpus Antiphonalium Officii.* 5 vols. Rome, 1963–1979.


## Liturgical Prayers

Gelasian Sacramentary, or the *Gelasianum:* Mohlberg, L. C., L. Eizenhöfer, and P. Siffrin, eds.. *Liber sacramentorum Romanae aecclesiae ordinis anni circuli.* Rome, 1960.

Sacramentary of Gellone, or the *Gellonense.* Dumas, A., ed. *Liber Sacramentorum Gellonensis.* CCSL 159. Turnhout, 1981.

Sacramentary of Padua, or the *Paduense:* Catella, Alceste, Ferdinando Dell'Oro, Aldo Martini, and Fabrizio Crivello, eds. *Liber Sacramentorum Paduensis.* Rome, 2005.

Gregorian Sacramentary of Hadrian I, or the *Hadrianum:* Deshusses, J., ed.

*Le sacramentaire grégorien, ses principales formes d'aprés les plus anciens man-uscripts.* 3 vols. Fribourg, 1971–1982.

The evidence of the sacramentaries is also conveniently surveyed in de Pu-niet, P. *Omnia sacramentaria synoptice descripta.* Rome, 1938.

## Other Liturgical Sources

Canon of the Mass, or *Canon Romanus:* Botte, Bernard, ed. *Le canon de la messe romaine.* Louvain, 1935.

Roman *ordines:* Andrieu, Michel, ed. *Les Ordines Romani du haut moyen âge.* 5 vols. Louvain, 1931–1961.

### Select Secondary Literature

Cabaniss, Allen. *Amalarius of Metz.* Amsterdam, 1954.

Chazelle, Celia. "Amalarius's *Liber Officialis:* Spirit and Vision in Carolin-gian Liturgical Thought." In *Seeing the Invisible in Late Antiquity and the Early Middle Ages,* edited by Giselle de Nie, Karl F. Morrison, and Marco Mostert, 327–57. Turnhout, 2005.

Cristiani, Marta. "Il 'Liber Officialis' di Amalario di Metz e la dottrina del 'corpus triforme': Simbolismo liturgico e mediazioni culturali." In *Culto cristiano, politica imperiale carolingia,* 121–167. Todi, 1979.

Diósi, Dávid. *Amalarius Fortunatus in der Trierer Tradition: Eine quellenkri-tische Untersuchung der trierischen Zeugnisse über einen Liturgiker der Karo-lingerzeit.* Münster, 2006.

Ekenberg, Anders. *Cur cantatur? Die Funktionen des liturgischen Gesanges nach den Autoren der Karolingerzeit.* Stockholm, 1987.

Jones, Christopher A. *A Lost Work by Amalarius of Metz.* London, 2001.

Kolping, Adolf. "Amalar von Metz und Florus von Lyon: Zeugen eiens Wandels im liturgischen Mysterienverständnis in der Karolingerzeit." *Zeitschrift für katholische Theologie* 73 (1951): 424–64.

Meßner, Reinhard. "Zur Hermeneutik allegorischer Liturgieerklärung in Ost und West." *Zeitschrift für katholische Theologie* 115 (1993): 285–319.

Steck, Wolfgang. *Der Liturgiker Amalarius: Eine quellenkritische Untersu-chung zu Leben und Werk eines Theologen der Karolingerzeit.* Munich, 2000.

Vogel, Cyrille. *Medieval Liturgy: An Introduction to the Sources.* Washington, D.C., 1986.

Zechiel-Eckes, Klaus. *Florus von Lyon als Kirchenpolitiker und Publizist.* Stuttgart, 1999.

# Index

The Proem, Preface, and Books 1 and 2 appear in volume 1 (DOML 35).